A Concordance
of the
Pilgrim Hymnal

compiled by

Robert F. Klepper

The Scarecrow Press, Inc.
Metuchen, N.J., & London
1989

British Library Cataloguing-in-Publication data available

Library of Congress Cataloging-in-Publication Data

Klepper, Robert F.
  A concordance of the Pilgrim hymnal / compiled by Robert F.
Klepper.
     p.   cm.
  ISBN 0-8108-2253-9
  1. Pilgrim hymnal--Concordances.   2. Conagregational churches--
Hymns--Concordances.   3. Hymns, English--Concordances.
4. Pilgrim hymnal. I. Title.
M2123.P6   1958 Suppl.
264'.05802--dc20   89-10597

in memory of

Judith

PREFACE

The Pilgrim Hymnal Concordance relates specifically to the Pilgrim Hymnal published by Pilgrim Press in 1958. It provides information on the entire text of the hymns and responses and functions in similar fashion for the hymnal as the Bible Concordance does for the Bible.

It provides aid for identifying phrases. It helps enlarge concepts and promotes idea associations. The poetry of our hymns uplifts us by expressions of the meaning of our church seasons and such themes as hope, joy, justice, peace, wisdom, and other aspects of the spiritual life. This book brings us in touch with poets and their inspirations.

FORMAT

The format of information is as follows:

Hymn No.	Verse No.	Phrase
306	5	And hearts are brave again, and arms are strong

(In the verse column: T = title, R = refrain)

USAGES

1. Selecting hymns. A purpose of this book is to locate hymns which relate to specific themes for meditations, sermons, and church programs. This concordance is more complete than the hymnal's topical index because it includes not only first lines but all verses of each hymn.

2. Finding phrases. For instance, you may remember "all our joy is touched with pain," and you want the full statement and context. This phrase is not a part of the title and so will not be in a hymnal index. The phrase can be found by looking in this concordance for the words, "joy," "touched," or "pain." Under either word (choose the one likely to have the fewest entries), one discovers that the above phrase is from Hymn No. 98 and the title is "My God, I Thank Thee Who Hast Made."

3. Enlarging concepts. There are twenty-eight references to the word "wisdom" in the Pilgrim Hymnal. Studying these phrases reveals at least these themes: Praise to God for wisdom; God as the Source of wisdom; Wisdom as a guiding force; the meaning of true wisdom; limits of human wisdom; prayer for wisdom. Usually it is helpful to look up the related word forms, such as "wisdom's" (one reference) and "wise" (thirteen references). Synonyms of a word broaden the scope of search. There is also value in checking the variations of verbs.

INDEXES

Two indexes compare the numbers of the hymns from the Pilgrim Hymnal with those in The Hymnal of Evangelical and Reformed tradition. The numbers are in sequence and where there is an omission, it means there is no corresponding number in the other hymnal. Parentheses indicate different tune (pp. 767-770).

A third index is a "write-in" index, so that this concordance can be useful to those who use other hymnals. The blanks can be filled with the corresponding numbers from any hymnal of choice (pp. 771-773).

The final index is for hymn titles. This identifies hymn numbers without the necessity of turning to the hymn book itself (pp. 774-784).

ACKNOWLEDGMENT

This book is dedicated to Judith French Klepper (Judith Mustin French before our marriage in 1973). She was a Commissioned Worker of the United Church of Christ and a Certified Specialist in Church Education when she died in 1982. This volume is dedicated to her in celebration of the years of life we shared.

Robert F. Klepper
Bella Vista, Arkansas

269	T,1	I Love Thy Kingdom, Lord, The house of thine abode
271	1	The eternal arms, their dear abode, We make our habitation
354	T,1	Who Trusts in God, a Strong Abode
354	1	strong abode In heaven and earth possesses
355	T,1	Who Trusts in God, a Strong Abode (words same as no. 354)
389	4	And at our Father's loved abode Our souls arrive in peace

abound

23	2	God's praises sound, As in his light ... ye do abound
23	2	in his light with sweet delight Ye do abound
98	2	I thank thee, too, that thou hast made Joy to abound
202	4	Blessings abound where'er he reigns
210	3	Let the healing streams abound, Make and keep me pure within
421	3	Abound with love and solace for the day
430	2	With joy and peace thou shalt abound

about

312	4	And all the virgins bear their part, Sitting about her feet
319	2	Just as I am, though tossed about
343	1	But God is round about me, And can I be dismayed

above

6	T,1	O Worship the King, All Glorious Above
7	2	Thy justice like mountains high soaring above
8	1	Opening to the sun above
19	1	Angels round his throne above
20	T,1	Sing Praise to God Who Reigns Above
23	4	My soul, bear thou thy part, Triumph in God above
25	2	Though high above all praise, Above all blessing high
32	5	Praise him above, ye heavenly host
50	5	We lose ourselves in heaven above
52	2	Stars ... shine out above, Telling still the ancient story
56	4	Praise him above, ye heavenly host
66	4	Friends on earth and friends above
66	6	For thy Church that evermore Lifteth holy hands above
67	T,1	God of Earth, the Sky, the Sea, Maker of all above, below
69	1	Praise him, all ye hosts above, Ever bright and fair in love
86	1	Whose stars serenely burn Above this earth's confusion
86	4	Inspire us from above With joy and strength for duty
89	4	Lord of all life, below, above
92	3	Thy calmness bends serene above, My restlessness to still
121	T,1	From Heaven Above to Earth I Come
127	1	mystery ...Which hosts of angels chanted from above
129	2	Above its sad and lowly plains They bend on hovering wing
132	2	Sing, all ye citizens of heaven above
134	1	Above thy deep and dreamless sleep The silent stars go by
134	2	For Christ is born of Mary, And gathered all above
142	4	Lead us all with hearts aflame Unto the joys above us
152	1	Above the stable while the angels sing
152	3	While birds and flowers and sky above are preaching
187	3	Now above the sky he's King ... Where the angels ever sing
187	4	Sing we to our God above ... Praise eternal as his love
193	3	Bring us safe through Jordan To thy home above
199	2	Rich wounds, yet visible above, In beauty glorified
200	3	The joy of all who dwell above, The joy of all below

204	2	When he had purged our stains, he took his seat above
206	4	All honor and blessing with angels above
218	2	Above the storms of passion, the murmurs of self-will
223	3	By saints below and saints above
228	3	Serve thee as thy hosts above
230	2	Our outward lips confess the Name All other names above
231	2	blessed unction from above Is comfort, life and fire of love
238	1	With light and comfort from above
241	3	let thy Church on earth become Blest as the Church above
247	1	All in heaven above adore thee
247	2	Hark, the glad celestial hymn Angel choirs above are raising
252	3	It shineth like a beacon Above the darkling world
259	4	O Father, Son, and Spirit, send Us increase from above
270	1	above all the soul distressed, Longing for rest everlasting
270	2	High above earth his temple stands
272	1	The fellowship of kindred minds Is like to that above
292	1	And having with us him that pleads above
297	T,1	O God, Above the Drifting Years
299	2	Give power and unction from above
302	2	And died on earth that man might live above
305	2	And thousand hearts ascending In gratitude above
308	4	High above the restless tides Stands their city on the hill
317	T,1	I Love to Tell the Story Of unseen things above
318	1	Raised my low self above, Won by thy deathless love
330	2	Thou dwellest in unshadowed light, All sin and shame above
334	1,3	revealing Of trust and strength and calmness from above
337	2	Far, far above thy thought His counsel shall appear
339	3	High above all praises praising For the gift of Christ
341	3	O sabbath rest by Galilee, O calm of hills above
346	4	To sing the songs of victory With faithful souls above
348	4	Oh, bear me safe above, a ransomed soul
352	2	Above the level of the former years
354	1	Who looks in love to Christ above No fear
363	4	That word above all earthly powers ... abideth
407	2	Above all boons, I pray, Grant me thy voice to hear
413	3	Come, O Christ, and reign above us
423	1	Where sounds the cries of race and clan Above the noise
423	1	Above the noise of selfish strife
423	6	Till glorious from thy heaven above Shall come the city
437	2	My heart with rapture thrills Like that above
440	1	For purple mountain majesties Above the fruited plain
441	3	God within the shadow Keeping watch above his own
460	R	All good gifts around us Are sent from heaven above
469	3	Above the requiem, Dust to dust, Shall rise our psalm
486	1	Birds above me fly, Flowers bloom below
487	T,1	Praise Our God Above For his boundless love
488	2	The shepherds feared and trembled When lo, above the earth
499	2	To him, enthroned above all height ... praises bring
514	1	Praise him above, ye heavenly host
515	1	Praise him above, ye heavenly host
539	1	With the Holy Spirit's favor Rest upon us from above
562	3	For the Lord is a great God and a great King above all gods
569	1-6	Praised and exalted above all for ever
575	2	blessed unction from above Is comfort, life and fire of love

Abraham
| 14 | T,1, | The God of Abraham Praise, All praised be his name |
| 570 | 9 | as he promised to our forefathers, Abraham and his seed |

abreast
| 441 | 2 | Who would keep abreast of truth |

abroad
33	3	Lest from thee we stray abroad, Stay our wayward feet,O Lord
68	1	spread the flowing seas abroad, And built the lofty skies
104	3	For the glory of the Lord Now o'er earth is shed abroad
192	T,1	The Day of Resurrection, Earth, tell it out abroad
203	3	Spread abroad the victor's fame
206	1	And publish abroad his wonderful name
223	2	spread through all the earth abroad The honors of thy name
240	3	Come, shed abroad a Savior's love, & that shall kindle ours
264	3	And tempests are abroad
299	3	Breathe thou abroad like morning air Till hearts ... beat
454	2	By day, by night, at home abroad, Still we are guarded
455	3	And though abroad the sharp winds blow

absent
| 106 | 1 | Though absent long, your Lord is nigh |

absolve
| 426 | 4 | From ease and plenty save us, From pride of place absolve |

abstain
| 148 | 2 | Shall not we thy sorrow share...from earthly joys abstain |

abundance
231	3	With the abundance of thy grace
575	3	Anoint and cheer our soiled face with the abundance
575	3	abundance of thy grace

abundant
| 26 | 3 | Let our lives express Our abundant thankfulness |

abuse
| 170 | 1 | With sore abuse and scorn |

accent
| 17 | 2 | tell the story In accent strong, with voices free |

accents
192	2	And, listening to his accents, May hear so calm and plain
218	2	O Let me hear thee speaking In accents clear and still
329	3	O Jesus, thou art pleading In accents meek and low

accept
155	3	Thou didst accept their praises, Accept the prayers we bring
221	3	My Lord, my Life, my Way, my End, Accept the praise I bring
255	4	The thoughts within my heart, Accept, O Lord
255	4	Accept, O Lord, for thou my Rock And my Redeemer art
321	T,1	My God, Accept My Heart This Day, And make it always thine

460	3	Accept the gifts we offer, For all thy love imparts
477	4	Accept the work our hands have wrought
477	4	Accept, O God, this earthly shrine
492	1	Accept our heartfelt praise

acceptable

| 522 | 1 | Be acceptable in thy sight, O Lord |
| 523 | 1 | Be acceptable in thy sight, O Lord |

acceptation

| 519 | T,1 | To My Humble Supplication, Lord give ear and acceptation |

acclamation

| 203 | 4 | Hark, those bursts of acclamation |

accord

26	1	Praise him with a glad accord...with lives of noblest worth
33	1	So to thee with one accord Lift we up our Hearts, O Lord
33	5	Thee would we with one accord Praise and magnify, O Lord
60	1	With one accord our parting hymn of praise
147	4	Let every tongue confess with one accord
156	1	Draw nigh ... Thy faithful people cry with one accord
184	4	And sing today with one accord
189	T,1	Lift Up Your Hearts, Ye People, In songs of glad accord
237	4	Earth's bitter voices drown In one deep ocean of accord
247	2	Fill the heavens with sweet accord, Holy, holy, holy Lord
262	3	Confessing, in a world's accord, The inward Christ
295	3	With one accord
304	1	Lift up your hearts in jubilant accord
352	1	Lift up your hearts, E'en so, with one accord
352	4	Still shall those hearts respond, with full accord
383	1	Gifts in differing measure, Hearts of one accord
525	1	Give we all, with one accord, Glory to our common Lord

according

284	T,1	According to Thy Gracious Word, In meek humility
285	T,1	According to Thy Gracious Word (same words as 284)
357	6	That mind and soul, according well, May make one music
572	1	according to thy word

accords

| 270 | 3 | Jesus his grace to us accords |

acknowledge

| 559 | T,1 | We Praise Thee, O God, we acknowledge thee to be the Lord |
| 559 | 5 | holy Church throughout all the world doth acknowledge thee |

across

51	1	Shadows of the evening Steal across the sky
161	1	Across our restless living The light streams from his cross
386	4	And daylight breaks across the morning sky
432	3	Thy hand has led across the hungry sea The eager peoples
440	2	A thoroughfare for freedom beat Across the wilderness
443	4	In the beauty of the lilies Christ was born across the sea
453	2	Ring, happy bells, across the snow

480	2	moon ... That sails across the sky at night
484	2	Some fish in mighty rivers, Some hunt across the snow
510	1	Shadows of the evening Steal across the sky

act

164	4	In this dread act your strength is tried
173	2	As the dread act of sacrifice began
416	T,1	Christian, Rise and Act Thy Creed
490	2	Teach us where'er we live, To act as in thy sight

action

| 356 | 2 | It has no spring of action sure, It varies with the wind |
| 401 | 4 | Who sweeps a room ... Makes that and the action fine |

actions

150	3	By words and signs and actions, thus Still seeking
245	1	with actions bold and meek Would for Christ my Savior speak
245	2	And with actions brotherly Speak my Lord's sincerity
558	2	What love through all his actions ran

active

| 41 | 1 | Active and watchful, stand we all before thee |

acts

| 332 | 2 | Acts unworthy, deeds unthinking |

Adam

| 82 | 3 | The sons of Adam in distress Fly to the shadow of thy wing |

add

| 69 | 2 | Those to whom the arts belong Add their voices to the song |

address

| 459 | T,1 | With Songs and Honors Sounding Loud Address the Lord on high |

addressed

| 146 | 5 | angels ... who thus Addressed their joyful song |

adds

| 157 | 3 | Adds more luster to the day |

adeste

| 133 | T,1 | Adeste Fideles |

adopt

| 321 | 3 | Anoint me with thy heavenly grace, Adopt me for thine own |

adorable

| 559 | 6 | thine adorable, true and only Son |

adoration

15	1	Join me in glad adoration
37	2	Alone with thee in breathless adoration
63	2	Thanks we give and adoration For thy Gospel's joyful sound
126	4	Richer by far is the heart's adoration

adoremus
133 R   Venite, adoremus ... Dominum

adores
266 2   One unseen Presence she adores, With silence, or with psalm

adoring
49 2   Thee, his incarnate Son, And Holy Spirit adoring
158 3   There adoring at his feet
247 4   And adoring bend the knee While we sing our praise to thee
249 5   O Triune God, with heart and voice adoring

adorn
475 3   all peoples ... That shall adorn thy dwelling place

adorned
114 2   Adorned with prayer and love and joy

adorning
126 1,5   Star of the east, the horizon adorning

adorns
200 1   A royal diadem adorns The mighty victor's brow
438 4   And spring adorns the earth no more

advancing
413 4   See the Christ-like host advancing
413 4   host advancing, High and lowly, great and small
427 1   Hark, the waking up of nations, Hosts advancing to the fray

advent
106 1   River and mountain-spring, Hark to the advent voice
108 2   And gladsome join the advent song
110 2   cheer Our spirits by thine advent here
115 4   Whose advent sets thy people free
156 2   And silently thy promised advent greet
325 3   New advent of the love of Christ

adventurers
308 2   Bold adventurers on the sea

aeterni
133 3   Patris aeterni Verbum caro factum

afar
89 T,1   Lord of All Being, Throned Afar
90 T,1   Lord of All Being, Throned Afar (same words as No. 89)
117 3   Brighter visions beam afar
138 2   Glories stream from heaven afar
143 T,1   We Thee Kings of Orient Are, Bearing gifts we traverse afar
305 1   Each breeze that sweeps the ocean Brings tidings from afar
388 1   His blood-red banner streams afar
502 2   O may we echo on the song afar

affection
185 3   Comes to glad Jerusalem Who with true affection

affections
324 2   Nail my affections to the cross

affiance
373 3   His truth be thine affiance, When faint and desolate

afflicted
163 1   By foes derided, by thine own rejected, O most afflicted

afford
  33 2   Strength unto our souls afford From thy living Bread, O Lord
259 2   And grow it shall, our glorious sun More fervid rays afford
342 1   No tender voice like thine Can peace afford
539 2   possess in sweet communion Joys which earth cannot afford

affords
200 2   The highest place that heaven affords Is his ... by right
203 4   O what joy the sight affords

affright
118 1   Ye shepherds, shrink not with affright
122 3   Fear not, then, said the angel, Let nothing you affright
467 3   Nought shall affright us, on thy goodness leaning

aflame
142 4   Lead us all with hearts aflame Unto the joys above us
432 4   For hearts aflame to serve thy destined good
436 3   In ire and exultation Aflame with faith and free

aflaring
422 2   When through the night the furnace fires aflaring

afoot
398 3   afoot on dusty highways

afraid
  78 2   afraid his power shall fail When comes thy evil day
444 2   Bring to our troubled minds, uncertain and afraid

afresh
287 2   Here taste afresh the calm of sin forgiven
557 2   Here taste afresh the calm of sin forgiven

after
222 1   Thirsting after thee, Thine I am, O spotless Lamb
263 3   And hereafter in thy glory Evermore with thee to reign
352 4   Then, as the trumpet call, in after years
378 4   or after we have striven, Peace in thy heaven
451 2   Age after age their tragic empires rise

afterward
408 T,1   I sought the Lord, and afterward I knew
578 T,1   I Sought the Lord, and Afterward I Knew

again

2	1	And peace shall reign on earth again
9	2	He brought us to his fold again
15	4	Let the Amen Sound from his people again
34	3	To give and give, and give again, What God hath given thee
42	1	Mists fold away, Gray wakes to green again
42	1	Beauty is seen again
42	1	Gold and serene again Dawneth the day
46	T,1	Again, as Evening's Shadow Falls
46	4	Life's tumult we must meet again
60	T,1	Savior, Again to Thy Dear Name we raise
61	T,1	God Be With You Till We Meet Again (also vs. 1-4)
62	T,1	God Be With You Till We Meet Again (same words as No. 61)
84	2	My soul he doth restore again
92	1	I feel thy strong and tender love, And all is well again
127	4	Till man's first heavenly state again takes place
143	2	Gold I bring to crown him again
150	5	For us he rose from death again
162	5	Then to life I turn again, Learning all the worth of pain
173	1	Calls us to fellowship with God again
182	2	Lives again our glorious King
183	T,1	Christ the Lord Is Risen Again
188	T,1	Joy Dawned Again on Easter Day
202	5	Angels descend with songs again
204	R	Rejoice, again I say, rejoice
272	4	And hope to meet again
290	1	We turn unfilled to thee again
306	5	And hearts are brave again, and arms are strong
325	3	Shall we again refuse thee
352	3	Till, sent from God, they mount to God again
377	1	Soon again his arms will fold thee To his loving heart
420	1	That shall not weep again
422	1	Who in the clouds is pledged to come again
422	5	Living again the eternal gospel story
423	5	O tread the city's streets again
426	1	As once he spake in Zion, So now he speaks again
427	3	Sworn to yield, to waver, never, Consecrated, born again
444	5	Let there be light again, and set Thy judgments in the earth
447	1-3	Give peace, O God, give peace again
457	T,1	The Summer Days Are Come Again
457	3	The summer days are come again, The birds are on the wing
509	T,1	Again, as Evening's Shadow Falls

against

2	4	Do thou our troubled souls uplift Against the foe prevailing
332	2	Sinful thoughts & words unloving Rise against us one by one
382	1	Christ the royal Master Leads against the foe
385	2	Ye that are men now serve him Against unnumbered foes
419	2	spirit's sword to shield The weak against the strong
493	2	Stephen preached against the laws & by those laws was tried
558	1	arose Against the Son of God's delight
580	2	Shut not that gate against me, Lord, But let me enter in

age

4	4	His truth ... shall from age to age endure

19	2	Age to age and shore to shore ... praise him evermore
105	4	From age to age more glorious, All-blessing and all-blest
129	4	with the ever-circling years Comes round the age of gold
252	1	A lantern to our footsteps, Shines on from age to age
261	1	The true thy chartered free-men are, Of every age and clime
266	T,1	One Holy Church of God Appears Through every age and race
267	2	Never fails from age to age
291	2	Here our humblest homage pay we
304	1	From age to age his righteous reign appears
308	4	Lord and light of every age, By thy same sure counsel led
345	2	Bright youth and snow-crowned age
345	4	From youth to age, by night and day, In gladness and in woe
363	2	Lord Sabaoth his name, From age to age the same
376	2	And age comes on uncheered by faith and hope
407	4	All grace and glory be to thee From age to age eternally
411	1	Armed with thy courage, till the world is won
417	2	Who would sit down and sigh for a lost age of gold
417	2	Each old age of gold was an iron age too
427	1	In an age on ages telling, To be living is sublime
451	2	Age after age their tragic empires rise
470	1	Each age its solemn task may claim but once
508	2	The blended notes of age and youth

agents

293	3	By feeblest agents may our God fulfill His righteous will

ages

1	T,1,6	Our God Our Help In Ages Past, our hope for years to come
1	4	A thousand ages in thy sight Are like an evening gone
14	3	His love shall be our strength and stay, While ages roll
35	6	Be this the eternal song Through all the ages long
78	3	Supreme in wisdom as in power The Rock of ages stands
106	3	The sleep of ages break, And rise to liberty
109	2	Traveler, ages are its own, See it bursts o'er all the earth
173	1	O voice, which, through the ages interceding
236	T,1,5	Life of Ages, Richly Poured, Love of God unspent and free
249	2	O holy Father, who hast led thy children In all the ages
263	4	One in might, and One in glory, While unending ages run
267	1	On the Rock of Ages founded, What can shake thy sure repose
268	3	Glory, glory, thine the glory Through the ages evermore
316	2	Borne thy witness in all ages
328	3	The Lord is wonderful and wise, As all the ages tell
358	T,1,4	Rock of Ages, Cleft for me, Let me hide myself in thee
359	T,1,4	Rock of Ages (same words as no. 358)
382	4	This through countless ages Men and angels sing
383	T,1-3	Forward Through the Ages
417	2	Who would ... While the Lord of all ages is here
427	1	In an age on ages telling, To be living is sublime
427	3	Strike, let every nerve and sinew Tell on ages, tell for God
432	2	And, all the ages through, past crumbling throne
438	2	onward through all ages bear The memory of that holy hour
481	3	They lived not only in ages past
575	4	That through the ages all along This may be our endless song
583	T,1	Our God, Our Help in Ages Past (as no. 1 with descant)

ago

agony

agree

ah

aid

aids

aim

aims

air

123	1	Till the air Everywhere Now with joy is ringing
128	3	Cherubim and seraphim Thronged the air
142	5	While the choir with peals of glee Doth rend the air asunder
259	3	Upward we press, the air is clear, & the sphere-music heard
299	3	Breathe thou abroad like morning air Till hearts ... beat
450	2	On earth and fire and sea and air
455	2	His life within the keen air breathes
457	1	And deepening shade of summer woods, And glow of summer air
496	1	And the rockets' red glare, the bombs bursting in air
509	1	vesper hymn and vesper prayer Rise mingling on the holy air

alabaster
| 440 | 4 | Thine alabaster cities gleam, Undimmed by human tears |

alarm
| 91 | 5 | No nightly terrors shall alarm |

alarms
| 356 | 1 | I sink in life's alarms When by myself I stand |
| 433 | 3 | From war's alarms, from deadly pestilence |

alas
| 163 | 2 | Alas, my treason, Jesus, hath undone thee |

alert
| 434 | 2 | God send us men alert and quick ... precepts to translate |

alien
| 294 | 1 | No alien race, no foreign shore, No child unsought, unknown |

alight
| 45 | 1 | night Sets her evening lamps alight Through all the sky |

alike
35	1	Alike at work and prayer, To Jesus I repair
60	3	For dark and light are both alike to thee
424	2	All must aid alike to carry Forward one sublime design
469	2	One providence alike they share

alive
| 422 | 2 | Speak to the heart of love, alive and daring |

allegiance
| 316 | 3 | Now in grateful dedication Our allegiance we would own |

alleluia
12	1,2,R	alleluia, alleluia
19	1-4	Alleluia
30	1	Raise the glad strain, Alleluia
30	1	Cry out ... Virtues, archangels, angels' choirs, Alleluia
30	R	Alleluia, Alleluia, Alleluia, Alleluia
30	2	Lead their praises, Alleluia
30	3	Respond ... Ye patriarchs and prophets blest, Alleluia
30	3	All saints triumphant raise the song, Alleluia
64	1	Lift up your voice and with us sing Alleluia, Alleluia

64	R	O praise him, O praise him, Alleluia, Alleluia, Alleluia
64	2,5	O praise him, Alleluia
64	3	Make music for thy Lord to hear, Alleluia, Alleluia
64	4	Forgiving others, take your part, O sing ye, Alleluia
65	1-3	Alleluia
107	4	Alleluia, Alleluia, Alleluia, Lord Most High
138	2	Heavenly hosts sing alleluia, Christ the Savior is born
143	5	Alleluia, alleluia, Sounds through the earth and skies
147	R	Alleluia
180	T,1	Alleluia, Alleluia, Hearts to Heaven and voices raise
180	3	Alleluia, Alleluia, Glory be to God on high
180	3	Alleluia to the Savior Who has won the victory
180	3	Alleluia to the Spirit, Fount of love and sanctity
180	3	Alleluia, Alleluia, To the Triune Majesty
181	T,1	Alleluia, The Strife is O'er, the battle done
181	R	Alleluia, Alleluia, Alleluia ... Alleluia
182	R	Alleluia
182	1	Sons of men and angels say, Alleluia
182	1	Sing, ye heavens, and earth reply, Alleluia
183	R	Alleluia, Alleluia, Alleluia, Alleluia ... Alleluia
184	R	Alleluia, Alleluia, Alleluia
187	T,1	Jesus Christ Is Risen Today, Alleluia
187	R	Alleluia
191	R	Alleluia, Alleluia, Alleluia ... Alleluia
194	R	Hilariter, Hilariter ... Alleluia, Alleluia
205	R	Alleluia
291	1-3	Alleluia, Alleluia, Alleluia
306	R	Alleluia, Alleluia
469	R	Alleluia, Alleluia, Alleluia

alleluias

311	2	What rush of alleluias Fills all the earth and sky

alleluja

139	2	Durch der Engel Alleluja

alles

139	1	Alles schlaft, eisam wacht

alloy

119	3	So may we with holy joy Pure and free from sin's alloy

almighty

6	3	Almighty, thy power hath founded of old
7	1	Almighty, victorious, thy great name we praise
9	3	What lasting honors ...Almighty Maker, to thy name
15	T,1	Praise to the Lord, the Almighty, the King of creation
15	3	Ponder anew What the Almighty can do
20	2	What God's almighty power hath made, His ... mercy keepeth
28	T,1	We Worship Thee, Almighty Lord
56	1	keep me, King of kings Beneath thine own almighty wings
72	1	And publishes to every land the work of an almighty hand
91	1	Shall with almighty God abide
128	2	A stable place sufficed The Lord God almighty, Jesus Christ
206	2	God ruleth on high, almighty to save

228	3	Come, almighty to deliver, Let us all thy life receive
229	4	My dear almighty Lord, My Conqueror and my King
246	T,1	Come, Thou Almighty King
246	3	Thou who almighty art, Now rule in every heart
248	1	The righteous Judge of judges, The almighty King of kings
251	T,1,4	Holy, Holy, Holy, Lord God Almighty
333	T,1	Father Almighty, Bless Us With Thy Blessing
339	2	Daily doth the almighty giver Bounteous gifts on us bestow
378	1	Lord God almighty
387	3	Where the one almighty Father Reigns in love forevermore
429	2	O Savior, whose almighty word, The winds and waves ... heard
433	T,1	God of Our Fathers, Whose Almighty Hand
433	1	almighty hand Leads forth in beauty all the starry band
460	1	But it is fed and watered By God's almighty hand
473	T,1	O Lord, Almighty God, Thy Works Both great and wondrous be
474	T,1	O Lord, Almighty God, Thy Works (same words as no. 473)
505	1	And pay a grateful song of praise To heaven's almighty King
520	T,1	Almighty Father, Hear Our Prayer
526	1	O grant us peace, almighty Lord
554	3	O Lord God, heavenly King, God the Father almighty

alms

416	3	Let thine alms be hope and joy

alone

1	2	Sufficient is thine arm alone, And our defense is sure
3	1	Him alone God we own, Him, our God and Savior
9	1	Know that the Lord is God alone
20	4	The Lord is God, and he alone
37	2	Alone with thee, amid the mystic shadows
37	2	Alone with thee in breathless adoration
69	3	Holy, holy, holy One, Glory be to God alone
91	6	Because thy trust is God alone ... no evil shall ... come
95	5	Thou in thy everlasting seat Remainest God alone
97	3	When we are strong, Lord, leave us not alone, Our refuge be
103	4	By thine own eternal Spirit Rule in all our hearts alone
109	2	Watchman, will its beams alone Gild the spot
113	4	things celestial thee shall own ...terrestrial, Lord alone
159	T,1	Alone Thou Goest Forth, O Lord, In sacrifice to die
167	IV-1	Jesus, whelmed in fears unknown With our evil left alone
174	1	None can tell what pangs unknown Hold thee silent and alone
174	2	Left alone with human sin, Gloom around thee and within
178	1	The suffering Savior prays alone
207	3	Thou art the life, by which alone we live
210	2	Leave, ah, leave me not alone, Still support and comfort me
212	2	Thou alone to God canst win us
220	T,1	We Bear the Strain of Earthly Care, But bear it not alone
250	1	By whose mighty power alone All is made and wrought and done
263	1	Holy Zion's help forever, And her confidence alone
287	5	My strength is in thy might, thy might alone
291	1	Thou alone, our strong defender Liftest up thy people's head
294	2	Whom love, and love alone can know
318	3	Not for myself alone May my prayer be
325	3	seek the kingdom of thy peace, By which alone we choose thee
330	5	If there is aught of worth in me, It comes from thee alone

332	4	May we live to thee alone
339	1	God unknown, He alone Calls my heart to be his own
354	1	In thee alone, dear Lord, we own Sweet hope and consolation
357	1	By faith, and faith alone, embrace
358	2	All for sin could not atone, Thou must save and thou alone
360	5	Assured alone that life and death His mercy underlies
376	3	Blindly we stumble when we walk alone
383	3	Not alone we conquer, Not alone we fall
384	2	Ye may o'ercome through Christ alone & stand entire at last
385	3	Stand up, stand up for Jesus, Stand in his strength alone
394	1	are dependent on thy will and love alone
400	2	Now thee alone I seek, Give what is best
439	T,1	Not Alone for Mighty Empire
439	1	Not alone for bounteous harvests Lift we up our hearts
441	3	Though the cause of evil prosper ... truth alone is strong
449	3	To joy and suffer not alone
473	2	O Lord, and glorify thy name, For holy thou alone
535	1	All that we have is thine alone, A trust, O Lord, from thee
557	3	My strength is in my might, thy might alone

along
20	3	Then all my gladsome way along, I sing aloud thy praises
64	2	Ye clouds that sail in heaven along
108	2	Hallelujah, We haste along, An eager throng
129	3	Who toil along the climbing way With painful steps and slow
168	3	Along that sacred way where thou art leading
368	3	From the rocks along our way
575	4	That through the ages all along This may be our endless song

aloud
18	2	To thee all angels cry aloud
20	3	Then all my gladsome way along, I sing aloud thy praises
20	4	All ye who own his power, proclaim Aloud the wondrous story
174	3	Hark, that cry that peals aloud
174	3	peals aloud Upward through the whelming cloud
206	3	Let all cry aloud and honor the Son
435	2	And the city's crowded clangor Cries aloud for sin to cease
559	2	To thee all angels cry aloud, the heavens and all the powers

alpha
111	1	He is Alpha and Omega, He the source, the ending he
142	5	Alpha and Omega be, Let the organ thunder
228	2	Alpha and Omega be, End of faith as its beginning

already
362	2	Forget the steps already trod, And onward urge thy way
420	4	Already in the mind of God That city riseth fair

altar
117	4	Saints before the altar bending
145	2	And make thee there an altar
195	2	Crown him, ye martyrs of our God, Who from his altar call
232	5	My heart an altar, and thy love the flame
436	T,1	O God of Earth and Altar, Bow down and hear our cry
443	2	They have builded him an altar in the evening dews and damps

altars
89	5	Till all thy living altars claim One holy light
262	1	The rival altars that we raise

alway
263	2	And thy fullest benediction Shed within its walls alway
392	3	Teach us to rule ourselves alway

always
4	3	Praise, laud, and bless his name always
228	3	Thee we would be always blessing
232	4	Teach me to feel that thou art always nigh
249	5	Thy love and favor, kept to us always
321	T,1	My God, Accept My Heart This Day, And make it always thine
391	3	Thou mine inheritance, now and always
408	3	Always thou lovedst me
578	3	Always thou lovedst me

amazed
127	3	Amazed, the wondrous story they proclaim

amazing
177	4	Love so amazing, so divine, Demands my soul, my life, my all

amber
440	T,1	O Beautiful for Spacious Skies, For amber waves of grain

amen
15	4	Let the Amen Sound from his people again
52	R	Jubilate, Jubilate, Jubilate, Amen
202	5	And earth repeat the loud Amen
375	2	And holiness shall whisper The sweet amen of peace
585	T,1	Amen
586	T	Twofold Amen
587	T	Twofold Amen
588	T	Twofold Amen
589	T	Threefold Amen
590	T	Threefold Amen
591	T	Fourfold Amen
592	T	Twofold Amen
593	T	Threefold Amen
594	T	Sevenfold Amen

America
440	1	America, America, God shed his grace on thee
440	2	America, America, God mend thine every flaw
440	3	America, America, May God thy gold refine
440	4	America, America, God shed his grace on thee

amid
37	2	Alone with thee, amid the mystic shadows
131	1	It came, a floweret bright, Amid the cold of winter
162	2	There I walk amid the shades While the ... twilight fades
215	T,1	Lead, Kingly Light, amid the encircling gloom
314	2	Amid the battle's strife
356	3	It only stands unbent Amid the clashing strife

| 363 | 1 | Our helper he amid the flood Of mortal ills prevailing |
| 429 | 2 | And calm amid its rage didst sleep |

amidst
| 72 | 3 | no real voice nor sound Amidst their radiant orbs be found |
| 185 | 4 | But today amidst the twelve Thou didst stand, bestowing |

among
244	T,1	O Holy Spirit, Enter In, Among these hearts thy work begin
252	4	To bear among the nations Thy true light as of old
411	1	Grant us to march among thy faithful legions
423	5	Among these restless throngs abide
483	1	When Jesus was here among men

ample
| 126 | 4 | Vainly we offer each ample oblation |

ampler
| 297 | 4 | give us grace, through ampler years |

anchor
| 256 | 3 | Our anchor and our stay |

ancient
6	1	Our Shield and Defender, the Ancient of Days
7	1	Most blessed, most glorious, the Ancient of Days
52	2	Stars ... shine out above, Telling still the ancient story
55	6	Thy touch has still its ancient power
129	4	peace shall over all the earth Its ancient splendors fling
198	2	In Christ all races meet, Their ancient feuds forgetting
198	3	To heal its ancient wrong, Come, Prince of peace, and reign
246	1	Come, and reign over us, Ancient of Days
249	T,1	Ancient of Days, Who Sittest Throned in Glory
345	3	The psalms of ancient days
363	1	For still our ancient foe Doth seek to work us woe
366	1	Crown thine ancient church's story
431	2	Still stands thine ancient sacrifice ... a contrite heart
432	2	Thine ancient might destroyed the Pharaoh's boast
434	1	aim ... Not to defend some ancient creed
441	2	Time makes ancient good uncouth

Andrew
| 322 | 2 | As of old, Saint Andrew heart it By the Galilean lake |

anew
15	3	Ponder anew What the Almighty can do
58	2	May we, born anew like morning, To labor rise
165	1	For God doth make his world anew
233	1	Fill me with life anew, That I may love what thou dost love
416	1	Raise thy work and life anew

angel
111	2	Angel hosts, his praises sing
122	2	From God, our heavenly Father, A blessed angel came
122	3	Fear not, then, said the angel, Let nothing you affright
123	1	As I hear, Far and near, Sweetest angel voices

141	T,1	The First Nowell, the angel did say
146	1	The angel of the Lord came down, And glory shone around
191	3	angel clad in white they see, Who sat & spake unto the three
197	2	All the angel faces, All the hosts of light
199	2	No angel in the sky Can fully bear that sight
232	2	No angel visitant, no opening skies
247	2	Hark, the glad celestial hymn Angel choirs above are raising
309	2	And bright with many an angel, And all the martyr throng
456	2	And clearer sounds the angel hymn, Good will to men on earth
488	2	Rang out the angel chorus That hailed our Savior's birth

angel's

118	1	But hear the angel's warning

angelic

120	1	With the angelic host proclaim, Christ is born in Bethlehem
127	2	Who heard the angelic herald's voice

angelorum

133	1	Natum videte Regem angelorum
133	2	Cantet nunc io Chorus angelorum

angels

3	2	Angels, saints, their voices blending
3	3	Like the holy angels Who behold thy glory ... adore thee
7	4	Thine angels adore thee, all veiling their sight
8	2	Stars and angels sing around thee, Center of unbroken praise
13	1	Praise him, angels, in the height
16	4	Angels, help us to adore him, Ye behold him face to face
18	2	To thee all angels cry aloud
19	1	Angels round his throne above
23	T,1	Ye Holy Angels Bright, Who wait at God's right hand
24	1	Let men with angels sing before thee
24	1	Where we partake through faith victorious with angels
24	1	partake ... With angels round thy throne of light
30	1	Cry out ... Virtues, archangels, angels' choirs, Alleluia
32	2	with the angels bear thy part
32	2	angels ... Who all night long, unwearied, sing
35	4	To God, the Word, on high, The hosts of angels cry
45	3	Lord of angels, on our eyes Let eternal morning rise
59	2	Thine angels send us
73	T,1	Angels Holy, High and Lowly, Sing the praises of the Lord
108	3	And men and angels sing before thee
116	T,1	Angels We Have Heard on High Sweetly singing o'er the plains
116	3	Come to Bethlehem and see Him whose birth the angels sing
117	T,1	Angels, From the Realms of Glory
120	T,1,R	Hark, The Herald Angels Sing, Glory to the new-born King
121	4	While angels sing with pious mirth
126	2	Angels adore him, in slumber reclining
127	1	mystery ...Which hosts of angels chanted from above
128	3	Angels and archangels May have gathered there
129	1	From angels bending near the earth
129	1	The world in solemn stillness lay To hear the angels sing
129	2	And ever o'er its Babel sounds The blessed angels sing
129	3	O rest beside the weary road, And hear the angels sing
129	4	the whole world send back the song Which now the angels sing

132	1	Come and behold him, born the King of angels
132	2	Sing, choirs of angels, sing in exultation
134	2	While mortals sleep, the angels keep Their watch
134	4	We hear the Christmas angels The great glad tidings tell
136	4	On this day angels sing
140	1	Whom angels greet with anthems sweet
140	R	Whom shepherds guard and angels sing
146	5	throng Of angels praising God
146	5	angels ... who thus Addressed their joyful song
152	1	Above the stable while the angels sing
178	4	Is borne the song that angels know
182	1	Sons of men and angels say, Alleluia
183	1	Hark, the angels shout for joy, Singing evermore on high
187	3	Now above the sky he's King ... Where the angels ever sing
193	1	Angels in bright raiment Rolled the stone away
195	T,1	All Hail the Power of Jesus' Name, Let angels prostrate fall
202	5	Angels descend with songs again
203	2	Crown the Savior, angels, crown him
203	3	Saints and angels throng around him
206	3	The praises of Jesus the angels proclaim
206	4	All honor and blessing with angels above
215	3	And with the morn those angels faces smile
227	3	Jesus shines purer Than all the angels heaven can boast
229	1	That mortals ever knew, That angels ever bore
232	5	Teach me to love thee as thine angels love
248	1	From whom all hosts of angels Have life and power received
293	2	Claim the high calling angels cannot share
326	2	Heaven's arches rang when the angels sang
326	2	angels sang Proclaiming thy royal degree
326	5	When the heavens shall ring & the angels sing At thy coming
326	5	angels sing At thy coming to victory
351	3	Angels to beckon me Nearer, my God, to thee
382	4	This through countless ages Men and angels sing
461	3	Give his angels charge at last In the fire the tares to cast
461	4	Come, with all thine angels, come
499	2	Him day and night The united choirs of angels sing
559	2	To thee all angels cry aloud, the heavens and all the powers

angels'

30	1	Cry out ... Virtues, archangels, angels' choirs, Alleluia
65	3	Silent powers and angels' song ... All unto our God belong

anger

410	3	Love shall tread out the baleful fire of anger

angry

261	4	In vain the surge's angry shock, In vain the drifting sands
429	3	Who bad'st its angry tumult cease

anguish

162	4	See his anguish ... faith, Love triumphant still in death
163	3	Thy death of anguish and thy bitter passion For my salvation
170	1	How art thou pale with anguish
174	4	Lord, should fear & anguish roll Darkly o'er my sinful soul
178	3	Yet he that hath in anguish knelt Is not forsaken
424	3	Oft in error, oft in anguish

anguished
174 1   Darkness veils thine anguished face

animating
362 3   'Tis God's all-animating voice That calls thee from on high

announce
144 1   'Tis sent to announce a new-born king

announces
115 1   Baptist's cry Announces that the Lord is nigh

annoy
157 2   Hopes deceive and fears annoy

anoint
84 4   My head thou dost with oil anoint, And my cup overflows
231 3   Anoint and cheer our soiled face With ... thy grace
321 3   Anoint me with thy heavenly grace, Adopt me for thine own
470 2   Anoint them prophets
470 3   Anoint them priests, Strong intercessors they For pardon
470 4   Anoint them kings, Aye, kingly kings, O Lord
470 4   Anoint them with the Spirit of thy Son
575 3   Anoint and cheer our soiled face with the abundance

anointed
105 T,1   Hail to the Lord's Anointed, Great David's greater Son
174 3   Thou, the Father's only Son, Thou, his own anointed one
292 2   Look, Father, look on his anointed face

anointing
231 1   Thou the anointing Spirit art (also No. 575-1)

another
47 3   The dawn leads on another day
287 5   I have no help but thine, nor do I need Another arm
287 5   Another arm save thine to lean upon
472 3   Love one another more As they seek thee
506 1   Now is breaking O'er the earth another day
557 3   I have no help but thine, nor do I need Another arm
557 3   Another arm save thine to lean upon

answer
31 2   Comfort thy sorrows and answer thy prayerfulness
108 1   Hallelujah, Lo, great and small, We answer all
161 3   And make us brave and full of joy To answer to his call
333 1   Answer in love thy children's supplication
408 3   the whole Of love is but my answer, Lord, to thee
426 3   We heed, O Lord, thy summons, And answer, Here are we
426 4   Speak, and behold, we answer, Command, and we obey
443 3   O be swift, my soul, to answer him, be jubilant, my feet
578 3   the whole Of love is but my answer, Lord, to thee

answers
159 2   Till through our pity & our shame Love answers love's appeal

503	1	Where my soul in joyful duty Waits for him who answers
503	1	Waits for him who answers prayer

anthem

23	3	And onward as ye go Some joyful anthem sing
69	3	Men and women, young and old, Raise the anthem manifold
199	1	Hark, how the heavenly anthem drowns All music but its own
496	T,1	The National Anthem

anthems

30	4	O friends, in gladness let us sing, Supernal anthems echoing
140	1	Whom angels greet with anthems sweet
155	1	Our praise and prayer and anthems Before thee we present
310	3	Safely the anthems of Zion shall sing

anxious

76	3	Why should this anxious load Press down your weary mind
93	3	Bid my anxious fears subside
540	1	Calm with trust each anxious heart

any

380	2	ne'er from Christ By any lure or guile enticed
481	2	there's not any reason, no, not the least
481	2	not any reason ... Why I shouldn't be one too

anything

401	1	And what I do in anything To do it as for thee

anywhere

335	2	Have we trials and temptations, Is there trouble anywhere

apart

114	2	Make it a temple set apart From earthly use
114	2	set apart From earthly use for heaven's employ
224	3	Apart from thee all gain is loss, All labor vainly done
576	3	Where can I go apart from thee

apes

484	2	Some work in sultry forests Where apes swing to and fro

apostate

299	1	Descend on our apostate race

apostles

18	4	The apostles glorious company ... Thy constant praise recite
127	3	The first apostles of his infant fame
188	1	The Apostles saw their risen Lord
470	5	Make them apostles, Heralds of thy cross
559	4	The glorious company of the apostles praise thee

apostolic

247	3	Lo, the apostolic train Joins thy sacred name to hallow

appall

63	3	Fear of death shall not appall us
376	1	And doubts appall, and sorrows still increase

appeal
159 2   Love answers love's appeal

appear
  3 1   Let us now adore him, And with awe appear before him
110 1   mourns in lonely exile here Until the Son of God appear
117 4   Suddenly the Lord, descending, In his temple shall appear
148 4   That with thee we may appear At the eternal Eastertide
239 1   O Comforter, draw near, Within my heart appear
245 2   with wisdom kind and clear Let thy life in mine appear
267 3   Round each habitation hovering, See the cloud & fire appear
274 3   Till all before our God at length In Zion do appear
311 3   Appear, Desire of nations, Thine exiles long for home
337 2   Far, far above thy thought His counsel shall appear
351 3   There let the way appear Steps unto heaven
442 1   In each sharp crisis, Lord, appear
459 2   he bids the sun cut short his race, And wintry days appear
461 2   Then the full corn shall appear

appeared
146 5   spake the seraph, and forthwith Appeared a shining throng
219 1   Who once appeared in humblest guise below

appearing
 49 1   Our Savior Jesus Christ, Joyful in thine appearing
132 4   Word of the Father, now in flesh appearing

appears
 14 1   The one eternal God, Ere aught that now appears
266 T,1 One Holy Church of God Appears Through every age and race
297 1   And where the higher gain appears, We trace ... thy hand
304 1   From age to age his righteous reign appears
375 3   For gladness breaks like morning Where'er thy face appears

apple
269 2   Dear as the apple of thine eye, And graven on thy hand

appointed
105 1   Hail, in the time appointed, His reign on earth begun
174 2   Till the appointed time is nigh ... the Lamb of God may die
429 1   Its own appointed limits keep

approach
  4 3   Approach with joy his courts unto
 91 6   Nor plague approach thy guarded home

approaching
175 3   To see the approaching sacrifice

approved
 76 4   His goodness stands approved Down to the present day

April's
458 2   Praise him for his budding green, April's resurrection scene

arch
| 89 | 3 | Our rainbow arch, thy mercy's sign |

archangels
| 30 | 1 | Cry out ... Virtues, archangels, angels' choirs, Alleluia |
| 128 | 3 | Angels and archangels May have gathered there |

arches
| 86 | 3 | The deep-toned organ blast That rolls through arches dim |
| 326 | 2 | Heaven's arches rang when the angels sang |

ardent
| 272 | 2 | Before our Father's throne We pour our ardent prayers |

ardor
| 78 | 6 | With growing ardor onward move ... growing brightness shine |
| 239 | 1 | And visit it with thine own ardor glowing |

aright
131	2	To show God's love aright She bore to men a Savior
192	2	Our hearts be pure from evil, That we may see aright
235	3	Teach us to know our God aright
256	5	Lord, grant us all aright to learn The wisdom it imparts
336	5	We by thy Spirit, and thy Son, Shall pray, and pray aright
430	1	His will obey, him serve aright
521	2	That we may know thy name aright

arise
11	1	Let the Creator's praise arise
43	1	Sun of righteousness arise, Triumph o'er the shades of night
50	1	Oh, may no earth-born cloud arise To hide thee
50	1	no ... cloud arise To hide thee from thy servant's eyes
52	3	As the darkness deepens o'er us, Lo, eternal stars arise
68	3	clouds arise, and tempests blow, By order from thy throne
86	4	May thy fresh light arise Within each clouded heart
108	1	Awake, Jerusalem, arise
143	5	Glorious now behold him arise, King and God and Sacrifice
152	5	Let us arise, all meaner service scorning
304	3	And from his waiting Church new hopes arise
384	T,1	Soldiers of Christ, Arise And put your armor on
392	3	That we may bring, if need arise, no ... worthless sacrifice
433	1	Our grateful songs before thy throne arise
499	2	To him may all our thoughts arise In never-ceasing sacrifice

arm
1	2	Sufficient is thine arm alone, And our defense is sure
17	1	While o'er my life his strong arm he raises I shall sing
17	2	Sing, all ye nations, exalt the glory Of him whose arm
17	2	exalt the glory Of him whose arm doth valiantly
78	2	can an all-creating arm Grow weary or decay
222	2	In thine arm I rest me
287	5	I have no help but thine, nor do I need Another arm
287	5	Another arm save thine to lean upon
293	3	No arm so weak but may do service here
384	2	And take, to arm you for the fight, The panoply of God
385	3	The arm of flesh will fail you, Ye dare not trust your own

416	2	Arm their faltering wills to fight
427	2	Up, it is Jehovah's rally, God's own arm hath need of thine
429	1	Whose arm doth bind the restless wave
433	3	Be thy strong arm our ever sure defense
468	3	Beyond thy voice, thine arm, thy care
483	2	That his arm had been thrown around me
557	3	I have no help but thine, nor do I need Another arm
557	3	Another arm save thine to lean upon
570	6	He hath showed strength with his arm

armed

| 363 | 1 | And armed with cruel hate, On earth is not his equal |
| 411 | 1 | Armed with thy courage, till the world is won |

armies

| 311 | 1 | armies of the ransomed saints throng up the steeps of light |
| 439 | 3 | For the armies of the faithful |

armor

378	2	Lord, thou canst help when earthly armor faileth
384	T,1	Soldiers of Christ, Arise And put your armor on
385	3	Put on the gospel armor, Each piece put on with prayer

armored

| 366 | 4 | Gird our lives that they may be Armored |
| 366 | 4 | Armored with all Christ-like graces in the fight |

arms

29	1	Who, from our mothers' arms, Hath blessed us on our way
61	3	Put his arms unfailing round you
217	3	Your hands swift to welcome your arms to embrace
271	1	The eternal arms, their dear abode, We make our habitation
277	1	Let thine arms around them be
306	5	And hearts are brave again, and arms are strong
335	3	In his arms he'll take and shield thee
356	1	Imprison me within thine arms, And strong shall be my hand
367	4	Faint not nor fear, his arms are near
377	1	Soon again his arms will fold thee To his loving heart
422	3	Feels in his arms the vigor of the Lord

army

261	2	One holy Church, one army strong, One steadfast high intent
382	2	Like a mighty army Moves the Church of God
385	1	From victory unto victory His army shall he lead
388	4	A noble army, men and boys, The matron and the maid
559	5	The noble army of martyrs praise thee

arose

| 558 | 1 | When powers of earth and hell arose |
| 558 | 1 | arose Against the Son of God's delight |

around

8	2	Stars and angels sing around thee, Center of unbroken praise
35	3	Let all the earth around Ring joyous with the sound
36	2	New mercies, each returning day Hover around us
36	2	New mercies ... Hover around us while we pray

ascend
269	3	For her my tears shall fall, For her my prayers ascend
407	1	No eye can to thy throne ascend

ascended
47	1	To thee our morning hymns ascended

ascending
3	2	Holy, holy, holy, Hear the hymn ascending
259	3	The valleys passed, ascending still
305	2	And thousand hearts ascending In gratitude above
508	1	Once more to thee our hymns ascending

ascends
109	2	Higher yet that star ascends

ascent
388	4	They climbed the steep ascent of heaven

ascribe
195	4	To him all majesty ascribe

ascribing
206	2	Ascribing salvation to Jesus, our King

ashes
239	2	To dust and ashes in its heat consuming
410	3	And in its ashes plant the tree of peace
426	3	Our strength is dust and ashes, Our years a passing hour

aside
287	2	Here would I lay aside each earthly load
348	3	Nor let me every stray From thee aside
367	3	Cast care aside, lean on thy guide
395	2	And scarcely can we turn aside For one brief hour of prayer
557	2	Here would I lay aside each earthly load

ask
21	T,1	We Gather Together to ask the Lord's blessing
89	4	Before thy ever-blazing throne We ask no luster of our own
160	3	I ask no other sunshine than The sunshine of his face
174	3	Thou dost ask him -- can it be, Why has thou forsaken me
215	1	I do not ask to see The distant scene
222	1	I will ... Ask for nought beside thee
232	2	I ask no dreams, no prophet ecstasies
263	3	Here vouchsafe to all thy servants What they ask of thee
263	3	What they ask of thee to gain
291	2	Thou art here, we ask not how
363	2	Dost ask who that may be, Christ Jesus, it is he
368	2	Not forever in green pastures Do we ask our way to be
399	4	I dare not ask to fly from thee
412	3	with the task sufficient strength, Show us thy will, we ask
493	4	No shield I ask, no faithful friend, No vengeance, no reward

asleep
137	1	The little Lord Jesus, asleep on the hay

aspiring
   362 3   'Tis his own hand presents the prize To thine aspiring eye

ass
   125 1   Ox and ass before him bow, And he is in the manger now
   136 2   Ox and ass beside him From the cold would hide him
   140 2   Why lies he in such mean estate Where ox and ass are feeding

assail
    91 3   No fatal stroke shall thee assail
   148 3   And if Satan, vexing sore, Flesh or spirit should assail
   222 2   Sin and hell ... With their heaviest storms assail us
   354 2   And worldly scorn assail us
   366 2   hosts of evil round us Scorn thy Christ assail his ways

assailed
   416 4   Freest faith assailed in vain

assaileth
   378 2   Lord, thou canst save when sin itself assaileth

assemble
   377 2   Though the sea his waves assemble And in fury fall on thee

asses
   142 2   Cradled in a stall was he with sleeply cows and asses

assigned
   406 2   task thy wisdom hath assigned, O let me cheerfully fulfill

assist
    23 1   Assist our song, For else the theme Too high doth seem
   223 2   My gracious Master and my God, Assist me to proclaim

assisted
   127 4   Treading his steps, assisted by his grace

assuage
   267 2   Ever flows their thirst to assuage

assuaging
   378 3   Peace, in our hearts, our evil thoughts assuaging

assurance
   168 2   Yet give us strength to trust the sweet assurance
   168 2   assurance That thou, O Lord, art greater than our heart
   465 2   O perfect Life, be thou their full assurance
   465 2   assurance Of tender charity and stadfast faith

assure
   470 2   their lips make eloquent To assure the right

assured
   360 5   Assured alone that life and death His mercy underlies

astray

122	1	To save us all from Satan's power When we were gone astray
168	1	salvation Which thou has won for us who went astray
229	3	O let my feet ne'er run astray
314	3	Nor let me go astray
327	2	Seek us when we go astray
376	1	Without thy guiding hand we go astray
470	3	Ah, if with them the world might pass astray
470	3	pass astray Into the dear Christ's life of sacrifice

asunder

142	5	While the choir with peals of glee Doth rend the air asunder

atone

358	2	All for sin could not atone, Thou must save and thou alone

atremble

377	2	Though thou cry, with heart atremble, O my Savior, succor me

attain

153	4	An Easter of unending joy We may attain at last

attend

15	3	Surely his goodness and mercy here daily attend thee
58	1	Holy dreams and hopes attend us, This live-long night
241	T,1,4	Spirit Divine, Attend our Prayers
246	2	Gird on thy mighty sword, Our prayer attend
374	3	Or should pain attend me On my path below

attends

11	2	Eternal truth attends thy word

attent

470	2	Make their ears attent To thy divinest speech

aught

14	1	The one eternal God, Ere aught that now appears
109	a	Aught of joy or hope foretell
313	2	Not with the hope of gaining aught, Not seeking a reward
330	5	If there is aught of worth in me, It comes from thee alone
331	1	Nor should I aught withhold, Dear Lord, from thee

aula

133	2	Cantet nunc aula caelistium

aus

139	3	Lieb' aus deinmem gottlichen Mund

author

437	4	Our father's God, to thee Author of Liberty, To thee we sing

autumn

462	2	All that liberal autumn pours From her rich ... stores
464	3	All that liberal autumn pours From her rich ... stores
487	1	Pearly rice and corn, Fragrant autumn morn

avert

2	4	Avert our woes and calm our dread

avowed

371	1	His first avowed intent To be a pilgrim

await

309	1	I know not, O I know not, What joys await us there

awaits

303	1	thanks ... That work awaits our hands and feet
375	3	The crown awaits the conquest, Lead on, O God of might

awake

32	T,1	Awake, My Soul, and With the Sun
34	T,1	Awake, Awake to Love and Work, The lark is in the sky
34	1	The fields are wet with diamond dew, The worlds awake to cry
56	3	To serve my God when I awake
69	1	Heaven & earth, awake & sing, God is good and therefore King
75	1	Wake, my soul, awake & sing, Now thy grateful praises bring
106	3	Lands of the East, awake, Soon shall your sons be free
108	T,1	Wake, Awake, for Night is Flying
108	1	Awake, Jerusalem, arise
127	T,1	Christians, Awake, Salute the Happy Morn
199	1	Awake, my soul, and sing Of him who died for thee
362	T,1	Awake, My Soul, Stretch Every nerve
386	3	Till clearer light our slumbering souls awake
437	3	Let mortal tongues awake, Let all that breathe partake
470	2	their hearts awake To human need

awaken

446	2	Bid not thy wrath in its terrors awaken

awakening

35	T,1	When Morning Gilds the Skies, My heart awakening cries

awakes

42	3	Splendor he makes on earth, Color awakes on earth
137	2	The cattle are lowing, the baby awakes
198	1	New life, new hope awakes Where'er men own his sway
201	1	When beauty gilds the eastern hills And life to joy awakes

awaking

37	3	So does this blessed consciousness, awaking, Breathe

away

1	5	Time, like an ever-rolling stream, Bears all its sons away
8	1	Drive the dark of doubt away
42	1	Mists fold away, Gray wakes to green again
47	3	Nor dies the strain of praise away
47	5	So be it, Lord, thy throne shall never ... pass away
47	5	Like earth's proud empires, pass away

63	3	when thy love shall call us, Savior, from the world away
76	4	I'll drop my burden at his feet, And bear a song away
96	2	His hand can turn my griefs away
100	3	Far as east from west is distant He hath put away our sin
105	1	To take away transgression, And rule in equity
107	3	powers of hell may vanish As the darkness clears away
128	2	Heaven and earth shall flee away When he comes to reign
137	T,1	Away in a Manger, no crib for a bed
158	1	Turn not from his griefs away
167	IV-2	When we vainly seem to pray, And our hope seems far away
171	T,1	There Is a Green Hill Far Away, Without a city wall
172	T,1	There Is a Green Hill Far Away (same words as No. 171)
193	1	Angels in bright raiment Rolled the stone away
209	2	Earth's joys grow dim, its glories pass away
221	1	And drives away his fear
228	2	Take away the love of sinning
232	2	But take the dimness of my soul away
290	4	Chase the dark night of sin away
293	3	Away with gloomy doubts and faithless fear
314	1	And purge away my sin
315	4	O welcome voice of Jesus, Which drives away our doubt
348	1	Take all my guilt away
348	3	Wipe sorrow's tears away
371	3	Then fancies, flee away, I'll fear not what men say
398	3	Walk thou beside us lest the tempting byways Lure us away
398	3	Lure us away from thee to endless night
431	3	Far-called, our navies melt away
436	1	Take not thy thunder from us, But take away our pride
461	3	From his field shall in that day All offenses purge away
468	1	we must not say that those are dead who pass away
528	2	Cast me not away from thy presence
554	5	That takest away the sins of the world, have mercy upon us
554	6	that takest away the sins of the world, receive our prayer
555	T,1	O Lamb of God, that takest away the sins of the world
556	1	that takest away the sins of the world
570	8	and the rich he hath sent empty away
576	4	And far away my dwelling make

awe

3	1	Let us now adore him, And with awe appear before him
123	3	Here let all, Great and small, Kneel in awe and wonder
132	3	we would embrace thee, with love and awe
431	4	Wild tongues that have not thee in awe
499	1	Serve him with awe, with reverence, love
562	8	let the whole earth stand in awe of him

aweful

9	T,1	Before Jehovah's Aweful Throne
10	T,1	Before Jehovah's Aweful Throne (same as Hymn No. 9)
292	3	And by this food, so aweful and so sweet Deliver us
325	2	aweful love ... found no room In life where sin denied thee
427	T,1	We Are Living, We Are Dwelling In a grand and aweful time

174	T,1	Throned Upon the Awful Tree
431	1	Beneath whose awful hand we hold Dominion over palm and pine
576	2	O wondrous knowledge, awful might

awhile
53	3	Awhile his mortal blindness May miss God's lovingkindness
164	T,1	O Come and Mourn with Me Awhile
205	1	Christ, awhile to mortals given
215	3	faces smile Which I have loved long since, and lost awhile
395	1	And met within thy holy place To rest awhile with thee

awoke
| 304 | 2 | and eager hearts awoke to greet the day |

aye
14	1,3	Who was, and is, and is to be, For aye the same
15	4	Gladly for aye we adore him
70	R	For his mercies aye endure, Ever faithful, ever sure
184	2	The Lord of life is risen for aye
470	4	Anoint them kings, Aye, kingly kings, O Lord
502	2	All hail to him, the mighty God, for aye

babe
127	4	trace we the babe, Who hath retrieved our loss
127	4	Trace we the babe ... his poor manger to his bitter cross
140	R	Haste, haste to bring him laud, The babe, the son of Mary
146	4	The heavenly babe you there shall find
146	4	babe ... To human view displayed
149	T,1	I Know Not How That Bethlehem's Babe Could in the Godhead be

Babel
| 129 | 2 | And ever o'er its Babel sounds The blessed angels sing |

baby
| 137 | 2 | The cattle are lowing, the baby awakes |
| 482 | 2 | Mary's little baby, sleep, sweetly sleep |

back
112	1	Look not back, the past regretting
116	1	And the mountains in reply Echo back their joyous strains
129	4	the whole world send back the song Which now the angels sing
161	2	The hopes that lead us onward, The fears that hold us back
197	3	Brought it back victorious, When from death he passed
236	4	Hurling floods of tyrant wrong From the sacred limits back
343	2	Wherever he may guide me, No want shall turn me back
398	4	We render back the love thy mercy gave us
399	1	I give thee back the life I owe
441	2	With the cross that turns not back
451	T,1	Turn Back, O Man, Forswear Thy Foolish Ways

backward
| 378 | 4 | Grant us thy help til backward they are driven |

bad'st
| 429 | 3 | Who bad'st its angry tumult cease |

baleful
410   3   Love shall tread out the baleful fire of anger

ball
72   3   Move round the dark terrestrial ball
195   4   Let every kindred, every tribe, On this terrestrial ball

balm
20   1   With healing balm my soul he fills
60   4   Our balm in sorrow, and our stay in strife
217   4   Whose voice is contentment, whose presence is balm
354   1   Our shield from foes, our balm for woes
405   3   Some balm of peace for eyes Blinded with tears

band
261   2   One working band, one harvest song, One King omnipotent
387   1   Onward goes the pilgrim band
388   3   A glorious band, the chosen few On whom the Spirit came
433   1   almighty hand Leads forth in beauty all the starry band
433   1   starry band Of shining worlds in splendor through the skies

bands
146   4   All meanly wrapped in swathing bands, And in a manger laid

bane
157   4   Bane and blessing, pain and pleasure ... are sanctified

baneful
386   2   darkness ... lulls our spirits with its baneful spell

banish
39   3   To banish sin from our delight
41   2   Banish our weakness, health and wholeness sending

banished
424   1   Wrong is banished from its borders

bank
115   T,1   On Jordan's Bank the Baptist's Cry

banner
61   4   Keep love's banner floating o'er you
252   3   It floateth like a banner Before God's hosts unfurled
267   3   deriving from their banner Light by night and shade by day
296   T,1-4 Fling Out the Banner
298   3   March we forth ... With the banner of Christ unfurled
345   1   Your festal banner wave on high, The cross of Christ
385   1   Lift high his royal banner, It must not suffer loss
388   1   His blood-red banner streams afar
496   1   O say does that star-spangled banner yet wave
496   2   And the star-spangled banner in triumph shall wave

banners
382   1   Forward into battle, See his banners go

battle's
314 2   Amid the battle's strife

battlefield
359 2   in the darkest battlefield Thou shalt know where to strike

battlements
264 2   We mark her goodly battlements, And her foundations strong

battles
22 2   And with thy help, O Lord, life's battles we win

battleship
439 2   Not for battleship and fortress ... conquests of the sword

battling
308 3   strong, yet battling for the weak

beacon
252 3   It shineth like a beacon Above the darkling world

beam
39 2   The Spirit's sanctifying beam Upon our earthly senses stream
64 1   Thou burning sun with golden beam
117 3   Brighter visions beam afar
357 5   A beam in darkness, let it grow

beamest
145 1   Thou beamest forth in truth and light

beaming
109 1   See that glory-beaming star
119 1   Leading onward, beaming bright
157 3   When the sun of bliss is beaming Light and love upon my way

beams
43 2   Joyless is the day's return Till thy mercy's beams I see
109 2   Watchman, will its beams alone Gild the spot
138 3   Radiant beams from thy holy face
144 T,1   What Star Is This, With Beams So Bright
161 1   And by its clear, revealing beams We measure gain and loss
212 2   Till thy Spirit breaks our night With the beams of truth
212 2   With the beams of truth unclouded

bear
19 4   Strings and voices, hands and hearts ... bear your parts
19 4   In the concert bear your parts
20 3   Both soul and body bear your part
23 4   My soul, bear thou thy part, Triumph in God above
31 2   High on his heart he will bear it for thee
32 2   with the angels bear thy part
39 4   And give us grace our wrongs to bear
54 2   May we and all who bear thy name ...thy cross proclaim

64	4	Ye who long pain and sorrow bear, Praise God
69	3	let children's happy hearts In this worship bear their parts
76	4	I'll drop my burden at his feet, And bear a song away
77	1	Bear patiently the cross of grief or pain
83	1	And bear thee through the evil days
99	4	We read thee best in him who came To bear for us the cross
99	4	To bear for us the cross of shame
112	3	Ours to bear the faithful witness
121	1	To bear good news to every home
154	2	We cannot understand the woe Thy love was pleased to bear
158	2	Learn of Christ to bear the cross
171	2	We may not know, we cannot tell What pains he had to bear
199	2	No angel in the sky Can fully bear that sight
201	2	Not as of old a little child To bear, and fight, and die
220	T,1	We Bear the Strain of Earthly Care, But bear it not alone
222	3	Yea, whate'er we here must bear
232	4	Teach me the struggles of the soul to bear
242	3	By thee may I strongly live, Bravely bear, and nobly strive
246	3	Thy sacred witness bear In this glad hour
252	4	To bear among the nations Thy true light as of old
272	3	We share each other's woes, Each other's burdens bear
286	3	One name we bear, one bread of life we break
293	2	To young and old the gospel gladness bear
295	3	With us the cross to bear, For Christ our Lord
302	3	Give of thy sons to bear the message glorious
312	4	And all the virgins bear their part, Sitting about her feet
329	1	Shame on us, Christian brothers, His name and sign who bear
330	2	That thou shouldst bear our sin and shame, How can I tell
335	1	All our sins and griefs to bear
335	1	Oh, what needless pain we bear
347	2	Help us, through good report & ill, Our daily cross to bear
348	4	Oh, bear me safe above, a ransomed soul
392	2	Teach us to bear the hope in youth With steadfastness
406	4	Give me to bear thy easy yoke
416	2	Thou canst help their load to bear
418	1	Tell me thy secret, help be bear The strain of toil
426	2	Whom shall I send to shatter The fetters which they bear
438	2	onward through all ages bear The memory of that holy hour
445	2	His conquering cross no kingdom wills to bear

bearer

| 30 | 2 | bearer of the eternal Word, Most gracious, magnify the Lord |

bearers

| 409 | 1 | workers, Burden-bearers of the earth |

bearest

| 159 | 2 | Our sins, not thine, thou bearest, Lord |

bearing

143	T,1	We Thee Kings of Orient Are, Bearing gifts we traverse afar
158	2	See him meekly bearing all
245	3	Ever by a mighty hope, Pressing on and bearing up
491	4	Bearing his cross in service glad and free

bears

1	5	Time, like an ever-rolling stream, Bears all its sons away
16	3	In his hands he gently bears us
76	2	hand which bears all nature up Shall guide his children well
388	1	Who patient bears his cross below, He follows in his train

beast

175	1	Thy humble beast pursues his road
481	2	And one was slain by a fierce wild beast

beasts

126	2	Low lies his head with the beasts of the stall
142	2	But the very beasts could see that he all men surpasses

beat

42	3	Hear we no beat of drums, Fanfare nor cry
198	2	To plough-share beat the sword, To pruning-hook the spear
299	3	Breathe thou abroad like morning air Till hearts ... beat
299	3	Till hearts of stone begin to beat
365	1	O how our hearts beat high with joy
440	2	A thoroughfare for freedom beat Across the wilderness

beaten

158	2	Beaten, bound, reviled, arraigned

beauteous

109	1	Watchman, does its beauteous ray ... joy or hope foretell
118	T,1	Break Forth, O Beauteous Heavenly Light
156	2	The consecration of thy beauteous feet

beautiful

124	1	Ah, ah, beautiful is the mother
124	1	Ah, ah, beautiful is her son
404	2	Take my feet and let them be Swift and beautiful for thee
440	T,1	O Beautiful for Spacious Skies, For amber waves of grain
440	2	O beautiful for pilgrim feet
440	3	O beautiful for heroes proved In liberating strife
440	4	O beautiful for patriot dream That sees beyond the years
456	T,1	All Beautiful the March of Days, As seasons come and go
478	T,R	All Things Bright and Beautiful, All creatures great & small
490	3	Teach us to love the true, The beautiful and pure

beauty

31	T,1	Worship the Lord in the Beauty of Holiness
31	3	Truth in its beauty, and love in its tenderness
42	1	Beauty is seen again
53	2	For joy of beauty not his own
66	T,1	For the Beauty of the Earth, For the beauty of the skies
66	2	For the beauty of each hour Of the day and of the night
86	3	All beauty speaks of thee, The mountains and the rivers
86	4	Thou hidden fount of love, Of Peace, and truth and beauty
98	1	So full of splendor and of joy, Beauty and light
143	R	star of wonder, star of night, Star with royal beauty bright

199	2	Rich wounds, yet visible above, In beauty glorified
201	1	When beauty gilds the eastern hills And life to joy awakes
201	4	Christ, our King, in beauty comes, And we his face shall see
201	5	morning dawns, And light and beauty brings
341	4	And let our ordered lives confess The beauty of thy peace
407	3	And, pure in heart, behold Thy beauty while I live
433	1	almighty hand Leads forth in beauty all the starry band
443	4	In the beauty of the lilies Christ was born across the sea
444	T,1	O Day of God, Draw Nigh In beauty and in power
455	2	His beauty paints the crimson dawn
456	3	O thou from whose unfathomed law The year in beauty flows
475	3	The beauty of the oak and pine
476	4	men of skill Who builded homes of beauty
503	T,1	Open Now Thy Gates of Beauty, Zion, let me enter there
562	8	O worship the Lord in the beauty of holiness

because

86	2	It is because thou art We're driven to the quest
91	6	Because thy trust is God alone ... no evil shall ... come
313	1	not because I hope for heaven thereby
313	1	Nor yet because who love thee not Are lost eternally
313	3	love ... Solely because thou art my God, And my eternal King
317	1	I love to tell the story, Because I know it's true
319	4	Because thy promise I believe
335	1	All because we do not carry Everything to God in prayer
422	4	When all the world looks up because of him

beckon

351	3	Angels to beckon me Nearer, my God, to thee

beckoning

303	3	We see the beckoning vision flame

become

203	1	Crowns become the victor's brow
239	3	For none can guess its grace, Till he become the place
241	3	let thy Church on earth become Blest as the Church above
276	4	And human life become divine
434	2	Until the laws of Christ become The laws and habits of

becomes

35	2	The night becomes as day, When from the heart we say

bed

119	2	As with joyful steps they sped To that lowly manger-bed
121	3	Ah, dearest Jesus, holy child, Make thee a bed
121	3	Make thee a bed, soft, undefiled Within my heart
136	3	Kneeling low by his bed, Lay their gifts before him
137	T,1	Away in a Manger, no crib for a bed

beds

230	5	The healing of his seamless dress Is by our beds of pain

been

15	2	Hast thou not seen How thy desires e'er have been Granted
22	2	Through life's storm and tempest our guide hast thou been
55	5	Thou hast been troubled, tempted, tried
100	3	Like the pity of a father Hath the Lord's compassion been
111	1	Of the things that are, that have been
191	4	And yet whose faith hath constant been
343	3	Bright skies ... Where the dark clouds have been
381	3	Of patient & courageous heart, As all true saints have been
413	2	Freely have thy gifts been granted
483	1	I should like to have been with him then
483	2	I wish that his hands had been placed on my head
483	2	That his arm had been thrown around me
568	3	which have been since the world began

befall

58	2	Strong through thee whate'er befall us, O God most wise
391	4	Heart of my own heart, whatever befall

befits

104	3	true and humble, As befits his holy reign

before

1	3	Before the hills in order stood, Or earth received her frame
1	4	Short as the watch that ends the night Before the rising sun
3	1	Let us now adore him, And with awe appear before him
4	1	Come ye before him and rejoice
8	1	Hearts unfold like flowers before thee
9	T,1	Before Jehovah's Aweful Throne
10	T,1	Before Jehovah's Aweful Throne (same as Hymn No. 9)
13	1	Sun and moon, rejoice before him
15	4	All ... life and breath, come now with praises before him
16	4	Sun and moon, bow down before him
22	1	We lay it before thee, we kneel and adore thee
24	1	Let men with angels sing before thee
26	T,1	O Be Joyful in the Lord, Sing before him, all the earth
26	1	Sons of every land, Humbly now before him stand
31	1	Bow down before him, his glory proclaim
41	1	Active and watchful, stand we all before thee
59	2	Let evil thoughts and spirits flee before us
61	4	Smite death's threatening wave before you
74	1	Humbly now we bow before thee
74	4	Thou whose purpose moves before us Toward the goal
79	4	Thy cross before to guide me
89	4	Before thy ever-blazing throne We ask no luster of our own
94	2	Before my infant heart conceived From whom those comforts
95	1	Before him righteousness shall go, His royal harbinger
95	4	all shall frame To bow them low before thee, Lord
98	4	A yearning for a deeper peace Not known before
105	3	Before him on the mountains Shall peace, the herald, go
108	3	And men and angels sing before thee
111	2	Powers, dominions, bow before him
117	4	Saints before the altar bending

119	2	There to bend the knee before Him who heaven and earth adore
125	1	Ox and ass before him bow, And he is in the manger now
136	3	Kneeling low by his bed, Lay their gifts before him
148	3	Thou, his vanquisher before, Grant we may not faint nor fail
152	1	Haste, let us lay our gifts before the King
152	4	At even-tide before the sun was set
155	1	The people of the Hebrews With palms before thee went
155	1	Our praise and prayer and anthems Before thee we present
155	2	To thee, before thy passion, They sang their hymns of praise
161	T,1	Before the Cross of Jesus Our lives are judged today
209	5	Hold thou thy cross before my closing eyes
213	1	Unknown waves before me roll
228	4	Till we cast our crowns before thee
229	4	behold I sit In willing bonds before thy feet
244	1	We before thee For that precious gift implore thee
247	1	Lord of all, we bow before thee
251	2	Cherubim and seraphim falling down before thee
252	3	It floateth like a banner Before God's hosts unfurled
258	3	When the storms are o'er us And dark clouds before us
269	2	I love thy Church, O God, Her walls before they stand
272	2	Before our Father's throne We pour our ardent prayers
274	3	Till all before our God at length In Zion do appear
305	2	See all the nations bending Before the God we love
306	1	Who thee by faith before the world confessed
310	4	Low before him with our praises we fall
321	2	Before the cross of him who died, Behold, I prostrate fall
325	4	We bring our hearts before thy cross To finish thy salvation
332	1	Low before thy throne we fall
340	1	Such happy, simple fisher-folk, Before the Lord came down
340	2	Contented, peaceful fishermen, Before they ever knew ... God
340	2	Before they every knew The peace of God
343	3	Green pastures are before me, Which yet I have not seen
344	2	Thou didst tread this earth before us
357	6	May make one music as before
367	2	Life with its way before us lies
382	1,R	With the cross of Jesus Going on before
387	1	Clear before us through the darkness Gleams ... light
389	2	Our vows, our prayers, we now present Before thy throne
389	2	Before thy throne of grace
402	4	And bring all heaven before our eyes
417	1	The night is darkest before the morn
422	5	God in a workman's jacket as before
433	1	Our grateful songs before thy throne arise
443	3	He is sifting out the hearts of men before his judgment seat
454	3	And, peaceful, leave before thy feet
465	1	Lowly we kneel in prayer before thy throne
367	2	When fond hopes fail and skies are dark before us
470	5	And stand at last with joy before thy face
471	1	For saints of old, who made their vows before thee
467	2	When fond hopes fail and skies are dark before us
493	1	He bore no shield before his face, No weapon in his hand
499	1	And silent bow before his face
503	2	Gracious God, I come before thee

507	T,1	To Thee Before the Close of Day
508	T,1	Before the Day Draws Near Its Ending
508	2	Before thy feet, abashed and lowly
520	1	and bless all souls that wait before thee
524	1	make thy way plain before my face
537	1	Thine own before thy feet we lay
540	T,1	Father, Give Thy Benediction, Give thy peace before we part
558	2	Before the mournful scene began, He took the bread
562	2	Let us come before his presence with thanksgiving
562	6	and kneel before the Lord our maker
565	1	and come before his presence with a song
568	8	In holiness and righteousness before him
568	9	shalt go before the face of the Lord to prepare his ways
572	3	Which thou hast prepared before the face of all people
580	1	Lamenting all their sinful lives, Before thy mercy gate

beforehand

408	3	For thou wert long beforehand with my soul

befriend

15	3	If with his love he befriend thee
327	2	We are thine, do thou befriend us

befriended

2	T,1	All Glory Be to God on High Who hath our race befriended

began

60	2	With thee began, with thee shall end the day
86	1	plan ... in which the world began, Endures, and shall endure
111	T,1	Of the Father's Love Begotten, Ere the world began to be
173	2	As the dread act of sacrifice began
257	3	So when thy truth began its race, It touched and glanced on
439	4	Strong as when her life began
558	2	Before the mournful scene began, He took the bread
568	3	which have been since the world began

begin

114	4	Let new and nobler life begin
146	6	Good will henceforth from heaven to men Begin & never cease
175	2	O Christ, thy triumphs now begin
175	2	thy triumphs now begin O'er captive death and conquered sin
192	3	Now let the heavens be joyful, Let earth her song begin
244	T,1	O Holy Spirit, Enter In, Among these hearts thy work begin
299	3	Till hearts of stone begin to beat
461	1	All is safely gathered in Ere the winter storms begin
462	1	All is safely gathered in Ere the winter storms begin

beginning

21	2	So from the beginning the fight we were winning
100	4	As it was without beginning, So it lasts without an end
197	1	Who from the beginning Was the mighty Word
228	2	Alpha and Omega be, End of faith as its beginning
511	1	As it was in the beginning, is now, and ever shall be

512	1	As it was in the beginning, is now, and ever shall be
512	1	As it was in the beginning, is now, and ever shall be
562	R	As it was in the beginning, is now, and ever shall be
565	R	As it was in the beginning, is now, and ever shall be
568	R	As it was in the beginning, is now, and ever shall be

begotten

2	3	O Jesus Christ, our God and Lord, Begotten of the Father
111	T,1	Of the Father's Love Begotten, Ere the world began to be
291	1	First-begotten from the dead
554	4	O Lord, the only begotten Son, Jesus Christ

begun

42	4	And for mankind at last Day has begun
105	1	Hail, in the time appointed, His reign on earth begun
127	1	With them the joyful tidings first begun
127	1	tidings first begun of God incarnate and the Virgin's Son
181	1	The victory of life is won, The song of triumph has begun
331	2	Some work of love begun, Some deed of kindness done
362	4	Blest Savior, introduced by thee, Have I my race begun
387	3	One the conflict, one the peril, One the march in God begun

behavior

| 249 | 3 | Stilling the rude wills of men's wild behavior |

beheld

| 421 | 2 | But often in some far off Galilee Beheld thee fairer |
| 421 | 2 | Beheld thee fairer yet while serving thee |

behest

| 47 | 1 | The darkness falls at thy behest |

behind

42	4	Now shall you find at last Night's left behind at last
87	3	Behind a frowning providence He hides a smiling face
427	2	Will ye play then, will ye dally Far behind the battle line
441	3	behind the dim unknown, Standeth God within the shadow

behold

2	3	Thou Lamb of God, enthroned on high Behold our need
3	3	Like the holy angels Who behold thy glory ... adore thee
16	4	Angels, help us to adore him, Ye behold him face to face
23	2	And now, from sin released, Behold the Savior's face
67	4	Thee in man's spirit we behold
85	2	Behold, he that keeps Israel, He slumbers not, nor sleeps
92	4	Thy hand in all things I behold, and all things in thy hand
114	1	Behold the King of glory waits
119	T,1	As With Gladness Men of Old Did the guiding star behold
120	2	Late in time behold him come, Offspring of the Virgin's womb
127	2	Behold, I bring good tidings of a Savior's birth
131	2	With Mary we behold it, The Virgin Mother kind
132	1	Come and behold him, born the King of angels
143	5	Glorious now behold him arise, King and God and Sacrifice

beholdest

beholding

being

beings

believe

believed

believer's

believers

believeth

258	1	Who its truth believeth Light and joy receiveth

believing

328	1	O come to him, come now to him With a believing mind
357	1	Believing where we cannot prove
377	4	Zion, if thou die believing, Heaven's path shall open lie

bells

270	1	Bells still are chiming and calling
453	T,1	Ring Out, Wild Bells, to the wild sky
453	1	Ring out, wild bells, and let him die
453	2	Ring, happy bells, across the snow

belong

65	3	Silent powers and angels' song ... All unto our God belong
69	2	Those to whom the arts belong Add their voices to the song
224	2	To thee our full humanity, Its joys and pains belong
295	4	Inspired with hope and praise, To Christ belong
475	4	To thee they all belong ... treasures of the earth and sea

belongs

49	3	To thee of right belongs All praise of holy songs
135	2	Whate'er we have belongs to thee

beloved

108	2	Ah, come thou blessed One, God's own beloved Son
128	3	his mother ... Worshipped the beloved With a kiss
275	2	The brothers of thy well-beloved Son
279	T,1	Blessed Jesus, Here Are We, Thy beloved word obeying

below

11	T,1	From All That Dwell Below the Skies
12	T,1	From All That Dwell Below the Skies (No. 11 with alleluias)
19	1	Saints within his courts below
23	3	Ye saints who toil below, Adore your heavenly King
32	5	Praise him, all creatures here below
56	4	Praise him, all creatures here below
67	T,1	God of Earth, the Sky, the Sea, Maker of all above, below
68	3	not a plant or flower below But makes thy glories known
77	2	His voice who ruled them while he dwelt below
89	4	Lord of all life, below, above
99	3	We read thee in the earth below
200	3	The joy of all who dwell above, The joy of all below
219	1	Who once appeared in humblest guise below
223	3	By saints below and saints above
374	3	Or should pain attend me On my path below
388	1	Who patient bears his cross below, He follows in his train
459	1	To cheer the plains below
486	1	Birds above me fly, Flowers bloom below
514	1	Praise him, all creatures here below
515	1	Praise him, all creatures here below

bend

113	4	At thy great name exalted now All knees must bend
113	4	All knees must bend, all hearts must bow
119	2	There to bend the knee before Him who heaven and earth adore
129	2	Above its sad and lowly plains They bend on hovering wing
247	4	And adoring bend the knee While we sing our praise to thee
366	3	Bend our pride to thy control

bended

| 116 | 3 | Come adore on bended knee Christ the Lord, the new-born King |
| 400 | 1 | Hear thou the prayer I make On bended knee |

bending

117	4	Saints before the altar bending
129	1	From angels bending near the earth
129	3	ye, beneath life's crushing load Whose forms are bending low
305	2	See all the nations bending Before the God we love

bends

| 92 | 3 | Thy calmness bends serene above, My restlessness to still |
| 199 | 2 | But downward bends his burning eye At mysteries so bright |

beneath

45	2	Lord of life, beneath the dome Of the universe, thy home
56	1	O keep me, King of kings Beneath thine own almighty wings
91	4	Beneath his wings shalt thou confide
129	3	ye, beneath life's crushing load Whose forms are bending low
160	T,1	Beneath the Cross of Jesus I fain would take my stand
194	2	Then shout beneath the racing skies
266	2	Beneath the pine or palm
309	1	Beneath thy contemplation Sink heart and voice oppressed
354	2	Nor shades of death, nor hell beneath, Our souls ... sever
381	2	Whether beneath was flinty rock Or yielding grassy sod
419	1	Whose life ... is freely poured On all beneath the sun
431	1	Beneath whose awful hand we hold Dominion over palm and pine
438	T,1	O God, Beneath Thy Guiding Hand
493	3	Fell crushed beneath the stones

benediction

263	2	And thy fullest benediction Shed within its walls alway
315	1	It tells of benediction, Of pardon, grace and peace
540	T,1	Father, Give Thy Benediction, Give thy peace before we part

bent

249	1	To thee all knees are bent, all voices pray
381	2	Unstayed by pleasures, still they bent Their zealous course
381	2	they bent Their zealous course to God

bereft

| 174 | 4 | Thou, who once wast thus bereft |
| 416 | 4 | Perfect love bereft of fear |

beseech

| 301 | 1-5 | We beseech thee, hear us |

532	1	Son of God, we beseech thee to hear us
532	1	We beseech thee to hear us, O Lord
544	1	and write all these thy laws in our hearts, we beseech thee

beset

354	2	Though Satan's wrath beset our path
371	2	Who so beset him round With dismal stories

beside

21	2	Beside us to guide us, our God with us joining
79	4	I fear no ill With thee, dear Lord, beside me
92	2	Shamed by its failures or its fears, I sink beside the road
129	3	O rest beside the weary road, And hear the angels sing
136	2	Ox and ass beside him From the cold would hide him
220	1	Beside us walks our brother Christ, & makes our task his own
220	3	The tasks he gives are those he gave Beside the restless sea
222	1	I will ... Ask for nought beside thee
251	3	Only thou art holy, there is none beside thee Perfect
254	1	As thou didst break the loaves Beside the sea
325	2	a nation's pride o'erthrown, Went down to dust beside thee
333	2	To pastures green beside the peaceful waters
341	2	In simple trust like theirs who heard, Beside the Syrian sea
343	2	My shepherd is beside me, And nothing can I lack
360	4	And so beside the silent sea I wait the muffled oar
398	3	Walk thou beside us lest the tempting byways Lure us away
446	3	Falsehood and wrong shall not tarry beside thee

bespeaks

311	2	What ringing of a thousand harps Bespeaks the triumph nigh

best

31	2	Guiding thy steps as may best for thee be
55	4	they who fain would serve thee best Are conscious most
55	4	who serve thee best .... Are conscious most of wrong within
77	1	thy best, thy heavenly friend Through thorny ways leads
98	4	I thank thee, Lord, that thou hast kept The best in store
99	4	We read thee best in him who came To bear for us the cross
126	T,1,5	Brightest and Best of the Sons of the Morning
161	3	We crave the power to do thy will With him who did it best
253	1	All the best we have we owe thee
290	1	From the best bliss that earth imparts, We turn unfilled
317	2	I love to tell the story, For those who know it best
322	5	Serve and love thee best of all
352	3	Low lies the best till lifted up to heaven
376	4	Through joy or sorrow, as thou deemest best
388	1	Who best can drink the cup of woe, Triumphant over pain
391	1	Thou my best thought, by day or by night
400	2	Now thee alone I seek, Give what is best
409	3	Jesus, thou divine companion, Help us all to work our best
442	2	In best and worst reveal us

bestow

169	2	He came from his blest throne, salvation to bestow
339	2	Daily doth the almighty giver Bounteous gifts on us bestow

bestowed
94	2	Unnumbered comforts to my soul Thy tender care bestowed
471	1	For all thy gifts bestowed upon our race

bestoweth
79	5	Thy unction grace bestoweth

bestowing
185	4	But today amidst the twelve Thou didst stand, bestowing
239	1	And kindle it, thy holy flame bestowing

Bethel
351	4	Out of my stony griefs Bethel I'll raise
389	T,1	O God of Bethel, by Whose Hand Thy people still are fed

Bethlehem
116	3	Come to Bethlehem and see Him whose birth the angels sing
120	1	With the angelic host proclaim, Christ is born in Bethlehem
122	2	How that in Bethlehem was born The Son of God by name
127	3	To Bethlehem straight the enlightened shepherds ran
132	1	O come ye, O come ye to Bethlehem
133	1	Laeti triumphantes, Venite, venite in Bethlehem
134	T,1	O Little Town of Bethlehem, How still we see thee lie
134	4	O holy Child of Bethlehem, Descend to us, we pray
136	2	Bethlehem saw his birth
141	4	O'er Bethlehem it took its rest

Bethlehem's
143	2	Born a king on Bethlehem's plain
149	T,1	I Know Not How That Bethlehem's Babe Could in the Godhead be
326	1	But in Bethlehem's home there was found no room

Bethlem
142	3	All the little boys he killed At Bethlem in his fury

betide
83	1	He'll give thee strength whate'er betide thee

betrayed
150	4	For us to wicked men betrayed
452	3	What skill and science slowly gain Is soon ... betrayed
452	3	Is soon to evil ends betrayed
558	1	And friends betrayed him to his foes

better
224	3	The solemn shadow of thy cross Is better than the sun
259	1	No, let a new and better hope Within our hearts be stirred
445	4	O give us brother love for better seeing Thy Word made flesh

between
292	2	lo, between our sins and their reward, We set the passion
439	1	Standing in the living present, Memory and hope between

| 496 | 2 | stand Between their loved homes and the war's desolation |
| 569 | 4 | and dwellest between the cherubim |

bewildering

| 249 | 2 | Through seas dry-shod, through weary wastes bewildering |

beyond

14	1	The First, the Last, beyond all thought His timeless years
99	1	Beyond all knowledge and all thought
141	2	Shining in the east, beyond them far
248	2	Beyond our ken thou shinest, The everlasting Light
254	1	Beyond the sacred page I seek thee, Lord
256	2	Our guide & chart, wherein we read Of realms beyond the sky
269	4	Beyond my highest joy I prize her heavenly ways
303	3	Beyond the present sin and shame
303	3	Beyond ... Wrong's bitter, cruel, scorching blight
309	1	What radiancy of glory, What bliss beyond compare
360	3	I only know I cannot drift Beyond his love and care
388	2	martyr first, whose eagle eye Could pierce beyond the grave
440	4	O beautiful for patriot dream That sees beyond the years
468	3	Not wandering in unknown despair Beyond thy voice
468	3	Beyond thy voice, thine arm, thy care

bid

42	4	Bid then farewell to sleep Rise up and run
60	4	Then, when thy voice shall bid our conflict cease
93	3	Bid my anxious fears subside
105	2	To help the poor and needy, And bid the weak be strong
110	4	Bid envy, strife and quarrels cease
232	3	Hast thou not bid us love thee, God and King
348	3	Be thou my guide, Bid darkness turn to day
405	4	And when earth's labors cease, Bid us depart in peace
413	3	Bid its cruel discords cease
446	2	Bid not thy wrath in its terrors awaken

bidd'st

| 319 | 1 | And that thou bidd'st me come to thee |
| 429 | 1 | Who bidd'st the mighty ocean deep Its ... limits keep |

biddest

| 279 | 1 | Now these children come to thee As thou biddest |
| 279 | 1 | As thou biddest in thy saying |

bidding

| 104 | 2 | Bidding all men to repentance Since the kingdom now is here |

bide

| 54 | 1 | with us bide, Thou that canst never set in night |

bids

47	4	The sun that bids us rest is waking Our brethren
420	4	bids us seize the whole of life And build its glory there
459	2	he bids the sun cut short his race, And wintry days appear
459	3	He calls the warmer gales to blow And bids the spring return

big

87	2	The clouds ye so much dread Are big with mercy

bind

86	2	we ... Have tried, with thoughts uncouth ... to bind thee
86	2	we ... Have tried ... In feeble words to bind thee
110	4	Desire of nations, bind All peoples in one heart and mind
301	2	And the broken-hearted bind
429	1	Whose arm doth bind the restless wave
436	3	Bind all our lives together, Smite us and save us all
466	3	O spirit, who dost bind Our hearts in unity

binding

263	1	Binding all the Church in one
414	2	His service is the golden cord Close-binding all mankind

binds

8	4	Brother love binds man to man
272	T,1	Blest Be the Tie That Binds Our hearts in Christian love
273	T,1	Blest Be the Tie That Binds (same words as no. 272)
304	4	Church ... binds the ransomed nations 'neath the sun
419	1	Whose purpose binds the starry spheres
419	1	binds the starry spheres In one stupendous whole

bird

8	2	Chanting bird & flowing fountain call us to rejoice in thee
37	1	When the bird waketh, and the shadows flee
38	1	Blackbird has spoken Like the first bird
478	1	Each little flower that opens, Each little bird that sings

birds

152	3	While birds and flowers and sky above are preaching
194	1	The birds do sing on every bough
326	3	The foxes found rest, and the birds their nest In the shade
457	3	The summer days are come again, The birds are on the wing
460	2	The winds and waves obey him, By him the birds are fed
485	2	The birds their carols raise
486	1	Birds above me fly, Flowers bloom below

birth

66	1	For the love which from our birth Over and around us lies
72	2	Repeats the story of her birth
74	1	Bringing suns and stars to birth
109	2	Gild the spot that gave them birth
116	3	Come to Bethlehem and see Him whose birth the angels sing
117	1	Ye who sang creation's story Now proclaim Messiah's birth
121	2	This little child, of lowly birth, Shall be the joy
127	2	Behold, I bring good tidings of a Savior's birth
134	2	O morning stars, together Proclaim the holy birth
136	2	Bethlehem saw his birth
138	3	With the dawn of redeeming grace, Jesus, Lord, at thy birth
260	2	Her charter of salvation, One Lord, one faith, one birth
326	2	But in lowly birth didst thou come to earth
392	+1	Land of our birth, we pledge to thee Our love and toil

392	+2	Land of our birth, our faith, our pride
392	+2	Land of our birth ... For whose dear sake our fathers died
395	5	Then let us prove our heavenly birth In all we do and know
409	1	By thy lowly human birth Thou hast come to join the workers
413	1	Son of man, whose birth incarnate Hallows all our human race
444	5	O Day of God, draw nigh As at creation's birth
449	1	Let broad humanity have birth
458	5	Praise for happy dreams of birth Brooding in the quiet earth
488	2	Rang out the angel chorus That hailed our Savior's birth

bitter

127	4	Trace we the babe ... his poor manger to his bitter cross
143	4	Myrrh is mine, its bitter perfume
158	1	Watch with him one bitter hour
162	4	There behold his agony, Suffered on the bitter tree
163	3	Thy death of anguish and thy bitter passion For my salvation
168	4	Until thou see thy bitter travail's ending
174	4	Teach me by that bitter cry In the gloom to know thee nigh
185	1	Loosed from Pharaoh's bitter yoke Jacob's sons and daughters
237	4	Earth's bitter voices drown In one deep ocean of accord
303	3	Beyond ... Wrong's bitter, cruel, scorching blight
330	4	I cannot look upon his face For shame, for bitter shame
392	6	And mirth that has no bitter springs
398	2	To heal earth's wounds and end her bitter strife
420	2	And bitter lips in blind despair Cry
435	1	Purge this land of bitter things
452	1	in bitter need Thy children lift their cry to thee

bitterness

207	4	No harshness hast thou and no bitterness
209	4	Ills have no weight, and tears no bitterness
265	2	Let all past bitterness Now and forever cease

black

42	1	Black turns to gray, Bird-song the valley fills

blackbird

38	1	Blackbird has spoken Like the first bird

blade

381	1	My faith, it is a weapon stout, The soldier's trusty blade
461	2	First the blade, and then the ear

blameless

113	3	child Of Mary, blameless mother mild
301	3	Blameless witnesses for thee

blast

1	1	Our shelter from the stormy blast, And our eternal home
86	3	The deep-toned organ blast That rolls through arches dim

blaze

308	2	Toilers at the furnace-blaze

399	2	That in thy sunshine's blaze its day May brighter, fairer be
442	2	Shed on our souls a blaze of light

blazing
| 89 | 4 | Before thy ever-blazing throne We ask no luster of our own |

blazoned
| 421 | 1 | lead To blazoned heights and down the slopes of need |
| 427 | 2 | Now, the blazoned cross unfolding |

bleak
128	T,1	In the bleak Midwinter, Frosty wind made moan
128	1	In the bleak midwinter, Long ago
128	2	In the bleak midwinter A stable place sufficed

bled
| 472 | 4 | O Christ, the Church's head, Who for us all has bled |
| 472 | 4 | bled That we might live |

bleed
| 166 | 3 | When with wrong our spirits bleed, Hear us, holy Jesus |

bleeding
143	4	Sorrowing, sighing, bleeding, dying
424	3	Oft with bleeding hands and tears
441	2	Jesus' bleeding feet I track, Toiling up new Calvaries ever

blend
| 382 | 4 | Blend with ours your voices In the triumph song |

blended
| 508 | 2 | The blended notes of age and youth |

blending
3	2	Angels, saints, their voices blending
52	1	Let our vesper hymn be blending With the holy calm around
344	3	Love with every passion blending

bless
4	3	Praise, laud, and bless his name always
16	2	same forever, Slow to chide and swift to bless
22	1	We bless thy holy name, glad praises we sing
22	2	We worship thee, God of our fathers, we bless thee
25	T,1	Stand Up and Bless the Lord, Ye people of his choice
25	1	Stand up & bless the Lord your God with heart & soul & voice
25	4	Stand up and bless the Lord, The Lord your God adore
25	4	Stand up and bless his glorious name Henceforth for evermore
50	5	Come near and bless us when we wake
60	1	We stand to bless thee ere our worship cease
64	5	Let all things their creator bless
97	2	With thee to bless, the darkness shines as light
99	5	We read thy power to bless and save
99	5	bless and save E'en in the darkness of the grave
100	T,1	O My Soul, Bless God, the Father

100	1	All within me bless his name
100	6	Bless the Father, all his creatures, Ever under his control
100	6	All throughout his vast dominion Bless the Father, O my soul
145	2	Toward thee longing Doth possess me, turn and bless me
184	4	Thy name we bless, O risen Lord
209	4	I fear no foe, with thee at hand to bless
212	3	Hear, and bless our prayers and praises
229	2	Great Prophet of my God, My tongue would bless thy name
246	2	Come, and thy people bless, And give thy word success
254	2	Bless thou the truth, dear Lord, To me, to me
254	2	As thou didst bless the bread By Galilee
268	3	Bless thy Church's new endeavor
271	3	Bless the same boundless Giver
276	3	dwell thou ... to guide and bless
332	5	Heavenly Father, bless thy children
333	T,1	Father Almighty, Bless Us With Thy Blessing
342	R	O bless me now, my Savior, I come to thee
372	3	For I will be near thee, thy troubles to bless
407	4	And let thy mercy bless Thy servant more and more
409	3	Bless us in our daily labor, Lead us to our sabbath rest
466	1	Bless thou all parents, guarding well, With constant love
466	2	Our children bless, in every place
468	4	And bless thee for the love which gave Thy Son
470	T,1	God of the Prophets, bless the prophets' sons
484	3	God bless the men and women Who serve him over-sea
520	1	and bless all souls that wait before thee
538	T,1	Bless Thou the Gifts our hands have brought
538	1	Bless thou the work our hearts have planned
542	T,1	Sweet Savior, Bless Us Ere We Go
554	2	We praise thee, we bless thee, we worship thee
559	13	O Lord, save thy people and bless thine heritage

blessed

7	1	Most blessed, most glorious, the Ancient of Days
23	2	Ye blessed souls at rest, Who ran this earthly race
29	1	Who, from our mothers' arms, Hath blessed us on our way
29	2	With ever joyful hearts And blessed peace to cheer us
37	3	So does this blessed consciousness, awaking, Breathe
41	3	All holy Father, Son and equal Spirit, Trinity blessed
77	3	All safe and blessed we shall meet at last
108	2	Ah, come thou blessed One, God's own beloved Son
122	2	From God, our heavenly Father, A blessed angel came
125	2	He hath oped the heavenly door, And man is blessed evermore
127	3	And found, with Joseph and the blessed maid, Her Son
129	2	And ever o'er its Babel sounds The blessed angels sing
155	2	Who in the Lord's name cometh, The King and blessed One
212	T,1	Blessed Jesus, at Thy Word, We are gathered all to hear thee
231	2	blessed unction from above Is comfort, life and fire of love
247	3	And the blessed martyrs follow
248	3	I walk secure and blessed In every clime or coast
249	1	Thy love has blessed the wide world's wondrous story
249	1	blessed ... With light and life since Eden's dawning day
251	1,4	God in three persons, blessed Trinity
263	3	What they gain from thee forever With the blessed to retain

277	1	Grant to them thy dearest blessing
278	1	So give this child of thine, we pray Thy grace and blessing
278	1	Thy grace and blessing day by day
286	2	Thou at the table, blessing, yet dost stand
305	2	And seek the Savior's blessing, A nation in a day
333	T,1	Father Almighty, Bless Us With Thy Blessing
344	1	Yet possessing every blessing, If our God our Father be
395	3	On homeliest work thy blessing falls
430	2	Glad shalt thou be, with blessing crowned
438	2	Thy blessing came, and still its power Shall onward
459	1	He sends his showers of blessing down To cheer the plains
510	2	With thy tenderest blessing May our eyelids close
526	1	O let thy children share thy blessing from on high

blessings

32	5	Praise God from whom all blessings flow
34	1	Their blessings on the Lord of life, As he goes meekly by
50	4	Watch by the sick, enrich the poor with blessings
50	4	With blessings from thy boundless store
56	1	All praise to thee ... For all the blessings of the light
56	4	Praise God, from whom all blessings flow
87	2	clouds ... shall break In blessings on your head
134	3	So God imparts to human hearts The blessings of his heaven
202	3	And infant voices shall proclaim their early blessings
202	3	Their early blessings on his name
202	4	Blessings abound where'er he reigns
462	2	All the blessings of the field
462	3	Source whence all our blessings flow
464	2	For the blessings of the field
464	3	Source whence all our blessings flow
514	1	Praise God from whom all blessings flow
515	1	Praise God from whom all blessings flow

blest

8	3	Thou art giving and forgiving, Ever blessing, ever blest
26	1	Praise him with a glad accord & with lives of noblest worth
30	3	Respond ... Ye patriarchs and prophets blest, Alleluia
49	1	The eternal splendor wearing, Celestial, holy, blest
81	3	How blest are they, and only they, Who in his truth confide
105	4	From age to age more glorious, All-blessing and all-blest
169	2	He came from his blest throne, salvation to bestow
191	4	How blest are they who have not seen
214	T,1	Blest Are the Pure in Heart For they shall see our God
215	3	So long thy power hath blest me
225	2	Nor can the memory find A sweeter sound than thy blest name
238	4	To be with him for ever blest
241	3	let thy Church on earth become Blest as the Church above
250	3	Blest and Holy Trinity, Praise forever be to thee
257	2	But the blest volume thou hast writ Reveals thy justice
257	4	Till Christ has all the nations blest
260	3	Till with the vision glorious, Her longing eyes are blest
269	1	Church our blest Redeemer saved With his own precious blood
272	T,1	Blest Be the Tie That Binds Our hearts in Christian love

273	T,1	Blest Be the Tie That Binds (same words as no. 272)
274	4	That man is truly blest Who only on thee doth rely
281	2	Vine of heaven, thy love supplies ... blest cup of sacrifice
286	3	One Church united in communion blest
290	3	Blest when our faith can hold thee fast
305	3	Blest river of salvation, Pursue thy onward way
306	1	Thy name, O Jesus, be forever blest
306	4	O blest communion, fellowship divine
309	T,1	Jerusalem the Golden, with milk and honey blest
309	4	Who art, with God the Father And Spirit, ever blest
310	1	God shall be all, and in all ever blest
312	3	Ten thousand times that man were blest ... this music hear
316	2	Thou hast blest us with thy favor
328	3	with his light thou shalt be blest, Therein to work and live
348	4	Blest Savior, then, in love, Fear and distrust remove
362	4	Blest Savior, introduced by thee, Have I my race begun
365	2	And blest would be their children's fate If they ... die for
359	3	Thrice blest is he to whom is given The instinct
359	4	Blest too is he who can divine Where real right doth lie
463	4	Glory to the Father, Son, And blest Spirit, Three in One
469	4	Living or dying, they are blest
496	2	Blest with victory and peace, may the heaven-rescued land
558	2	He took the bread and blest and brake

blight

303	3	Beyond ... Wrong's bitter, cruel, scorching blight
352	2	The mist of doubt, the blight of love's decay
441	1	God's new messiah, Offering each the bloom or blight

blind

44	1	love's blind instinct made them bold to crave thy presence
87	4	Blind unbelief is sure to err And scan his work in vain
169	4	He made the lame to run, He gave the blind their sight
301	2	May she guide the poor and blind
319	3	Just as I am, poor, wretched, blind
420	2	And bitter lips in blind despair Cry

blinded

231	2	Enable with perpetual light The dullness of... blinded sight
405	3	Some balm of peace for eyes Blinded with tears
575	2	The dullness of our blinded sight

blindfold

359	4	seems Wrong to man's blindfold eye

blindly

376	3	Blindly we stumble when we walk alone
386	1	night Through which we blindly stumble to the day

blindness

53	3	Awhile his mortal blindness May miss God's lovingkindness
445	1	Light to man's blindness, O be thou our aid

bliss

35	5	In heaven's eternal bliss The loveliest strain is this
98	3	So that earth's bliss may be our guide, And not our chain
125	2	Now ye hear of endless bliss, Jesus Christ was born for this
128	3	But his mother only, In her maiden bliss
157	3	When the sun of bliss is beaming Light and love upon my way
217	1	Your bliss in our hearts, Lord, at the break of the day
269	5	brightest glories earth can yield & brighter bliss of heaven
290	1	From the best bliss that earth imparts, We turn unfilled
309	1	What radiancy of glory, What bliss beyond compare

blithe

73	4	Each blithe voice its free song singing

blood

2	4	For us the Savior's blood was shed
107	2	Lord of lords, in human vesture, In the body and the blood
166	T,1	Jesus, in Thy Dying Woes, Even while thy life-blood flows
167	V-1	While thy wounds thy life-blood drain
171	3	we might go at last to heaven, Saved by his precious blood
171	4	And trust in his redeeming blood, And try his works to do
177	2	I sacrifice them to his blood
178	3	The Man of Sorrows weeps in blood
236	3	Pulsing in the hero's blood
260	1	With his own blood he bought her, And for her life he died
269	1	Church our blest Redeemer saved With his own precious blood
280	2	There sup with us in love divine, Thy body and thy blood
319	1	But that thy blood was shed for me
358	1	Let the water & the blood, From thy riven side which flowed
422	2	Shooting out tongues of flame like leaping blood
450	2	strong To spill no drop of blood
452	4	For us his tears and blood were spent
453	4	Ring out false pride in place and blood
558	3	'Tis the new covenant in my blood
559	11	servants whom thou hast redeemed with thy precious blood

bloom

441	1	God's new messiah, Offering each the bloom or blight
486	1	Birds above me fly, Flowers bloom below

blooming

131	T,1	Lo, How a Rose E'er Blooming From tender stem hath sprung
227	2	woodlands Robed in the blooming garb of spring

blossom

7	3	We blossom and flourish as leaves on the tree
95	2	Truth from the earth, like a flower, Shall bud and blossom

blossoms

399	4	from the ground ... blossoms red Life that shall endless be

blow

67	2	When lightnings flash and storm-winds blow ... is thy power

68	3	clouds arise, and tempests blow, By order from thy throne
455	1	Through leafless boughs the sharp winds blow
455	3	And though abroad the sharp winds blow
459	3	He calls the warmer gales to blow And bids the spring return

bloweth

| 328 | 2 | thou shalt surely feel His wind, that bloweth healthily |

blue

| 51 | 3 | Guard the sailors tossing On the deep blue sea |
| 72 | 1 | blue ethereal sky And spangled heavens, a shining frame |

board

| 286 | 1 | Thyself at thine own board make manifest in ...our sacrament |

boast

177	2	Forbid it, Lord, that I should boast
194	4	Our God most high, our joy and boast
227	3	Jesus shines purer Than all the angels heaven can boast
425	T,1	Men, Whose Boast It Is that ye Come of fathers brave & free
431	5	For frantic boast and foolish word, Thy mercy
432	2	Thine ancient might destroyed the Pharaoh's boast

boastings

| 431 | 4 | Such boastings as the Gentiles use Or lesser breeds |

boasts

| 449 | 1 | Let there be deeds, instead of boasts |

bodies

| 270 | 2 | to abide on earth with men, Built in our bodies his temple |

body

20	3	Both soul and body bear your part
59	2	In soul and body, thou from harm defend us
107	2	Lord of lords, in human vesture, In the body and the blood
183	1	Kept the folded grave-clothes Where the body lay
280	2	There sup with us in love divine, Thy body and thy blood
284	2	Thy body, broken for my sake, My bread from heaven shall be
286	2	This is my body, so thou givest yet
286	3	One body we, one body who partake
330	3	And not unworthy for my sake A mortal body deem
354	3	O God, renew with heavenly dew Our body, soul and spirit
363	4	The body they may kill, God's truth abideth still
382	2	We are not divided, All one body we
435	3	Cleanse the body of this nation Through the ... Lord
558	3	'This is my body, broke for sin

boisterous

| 213 | 2 | Boisterous waves obey thy will |

bold

| 44 | 1 | love's blind instinct made them bold to crave thy presence |

44	1	bold To crave thy presence through the night
245	1	with actions bold and meek Would for Christ my Savior speak
268	3	For thy kingdom make us bold
304	2	Till saint and martyr sped the venture bold
306	3	O may thy soldiers, faithful, true and bold Fight
308	2	Bold adventurers on the sea
380	1	Who 'gainst enthroned wrong Stood confident and bold
412	3	Give us a conscience bold and good, Give us a purpose true
428	2	Thus saith the Lord, bold Moses said

bombs
496	1	And the rockets' red glare, the bombs bursting in air

bond
106	5	City of God, the bond are free
276	2	The common home of rich and poor, Of bond and free
308	2	Prince and peasant, bond and free
448	2	One in the bond of peace

bondage
198	1	Freedom her bondage breaks, And night is turned to day
254	2	Then shall all bondage cease, All fetters fall
428	3	No more in bondage shall they toil

bonds
229	4	behold I sit In willing bonds before thy feet
324	1	O burst these bonds, and set it free
413	4	Liked in bonds of common service For the common Lord of all
426	1	Whom shall I send to loosen The bonds of shame and greed
450	4	For man shall be at one with God in bonds of firm necessity
452	4	That from our bonds we might be freed

bones
493	3	had no curse nor vengeful cry For those who broke his bones

book
236	4	Consecrating art and song, Holy book and pilgrim track
253	T,1	Book of Books, Our People's Strength

books
253	T,1	Book of Books, Our People's Strength

boons
407	2	Above all boons, I pray, Grant me thy voice to hear

borders
424	1	Wrong is banished from its borders
432	1	stand Here in the borders of our promised land

bore
131	2	To show God's love aright She bore to men a Savior
150	2	for us he bore His holy fast, and hungered sore
150	4	He bore the shameful cross and death

born

180	2	Christ from death to life is born
295	4	The new-born souls, whose days Reclaimed from error's ways
296	2	And nations, crowding to be born, Baptize their spirits
314	1	From earth-born passions set me free
416	4	Born in heaven and radiant here
417	1	When the pain is sorest the child is born
427	3	Sworn to yield, to waver, never, Consecrated, born again
428	2	If not I'll smite your first-born dead
443	4	In the beauty of the lilies Christ was born across the sea
488	R	Go, tell it on the mountain That Jesus Christ is born
488	3	Down in a lowly manger The humble Christ was born
559	8	Thou didst humble thyself to be born of a virgin

borne
178	4	'Tis midnight, and from heavenly plains Is borne the song
178	4	Is borne the song that angels know
316	2	Borne thy witness in all ages

borrow
170	3	What language shall I borrow To thank thee, dearest friend

borrowed
399	2	My heart restores its borrowed ray

borrows
68	3	While all that borrows life from thee Is ever in thy care

bosom
210	T,1	Jesus, Lover of My Soul, Let me to thy bosom fly
356	3	When on thy bosom it has leant And found in thee its life
443	4	With a glory in his bosom that transfigures you and me

bosoms
327	3	Blessed Lord and only Savior, With thy love our bosoms fill
347	3	And kindness in our bosoms dwell As free and true as thine

both
7	3	To all, life thou givest to both great and small
18	2	Both cherubim and seraphim, Continually do cry
20	3	Both soul and body bear your part
60	3	For dark and light are both alike to thee
64	3	That givest man both warmth and light
141	2	And so it continued both day and night
182	5	Praise to thee by both be given
248	3	O God, thou doest all things, All things both new and old
250	3	We all confess the Holy Ghost Who from both fore'er proceeds
294	T,1	Eternal God, Whose Power Upholds Both flower & flaming star
365	4	Faith of our fathers, we will love Both friend and foe
365	4	love Both friend and foe in all our strife
414	4	In Christ now meet both East and West
473	T,1	O Lord, Almighty God, Thy Works Both great and wondrous be
575	4	Teach us to know the Father, Son, And thee, of both to be
575	4	And thee, of both, to be but one
576	5	To thee both night and day are bright

bough
194	1	The birds do sing on every bough

boughs
455	1	Through leafless boughs the sharp winds blow
455	2	And clothes the boughs with glittering wreaths

bought
260	1	With his own blood he bought her, And for her life he died
292	1	love That bought us, once for all, on Calvary's tree
327	1	Blessed Jesus, Thou hast bought us, thine we are

bound
158	2	Beaten, bound, reviled, arraigned
242	4	Be my law, and I shall be Firmly bound, forever free
325	1	Upon a cross they bound thee
366	2	From the fears that long have bound us Free our hearts
383	3	Bound by God's far purpose In one living whole
452	2	Our souls are bound In iron chains of fear and pride
459	2	The liquid streams forbear to flow, In icy fetters bound

bounding
352	3	Low lie the bounding heart, the teeming brain

boundless
2	2	Thy boundless power o'er all things reigns
18	5	That thou eternal Father art, Of boundless majesty
50	4	With blessings from thy boundless store
106	2	He comes to reign with boundless sway
271	3	Bless the same boundless Giver
315	4	Of love so free and boundless, To come, dear Lord, to thee
367	3	His boundless mercy will provide
422	2	Sing of the boundless energy of God
487	T,1	Praise Our God Above For his boundless love
508	2	O boundless Mercy pardoning all
539	1	And the Father's boundless love

bounds
475	1	glory fills The bounds of the eternal hills

bounteous
29	2	O may this bounteous God Through all our life be near us
73	4	Praise him ever, bounteous giver
339	2	Daily doth the almighty giver Bounteous gifts on us bestow
433	3	Thy bounteous goodness nourish us in peace
439	1	Not alone for bounteous harvests Lift we up our hearts
462	2	All that spring with bounteous hand Scatters
463	4	Glory to our bounteous King, Glory let creation sing
464	1	Bounteous source of every joy
464	3	All that spring with bounteous hand Scatters

bountiful
6	4	Thy bountiful care, what tongue can recite

bounty

26	1	Raise your voice and rejoice In the bounty of his hand
413	2	We but stewards of thy bounty, Held in solemn trust for thee
454	2	By his incessant bounty fed, By his unerring counsel led

bow

3	2	Bow thine ear To us here
9	1	Ye nations bow with sacred joy
16	4	Sun and moon, bow down before him
31	1	Bow down before him, his glory proclaim
46	3	O God, our Light, to thee we bow
74	1	Humbly now we bow before thee
75	4	To thy sway all creatures bow
95	4	all shall frame To bow them low before thee, Lord
104	2	And the hills bow down to greet him
111	2	Powers, dominions, bow before him
113	4	All knees must bend, all hearts must bow
125	1	Ox and ass before him bow, And he is in the manger now
175	4	Bow thy meek head to mortal pain
197	T,1	At the Name of Jesus Every knee shall bow
203	1	Every knee to him shall bow
247	1	Lord of all, we bow before thee
291	2	Here in loving reverence bow
331	1	In love my soul would bow, My heart fulfill its vow
386	3	Lighten our darkness when we bow the knee To all the gods
436	T,1	O God of Earth and Altar, Bow down and hear our cry
458	1	Hearts, bow down, & voices, sing Praises to the glorious One
458	6	Hearts, bow down and voices, sing Praise and love
499	1	And silent bow before his face
509	3	O God, our Light, to thee we bow
521	1	Our hearts in true devotion bow

bowed

249	2	To thee in reverent love, our hearts are bowed
332	3	While in prayer we bowed the knee
388	3	They bowed their necks the death to feel

bower

95	2	justice, from her heavenly bower, Look down on mortal men

boy

142	T,1	Unto Us a Boy Is Born, The King of all creation

boyhood

412	1	We thank thee for thy boyhood faith
412	1	boyhood faith That shone thy whole life through

boys

142	3	All the little boys he killed At Bethlem in his fury
388	4	A noble army, men and boys, The matron and the maid

brain

308	3	strong in heart and hand and brain

| 352 | 3 | Low lie the bounding heart, the teeming brain |
| 450 | 3 | In every heart and brain shall throb the pulse of one |

brake

| 558 | 2 | He took the bread and blest and brake |

brandished

| 388 | 3 | They met the tyrant's brandished steel, The lion's gory mane |

brave

161	3	And make us brave and full of joy To answer to his call
306	5	And hearts are brave again, and arms are strong
308	T,1	For the Brave of Every Race
419	3	The faith that makes men brave
425	T,1	Men, Whose Boast It Is that ye Come of fathers brave & free
450	2	They shall be gentle, brave, and strong
465	2	Of patient hope, and quiet, brave endurance
476	2	Praise we the wise and brave and strong
481	1	saints of God Patient and brave and true
489	1	I would be brave, for there is much to dare
490	3	But give us grace to stand Decided, brave, and strong
491	2	Fill thou our hearts with zeal in every brave endeavor
496	1-2	O'er the land of the free and the home of the brave

bravely

| 242 | 3 | By thee may I strongly live, Bravely bear, and nobly strive |

brawn

| 486 | 1 | Comes the eastern sun Like a man of brawn |
| 486 | 1 | Like a man of brawn Set his course to run |

bread

33	2	Strength unto our souls afford From thy living Bread, O Lord
93	1	Bread of heaven, Feed me till I want no more
97	3	Be thou for us in life our daily bread
254	T,1	Break Thou the Bread of Life, Dear Lord, to me
254	2	As thou didst bless the bread By Galilee
256	2	Bread of our souls, whereon we feed
266	4	With Bread of life earth's hunger feed
280	T,1	Be Known to Us in Breaking Bread, But do not then depart
280	2	That living bread, that heavenly wine, Be our immortal food
281	T,1	Bread of Heaven, on Thee We Feed
281	1	Ever may our souls be fed With this true and living bread
282	T,1	Bread of the World in Mercy Broken
283	T,1	Bread of the World, in Mercy Broken (like 282 in 2 verses)
284	2	Thy body, broken for my sake, My bread from heaven shall be
286	1	In this our sacrament of bread and wine
286	3	One name we bear, one bread of life we break
286	4	Be known to us in breaking of the bread
287	2	Here would I feed upon the bread of God
287	4	The bread and wine remove, but thou art here
288	T,1	Let us Break Bread Together on our knees
289	1	Giving in Christ the bread eternal

289	2	As grain ... Was in this broken bread made one
291	1	Jesus, true and living Bread
389	3	Give us each day our daily bread, And raiment fit provide
398	2	Bringing to hungry souls the bread of life
403	2	Lo, the Bread of heaven is broken in the sacrament of life
409	2	Thou, the Bread of heaven, art broken In the sacrament
460	2	Much more, to us his children, He gives our daily bread
486	2	Give me daily bread While I do my part
557	2	Here would I feed upon the bread of God
558	2	Before the mournful scene began, He took the bread
558	2	He took the bread and blest and brake

break

82	1	Thy truth shall break through every cloud That veils
87	2	clouds ... shall break In blessings on your head
105	1	He comes to break oppression, to set the captive free
106	3	The sleep of ages break, And rise to liberty
106	4	Unvisited, unblest, Break forth to swelling song
118	T,1	Break Forth, O Beauteous Heavenly Light
191	2	That Easter morn at break of day, The faithful women went
217	1	Your bliss in our hearts, Lord, at the break of the day
219	1	Sin to rebuke, to break the captive's chain
254	T,1	Break Thou the Bread of Life, Dear Lord, to me
254	1	As thou didst break the loaves Beside the sea
259	R	The Lord hath yet more light and truth To break forth
259	R	To break forth from his Word
265	1	Break every bar that holds Thy flock in diverse folds
286	3	One name we bear, one bread of life we break
288	T,1	Let us Break Bread Together on our knees
315	2	But morning brings us gladness, And songs the break of day
425	2	Is true freedom but to break Fetters for our own dear sake
437	3	Let rocks their silence break, The sound prolong
470	2	and every evil break

breakers

213	3	When at last I near the shore And the fearful breakers roar

breaketh

37	T,1	Still, Still With Thee, when purple morning breaketh
42	2	Soundless and bright for us Breaketh God's morn
275	3	One with the joy that breaketh into song

breaking

75	2	See the glorious orb of day Breaking through the clouds
75	2	Breaking through the clouds his way
118	1	The power of Satan breaking, Our peace eternal making
280	T,1	Be Known to Us in Breaking Bread, But do not then depart
286	4	Be known to us in breaking of the bread
305	T,1	The Morning Light Is Breaking, The darkness disappears
506	1	Now is breaking O'er the earth another day

breaks

42	3	Suddenly breaks on earth Light from the sky

53	2	all the heavenly splendor Breaks forth in starlight tender
67	3	when the morning breaks in power, We hear thy word
198	1	Freedom her bondage breaks, And night is turned to day
201	1	And light triumphant breaks
209	5	Heaven's morning breaks, and earth's vain shadows flee
212	2	Till thy Spirit breaks our night With the beams of truth
375	3	For gladness breaks like morning Where'er thy face appears
386	4	And daylight breaks across the morning sky
486	T,1	Golden Breaks the Dawn

breast

50	2	Forever on my Savior's breast
115	2	Then cleansed be every Christian breast
197	4	To the throne of God-head, To the Father's breast
213	3	Then, while leaning on thy breast
221	2	And calms the troubled breast
225	1	thought of thee With sweetness fills my breast
228	2	O breathe thy loving Spirit Into every troubled breast
294	2	O God of love, whose spirit wakes In every human breast
349	3	And drove thee from my breast
377	2	Zion, calm the breast that quaketh
441	2	Who would keep abreast of truth
458	5	Snow that falls on nature's breast

breasted

73	2	Mighty mountains, purple breasted

breath

15	4	All ... life and breath, come now with praises before him
17	2	All that hath life and breath, tell the story
150	4	For us gave up his dying breath
169	3	Then, Crucify, Is all their breath
233	T,1-4	Breathe on Me, Breath of God
234	T,1	Breathe on Me, Breath of God (same words as no. 233)
284	3	Yea, while a breath, a pulse remains, Will I remember thee
358	4	While I draw this fleeting breath
400	3	Then shall my latest breath Whisper thy praise
457	1	golden wealth of ripening grain And breath of clover fields

breathe

19	4	All that breathe, your Lord adore ... praise him evermore
37	3	So does this blessed consciousness, awaking, Breathe
37	3	Breathe each day nearness unto thee and heaven
228	2	O breathe thy loving Spirit Into every troubled breast
233	T,1-4	Breathe on Me, Breath of God
234	T,1	Breathe on Me, Breath of God (same words as no. 233)
299	3	Breathe thou abroad like morning air Till hearts ... beat
318	1	Breathe into every wish Thy will divine
341	5	Breathe through the pulses of desire Thy coolness & thy balm
344	2	Savior, breathe forgiveness o'er us
425	1	If there breathe on earth a slave, Are ye truly free & brave
437	3	Let mortal tongues awake, Let all that breathe partake

breathed
173 1   Breathed in the hour of loneliness and pain

breathes
6 4   It breathes in the air, it shines in the light
143 4   Myrrh ... Breathes a life of gathering gloom
316 1   Man, created in thine image, Lives nor breathes without
316 1   Lives nor breathes without thine aid
455 2   His life within the keen air breathes

breathing
236 3   Breathing in the thinker's creed

breathless
37 2   Alone with thee in breathless adoration

breeds
431 4   Such boastings as the Gentiles use Or lesser breeds
431 4   Or lesser breeds without the law
432 3   from the breeds of earth thy silent sway Fashions the nation

breeze
106 2   Pent be each warring breeze, Lulled be your restless waves
305 1   Each breeze that sweeps the ocean Brings tidings from afar
437 3   Let music swell the breeze

breezes
460 1   The breezes and the sunshine, And soft, refreshing rain

brethren
47 4   The sun that bids us rest is waking Our brethren
47 4   Our brethren 'neath the western sky
123 2   Brethren, come, from all doth grieve you You are freed
219 1   To call thy brethren forth from want and woe
347 4   Or brethren faithless prove
429 4   O Trinity of love and power, Our brethren shield

brethren's
347 2   Our brethren's grief to share

bride
260 1   From heaven he came and sought her To be his holy bride

bridegroom
108 1   Rise up, with willing feet Go forth, the Bridegroom meet

bridge
494 1   And hearts creative bridge the human rift

brief
287 3   prolong The brief, bright hour of fellowship with thee
395 2   And scarcely can we turn aside For one brief hour of prayer

bright
23	T,1	Ye Holy Angels Bright, Who wait at God's right hand
30	1	Bright seraphs, cherubim and thrones, Raise the glad strain
37	4	So shall it be at last, in that bright morning
39	T,1	O Splendor of God's Glory Bright
40	T,1	O Splendor of God's Glory Bright (same words as No. 39)
42	2	Soundless and bright for us Breaketh God's morn
51	3	Grant to little children Visions bright of thee
64	3	Thou fire so masterful and bright
69	1	Praise him, all ye hosts above, Ever bright and fair in love
70	4	moon to shine by night 'Mid her spangled sisters bright
77	2	All now mysterious shall be bright at last
98	T,1	My God, I Thank Thee, Who Hast Made The earth so bright
113	3	not in splendor bright As monarch, but the humble child
119	1	Leading onward, beaming bright
122	3	This day is born a Savior, Of a pure virgin bright
123	3	Hail the star That from far Bright with hope is burning
131	1	It came, a floweret bright, Amid the cold of winter
136	3	God's bright star, o'er his head, Wise men three to him led
138	1	All is calm, all is bright Round yon virgin mother and child
144	T,1	What Star Is This, With Beams So Bright
145	T,1	O Morning Star, How Fair and Bright
170	1	How does that visage languish Which once was bright as morn
185	3	Now the queen of seasons, bright With the day of splendor
189	2	Now let the earth be joyful In spring-time's bright array
193	1	Angels in bright raiment Rolled the stone away
194	T,1	The Whole Bright World Rejoices Now
198	1	The day-star clear and bright Of every man and nation
199	2	But downward bends his burning eye At mysteries so bright
261	3	How rise thy towers, serene & bright To meet the dawning day
276	2	And warm and bright and good to all
277	3	behold thy kingdom glorious, In our world so bright and fair
287	3	prolong The brief, bright hour of fellowship with thee
290	4	Make all our moments calm and bright
309	2	And bright with many an angel, And all the martyr throng
343	3	Bright skies will soon be o'er me
343	3	Bright skies ... Where the dark clouds have been
345	2	Bright youth and snow-crowned age
351	4	Then, with my waking thoughts Bright with thy praise
391	4	May I reach heaven's joys, O bright heaven's Sun
401	3	Will not grow bright and clean
437	4	Long may our land be bright With freedom's holy light
460	3	We thank thee, then, O Father, For all things bright & good
478	T,R	All Things Bright and Beautiful, All creatures great & small
480	1	Jesus saw The same bright sun that shines today
481	3	The world is bright with the joyous saints
486	2	Bright skies overhead, Gladness in my heart
490	4	Spirit of Christ, do thou Our first bright days inspire
496	1	Whose broad stripes & bright stars through the perilous fight
576	5	To thee both night and day are bright

bright'ning
33	T,1	As the Sun Doth Daily Rise Bright'ning all the morning skies

brighten
167 VI-3 Brighten all our heavenward way With an ever holier ray

brightened
405 2 Toilsome and gloomy ways Brightened with song

brightening
387 2 Brightening all the path we tread

brightens
465 3 Grant them the joy which brightens earthly sorrow
478 2 The sunset, and the morning That brightens up the sky

brighter
117 3 Brighter visions beam afar
201 3 O brighter than the rising morn When he, victorious, rose
201 4 brighter than that glorious morn Shall this fair morning be
227 3 And all the twinkling starry host, Jesus shines brighter
269 5 brightest glories earth can yield & brighter bliss of heaven
399 2 That in thy sunshine's blaze its day May brighter, fairer be
456 2 The solemn splendors of the night Burn brighter
456 2 Burn brighter through the cold

brightest
98 3 That shadows fall on brightest hours, That thorns remain
126 T,1,5 Brightest and Best of the Sons of the Morning
269 5 brightest glories earth can yield & brighter bliss of heaven

brightly
244 1 Around and in us brightly shine

brightness
78 6 With growing ardor onward move ... growing brightness shine
145 2 Thou heavenly Brightness, Light divine
235 2 Lord, by the brightness of thy light ... men unite
314 4 That when this life is past ... the eternal brightness see
314 4 I may the eternal brightness see, And share thy joy at last
407 1 Nor mind thy brightness comprehend

brimful
340 2 peace of God that filled their hearts Brimful, & broke them

bring
16 1 To his feet thy tribute bring
22 1 In grateful devotion our tribute we bring
36 5 Room to deny ourselves - a road To bring us daily nearer God
41 2 Bring us to heaven, where thy saints united Joy
46 3 Give deeper calm than night can bring
75 1 Wake, my soul, awake & sing, Now thy grateful praises bring
103 3 Born to reign in us forever, Now thy gracious kingdom bring
119 3 All our costliest treasures bring, Christ, to thee
119 3 treasures bring, Christ, to thee, our heavenly King
119 4 Bring our ransomed souls at last Where they need no star

bringer

| 411 | 3 | O Prince of peace, thou bringer of good tidings |
| 577 | R | Creator of the earth and heaven, Thou bringer of salvation |

bringest

| 39 | 1 | O thou that bringest light from light |
| 333 | 2 | Shepherd of souls who bringest all who seek thee To pastures |

bringing

74	1	Bringing suns and stars to birth
253	1	Bringing freedom, spreading truth
304	4	To east and west his kingdom bringing near
398	2	Bringing to hungry souls the bread of life

brings

52	1	Now ... Brings the night its peace profound
106	1	He judgment brings and victory
109	1	traveler, yes, it brings the day, Promised day of Israel
115	1	Come then and hearken, for he brings Glad tidings
120	3	Light and life to all he brings
140	3	The King of kings salvation brings
165	3	And sin is slain, and death brings life
201	5	morning dawns, And light and beauty brings
203	2	Rich the trophies Jesus brings
305	1	Each breeze that sweeps the ocean Brings tidings from afar
310	2	Vision of peace, that brings joy evermore
315	2	But morning brings us gladness, And songs the break of day
435	2	For the hour that brings release
498	T,1	Each Morning Brings us fresh outpoured The loving-kindness

broad

150	T,1	O Love, How Deep, How Broad, How High
150	5	For love so deep, so high, so broad
151	T,1	O Love, How Deep, How Broad, How High (same words no. 150)
261	T,1	City of God, How Broad and Far Outspread thy walls sublime
448	4	Till rise in ordered plan On firm foundations broad
449	1	Let broad humanity have birth
458	4	Praise for hills and valleys broad
496	1	Whose broad stripes & bright stars through the perilous fight

broadening

| 418 | 4 | Far down the future's broadening way |
| 432 | 3 | Fashions the nation of the broadening day |

broader

| 101 | 2 | love of God is broader Than the measure of man's mind (102-3 |

broke

340	2	peace of God that filled their hearts Brimful, & broke them
493	3	had no curse nor vengeful cry For those who broke his bones
558	3	'This is my body, broke for sin

broken

| 13 | 1 | Laws which never shall be broken for their guidance |

38	T,1	Morning Has Broken, Like the first morning
104	3	all flesh shall see the token That his word is never broken
180	2	Now the iron bars are broken
183	1	Christ hath broken every chain
267	1	He whose word cannot be broken Formed thee for his own abode
282	T,1	Bread of the World in Mercy Broken
282	1	Look on the heart by sorrow broken
283	T,1	Bread of the World, in Mercy Broken (like 282 in 2 verses)
284	2	Thy body, broken for my sake, My bread from heaven shall be
289	2	As grain ... Was in this broken bread made one
336	3	God of all grace, we come to thee With broken ... hearts
336	3	With broken, contrite hearts
357	4	They are but broken lights of thee
403	2	Lo, the Bread of heaven is broken in the sacrament of life
409	2	Thou, the Bread of heaven, art broken In the sacrament
432	2	past crumbling throne And broken fetter, thou hast brought
494	1	waiting till love can raise the broken stone
529	T,1	The Sacrifices of God are a broken spirit
529	1	A broken and a contrite heart, O God, thou wilt not despise

brood

429	3	O Holy Spirit, who didst brood Upon the chaos dark and rude

brooding

458	5	Praise for happy dreams of birth Brooding in the quiet earth

brook

256	1	Brook by the traveler's way

brother

8	3	Thou our Father, Christ our Brother
8	4	Brother love binds man to man
66	4	For the joy of human love, Brother, sister, parent, child
220	1	Beside us walks our brother Christ, & makes our task his own
220	4	Our brotherhood still rests in him, The brother of us all
275	2	As one with him, our brother and our friend
387	1	Brother clasps the hand of brother
410	T,1	O Brother Man, Fold to the Heart thy brother
445	4	O give us brother love for better seeing Thy Word made flesh
495	3	Brother, do you love my Jesus

brother's

425	1	If ye do not feel the chain when it works a brother's pain
449	3	Give us the peace of vision clear To see our brother's good
449	3	our brother's good our own

brotherhood

122	4	And with true love and brotherhood Each other now embrace
220	4	Our brotherhood still rests in him, The brother of us all
300	2	Bring in the day of brotherhood, And end the night of wrong
308	1	Brotherhood and sisterhood Of earth's age-long chivalry
346	1	One brotherhood in heart are we, And one our Lord and King
420	3	Whose ways are brotherhood
432	4	Then, for thy grace to grow in brotherhood

439	4	Till it find its full fruition In the brotherhood of man
440	1,4	And crown thy good with brotherhood From sea to shining sea
476	4	rich in art, made richer still The brotherhood of duty

brotherly
| 245 | 2 | And with actions brotherly Speak my Lord's sincerity |

brothers
268	T,1	Lord, We Thank Thee for Our Brothers
275	2	The brothers of thy well-beloved Son
300	4	As brothers of the Son of man Rise up, O men of God
329	1	Shame on us, Christian brothers, His name and sign who bear
340	4	brothers, pray for but one thing, The marvelous peace of God
378	3	Peace, in thy Church, where brothers are engaging
382	2	Brothers, we are treading Where the saints have trod
414	3	Join hands, then, brothers of the faith
425	2	share All the chains our brothers wear

brought
9	2	And when, like wandering sheep we strayed, He brought us
9	2	He brought us to his fold again
36	1	Through sleep and darkness safely brought
79	3	on his shoulder gently laid, And home rejoicing brought me
108	3	No vision ever brought ... such great glory
122	2	And unto certain shepherds Brought tidings of the same
149	1	I only know the manger child Has brought God's life to me
149	2	I only know its matchless love Has brought God's love to me
163	2	Who was the guilty, Who brought this upon thee
185	1	God hath brought his Israel Into joy from sadness
192	1	Our Christ hath brought us over With hymns of victory
197	3	Brought it back victorious, When from death he passed
271	1	We bring thee, Lord, the praise they brought
411	3	Light for the path of life, and God brought near
432	2	past crumbling throne And broken fetter, thou hast brought
432	2	thou hast brought thine own
472	1	Our willing offerings brought This work to share
538	T,1	Bless Thou the Gifts our hands have brought

brow
165	1	On the Redeemer's thorn-crowned brow ... that dawn we view
178	T,1	'Tis Midnight, and on Olive's Brow
200	1	A royal diadem adorns The mighty victor's brow
203	1	Crowns become the victor's brow
325	1	New thorns to pierce that steady brow
329	2	And thorns thy brow encircle, And tears thy face have marred

brown
| 340 | T,1 | They Cast Their Nets in Galilee Just off the hills of brown |

buckler
| 91 | 4 | His faithfulness shall ever be a shield & buckler unto thee |

bud
| 95 | 2 | Truth from the earth, like a flower, Shall bud and blossom |
| 366 | 1 | Bring to bud her glorious flower |

budding
458	2	Praise him for his budding green, April's resurrection scene

buds
66	5	Graces, human and divine, Flowers of earth & buds of heaven

build
297	4	give us grace ... To build the kingdom yet to be
325	4	O wounded hands of Jesus, build In us thy new creation
392	1	That they may build from age to age An undefiled heritage
412	2	Build us a tower of Christ-like height
412	2	Build us a tower ... That we the land may view
420	3	Give us, O God, the strength to build The city
420	4	bids us seize the whole of life And build its glory there
444	3	And finely build for days to come Foundations that endure
449	4	That useful labor yet may build Its homes with love
494	2	Teach us to build
494	3	We build with thee

builded
28	2	Upon a mountain builded high
424	3	And the work that we have builded
443	2	They have builded him an altar in the evening dews and damps
476	4	men of skill Who builded homes of beauty

builder
412	2	O Carpenter of Nazareth, Builder of life divine

builders
424	2	We are builders of that city

building
424	2	All our lives are building stones
445	3	Building proud towers which shall not reach to heaven
472	1	Building for thine employ This house of prayer
494	T,1	We Would Be Building temples still undone
494	1	We would be building, Master,
494	3	O keep us building Master

builds
83	1	Who trusts in God's unchanging love Builds on the rock
83	1	Builds on the rock that nought can move
431	5	All valiant dust that builds on dust

built
68	1	spread the flowing seas abroad, And built the lofty skies
207	5	Our faith is built upon thy promise free
270	T,1	Built on the Rock the Church doth stand
270	2	to abide on earth with men, Built in our bodies his temple
281	2	Thou our life, O let us be Rooted, grafted, built on thee
451	2	Built while they dream, and in that dreaming weep
475	2	Built on the precious Cornerstone

bulwark
363 T,1 A Mighty Fortress Is Our God, A bulwark never failing

bulwarks
434 4 These are the bulwarks of the state

burden
31 2 Low at his feet lay the burden of carefulness
46 2 Lay down the burden and the care
76 4 I'll drop my burden at his feet, And bear a song away
160 1 And the burden of the day
509 2 Lay down the burden and the care

burdened
26 3 Enter now his holy gate, Let our burdened hearts be still
230 6 The last low whispers of our dead Are burdened with his name
405 3 Some word of hope for hearts Burdened with fears
423 3 From woman's grief, man's burdened toil

burdens
76 1 Come, cast your burdens on the Lord
272 3 We share each other's woes, Each other's burdens bear
421 3 And, 'neath the burdens there, thy sovereignty Has held

buried
308 1 Whose forgotten resting place Rolling years have buried deep

burn
44 2 Did not their hearts within them burn
72 2 Whilst all the stars that round her burn ... confirm
86 1 Whose stars serenely burn Above this earth's confusion
89 5 And kindling hearts that burn for thee
239 2 O let it freely burn, Till earthly passions turn To dust
456 2 The solemn splendors of the night Burn brighter
456 2 Burn brighter through the cold

burning
64 1 Thou burning sun with golden beam
69 2 Prophets burning with his word
123 3 Hail the star That from far Bright with hope is burning
160 1 From the burning of the noon-tide heat
199 2 But downward bends his burning eye At mysteries so bright
244 2 Let thy dear word ... Be so within us burning
253 3 Light of knowledge, ever burning, Shed on us
441 2 By the light of burning martyrs, Jesus' ... feet I track
506 2 Ready burning Be the incense of thy powers

burnished
252 4 O make thy Church, dear Savior, A lamp of burnished gold

burns
361 2 Have faith in God, my mind, Though oft thy light burns low
387 1 Gleams and burns the guiding light

burst

185	2	'Tis the spring of souls today, Christ hath burst his prison
324	1	O burst these bonds, and set it free

bursting

496	1	And the rockets' red glare, the bombs bursting in air

bursts

109	2	Traveler, ages are its own, See it bursts o'er all the earth
203	4	Hark, those bursts of acclamation

business

395	2	Around us rolls the ceaseless tide Of business, toil, & care

busy

378	3	Peace, when the world its busy war is waging

byways

398	3	Walk thou beside us lest the tempting byways Lure us away

call

8	2	Field and forest, vale and mountain ... call us to rejoice
8	2	Flowery meadow, flashing sea ... call us to rejoice
8	2	Chanting bird & flowing fountain call us to rejoice in thee
60	4	Call us, O Lord, to thine eternal peace
63	3	when thy love shall call us, Savior, from the world away
108	1	We follow where thy voice shall call
113	1	We pray thee, hear us when we call
161	3	And make us brave and full of joy To answer to his call
195	2	Crown him, ye martyrs of our God, Who from his altar call
197	1	'Tis the Father's pleasure We should call him Lord
219	1	To call thy brethren forth from want and woe
220	4	o'er the centuries still we hear The Master's winsome call
224	1	We own thy sway, we hear thy call
235	3	And call him Father from the heart
263	2	To this temple, where we call thee, Come, O Lord of hosts
290	2	Thou savest those that on thee call
299	4	The name of Jesus glorify Till every kindred call him Lord
305	2	While sinners, now confessing, The gospel call obey
326	5	Let thy voice call me home, saying, Yet there is room
332	1	Our misdeeds to thee confessing, On thy name we humbly call
339	3	Christ doth call One and all, Ye who follow shall not fall
352	4	Then, as the trumpet call, in after years
372	3	When through the deep waters I call thee to go
383	1-3	At the call divine
385	2	Stand Up, stand up for Jesus, The trumpet call obey
392	1	O help thy children when they call
443	3	trumpet that shall never call retreat
444	2	The quiet of a steadfast faith, Calm of a call obeyed
472	2	shrine Where thy pure light may shine, O hear our call
570	3	For behold, from henceforth all generations shall call me
570	3	all generations shall call me blessed

called

60	2	That in this house have called upon thy name
81	2	When in distress to him I called, He to my rescue came
272	4	When we are called to part It give us inward pain
388	2	Who saw his Master in the sky, And called on him to save
411	4	Lord God, whose grace has called us to thy service
424	2	Whether humble or exalted, All are called to task divine
431	3	Far-called, our navies melt away
447	3	None ever called on thee in vain
483	1	How he called little children as lambs to his fold
568	9	And thou, child, shalt be called the prophet of the Highest

callest

326	5	When thou comest and callest me

calleth

152	5	Still as of old he calleth, Follow me

calling

53	1	On God, Our Maker, calling ... the Giver good
124	1	Christ is born and Mary's calling
167	II-2	Calling humbly on thy name, Hear us, holy Jesus
270	1	Bells still are chiming and calling
270	1	Calling the young and old to rest
293	2	Claim the high calling angels cannot share
341	2	The gracious calling of the Lord
426	T,1	The Voice of God Is Calling Its summons unto men
471	2	Confirm in him his high and holy calling

calls

58	2	Gird us for the task that calls us
125	3	Calls you one & calls you all, To gain his everlasting hall
173	1	Calls us to fellowship with God again
205	3	Still he calls mankind his own
303	1	thanks ... That battle calls our marshaled ranks
315	4	Which calls us, very sinners, Unworthy though we be
322	T,1	Jesus Calls Us, O'er the Tumult
322	3	Jesus calls us from the worship of the vain world's
322	4	Still he calls in cares and pleasures
322	5	Jesus calls us, by thy mercies, Savior, may we hear thy call
323	T,1	Jesus Calls Us, O'er the Tumult (same words as no. 322)
339	1	God unknown, He alone Calls my heart to be his own
362	3	'Tis God's all-animating voice That calls thee from on high
385	3	Where duty calls, or danger, Be never wanting there
431	5	And guarding, calls not thee to guard
459	3	He calls the warmer gales to blow And bids the spring return
504	1	He calls the hours his own

calm

2	4	Avert our woes and calm our dread
37	2	In the calm dew and freshness of the morn
46	3	Give deeper calm than night can bring
51	2	Jesus, give the weary Calm and sweet repose
52	1	Let our vesper hymn be blending With the holy calm around
67	3	We feel thy calm at evening's hour
138	1	All is calm, all is bright Round yon virgin mother and child

192	2	And, listening to his accents, May hear so calm and plain
207	5	Lord, give us peace, and make us calm and sure
217	4	Lord of all gentleness, Lord of all calm
287	2	Here taste afresh the calm of sin forgiven
290	4	Make all our moments calm and bright
341	3	O sabbath rest by Galilee, O calm of hills above
341	5	O still, small voice of calm
349	T,1	O For a Closer Walk With God, A calm and heavenly frame
349	5	So shall my walk be close with God, Calm and serene my frame
377	2	Zion, calm the breast that quaketh
378	3	Calm thy foes' raging
429	2	And calm amid its rage didst sleep
444	2	The quiet of a steadfast faith, Calm of a call obeyed
449	2	Within our passioned hearts instill The calm
449	2	The calm that endeth strain and strife
467	2	Comes with its calm the thought that thou art o'er us
509	3	Give deeper calm than night can bring
510	2	Jesus, give the weary Calm and sweet repose
540	1	Calm with trust each anxious heart
557	2	Here taste afresh the calm of sin forgiven

calming
| 249 | 3 | And calming passion's fierce and stormy gales |

calmness
| 92 | 3 | Thy calmness bends serene above, My restlessness to still |
| 334 | 1,3 | revealing Of trust and strength and calmness from above |

calms
| 221 | 2 | And calms the troubled breast |
| 465 | 3 | Grant them the peace which calms all earthly strife |

calvaries
| 441 | 2 | Jesus' bleeding feet I track, Toiling up new Calvaries ever |

calvary
147	3	Humbling thyself to death on Calvary
162	3	Hill of Calvary, I go To thy scenes of fear and woe
326	4	They bore thee to Calvary
348	T,1	My Faith Looks Up to Thee, Thou Lamb of Calvary
374	2	Or, in darker semblance, Cross-crowned Calvary

calvary's
149	2	know not how ... Calvary's cross A world from sin could free
158	3	Calvary's mournful mountain climb
165	2	from the cross on Calvary's height Gleams of eternity appear
292	1	love That bought us, once for all, on Calvary's tree

cam'st
| 147 | 2 | Thou cam'st to us in lowliness of thought |
| 325 | T,1 | Lord Christ, When First Thou cam'st to men |

came
81	2	When in distress to him I called, He to my rescue came
99	4	We read thee best in him who came To bear for us the cross
122	2	From God, our heavenly Father, A blessed angel came

129	T,1	It Came Upon the Midnight Clear, that glorious song of old
131	1	It came, a floweret bright, Amid the cold of winter
136	2	His the doom, ours the mirth When he came down to earth
141	3	And by the light of that same star Three wise men came
141	3	Three wise men came from country far
142	1	Came he to a world forlorn, the Lord of every nation
142	4	Now may Mary's son, who came So long ago to love us
146	1	The angel of the Lord came down, And glory shone around
169	2	He came from his blest throne, salvation to bestow
197	3	From the lips of sinners, Unto whom he came
199	3	And rose victorious in the strife For those he came to save
229	2	By thee the joyful news Of our salvation came
230	2	Love only knoweth whence it came, And comprehendeth love
253	2	Til they came, who told the story Of the Word
260	1	From heaven he came and sought her To be his holy bride
264	T,1	O Where Are Kings and Empires Now Of old that went and came
330	4	So, Love itself in human form, For love of me he came
340	1	Such happy, simple fisher-folk, Before the Lord came down
388	3	A glorious band, the chosen few On whom the Spirit came
438	2	Thy blessing came, and still its power Shall onward
438	3	Laws, freedom, truth, and faith in God Came with those
438	3	Came with those exiles o'er the waves

camel
| 484 | 1 | wade through rice fields And watch the camel trains |

camest
113	3	When the old world drew on toward night, Thou camest
326	1	When thou camest to earth for me
326	4	Thou camest, O Lord, with the living word

camps
| 443 | 2 | have seen him in the watchfires of a hundred circling camps |

can
6	4	Thy bountiful care, what tongue can recite
9	1	He can create, and he destroy
15	3	Ponder anew What the Almighty can do
46	3	Give deeper calm than night can bring
46	3	Give sweeter songs than lips can sing
55	5	Thy kind but searching glance can scan the very wounds
55	6	No word from thee can fruitless fall
68	3	And everywhere that man can be, Thou, God, art present there
78	2	can an all-creating arm Grow weary or decay
83	1	Builds on the rock that nought can move
86	2	Till truth from falsehood part, Our souls can find no rest
96	2	His hand can turn my griefs away
112	3	witness Which can shape the world to fitness
128	4	what can I give him, Poor as I am
128	4	Yet what I can I give him - Give my heart
160	2	Upon that cross of Jesus Mine eye at times can see
173	4	Teach us to know the love which can forgive
174	1	None its lines of woe can trace
174	1	None can tell what pangs unknown Hold thee silent and alone
174	3	Thou dost ask him -- can it be, Why has thou forsaken me
188	3	From every weapon death can wield Thine own ... shield

199	2	No angel in the sky Can fully bear that sight
209	3	What but thy grace can foil the tempter's power
209	3	Who like thyself my guide and stay can be
225	2	No voice can sing, no heart can frame
225	2	Nor can the memory find A sweeter sound than thy blest name
225	4	Ah, this Nor tongue nor pen can show
227	3	Jesus shines purer Than all the angels heaven can boast
230	3	For him no depths can drown
231	3	Where thou art guide no ill can come
239	3	For none can guess its grace, Till he become the place
245	4	And whatever I can be Give to him who gave me thee
253	1	Shedding light that none can measure
258	4	Who can tell the pleasure, Who recount the treasure
267	1	On the Rock of Ages founded, What can shake thy sure repose
267	2	Who can faint, while such a river Ever flows
269	5	brightest glories earth can yield & brighter bliss of heaven
290	3	Blest when our faith can hold thee fast
294	2	Whom love, and love alone can know
298	4	All we can do is nothing worth Unless God blesses the deed
310	2	Wish and fulfillment can severed be ne'er
310	3	We, where no trouble distraction can bring
330	2	That thou shouldst bear our sin and shame, How can I tell
330	2	How can I tell such love
333	3	Father of mercy, from thy watch & keeping No place can part
333	3	No place can part, nor hour of time remove us
335	2	Can we find a friend so faithful
342	1	No tender voice like thine Can peace afford
343	1	But God is round about me, And can I be dismayed
343	2	My shepherd is beside me, And nothing can I lack
344	3	Pleasure that can never cloy
344	3	provided, pardoned, guided, Nothing can our peace destroy
358	2	Not the labors of my hands Can fulfill thy law's demands
360	2	I can but give the gifts he gave, & plead his love for love
360	4	No harm from him can come to me On ocean or on shore
361	3	neither life nor death can pluck His children from his hands
363	3	His rage we can endure, For lo, his doom is sure
359	3	The instinct that can tell That God is on the field
359	4	Blest too is he who can divine Where real right doth lie
372	1	What more can he say than to you he hath said
373	2	What terror can confound me With God at my right hand
382	3	Gates of hell can never 'Gainst that Church prevail
388	1	Who best can drink the cup of woe, Triumphant over pain
394	2	He can give me victory o'er all that threatens me
395	2	And scarcely can we turn aside For one brief hour of prayer
401	3	All may of thee partake, Nothing can be so mean
407	1	No eye can to thy throne ascend
417	2	And those who can suffer can dare
443	2	I can read his righteous sentence by the dim & flaring lamps
445	2	And sharing not our griefs, no joy can share
481	3	You can meet them in school, or in lanes, or at sea
482	2	We will serve you all we can, Darling, darling little man
494	1	waiting till love can raise the broken stone
496	1	O say can you see by the dawn's early light
504	2	Hosanna in the highest strains The Church on earth can raise
506	1	See thou render All thy feeble strength can pay
509	3	Give deeper calm than night can bring

509	3	Give sweeter songs than lips can sing
575	3	Where thou art guide no ill can come
576	3	Where can I go apart from thee

Canaan's

| 93 | 3 | Land me safe on Canaan's side |

cannot

46	4	We cannot at the shrine remain
50	3	For without thee I cannot live
55	2	What if thy form we cannot see
95	1	His footsteps cannot err
128	2	Our God, heaven cannot hold him, Nor earth sustain
145	2	Thy member, ever joined to thee In love that cannot falter
154	2	We cannot understand the woe Thy love was pleased to bear
163	4	Therefore, kind Jesus, since I cannot pay thee
171	2	We may not know, we cannot tell What pains he had to bear
184	3	That love, that life which cannot die
204	3	His kingdom cannot fail, He rules o'er earth and heaven
222	2	Foes who would molest me Cannot reach me here
267	1	He whose word cannot be broken Formed thee for his own abode
270	2	Yet he whom heavens cannot contain Chose to abide on earth
293	2	Claim the high calling angels cannot share
315	1	Of joy that hath no ending, Of love which cannot cease
330	4	I cannot look upon his face For shame, for bitter shame
343	3	My hope I cannot measure, The path to life is free
356	2	It cannot freely move Till thou hast wrought its chain
357	1	Believing where we cannot prove
357	5	We have but faith, we cannot know
360	3	I only know I cannot drift Beyond his love and care
382	3	We have Christ's own promise, And that cannot fail
392	5	Teach us the strength that cannot seek ... to hurt the weak
392	5	cannot seek By deed or thought, to hurt the weak
399	3	I cannot close my heart to thee
401	5	that which God doth touch and own cannot for less be told
539	2	possess in sweet communion Joys which earth cannot afford
576	2	My words from thee I cannot hide

canopy

| 6 | 2 | Whose robe is the light, whose canopy space |

canst

54	1	with us bide, Thou that canst never set in night
78	3	him thou canst not see, nor trace the working of his hands
212	2	Thou alone to God canst win us
213	2	As a mother stills her child, Thou canst hush the ocean wild
292	3	Most patient Savior who canst love us still
361	2	God's mercy holds a wiser plan Than thou canst fully know
378	2	Lord, thou canst help when earthly armor faileth
378	2	Lord, thou canst save when sin itself assaileth
416	2	Thou canst help their load to bear
416	2	Thou canst bring inspiring light
418	4	In peace that only thou canst give
426	3	But thou canst use our weakness To magnify thy power

469	2	They rest within thy sheltering care
471	4	Tending with care the lambs within the fold
479	1	For rest and food and loving care
487	2	God's care like a cloak Wraps us country folk
489	1	I would be pure,for there are those who care
492	T,1	O Gracious God, Whose Constant Care
492	1	whose constant care Supplies our golden days
506	2	God hath tended With his care thy helpless hours
509	2	Lay down the burden and the care

cared
| 381 | 2 | They cared not, but with force unspent ... they onward went |

careful
| 392 | 2 | With steadfastness and careful truth |

carefulness
| 31 | 2 | Low at his feet lay the burden of carefulness |

cares
207	1	I pray thee from our hearts all cares to take
217	1	Whose trust, ever child-like, no cares could destroy
269	3	To her my cares and toils be given
269	3	Till toils and cares shall end
272	2	Our comforts and our cares
322	4	Still he calls in cares and pleasures
467	2	When the vain cares that vex our life increase

caro
| 133 | 3 | Patris aeterni Verbum caro factum |

carol
| 268 | 2 | Sweet the psalm and sweet the carol When our song is raised |

carols
| 485 | 2 | The birds their carols raise |

carpenter
| 409 | 1 | Thou, the carpenter of Nazareth, Toiling for thy daily bread |
| 412 | 2 | O Carpenter of Nazareth, Builder of life divine |

carry
335	1	What a privilege to carry Everything to God in prayer
335	1	All because we do not carry Everything to God in prayer
424	2	All must aid alike to carry Forward one sublime design

case
| 312 | 2 | Most happy is their case |

casket
| 252 | 2 | It is the golden casket Where gems of truth are stored |

cast
6	3	And round it hath cast, like a mantle, the sea
20	4	Cast each false idol from his throne
64	4	Praise God and on him cast your care

76	1	Come, cast your burdens on the Lord
134	4	Cast out our sin and enter in, Be born in us today
198	3	Cast out our pride and shame That hinder to enthrone thee
228	4	Till we cast our crowns before thee
276	4	Thy perfect love cast out all fear
290	3	Where'er our changeful lot is cast
315	4	And whosoever cometh I will not cast him out
340	T,1	They Cast Their Nets in Galilee Just off the hills of brown
367	3	Cast care aside, lean on thy guide
374	3	Grant that I may ever Cast my care on thee
380	1	Who, thrust in prison or cast to flame
380	1	cast to flame, Still made their glory in thy name
390	3	Why restless, why cast down, my soul
433	2	In this free land by thee our lot is cast
467	4	Be not cast down, disquieted in vain
470	1	Elijah's mantle o'er Elisha cast
528	2	Cast me not away from thy presence

casteth

449	3	The love that casteth out all fear

casting

251	2	Casting down their golden crowns around the glassy sea

catch

423	2	We catch the vision of thy tears

cattle

137	2	The cattle are lowing, the baby awakes

caught

108	3	No ear hath ever caught Such great glory

cause

110	3	knowledge show, And cause us in her ways to go
372	2	I'll strengthen thee, help thee, and cause thee to stand
441	1	Some great cause, God's new messiah
441	3	Though the cause of evil prosper ... truth alone is strong
493	2	He had no friend to plead his cause
493	4	Let me, O Lord, thy cause defend, A knight without a sword
496	2	Then conquer we must, when our cause it is just

caused

70	3	He the golden-tressed sun Caused all day his course to run
337	2	When fully he the work hath wrought that caused ... fear
337	2	That caused thy needless fear

causes

179	R	Oh, Sometimes it causes me to tremble, tremble, tremble

caves

106	2	Isles of the southern seas, Deep in your coral caves

cease

9	5	thy truth must stand When rolling years shall cease to move
21	1	The wicked oppressing now cease from distressing
60	1	We stand to bless thee ere our worship cease
60	4	Then, when thy voice shall bid our conflict cease
78	5	Mere human power shall fast decay, And youthful vigor cease
109	3	Watchman, let thy wanderings cease
110	4	Bid envy, strife and quarrels cease
146	6	Good will henceforth from heaven to men Begin & never cease
254	2	Then shall all bondage cease, All fetters fall
265	2	Let all past bitterness Now and forever cease
294	2	Till greed and hate shall cease
315	1	Of joy that hath no ending, Of love which cannot cease
336	2	We perish if we cease from prayer
341	4	Drop thy still dews of quietness, Till ... strivings cease
341	4	Till all our strivings cease
357	4	They have their day and cease to be
375	2	Lead on, O King eternal, Till sin's fierce war shall cease
380	4	Not long the conflict, soon The holy war shall cease
389	4	Till all our wanderings cease
405	4	And when earth's labors cease, Bid us depart in peace
410	3	clangor Of wild war music o'er the earth shall cease
413	3	Bid its cruel discords cease
429	3	Who bad'st its angry tumult cease
435	2	And the city's crowded clangor Cries aloud for sin to cease
444	4	That war may haunt the earth no more And desolation cease
447	1	Make wars throughout the world to cease
449	4	Let woe and waste of warfare cease

ceaseless

107	4	As with ceaseless voice they cry
275	T,1	Eternal Ruler of the Ceaseless Round Of circling planets
395	2	Around us rolls the ceaseless tide Of business, toil, & care
404	1	Let them flow in ceaseless praise

ceaselessly

3	3	May I ceaselessly adore thee

ceasing

143	2	King forever, ceasing never Over us all to reign
206	4	And thanks never ceasing and infinite love
228	3	Pray and praise thee without ceasing
499	2	To him may all our thoughts arise In never-ceasing sacrifice

celebrate

558	5	Jesus, thy feast we celebrate

celestial

49	1	The eternal splendor wearing, Celestial, holy, blest
79	2	where the verdant pastures grow With food celestial feedeth
113	4	things celestial thee shall own ...terrestrial, Lord alone
231	1	And lighten with celestial fire
247	2	Hark, the glad celestial hymn Angel choirs above are raising
575	1	And lighten with celestial fire

cell
46   4   in the spirit's secret cell May hymn & prayer forever dwell

center
8   2   Stars and angels sing around thee, Center of unbroken praise
89   1   Center and soul of every sphere

central
197 4   Through all ranks of creatures, To the central height

centuries
220 4   o'er the centuries still we hear The Master's winsome call

certain
122 2   And unto certain shepherds Brought tidings of the same
141 1   Was to certain poor shepherds in fields as they lay

chain
98   3   So that earth's bliss may be our guide, And not our chain
183 1   Christ hath broken every chain
219 1   Sin to rebuke, to break the captive's chain
271 3   Unbroken be the golden chain, Keep on the song forever
356 2   It cannot freely move Till thou hast wrought its chain
425 1   If ye do not feel the chain when it works a brother's pain

chained
365 2   Our fathers, chained in prisons dark, Were still ... free

chains
202 4   The prisoner leaps to lose his chains
377 4   Though in chains thou now art grieving
425 2   No, true freedom is to share All the chains
425 2   share All the chains our brothers wear
452 2   Our souls are bound In iron chains of fear and pride

chalice
79   5   O what transport of delight From thy pure chalice floweth

challenge
419 2   One in the holy fellowship Of those who challenge wrong

challenges
420 4   Lo, how its splendor challenges The souls that greatly dare

chamber
121 3   heart, that it may be A quiet chamber kept for thee

chance
339 1   Me through change and chance he guideth

change
77   1   In every change he faithful will remain
77   3   when change and tears are past
209 2   Change and decay in all around I see
339 1   Me through change and chance he guideth

343	T,1	In Heavenly Love Abiding, No change my heart shall fear
459	2	His steady counsels change the face Of the declining year
494	2	Ribbed with the steel that time and change doth mock

changed
| 228 | 4 | Changed from glory into glory |

changeful
| 290 | 3 | Where'er our changeful lot is cast |

changeless
6	3	Hath stablished it fast by a changeless decree
14	2	Established is his law, And changeless it shall stand
26	4	Evermore, as of yore, Shall his changeless truth endure
52	2	Stars ... Telling ... Their Creator's changeless love
99	2	Changeless, eternal, infinite
348	2	O may my love to thee Pure, warm and changeless be
348	2	Pure, warm, and changeless be, A living fire

changes
2	2	O Father, that thy rule is just And wise, and changes never
97	2	And faith's fair vision changes into sight
165	T,1	Sunset to Sunrise Changes Now
343	1	And safe is such confiding, For nothing changes here

changest
| 209 | 2 | O thou who changest not, abide with me |

changeth
| 7 | 3 | And wither and perish, but naught changeth thee |
| 367 | 4 | He changeth not, and thou art dear |

changing
81	T,1	Through All the Changing Scenes of life
257	2	The rolling sun, the changing light, And nights and days
266	1	Unwasted by the lapse of years, Unchanged by changing place
454	4	Adored through all our changing days
456	3	In ever changing words of light, The wonder of thy name
459	3	The changing wind, the flying cloud, Obey his mighty word

chant
| 35 | 2 | The powers of darkness fear, When this sweet chant they hear |
| 111 | 3 | Hymn & chant and high thanksgiving And unwearied praises be |

chanted
| 127 | 1 | mystery ...Which hosts of angels chanted from above |

chanting
8	2	Chanting bird & flowing fountain call us to rejoice in thee
345	4	Yes, on through life's long path, Still chanting as ye go
508	2	And through the swell of chanting voices

chaos
| 429 | 3 | O Holy Spirit, who didst brood Upon the chaos dark and rude |

charge
461 3   Give his angels charge at last In the fire the tares to cast

charging
427 2   Worlds are charging, heaven beholding

chariot
108 1   His chariot wheels are nearer rolling

chariots
6 2   His chariots of wrath the deep thunder-clouds form

charity
265 2   And all our souls possess Thy charity
301 4   May she one in doctrine be, One in truth and charity
382 2   One in hope and doctrine, One in charity
465 2   assurance Of tender charity and steadfast faith
470 3   For pardon, and for charity and peace
527 1   Enrich ... With faith, with hope, with charity

charm
177 2   All the vain things that charm me most
374 2   With forbidden pleasures Would this vain world charm

charming
124 3   Look and see how charming is Jesus

chart
213 1   Chart and compass come from thee, Jesus, Savior, pilot me
252 3   It is the chart and compass That o'er life's surging sea
256 2   Our guide & chart, wherein we read Of realms beyond the sky

charter
260 2   Her charter of salvation, One Lord, one faith, one birth

chartered
261 1   The true thy chartered free-men are, Of every age and clime

chase
290 4   Chase the dark night of sin away
390 1   When heated in the chase

chasing
387 2   Chasing far the gloom and terror

chastened
467 3   Chastened by pain we learn life's deeper meaning

chastening
446 4   earth by thy chastening Yet shall ... be restored

chastens
21 1   He chastens and hastens his will to make known

cheeks
124 3   How he is white, his cheeks are rosy

cheer

29	2	With ever joyful hearts And blessed peace to cheer us
54	T,1	Now Cheer Our Hearts This Eventide, Lord Jesus Christ
110	2	O Come, thou Day-spring, come and cheer Our spirits
110	2	cheer Our spirits by thine advent here
150	2	To guide, to strengthen, and to cheer
167	II-3	Cheer our souls with hope divine, Hear us, holy Jesus
167	VI-2	Save us in our soul's distress, Be our help to cheer & bless
231	3	Anoint and cheer our soiled face With ... thy grace
258	2	When our foes are near us, Then thy word doth cheer us
274	3	With joy and gladsome cheer
315	2	O loving voice of Jesus, Which comes to cheer the night
411	3	Teach us to speak thy word of hope and cheer
459	1	He sends his showers of blessing down To cheer the plains
459	1	To cheer the plains below
575	3	Anoint and cheer our soiled face with the abundance

cheerful

4	1	Sing to the Lord with cheerful voice
83	2	Only be still, and wait his leisure in cheerful hope
94	3	Nor in the least a cheerful heart that tastes those gifts
333	2	Tenderest guide, in ways of cheerful duty, Lead us
505	1	And joy to see the cheerful light That riseth in the east

cheerfully

312	5	There Magdalen hath left her moan And cheerfully doth sing
406	2	task thy wisdom hath assigned, O let me cheerfully fulfill

cheering

315	3	O cheering voice of Jesus, Which comes to aid our strife

cheerless

43	2	Dark and cheerless is the morn Unaccompanied by thee

cheers

89	2	Star of our hope, thy softened light Cheers
89	2	Cheers the long watches of the night

cherish

227	1	O thou of God and man the Son, Thee will I cherish
245	4	Separate from sin, I would Choose & cherish all things good

cherubim

18	2	Both cherubim and seraphim, Continually do cry
28	4	while cherubim reply to seraphim
30	1	Bright seraphs, cherubim and thrones, Raise the glad strain
30	2	O higher than the cherubim, More glorious than the seraphim
107	4	Cherubim, with sleepless eye
128	3	Cherubim and seraphim Thronged the air
247	2	Cherubim and seraphim In unceasing chorus praising
251	2	Cherubim and seraphim falling down before thee
559	2	To thee cherubim and seraphim continually do cry
569	4	and dwellest between the cherubim

chide

16	2	same forever, Slow to chide and swift to bless

child

66	4	For the joy of human love, Brother, sister, parent, child
74	2	Child of earth, yet full of yearning
103	3	Born thy people to deliver, Born a child, and yet a king
113	3	not in splendor bright As monarch, but the humble child
113	3	child Of Mary, blameless mother mild
118	1	This child, now weak in infancy, Our confidence ... shall be
121	2	To you, this night, is born a child
121	2	a child Of Mary, chosen mother mild
121	2	This little child, of lowly birth, Shall be the joy
121	3	Ah, dearest Jesus, holy child, Make thee a bed
124	2	It is wrong when the child is sleeping
124	3	Hush, hush, see how the child is sleeping
132	3	Child, for us sinners poor and in the manger
134	4	O holy Child of Bethlehem, Descend to us, we pray
140	T,1	What Child Is This, Who, Laid to Rest
149	1	I only know the manger child Has brought God's life to me
201	2	Not as of old a little child To bear, and fight, and die
213	2	As a mother stills her child, Thou canst hush the ocean wild
278	1	So give this child of thine, we pray Thy grace and blessing
294	1	No alien race, no foreign shore, No child unsought, unknown
407	2	From sin thy child in mercy free
417	1	When the pain is sorest the child is born
451	1	Yet thou, her child, whose head is crowned with flame
466	2	O Christ, thyself a child Within an earthly home
480	3	He is my Father, who will keep His child through every day
568	9	And thou, child, shalt be called the prophet of the Highest

childhood

230	6	prayers ... Our lips of childhood frame

childhood's

423	3	From tender childhood's helplessness

children

6	5	Frail children of dust, and feeble as frail
51	3	Grant to little children Visions bright of thee
60	3	from harm and danger keep thy children free
76	2	hand which bears all nature up Shall guide his children well
100	4	To ... children's children ever ... his righteousness extend
136	1	With the song children sing To the Lord, Christ our King
155	1,3	To whom the lips of children Made sweet hosannas ring
249	2	O holy Father, who hast led thy children In all the ages
275	2	We are of thee, the children of thy love
275	3	One in the power that makes the children free
277	2	Thou didst receive the children to thyself so tenderly
277	3	Grant to us a deep compassion For thy children everywhere
279	1	Now these children come to thee As thou biddest
301	3	May her scattered children be From reproach of evil free
327	2	Blessed Jesus, Hear thy children when they pray
329	3	I died for you, my children, And will ye treat me so
332	5	Heavenly Father, bless thy children
361	3	neither life nor death can pluck His children from his hands
392	1	O help thy children when they call
397	1	As thou hast sought, so let me seek Thy erring children

397	1	Thy erring children lost and lone
438	4	And here thy name, O God of love ... children shall adore
438	4	thy name ... Their children's children shall adore
449	4	God, give thy wayward children peace
452	1	in bitter need Thy children lift their cry to thee
460	2	Much more, to us his children, He gives our daily bread
466	2	Our children bless, in every place
483	1	How he called little children as lambs to his fold
484	1	Where children wade through rice fields
484	2	Remember all God's children Who yet have never heard
508	2	With one last prayer thy children fall
526	1	O let thy children share thy blessing from on high

children's
69	3	let children's happy hearts In this worship bear their parts
100	4	To ... children's children ever ... his righteousness extend
333	1	Answer in love thy children's supplication
365	2	And blest would be their children's fate If they ... die for
366	3	Cure thy children's warring madness
438	4	thy name ... Their children's children shall adore

chill
| 455 | 3 | And skies are chill, and frosts are keen |

chiming
| 270 | 1 | Bells still are chiming and calling |

chivalry
| 308 | 1 | Brotherhood and sisterhood Of earth's age-long chivalry |

choice
| 25 | T,1 | Stand Up and Bless the Lord, Ye people of his choice |
| 441 | 1 | choice goes by forever "Twixt that darkness and that light |

choir
| 142 | 5 | While the choir with peals of glee Doth rend the air asunder |
| 312 | 3 | There David stands with harp in hand As master of the choir |

choirs
30	1	Cry out ... Virtues, archangels, angels' choirs, Alleluia
108	3	Where we shall join the choirs immortal
123	1	Christ is born, their choirs are singing
132	2	Sing, choirs of angels, sing in exultation
247	2	Hark, the glad celestial hymn Angel choirs above are raising
499	2	Him day and night The united choirs of angels sing

choose
215	2	I loved to choose and see my path, but now Lead thou me on
238	2	And make us know and choose thy way
245	4	Separate from sin, I would Choose & cherish all things good
325	3	seek the kingdom of thy peace, By which alone we choose thee
337	2	Leave to this sovereign sway To choose and to command
425	3	They are slaves who will not choose Hatred, scoffing & abuse

chooseth
| 214 | 3 | for his dwelling and his throne Chooseth the pure in heart |

125	1	Christ is born today
125	2	Now ye hear of endless bliss, Jesus Christ was born for this
125	2	Christ was born for this
125	3	Jesus Christ was born to save
125	3	Christ was born to save
127	2	This day is born a Savior, Christ the Lord
128	2	A stable place sufficed The Lord God almighty, Jesus Christ
132	R	O come, let us adore him ... Christ the Lord
134	2	For Christ is born of Mary, And gathered all above
134	3	Where meek souls will receive him ... Christ enters in
134	3	still The dear Christ enters in
136	1	With the song children sing To the Lord, Christ our King
136	4	Praising Christ, heaven's King
138	2	Heavenly hosts sing alleluia, Christ the Savior is born
139	2	Tont es laut von fern und nah, Christ der Retter ist da
139	3	Christ, in deiner Geburt
140	R	This, this is Christ the King
144	4	To Christ, revealed in earthly night
146	3	The Savior, who is Christ the Lord
147	4	confess ... that Jesus Christ is Lord
149	3	I only know a living Christ, Our immortality
152	2	The Christ of God, the Life, the Truth, the Way
157	T,1,5	In the Cross of Christ I Glory
158	1	Learn of Jesus Christ to pray
158	2	Learn of Christ to bear the cross
158	3	It is finished, hear him cry, Learn of Jesus Christ to die
169	2	and none The longed-for Christ would know
173	3	The souls for whom Christ prays to Christ are given
175	2	O Christ, thy triumphs now begin
175	4	Then take, O Christ, thy power, and reign
177	2	Save in the death of Christ, my God
180	1	Jesus Christ, the King of glory, Now is risen from the dead
180	2	Christ from death to life is born
180	2	Christ has triumphed, & we conquer By his mighty enterprise
181	2	But Christ their legions hath dispersed
182	T,1	Christ the Lord Is Risen Today
182	3	Christ has opened Paradise
182	4	Soar we now where Christ has led
183	T,1	Christ the Lord Is Risen Again
183	1	Christ hath broken every chain
185	2	'Tis the spring of souls today, Christ hath burst his prison
187	T,1	Jesus Christ Is Risen Today, Alleluia
187	2	Unto Christ, our heavenly King
189	1	And in your adoration Praise Christ, your risen Lord
189	2	O, sing in exultation To Christ, your risen King
192	1	Our Christ hath brought us over With hymns of victory
192	3	For Christ the Lord is risen, Our joy that hath no end
198	T,1	Christ Is the World's True Light, Its captain of salvation
198	2	In Christ all races meet, Their ancient feuds forgetting
198	2	When Christ is throned as Lord, Men shall forsake their fear
201	4	Christ, our King, in beauty comes, And we his face shall see
201	5	Hail, Christ the Lord, thy people pray
205	1	Christ, awhile to mortals given
205	2	Christ hath vanquished death and sin
220	1	Beside us walks our brother Christ, & makes our task his own
230	3	To bring the Lord Christ down

238	3	Lead us to Christ, the living Way
244	2	By thy power Christ confessing, Let us win his grace
245	1	with actions bold and meek Would for Christ my Savior speak
250	2	We all believe in Jesus Christ, Son of God and Mary's son
252	2	It is the heaven-drawn picture of Christ, the living Word
252	3	Still guides, O Christ, to thee
257	4	Till Christ has all the nations blest
260	T,1	The Church's One Foundation Is Jesus Christ her Lord
262	3	Confessing, in a world's accord, The inward Christ
262	3	The inward Christ, the living Word
263	T,1	Christ Is Made the Sure Foundation
263	1	Christ the head and cornerstone
268	3	One our Christ and one our gospel
276	3	And dwell thou with us in this place, Thou and thy Christ
278	T,1	Lord Jesus Christ, Our Lord Most Dear
289	1	Giving in Christ the bread eternal
294	3	O God of righteousness and grace, Seen in the Christ thy Son
294	3	Till Christ is formed in all mankind And every land is thine
295	T,1-4	Christ for the World We Sing, The world to Christ we bring
295	1	Sinsick and sorrow-worn, Whom Christ doth heal
295	3	With us the cross to bear, For Christ our Lord
295	4	Inspired with hope and praise, To Christ belong
298	3	March we forth ... With the banner of Christ unfurled
300	4	Lift high the cross of Christ Tread where his feet have trod
304	1	From land to land the love of Christ is told
318	T,1	Draw Thou My Soul, O Christ, Closer to thine
318	1	Ever, O Christ, through mine Let thy life shine
318	2	Lead forth my soul, O Christ, One with thine own
318	3	Lift thou thy world, O Christ, Closer to thee
321	2	Let every sin be crucified, Let Christ be all in all
325	T,1	Lord Christ, When First Thou cam'st to men
325	3	New advent of the love of Christ
339	3	High above all praises praising For the gift of Christ
339	3	For the gift of Christ his Son
339	3	Christ doth call One and all, Ye who follow shall not fall
345	1	Your festal banner wave on high, The cross of Christ
345	1	The cross of Christ your King
354	1	Who looks in love to Christ above No fear
363	2	Dost ask who that may be, Christ Jesus, it is he
366	2	hosts of evil round us Scorn thy Christ assail his ways
367	1	Christ is thy strength, and Christ thy right
367	2	Christ is the path, and Christ the prize
367	3	Trust, and thy trusting soul shall prove Christ is its life
367	3	Christ is its life, and Christ its love
367	4	Only believe, and thou shalt see That Christ is all in all
376	1	Lead us through Christ, the true and living Way
380	2	Heroic warriors, ne'er from Christ ... enticed
380	2	ne'er from Christ By any lure or guile enticed
382	1	Christ the royal Master Leads against the foe
382	4	Glory, laud and honor Unto Christ the King
384	T,1	Soldiers of Christ, Arise And put your armor on
384	2	Ye may o'ercome through Christ alone & stand entire at last
385	1	Till every foe is vanquished, And Christ is Lord indeed
394	2	Jesus Christ is filling all the heart of me
394	2	Jesus Christ is filling all my heart
398	1	thou Christ of great compassion

398	5	O Christ, o'er death victorious
400	T,1,R	More Love to Thee, O Christ, More love to thee
400	1	This is my earnest plea, More love, O Christ, to thee
400	2	This all my prayer shall be, More love, O Christ, to thee
400	3	This still its prayer shall be, More Love, O Christ, to thee
403	1	who love and ... labor follow in the way of Christ
407	3	And thee, O Christ, my Savior, praise
411	1	purpose never swerving Leads toward the day of Jesus Christ
411	1	Leads to the day of Jesus Christ thy Son
413	3	Come, O Christ, and reign above us
414	T,1	In Christ There Is No East or West, In him no South or North
414	4	In Christ now meet both East and West
415	T,1	In Christ There Is No East or West (words as no. 414)
420	1	O holy city ... Where Christ, the Lamb, doth reign
420	2	Cry, Christ hath died in vain
427	3	O for Christ at least be men
434	1	But to live out the laws of Christ In every thought
434	2	Until the laws of Christ become The laws and habits of
443	4	In the beauty of the lilies Christ was born across the sea
453	5	Ring in the Christ that is to be
466	2	O Christ, thyself a child Within an earthly home
470	4	Theirs, by sweet love, for Christ a kingdom won
472	4	O Christ, the Church's head, Who for us all has bled
488	R	Go, tell it on the mountain That Jesus Christ is born
488	3	Down in a lowly manger The humble Christ was born
490	4	Spirit of Christ, do thou Our first bright days inspire
491	3	Teach us to know the way of Jesus Christ, our Master
521	T,1	Lord Jesus Christ, Be Present Now
525	T,1	Come, & Let Us Sweetly Join Christ to praise in hymns divine
539	T,1	May the Grace of Christ our Savior
545	T,1	Lord, Have Mercy Upon Us, Christ have mercy upon us
548	T,1	Thanks Be to Thee, O Christ, for this thy holy gospel
548	T,1	Praise Be to Thee, O Christ
554	4	O Lord, the only begotten Son, Jesus Christ
554	9	Thou only, O Christ, with the Holy Ghost, art most high
556	T,1	O Christ, Thou Lamb of God
559	7	Thou art the King of glory, O Christ
582	T,1	Christ the Lord Is Risen Today (as no. 182 with descant)

Christ's

20	4	ye who name Christ's holy name, Give God all praise & glory
214	1	Their soul is Christ's abode
382	3	We have Christ's own promise, And that cannot fail
427	3	Sworn to be Christ's soldiers ever
470	3	pass astray Into the dear Christ's life of sacrifice

Christendom

183	3	through Christendom it rings That the Lamb is King of kings

Christian

28	3	And all rejoice with Christian heart and voice
115	2	Then cleansed be every Christian breast
125	T,1-3	Good Christian Men, Rejoice, With heart and soul and voice
140	2	Good Christian, fear
184	T,1	Good Christian Men Rejoice and Sing
259	4	Enlarge, expand all Christian souls To comprehend thy love

272	T,1	Blest Be the Tie That Binds Our hearts in Christian love
304	3	One Christian fellowship of love abides
322	1	Saying, Christian, follow me
322	3	Saying, Christian, love me more
322	4	Christian, love me more than these
329	1	Shame on us, Christian brothers, His name and sign who bear
353	T,1	Lord, I Want to Be a Christian
364	T,1	Christian, Dost Thou See Them On the holy ground
364	1	Christian, up and smite them, Counting gain but loss
364	2	Christian, dost thou feel them, How they work within
364	2	Christian, never tremble, Never be downcast
364	3	Christian, dost thou hear them, How they speak thee fair
382	T,1,R	Onward, Christian Soldiers, Marching as to war
416	T,1	Christian, Rise and Act Thy Creed
475	1	And yet vouchsafes in Christian lands To dwell in temples

Christians
| 127 | T,1 | Christians, Awake, Salute the Happy Morn |

Christly
| 414 | 4 | All Christly souls are one in him |

Christmas
122	1	Remember Christ, our Savior, Was born on Christmas Day
122	4	This holy tide of Christmas Doth bring redeeming grace
134	4	We hear the Christmas angels The great glad tidings tell
488	3	And God sent us salvation That blessed Christmas morn

church
3	2	Hear, O Christ the praises That thy Church how raises
18	5	The holy Church throughout the world, O Lord, confesses thee
28	2	Thy Church doth in thy strength rely
28	2	Thy Church ... standeth sure while earth and time endure
47	2	We thank thee that thy Church, unsleeping
66	6	For thy Church that evermore Lifteth holy hands above
108	1	He comes, O Church, lift up thine eyes
193	2	Let his church with gladness Hymns of triumph sing
223	3	The Church in earth and heaven
241	3	let thy Church on earth become Blest as the Church above
247	3	from morn to set of sun Through the Church the song goes on
252	2	The Church from her dear Master Received the gift divine
252	4	O make thy Church, dear Savior, A lamp of burnished gold
260	3	And the great Church victorious Shall be the Church at rest
261	2	One holy Church, one army strong, One steadfast high intent
262	2	One Church for all humanity
263	1	Binding all the Church in one
264	1	Lord, thy Church is praying yet, A thousand years the same
264	3	For not like kingdoms of the world Thy holy Church, O God
266	T,1	One Holy Church of God Appears Through every age and race
266	4	O living Church, thine errand speed
268	1	Churches in thy Church rejoice
269	1	Church our blest Redeemer saved With his own precious blood
269	2	I love thy Church, O God, Her walls before they stand
270	T,1	Built on the Rock the Church doth stand
270	1	the Church doth stand Even when steeples are falling

286	3	One Church united in communion blest
289	2	Watch o'er thy Church, O Lord, in mercy
289	2	So from all lands thy Church be gathered Into thy kingdom
289	2	thy Church be gathered Into thy kingdom by thy Son
300	3	The Church for you doth wait
301	T,1	Jesus, With Thy Church Abide
304	3	And from his waiting Church new hopes arise
304	4	Rejoice, rejoice, his Church on earth is one
304	4	Church ... binds the ransomed nations 'neath the sun
378	3	Peace, in thy Church, where brothers are engaging
382	2	Like a mighty army Moves the Church of God
382	3	But the Church of Jesus Constant will remain
382	3	Gates of hell can never 'Gainst that Church prevail
439	2	For the home, the church, the school
477	1	Thy Church shall stand as stands thy word
481	3	In church, or in trains, or in shops, or at tea
504	2	Hosanna in the highest strains The Church on earth can raise
559	5	holy Church throughout all the world doth acknowledge thee

church's
260	T,1	The Church's One Foundation Is Jesus Christ her Lord
268	3	Bless thy Church's new endeavor
366	1	Crown thine ancient church's story
378	1	Hear and receive thy Church's supplication,
472	4	O Christ, the Church's head, Who for us all has bled

churches
| 265 | 2 | Lord, set thy churches free From foolish rivalry |
| 268 | 1 | Churches in thy Church rejoice |

circle
69	2	Kings of knowledge and of law, To the glorious circle draw
329	2	And thorns thy brow encircle, And tears thy face have marred
455	3	Home closer draws her circle now

circling
97	T,1	God of Our Life, Through All the Circling Years
98	2	So many gentle thoughts and deeds Circling us round
129	4	with the ever-circling years Comes round the age of gold
215	T,1	Lead, Kingly Light, amid the encircling gloom
275	T,1	Eternal Ruler of the Ceaseless Round Of circling planets
275	1	round Of circling planets singing on their way
443	2	have seen him in the watchfires of a hundred circling camps
448	T,1	Thy Kingdom Come, O Lord, Wide-circling as the sun

cities
| 440 | 4 | Thine alabaster cities gleam, Undimmed by human tears |
| 484 | 1 | In strange and lovely cities, Or roam the desert sands |

citizens
| 132 | 2 | Sing, all ye citizens of heaven above |

city
74	3	Soaring spire and ruined city ... our hopes & failures show
106	5	City of God, the bond are free
171	T,1	There Is a Green Hill Far Away, Without a city wall

clasps

387	1	Brother clasps the hand of brother

class

439	4	From the strife of class and faction Make our nation free

clause

401	4	A servant with this clause Makes drudgery divine

clay

9	2	His sovereign power without our aid Made us of clay
9	2	Made us of clay and formed us men
232	2	No sudden rending of the veil of clay

clean

324	2	Hallow each thought, let all within Be clean
324	2	Be clean, as thou, my Lord, art clean
401	3	Will not grow bright and clean
407	3	Clean hands in holy worship raise
528	T,1	Create in Me a Clean Heart, O God
531	1	O God, make clean our hearts within us
533	1	O God, make clean our hearts within us

cleanly

392	3	Controlled and cleanly night and day

cleanse

237	3	And cleanse them of their hate and strife
318	3	Cleanse it from guilt and wrong, Teach it salvation's song
319	4	Wilt welcome, pardon, cleanse, relieve
358	1	Be of sin the double cure, Cleanse me from its guilt & power
435	3	Cleanse the body of this nation Through the ... Lord

cleansed

115	2	Then cleansed be every Christian breast
289	2	Cleansed and conformed unto thy will
407	3	That, cleansed from stain of sin, I may meet homage give

clear

64	3	Thou flowing water, pure and clear
67	4	But higher far, and far more clear Thee in man's spirit
129	T,1	It Came Upon the Midnight Clear, that glorious song of old
161	1	And by its clear, revealing beams We measure gain and loss
161	1	On all, the judgment of the cross Falls steady, clear & sure
198	1	The day-star clear and bright Of every man and nation
208	1	Let thy clear light forever shine
218	2	O Let me hear thee speaking In accents clear and still
224	4	But dim or clear, we own in thee The light ... truth ... way
242	1	Wake my spirit, clear my sight
245	2	with wisdom kind and clear Let thy life in mine appear
259	3	Upward we press, the air is clear, & the sphere-music heard
304	4	When o'er the strife of nations sounding clear Shall ring
387	1	Clear before us through the darkness Gleams ... light
418	2	move By some clear, winning word of love
434	3	strong and true, With vision clear and mind equipped
442	1	Forgive, and show our duty clear

449	3	Give us the peace of vision clear To see our brother's good
455	1	snow Has left the heavens all coldly clear
508	2	O Light all clear, O Truth most holy

clearer
| 386 | 3 | Till clearer light our slumbering souls awake |
| 456 | 2 | And clearer sounds the angel hymn, Good will to men on earth |

clearest
| 108 | 3 | With harp and cymbal's clearest tone |
| 255 | 2 | The Lord's commandments all are pure & clearest light impart |

clearly
| 73 | 3 | Silver fountain, clearly gushing |

clears
| 107 | 3 | powers of hell may vanish As the darkness clears away |
| 337 | 1 | Through waves and clouds and storms He gently clears the way |

cleave
| 403 | 1 | cleave the wood, and there am I |
| 435 | 3 | Cleave our darkness with thy sword |

cleaving
| 73 | 2 | Peaks cloud-cleaving snowy crested |
| 351 | 5 | Or if on joyful wing Cleaving the sky |

cleft
| 358 | T,1,4 | Rock of Ages, Cleft for me, Let me hide myself in thee |

climb
158	3	Calvary's mournful mountain climb
230	3	We may not climb the heavenly steeps
259	3	Our souls would higher climb

climbed
| 388 | 4 | They climbed the steep ascent of heaven |
| 388 | 4 | They climbed ... Through peril, toil, and pain |

climbing
| 129 | 3 | Who toil along the climbing way With painful steps and slow |
| 495 | T,1 | We Are Climbing Jacob's Ladder |

clime
| 248 | 3 | I walk secure and blessed In every clime or coast |
| 261 | 1 | The true thy chartered free-men are, Of every age and clime |

cling
| 232 | 3 | I see thy cross -- there teach my heart to cling |
| 358 | 3 | Nothing in my hand I bring, Simply to thy cross I cling |

clings
| 360 | 1 | To one fixed trust my spirit clings, I know that God is good |

cloak
| 487 | 2 | God's care like a cloak Wraps us country folk |

close
44	1,2	O leave us not at close of day
51	2	With thy tenderest blessing May our eyelids close
56	3	And with sweet sleep mine eye-lids close
153	1	Teach us ... to mourn our sins, And close by thee to stay
209	2	Swift to its close ebbs out life's little day
349	5	So shall my walk be close with God, Calm and serene my frame
358	4	When mine eyes shall close in death
399	3	I cannot close my heart to thee
454	1	That mercy crowns it till it close
507	T,1	To Thee Before the Close of Day
510	2	With thy tenderest blessing May our eyelids close

closed
329	T,1	O Jesus, Thou Art Standing Outside the fast-closed door
340	4	peace of God, it is no peace, But strife closed in the sod

closer
318	T,1	Draw Thou My Soul, O Christ, Closer to thine
318	3	Lift thou thy world, O Christ, Closer to thee
349	T,1	O For a Closer Walk With God, A calm and heavenly frame
350	T,1	O for a Closer Walk With God (same words as no. 349)
418	3	Teach me thy patience, still with thee In closer
418	3	In closer, dearer company
455	3	Home closer draws her circle now

closes
405	4	Thus, in thy service, Lord, Till eventide Closes the day
405	4	Till eventide Closes the day of life, May we abide

closeth
53	T,1	The Duteous Day Now Closeth, Each flower and tree reposeth

closing
59	T,1	Now God Be With Us, for the night is closing
209	5	Hold thou thy cross before my closing eyes

clothe
239	2	And clothe me round, the while my path illuming
459	2	descend and clothe the ground

clothes
183	1	Kept the folded grave-clothes Where the body lay
455	2	And clothes the boughs with glittering wreaths

cloud
42	2	Out of the cloud and strife Sunrise is born
50	1	Oh, may no earth-born cloud arise To hide thee
50	1	no ... cloud arise To hide thee from thy servant's eyes
82	1	Thy truth shall break through every cloud That veils
174	3	peals aloud Upward through the whelming cloud
209	3	Through cloud and sunshine, O abide with me
249	2	led ... with the fire and cloud
256	3	Pillar of fire through watches dark, & radiant cloud by day

267	3	Round each habitation hovering, See the cloud & fire appear
362	2	A cloud of witnesses around Hold thee in full survey
453	1	The flying cloud, the frosty light
459	3	The changing wind, the flying cloud, Obey his mighty word

clouded

86	4	May thy fresh light arise Within each clouded heart

clouds

6	2	His chariots of wrath the deep thunder-clouds form
7	2	Thy clouds which are fountains of goodness and love
8	1	Melt the clouds of sin and sadness
64	2	Ye clouds that sail in heaven along
68	3	clouds arise, and tempests blow, By order from thy throne
75	2	See the glorious orb of day Breaking through the clouds
75	2	Breaking through the clouds his way
87	2	The clouds ye so much dread Are big with mercy
87	2	clouds ... shall break In blessings on your head
89	3	All, save the clouds of sin, are thine
110	2	Disperse the gloomy clouds of night
119	4	need no star to guide, Where no clouds thy glory hide
252	4	Till, clouds and darkness ended, They see thee face to face
258	3	When the storms are o'er us And dark clouds before us
337	1	Through waves and clouds and storms He gently clears the way
343	3	Bright skies ... Where the dark clouds have been
422	1	Who in the clouds is pledged to come again
459	1	Over the heavens he spreads his clouds

cloudy

93	2	Let the fire & cloudy pillar Lead me all my journey through

cloven

129	2	Still through the cloven skies they come

clover

457	1	golden wealth of ripening grain And breath of clover fields

cloy

344	3	Pleasure that can never cloy

coast

248	3	I walk secure and blessed In every clime or coast

coat

482	1	We will lend a coat of fur, We will rock you

cold

106	3	On your far hills, long cold and gray, Has dawned
126	2	Cold on his cradle the dew-drops are shining
131	1	It came, a floweret bright, Amid the cold of winter
136	2	Ox and ass beside him From the cold would hide him
141	1	On a cold winter's night that was so deep
143	4	Sealed in a stone-cold tomb
221	1	Weak is the effort of my heart, And cold my warmest thought
240	1	Kindle a flame of sacred love In these cold hearts of ours
348	4	When death's cold, sullen stream Shall e'er me roll

370	3	E'en death's cold wave, I will not flee
455	4	O God, who givest the winter's cold As well as summer's
456	2	Burn brighter through the cold
478	3	The cold wind in the winter, The pleasant summer sun
579	2	Seed-time, harvest, cold, and heat shall their yearly round

coldly

455	1	snow Has left the heavens all coldly clear

color

42	3	Splendor he makes on earth, Color awakes on earth

colors

478	1	He made their glowing colors, He made their tiny wings

come

1	T,1,6	Our God Our Help In Ages Past, our hope for years to come
2	1	To us no harm shall now come nigh
4	1	Come ye before him and rejoice
15	4	All ... life and breath, come now with praises before him
33	2	For from thee come all things good
34	2	Come, let thy voice be one with theirs
34	2	So let the love of Jesus come And set thy soul ablaze
50	5	Come near and bless us when we wake
76	1	Come, cast your burdens on the Lord
85	1	From whence doth come mine aid
91	6	Because thy trust is God alone ... no evil shall ... come
95	T,1	The Lord Will Come and Not Be Slow
95	4	The nations all whom thou hast made Shall come
103	T,1	Come, Thou Long-Expected Jesus, Born to set thy people free
105	3	He shall come down like showers Upon the fruitful earth
106	5	Lo, from the North we come, From East, and West, and South
106	5	We come to live and reign in thee
108	2	Her star is risen, her light is come
108	2	Ah, come thou blessed One, God's own beloved Son
109	3	Traveler, lo, the Prince of peace ... Son of God is come
110	T,1	O Come, O Come Emmanuel, And ransom captive Israel
110	R	Rejoice, Rejoice, Emmanuel Shall come to thee, O Israel
110	2	O Come, thou Day-spring, come and cheer Our spirits
110	3	O come, thou Wisdom from on high
114	3	Redeemer, come, I open wide My heart to thee
114	4	So come, my Sovereign, enter in
115	1	Come then and hearken, for he brings Glad tidings
115	2	let us each our hearts prepare For Christ to come and enter
116	3	Come to Bethlehem and see Him whose birth the angels sing
116	3	Come adore on bended knee Christ the Lord, the new-born King
117	R	Come and worship, Worship Christ, the new-born King
120	2	Late in time behold him come, Offspring of the Virgin's womb
121	T,1	From Heaven Above to Earth I Come
123	2	Brethren, come, from all doth grieve you You are freed
123	3	Come, then, let us hasten yonder
124	3	Softly to the little stable, Softly for a moment come
129	2	Still through the cloven skies they come
129	3	Look now, for glad and golden hours Come swiftly on the wing
130	T,1	Joy to the World, The Lord Is Come
132	T,1	O Come, All Ye Faithful, joyful and triumphant

328	1	O come to him, come now to him With a believing mind
336	T,1	O Thou by Whom we Come to God, The Life, the Truth, the Way
336	3	God of all grace, we come to thee With broken ... hearts
342	R	O bless me now, my Savior, I come to thee
342	3	Come quickly, and abide Or life is vain
346	T,1	Come, Let Us Join with Faithful Souls
358	3	Naked, come to thee for dress
360	4	No harm from him can come to me On ocean or on shore
375	T,1	Lead On, O King Eternal, The day of march has come
402	2	Such ever bring thee where they come
409	1	By thy lowly human birth Thou hast come to join the workers
411	4	Until in all the earth thy kingdom come
413	3	Come, O Christ, and reign above us
416	4	Come then, law divine, and reign
420	1	Within whose four-square walls shall come No night
422	1	Who in the clouds is pledged to come again
422	5	Then will he come with meekness for his glory
423	6	Till glorious from thy heaven above Shall come the city
423	6	Shall come the city of our God
425	T,1	Men, Whose Boast It Is that ye Come of fathers brave & free
428	3	Let them come out with Egypt's spoil
430	2	Until thou see God's kingdom come
442	3	Lo, fearing nought we come to thee
444	1	Come with thy ... judgment now To match our present hour
444	1	Come with thy timeless judgment now
444	3	And finely build for days to come Foundations that endure
445	1-4	Thy kingdom come, O Lord, thy will be done
448	T,1	Thy Kingdom Come, O Lord, Wide-circling as the sun
456	T,1	All Beautiful the March of Days, As seasons come and go
457	T,1	The Summer Days Are Come Again
457	3	The summer days are come again, The birds are on the wing
461	T,1	Come, Ye Thankful People, Come
461	1	Come to God's own temple, come, Raise the song of harvest
461	3	For the Lord our God shall come And shall take his harvest
461	4	Even so, Lord, quickly come To thy final harvest home
461	4	Come, with all thine angels, come
462	T,1	Come, Ye Thankful People Come (different vs. 2-3)
462	1,3	Come to God's own temple, come
462	3	Come, then, thankful people, come, Raise the song of harvest
466	2	With heart still undefiled, Thou didst to manhood come
444	3	finely build for days to come Foundations that endure
472	2	Come, thou, O Lord divine, Make this thy holy shrine
477	2	Come, fix thy glorious presence here
477	3	Come, with thy Spirit and thy power
483	2	Let the little ones come unto me
484	3	Shall understand his kingdom And come into his grace
490	4	And be by thee prepared For larger years to come
494	3	When to our ears there come divine commands
503	2	Gracious God, I come before thee
503	2	Come thou also unto me
506	T,1	Come, My Soul, Thou Must Be Waking
506	1	Come to him who made this splendor
525	T,1	Come, & Let Us Sweetly Join Christ to praise in hymns divine
530	T,1	O Thou by Whom We Come to God, The Life, the Truth, the Way
536	T,1	All Things Come of Thee, O Lord
559	11	We believe that thou shalt come to be our judge

562	T,1	O Come, Let Us Sing unto the Lord
562	2	Let us come before his presence with thanksgiving
562	6	O come, let us worship and fall down
565	1	and come before his presence with a song
575	T,1	Come, Holy Ghost, Our Souls Inspire
575	3	Where thou art guide no ill can come

comes

42	3	When Christ the herald comes Quietly nigh
78	2	afraid his power shall fail When comes thy evil day
105	1	He comes to break oppression, to set the captive free
105	2	He comes with succor speedy To those who suffer wrong
106	2	He comes to reign with boundless sway
108	1	He comes, O Church, lift up thine eyes
108	2	For her Lord comes down all glorious
112	2	Like the sheltering tree that groweth, Comes the life
112	2	Comes the life eternal here
112	3	Comes the Lord when strikes the hour
128	2	Heaven and earth shall flee away When he comes to reign
129	4	with the ever-circling years Comes round the age of gold
185	3	With the royal feast of feasts, Comes its joy to render
185	3	Comes to glad Jerusalem Who with true affection
201	4	Christ, our King, in beauty comes, And we his face shall see
253	1	Wisdom comes to those who know thee
293	4	glad sound comes with the setting sun, Well done, well done
315	1	O blessed voice of Jesus, Which comes to hearts oppressed
315	2	O loving voice of Jesus, Which comes to cheer the night
315	3	O cheering voice of Jesus, Which comes to aid our strife
330	5	If there is aught of worth in me, It comes from thee alone
357	5	And yet we trust it comes from thee
365	3	And through the truth that comes from God Mankind ... free
375	2	But deeds of love and mercy, The heavenly kingdom comes
376	2	And age comes on uncheered by faith and hope
441	T,1	Once to Every Man and Nation Comes the moment to decide
467	2	Comes with its calm the thought that thou art o'er us
484	2	The truth that comes from Jesus, The glory of his Word
486	1	Comes the eastern sun Like a man of brawn
494	3	O grant enduring worth Until the heavenly kingdom comes
494	3	Until the heavenly kingdom comes on earth

comest

| 326 | 5 | my heart shall rejoice, Lord Jesus, When thou comest |
| 326 | 5 | When thou comest and callest me |

cometh

59	2	The morning cometh, watch, Protector, o'er us
85	1	My safety cometh from the Lord, Who heaven & earth hath made
155	2	Who in the Lord's name cometh, The King and blessed One
315	4	And whosoever cometh I will not cast him out
364	1	In the strength that cometh By the holy cross
467	1	Dark though the night, joy cometh with the morrow
562	9	For he cometh, for he cometh to judge the earth

comfort

| 31 | 2 | Comfort thy sorrows and answer thy prayerfulness |
| 51 | 4 | Comfort every sufferer Watching late in pain |

79	4	Thy rod and staff my comfort still
82	3	grace Whence all our hope and comfort spring
84	3	thy rod And staff me comfort still
104	T,1	Comfort, Comfort Ye My People
104	1	Comfort those who sit in darkness
122	R	O tidings of comfort and joy
173	2	O word of comfort, through the silence stealing
210	2	Leave, ah, leave me not alone, Still support and comfort me
231	2	blessed unction from above Is comfort, life and fire of love
238	1	With light and comfort from above
258	5	Word of life, supplying Comfort to the dying
370	1	O words with heavenly comfort fraught
392	5	That, under thee, we may possess Man's strength to comfort
392	5	Man's strength to comfort man's distress
436	2	From all the easy speeches That comfort cruel men
482	2	Sleep in comfort, slumber deep, We will rock you
575	2	blessed unction from above Is comfort, life and fire of love

comforter

2	4	O Holy Spirit, precious Gift, Thou Comforter unfailing
239	1	O Comforter, draw near, Within my heart appear
246	3	Come, holy Comforter
559	6	also the Holy Ghost, the Comforter

comfortless

| 183 | 2 | He who bore all pain and loss Comfortless upon the cross |

comforts

94	2	Unnumbered comforts to my soul Thy tender care bestowed
94	2	Before my infant heart conceived From whom those comforts
94	2	From whom those comforts flowed
209	1	When other helpers fail, and comforts flee
250	3	Who upholds and comforts us in all trials, fears, and needs
272	2	Our comforts and our cares
328	1	His comforts, they shall strengthen thee

coming

60	3	Grant us thy peace, Lord, through the coming night
97	3	God of the coming years, through paths unknown we follow
131	1	Of Jesse's lineage coming As men of old have sung
134	3	No ear may hear his coming, But in this world of sin
248	2	And in the coming glory Thou shalt be Sovereign Lord
268	2	God be praise for congregations Coming side by side to thee
326	5	When the heavens shall ring & the angels sing At thy coming
326	5	angels sing At thy coming to victory
422	1	Peals like a trumpet promise of his coming
443	T,1	Mine Eyes Have Seen the Glory of the coming of the Lord

command

9	5	Wide as the world is thy command
23	1	Or through the realms of light Fly at your Lord's command
68	1	The moon shines full at his command, And all the stars obey
112	1	Rise, and join the Lord's command
144	2	To read in heaven the Lord's command
308	3	True and faithful to command, Swift and fearless to obey
337	2	Leave to this sovereign sway To choose and to command

339	2	Love doth stand At his hand, Joy doth wait on his command
406	3	And labor on at thy command, And offer all my works to thee
426	4	Speak, and behold, we answer, Command, and we obey

commanding

| 70 | 2 | He, with all commanding might, Filled the new-made earth |

commandments

100	5	Unto those who still remember His commandments and obey
255	2	The Lord's commandments all are pure & clearest light impart
419	2	And steadfastly pursue the way Of thy commandments still

commands

| 76 | T,1 | How Gentle God's Commands, How kind his precepts are |
| 494 | 3 | When to our ears there come divine commands |

commending

| 168 | 4 | And, to thy Father's hands thy soul commending |

commit

394	1	I commit my spirit unto thee
394	2	Sinful, I commit myself to thee
454	3	future, all to us unknown, We to thy guardian care commit

common

36	5	The trivial round, the common task, Will furnish all
36	5	the common task, Will furnish all we ought to ask
220	3	The common hopes that makes us men Were his in Galilee
276	2	The common home of rich and poor, Of bond and free
276	2	common home of ... great and small
396	2	Praise in the common things of life, Its goings out and in
403	2	Lo, the Prince of common welfare dwells within the market
413	4	Liked in bonds of common service For the common Lord of all
453	4	Ring in the common love of good
525	1	Give we all, with one accord, Glory to our common Lord

commonwealth

| 448 | 4 | The commonwealth of man, The city of our God |

commotion

| 305 | 1 | Of nations in commotion, Prepared for Zion's war |

communion

260	4	And mystic sweet communion With those whose rest is won
269	4	Her sweet communion, solemn vows, Her hymns of love & praise
286	3	One Church united in communion blest
306	4	O blest communion, fellowship divine
414	2	In him shall true hearts ... Their high communion find
539	2	possess in sweet communion Joys which earth cannot afford

companion

409	T,1	Jesus, Thou Divine Companion
409	3	Jesus, thou divine companion, Help us all to work our best
492	3	Companion of this sacred hour, Renew

company
18	4	The apostles glorious company ... Thy constant praise recite
268	1	Making strong our company
418	3	In closer, dearer company
419	2	One in the patient company Of those who heed thy will
559	4	The glorious company of the apostles praise thee

compare
| 309 | 1 | What radiancy of glory, What bliss beyond compare |

compass
213	1	Chart and compass come from thee, Jesus, Savior, pilot me
252	3	It is the chart and compass That o'er life's surging sea
364	1	How the powers of darkness Compass thee around

compassion
100	3	Like the pity of a father Hath the Lord's compassion been
159	4	Give us compassion for thee, Lord
173	2	O infinite compassion, still revealing ... forgiveness
228	1	Jesus, thou art all compassion
277	3	Grant to us a deep compassion For thy children everywhere
398	1	thou Christ of great compassion
423	4	Yet long these multitudes to see The sweet compassion
423	4	The sweet compassion of thy face

complaining
| 409 | 2 | They who work without complaining Do the holy will of God |

complete
158	3	Mark that miracle of time, God's own sacrifice complete
168	4	The world redeemed, the will of God complete
198	2	the whole round world complete, From sunrise to its setting
579	2	Shall their yearly round complete

completeness
| 38 | 2 | Sprung in completeness Where his feet pass |

completing
| 253 | 2 | Many diverse scrolls completing |

compose
| 177 | 3 | Or thorns compose so rich a crown |

comprehend
| 259 | 4 | Enlarge, expand all Christian souls To comprehend thy love |
| 407 | 1 | Nor mind thy brightness comprehend |

comprehendeth
| 230 | 2 | Love only knoweth whence it came, And comprehendeth love |

comrades
| 411 | 2 | One make us all, true comrades in thy service |
| 450 | 3 | Inarmed shall live as comrades free |

conceit
| 386 | 2 | Lighten our darkness of our self-conceit |

conceived

94	2	Before my infant heart conceived From whom those comforts

concert

19	4	In the concert bear your parts
111	2	Every voice in concert ring, Evermore and evermore

concord

35	3	Ye nations of mankind, In this your concord find

condemned

105	2	Whose souls, condemned and dying, Were precious in his sight

conferred

259	4	And make us to go on, to know With nobler powers conferred

confess

18	T,1	O God, We Praise Thee,and Confess
26	3	All our days, all our ways, shall our Father's love confess
147	4	Let every tongue confess with one accord
147	4	confess ... that Jesus Christ is Lord
160	2	And from my smitten heart with tears Two wonders I confess
197	1	Every tongue confess him King of glory now
230	2	Our outward lips confess the Name All other names above
250	3	We all confess the Holy Ghost Who from both fore'er proceeds
257	2	nights and days thy power confess
341	4	And let our ordered lives confess The beauty of thy peace

confessed

306	1	Who thee by faith before the world confessed

confesses

18	5	The holy Church throughout the world, O Lord, confesses thee

confessing

22	3	Our sins now confessing, we pray for thy blessing
244	2	By thy power Christ confessing, Let us win his grace
262	3	Confessing, in a world's accord, The inward Christ
305	2	While sinners, now confessing, The gospel call obey
332	1	Our misdeeds to thee confessing, On thy name we humbly call

confide

81	3	How blest are they, and only they, Who in his truth confide
91	4	Beneath his wings shalt thou confide
363	2	Did we in our own strength confide, Our striving would be

confidence

77	2	Thy hope, thy confidence let nothing shake
118	1	This child, now weak in infancy, Our confidence ... shall be
118	1	Our confidence and joy shall be
263	1	Holy Zion's help forever, And her confidence alone
336	4	A strong, desiring confidence To hear thy voice and live

confident

380	1	Who 'gainst enthroned wrong Stood confident and bold

confiding
343 1   And safe is such confiding, For nothing changes here

confined
236 2   Never was to chosen race That unstinted tide confined
259 1   By notions of our day and sect, Crude, partial and confined
402 2   thou, within no walls confined, Inhabitest the humble mind

confirm
72 2   Whilst all the stars that round her burn ... confirm
72 2   And all the planets in their turn, Confirm the tidings
72 2   Confirm the tidings as they roll
440 2   Confirm thy soul in self control, Thy liberty in law
471 2   Confirm in him his high and holy calling

conflict
60 4   Then, when thy voice shall bid our conflict cease
158 1   Your Redeemer's conflict see
167 VII-1 Jesus, all thy labor vast, All thy woe and conflict past
168 1   In all the conflict of thy sore temptation
222 2   Sin and hell in conflict fell
319 2   With many a conflict, many a doubt
380 4   Not long the conflict, soon The holy war shall cease
385 2   Forth to the mighty conflict, In this his glorious day
387 3   One the conflict, one the peril, One the march in God begun
398 1   Speak to our fearful hearts by conflict rent

conflicts
384 2   That, having all things done, And all your conflicts past

conformed
289 2   Cleansed and conformed unto thy will

confound
61 3   When life's perils thick confound you
371 2   Do but themselves confound, His strength the more is.
373 2   What terror can confound me With God at my right hand

confounded
442 3   Though by our fault confounded
445 3   Envious of heart, blind-eyed, with tongues confounded
559 16   O Lord, in thee have I trusted, let me never be confounded

confusion
86 1   Whose stars serenely burn Above this earth's confusion

congregation
21 3   Let thy congregation escape tribulation
206 2   The great congregation his triumph shall sing

congregations
268 2   God be praise for congregations Coming side by side to thee

conquer

153	2	O give us strength in thee to fight, In thee to conquer sin
180	2	Christ has triumphed, & we conquer By his mighty enterprise
296	4	We conquer only in that sign
347	4	Then, like thine own, be all our aim To conquer them by love
383	3	Not alone we conquer, Not alone we fall
398	5	Who by this sign didst conquer grief and pain
496	2	Then conquer we must, when our cause it is just

conquered

175	2	thy triumphs now begin O'er captive death and conquered sin
309	3	And they, who with their leader, Have conquered in the fight

conquering

193	T,1,R	Thine Is the Glory, Risen, conquering Son
445	2	His conquering cross no kingdom wills to bear

conqueror

229	4	My dear almighty Lord, My Conqueror and my King
356	1	Force me to render up my sword, And I shall conqueror be
384	1	Who in the strength of Jesus trusts Is more than conqueror
477	3	The Conqueror, Once the Crucified

conquerors

193	3	Make us more than conquerors, Through thy deathless love

conquest

78	4	He gives the conquest to the weak
375	1	Henceforth in fields of conquest Thy tents shall be our home
375	3	The crown awaits the conquest, Lead on, O God of might

conquests

439	2	Not for battleship and fortress ... conquests of the sword
439	2	But for conquests of the spirit Give we thanks ... O Lord

conscience

242	4	Holy Spirit, Right divine, King within my conscience reign
365	2	Were still in heart and conscience free
412	3	Give us a conscience bold and good, Give us a purpose true

conscious

55	4	they who fain would serve thee best Are conscious most
55	4	who serve thee best .... Are conscious most of wrong within
74	4	Conscious of our human need

consciousness

37	1	lovelier ... Dawns the sweet consciousness, I am with thee
37	3	So does this blessed consciousness, awaking, Breathe

consecrated

404	T,1	Take My Life and Let It Be Consecrated, Lord, to thee
427	3	Sworn to yield, to waver, never, Consecrated, born again

content

83	2	with heart content To take whate'er thy Father's pleasure
96	2	And take, content, What he hath sent
160	3	Content to let the world go by, To know no gain nor loss
370	2	Content whatever lot I see, Since 'tis my God that leadeth
420	2	O shame to us who rest content While lust and greed for gain

contented

340	2	Contented, peaceful fishermen, Before they ever knew ... God

contentment

217	4	Whose voice is contentment, whose presence is balm

continent

47	3	As o'er each continent and island The dawn leads on

continents

298	2	Give ear to me, ye continents, Ye isles, give ear to me

continually

18	2	To thee, the powers on high ... Continually do cry
18	2	Both cherubim and seraphim, Continually do cry
559	2	To thee cherubim and seraphim continually do cry

continue

168	1	We would continue with thee day by day

continued

141	2	And so it continued both day and night

contrite

225	3	O hope of every contrite heart, O joy of all the meek
336	3	With broken, contrite hearts
431	2	Still stands thine ancient sacrifice ... a contrite heart
431	2	An humble and a contrite heart
529	1	A broken and a contrite heart, O God, thou wilt not despise

control

32	4	Direct, control, suggest, this day All I design or do or say
100	6	Bless the Father, all his creatures, Ever under his control
218	2	O speak to reassure me, To hasten or control
366	3	Bend our pride to thy control
440	2	Confirm thy soul in self control, Thy liberty in law

controlled

392	3	Controlled and cleanly night and day

convey

257	3	Sun, moon, and stars convey thy praise Round the whole earth

convict

442	1	Convict us now, if we rebel, Our nation judge, and shame it

conviction

540	1	Still our minds with truth's conviction

cool
328   1   Like flowing waters cool

cooling
390   T,1   As Pants the Hart for cooling streams

coolness
341   5   Breathe through the pulses of desire Thy coolness & thy balm

cope
303   4   And still with haughty foes must cope

coral
106   2   Isles of the southern seas, Deep in your coral caves

cord
414   2   His service is the golden cord Close-binding all mankind

corn
459   1   And corn in valleys grow
461   2   Then the full corn shall appear
487   1   Pearly rice and corn, Fragrant autumn morn

corners
562   4   In his hand are all the corners of the earth

cornerstone
263   1   Christ the head and cornerstone
475   2   Built on the precious Cornerstone

cost
34   3   To spend thyself nor count the cost
295   2   Redeemed at countless cost From dark despair

costliest
119   3   All our costliest treasures bring, Christ, to thee

costly
126   3   Say, shall we yield him, in costly devotion
405   T,1   Master, No Offering Costly and Sweet

cot
426   2   I hear my people crying In cot and mine and slum

couch
326   3   But thy couch was the sod ... In the deserts of Galilee

could
44   2   They could not let the Stranger go
142   2   But the very beasts could see that he all men surpasses
149   T,1   I Know Not How That Bethlehem's Babe Could in the Godhead be
149   2   know not how ... Calvary's cross A world from sin could free
149   3   know not how that Joseph's tomb Could solve death's mystery
169   5   In whose sweet praise I all my days Could gaily spend
217   1   Whose trust, ever child-like, no cares could destroy
256   4   Without thee how could earth be trod, Or heaven ... be won

297	4	faith like theirs Who served the days they could not see
358	2	Could my zeal no respite know, Could my tears forever flow
358	2	All for sin could not atone, Thou must save and thou alone
388	2	martyr first, whose eagle eye Could pierce beyond the grave

counsel

308	4	Lord and light of every age, By thy same sure counsel led
337	2	Far, far above thy thought His counsel shall appear
454	2	By his incessant bounty fed, By his unerring counsel led

counsellor

229	3	Be thou my counsellor, My pattern and my guide

counsels

61	1	By his counsels guide, uphold you
459	2	His steady counsels change the face Of the declining year

count

34	3	To spend thyself nor count the cost
177	1	My richest gain I count but loss
330	T,1	One Who Is All Unfit to Count As scholar in thy school
451	1	Old now is earth, and none may count her days
470	5	Inspired of thee, may they count all but loss

counting

364	1	Christian, up and smite them, Counting gain but loss

countless

29	1	With countless gifts of love, And still is ours today
36	3	New treasures still, of countless price, God will provide
295	2	Redeemed at countless cost From dark despair
382	4	This through countless ages Men and angels sing
508	1	Thy name is blessed by countless numbers

country

141	3	Three wise men came from country far
309	4	O sweet and blessed country, The home of God's elect
309	4	O sweet and blessed country, that eager hearts expect
437	T,1	My Country, 'Tis of Thee
437	2	My native country, thee, Land of the noble free
440	3	Who more than self their country loved
487	2	God's care like a cloak Wraps us country folk

counts

337	1	God hears thy sighs and counts thy tears

courage

78	4	And courage in the evil hour His heavenly aids impart
87	2	Ye fearful saints, fresh courage take
161	2	The courage that we lack
173	3	When courage fails us, and when faith is dim
366	1	Grant us wisdom ... courage, For the facing of his hour
366	2	Grant us wisdom ... courage For the living of these days
366	3	Grant us wisdom ... courage, Lest we miss thy kingdom's goal
366	4	Grant us wisdom ... courage, That we fail not man nor thee
366	5	Grant us wisdom ... courage, Serving thee whom we adore

373	3	Place on the Lord reliance, My soul, with courage wait
377	1	And with courage play thy part
380	3	'Gainst lies and lusts & wrongs, Let courage rule our souls
385	2	Let courage rise with danger, & strength to strength oppose
409	1	By thy patience and thy courage, Thou hast taught us
411	1	Armed with thy courage, till the world is won

courageous

| 381 | 3 | Of patient & courageous heart, As all true saints have been |
| 434 | 3 | God send us men of steadfast will, Patient, courageous |

courageously

| 368 | 1 | But for strength that we may ever Live ... courageously |
| 368 | 1 | Live our lives courageously |

course

36	3	If on our daily course our mind Be set to hallow all we find
70	3	He the golden-tressed sun Caused all day his course to run
73	4	Each glad soul its free course winging
109	2	Traveler, blessedness and light ... its course portends
109	2	Peace and truth its course portends
381	2	Unstayed by pleasures, still they bent Their zealous course
381	2	they bent Their zealous course to God
486	1	Like a man of brawn Set his course to run

courts

4	3	Approach with joy his courts unto
9	4	earth, with her ten thousand tongues Shall fill thy courts
9	4	Shall fill thy courts with sounding praise
19	1	Saints within his courts below
31	3	Fear not to enter his courts in the slenderness of the poor
472	5	Still may these courts proclaim the glory of thy name
565	3	and into his courts with praise

covenant

100	5	Unto such as keep his covenant And are steadfast in his way
105	4	The tide of time shall never His covenant remove
558	3	'Tis the new covenant in my blood
568	5	and to remember his holy covenant

cover

104	1	Tell her that her sins I cover, And her warfare now is over
210	2	Cover my defenseless head With the shadow of thy wing
210	3	Grace to cover all my sin
298	1-4	As the waters cover the sea
576	5	If deepest darkness cover me

covering

267	3	For a glory and a covering, Showing that the Lord is near
389	4	Oh, spread thy covering wings around
445	1	Through the thick darkness covering every nation

cows

| 142 | 2 | Cradled in a stall was he with sleeply cows and asses |

177	T,1	When I Survey the Wondrous Cross
177	1	cross On which the Prince of glory died
180	1	He who on the cross as Savior For the world's salvation bled
182	4	Ours the cross, the grave, the skies
183	2	He who bore all pain and loss Comfortless upon the cross
187	1	Who did once upon the cross ... Suffer to redeem our loss
187	2	Who endured the cross and grave ... Sinners to redeem & save
200	4	To them the cross, with all its shame ... is given
200	4	To them the cross ... With all its grace, is given
209	5	Hold thou thy cross before my closing eyes
224	3	The solemn shadow of thy cross Is better than the sun
232	3	I see thy cross -- there teach my heart to cling
250	2	By whose cross and death are we Rescued from all misery
268	1	With the cross our only standard Let us sing
281	2	To thy cross we look and live
295	3	With us the cross to bear, For Christ our Lord
296	1	The cross on which the Savior died
296	3	Our glory only in the cross, Our only hope, the Crucified
299	4	The triumphs of the cross record
300	4	Lift high the cross of Christ Tread where his feet have trod
304	3	But on the cross God's love reveals his power
321	2	Before the cross of him who died, Behold, I prostrate fall
324	2	Nail my affections to the cross
325	1	Upon a cross they bound thee
325	4	We bring our hearts before thy cross To finish thy salvation
345	1	Your festal banner wave on high, The cross of Christ
345	1	The cross of Christ your King
347	T,1	Lord, As to Thy Dear Cross we flee, And plead to be forgiven
347	2	Help us, through good report & ill, Our daily cross to bear
351	1	E'en though it be a cross That raiseth me
358	3	Nothing in my hand I bring, Simply to thy cross I cling
361	3	Have faith in God, my soul, His cross forever stands
364	1	In the strength that cometh By the holy cross
375	3	Thy cross is lifted o'er us, We journey in its light
382	1,R	With the cross of Jesus Going on before
385	T,1	Stand Up, Stand Up for Jesus, Ye soldiers of the cross
388	1	Who patient bears his cross below, He follows in his train
388	3	And mocked the cross and flame
398	4	who by thy cross didst save us
399	4	O Cross that liftest up my head
423	T,1	Where Cross the Crowded Ways of Life
427	2	Now, the blazoned cross unfolding
441	2	With the cross that turns not back
445	2	His conquering cross no kingdom wills to bear
470	5	Make them apostles, Heralds of thy cross
471	5	He learns at length the triumph of the cross
472	4	Thy cross we lift on high This house to glorify
491	4	Bearing his cross in service glad and free
495	1-4	Soldiers of the cross

crossed

| 438 | 1 | Our exiled fathers crossed the sea |

crosses

| 494 | 1 | O'er crumbling walls their crosses scarcely lift |

crowd

9	4	We'll crowd thy gates with thankful songs
392	4	uncowed By fear or favor of the crowd

crowded

423	T,1	Where Cross the Crowded Ways of Life
435	2	And the city's crowded clangor Cries aloud for sin to cease

crowding

296	2	And nations, crowding to be born, Baptize their spirits

crowds

3	2	See the crowds the throne surrounding

crown

114	4	Thy Holy Spirit guide us on Until the glorious crown be won
143	2	Gold I bring to crown him again
170	1	Now scornfully surrounded With thorns thy only crown
177	3	Or thorns compose so rich a crown
195	R	And crown him Lord of all
195	2	Crown him, ye martyrs of our God, Who from his altar call
197	5	Crown him as your captain In temptation's hour
199	T,1	Crown Him With Many Crowns, The Lamb upon his throne
199	2	Crown him the Lord of love, Behold his hands and side
199	3	Crown him the Lord of life, Who triumphed o'er the grave
199	4	Crown him the Lord of years, The potentate of time
202	2	And praises throng to crown his head
203	1-3	Crown him, crown him
203	2	Crown the Savior, angels, crown him
203	2	Crown the Savior King of kings
203	4	crown him King of kings, and Lord of lords
227	1	Thee will I honor, Thou, my soul's glory, joy and crown
228	1	All thy faithful mercies crown
237	3	Send down thy love, thy life, Our lesser lives to crown
249	5	Praise we the goodness that doth crown our days
306	3	And win with them the victor's crown of gold
310	1	Crown for the valiant, to weary ones rest
326	T,1	Thou Didst Leave Thy Throne and thy kingly crown
326	4	But with mocking scorn and with crown of thorn they bore
356	3	It must its crown resign
362	1	A heavenly race demands thy zeal, And an immortal crown
366	1	Crown thine ancient church's story
367	1	Lay hold on life, & it shall be Thy joy and crown eternally
375	3	The crown awaits the conquest, Lead on, O God of might
380	4	Look up, the victor's crown at length
385	4	To him that overcometh A crown of life shall be
388	T,1	The Son of God Goes Forth to War, A kingly crown to gain
435	3	Crown, O God, thine own endeavor
440	1,4	And crown thy good with brotherhood From sea to shining sea
459	1	He makes the grass the mountains crown
470	4	Theirs not a jeweled crown, a blood-stained sword
493	4	that the stones of earthly shame A jewelled crown may seem

crowned

18	4	prophets crowned with light, with all the martyrs noble host
165	1	On the Redeemer's thorn-crowned brow ... that dawn we view

200	T,1	The Head That Once Was Crowned With Thorns
200	1	Is crowned with glory now
201	2	But crowned with glory like the sun
203	3	Sinners in derision crowned him
312	2	Thy saints are crowned with glory great
325	1	By thorns with which they crowned thee
345	2	Bright youth and snow-crowned age
362	4	crowned with victory, at thy feet I'll lay my honors down
374	2	Or, in darker semblance, Cross-crowned Calvary
430	2	Glad shalt thou be, with blessing crowned
451	1	Yet thou, her child, whose head is crowned with flame

crowns

199	T,1	Crown Him With Many Crowns, The Lamb upon his throne
203	1	Crowns become the victor's brow
228	4	Till we cast our crowns before thee
251	2	Casting down their golden crowns around the glassy sea
382	3	Crowns and thrones may perish, Kingdoms rise and wane
454	1	That mercy crowns it till it close
464	1	praise For the love that crowns our days

crucified

106	4	Yet lives and reigns, the Crucified
163	2	I crucified thee
164	1-3	Jesus, our Lord, is crucified
171	1	Where the dear Lord was crucified, Who died to save us all
179	T,1	Were You There when they crucified my Lord
296	3	Our glory only in the cross, Our only hope, the Crucified
321	2	Let every sin be crucified, Let Christ be all in all
340	3	Peter, who hauled the teeming net, Head down was crucified
477	3	The Conqueror, Once the Crucified

crucify

| 169 | 3 | Then, Crucify, Is all their breath |

crude

| 259 | 1 | By notions of our day and sect, Crude, partial and confined |

cruel

303	3	Beyond ... Wrong's bitter, cruel, scorching blight
363	1	And armed with cruel hate, On earth is not his equal
413	3	Bid its cruel discords cease
436	2	From all the easy speeches That comfort cruel men

crumbled

| 270 | 1 | Crumbled have spires in every land |

crumbling

432	2	And, all the ages through, past crumbling throne
432	2	past crumbling throne And broken fetter, thou hast brought
494	1	O'er crumbling walls their crosses scarcely lift

crushed

| 493 | 3 | When Stephen, young and doomed to die, Fell crushed |
| 493 | 3 | Fell crushed beneath the stones |

crushing

129	3	ye, beneath life's crushing load Whose forms are bending low

cry

2	3	hear our cry, Have mercy on us, Jesus
18	2	To thee all angels cry aloud
18	2	To thee, the powers on high ... Continually do cry
18	2	Both cherubim and seraphim, Continually do cry
30	1	Cry out, dominion, princedoms, powers
30	1	Cry out ... Virtues, archangels, angels' choirs, Alleluia
35	4	To God, the Word, on high, The hosts of angels cry
42	3	Hear we no beat of drums, Fanfare nor cry
65	1	Let the whole creation cry
65	2	Earth and sea cry, God is good
69	T,1	Let the Whole Creation Cry, Glory to the Lord on high
104	2	Oh, that warning cry obey, Now prepare for God a way
107	4	As with ceaseless voice they cry
115	T,1	On Jordan's Bank the Baptist's Cry
115	1	Baptist's cry Announces that the Lord is nigh
156	1	Draw nigh ... Thy faithful people cry with one accord
158	3	It is finished, hear him cry, Learn of Jesus Christ to die
169	3	And for his death They thirst and cry
174	3	Hark, that cry that peals aloud
174	4	Teach me by that bitter cry In the gloom to know thee nigh
175	1	Hark, all the tribes hosanna cry
183	2	Lives in glory now on high, Pleads for us and hears our cry
206	3	Let all cry aloud and honor the Son
212	3	Hear the cry thy people raises
332	5	Loving Savior, Holy Spirit, Hear and heed our humble cry
377	2	Though thou cry, with heart atremble, O my Savior, succor me
400	3	This be the parting cry My heart shall raise
420	2	And bitter lips in blind despair Cry
420	2	Cry, Christ hath died in vain
429	1-3	O hear us when we cry to thee, For those in peril on the sea
432	4	God of thy people, hear us cry to thee
436	T,1	O God of Earth and Altar, Bow down and hear our cry
451	3	Peals forth in joy man's old undaunted cry
452	1	in bitter need Thy children lift their cry to thee
493	3	had no curse nor vengeful cry For those who broke his bones
526	T,1	O Thou Who Hearest Prayer, Give ear unto our cry
559	2	To thee all angels cry aloud, the heavens and all the powers
559	2	To thee cherubim and seraphim continually do cry

crying

108	1	The watchmen on the heights are crying
137	2	But little Lord Jesus, no crying he makes
426	2	I hear my people crying In cot and mine and slum

crystal

93	2	Open now the crystal fountain
456	1	The crystal of the snow
456	3	Thyself the vision passing by In crystal and in rose

cumbered

335	3	Are we weak and heavy laden, Cumbered with a load of care

cup

84	4	My head thou dost with oil anoint, And my cup overflows
281	2	Vine of heaven, thy love supplies ... blest cup of sacrifice
284	2	Thy testamental cup I take, And thus remember thee
286	2	Faith still receives the cup as from thy hand
388	1	Who best can drink the cup of woe, Triumphant over pain
423	4	The cup of water given for thee Still holds the freshness
457	2	We know who giveth all the good That doth our cup o'erbrim
558	3	Then took the cup and blessed the wine

cure

154	1	sick to cure, the lost to seek, To raise up them that fall
358	1	Be of sin the double cure, Cleanse me from its guilt & power
366	3	Cure thy children's warring madness

curse

449	2	Purge us from lusts that curse and kill
493	3	had no curse nor vengeful cry For those who broke his bones

cut

459	2	he bids the sun cut short his race, And wintry days appear

cymbal's

108	3	With harp and cymbal's clearest tone

cymbals

24	1	Let harps and cymbals now unite

da

139	2	Tont es laut von fern und nah, Christ der Retter ist da
139	3	Da uns schlagt die rettende Stund'

daily

15	3	Surely his goodness and mercy here daily attend thee
32	1	Thy daily stage of duty run
33	T,1	As the Sun Doth Daily Rise Bright'ning all the morning skies
33	4	While we daily search thy Word, Wisdom true impart, O Lord
36	3	If on our daily course our mind Be set to hallow all we find
36	5	Room to deny ourselves - a road To bring us daily nearer God
61	2	Daily manna still provide you
94	3	Ten thousand precious gifts My daily thanks employ
97	3	Be thou for us in life our daily bread
150	3	For us his daily works he wrought
339	2	Daily doth the almighty giver Bounteous gifts on us bestow
347	2	Help us, through good report & ill, Our daily cross to bear
377	1	Thou art daily in his keeping, And thine every care is his
389	3	Give us each day our daily bread, And raiment fit provide
395	T,1	Behold Us, Lord, a Little Space From daily tasks set free
405	2	Daily our lives would show Weakness made strong
406	T,1	Forth in Thy Name, O Lord, I Go, My daily labor to pursue
409	1	Thou, the carpenter of Nazareth, Toiling for thy daily bread
409	2	Thou the peace that passeth knowledge Dwellest in the daily
409	2	Thou ... Dwellest in the daily strife
409	3	Bless us in our daily labor, Lead us to our sabbath rest
460	2	Much more, to us his children, He gives our daily bread
486	2	Give me daily bread While I do my part

dale
421	4	O'er hill and dale in saffron flame and red

dally
427	2	Will ye play then, will ye dally Far behind the battle line

damnation
436	2	From sleep and from damnation, Deliver us, good Lord

damps
443	2	builded him an altar in the evening dews and damps

danger
60	3	from harm and danger keep thy children free
123	2	Doth entreat, Flee from woe and danger
277	1	From all danger keep them free
368	4	Through endeavor, failure, danger, Father, be ...at our side
385	2	Let courage rise with danger, & strength to strength oppose
385	3	Where duty calls, or danger, Be never wanting there
491	3	And through life's darkness, danger, and disaster

danger's
429	4	shield in danger's hour From rock and tempest, fire and foe

dare
50	3	For without thee I dare not die
161	2	Our will to dare great things for God
167	III-2	May we in thy sorrows share, And for thee all perils dare
295	3	With us the work to share, With us reproach to dare
346	2	Faithful are all who ... dare the truth to tell
385	3	The arm of flesh will fail you, Ye dare not trust your own
399	4	I dare not ask to fly from thee
417	2	And those who can suffer can dare
420	4	Lo, how its splendor challenges The souls that greatly dare
425	3	slaves who dare not be In the right with two or three
450	2	dare All that may plant man's lordship firm On earth
489	1	I would be brave, for there is much to dare

dares
293	1	Who dares stand idle on the harvest plain
359	4	dares to take the side that seems Wrong to man's ... eye

daring
422	2	Speak to the heart of love, alive and daring
492	2	For prophet voices gladly heard, For daring dreams

dark
6	2	And dark is his path on the wings of the storm
8	1	Drive the dark of doubt away
43	2	Dark and cheerless is the morn Unaccompanied by thee
60	3	For dark and light are both alike to thee
72	3	Move round the dark terrestrial ball
79	4	In death's dark vale I fear no ill
84	3	Yea, though I walk in death's dark vale
96	1	Though dark my road, He holds me that I shall not fall
110	2	And death's dark shadows put to flight

134	1	Yet in thy dark streets shineth The everlasting Light
158	T,1	Go to Dark Gethsemane, Ye that feel the tempter's power
185	2	All the winter of our sins, Long and dark, is flying
185	4	Neither might the gates of death, Nor the tomb's dark portal
189	1	For he hath won the victory O'er sin and death's dark night
215	1	The night is dark and I am far from home, Lead thou me on
252	1	O Truth unchanged, unchanging, O Light of our dark sky
256	3	Pillar of fire through watches dark, & radiant cloud by day
258	3	When the storms are o'er us And dark clouds before us
290	4	Chase the dark night of sin away
295	2	Redeemed at countless cost From dark despair
297	3	The torch of their devotion lent, Lightens the dark
297	3	Lightens the dark that round us lies
343	3	Bright skies ... Where the dark clouds have been
348	3	While life's dark maze I tread, And griefs around me spread
365	2	Our fathers, chained in prisons dark, Were still ... free
398	4	save us From death and dark despair, from sin and guilt
423	2	On shadowed thresholds dark with fears
429	3	O Holy Spirit, who didst brood Upon the chaos dark and rude
447	2	Remember not our sin's dark stain
467	1	Dark though the night, joy cometh with the morrow
367	2	When fond hopes fail and skies are dark before us
467	2	When fond hopes fail and skies are dark before us
542	1	Through life's long day and death's dark night
558	T,1	Twas on That Dark and Doleful Night

darkened

147	1	That in our darkened hearts thy grace might shine
237	1	Too long the darkened way we've trod
421	3	We've felt thy touch in sorrow's darkened way
467	4	Yet shall thou praise him, when these darkened furrows

darkens

81	1	That veils and darkens thy designs

darker

374	2	Or, in darker semblance, Cross-crowned Calvary

darkest

98	2	That in the darkest spot of earth Some love is found
159	3	This is earth's darkest hour
359	2	in the darkest battlefield Thou shalt know where to strike
417	1	The night is darkest before the morn

darkling

252	3	It shineth like a beacon Above the darkling world
259	2	Darkling our great forefathers went The first steps

darkly

174	4	Lord, should fear & anguish roll Darkly o'er my sinful soul

darkness

35	2	The powers of darkness fear, When this sweet chant they hear
36	1	Through sleep and darkness safely brought
47	1	The darkness falls at thy behest
52	3	As the darkness deepens o'er us, Lo, eternal stars arise

97	1	With each new day, when morning lifts the veil
106	3	Has dawned the everlasting day
109	1	traveler, yes, it brings the day, Promised day of Israel
119	4	Holy Jesus, every day Keep us in the narrow way
122	1	Remember Christ, our Savior, Was born on Christmas Day
122	3	This day is born a Savior, Of a pure virgin bright
127	2	This day hath God fulfilled his promised word
127	2	This day is born a Savior, Christ the Lord
136	T,1	On This Day Earth Shall Ring
136	4	On this day angels sing
141	2	And so it continued both day and night
146	3	To you, in David's town, this day Is born of David's line
152	2	Light of the village life from day to day
157	3	Adds more luster to the day
160	1	And the burden of the day
167	VI-3	Till we pass to perfect day, Hear us, holy Jesus
168	1	We would continue with thee day by day
169	3	Resounding all the day Hosannas to their king
185	3	Now the queen of seasons, bright With the day of splendor
187	1	Our triumphant holy day
188	T,1	Joy Dawned Again on Easter Day
189	2	Let hearts downcast and lonely Rejoice this Easter day
191	2	That Easter morn at break of day, The faithful women went
191	5	On the most holy day of days, Our hearts and voices, Lord
192	T,1	The Day of Resurrection, Earth, tell it out abroad
198	1	Freedom her bondage breaks, And night is turned to day
205	T,1	Hail the Day That Sees Him Rise
207	2	Shine on us with the light of thy pure day
209	2	Swift to its close ebbs out life's little day
215	2	I loved the garish day
217	1	Your bliss in our hearts, Lord, at the break of the day
217	2	Your strength in our hearts, Lord, at the noon of the day
217	3	Your love in our hearts, Lord, at the eve of the day
217	4	Your peace in our hearts, Lord, at the end of the day
219	2	Yet hoping ever for the perfect day
249	1	blessed ... With light and life since Eden's dawning day
256	3	Pillar of fire through watches dark, & radiant cloud by day
259	1	By notions of our day and sect, Crude, partial and confined
259	2	'Twas but the dawning yet to grow Into the perfect day
267	3	deriving from their banner Light by night and shade by day
275	1	from the night profound Into the glory of the perfect day
278	1	Thy grace and blessing day by day
281	1	Day by day with strength supplied Through the life of him
300	2	Bring in the day of brotherhood, And end the night of wrong
304	2	and eager hearts awoke to greet the day
305	2	And seek the Savior's blessing, A nation in a day
311	2	O day, for which creation And all its tribes were made
315	2	But morning brings us gladness, And songs the break of day
321	T,1	My God, Accept My Heart This Day, And make it always thine
322	1	Day by day his sweet voice soundeth
331	2	That each departing day Henceforth may see Some work of love
337	1	Soon end in joyous day
345	4	From youth to age, by night and day, In gladness and in woe
345	5	toil Till dawns the golden day
348	1	Oh, let me from this day Be wholly thine
348	3	Be thou my guide, Bid darkness turn to day

451	1	Old now is earth, and none may count her days
454	4	Adored through all our changing days
455	4	And keep us through life's wintry days
456	T,1	All Beautiful the March of Days, As seasons come and go
457	T,1	The Summer Days Are Come Again
457	3	The summer days are come again, The birds are on the wing
459	2	he bids the sun cut short his race, And wintry days appear
464	1	praise For the love that crowns our days
464	1	Singing thus through all our days
472	5	though ... all our earthly days Will soon be o'er
490	T,1	Now in the Days of Youth, When life flows fresh and free
490	1	Through all our days, in all our ways, Our ... Father's will
490	4	Spirit of Christ, do thou Our first bright days inspire
492	1	whose constant care Supplies our golden days
501	2	And so let all our days
568	8	all the days of our life

days'

185	2	And from three days' sleep in death As a sun hath risen

dayspring

568	11	whereby the Dayspring from on high hath visited us

dead

180	1	Jesus Christ, the King of glory, Now is risen from the dead
181	3	He rises glorious from the dead
230	6	The last low whispers of our dead Are burdened with his name
282	1	And in whose death our sins are dead
291	1	First-begotten from the dead
399	4	I lay in dust life's glory dead
428	2	If not I'll smite your first-born dead
455	1	And all the earth lies dead and drear
468	1	we must not say that those are dead who pass away
468	2	well we know where'er they be, Our dead are living unto thee
468	3	Not left to lie like fallen tree, Not dead, but living
468	3	Not dead, but living unto thee
469	1	Safe in thine own eternity Our dead are living unto thee

deadly

91	5	No deadly shaft by day shall harm
170	2	Mine, mine was the transgression, But thine the deadly pain
433	3	From war's alarms, from deadly pestilence

deals

100	2	Who with thee so kindly deals

dear

36	6	Only, O Lord, in thy dear love Fit us for perfect rest above
50	T,1	Sun of My Soul, Thou Savior Dear
56	2	Forgive me, Lord, for thy dear Son, The ill that I this day
59	4	But thy dear presence will not leave them lonely
60	T,1	Savior, Again to Thy Dear Name we raise
79	4	I fear no ill With thee, dear Lord, beside me
92	4	Enfolded deep in thy dear love, Held in thy law, I stand
103	2	Dear desire of every nation, Joy of every longing heart

134	3	still The dear Christ enters in
148	4	Keep, O keep us, Savior dear, Ever constant by thy side
156	3	for here Thou hast a temple, too, as Zion dear
156	3	O enter in, dear Lord, unbar the door
169	5	Never was love, dear King, Never was grief like thine
171	1	Where the dear Lord was crucified, Who died to save us all
208	T,1	Dear Master, In Whose Life I See
229	4	My dear almighty Lord, My Conqueror and my King
244	2	Let thy dear word 'mid doubt and strife
244	2	Let thy dear word ... Be so within us burning
252	2	The Church from her dear Master Received the gift divine
252	4	O make thy Church, dear Savior, A lamp of burnished gold
254	T,1	Break Thou the Bread of Life, Dear Lord, to me
254	2	Bless thou the truth, dear Lord, To me, to me
269	2	Dear as the apple of thine eye, And graven on thy hand
271	1	The eternal arms, their dear abode, We make our habitation
271	3	Safe in the same dear dwelling place
274	1	how dear The pleasant tabernacles are Where thou dost dwell
278	T,1	Lord Jesus Christ, Our Lord Most Dear
309	4	Jesus, in mercy bring us To that dear land of rest
315	4	Of love so free and boundless, To come, dear Lord, to thee
322	2	Leaving all for his dear sake
329	3	Dear Savior, enter, enter, And leave us nevermore
331	1	Nor should I aught withhold, Dear Lord, from thee
334	3	Now, Father, now, in thy dear presence kneeling
341	T,1	Dear Lord and Father of Mankind, Forgive our foolish ways
347	T,1	Lord, As to Thy Dear Cross we flee, And plead to be forgiven
354	1	In thee alone, dear Lord, we own Sweet hope and consolation
367	4	He changeth not, and thou art dear
392	+2	Land of our birth ... For whose dear sake our fathers died
405	1-4	Dear Lord, to thee, Dear Lord, to thee
408	2	As thou, dear Lord, on me
425	2	Is true freedom but to break Fetters for our own dear sake
470	3	pass astray Into the dear Christ's life of sacrifice
481	2	They loved their Lord so dear, so dear
578	2	not so much that I ... As thou, dear Lord, on me

dearer

| 126 | 4 | Dearer to God are the prayers of the poor |
| 418 | 3 | In closer, dearer company |

dearest

121	3	Ah, dearest Jesus, holy child, Make thee a bed
167	III-1	And thy dearest human friend, Hear us, holy Jesus
170	3	What language shall I borrow To thank thee, dearest friend
219	3	And they who dearest hope and deepest pray Toil
277	1	Grant to them thy dearest blessing
349	4	The dearest idol I have known, Whate'er that idol be

dearly

3	3	Seek to do most nearly What thou lovest dearly
132	3	Who would not love thee, loving us so dearly
171	4	O dearly, dearly has he love, And we must love him too

death

| 13 | 2 | Sin and death shall not prevail |

death's

53	3	when life's day is over Shall death's fair night discover
61	4	Smite death's threatening wave before you
79	4	In death's dark vale I fear no ill
84	3	Yea, though I walk in death's dark vale
110	2	And death's dark shadows put to flight
149	3	know not how that Joseph's tomb Could solve death's mystery
181	4	From death's dread sting thy servants free
189	1	For he hath won the victory O'er sin and death's dark night
209	4	Where is death's sting, where, grave, thy victory
348	4	When death's cold, sullen stream Shall e'er me roll
370	3	E'en death's cold wave, I will not flee
542	1	Through life's long day and death's dark night
576	3	In death's abode? Lo, thou art there

deathless

193	3	Make us more than conquerors, Through thy deathless love
253	3	Shed on us thy deathless learning
318	1	Raised my low self above, Won by thy deathless love
356	2	Enslave it ... And deathless it shall reign
439	3	For the glory that illumines Patriot souls of deathless fame

debt

425	2	with leathern hearts, forget That we owe mankind a debt

decay

78	2	can an all-creating arm Grow weary or decay
78	5	Mere human power shall fast decay, And youthful vigor cease
209	2	Change and decay in all around I see
352	2	The mist of doubt, the blight of love's decay

deceive

96	2	He never will deceive me, He leads me by the proper path
157	2	Hopes deceive and fears annoy

decide

81	3	Oh make but trial of his love, Experience will decide
441	T,1	Once to Every Man and Nation Comes the moment to decide
441	1	decide In the strife of truth with falsehood, For the good

decided

490	3	But give us grace to stand Decided, brave, and strong

decked

309	2	The pastures of the blessed Are decked in glorious sheen

declare

75	1	All their maker's praise declare
257	T,1	The Heavens Declare Thy Glory, Lord
485	2	morning light, the lily white, Declare their Maker's praise

decline

321	1	No more from thee decline

declining

459	2	His steady counsels change the face Of the declining year

decree

   6   3   Hath stablished it fast by a changeless decree

decreed

 144   2   'Tis now fulfilled what God decreed

dedicate

 501   1   And unto thee we dedicate The first fruits of the day

dedication

 316   3   Now in grateful dedication Our allegiance we would own

deed

 166   3   O may we, who mercy need, Be like thee in heart and deed
 236   3   Nerving simplest thought and deed
 298   4   All we can do is nothing worth Unless God blesses the deed
 331   2   Some work of love begun, Some deed of kindness done
 392   5   cannot seek By deed or thought, to hurt the weak
 396   2   Praise in each duty and each deed, However small or mean
 409   3   Every deed of love and kindness Done to man is done to thee
 410   1   Each smile a hymn, each kindly deed a prayer
 411   2   One with the Father, thought and deed and word
 416   1   Let thy prayer be in thy deed
 434   1   In every thought and word and deed
 452   1   We wait thy liberating deed To signal hope and set us free
 475   2   May be in very deed thine own
 494   2   upon the solid rock We set the dream that hardens into deed

deeds

  98   2   So many gentle thoughts and deeds Circling us round
 208   2   O thou whose deeds and dreams were one
 332   2   Acts unworthy, deeds unthinking
 375   2   But deeds of love and mercy, The heavenly kingdom comes
 405   2   Some deeds of kindness done, Some souls by patience won
 449   1   Let there be deeds, instead of boasts
 492   3   grant us power That worthy thoughts in deeds may flower

deem

 330   3   And not unworthy for my sake A mortal body deem

deemest

 376   4   Through joy or sorrow, as thou deemest best

deep

   6   2   His chariots of wrath the deep thunder-clouds form
  14   2   law ... Deep writ upon the human heart, On sea, or land
  51   3   Guard the sailors tossing On the deep blue sea
  73   3   From the mountain's deep vein poured
  82   2   Thy judgments are a mighty deep
  92   4   Enfolded deep in thy dear love, Held in thy law, I stand
  99   2   O love of God, how deep and great, Far deeper than ... hate
 106   2   Isles of the southern seas, Deep in your coral caves
 108   2   Her heart with deep delight is springing
 113   2   To thee the travail deep was known
 134   1   Above thy deep and dreamless sleep The silent stars go by
 141   1   On a cold winter's night that was so deep

145	2	O deep within my heart now shine
150	T,1	O Love, How Deep, How Broad, How High
150	6	All glory to our Lord and God For love to deep
150	5	For love so deep, so high, so broad
151	T,1	O Love, How Deep, How Broad, How High (same words no. 150)
152	4	Divine and human, in his deep revealing
237	4	Earth's bitter voices drown In one deep ocean of accord
277	3	Grant to us a deep compassion For thy children everywhere
297	2	And seed laid deep in sacred soil Yields harvests
334	1	For we are weak, and need some deep revealing
334	3	Now make us strong, we need thy deep revealing
336	4	Give deep humility, the sense Of godly sorrow give
372	3	When through the deep waters I call thee to go
429	1	Who bidd'st the mighty ocean deep Its ... limits keep
429	2	Who walkedst on the foaming deep
432	1	Through whose deep purpose stranger thousands stand Here
439	1	Lord, we would with deep thanksgiving Praise thee most for
482	2	Sleep in comfort, slumber deep, We will rock you

deepening

| 457 | 1 | And deepening shade of summer woods, And glow of summer air |

deepens

52	3	As the darkness deepens o'er us, Lo, eternal stars arise
209	1	The darkness deepens, Lord, with me abide
456	2	Love deepens round the hearth

deeper

46	3	Give deeper calm than night can bring
98	4	A yearning for a deeper peace Not known before
99	2	O love of God, how deep and great, Far deeper than ... hate
99	2	love of God ... Far deeper than man's deepest hate
162	1	When for deeper faith I seek
224	2	The wrong of man to man on thee Inflicts a deeper wrong
341	1	In deeper reverence, praise
467	3	Chastened by pain we learn life's deeper meaning
509	3	Give deeper calm than night can bring

deepest

3	1	Prostrate lie with deepest reverence
99	2	love of God ... Far deeper than man's deepest hate
212	2	All our knowledge, sense and sight Lie in deepest darkness
212	2	Lie in deepest darkness shrouded
219	3	And they who dearest hope and deepest pray Toil
372	3	And sanctify to thee thy deepest distress
576	5	If deepest darkness cover me

deeply

| 75 | 4 | Write thou deeply in my heart What I am, and what thou art |

deeps

| 230 | 3 | In vain we search the lowest deeps |

defame

| 347 | 4 | Should friends misjudge, or foes defame |

defend

15	3	Lord, who doth prosper thy work and defend thee
58	1	May thine angel-guards defend us
59	2	In soul and body, thou from harm defend us
327	2	Keep thy flock, from sin defend us
371	3	Since, Lord, thou dost defend Us with thy Spirit
434	1	aim ... Not to defend some ancient creed
493	4	Let me, O Lord, thy cause defend, A knight without a sword

defender

6	1	Our Shield and Defender, the Ancient of Days
6	5	Our Maker, Defender, Redeemer and Friend
21	3	And pray that thou still our defender wilt be
291	1	Thou alone, our strong defender Liftest up thy people's head

defense

1	2	Sufficient is thine arm alone, And our defense is sure
235	3	Thou strong Defense, thou holy Light
433	3	Be thy strong arm our ever sure defense

defenseless

| 210 | 2 | Cover my defenseless head With the shadow of thy wing |

defied

| 446 | 3 | man hath defied thee, Yet to eternity standeth thy word |

degree

| 326 | 2 | angels sang Proclaiming thy royal degree |

deign

| 244 | 1 | Thy temple deign to make us |
| 286 | T,1 | Come, Risen Lord, and deign to be our guest |

deinem

| 139 | 3 | Lieb' aus deinem gottlichen Mund |

deiner

| 139 | 3 | Christ, in deiner Geburt |

deity

| 120 | 2 | Veiled in flesh the God-head see, Hail the incarnate Deity |
| 143 | 3 | Frankincense to offer have I, Incense owns a deity nigh |

delay

| 303 | 4 | What though the kingdom long delay |

delayeth

| 112 | T,1 | Ah! Think Not the Lord Delayeth |

delight

23	2	in his light with sweet delight Ye do abound
39	3	To banish sin from our delight
79	5	O what transport of delight From thy pure chalice floweth
81	4	Make you his service your delight
108	2	Her heart with deep delight is springing
392	6	Teach us delight in simple things And mirth

480	2	He used to see in Galilee, And watch it with delight
490	2	And do what thou wouldst have us do With radiant delight
558	1	arose Against the Son of God's delight

delightest

| 155 | 3 | Who in all good delightest, Thou good and gracious King |

delighteth

| 339 | 2 | His desire our soul delighteth |

delights

| 336 | 3 | Give, what thine eye delights to see, Truth |

deliver

103	3	Born thy people to deliver, Born a child, and yet a king
228	3	Come, almighty to deliver, Let us all thy life receive
292	3	And by this food, so aweful and so sweet Deliver us
292	3	Deliver us from every touch of ill
436	2	From sleep and from damnation, Deliver us, good Lord
442	3	Deliver us from evil
532	T,1	Have Mercy Upon Us, Good Lord, deliver us
559	8	When thou tookest upon thee to deliver man

delivered

568	7	That we being delivered out of the hand our enemies
577	T,1	Great God Who Hast Delivered Us
577	1	delivered us By thy great love and mighty power
577	1	delivered us ... In many an evil hour

deliverer

| 93 | 2 | Strong Deliverer, Be thou still my strength and shield |

demand

| 107 | 1 | Our full homage to demand |

demands

177	4	Love so amazing, so divine, Demands my soul, my life, my all
358	2	Not the labors of my hands Can fulfill thy law's demands
362	1	A heavenly race demands thy zeal, And an immortal crown

denial

| 374 | 1 | Lest by base denial I depart from thee |
| 471 | 5 | Be in his will, his strength for self denial |

denied

| 163 | 2 | 'Twas I, Lord Jesus, I it was denied thee |
| 325 | 2 | aweful love ... found no room In life where sin denied thee |

deny

| 36 | 5 | Room to deny ourselves - a road To bring us daily nearer God |

deo

116	R	Gloria in excelsis Deo
133	2	Gloria in Excelsis Deo
136	R	Ideo ... Ideo gloria in excelsis Deo

depart

238	2	That we from thee may ne'er depart
246	3	And ne'er from us depart, Spirit of power
280	T,1	Be Known to Us in Breaking Bread, But do not then depart
374	1	Lest by base denial I depart from thee
405	4	And when earth's labors cease, Bid us depart in peace
431	2	The captains and the kings depart
491	3	Oh, may we never from his side depart
572	T,1	Lord, Now Lettest Thou Thy Servant Depart in peace

departed

558	4	Meet at my table and record The love of your departed Lord

departing

331	2	That each departing day Henceforth may see Some work of love
393	1	God be at mine end, And at my departing
543	1	God be at mine end, and at my departing

departs

494	3	And all the pride of sinful will departs

dependent

394	1	are dependent on thy will and love alone

deplore

366	5	Save us from weak resignation to the evils we deplore

depressed

454	4	In scenes exalted or depressed, Thou art our joy & ... rest

depth

8	3	Well-spring of the joy of living, Ocean depth of happy rest
35	5	Let air, and sea, and sky From depth to height reply
497	1	And in the depth be praise
576	2	Unfathomed depth, unmeasured height

depths

230	3	For him no depths can drown
397	3	And wing my words, that they may reach The hidden depths
397	3	The hidden depths of many a heart
399	1	that in thine ocean depths its flow May richer, fuller be
422	3	When in the depths the patient miner striving
569	4	Blessed art thou that beholdest the depths

deride

164	2	While soldiers scoff and foes deride

derided

163	1	By foes derided, by thine own rejected, O most afflicted
445	2	By wars and tumults love is mocked, derided

derision

203	3	Sinners in derision crowned him

deriving

267	3	deriving from their banner Light by night and shade by day

descend

134	4	O holy Child of Bethlehem, Descend to us, we pray
202	5	Angels descend with songs again
232	T,1	Spirit of God, Descend Upon My Heart
241	1,4	Descend with all thy gracious powers
246	2	Spirit of holiness, On us descend
275	2	Descend, O Holy Spirit, like a dove Into our hearts
275	2	Descend ... that we may be as one
299	1	Descend on our apostate race
459	2	His hoary frost, his fleecy snow, Descend
459	2	descend and clothe the ground

descended

232	5	The baptism of the heaven-descended Dove
250	2	Who descended from his throne And for us salvation won

descendeth

107	1	blessing in his hand, Christ our God to earth descendeth
107	3	the Light of light descendeth From the realms of endless day
271	2	Their song to us descendeth

descending

52	T,1	Now on Land and Sea Descending
117	4	Suddenly the Lord, descending, In his temple shall appear
344	3	Spirit of our God, descending, Fill our hearts

descends

6	4	It streams from the hills, it descends to the plain
44	1	As night descends, we too would pray

desert

104	2	Hark, the voice of one that crieth in the desert far & near
229	3	And through this desert land, Still keep me near thy side
344	2	Lone and dreary, faint and weary, Through the desert
344	2	Through the desert thou didst go
372	5	I will not, I will not desert to his foes
484	1	In strange and lovely cities, Or roam the desert sands

deserts

326	3	But thy couch was the sod ... In the deserts of Galilee

deserve

170	2	Lo, here I fall, my Savior, 'Tis I deserve thy place

deserving

83	2	whate'er thy Father's ... and all deserving love have sent
83	3	though undeserving, Thou yet shalt find it true for thee
163	4	Think on thy pity and thy love unswerving, Not my deserving

design

32	4	Direct, control, suggest, this day All I design or do or say
372	4	I only design Thy dross to consume and thy gold to refine
412	2	Who shapest man to God's own law, Thyself the fair design
424	2	All must aid alike to carry Forward one sublime design

designs
81 1 That veils and darkens thy designs

desire
103 2 Dear desire of every nation, Joy of every longing heart
110 4 Desire of nations, bind All peoples in one heart and mind
117 3 Seek the great Desire of nations
242 2 Kindle every high desire, Perish self in thy pure fire
311 3 Appear, Desire of nations, Thine exiles long for home
339 2 His desire our soul delighteth
341 5 Breathe through the pulses of desire Thy coolness & thy balm
490 4 That we may live the life of love And loftiest desire
491 1 Hope and desire for noble lives and true

desires
15 2 Hast thou not seen How thy desires e'er have been Granted
15 2 desires ... Granted in what he ordaineth
402 4 To teach our faint desires to rise

desirest
460 3 And, what thou most desirest, Our humble, thankful hearts

desiring
336 4 A strong, desiring confidence To hear thy voice and live

desolate
373 3 His truth be thine affiance, When faint and desolate

desolation
444 4 That war may haunt the earth no more And desolation cease
496 2 stand Between their loved homes and the war's desolation

despair
277 3 May we see our human family Free from sorrow and despair
295 2 Redeemed at countless cost From dark despair
398 4 save us From death and dark despair, from sin and guilt
420 2 And bitter lips in blind despair Cry
426 2 I see my people falling In darkness and despair
468 3 Not wandering in unknown despair Beyond thy voice

despise
335 3 Do thy friends despise, forsake thee
529 1 A broken and a contrite heart, O God, thou wilt not despise

despite
201 3 left the lonesome place of death, Despite the rage of foes

destined
432 4 For hearts aflame to serve thy destined good

destroy
9 1 He can create, and he destroy
217 1 Whose trust, ever child-like, no cares could destroy
344 3 provided, pardoned, guided, Nothing can our peace destroy

destroyed

| 432 | 2 | Thine ancient might destroyed the Pharaoh's boast |

destruction

93	3	Death of death, and hell's destruction land me safe
100	1	Who redeems thee from destruction
100	2	Who redeems thee from destruction

devils

| 363 | 3 | And though this world, with devils filled |

devotion

22	1	In grateful devotion our tribute we bring
126	3	Say, shall we yield him, in costly devotion
240	2	Hosannas languish on our tongues, And our devotion dies
297	3	The torch of their devotion lent, Lightens the dark
521	1	Our hearts in true devotion bow

dew

6	4	And sweetly distills in the dew and the rain
32	3	Disperse my sins as morning dew
34	1	The fields are wet with diamond dew, The worlds awake to cry
37	2	In the calm dew and freshness of the morn
354	3	O God, renew with heavenly dew Our body, soul and spirit

dewfall

| 38 | 2 | Like the first dewfall On the first grass |

dews

50	2	When the soft dews of kindly sleep
341	4	Drop thy still dews of quietness, Till ... strivings cease
405	3	Some dews of mercy shed, Some wayward footsteps led
443	2	They have builded him an altar in the evening dews and damps

diadem

| 195 | 1 | Bring forth the royal diadem |
| 200 | 1 | A royal diadem adorns The mighty victor's brow |

diamond

| 34 | 1 | The fields are wet with diamond dew, The worlds awake to cry |

did

4	2	Without our aid he did us make
44	2	Did not their hearts within them burn
44	2	Did not their spirits inly yearn
119	T,1	As With Gladness Men of Old Did the guiding star behold
141	T,1	The First Nowell, the angel did say
161	3	We crave the power to do thy will With him who did it best
169	2	Who at my need His life did spend
177	3	Did e'er such love and sorrow meet
187	1	Who did once upon the cross ... Suffer to redeem our loss
271	2	The Spirit who in them did sing To us his music lendeth
330	3	Ah, did not he the heavenly throne A little thing esteem
363	2	Did we in our own strength confide, Our striving would be
388	2	He prayed for them that did the wrong

| 412 | 1 | Who with the eyes of early youth Eternal things did see |
| 412 | 1 | Did ye not know it is my work My Father's work to do |

didst

147	1	Didst yield the glory that of right was thine
153	T,1	For us didst fast and pray
153	2	As thou with Satan didst contend, And didst the victory win
154	T,1	O thou Who Through This Holy Week Didst suffer for us all
155	3	Thou didst accept their praises, Accept the prayers we bring
168	3	Which thou didst take to save our souls from loss
185	4	But today amidst the twelve Thou didst stand, bestowing
207	1	Who pain didst undergo for my poor sake
254	1	As thou didst break the loaves Beside the sea
254	2	As thou didst bless the bread By Galilee
277	2	Thou didst receive the children to thyself so tenderly
289	1	Thou, Lord, didst make all for thy pleasure
289	1	Didst give man food for all his days
326	T,1	Thou Didst Leave Thy Throne and thy kingly crown
326	2	But in lowly birth didst thou come to earth
344	2	Thou didst tread this earth before us
344	2	Thou didst feel its keenest woe
344	2	Through the desert thou didst go
394	1	All these were thine, Lord, thou didst give them all to me
398	4	who by thy cross didst save us
398	5	Who by this sign didst conquer grief and pain
408	2	Thou didst reach forth thy hand and mine enfold
412	3	O thou who didst the vision send And gives to each his task
429	2	And calm amid its rage didst sleep
429	3	O Holy Spirit, who didst brood Upon the chaos dark and rude
466	2	With heart still undefiled, Thou didst to manhood come
559	8	Thou didst humble thyself to be born of a virgin
559	9	Thou didst open the kingdom of heaven to all believers
578	2	Thou didst reach forth thy hand and mine enfold

die

50	3	For without thee I dare not die
99	4	Our life to live, our death to die
120	3	Mild he lays his glory by, Born that man no more may die
158	3	It is finished, hear him cry, Learn of Jesus Christ to die
159	T,1	Alone Thou Goest Forth, O Lord, In sacrifice to die
169	1	take Frail flesh and die
174	2	Till the appointed time is nigh ... the Lamb of God may die
175	2	In lowly pomp ride on to die
184	3	That love, that life which cannot die
199	3	Who died, eternal life to bring, & lives that death may die
201	2	Not as of old a little child To bear, and fight, and die
233	4	So shall I never die
357	2	He thinks he was not made to die
358	3	Foul, I to the fountain fly, Wash me, Savior, or I die
365	2	And blest would be their children's fate If they ... die for
365	2	If they, like them, should die for thee
377	4	Though a tortured slave thou die
377	4	Zion, if thou die believing, Heaven's path shall open lie
386	4	And in the midnight lay us down to die
436	1	Our earthly rulers falter, Our people drift and die

443	4	As he died to make men holy, let us die to make men free
450	4	Though pain and passion may not die
453	1	Ring out, wild bells, and let him die
493	3	When Stephen, young and doomed to die, Fell crushed

died

106	4	High raise the note, that Jesus died, Yet lives and reigns
171	1	Where the dear Lord was crucified, Who died to save us all
171	3	He died that we may be forgiven, He died to make us good
177	1	cross On which the Prince of glory died
199	1	Awake, my soul, and sing Of him who died for thee
199	3	His glories now we sing Who died and rose on high
`199	3	Who died, eternal life to bring, & lives that death may die
199	4	All hail, Redeemer, hail, For thou hast died for me
260	1	With his own blood he bought her, And for her life he died
281	1	strength supplied through the life of him who died
296	1	The cross on which the Savior died
302	2	And died on earth that man might live above
321	2	Before the cross of him who died, Behold, I prostrate fall
329	3	I died for you, my children, And will ye treat me so
340	3	Young John ... Homeless, in Patmos died
348	2	As thou hast died for me, Oh, may my love to thee
383	2	Poets sung its glory, Heroes for it died
392	+2	Land of our birth ... For whose dear sake our fathers died
420	2	Cry, Christ hath died in vain
437	1	Land where my fathers died, Land of the pilgrim's pride
443	4	As he died to make men holy, let us die to make men free
481	1	Who toiled and fought and lived and died for the Lord

dies

1	5	They fly, forgotten, as a dream Dies at the opening day
47	3	Nor dies the strain of praise away
52	2	Soon as dies the sunset glory, Stars of heaven shine out
167	II-1	Jesus, pitying the sighs Of the thief, who near thee dies
240	2	Hosannas languish on our tongues, And our devotion dies
304	3	Low lies man's pride and human wisdom dies
431	2	The tumult and the shouting dies

differences

| 268 | 3 | Hallowed be thy name forever, Heal our differences of old |

differing

| 224 | 4 | We faintly hear, we dimly see, In differing phrase we pray |
| 383 | 1 | Gifts in differing measure, Hearts of one accord |

differs

| 196 | T,1 | All Hail the Power of Jesus' Name (R differs from no. 195) |

dim

86	3	The deep-toned organ blast That rolls through arches dim
173	3	When courage fails us, and when faith is dim
209	2	Earth's joys grow dim, its glories pass away
224	4	But dim or clear, we own in thee The light ... truth ... way
292	2	Our prayer so languid, and our faith so dim

343	2	His wisdom ever waketh, His sight is never dim
422	4	Toiling in twilight flickering and dim
441	3	behind the dim unknown, Standeth God within the shadow
443	2	I can read his righteous sentence by the dim & flaring lamps

dimly

| 224 | 4 | We faintly hear, we dimly see, In differing phrase we pray |

dimmed

| 178 | 1 | The star is dimmed that lately shone |
| 440 | 4 | Thine alabaster cities gleam, Undimmed by human tears |

dimness

| 232 | 2 | But take the dimness of my soul away |

dims

| 376 | 2 | While passion stains and folly dims our youth |

din

| 220 | 2 | Through din of market, whirl of wheels |

direct

| 32 | 4 | Direct, control, suggest, this day All I design or do or say |

directeth

| 258 | 3 | Then its light directeth, And our way protecteth |

directs

| 253 | 3 | Those whose wisdom still directs us |

disappear

| 287 | 4 | Too soon we rise, the symbols disappear |

disappears

| 305 | T,1 | The Morning Light Is Breaking, The darkness disappears |

disappointment

| 77 | 3 | When disappointment, grief, and fear are gone |

disaster

| 371 | T,1 | He Who Would Valiant Be 'Gainst all disaster |
| 491 | 3 | And through life's darkness, danger, and disaster |

disastrous

| 219 | 2 | Stumbling and falling in disastrous night |

discerning

| 258 | 6 | O, that we discerning Its most holy learning |

discernment

| 291 | 2 | Here for faith's discernment pray we |

discerns

| 508 | 2 | Thine ear discerns, thy love rejoices When hearts rise up |

disciple
178 2   E'en that disciple whom he loved Heeds not

disciples
403 1   Thus the first disciples found him

discords
413 3   Bid its cruel discords cease

discouraged
92 2   Discouraged in the work of life, Disheartened by its load
335 2   We should never be discouraged

discouragement
371 1   There's no discouragement Shall make him once relent

discover
53 3   when life's day is over Shall death's fair night discover
53 3   discover The fields of everlasting life

diseases
100 2   Who forgiveth thy transgressions, Thy diseases all who heals

disheartened
92 2   Discouraged in the work of life, Disheartened by its load

disloyalty
359 5   To doubt would be disloyalty, To falter would be sin

dismal
371 2   Who so beset him round With dismal stories

dismay
122 T,1   God Rest You Merry, Gentlemen, Let nothing you dismay

dismayed
337 T,1   Give to the Winds Thy Fears, Hope and be undismayed
343 1   But God is round about me, And can I be dismayed
372 2   Fear not, I am with thee, oh, be not dismayed

dismiss
63 T,1   Lord, Dismiss Us With Thy Blessing

dispel
55 3   A Savior Christ, our woes dispel

dispels
222 2   God dispels our fear

disperse
32 3   Disperse my sins as morning dew
110 2   Disperse the gloomy clouds of night

dispersed
181 2   But Christ their legions hath dispersed

display
43	3	More and more thyself display, Shining to the perfect day
72	1	The unwearied sun, from day to day ... power display
72	1	sun ... Does his creator's power display
238	2	The light of truth to us display

displayed
68	2	Lord, how thy wonders are displayed, Where'er I turn my eye
74	2	Moon and stars, thy power displayed
146	4	babe ... To human view displayed

displease
169	4	Yet they at these Themselves displease, And 'gainst him rise

disposing
59	1	The light and darkness are of his disposing

disquieted
467	4	Be not cast down, disquieted in vain

distant
100	3	Far as east from west is distant He hath put away our sin
215	1	I do not ask to see The distant scene
296	2	distant lands Shall see from far the glorious sight
306	5	Steals on the ear the distant triumph song
484	3	Till all the distant people In every foreign place

distills
6	4	And sweetly distills in the dew and the rain

distraction
310	3	We, where no trouble distraction can bring

distress
16	2	favor To our fathers in distress
81	2	When in distress to him I called, He to my rescue came
82	3	The sons of Adam in distress Fly to the shadow of thy wing
167	VI-2	Save us in our soul's distress, Be our help to cheer & bless
372	3	And sanctify to thee thy deepest distress
392	5	Man's strength to comfort man's distress

distressed
270	1	above all the soul distressed, Longing for rest everlasting

distressing
21	1	The wicked oppressing now cease from distressing

distrust
348	4	Blest Savior, then, in love, Fear and distrust remove

diverse
55	1	O in what diverse pains they met ... what joy they went away
253	2	Many diverse scrolls completing
265	1	Break every bar that holds Thy flock in diverse folds

divide
436	1	The walls of gold entomb us, The swords of scorn divide

divided
247	4	While in essence only One, Undivided God we claim thee
382	2	We are not divided, All one body we
445	2	Races and peoples, lo, we stand divided

divides
304	3	Rejoice that while the sin of man divides

divine
8	3	Lift us to the joy divine
21	2	Ordaining, maintaining his kingdom divine
35	6	Be this, while life is mine, My canticle divine
43	3	Fill me, Radiancy divine, Scatter all my unbelief
66	5	Graces, human and divine, Flowers of earth & buds of heaven
72	3	singing ... The hand that made us is divine
115	3	And fill the world with love divine
126	3	Odors of Edom and offerings divine
145	2	Thou heavenly Brightness, Light divine
147	T,1	All Praise to Thee, for Thou, O King Divine
152	4	Divine and human, in his deep revealing
167	II-3	Cheer our souls with hope divine, Hear us, holy Jesus
169	5	Here might I stay and sing, No story so divine
177	4	Love so amazing, so divine, Demands my soul, my life, my all
228	T,1	Love Divine, All Loves Excelling
233	3	Until this earthly part of me Glows with thy fire divine
239	T,1	Come Down, O Love divine, Seek thou this soul of mine
241	T,1,4	Spirit Divine, Attend our Prayers
242	T,1	Holy Spirit, Truth Divine, dawn upon this soul of mine
242	2	Holy Spirit, Love divine, Glow within this heart of mine
242	3	Holy Spirit, Power divine, Fill and nerve this will of mine
242	4	Holy Spirit, Right divine, King within my conscience reign
243	T,1	Holy Spirit, Truth Divine (words same as no. 242)
244	1	Sun of the soul, thou Light divine
252	2	The Church from her dear Master Received the gift divine
276	4	And human life become divine
280	2	There sup with us in love divine, Thy body and thy blood
294	3	Inspire thy heralds of good news To live thy life divine
306	4	O blest communion, fellowship divine
318	1	Breathe into every wish Thy will divine
348	1	Savior divine, Now hear me while I pray
357	3	Thou seemest human and divine
359	4	Blest too is he who can divine Where real right doth lie
383	1-3	At the call divine
390	2	O when shall I behold thy face, Thou majesty divine
401	4	A servant with this clause Makes drudgery divine
409	T,1	Jesus, Thou Divine Companion
409	3	Jesus, thou divine companion, Help us all to work our best
412	2	O Carpenter of Nazareth, Builder of life divine
416	4	Come then, law divine, and reign
424	2	Whether humble or exalted, All are called to task divine
433	2	Thy love divine hath led us in the past
433	4	Fill all our lives with love and grace divine
440	3	Till all success be nobleness, And every gain divine

472	2	Come, thou, O Lord divine, Make this thy holy shrine
491	1	With light and love divine our souls endue
494	3	When to our ears there come divine commands
521	1	Thy Spirit send with grace divine
576	4	And my support thy power divine

divinest

470	2	Make their ears attent To thy divinest speech

do

2	4	Do thou our troubled souls uplift Against the foe prevailing
2	4	Do thou in faith sustain us
3	3	in all, Great and small, Seek to do ... what thou lovest
3	3	Seek to do most nearly What thou lovest dearly
4	T,1	All People That on Earth Do Dwell
4	3	Praise ... for it is seemly so to do
5	T,1	All People That on Earth Do Dwell (same as No. 4)
6	5	In thee do we trust, nor find thee to fail
15	3	Ponder anew What the Almighty can do
18	2	To thee, the powers on high ... Continually do cry
18	2	Both cherubim and seraphim, Continually do cry
21	3	We all do extol thee, thou leader triumphant
23	2	God's praises sound, As in his light ... ye do abound
23	2	in his light with sweet delight Ye do abound
32	4	Direct, control, suggest, this day All I design or do or say
39	4	To guide whate'er we nobly do, With love all envy to subdue
83	3	So do thine own part faithfully, And trust his word
112	1	Do you yet not understand
128	4	If I were a wiseman, I would do my part
135	2	Help us to do as thou hast willed
161	3	We crave the power to do thy will With him who did it best
163	4	I do adore thee, and will ever pray thee
166	2	For we know not what we do, Hear us, holy Jesus
171	4	And trust in his redeeming blood, And try his works to do
188	2	Do thou thyself our hearts possess
194	1	The birds do sing on every bough
208	2	Though what I dream and what I do
208	2	what I dream ... do ... In all my days are often two
215	1	I do not ask to see The distant scene
233	1	And do what thou wouldst do
233	2	Until with thee I will one will To do and to endure
266	3	And feet on mercy's errands swift Do make her pilgrimage
274	3	Till all before our God at length In Zion do appear
280	T,1	Be Known to Us in Breaking Bread, But do not then depart
284	1	This will I do, my dying Lord, I will remember thee
287	5	I have no help but thine, nor do I need Another arm
293	3	No arm so weak but may do service here
298	4	All we can do is nothing worth Unless God blesses the deed
308	4	Evermore their life abides Who have lived to do thy will
317	1	It satisfies my longings As nothing else would do
318	2	In thee my strength renew, Give me thy work to do
327	2	We are thine, do thou befriend us
327	3	Early let us seek thy favor, Early let us do thy will
335	1	All because we do not carry Everything to God in prayer
335	3	Do thy friends despise, forsake thee
347	2	Like thee, to do our Father's will

368	2	Not forever in green pastures Do we ask our way to be
370	1	Whate'er I do, where'er I be, Still 'tis God's hand
371	2	Do but themselves confound, His strength the more is.
394	1	Plans and my thoughts and everything I ever do are dependent
395	5	Then let us prove our heavenly birth In all we do and know
401	1	And what I do in anything To do it as for thee
406	1	only thee resolved to know In all I think or speak or do
409	2	They who work without complaining Do the holy will of God
412	1	Did ye not know it is my work My Father's work to do
412	2	And see like thee our noblest work Our Father's work to do
412	3	That it may be our highest joy Our Father's work to do
417	2	And the meekest of saints may find stern work to do
425	1	If ye do not feel the chain when it works a brother's pain
434	3	mind equipped His will to learn, his work to do
479	2	Help us to do the things we should
479	2	In all we do in work or play To grow more loving every day
480	1	It gave him light to do his work, And smiled upon his play
481	3	saints Who love to do Jesus' will
482	T,1	Little Jesus, Sweetly Sleep, do not stir
486	2	Give me daily bread While I do my part
490	2	And do what thou wouldst have us do With radiant delight
490	4	Spirit of Christ, do thou Our first bright days inspire
495	3	Brother, do you love my Jesus
552	1	It is meet and right so to do
557	3	I have no help but thine, nor do I need Another arm
558	4	Do this, he cried, till time shall end
559	2	To thee cherubim and seraphim continually do cry
580	2	A gate which opens wide to those That do lament their sin

doctor

| 481 | 1 | And one was a doctor, and one was a queen |

doctrine

| 301 | 4 | May she one in doctrine be, One in truth and charity |
| 382 | 2 | One in hope and doctrine, One in charity |

doctrines

| 235 | 4 | That we may love not doctrines strange |

does

37	3	So does this blessed consciousness, awaking, Breathe
72	1	sun ... Does his creator's power display
109	1	Watchman, does its beauteous ray ... joy or hope foretell
170	1	How does that visage languish Which once was bright as morn
293	1	And to each servant does the Master say, Go work today
409	3	Every task, however simple, Sets the soul that does it free
496	1	O say does that star-spangled banner yet wave

doest

| 248 | 3 | O God, thou doest all things, All things both new and old |

doing

| 59 | 3 | Let us serve thee, in all that we are doing |
| 410 | 2 | example Of him whose holy work was doing good |

doings
47   4   lips are making Thy wondrous doings heard on high
394 1   Wondrous are thy doings unto me

doleful
558 T,1 Twas on That Dark and Doleful Night

domain
247 1   Infinite thy vast domain, Everlasting is thy reign

dome
45   2   Lord of life, beneath the dome Of the universe, thy home

dominations
197 2   Thrones and dominations, Stars upon their way

dominion
30   1   Cry out, dominion, princedoms, powers
74   3   Thou hast given man dominion o'er the wonders of thy hand
100 6   All throughout his vast dominion Bless the Father, O my soul
111 3   Honor, glory, and dominion, And eternal victory, Evermore
431 1   Beneath whose awful hand we hold Dominion over palm and pine
435 1   Solace all its wide dominion With the healing of thy wings

dominions
111 2   Powers, dominions, bow before him

dominum
133 R   Venite, adoremus ... Dominum

done
19   3   All that he for man hath done ... sends us through his Son
29   1   Who wondrous things hath done, In whom his world rejoices
56   2   The ill that I this day have done
95   5   wonders great By thy strong hand are done
154 3   What shall we render to our God For all that he hath done
169 4   Why, what hath my Lord done, What makes this rage and spite
181 T,1 Alleluia, The Strife is O'er, the battle done
181 2   The powers of death have done their worst
182 3   Love's redeeming work is done
224 3   Apart from thee all gain is loss, All labor vainly done
268 2   Glory, glory, thine the power As in heaven thy will be done
293 4   glad sound comes with the setting sun, Well done, well done
294 3   By whom thy will was done
300 1   Have done with lesser things
331 2   Some work of love begun, Some deed of kindness done
334 2   Thou wilt sustain us till its work is done
336 5   Give these, and then thy will be done
339 3   Still from man to God eternal Sacrifice of praise be done
370 3   And when my task on earth is done
384 2   That, having all things done, And all your conflicts past
392 6   Forgiveness free of evil done
395 6   As thou wouldst have it done
405 2   Some deeds of kindness done, Some souls by patience won
409 3   Every deed of love and kindness Done to man is done to thee
413 4   grant our hope's fruition, Here on earth thy will be done

445	1-4	Thy kingdom come, O Lord, thy will be done
451	3	Nor till that hour shall God's whole will be done
458	1	All his year of wonder done
458	6	For his year of wonder done Praise to the all-glorious One
486	2	Jesus at my side Till the day is done

doom

136	2	His the doom, ours the mirth When he came down to earth
325	2	doomed to death must bring to doom The power which crucified
363	3	His rage we can endure, For lo, his doom is sure

doomed

| 325 | 2 | doomed to death must bring to doom The power which crucified |
| 493 | 3 | When Stephen, young and doomed to die, Fell crushed |

door

125	2	He hath oped the heavenly door, And man is blessed evermore
156	3	O enter in, dear Lord, unbar the door
329	T,1	O Jesus, Thou Art Standing Outside the fast-closed door
329	3	O Lord, with shame and sorrow We open now the door
439	2	For the open door to manhood, In a land the people rule
472	3	May all who seek this door, And saving grace implore

dost

2	2	Thou dost whate'er thy will ordains
2	3	And the lost sheep dost gather
84	4	My head thou dost with oil anoint, And my cup overflows
159	3	but thou Dost light and life restore
174	3	Thou dost ask him -- can it be, Why has thou forsaken me
231	1	Who dost thy seven-fold gifts impart
233	1	Fill me with life anew, That I may love what thou dost love
235	2	Thou in the faith dost men unite of every land ... tongue
248	3	Thou to the meek and lowly Thy secrets dost unfold
274	1	how dear The pleasant tabernacles are Where thou dost dwell
274	1	Where thou dost dwell so near
286	2	Thou at the table, blessing, yet dost stand
344	2	All our weakness thou dost know
363	2	Dost ask who that may be, Christ Jesus, it is he
364	T,1	Christian, Dost Thou See Them On the holy ground
364	2	Christian, dost thou feel them, How they work within
364	3	Christian, dost thou hear them, How they speak thee fair
371	3	Since, Lord, thou dost defend Us with thy Spirit
397	3	The precious things thou dost impart
398	5	Thou art our Lord, Thou dost forever reign
413	1	For thine own dost ever plead
442	2	When all our lack thou dost survey
465	1	Whom thou for evermore dost join in one
466	1	Who dost in love proclaim Each family thine own
466	3	O spirit, who dost bind Our hearts in unity
467	3	And in our weakness thou dost make us strong
575	1	Who dost thy seven-fold gifts impart
576	T,1	Lord, Thou Hast Searched Me and dost know Where'er I rest

doth

| 4 | 2 | We are his folk, he doth us feed |
| 4 | 2 | And for his sheep he doth us take |

15	3	Lord, who doth prosper thy work and defend thee
17	2	exalt the glory Of him whose arm doth valiantly
23	1	Assist our song, For else the theme Too high doth seem
23	1	Too high doth seem For mortal tongue
28	2	Thy Church doth in thy strength rely
33	T,1	As the Sun Doth Daily Rise Bright'ning all the morning skies
49	3	Thee ... O Most High, The world doth glorify
49	3	Thee ... The world doth glorify And shall exalt forever
67	1	Thy present life through all doth flow
70	5	All things living he doth feed
74	2	From thy ways so often turning, Yet thy love doth seek him
74	2	Yet thy love doth seek him still
77	2	thy God doth undertake To guide the future as ... the past
84	2	My soul he doth restore again
84	2	me to walk doth make Within the paths of righteousness
85	1	From whence doth come mine aid
85	3	the Lord thy shade On thy right hand doth stay
93	2	fountain, Whence the healing stream doth flow
96	1	I will be still, whate'er he doth
122	4	This holy tide of Christmas Doth bring redeeming grace
123	2	Doth entreat, Flee from woe and danger
123	2	Brethren, come, from all doth grieve you You are freed
142	5	While the choir with peals of glee Doth rend the air asunder
145	2	Toward thee longing Doth possess me, turn and bless me
165	1	For God doth make his world anew
182	2	Dying once, ye all doth save
191	3	Your Lord doth go to Galilee
202	1	sun Doth his successive journeys run
214	3	Still to the lowly soul He doth himself impart
249	5	Praise we the goodness that doth crown our days
258	2	When our foes are near us, Then thy word doth cheer us
270	T,1	Built on the Rock the Church doth stand
270	1	the Church doth stand Even when steeples are falling
270	3	His truth doth hallow the temple
274	2	Happy, whose strength in thee doth hide
274	4	That man is truly blest Who only on thee doth rely
295	1	Sinsick and sorrow-worn, Whom Christ doth heal
300	3	The Church for you doth wait
312	5	There Magdalen hath left her moan And cheerfully doth sing
312	5	With blessed saints, whose harmony In every street doth ring
339	T,1	All My Hope on God Is Founded, He doth still my trust renew
339	2	Daily doth the almighty giver Bounteous gifts on us bestow
339	2	Love doth stand At his hand, Joy doth wait on his command
339	3	Christ doth call One and all, Ye who follow shall not fall
363	1	For still our ancient foe Doth seek to work us woe
359	4	Blest too is he who can divine Where real right doth lie
390	2	For thee, my God, the living God, My thirsty soul doth pine
401	5	that which God doth touch and own cannot for less be told
420	1	O holy city ... Where Christ, the Lamb, doth reign
429	1	Whose arm doth bind the restless wave
456	3	Day unto day doth utter speech, And night to night proclaim
457	2	We know who giveth all the good That doth our cup o'erbrim
461	1	God, our Maker, doth provide For our wants to be supplied
462	1	God, our Maker, doth provide For our wants to be supplied
494	2	Ribbed with the steel that time and change doth mock
559	1	All the earth doth worship thee, The Father everlasting

| 559 | 5 | holy Church throughout all the world doth acknowledge thee |
| 570 | T,1 | My Soul Doth Magnify the Lord |

double
| 358 | 1 | Be of sin the double cure, Cleanse me from its guilt & power |

doubt
8	1	Drive the dark of doubt away
83	2	Nor doubt our inmost wants are known To him
109	3	Doubt and terror are withdrawn
193	3	No more we doubt thee, Glorious Prince of life
232	4	To check the rising doubt, the rebel sigh
244	2	Let thy dear word 'mid doubt and strife
315	4	O welcome voice of Jesus, Which drives away our doubt
319	2	With many a conflict, many a doubt
334	2	Lord, we have wandered forth through doubt and sorrow
352	2	The mist of doubt, the blight of love's decay
359	5	To doubt would be disloyalty, To falter would be sin
387	T,1	Through the Night of Doubt and Sorrow
469	4	No more by fear and doubt oppressed

doubts
| 293 | 3 | Away with gloomy doubts and faithless fear |
| 376 | 1 | And doubts appall, and sorrows still increase |

dove
232	5	The baptism of the heaven-descended Dove
238	T,1	Come, Gracious Spirit, Heavenly Dove
240	T,1,3	Come, Holy Spirit, Heavenly Dove
241	3	Come as the dove, and spread thy wings
275	2	Descend, O Holy Spirit, like a dove Into our hearts
349	3	Return, O holy Dove, return, Sweet messenger of rest

down
16	4	Sun and moon, bow down before him
31	1	Bow down before him, his glory proclaim
46	2	Lay down the burden and the care
76	3	Why should this anxious load Press down your weary mind
76	4	His goodness stands approved Down to the present day
84	1	He makes me down to lie In pastures green
95	2	justice, from her heavenly bower, Look down on mortal men
104	2	And the hills bow down to greet him
105	3	He shall come down like showers Upon the fruitful earth
108	2	For her Lord comes down all glorious
136	2	His the doom, ours the mirth When he came down to earth
137	1	The little Lord Jesus laid down his sweet head
137	1	The stars in the sky looked down where he lay
137	2	I love thee, Lord Jesus, look down from the sky
146	1	The angel of the Lord came down, And glory shone around
170	1	With grief and shame weighed down
175	3	The winged squadrons of the sky Look down
175	3	Look down with sad and wondering eye To see
177	3	Sorrow and love flow mingled down
184	4	The life laid down, the life restored
206	3	Fall down on their faces and worship the Lamb
228	1	Joy of heaven, to earth come down

230	3	To bring the Lord Christ down
237	T,1	Send Down Thy Truth, O God, Too long the shadows frown
237	1	Thy truth, O Lord, send down
237	2	Send down thy Spirit free
237	2	Thy Spirit, O send down
237	3	Send down thy love, thy life, Our lesser lives to crown
237	3	Thy living love send down
237	4	Send down thy peace, O Lord
237	4	Thy peace, O God, send down
239	T,1	Come Down, O Love divine, Seek thou this soul of mine
251	2	Casting down their golden crowns around the glassy sea
251	2	Cherubim and seraphim falling down before thee
259	3	And look down from supernal heights On all the by-gone time
325	2	a nation's pride o'erthrown, Went down to dust beside thee
340	1	Such happy, simple fisher-folk, Before the Lord came down
340	3	Peter, who hauled the teeming net, Head down was crucified
351	2	Though like the wanderer, The sun gone down
362	4	crowned with victory, at thy feet I'll lay my honors down
384	3	Tread all the powers of darkness down
386	4	And in the midnight lay us down to die
390	3	Why restless, why cast down, my soul
417	2	Who would sit down and sigh for a lost age of gold
418	4	In hope that sends a shining ray Far down
418	4	Far down the future's broadening way
421	1	lead To blazoned heights and down the slopes of need
428	R	Go down, Moses, 'Way down in Egypt's land
436	T,1	O God of Earth and Altar, Bow down and hear our cry
458	1	Hearts, bow down, & voices, sing Praises to the glorious One
458	6	Hearts, bow down and voices, sing Praise and love
459	1	He sends his showers of blessing down To cheer the plains
467	4	Be not cast down, disquieted in vain
488	3	Down in a lowly manger The humble Christ was born
509	2	Lay down the burden and the care
562	6	O come, let us worship and fall down
570	7	He hath put down the mighty from their seat

downcast

189	2	Let hearts downcast and lonely Rejoice this Easter day
364	2	Christian, never tremble, Never be downcast

downward

199	2	But downward bends his burning eye At mysteries so bright

drain

167	V-1	While thy wounds thy life-blood drain

draw

15	1	All ye who hear, Now to his temple draw near
55	2	Once more 'tis eventide, and we ... draw near
55	2	we, Oppressed with various ills, draw near
69	2	Kings of knowledge and of law, To the glorious circle draw
156	T,1	Draw Nigh to Thy Jerusalem, O Lord
156	1	Draw nigh ... Thy faithful people cry with one accord
239	1	O Comforter, draw near, Within my heart appear
291	3	Draw us in the Spirit's tether
292	3	And so we come, O draw us to thy feet

318	T,1	Draw Thou My Soul, O Christ, Closer to thine
358	4	While I draw this fleeting breath
444	T,1	O Day of God, Draw Nigh In beauty and in power
444	5	O Day of God, draw nigh As at creation's birth

drawing

51	T,1	Now the Day Is Over, Night is drawing nigh
114	1	The King of kings is drawing near
298	1	God is working his purpose out, And the time is drawing near
510	T,1	Now the Day Is Over, Night is drawing nigh

drawn

| 212 | 1 | Drawn from earth to love thee solely |
| 252 | 2 | It is the heaven-drawn picture of Christ, the living Word |

draws

293	2	The night draws nigh
298	1,4	Nearer & nearer draws the time ... time that shall surely be
455	3	Home closer draws her circle now
508	T,1	Before the Day Draws Near Its Ending

dread

2	4	Avert our woes and calm our dread
87	2	The clouds ye so much dread Are big with mercy
146	2	Fear not, said he, for mighty dread had seized
146	2	mighty dread Had seized their troubled mind
164	4	In this dread act your strength is tried
173	2	As the dread act of sacrifice began
174	2	Silent through those three dread hours
181	4	From death's dread sting thy servants free
477	1	Nor fear the storm, nor dread the shock
577	1	Make manifest in this dread time Thy power supreme

dream

1	5	They fly, forgotten, as a dream Dies at the opening day
208	2	Though what I dream and what I do
208	2	what I dream ... do ... In all my days are often two
348	4	When ends life's transient dream
420	3	city that hath stood Too long a dream, whose laws are love
440	4	O beautiful for patriot dream That sees beyond the years
451	2	Built while they dream, and in that dreaming weep
493	4	And in my soul a dream
494	2	upon the solid rock We set the dream that hardens into deed
494	3	may our hands Ne'er falter when the dream is in our hearts

dreamers

| 417 | 1 | All dreamers toss and sigh |

dreaming

| 386 | 3 | And worship, dreaming that we worship thee |
| 451 | 2 | Built while they dream, and in that dreaming weep |

dreamless

| 134 | 1 | Above thy deep and dreamless sleep The silent stars go by |
| 468 | 3 | Not wrapped in dreamless sleep profound |

dreams

58	1	Holy dreams and hopes attend us, This live-long night
124	3	Hush, hush, see how he smiles in dreams
208	2	O thou whose deeds and dreams were one
232	2	I ask no dreams, no prophet ecstasies
351	2	Yet in my dreams I'd be Nearer, my God, to thee
458	5	Praise for happy dreams of birth Brooding in the quiet earth
492	2	For prophet voices gladly heard, For daring dreams

drear

306	2	Thou, in the darkness drear, their one true light
455	1	And all the earth lies dead and drear

dreary

344	2	Lone and dreary, faint and weary, Through the desert

dress

230	5	The healing of his seamless dress Is by our beds of pain
358	3	Naked, come to thee for dress

drew

113	3	When the old world drew on toward night, Thou camest
141	4	This star drew nigh to the northwest

drift

360	3	I only know I cannot drift Beyond his love and care
436	1	Our earthly rulers falter, Our people drift and die

drifting

261	4	In vain the surge's angry shock, In vain the drifting sands
297	T,1	O God, Above the Drifting Years

drink

287	2	Here drink with thee the royal wine of heaven
288	2	Let us drink wine together on our knees
388	1	Who best can drink the cup of woe, Triumphant over pain
557	2	Here drink with thee the royal wine of heaven

drive

8	1	Drive the dark of doubt away

driven

86	2	It is because thou art We're driven to the quest
378	4	Grant us thy help til backward they are driven

drives

221	1	And drives away his fear
315	4	O welcome voice of Jesus, Which drives away our doubt

driving

220	2	Through ... thrust of driving trade We follow

drop

76	4	I'll drop my burden at his feet, And bear a song away
341	4	Drop thy still dews of quietness, Till ... strivings cease
450	2	strong To spill no drop of blood

drops
126   2   Cold on his cradle the dew-drops are shining

dross
324   2   Wash out its stains, refine its dross
372   4   I only design Thy dross to consume and thy gold to refine

drove
349   3   I hate the sins that made thee mourn And drove thee
349   3   And drove thee from my breast

drown
230   3   For him no depths can drown
237   4   Earth's bitter voices drown In one deep ocean of accord

drowns
199   1   Hark, how the heavenly anthem drowns All music but its own

drudgery
401   4   A servant with this clause Makes drudgery divine

drums
42   3   Hear we no beat of drums, Fanfare nor cry
375   2   not with swords' loud clashing Nor roll of stirring drums

drunk
431   4   If drunk with sight of power, we loose Wild tongues

dry
562   5   and his hands prepared the dry land

dull
32   1   Shake off dull sloth

dullness
231   2   Enable with perpetual light The dullness of... blinded sight
575   2   Enable with perpetual light The dullness
575   2   The dullness of our blinded sight

dumb
284   4   when these failing lips grow dumb, And mind and memory flee
341   5   Let sense be dumb, let flesh retire
426   2   No field or mart is silent, No city street is dumb

dune
431   3   On dune and headland sinks the fire

dungeon
365   1   living still In spite of dungeon, fire, and sword

durch
139   2   Durch der Engel Alleluja

dust
6   5   Frail children of dust, and feeble as frail

239	2	O let it freely burn, Till earthly passions turn To dust
239	2	To dust and ashes in its heat consuming
325	2	a nation's pride o'erthrown, Went down to dust beside thee
325	4	Our pride is dust, our vaunt is stilled
357	2	Thou wilt not leave us in the dust
399	4	I lay in dust life's glory dead
426	3	Our strength is dust and ashes, Our years a passing hour
431	5	All valiant dust that builds on dust
469	3	Above the requiem, Dust to dust, Shall rise our psalm

dusty
| 398 | 3 | afoot on dusty highways |

duteous
| 53 | T,1 | The Duteous Day Now Closeth, Each flower and tree reposeth |
| 508 | 1 | Whose duteous service never slumbers |

duties
| 441 | 2 | New occasions teach new duties |

duty
32	1	Thy daily stage of duty run
86	4	Inspire us from above With joy and strength for duty
333	2	Tenderest guide, in ways of cheerful duty, Lead us
385	3	Where duty calls, or danger, Be never wanting there
396	2	Praise in each duty and each deed, However small or mean
442	1	Forgive, and show our duty clear
476	4	rich in art, made richer still The brotherhood of duty
503	1	Where my soul in joyful duty Waits for him who answers

dwell
4	T,1	All People That on Earth Do Dwell
5	T,1	All People That on Earth Do Dwell (same as No. 4)
11	T,1	From All That Dwell Below the Skies
12	T,1	From All That Dwell Below the Skies (No. 11 with alleluias)
46	4	in the spirit's secret cell May hymn & prayer forever dwell
76	2	While providence supports, Let saints securely dwell
120	2	Pleased as man with men to dwell, Jesus our Emmanuel
156	3	And in that temple dwell forevermore
200	3	The joy of all who dwell above, The joy of all below
202	3	People and realms of every tongue Dwell on his love
202	3	Dwell on his love with sweetest song
207	4	That we may dwell in perfect unity
214	2	To dwell in lowliness with men, their pattern and their King
238	4	holiness, the road That we must take to dwell with God
245	T,1	Gracious Spirit, Dwell With Me, I myself would gracious be
245	2	Truthful Spirit, dwell with me, I myself would truthful be
245	3	Mighty Spirit, dwell with me, I myself would mighty be
245	4	Holy Spirit, dwell with me, I myself would holy be
260	4	Like them, the meek and lowly, On high may dwell with thee
274	1	how dear The pleasant tabernacles are Where thou dost dwell
274	1	Where thou dost dwell so near
276	3	And dwell thou with us in this place, Thou and thy Christ
276	3	dwell thou ... to guide and bless
294	2	kindness dwell in human hearts And all the earth find peace

347	3	And kindness in our bosoms dwell As free and true as thine
357	6	But more of reverence in us dwell
407	2	And let me dwell in light with thee
424	1	Only righteous men and women Dwell within its gleaming wall
444	3	Bring justice to our land, That all may dwell secure
466	1	guarding well ... The homes in which thy people dwell
475	1	And yet vouchsafes in Christian lands To dwell in temples
475	1	To dwell in temples made with hands
524	1	For it is thou, Lord, thou, Lord only, that makest me dwell
524	1	thou, Lord, only, that makest me dwell in safety

dwellers

| 16 | 4 | Sun and moon ... Dwellers in all time and space |

dwellest

330	2	Thou dwellest in unshadowed light, All sin and shame above
409	2	Thou the peace that passeth knowledge Dwellest in the daily
409	2	Thou ... Dwellest in the daily strife
569	4	and dwellest between the cherubim

dwelling

84	5	And in God's house for evermore My dwelling place shall be
214	3	for his dwelling and his throne Chooseth the pure in heart
228	1	Fix in us thy humble dwelling
239	3	the place Wherein the Holy Spirit makes his dwelling
270	2	Surely in temples made with hands, God ... is not dwelling
270	2	God, the Most High, is not dwelling
270	3	E'en in the lowliest dwelling
271	3	Safe in the same dear dwelling place
391	2	Thou in me dwelling, and I with thee one
427	T,1	We Are Living, We Are Dwelling In a grand and aweful time
466	3	That every home ... May be the dwelling place of peace
466	3	every home, by this release, May be the dwelling place
475	3	all peoples ... That shall adorn thy dwelling place
576	3	In heaven. It is thy dwelling fair
576	4	And far away my dwelling make

dwellings

| 274 | T,1 | How Lovely Are Thy Dwellings Fair, O Lord of hosts |

dwells

403	2	Lo, the Prince of common welfare dwells within the market
403	2	dwells within the market strife
410	1	Where pity dwells, the peace of God is there

dwelt

| 1 | 2 | Under the shadow of thy throne Thy saints have dwelt secure |
| 77 | 2 | His voice who ruled them while he dwelt below |

dying

45	T,1	Day is Dying in the West, Heaven is touching earth with rest
105	2	Whose souls, condemned and dying, Were precious in his sight
143	4	Sorrowing, sighing, bleeding, dying
150	4	For us gave up his dying breath

e'en

e'er

each

253	2	Each his word from God repeating
267	3	Round each habitation hovering, See the cloud & fire appear
272	3	We share each other's woes, Each other's burdens bear
272	3	And often for each other flows The sympathizing tear
286	4	One with each other, Lord, for one in thee
287	2	Here would I lay aside each earthly load
293	1	And to each servant does the Master say, Go work today
305	1	Each breeze that sweeps the ocean Brings tidings from afar
322	3	From each idol that would keep us
324	2	Hallow each thought, let all within Be clean
331	2	That each departing day Henceforth may see Some work of love
334	2	And thou hast made each step an onward one
334	2	And we will ever trust each unknown morrow
361	1	God will fulfil in every part Each promise he has made
383	3	In each loss or triumph Lose or triumph all
385	3	Put on the gospel armor, Each piece put on with prayer
389	3	Through each perplexing path of life
389	3	Give us each day our daily bread, And raiment fit provide
396	2	Praise in each duty and each deed, However small or mean
410	1	To worship rightly is to love each other
410	1	Each smile a hymn, each kindly deed a prayer
410	2	Each loving life a psalm of gratitude
412	3	O thou who didst the vision send And gives to each his task
417	2	Each old age of gold was an iron age too
441	1	God's new messiah, Offering each the bloom or blight
442	T,1	Thou Judge by Whom Each Empire Fell
442	1	In each sharp crisis, Lord, appear
452	2	Our faces from each other hide
458	4	Each the table of our God
466	1	Who dost in love proclaim Each family thine own
470	1	Each age its solemn task may claim but once
470	1	Make each one nobler, stronger than the last
478	1	Each little flower that opens, Each little bird that sings
492	2	We thank thee, Father, for each word
492	2	Each thought-revealing truth
492	3	Renew in us each day Our lofty purpose
498	T,1	Each Morning Brings us fresh outpoured The loving-kindness
539	2	Thus may we abide in union with each other and the Lord
540	1	Calm with trust each anxious heart
557	2	Here would I lay aside each earthly load

eager

108	2	Hallelujah, We haste along, An eager throng
161	1	The meaning of our eager strife Is tested by his Way
304	2	and eager hearts awoke to greet the day
309	4	O sweet and blessed country, that eager hearts expect
315	3	The foe is stern and eager, The fight is fierce and long
432	3	Thy hand has led across the hungry sea The eager peoples
432	3	The eager peoples flocking to be free

eagerness

217	2	Lord of all eagerness, Lord of all faith

eagle

74	3	Made him fly with eagle pinion, Master over sea and land
388	2	martyr first, whose eagle eye Could pierce beyond the grave

eagle's

73	2	Crag where eagle's pride hath soared

ear

3	2	Bow thine ear To us here
24	1	No mortal eye hath seen, No mortal ear hath heard such
24	1	No mortal ear hath heard such wondrous things
66	3	For the joy of ear and eye, For the heart and mind's delight
72	3	In reason's ear they all rejoice
108	3	No ear hath ever caught Such great glory
221	T,1	How Sweet the Name of Jesus Sounds In a believer's ear
298	2	Give ear to me, ye continents, Ye isles, give ear to me
306	5	Steals on the ear the distant triumph song
461	2	First the blade, and then the ear
508	2	Thine ear discerns, thy love rejoices When hearts rise up
519	T,1	To My Humble Supplication, Lord give ear and acceptation
526	T,1	O Thou Who Hearest Prayer, Give ear unto our cry

earliest

59	3	Our earliest thoughts be thine when morning wakes us
502	T,1	We Praise Thee, Lord, with earliest morning ray

early

152	5	We would see Jesus in the early morning
202	3	And infant voices shall proclaim their early blessings
202	3	Their early blessings on his name
251	1	Early in the morning our song shall rise to thee
327	3	Early let us seek thy favor, Early let us do thy will
412	1	Who with the eyes of early youth Eternal things did see
496	1	O say can you see by the dawn's early light

earnest

387	2	One the earnest looking forward
400	1	This is my earnest plea, More love, O Christ, to thee
425	2	And, with heart and hand, to be Earnest to make others free

ears

212	3	Open thou our ears and heart
352	4	Lift up your hearts, rings pealing in our ears
461	3	But the fruitful ears to store In his garner evermore
470	2	Make their ears attent To thy divinest speech
485	1	And to my listening ears, All nature sings
494	3	When to our ears there come divine commands

earth

1	3	Before the hills in order stood, Or earth received her frame
2	1	And peace shall reign on earth again
4	T,1	All People That on Earth Do Dwell
5	T,1	All People That on Earth Do Dwell (same as No. 4)
6	3	The earth with its store of wonders untold
8	2	Earth and heaven reflect thy rays
9	4	earth, with her ten thousand tongues Shall fill thy courts
13	2	Heaven and earth and all creation Laud and magnify his name
18	1	By all the earth adored
19	2	Earth to heaven, and heaven to earth ...tell his wonders
26	T,1	O Be Joyful in the Lord, Sing before him, all the earth

28	1	word When it goes forth from heaven o'er all the earth
28	2	Thy Church ... standeth sure while earth and time endure
29	3	The one eternal God, Whom earth and heaven adore
35	3	Let all the earth around Ring joyous with the sound
42	3	Splendor he makes on earth, Color awakes on earth
42	3	Suddenly breaks on earth Light from the sky
45	T,1	Day is Dying in the West, Heaven is touching earth with rest
45	R	Heaven and earth are full of thee
45	R	Heaven and earth are praising thee, O Lord most high
47	2	While earth rolls onward into light
54	2	Thy gift of peace on earth secure
58	T,1	God That Madest Earth and Heaven, Darkness and light
59	4	We have no refuge, none on earth to aid us
65	1	Earth repeat the songs of heaven
65	2	Earth and sea cry, God is good
66	T,1	For the Beauty of the Earth, For the beauty of the skies
66	4	Friends on earth and friends above
66	5	Graces, human and divine, Flowers of earth & buds of heaven
67	T,1	God of Earth, the Sky, the Sea, Maker of all above, below
68	2	goodness of the Lord, That filled the earth with food
69	1	Heaven & earth, awake & sing, God is good and therefore King
70	2	He, with all commanding might, Filled the new-made earth
72	2	nightly, to the listening earth, Repeats the story
73	1	Earth and sky, all living nature ... praise
74	1	full of wonder Is thy name o'er all the earth
74	2	Child of earth, yet full of yearning
75	T,1	Heaven and Earth, and Sea and Air
75	3	See how he hath everywhere made this earth so rich and fair
78	1	throne of him Who formed the earth and sky
85	1	My safety cometh from the Lord, Who heaven & earth hath made
95	2	Truth from the earth, like a flower, Shall bud and blossom
95	3	Rise, God, judge thou the earth in might
95	3	This wicked earth redress
98	T,1	My God, I Thank Thee, Who Hast Made The earth so bright
98	2	That in the darkest spot of earth Some love is found
99	3	We read thee in the earth below
103	2	Hope of all the earth thou art
104	3	For the glory of the Lord Now o'er earth is shed abroad
105	1	Hail, in the time appointed, His reign on earth begun
105	3	He shall come down like showers Upon the fruitful earth
107	1	blessing in his hand, Christ our God to earth descendeth
107	2	King of kings, yet born of Mary, As of old on earth he stood
111	2	Let no tongue on earth be silent
117	1	Wing your flight o'er all the earth
119	2	There to bend the knee before Him who heaven and earth adore
120	1	Peace on earth, and mercy mild
120	3	Born to raise the sons of earth ...to give them second birth
121	T,1	From Heaven Above to Earth I Come
121	2	Shall be the joy of all your earth
121	4	A glad new year to all the earth
127	2	To you and all the nations upon earth
128	1	Earth stood hard as iron, Water like a stone
128	2	Our God, heaven cannot hold him, Nor earth sustain
128	2	Heaven and earth shall flee away When he comes to reign
129	1	From angels bending near the earth
129	1	Peace on the earth, good will to men

326	2	But in lowly birth didst thou come to earth
344	2	Thou didst tread this earth before us
354	1	strong abode In heaven and earth possesses
363	1	And armed with cruel hate, On earth is not his equal
369	1	of all things on earth least like What men agree to praise
370	3	And when my task on earth is done
378	4	Grant peace on earth
395	5	And claim the kingdom of the earth For thee and not thy foe
407	1	All things in earth and heaven Are lustered by thy ray
409	1	workers, Burden-bearers of the earth
410	2	So shall the wide earth seem our Father's temple
410	3	clangor Of wild war music o'er the earth shall cease
411	4	Until in all the earth thy kingdom come
413	4	grant our hope's fruition, Here on earth thy will be done
414	1	fellowship of love Throughout the whole wide earth
414	4	one in him throughout the whole wide earth
425	1	If there breathe on earth a slave, Are ye truly free & brave
432	3	from the breeds of earth thy silent sway Fashions the nation
436	T,1	O God of Earth and Altar, Bow down and hear our cry
438	4	And spring adorns the earth no more
444	4	That war may haunt the earth no more And desolation cease
444	5	Let there be light again, and set Thy judgments in the earth
446	2	earth hath forsaken Thy ways all holy, and slighted thy word
446	4	earth by thy chastening Yet shall ... be restored
449	1	Let there be wisdom on the earth
450	2	dare All that may plant man's lordship firm On earth
450	2	On earth and fire and sea and air
451	1	Old now is earth, and none may count her days
451	2	Earth might be fair and all men glad and wise
451	3	Earth shall be fair, and all her people one
451	3	Now, even now, once more from earth to sky Peals forth
451	3	Earth shall be fair, and all her folk be one
455	1	And all the earth lies dead and drear
457	1	One more the glad earth yields Her golden wealth
475	4	To thee they all belong ... treasures of the earth and sea
485	3	God reigns, let the earth be glad
486	1	Through the earth and sky God's great mercies flow
488	2	The shepherds feared and trembled When lo, above the earth
494	3	Until the heavenly kingdom comes on earth
503	2	Where we find thee and adore thee, There a heaven on earth
503	2	There a heaven on earth must be
504	1	Let heaven rejoice, let earth be glad
504	2	Hosanna in the highest strains The Church on earth can raise
506	1	Now is breaking O'er the earth another day
508	1	And evening steals o'er earth and sky
539	2	possess in sweet communion Joys which earth cannot afford
550	1	Heaven and earth are full of thy glory
551	1	Heaven and earth are full of thy glory
553	1	Heaven and earth are full of thy glory
554	1	and on earth peace, good will towards men
558	1	When powers of earth and hell arose
559	1	All the earth doth worship thee, The Father everlasting
559	3	heaven and earth are full of the majesty of thy glory
562	4	In his hand are all the corners of the earth
562	8	let the whole earth stand in awe of him

ease
58	2	Let not ease and self enthrall us
368	1	Not for ease that prayer shall be
426	4	From ease and plenty save us, From pride of place absolve

east
100	3	Far as east from west is distant He hath put away our sin
106	3	Lands of the East, awake, Soon shall your sons be free
106	5	Lo, from the North we come, From East, and West, and South
126	1,5	Star of the east, the horizon adorning
141	2	They looked up and saw a star Shining in the east
141	2	Shining in the east, beyond them far
298	2	utmost east to utmost west, Where'er man's foot hath trod
304	4	To east and west his kingdom bringing near
414	T,1	In Christ There Is No East or West, In him no South or North
414	4	In Christ now meet both East and West
415	T,1	In Christ There Is No East or West (words as no. 414)
505	1	And joy to see the cheerful light That riseth in the east

Easter
153	4	An Easter of unending joy We may attain at last
180	2	Glorious life, and life immortal On this holy Easter morn
188	T,1	Joy Dawned Again on Easter Day
189	2	Let hearts downcast and lonely Rejoice this Easter day
191	2	That Easter morn at break of day, The faithful women went

eastern
144	2	And lo, the eastern sages stand to read in heaven
201	1	When beauty gilds the eastern hills And life to joy awakes
486	1	Comes the eastern sun Like a man of brawn

Eastertide
| 148 | 4 | That with thee we may appear At the eternal Eastertide |
| 188 | 3 | O Lord of all, with us abide In this our joyful Eastertide |

easy
| 406 | 4 | Give me to bear thy easy yoke |
| 436 | 2 | From all the easy speeches That comfort cruel men |

eat
| 558 | 3 | Receive and eat the living food |
| 558 | 5 | Till thou return and we shall eat The marriage supper |

ebbing
| 230 | 1 | Forever shared, forever whole, A never-ebbing sea |

ebbs
| 209 | 2 | Swift to its close ebbs out life's little day |

echo
| 116 | 1 | And the mountains in reply Echo back their joyous strains |
| 502 | 2 | O may we echo on the song afar |

echoes
| 397 | 1 | speak In living echoes of thy tone |

echoing
30 4   let us sing Supernal anthems echoing, Alleluia

ecstasies
232 2   I ask no dreams, no prophet ecstasies

Eden
38 3   Born of the one light Eden saw play

Eden's
249 1   blessed ... With light and life since Eden's dawning day

Edom
126 3   Odors of Edom and offerings divine

effort
221 4   Weak is the effort of my heart, And cold my warmest thought

Egypt's
428 T,1   When Israel Was in Egypt's Land
428 R   Go down, Moses, 'Way down in Egypt's land
428 3   Let them come out with Egypt's spoil

einsam
139 1   Alles schlaft, einsam wacht

elation
38 3   Praise with elation, Praise every morning
325 4   We wait thy revelation

elect
260 2   Elect from every nation, Yet one o'er all the earth
309 4   O sweet and blessed country, The home of God's elect
311 3   Fill up the roll of thine elect, Then take thy power & reign

Elijah's
470 1   Elijah's mantle o'er Elisha cast

Elisha
470 1   Elijah's mantle o'er Elisha cast

eloquent
470 2   their lips make eloquent To assure the right

else
23 1   Assist our song, For else the theme Too high doth seem
81 4   Fear him, ye saints, and ... then Have nothing else to fear
317 1   It satisfies my longings As nothing else would do
391 1   Nought be all else to me save that thou art

embrace
45 2   Gather us who seek thy face To the fold of thy embrace
122 4   And with true love and brotherhood Each other now embrace
132 3   we would embrace thee, with love and awe
217 3   Your hands swift to welcome your arms to embrace

357 1   Whom we, that have not seen thy face, By faith ... embrace
357 1   By faith, and faith alone, embrace

embracing
99 3   wide-embracing, wondrous love, We read thee in the sky above

emerge
297 2   From out their tireless prayer and toil Emerge the gifts
297 2   Emerge the gifts that time has proved

Emmanuel
110 T,1   O Come, O Come Emmanuel, And ransom captive Israel
110 R   Rejoice, Rejoice, Emmanuel Shall come to thee, O Israel
120 2   Pleased as man with men to dwell, Jesus our Emmanuel
134 4   O come to us, abide with us, Our Lord Emmanuel

empire
439 T,1   Not Alone for Mighty Empire
442 T,1   Thou Judge by Whom Each Empire Fell
442 1   empire fell ... When pride of power o'ercame it

empires
47 5   Like earth's proud empires, pass away
264 T,1   O Where Are Kings and Empires Now Of old that went and came
451 2   Age after age their tragic empires rise

employ
94 3   Ten thousand precious gifts My daily thanks employ
114 2   set apart From earthly use for heaven's employ
130 2   Let men their songs employ
416 3   And thy worship God's employ
464 1   Let thy praise our tongues employ
472 1   Building for thine employ This house of prayer

empty
391 3   Riches I heed not, nor man's empty praise
570 8   and the rich he hath sent empty away

enable
231 2   Enable with perpetual light The dullness of... blinded sight
575 2   Enable with perpetual light The dullness

encamp
373 2   Though hosts encamp around me, Firm in the fight I stand

encircle
329 2   And thorns thy brow encircle, And tears thy face have marred

encircling
215 T,1   Lead, Kingly Light, amid the encircling gloom

encompass
421 1   They reach thy throne, encompass land and sea

end
6 5   Thy mercies how tender, how firm to the end

23	4	all thy days Till life shall end...filled with thy praise
45	3	and shadows end
60	2	With thee began, with thee shall end the day
77	1	Through thorny ways leads to a joyful end
100	4	As it was in the beginning, So it lasts without an end
167	III-1	Jesus, loving to the end Her whose heart thy sorrows rend
170	3	For this thy dying sorrow, Thy pity without end
192	3	For Christ the Lord is risen, Our joy that hath no end
217	4	Your peace in our hearts, Lord, at the end of the day
218	T,1	O Jesus, I Have Promised, To serve thee to the end
218	3	And, Jesus, I have promised, To serve thee to the end
221	3	My Lord, my Life, my Way, my End, Accept the praise I bring
228	2	Alpha and Omega be, End of faith as its beginning
269	3	Till toils and cares shall end
300	2	Bring in the day of brotherhood, And end the night of wrong
312	1	When shall my sorrows have an end
337	1	Wait thou his time, so shall this night Soon end
337	1	Soon end in joyous day
364	4	And the end of sorrow shall be near my throne
371	3	We know we at the end Shall life inherit
393	1	God be at mine end, And at my departing
398	2	To heal earth's wounds and end her bitter strife
471	3	He sees the glory that shall end our night
500	2	Praise him through time, till time shall end
511	1	world without end
512	1	world without end
513	1	world without end
517	1	teach me...the way...And I shall keep it safe unto the end
543	1	God be at mine end, and at my departing
558	4	So this, he cried, till time shall end
559	14	we worship thy name ever, world without end
562	R	world without end
565	R	world without end

endeavor

268	3	Bless thy Church's new endeavor
271	3	The same sweet theme endeavor
368	4	Through endeavor, failure, danger, Father, be ...at our side
372	5	That soul, though all hell should endeavor to shake
435	3	Crown, O God, thine own endeavor
491	2	Fill thou our hearts with zeal in every brave endeavor

ended

2	1	The strife at last is ended
42	2	Swift grows the light for us, Ended is night for us
47	T,1,	The Day Thou Gavest, Lord, Is Ended
48	T,1	The Day Thou Gavest, Lord, Is Ended (same words as No. 47)
252	4	Till, clouds and darkness ended, They see thee face to face
380	4	Faith's warfare ended, won The home of endless peace
506	2	For the night is safely ended
579	T,1	Summer Ended, Harvest O'er, Lord, to thee our song we pour

endeth

271	2	We raise it high, we send it on, The song that never endeth
449	2	The calm that endeth strain and strife

ending

41	2	Joy without ending
111	1	He is Alpha and Omega, He the source, the ending he
168	4	Until thou see thy bitter travail's ending
315	1	Of joy that hath no ending, Of love which cannot cease
433	4	Lead us from night to never-ending day
465	1	That theirs may be the love which knows no ending
508	T,1	Before the Day Draws Near Its Ending

endless

1	3	From everlasting thou art God, To endless years the same
30	3	Respond, ye souls in endless rest
63	3	may we ever Reign with thee in endless day
107	3	the Light of light descendeth From the realms of endless day
125	2	Now ye hear of endless bliss, Jesus Christ was born for this
144	4	To God the Holy Ghost we raise An endless song
144	4	And endless song of thankful praise
193	1,R	Endless is the victory Thou o'er death hast won
202	2	For him shall endless prayer be made
310	1	Those endless sabbaths the blessed ones see
312	6	see Thine endless joy, and of the same Partaker ever be
380	4	Faith's warfare ended, won The home of endless peace
398	3	Lure us away from thee to endless night
399	4	from the ground ... blossoms red Life that shall endless be
407	T,1	O Light That Knew No Dawn, that shines to endless day
484	1	Or farm the mountain pastures, Or till the endless plains
575	4	That through the ages all along This may be our endless song

ends

1	4	Short as the watch that ends the night Before the rising sun
348	4	When ends life's transient dream
392	4	Teach us to look in all our ends On thee
452	3	Is soon to evil ends betrayed
498	1	It ends not as the day goes past

endue

471	2	Endue him with thy wisdom, love, and power
475	3	Endue all peoples with thy grace
491	1	With light and love divine our souls endue

endued

260	2	And to one hope she presses, With every grace endued
384	2	With all his strength endued

endurance

168	2	We would not leave thee, though our weak endurance
168	2	our weak endurance Make us unworthy here to take our part
465	2	Of patient hope, and quiet, brave endurance

endure

4	4	His truth ... shall from age to age endure
26	4	Evermore, as of yore, Shall his changeless truth endure
28	2	Thy Church ... standeth sure while earth and time endure
54	2	And for thy truth the world endure
70	R	For his mercies aye endure, Ever faithful, ever sure
207	5	That in thy strength we evermore endure

233	2	Until with thee I will one will To do and to endure
255	3	The fear of God is undefiled And ever shall endure
363	3	His rage we can endure, For lo, his doom is sure
444	3	And finely build for days to come Foundations that endure
463	1-3	For his mercies still endure, Ever faithful, ever sure
490	3	And let us not for one short hour An evil thought endure
579	2	For the promise ever sure that, while heaven & earth endure

endured

| 187 | 2 | Who endured the cross and grave ... Sinners to redeem & save |
| 187 | 3 | the pains which he endured ... Our salvation have procured |

endures

| 86 | 1 | plan ... in which the world began, Endures, and shall endure |

endureth

| 565 | 4 | his truth endureth from generation to generation |

enduring

| 494 | 3 | O grant enduring worth Until the heavenly kingdom comes |

enemies

| 568 | 4 | That we should be saved from our enemies |
| 568 | 7 | That we being delivered out of the hand our enemies |

energy

| 422 | 2 | Sing of the boundless energy of God |

enfold

197	5	Let his will enfold you In its light and power
277	1	Now enfold them in thy goodness
408	2	Thou didst reach forth thy hand and mine enfold
455	4	Us warmly in thy love enfold
578	2	Thou didst reach forth thy hand and mine enfold

enfolded

| 92 | 4 | Enfolded deep in thy dear love, Held in thy law, I stand |

engaging

| 378 | 3 | Peace, in thy Church, where brothers are engaging |

Engel

| 139 | 2 | Durch der Engel Alleluja |

engines

| 422 | T,1 | When Through the Whirl of Wheels, and engines humming |

enjoy

| 167 | III-2 | And enjoy thy tender care, Hear us, holy Jesus |

enlarge

| 259 | 4 | Enlarge, expand all Christian souls To comprehend thy love |

enlightened

| 127 | 3 | To Bethlehem straight the enlightened shepherds ran |

enough

98	4	We have enough, yet not too much To long for more
215	1	one step enough for me
287	5	It is enough, my Lord, enough indeed
557	3	It is enough, my Lord, enough indeed

enrich

50	4	Watch by the sick, enrich the poor with blessings
527	T,1	Enrich, Lord, Heart, Mouth, Hands in Me
527	1	Enrich ... With faith, with hope, with charity

enslave

356	2	Enslave it with thy matchless love
356	2	Enslave it ... And deathless it shall reign

enter

4	3	O enter then his gates with praise
26	3	Enter now his holy gate, Let our burdened hearts be still
31	3	Fear not to enter his courts in the slenderness of the poor
114	4	So come, my Sovereign, enter in
115	2	let us each our hearts prepare For Christ to come and enter
134	4	Cast out our sin and enter in, Be born in us today
156	3	O enter in, dear Lord, unbar the door
228	1	Visit us with thy salvation, Enter every trembling heart
244	T,1	O Holy Spirit, Enter In, Among these hearts thy work begin
329	3	Dear Savior, enter, enter, And leave us nevermore
503	T,1	Open Now Thy Gates of Beauty, Zion, let me enter there
503	2	To my heart O enter thou, Let it be thy temple now
580	2	Shut not that gate against me, Lord, But let me enter in

entered

141	5	Then entered in those wise men three

enterprise

180	2	Christ has triumphed, & we conquer By his mighty enterprise

enters

134	3	Where meek souls will receive him ... Christ enters in
134	3	still The dear Christ enters in
205	1	Enters now the highest heaven
222	3	For the Lord of gladness, Jesus, enters in

enthrall

58	2	Let not ease and self enthrall us

enthralled

421	3	Has held our hearts enthralled while serving thee

enthrone

140	3	Let loving hearts enthrone him
197	5	In your hearts enthrone him, There let him subdue All
198	3	Cast out our pride and shame That hinder to enthrone thee
203	2	In the seat of power enthrone him

enthroned

2	3	Thou Lamb of God, enthroned on high Behold our need

ergo
  133 3   Ergo qui natus Die hodierna

err
   87 4   Blind unbelief is sure to err And scan his work in vain
   95 1   His footsteps cannot err

errand
  266 4   O living Church, thine errand speed
  426 3   Send us upon thine errand, Let us thy servants be

errands
  266 3   And feet on mercy's errands swift Do make her pilgrimage

erring
  397 1   As thou hast sought, so let me seek Thy erring children
  397 1   Thy erring children lost and lone

error
  424 3   Oft in error, oft in anguish

error's
  295 4   The new-born souls, whose days Reclaimed from error's ways
  376 2   Unhelped by thee, in error's maze we grope

erst
  139 2   Hirten erst kundgemacht

es
  139 2   Tont es laut von fern und nah, Christ der Retter ist da

escape
   21 3   Let thy congregation escape tribulation

espy
  401 2   Or if he pleaseth through it pass, And then the heaven espy

essence
  247 4   While in essence only One, Undivided God we claim thee

established
   14 2   Established is his law, And changeless it shall stand

estate
  140 2   Why lies he in such mean estate Where ox and ass are feeding

esteem
  330 3   Ah, did not he the heavenly throne A little thing esteem

eternal
    1 1   Our shelter from the stormy blast, And our eternal home
    1 6   Be thou our guard while troubles last, and our eternal home
   11 2   Eternal are thy mercies, Lord
   11 2   Eternal truth attends thy word
   14 1   The one eternal God, Ere aught that now appears
   14 3   He hath eternal life Implanted in the soul

18	5	That thou eternal Father art, Of boundless majesty
29	3	The one eternal God, Whom earth and heaven adore
30	2	bearer of the eternal Word, Most gracious, magnify the Lord
32	2	sing High praise to the eternal King
35	5	In heaven's eternal bliss The loveliest strain is this
35	6	Be this the eternal song Through all the ages long
45	3	Lord of angels, on our eyes Let eternal morning rise
49	1	The eternal splendor wearing, Celestial, holy, blest
52	3	As the darkness deepens o'er us, Lo, eternal stars arise
60	4	Call us, O Lord, to thine eternal peace
82	T,1	High in the Heavens, Eternal God
86	3	Hints of the music vast Of thine eternal hymn
99	T,1	O Love of God, How Strong and True, Eternal and yet ever new
99	2	Changeless, eternal, infinite
101	2	heart of the Eternal Is most wonderfully kind (102-3)
103	4	By thine own eternal Spirit Rule in all our hearts alone
111	3	Honor, glory, and dominion, And eternal victory, Evermore
112	2	Comes the life eternal here
115	4	All praise, eternal Son, to thee
118	1	The power of Satan breaking, Our peace eternal making
148	4	That with thee we may appear At the eternal Eastertide
180	2	We with him to life eternal By his resurrection rise
187	4	Sing we to our God above ... Praise eternal as his love
191	4	For they eternal life shall win
192	1	From death to life eternal, From earth unto the sky
192	2	The Lord in rays eternal Of resurrection light
199	3	Who died, eternal life to bring, & lives that death may die
200	2	King of kings, and Lord of lords, And heaven's eternal light
202	4	The weary find eternal rest & all the sons of want are blest
205	2	Lift your heads, eternal gates
246	4	To the great One in Three Eternal praises be Hence evermore
261	4	Unharmed upon the eternal rock The eternal city stands
264	4	Unshaken as eternal hills, Immovable she stands
267	2	See ... streams of living waters Springing from eternal love
271	1	The eternal arms, their dear abode, We make our habitation
271	3	Rich with the same eternal grace
275	T,1	Eternal Ruler of the Ceaseless Round Of circling planets
287	1	Here grasp with firmer hand the eternal grace
289	1	Giving in Christ the bread eternal
294	T,1	Eternal God, Whose Power Upholds Both flower & flaming star
313	3	love ... Solely because thou art my God, And my eternal King
314	4	That when this life is past ... the eternal brightness see
314	4	I may the eternal brightness see, And share thy joy at last
339	3	Still from man to God eternal Sacrifice of praise be done
375	T,1	Lead On, O King Eternal, The day of march has come
375	1	And now, O King eternal, We lift our battle song
375	2	Lead on, O King eternal, Till sin's fierce war shall cease
375	3	Lead on, O King eternal, We follow, not with fears
384	1	God supplies Through his eternal Son
387	3	One the gladness of rejoicing On the far eternal shore
390	3	praise of him who is thy God, Thy health's eternal spring
406	4	And still to things eternal look
412	1	Who with the eyes of early youth Eternal things did see
413	T,1	Son of God, Eternal Savior, Source of life and truth & grace
422	5	Living again the eternal gospel story
429	T,1	Eternal Father, Strong to Save

435	T,1	Judge Eternal, Throned in Splendor
438	4	Till these eternal hills remove
445	T,1	Father Eternal, Ruler of Creation
465	3	morrow That dawns upon eternal love and life
475	1	glory fills The bounds of the eternal hills
501	2	O let heaven's eternal day Be thine eternal praise
557	1	Here grasp with firmer hand eternal grace
575	R	Praise to thy eternal merit, Father, Son and Holy Spirit

eternally

17	1	Be magnified eternally, Hallelujah, Hallelujah
108	3	Therefore will we, eternally, Sing hymns of joy and praise
313	1	Nor yet because who love thee not Are lost eternally
367	1	Lay hold on life, & it shall be Thy joy and crown eternally
385	4	He with the King of glory Shall reign eternally
407	4	All grace and glory be to thee From age to age eternally

eternity

9	5	Vast as eternity thy love
94	4	Through all eternity to thee A joyful song I'll raise
165	2	from the cross on Calvary's height Gleams of eternity appear
199	1	And hail him as thy matchless King Through all eternity
199	4	Thy praise shall never, never fail Throughout eternity
210	3	Spring thou up within my heart, Rise to all eternity
225	5	Jesus, be thou our glory now, And through eternity
233	4	But live with thee the perfect life Of thine eternity
246	4	And to eternity, Love and adore
276	1	And pray that this may be our home Until we touch eternity
331	3	My ransomed soul ... Through all eternity Offered to thee
341	3	The silence of eternity, Interpreted by love
446	3	man hath defied thee, Yet to eternity standeth thy word
469	1	Safe in thine own eternity Our dead are living unto thee

eternity's

| 94 | 4 | For, oh, eternity's too short To utter all thy praise |

ethereal

| 72 | 1 | blue ethereal sky And spangled heavens, a shining frame |

eve

| 50 | 3 | Abide with me from morn till eve |
| 217 | 3 | Your love in our hearts, Lord, at the eve of the day |

even

55	T,1	At Even, Ere the Sun Was Set
166	T,1	Jesus, in Thy Dying Woes, Even while thy life-blood flows
230	4	But warm, sweet, tender, even yet A present help is he
270	1	the Church doth stand Even when steeples are falling
451	3	Now, even now, once more from earth to sky Peals forth
461	4	Even so, Lord, quickly come To thy final harvest home

evening

1	4	A thousand ages in thy sight Are like an evening gone
20	2	By morning glow or evening shade His ... eye ne'er sleepeth
45	1	Wait and worship while the night sets her evening lamps
45	1	night Sets her evening lamps alight Through all the sky

49	2	Now, ere day fadeth quite, We see the evening light
51	1	Shadows of the evening Steal across the sky
55	6	Hear, in this solemn evening hour
64	2	Ye lights of evening, find a voice
72	2	Soon as the evening shades prevail The moon takes up .. tale
328	3	And he shall be to thee a rest When evening hours arrive
443	2	They have builded him an altar in the evening dews and damps
460	2	He paints the wayside flower, He lights the evening star
508	1	And evening steals o'er earth and sky
510	1	Shadows of the evening Steal across the sky

evening's

46	T,1	Again, as Evening's Shadow Falls
67	3	We feel thy calm at evening's hour
509	T,1	Again, as Evening's Shadow Falls

eventide

54	T,1	Now Cheer Our Hearts This Eventide, Lord Jesus Christ
55	2	Once more 'tis eventide, and we ... draw near
405	4	Thus, in thy service, Lord, Till eventide Closes the day
405	4	Till eventide Closes the day of life, May we abide

ever

8	3	Thou art giving and forgiving, Ever blessing, ever blest
8	4	Ever singing march we onward, Victors in the midst of strife
21	3	Thy name be ever praised, O Lord, make us free
23	3	praise him still Through good and ill, Who ever lives
29	2	With ever joyful hearts And blessed peace to cheer us
63	2	Ever faithful To the truth may we be found
63	3	may we ever Reign with thee in endless day
68	3	While all that borrows life from thee Is ever in thy care
69	1	Praise him, all ye hosts above, Ever bright and fair in love
70	R	For his mercies aye endure, Ever faithful, ever sure
73	3	Rolling river, praise him ever
73	4	Praise him ever, bounteous giver
91	4	His faithfulness shall ever be a shield & buckler unto thee
93	3	songs of praises, I will ever give to thee
99	T,1	O Love of God, How Strong and True, Eternal and yet ever new
100	4	To ... children's children ever ... his righteousness extend
100	6	Bless the Father, all his creatures, Ever under his control
108	3	No vision ever brought ... such great glory
108	3	No ear hath ever caught Such great glory
119	2	So may we with willing feet Ever seek thy mercy seat
129	2	And ever o'er its Babel sounds The blessed angels sing
135	2	O may we ever faithful be
145	2	Thy member, ever joined to thee In love that cannot falter
148	4	Keep, O keep us, Savior dear, Ever constant by thy side
150	5	The Trinity whom we adore For ever and for evermore
163	4	I do adore thee, and will ever pray thee
167	VI-3	Brighten all our heavenward way With an ever holier ray
173	4	O Intercessor, who art ever living To plead for ... souls
187	3	Now above the sky he's King ... Where the angels ever sing
215	2	I was not ever thus
217	1	Whose trust, ever child-like, no cares could destroy
219	2	Yet hoping ever for the perfect day
223	3	Glory to God and praise and love Be ever, ever given

229	1	That mortals ever knew, That angels ever bore
238	4	Fulness of joy for ever there
238	4	To be with him for ever blest
239	2	And let thy glorious light Shine ever on my sight
245	3	Ever by a mighty hope, Pressing on and bearing up
253	3	Light of knowledge, ever burning, Shed on us
255	3	The fear of God is undefiled And ever shall endure
263	4	Laud and honor to the Spirit, Ever Three and ever One
267	2	Who can faint, while such a river Ever flows
267	2	Ever flows their thirst to assuage
274	2	Happy, who in thy house reside, Where thee they ever praise
275	1	Rule in our hearts, that we may ever be Guided
275	2	As one with thee, to whom we ever tend, As one with him
281	1	Ever may our souls be fed With this true and living bread
287	4	thou art here, Nearer than ever, still my shield and sun
290	2	Thy truth unchanged hath ever stood
290	4	O Jesus, ever with us stay
309	2	The Prince is ever in them, The daylight is serene
309	4	Who art, with God the Father And Spirit, ever blest
310	1	God shall be all, and in all ever blest
310	4	Through whom, the Spirit, with these ever One
312	6	see Thine endless joy, and of the same Partaker ever be
316	2	In our hearts thou'rt ever near
318	1	Ever, O Christ, through mine Let thy life shine
321	4	Let every thought, and work, and word To thee be ever given
328	1	And he shall for thy spirit be A fountain ever full
331	3	Ever in joy or grief, My Lord, for thee
334	2	And we will ever trust each unknown morrow
340	2	Contented, peaceful fishermen, Before they ever knew ... God
368	1	But for strength that we may ever Live ... courageously
370	2	Nor ever murmur nor repine
374	3	Grant that I may ever Cast my care on thee
377	3	Yet, O Zion, have no fear, Ever is thy helper near
381	3	Thy spirit, Lord, to me impart, O make me what thou ever art
391	2	I ever with thee and thou with me, Lord
394	1	Plans and my thoughts and everything I ever do are dependent
402	2	Such ever bring thee where they come
403	2	But the lonely worker also finds him ever at his side
404	4	Take myself, and I will be Ever, only, all for thee
413	1	For thine own dost ever plead
427	3	Sworn to be Christ's soldiers ever
433	3	Be thy strong arm our ever sure defense
433	4	And glory, laud, and praise be ever thine
441	2	Jesus' bleeding feet I track, Toiling up new Calvaries ever
447	3	None ever called on thee in vain
456	3	In ever changing words of light, The wonder of thy name
463	1-3	For his mercies still endure, Ever faithful, ever sure
496	2	O thus be it ever when free men shall stand
511	1	As it was in the beginning, is now, and ever shall be
512	1	As it was in the beginning, is now, and ever shall be
512	1	As it was in the beginning, is now, and ever shall be
559	14	we worship thy name ever, world without end
562	R	As it was in the beginning, is now, and ever shall be
565	R	As it was in the beginning, is now, and ever shall be
568	R	As it was in the beginning, is now, and ever shall be

| 569 | 1-6 | Praised and exalted above all for ever |
| 579 | 2 | For the promise ever sure that, while heaven & earth endure |

everlasting

1	3	From everlasting thou art God, To endless years the same
16	1	Praise the everlasting King
18	1	That thou the only Lord And everlasting Father art
53	3	discover The fields of everlasting life
78	1	firm remains on high The everlasting throne of him
95	5	Thou in thy everlasting seat Remainest God alone
106	3	Has dawned the everlasting day
113	1	Thy People's Everlasting light
120	2	Christ, the everlasting Lord
125	3	Calls you one & calls you all, To gain his everlasting hall
134	1	Yet in thy dark streets shineth The everlasting Light
195	5	We'll join the everlasting song
200	4	Their name an everlasting name, Their joy the joy of heaven
247	1	Infinite thy vast domain, Everlasting is thy reign
248	2	Beyond our ken thou shinest, The everlasting Light
270	1	above all the soul distressed, Longing for rest everlasting
424	1	Everlasting light shines o'er it
477	1	Founded ... On thee, the everlasting Rock
559	1	All the earth doth worship thee, The Father everlasting
559	7	Thou art the everlasting Son of the Father
559	12	Make them ... numbered with thy saints in glory everlasting
565	4	For the Lord is gracious, his mercy is everlasting

everloving

| 313 | 2 | But as thyself hast loved me, O everloving Lord |

evermore

19	2	Age to age and shore to shore ... praise him evermore
19	4	All that breathe, your Lord adore ... praise him evermore
26	4	Evermore, as of yore, Shall his changeless truth endure
29	3	For thus it was, is now, And shall be evermore
39	3	Father of glory evermore
66	6	For thy Church that evermore Lifteth holy hands above
81	5	Be glory, as it was, is now, And shall be evermore
84	5	And in God's house for evermore My dwelling place shall be
111	1	And that future years shall see, Evermore and evermore
111	2	Every voice in concert ring, Evermore and evermore
111	3	Honor, glory, and dominion, And eternal victory, Evermore
119	1	So most gracious Lord, may we Evermore be led to thee
125	2	He hath oped the heavenly door, And man is blessed evermore
150	5	The Trinity whom we adore For ever and for evermore
153	3	Yea, evermore, in life and death, Jesus, with us abide
159	3	Then let all praise be given thee Who livest evermore
183	1	Hark, the angels shout for joy, Singing evermore on high
185	4	That thy peace which evermore Passeth human knowing
204	1	Rejoice, give thanks, and sing, And triumph evermore
207	5	That in thy strength we evermore endure
246	4	To the great One in Three Eternal praises be Hence evermore
251	2	thee Which wert and art and evermore shalt be
258	6	Lord, may love and fear thee, Evermore be near thee
260	3	She waits the consummation Of peace for evermore
263	3	And hereafter in thy glory Evermore with thee to reign

every

207	3	And give us strength in every trying hour
209	3	I need thy presence every passing hour
222	2	Though the earth be shaking, Every heart be quaking
225	3	O hope of every contrite heart, O joy of all the meek
228	1	Visit us with thy salvation, Enter every trembling heart
228	2	O breathe thy loving Spirit Into every troubled breast
235	2	Thou in the faith dost men unite of every land ... tongue
236	2	Thine is every time & place, Fountain sweet of heart & mind
238	1	O'er every thought and step preside
238	2	Plant holy fear in every heart
242	2	Kindle every high desire, Perish self in thy pure fire
246	3	Thou who almighty art, Now rule in every heart
248	3	I walk secure and blessed In every clime or coast
257	1	In every star thy wisdom shines
257	2	It touched and glanced on every land
260	2	Elect from every nation, Yet one o'er all the earth
260	2	And to one hope she presses, With every grace endued
261	1	The true thy chartered free-men are, Of every age and clime
265	1	Break every bar that holds Thy flock in diverse folds
266	T,1	One Holy Church of God Appears Through every age and race
270	1	Crumbled have spires in every land
271	1	We seek thee as thy saints have sought in every generation
292	3	Deliver us from every touch of ill
294	2	O God of love, whose spirit wakes In every human breast
294	3	Till Christ is formed in all mankind And every land is thine
299	4	The name of Jesus glorify Till every kindred call him Lord
302	2	Proclaim to every people, tongue & nation ... God ...is love
305	3	Flow thou to every nation, Nor in thy richness stay
308	T,1	For the Brave of Every Race
308	4	Lord and light of every age, By thy same sure counsel led
312	5	With blessed saints, whose harmony In every street doth ring
318	1	Breathe into every wish Thy will divine
321	2	Let every sin be crucified, Let Christ be all in all
321	4	Let every thought, and work, and word To thee be ever given
335	2	Jesus knows our every weakness
340	2	Before they every knew The peace of God
342	T,1	I Need Thee Every Hour, Most gracious Lord
342	R	I need thee, oh, I need thee, Every hour I need thee
342	2	I need thee every hour, Stay thou near by
342	3	I need thee every hour In joy or pain
342	4	I need thee every hour, Teach me thy will
344	1	Yet possessing every blessing, If our God our Father be
344	3	Love with every passion blending
346	3	Of every hearth to make a home, Of every home a heaven
348	3	Nor let me every stray From thee aside
352	3	Lift every gift that thou thyself hast given
361	1	God will fulfil in every part Each promise he has made
362	T,1	Awake, My Soul, Stretch Every nerve
377	1	Thou art daily in his keeping, And thine every care is his
377	3	Though the moving signs of heaven Wars presage in every land
378	1	Star of our night, and hope of every nation
384	3	Take every virtue, every grace, And fortify the whole
385	1	Till every foe is vanquished, And Christ is Lord indeed
396	T,1	Fill Thou My Life, O Lord my God, In every part with praise
396	3	Fill every part of me with praise
396	4	But all my life, in every step, Be fellowship with thee

402	1	And every place is hallowed ground
406	4	And every moment watch and pray
409	3	Every task, however simple, Sets the soul that does it free
409	3	Every deed of love and kindness Done to man is done to thee
427	3	Strike, let every nerve and sinew Tell on ages, tell for God
434	1	But to live out the laws of Christ In every thought
434	1	In every thought and word and deed
437	1	From every mountain side Let freedom ring
440	2	America, America, God mend thine every flaw
440	3	Till all success be nobleness, And every gain divine
441	T,1	Once to Every Man and Nation Comes the moment to decide
445	1	Through the thick darkness covering every nation
450	3	In every heart and brain shall throb the pulse of one
456	2	Life mounts in every throbbing vein
464	1	Bounteous source of every joy
466	2	Our children bless, in every place
466	3	In all our hearts such love increase, That every home
466	3	That every home ... May be the dwelling place of peace
466	3	every home, by this release, May be the dwelling place
470	2	and every evil break
471	5	Serving the world, until through every trial
478	3	The ripe fruits in the garden, He made them every one
479	2	In all we do in work or play To grow more loving every day
480	3	He is my Father, who will keep His child through every day
484	3	Till all the distant people In every foreign place
491	2	Fill thou our hearts with zeal in every brave endeavor
495	2	Every round goes higher, higher
576	2	I feel thy power on every side

everything

335	1	What a privilege to carry Everything to God in prayer
335	1	All because we do not carry Everything to God in prayer
394	1	Plans and my thoughts and everything I ever do are dependent

everywhere

68	3	And everywhere that man can be, Thou, God, art present there
75	3	See how he hath everywhere Made this earth so rich and fair
123	1	Till the air Everywhere Now with joy is ringing
277	3	Grant to us a deep compassion For thy children everywhere
414	2	true hearts everywhere Their high communion find
485	2	He speaks to me everywhere
488	T,R	Go, Tell It on the Mountain, Over the hills and everywhere

evil

51	4	Those who plan some evil, From their sin restrain
59	2	Let evil thoughts and spirits flee before us
78	2	afraid his power shall fail When comes thy evil day
78	4	And courage in the evil hour His heavenly aids impart
83	1	And bear thee through the evil days
91	6	Because thy trust is God alone ... no evil shall ... come
167	IV-1	Jesus, whelmed in fears unknown With our evil left alone
174	2	Wrestling with the evil powers
192	2	Our hearts be pure from evil, That we may see aright
266	4	Redeem the evil time
289	2	Save it from evil, guard it still
301	3	May her scattered children be From reproach of evil free

333	3	Give us thy good, and save us from our evil, Infinite Spirit
366	2	hosts of evil round us Scorn thy Christ assail his ways
378	3	Peace, in our hearts, our evil thoughts assuaging
392	6	Forgiveness free of evil done
441	1	For the good or evil side
441	3	Though the cause of evil prosper ... truth alone is strong
442	3	Deliver us from evil
452	3	Is soon to evil ends betrayed
470	2	and every evil break
486	2	Simple wants provide, Evil let he shun
490	3	And let us not for one short hour An evil thought endure
577	1	delivered us ... In many an evil hour

evils

324	3	No foes, no evils need I fear
363	3	And though this world, with devils filled
366	5	Save us from weak resignation to the evils we deplore

exalt

17	2	Sing, all ye nations, exalt the glory Of him whose arm
17	2	exalt the glory Of him whose arm doth valiantly
49	3	Thee ... The world doth glorify And shall exalt forever
81	2	Oh magnify the Lord with me, With me exalt his name

exalted

113	4	At thy great name exalted now All knees must bend
155	2	To thee, now high exalted, Our melody we raise
182	4	Following our exalted Head
183	3	He who slumbered in the grave Is exalted now to save
424	2	Whether humble or exalted, All are called to task divine
454	4	In scenes exalted or depressed, Thou art our joy & ... rest
569	1-6	Praised and exalted above all for ever
570	7	and hath exalted the humble and meek

example

410	2	Follow with reverent steps the great example Of him
410	2	example Of him whose holy work was doing good

excellent

82	3	My God, how excellent thy grace
372	1	foundation ... Is laid for your faith in his excellent word

excelling

228	T,1	Love Divine, All Loves Excelling
270	2	All earthly temples excelling

excelsis

116	R	Gloria in excelsis Deo
133	2	Gloria in Excelsis Deo
136	R	Ideo ... Ideo gloria in excelsis Deo

exile

110	1	mourns in lonely exile here Until the Son of God appear

exiled

438	1	Our exiled fathers crossed the sea

exiles
| 311 | 3 | Appear, Desire of nations, Thine exiles long for home |
| 438 | 3 | Came with those exiles o'er the waves |

expand
| 259 | 4 | Enlarge, expand all Christian souls To comprehend thy love |

expanses
| 456 | 2 | O'er white expanses sparkling pure The radiant morns unfold |

expect
| 309 | 4 | O sweet and blessed country, that eager hearts expect |

expectation
| 156 | 2 | with longing expectation seem to wait The consecration |
| 387 | 1 | Singing songs of expectation, Marching to the promised land |

expected
| 103 | T,1 | Come, Thou Long-Expected Jesus, Born to set thy people free |

expel
| 347 | 3 | Let grace our selfishness expel, Our earthliness refine |

experience
| 81 | 3 | Oh make but trial of his love, Experience will decide |

express
| 26 | 3 | Let our lives express Our abundant thankfulness |

extend
| 100 | 4 | To their children's children...his righteousnenss extend |

extol
21	3	We all do extol thee, thou leader triumphant
111	2	And extol our God and King
195	2	Extol the stem of Jesse's rod
206	1	The name, all victorious, of Jesus extol

exultation
132	2	Sing, choirs of angels, sing in exultation
189	2	O, sing in exultation To Christ, your risen King
436	3	In ire and exultation Aflame with faith and free

exulting
| 345 | 2 | Raise high your free, exulting song |

eye
20	2	By morning glow or evening shade His ... eye ne'er sleepeth
20	2	His watchful eye ne'er sleepeth
24	1	No mortal eye hath seen, No mortal ear hath heard such
66	3	For the joy of ear and eye, For the heart and mind's delight
68	2	Lord, how thy wonders are displayed, Where'er I turn my eye
107	4	Cherubim, with sleepless eye
145	2	Here in sadness Eye and heart long for thy gladness
160	2	Upon that cross of Jesus Mine eye at times can see
175	3	Look down with sad and wondering eye To see

199	2	But downward bends his burning eye At mysteries so bright
251	3	Though the eye of sinful man thy glory may not see
269	2	Dear as the apple of thine eye, And graven on thy hand
336	3	Give, what thine eye delights to see, Truth
362	3	'Tis his own hand presents the prize To thine aspiring eye
359	4	dares to take the side that seems Wrong to man's ... eye
359	4	seems Wrong to man's blindfold eye
388	2	martyr first, whose eagle eye Could pierce beyond the grave
401	2	A man that looks on glass On it may stay his eye
407	1	No eye can to thy throne ascend

eyed

445	3	Envious of heart, blind-eyed, with tongues confounded
491	3	Give us his clear-eyed faith, his fearless heart

eyelids

50	2	My wearied eyelids gently steep
51	2	With thy tenderest blessing May our eyelids close
510	2	With thy tenderest blessing May our eyelids close

eyes

7	1	In light inaccessible hid from our eyes
43	2	Till they inward light impart Glad my eyes and warm my heart
45	3	Lord of angels, on our eyes Let eternal morning rise
50	1	no ... cloud arise To hide thee from thy servant's eyes
58	2	When the constant sun returning Unseals our eyes
85	T,1	I to the Hills Will Lift Mine Eyes
86	4	And give us open eyes To see thee as thou art
108	1	He comes, O Church, lift up thine eyes
188	1	When to their longing eyes restored
209	5	Hold thou thy cross before my closing eyes
257	1	But when our eyes behold thy Word, We read thy name
260	3	Till with the vision glorious, Her longing eyes are blest
286	4	Then open thou our eyes, that we may see
292	1	That only offering perfect in thine eyes
358	4	When mine eyes shall close in death
367	2	Lift up thine eyes, and seek his face
393	1	God be in mine eyes, And in my looking
402	4	And bring all heaven before our eyes
405	3	Some balm of peace for eyes Blinded with tears
406	3	Thee ... Whose eyes my inmost substance see
412	1	Who with the eyes of early youth Eternal things did see
420	1	And where the tears are wiped from eyes That shall not weep
421	4	But in the eyes of men, redeemed and free
443	T,1	Mine Eyes Have Seen the Glory of the coming of the Lord
450	1	And light of knowledge in their eyes
468	T,1	God of the Living, in Whose eyes
468	1	in whose eyes Unveiled thy whole creation lies
493	2	And in his eyes a light ... God's daybreak to proclaim
543	1	God be in mine eyes and in my looking
572	2	For mine eyes have seen thy salvation

face

16	4	Angels, help us to adore him, Ye behold him face to face
23	2	And now, from sin released, Behold the Savior's face
45	2	Gather us who seek thy face To the fold of thy embrace

49	T,1	O Gladsome Light, O grace of God the Father's face
87	3	Behind a frowning providence He hides a smiling face
138	3	Radiant beams from thy holy face
144	3	Impels us on to seek thy face
160	3	I ask no other sunshine than The sunshine of his face
161	3	Yet humbly, in our striving, O God, we face its test
174	1	Darkness veils thine anguished face
201	4	Christ, our King, in beauty comes, And we his face shall see
225	1	But sweeter far thy face to see, And in thy presence rest
231	3	Anoint and cheer our soiled face With ... thy grace
252	4	Till, clouds and darkness ended, They see thee face to face
287	T,1	Here, O My Lord, I See Thee Face to Face
288	R	When I fall on my knees with my face to the rising sun
292	2	Look, Father, look on his anointed face
294	3	Whose life and death reveal thy face
312	2	They see God face to face
321	3	That I may see thy glorious face, And worship at thy throne
329	2	And thorns thy brow encircle, And tears thy face have marred
330	4	I cannot look upon his face For shame, for bitter shame
331	3	and when thy face I see, My ransomed soul shall be
357	1	Whom we, that have not seen thy face, By faith ... embrace
367	2	Lift up thine eyes, and seek his face
375	3	For gladness breaks like morning Where'er thy face appears
390	2	O when shall I behold thy face, Thou majesty divine
421	2	And marveled at the radiance of thy face
423	4	The sweet compassion of thy face
459	2	His steady counsels change the face Of the declining year
466	2	That they may all behold thy face
470	5	And stand at last with joy before thy face
480	2	The same white moon, with silver face ... He used to see
493	1	He bore no shield before his face, No weapon in his hand
499	1	And silent bow before his face
524	1	make thy way plain before my face
557	T,1	Here, O My Lord, I See Thee face to face
568	9	shalt go before the face of the Lord to prepare his ways
572	3	Which thou hast prepared before the face of all people
575	3	Anoint and cheer our soiled face with the abundance
580	T,1	O Lord, Turn Not Thy Face From Them, Who lie in woeful state

faces

107	4	Veil their faces to the presence
197	2	All the angel faces, All the hosts of light
206	3	Fall down on their faces and worship the Lamb
215	3	And with the morn those angels faces smile
215	3	faces smile Which I have loved long since, and lost awhile
452	2	Our faces from each other hide

facing

366	1	Grant us wisdom ... courage, For the facing of his hour

faction

439	4	From the strife of class and faction Make our nation free

factum

133	3	Patris aeterni Verbum caro factum

fades

162	2	There I walk amid the shades While the ... twilight fades
162	2	While the lingering twilight fades

fadeth

49	2	Now, ere day fadeth quite, We see the evening light

fail

6	5	In thee do we trust, nor find thee to fail
13	2	Never shall his promise fail
78	2	afraid his power shall fail When comes thy evil day
97	1	We own thy mercies, Lord, which never fail
199	4	Thy praise shall never, never fail Throughout eternity
204	3	His kingdom cannot fail, He rules o'er earth and heaven
208	1	All that I would, but fail, to be
209	1	When other helpers fail, and comforts flee
222	2	Jesus will not fail us
245	3	Mighty so as to prevail Where unaided man must fail
291	2	pray we Lest we fail to know thee now
354	2	Thy strength shall never fail us
366	4	Grant us wisdom ... courage, That we fail not man nor thee
374	3	Grant that I may never Fail thy hand to see
382	3	We have Christ's own promise, And that cannot fail
385	3	The arm of flesh will fail you, Ye dare not trust your own
386	4	Lighten our darkness when we fail at last
367	2	When fond hopes fail and skies are dark before us
491	2	never Falter or fail however long the strife
467	2	When fond hopes fail and skies are dark before us

failed

44	2	And though their Lord they failed to know

faileth

79	1	Whose goodness faileth never
79	6	so through all the length of days thy goodness faileth never
378	2	Lord, thou canst help when earthly armor faileth
577	1	That love that never faileth

failing

101	1	no place ... earth's failing Have such kindly judgment given
284	4	when these failing lips grow dumb, And mind and memory flee
363	T,1	A Mighty Fortress Is Our God, A bulwark never failing

fails

173	3	When courage fails us, and when faith is dim
267	2	Grace, which like the Lord, the Giver, Never fails
267	2	Never fails from age to age

failure

368	4	Through endeavor, failure, danger, Father, be ...at our side

failures

74	3	Soaring spire and ruined city ... our hopes & failures show
92	2	Shamed by its failures or its fears, I sink beside the road

fain

55	4	they who fain would serve thee best Are conscious most
86	2	Though we who fain would find thee
160	T,1	Beneath the Cross of Jesus I fain would take my stand
334	1	Fain would our souls feel all thy kindling love

faint

148	3	Thou, his vanquisher before, Grant we may not faint nor fail
267	2	Who can faint, while such a river Ever flows
295	1	The poor, and them that mourn, The faint and overborne
344	2	Lone and dreary, faint and weary, Through the desert
367	4	Faint not nor fear, his arms are near
373	3	His truth be thine affiance, When faint and desolate
402	4	To teach our faint desires to rise
435	3	Feed the faint and hungry peoples with the richness

fainted

222	1	Long my heart hath panted, Till it well-nigh fainted

fainting

78	4	He ... Supports the fainting heart
170	3	O make me thine forever, And should I fainting be
261	3	watchfires ... With never fainting ray
315	3	Come unto me, ye fainting, And I will give you life
348	2	May thy rich grace impart Strength to my fainting heart

faintly

224	4	We faintly hear, we dimly see, In differing phrase we pray

fair

39	4	To make ill-fortune turn to fair
53	3	when life's day is over Shall death's fair night discover
69	1	Praise him, all ye hosts above, Ever bright and fair in love
75	3	See how he hath everywhere Made this earth so rich and fair
97	2	And faith's fair vision changes into sight
145	T,1	O Morning Star, How Fair and Bright
145	1	Thou art holy, Fair and glorious, all victorious
188	1	The sun shone out with fair array
201	4	brighter than that glorious morn Shall this fair morning be
227	2	Fair are the meadows, Fairer still the woodlands
227	3	Fair is the sunshine, Fairer still the moonlight
274	T,1	How Lovely Are Thy Dwellings Fair, O Lord of hosts
275	3	One in our love of all things sweet and fair
364	3	Christian, dost thou hear them, How they speak thee fair
412	2	Who shapest man to God's own law, Thyself the fair design
420	4	Already in the mind of God That city riseth fair
451	2	Earth might be fair and all men glad and wise
451	3	Earth shall be fair, and all her people one
451	3	Earth shall be fair, and all her folk be one
479	1	And all that makes the day so fair
485	2	He shines in all that's fair
576	3	In heaven. It is thy dwelling fair

fairer

37	1	Fairer than morning, lovelier than daylight
37	4	O in that hour, fairer than daylight dawning

227	2	Fair are the meadows, Fairer still the woodlands
227	2	Jesus is fairer, Jesus is purer
227	3	Fair is the sunshine, Fairer still the moonlight
257	1	We read thy name in fairer lines
399	2	That in thy sunshine's blaze its day May brighter, fairer be
421	2	But often in some far off Galilee Beheld thee fairer
421	2	Beheld thee fairer yet while serving thee

fairest

| 227 | T,1 | Fairest Lord Jesus, Ruler of all nature |

faith

2	4	Do thou in faith sustain us
24	1	Where we partake through faith victorious with angels
52	3	Hope and faith and love rise glorious
97	2	Lead us by faith to hope's true promised land
161	2	The faith we keep in goodness
162	1	When for deeper faith I seek
162	3	When for stronger faith I seek
162	4	See his anguish ... faith, Love triumphant still in death
167	IV-3	Tell our faith that God is near, Hear us, holy Jesus
173	3	When courage fails us, and when faith is dim
191	4	And yet whose faith hath constant been
207	3	Sustain us by thy faith and by thy power
207	5	Our faith is built upon thy promise free
217	2	Lord of all eagerness, Lord of all faith
228	2	Alpha and Omega be, End of faith as its beginning
230	4	And faith has still its Olivet, And love its Galilee
235	2	Thou in the faith dost men unite of every land ... tongue
244	2	In thy pure love & holy faith From thee true wisdom learning
260	2	Her charter of salvation, One Lord, one faith, one birth
262	4	One hope, one faith, one love restore The seamless robe
268	1	Keeping faith with us and thee
286	2	Faith still receives the cup as from thy hand
289	1	Knowledge and faith and life immortal Jesus ... imparts
290	3	Blest when our faith can hold thee fast
292	2	Our prayer so languid, and our faith so dim
297	4	Fill thou our hearts with faith like theirs
297	4	faith like theirs Who served the days they could not see
301	1	While on earth her faith is tried
301	4	Winning all to faith in thee
303	4	A field for toil and faith and hope
306	1	Who thee by faith before the world confessed
346	1	Our song of faith to sing
346	4	O Lord of hosts, our faith renew
348	T,1	My Faith Looks Up to Thee, Thou Lamb of Calvary
357	1	Whom we, that have not seen thy face, By faith ... embrace
357	1	By faith, and faith alone, embrace
357	5	We have but faith, we cannot know
360	2	No offering of my own I have, Nor works my faith to prove
361	T,1	Have Faith in God, my heart, Trust and be unafraid
361	2	Have faith in God, my mind, Though oft thy light burns low
361	3	Have faith in God, my soul, His cross forever stands
365	T,1	Faith of Our Fathers
365	R	Faith of our fathers, holy faith, We will be true to thee
365	3	Faith of our fathers, God's great power shall win

365	4	Faith of our fathers, we will love Both friend and foe
366	2	Free our hearts to faith and praise
372	1	foundation ... Is laid for your faith in his excellent word
376	2	And age comes on uncheered by faith and hope
380	2	The sons of fathers we By whom our faith is taught
381	T,1	My Faith, It Is an Oaken Staff
381	1	faith ... The traveler's well-loved aid
381	1	My faith, it is a weapon stout, The soldier's trusty blade
381	3	My faith, it is an oaken staff, O let me on it lean
381	3	My faith, it is a trusty sword, May falsehood find it keen
383	2	For it we must labor, Till our faith is sight
387	2	One the faith which never tires
392	+2	Land of our birth, our faith, our pride
402	4	Here may we prove the power of prayer To strengthen faith
402	4	To strengthen faith and sweeten care
412	1	We thank thee for thy boyhood faith
412	1	boyhood faith That shone thy whole life through
414	3	Join hands, then, brothers of the faith
416	4	Freest faith assailed in vain
418	3	In work that keeps faith sweet and strong
419	3	The faith that makes men brave
432	4	For faith, and will to win what faith shall see
436	3	In ire and exultation Aflame with faith and free
438	3	Laws, freedom, truth, and faith in God Came with those
439	4	Keep her faith in simple manhood
444	2	The quiet of a steadfast faith, Calm of a call obeyed
465	2	assurance Of tender charity and steadfast faith
467	3	Low in the heart faith singeth still her song
471	3	Give him the faith that welcomes all the light
491	3	Give us his clear-eyed faith, his fearless heart
521	2	Make strong our faith, increase our light
527	1	Enrich ... With faith, with hope, with charity
538	1	Ours is the faith, the will, the thought

faith's

97	2	And faith's fair vision changes into sight
291	2	Here for faith's discernment pray we
380	4	Faith's warfare ended, won The home of endless peace

faithful

63	2	Ever faithful To the truth may we be found
70	R	For his mercies aye endure, Ever faithful, ever sure
77	1	In every change he faithful will remain
107	2	He will give to all the faithful His own self
112	3	Ours to bear the faithful witness
132	T,1	O Come, All Ye Faithful, joyful and triumphant
135	2	O may we ever faithful be
156	1	Draw nigh ... Thy faithful people cry with one accord
185	T,1	Come, Ye Faithful, Raise the Strain Of triumphant gladness
186	T,1	Come, Ye Faithful, Raise the Strain (same words as no. 185)
191	2	That Easter morn at break of day, The faithful women went
228	1	All thy faithful mercies crown
244	2	That we be faithful unto death
306	3	O may thy soldiers, faithful, true and bold Fight
308	2	Faithful stewards of the word
308	3	True and faithful to command, Swift and fearless to obey

410	3	Then shall all shackles fall, the stormy clangor Of ... war
508	2	With one last prayer thy children fall
562	6	O come, let us worship and fall down

fallen

128	1	Snow had fallen, snow on snow
425	3	They are slaves who fear to speak For the fallen & the weak
455	T,1	'Tis Winter Now, the Fallen Snow
468	3	Not left to lie like fallen tree, Not dead, but living

falling

53	1	Let us, as night is falling ... Give thanks to him
219	2	Stumbling and falling in disastrous night
251	2	Cherubim and seraphim falling down before thee
270	1	the Church doth stand Even when steeples are falling
426	2	I see my people falling In darkness and despair
471	2	We praise thee, Lord, that now the light is falling Here

falls

46	T,1	Again, as Evening's Shadow Falls
47	1	The darkness falls at thy behest
161	2	On all, the judgment of the cross Falls steady, clear & sure
209	T,1	Abide With Me, fast falls the even-tide
395	3	On homeliest work thy blessing falls
458	5	Snow that falls on nature's breast
509	T,1	Again, as Evening's Shadow Falls

false

20	4	Cast each false idol from his throne
398	1	Who by our own false hopes and aims are spent
453	2	Ring out the false, ring in the true
453	4	Ring out false pride in place and blood

falsehood

86	2	Till truth from falsehood part, Our souls can find no rest
381	3	My faith, it is a trusty sword, May falsehood find it keen
441	1	decide In the strife of truth with falsehood, For the good
446	3	Falsehood and wrong shall not tarry beside thee

falter

145	2	Thy member, ever joined to thee In love that cannot falter
359	5	To doubt would be disloyalty, To falter would be sin
436	1	Our earthly rulers falter, Our people drift and die
491	2	Give us the valiant spirit that shall never Falter
491	2	never Falter or fail however long the strife
494	3	may our hands Ne'er falter when the dream is in our hearts

faltering

| 92 | 3 | To nerve my faltering will |
| 416 | 2 | Arm their faltering wills to fight |

fame

| 127 | 3 | The first apostles of his infant fame |
| 203 | 3 | Spread abroad the victor's fame |

family

167	III-3	May we all thy loved ones be, All one holy family
277	3	May we see our human family Free from sorrow and despair
466	1	Who dost in love proclaim Each family thine own

famished

423	3	From famished souls, from sorrows' stress

famous

401	5	This is the famous stone That turneth all to gold
476	T,1	Now Praise We Great and Famous Men

fancies

371	3	Then fancies, flee away, I'll fear not what men say

fanfare

42	3	Hear we no beat of drums, Fanfare nor cry

fantasy

150	1	How passing thought and fantasy

far

67	4	But higher far, and far more clear Thee in man's spirit
92	1	The thought of thee is mightier far than sin and pain
92	1	mightier far than sin and pain and sorrow are
99	2	O love of God, how deep and great, Far deeper than ... hate
99	2	love of God ... Far deeper than man's deepest hate
100	3	Far as east from west is distant He hath put away our sin
104	2	Hark, the voice of one that crieth in the desert far & near
106	3	On your far hills, long cold and gray, Has dawned
110	3	And order all things, far and nigh
123	1	As I hear, Far and near, Sweetest angel voices
123	3	Hail the star That from far Bright with hope is burning
126	4	Richer by far is the heart's adoration
141	2	Shining in the east, beyond them far
141	3	Three wise men came from country far
167	IV-2	When we vainly seem to pray, And our hope seems far away
171	T,1	There Is a Green Hill Far Away, Without a city wall
172	T,1	There Is a Green Hill Far Away (same words as No. 171)
177	4	That were a present far too small
215	1	The night is dark and I am far from home, Lead thou me on
225	1	But sweeter far thy face to see, And in thy presence rest
231	3	Keep far our foes, give peace at home
239	3	Shall far outpass the power of human telling
261	T,1	City of God, How Broad and Far Outspread thy walls sublime
296	2	distant lands Shall see from far the glorious sight
299	4	Baptize the nations, far and nigh
332	3	Hearts that far from thee were straying
337	2	Far, far above thy thought His counsel shall appear
383	3	Bound by God's far purpose In one living whole
387	2	Chasing far the gloom and terror
387	3	One the gladness of rejoicing On the far eternal shore
418	4	In hope that sends a shining ray Far down
418	4	Far down the future's broadening way
421	2	But often in some far off Galilee Beheld thee fairer
427	2	Will ye play then, will ye dally Far behind the battle line

439	1	Stretching far o'er land and sea
460	2	He only is the maker Of all things near and far
575	3	Keep far our foes, give peace at home
576	4	And far away my dwelling make

farewell

| 42 | 4 | Bid then farewell to sleep Rise up and run |

farm

| 484 | 1 | Or farm the mountain pastures, Or till the endless plains |

farthest

| 266 | 2 | From oldest time, on farthest shores |

fashions

| 432 | 3 | from the breeds of earth thy silent sway Fashions the nation |
| 432 | 3 | Fashions the nation of the broadening day |

fast

6	3	Hath stablished it fast by a changeless decree
26	2	Standing fast to the last, By his hand our lives are stayed
78	5	Mere human power shall fast decay, And youthful vigor cease
124	2	Hush, hush, see how fast he slumbers
124	2	Hush, hush, see how fast he sleeps
150	2	for us he bore His holy fast, and hungered sore
153	T,1	For us didst fast and pray
209	T,1	Abide With Me, fast falls the even-tide
290	3	Blest when our faith can hold thee fast
329	2	O sin that hath no equal, So fast to bar the gate
364	2	Gird thee for the battle, Watch and pray and fast

fasting

| 148 | T,1 | Forty Days and Forty Nights Thou wast fasting in the wild |
| 148 | 2 | Fasting with unceasing prayer, Glad with thee to suffer pain |

fatal

| 91 | 3 | When fearful plagues around prevail, No fatal stroke shall |
| 91 | 3 | No fatal stroke shall thee assail |

fate

| 365 | 2 | And blest would be their children's fate If they ... die for |

fateful

| 443 | 1 | He hath loosed the fateful lightning of his ... swift sword |

Father

2	2	O Father, that thy rule is just And wise, and changes never
2	3	O Jesus Christ, our God and Lord, Begotten of the Father
7	4	Great Father of glory, pure Father of light
8	3	Thou our Father, Christ our Brother
8	4	Father love is reigning o'er us
17	2	servants of the Triune God, Father and Son and Spirit laud
18	1	That thou the only Lord And everlasting Father art
18	5	That thou eternal Father art, Of boundless majesty
29	3	All praise and thanks to God The Father now be given
30	4	To God the Father, God the Son ... the Spirit Three in One

197	1	'Tis the Father's pleasure We should call him Lord
197	4	To the throne of God-head, To the Father's breast
271	T,1	We Come Unto Our Father's God, Their Rock is our salvation
272	2	Before our Father's throne We pour our ardent prayers
303	2	As sons who know the Father's will
347	2	Like thee, to do our Father's will
389	4	And at our Father's loved abode Our souls arrive in peace
410	2	So shall the wide earth seem our Father's temple
412	1	Did ye not know it is my work My Father's work to do
412	2	And see like thee our noblest work Our Father's work to do
412	3	That it may be our highest joy Our Father's work to do
437	4	Our father's God, to thee Author of Liberty, To thee we sing
485	T,1-3	This Is My Father's World
490	1	Through all our days, in all our ways, Our ... Father's will
490	1	Our heavenly Father's will
490	4	And for the life ineffable Within the Father's home
539	1	And the Father's boundless love

fatherhood

466	T,1	O Father, by whose name All fatherhood is known

fathers

16	2	Praise him for this grace and favor To our fathers
16	2	favor To our fathers in distress
22	2	We worship thee, God of our fathers, we bless thee
259	2	Darkling our great forefathers went The first steps
297	1	The shrines our fathers founded stand
345	3	Send forth the hymns our fathers loved
365	T,1	Faith of Our Fathers
365	R	Faith of our fathers, holy faith, We will be true to thee
365	2	Our fathers, chained in prisons dark, Were still ... free
365	3	Faith of our fathers, God's great power shall win
365	4	Faith of our fathers, we will love Both friend and foe
380	2	The sons of fathers we By whom our faith is taught
389	1	Who through this earthly pilgrimage Hast all our fathers led
389	2	God of our fathers, be the God Of their succeeding race
392	+2	Land of our birth ... For whose dear sake our fathers died
425	T,1	Men, Whose Boast It Is that ye Come of fathers brave & free
431	T,1	God of Our Fathers, Known of Old
433	T,1	God of Our Fathers, Whose Almighty Hand
437	1	Land where my fathers died, Land of the pilgrim's pride
438	1	Our exiled fathers crossed the sea
447	2	The wonders that our fathers told
476	1	The fathers named in story
568	5	To perform the mercy promised to our forefathers
569	T,1	Blessed Art Thou, O Lord, God of our fathers
570	9	as he promised to our forefathers, Abraham and his seed

fault

442	3	Though by our fault confounded

faultless

508	1	In perfect love and faultless tone

favor

16	2	Praise him for this grace and favor To our fathers

16	2	favor To our fathers in distress
126	4	Vainly with gifts would his favor secure
170	2	Look on me with thy favor, Vouch-safe to me thy grace
249	5	Thy love and favor, kept to us always
316	2	Thou hast blest us with thy favor
327	3	Early let us seek thy favor, Early let us do thy will
374	1	Nor for fear or favor Suffer me to fall
392	4	uncowed By fear or favor of the crowd
507	1	Creator of the world, we pray That, with thy wonted favor
539	1	With the Holy Spirit's favor Rest upon us from above

fear

25	2	Who would not fear his holy name, And laud and magnify
31	3	Fear not to enter his courts in the slenderness of the poor
35	2	The powers of darkness fear, When this sweet chant they hear
63	3	Fear of death shall not appall us
77	3	When disappointment, grief, and fear are gone
79	4	In death's dark vale I fear no ill
79	4	I fear no ill With thee, dear Lord, beside me
81	4	Fear him, ye saints, and ... then Have nothing else to fear
84	3	Yet will I fear no ill, For thou art with me
107	1	And with fear and trembling stand
117	4	Watching long in hope and fear
122	3	Fear not, then, said the angel, Let nothing you affright
125	3	Now ye need not fear the grave
140	2	Good Christian, fear
142	3	Herod then with fear was filled
146	2	Fear not, said he, for mighty dread had seized
162	3	Hill of Calvary, I go To thy scenes of fear and woe
174	4	Lord, should fear & anguish roll Darkly o'er my sinful soul
193	2	Lovingly he greets thee, Scatters fear and gloom
209	4	I fear no foe, with thee at hand to bless
212	1	Now to seek and love and fear thee
213	3	May I hear thee say to me, Fear not, I will pilot thee
218	1	I shall not fear the battle If thou art by my side
221	1	And drives away his fear
222	2	God dispels our fear
238	2	Plant holy fear in every heart
255	3	The fear of God is undefiled And ever shall endure
258	6	Lord, may love and fear thee, Evermore be near thee
267	2	And all fear of want remove
276	4	Thy perfect love cast out all fear
293	3	Away with gloomy doubts and faithless fear
324	3	No foes, no evils need I fear
337	2	That caused thy needless fear
343	T,1	In Heavenly Love Abiding, No change my heart shall fear
348	4	Blest Savior, then, in love, Fear and distrust remove
354	1	Who looks in love to Christ above No fear
354	1	No fear his heart oppresses
354	2	While thou art near we will not fear
363	3	We will not fear, for God hath willed His truth to triumph
367	4	Faint not nor fear, his arms are near
371	3	Then fancies, flee away, I'll fear not what men say
372	2	Fear not, I am with thee, oh, be not dismayed
373	T,1	God Is My Strong Salvation, What foe have I to fear
374	1	Nor for fear or favor Suffer me to fall

377	3	Yet, O Zion, have no fear, Ever is thy helper near
380	2	taught To fear no ill, to fight The holy fight they fought
392	4	That we, with thee, may walk uncowed By fear
392	4	uncowed By fear or favor of the crowd
407	2	Thy grace, O Father, give, That I may serve with fear
416	4	Perfect love bereft of fear
425	3	They are slaves who fear to speak For the fallen & the weak
430	1	Fear not, O land, in God rejoice
445	3	In wrath and fear, by jealousies surrounded
449	3	The love that casteth out all fear
452	2	Our souls are bound In iron chains of fear and pride
468	4	That none might fear that world to see Where all are living
469	4	No more by fear and doubt oppressed
477	1	Nor fear the storm, nor dread the shock
568	7	might serve him without fear
570	5	mercy is on them that fear him throughout all generations

feared

488	2	The shepherds feared and trembled When lo, above the earth

fearful

87	2	Ye fearful saints, fresh courage take
91	3	When fearful plagues around prevail, No fatal stroke shall
213	3	When at last I near the shore And the fearful breakers roar
398	1	Speak to our fearful hearts by conflict rent

fearing

442	3	Lo, fearing nought we come to thee

fearless

308	3	True and faithful to command, Swift and fearless to obey
387	1	Stepping fearless through the night
491	3	Give us his clear-eyed faith, his fearless heart

fears

92	2	Shamed by its failures or its fears, I sink beside the road
93	3	Bid my anxious fears subside
97	1	In all the past ... our hopes & fears, Thy hand we see
103	1	From our fears and sins release us
134	1	The hopes and fears of all the years Are met in thee tonight
157	2	Hopes deceive and fears annoy
161	2	The hopes that lead us onward, The fears that hold us back
167	IV-1	Jesus, whelmed in fears unknown With our evil left alone
178	2	The Savior wrestles lone with fears
215	2	and, spite of fears, Pride ruled my will
250	3	Who upholds and comforts us in all trials, fears, and needs
272	2	Our fears, our hopes, our aims are one
319	2	Fightings and fears within, without
337	T,1	Give to the Winds Thy Fears, Hope and be undismayed
338	T,1	Give to the Winds Thy Fears (same words as no. 337 in 4 vs)
352	2	The mire of sin, the weight of guilty fears
366	2	From the fears that long have bound us Free our hearts
375	3	Lead on, O King eternal, We follow, not with fears
405	3	Some word of hope for hearts Burdened with fears
423	2	On shadowed thresholds dark with fears
465	2	With child-like trust that fears nor pain nor death

feast
185	3	With the royal feast of feasts, Comes its joy to render
282	1	And be thy feast to us the token That ... our souls are fed
286	1	Nay, let us be thy guests, the feast is thine
287	3	Here let me feast, and, feasting, still prolong
287	4	The feast, though not the love is past and gone
309	3	The shout of them that triumph, The song of them that feast
558	5	Jesus, thy feast we celebrate

feasting
| 287 | 3 | Here let me feast, and, feasting, still prolong |

feasts
| 185 | 3 | With the royal feast of feasts, Comes its joy to render |

fed
99	2	Self-fed, self-kindled like the light
281	1	Ever may our souls be fed With this true and living bread
282	1	And be thy feast to us the token That ... our souls are fed
282	1	That by thy grace our souls are fed
389	T,1	O God of Bethel, by Whose Hand Thy people still are fed
454	2	By his incessant bounty fed, By his unerring counsel led
460	1	But it is fed and watered By God's almighty hand
460	2	The winds and waves obey him, By him the birds are fed

fee
| 165 | 3 | And sons of earth hold heaven in fee |

feeble
6	5	Frail children of dust, and feeble as frail
16	3	Well our feeble frame he knows
86	2	we ... Have tried ... In feeble words to bind thee
87	3	Judge not the Lord by feeble sense
506	1	See thou render All thy feeble strength can pay

feeblest
| 293 | 3 | By feeblest agents may our God fulfill His righteous will |

feebly
| 306 | 4 | We feebly struggle, they in glory shine |

feed
4	2	We are his folk, he doth us feed
70	5	All things living he doth feed
93	1	Bread of heaven, Feed me till I want no more
256	2	Bread of our souls, whereon we feed
266	4	With Bread of life earth's hunger feed
267	3	Safe they feed upon the manna Which he gives them
281	T,1	Bread of Heaven, on Thee We Feed
287	2	Here would I feed upon the bread of God
327	1	In thy pleasant pastures feed us
344	1	Guard us, guide us, keep us, feed us
435	3	Feed the faint and hungry peoples with the richness
557	2	Here would I feed upon the bread of God

feedeth
79	2	where the verdant pastures grow With food celestial feedeth

feeding
458	3	Feeding, day and night, the grain

feel
55	2	We know and feel that thou art here
67	3	We feel thy calm at evening's hour
92	1	I feel thy strong and tender love, And all is well again
114	3	here, Lord, abide. Let me thy inner presence feel
158	T,1	Go to Dark Gethsemane, Ye that feel the tempter's power
159	2	Make us thy sorrow feel
232	4	Teach me to feel that thou art always nigh
257	4	That see the light or feel the sun
328	2	thou shalt surely feel His wind, that bloweth healthily
334	1	Fain would our souls feel all thy kindling love
334	3	Our spirits yearn to feel thy kindling love
344	2	Thou didst feel its keenest woe
364	2	Christian, dost thou feel them, How they work within
388	3	They bowed their necks the death to feel
399	3	And feel the promise is not vain that morn shall tearless be
416	3	Learning all his will to feel
425	1	If ye do not feel the chain when it works a brother's pain
499	1	Let all within us feel his power
576	2	I feel thy power on every side

feels
422	3	Feels in his arms the vigor of the Lord

feet
16	1	To his feet thy tribute bring
31	2	Low at his feet lay the burden of carefulness
33	3	Lest from thee we stray abroad, Stay our wayward feet,O Lord
38	2	Sprung in completeness Where his feet pass
76	4	I'll drop my burden at his feet, And bear a song away
78	6	They with unwearied feet shall tread the path of life divine
107	4	At his feet the six-winged seraph
108	1	Rise up, with willing feet Go forth, the Bridegroom meet
119	2	So may we with willing feet Ever seek thy mercy seat
154	3	Thy feet the path of suffering trod
156	2	The consecration of thy beauteous feet
158	3	There adoring at his feet
168	4	Thou lay the work he gave thee at his feet
177	3	See, from his head, his hands, his feet, Sorrow and love
195	5	O that, with yonder sacred throng, We at his feet may fall
215	1	Keep thou my feet
229	3	O let my feet ne'er run astray
229	4	behold I sit In willing bonds before thy feet
256	T,1	Lamp of Our Feet, Whereby We Trace Our path
266	3	And feet on mercy's errands swift Do make her pilgrimage
292	3	And so we come, O draw us to thy feet
300	4	Lift high the cross of Christ Tread where his feet have trod
303	1	thanks ... That work awaits our hands and feet
312	4	And all the virgins bear their part, Sitting about her feet
352	1	Here at thy feet none other may we see

fern
139   2   Tont es laut von fern und nah, Christ der Retter ist da

fervent
295   2   With fervent prayer
490   1   Our fervent gift receive, And fit us to fulfill
542   1   With lowly love and fervent will

fervid
259   2   And grow it shall, our glorious sun More fervid rays afford

festal
345   1   Your festal banner wave on high, The cross of Christ

fetter
432   2   past crumbling throne And broken fetter, thou hast brought

fetters
254   2   Then shall all bondage cease, All fetters fall
425   2   Is true freedom but to break Fetters for our own dear sake
426   2   Whom shall I send to shatter The fetters which they bear
459   2   The liquid streams forbear to flow, In icy fetters bound

feud
453   3   Ring out the feud of rich and poor

feuds
198   2   In Christ all races meet, Their ancient feuds forgetting

fevered
413   3   Quench our fevered thirst of pleasure

few
388   3   A glorious band, the chosen few On whom the Spirit came
402   3   Great Shepherd of thy chosen few ... mercies here renew

fideles
133   T,1   Adeste Fideles

field
8   2   Field and forest, vale and mountain ... call us to rejoice
65   2   Creatures of the field and flood
143   1   Field and fountain, moor and mountain, Following yonder star
303   4   A field for toil and faith and hope
359   3   The instinct that can tell That God is on the field
359   3   God is on the field when he Is most invisible
426   2   No field or mart is silent, No city street is dumb
456   1   And laid a silent loveliness On hill and wood and field
457   2   For summer joy in field and wood We lift our song to him
461   2   All the world is God's own field
461   3   From his field shall in that day All offenses purge away
462   2   All the blessings of the field
464   2   For the blessings of the field
487   2   Praise him, field and flower, Praise his mighty power
579   1   For the valley's golden yield ... fruits of tree and field

fields

34	1	The fields are wet with diamond dew, The worlds awake to cry
53	3	discover The fields of everlasting life
117	2	Shepherds in the fields abiding
130	2	While fields and floods, rocks, hills and plains Repeat
141	1	Was to certain poor shepherds in fields as they lay
141	1	In fields where they lay keeping their sheep
375	1	Henceforth in fields of conquest Thy tents shall be our home
457	1	golden wealth of ripening grain And breath of clover fields
459	3	The fields no longer mourn
460	T,1	We Plow the Fields and Scatter The good seed on the land
484	1	Where children wade through rice fields
484	1	wade through rice fields And watch the camel trains

fierce

249	3	And calming passion's fierce and stormy gales
306	5	And when the strife is fierce, the warfare long
315	3	The foe is stern and eager, The fight is fierce and long
375	2	Lead on, O King eternal, Till sin's fierce war shall cease
481	2	And one was slain by a fierce wild beast

fiercest

175	4	Thy last and fiercest strife is nigh

fiery

372	4	When through fiery trials thy pathway shall lie

fight

21	2	So from the beginning the fight we were winning
153	2	O give us strength in thee to fight, In thee to conquer sin
182	3	Fought the fight, the battle won
201	2	Not as of old a little child To bear, and fight, and die
203	1	From the fight returned victorious
298	3	Fight we the fight with sorrow and sin
306	2	Thou, Lord, their captain in the well-fought fight
306	3	O may thy soldiers, faithful, true and bold Fight
306	3	Fight as the saints who nobly fought of old
311	1	'Tis finished, all is finished, their fight with death & sin
315	3	The foe is stern and eager, The fight is fierce and long
366	4	Christ-like graces in the fight to set men free
367	T,1	Fight the Good Fight with all thy might
371	2	No foes shall stay his might, Though he with giants fight
373	2	Though hosts encamp around me, Firm in the fight I stand
380	2	taught To fear no ill, to fight The holy fight they fought
384	2	And take, to arm you for the fight, The panoply of God
384	3	From strength to strength go on, Wrestle and fight and pray
416	2	Arm their faltering wills to fight
427	2	Thou hast but an hour to fight
496	1	broad stripes and bright stars through the perilous fight

fighting

69	2	Warriors fighting for the Lord

fightings

319	2	Fightings and fears within, without

fill

8	1	Giver of immortal gladness, Fill us with the light of day
9	4	shall fill thy courts with sounding praise
32	3	with thyself my spirit fill
43	3	Fill me, Radiancy divine, Scatter all my unbelief
63	1	Fill our hearts with joy and peace
110	4	Fill the whole world with heaven's peace
115	3	fill the world with love divine
145	2	Fill me with joy and strength to be Thy member
233	1	Fill me with life anew, That I may love what thou dost love
242	3	Holy Spirit, Power divine, Fill and nerve this will of mine
247	2	Fill the heavens with sweet accord, Holy, holy, holy Lord
255	2	With joy they fill the heart
264	4	A mountain that shall fill the earth
297	4	Fill thou our hearts with faith like theirs
311	3	Fill up the roll of thine elect...take thy power and reign
316	2	Fill our hearts with prayer and praise
327	3	Blessed Lord and only Savior, with thy love our bosoms fill
344	3	Fill our heartrs with heavely joy
396	T,1	Fill Thou My Life, O Lord my God, In every part with praise
396	3	Fill every part of me with praise
397	4	fill me with thy fullness Lord, Until my very heart o'erflow
413	1	Fill us with thy love and pity
433	4	Fill all our lives with love and grace divine
468	4	gave Thy Son to fill a human grave
491	2	Fill thou our hearts with zeal in every brave endeavor

filled

18	3	The world is with the glory filled Of thy majestic sway
23	4	Let all thy days Till life shall end ... filled with praise
23	4	Till life shall end, Whate'er he send, Be filled with praise
68	2	goodness of the Lord, That filled the earth with food
70	2	He, with all commanding might, Filled the new-made earth
70	2	Filled the new-made world with light
142	3	Herod then with fear was filled
189	1	And filled the gloom and darkness With resurrection light
197	4	Filled it with the glory Of that perfect rest
298	1,4	When the earth shall be filled with the glory of God
298	2,3	That the earth may be filled with the glory of God
315	2	Our hearts are filled with sadness, And we had lost our way
340	2	peace of God that filled their hearts Brimful, & broke them
363	3	And though this world, with devils filled
449	4	homes with love and laughter filled
463	3	He hath filled the garner floor
503	1	place, Filled with solace, light, and grace
570	8	He hath filled the hungry with good things

filling

232	5	One holy passion filling all my frame
302	T,1	O Zion, Haste, Thy Mission High Fulfilling
394	2	Jesus Christ is filling all the heart of me
394	2	Jesus Christ is filling all my heart

fills

20	1	With healing balm my soul he fills
42	1	Black turns to gray, Bird-song the valley fills

final

find

466	3	Who teachest us to find The love from self set free
500	1	As in the dawn the shadows fly, We seem to find the now
500	1	We seem to find thee now more nigh
503	2	Where we find thee and adore thee, There a heaven on earth
509	2	May struggling hearts that seek release Here find the rest
509	2	Here find the rest of God's own peace
578	3	I find, I walk, I love, but O the whole Of love is

finds

403	2	But the lonely worker also finds him ever at his side

fine

401	4	Who sweeps a room ... Makes that and the action fine

finely

444	3	finely build for days to come Foundations that endure

finish

228	4	Finish, then, thy new creation
325	4	We bring our hearts before thy cross To finish thy salvation

finished

158	3	It is finished, hear him cry, Learn of Jesus Christ to die
303	2	thou hast not yet finished man ...we are in the making still
311	1	'Tis finished, all is finished, their fight with death & sin

fire

64	3	Thou fire so masterful and bright
93	2	Let the fire & cloudy pillar Lead me all my journey through
231	1	And lighten with celestial fire
231	2	blessed unction from above Is comfort, life and fire of love
233	3	Until this earthly part of me Glows with thy fire divine
241	2	Come as the fire and purge our hearts Like sacrificial flame
242	2	Kindle every high desire, Perish self in thy pure fire
249	2	led ... with the fire and cloud
256	3	Pillar of fire through watches dark, & radiant cloud by day
267	3	Round each habitation hovering, See the cloud & fire appear
299	2	Give tongues of fire and hearts of love
341	5	Speak through the earthquake, wind and fire
348	2	Pure, warm, and changeless be, A living fire
365	1	living still In spite of dungeon, fire, and sword
410	3	Love shall tread out the baleful fire of anger
429	4	shield in danger's hour From rock and tempest, fire and foe
431	3	On dune and headland sinks the fire
435	1	With thy living fire of judgment Purge this land
450	2	On earth and fire and sea and air
461	3	Give his angels charge at last In the fire the tares to cast
575	1	And lighten with celestial fire
575	2	blessed unction from above Is comfort, life and fire of love

fires

422	2	When through the night the furnace fires aflaring

firm

6	5	Thy mercies how tender, how firm to the end
9	5	Firm as a rock thy truth must stand
78	1	firm remains on high The everlasting throne of him
82	2	Forever firm thy justice stands
82	2	firm thy justice stands As mountains their foundations keep
345	5	Still lift your standard high, Still march in firm array
372	T,1	How Firm a Foundation, ye saints of the Lord
373	2	Though hosts encamp around me, Firm in the fight I stand
397	2	O strengthen me, that while I stand firm on the rock
448	4	Till rise in ordered plan On firm foundations broad
450	2	dare All that may plant man's lordship firm On earth
450	4	For man shall be at one with God in bonds of firm necessity

firmament

72	T,1	The Spacious Firmament on High
569	6	Blessed art thou in the firmament of heaven

firmer

287	1	Here grasp with firmer hand the eternal grace
557	1	Here grasp with firmer hand eternal grace

firmly

4	4	His truth at all times firmly stood
242	4	Be my law, and I shall be Firmly bound, forever free

first

14	1	The First, the Last, beyond all thought His timeless years
32	3	Guard my first springs of thought and will
38	T,1	Morning Has Broken, Like the first morning
38	1	Blackbird has spoken Like the first bird
38	2	Like the first dewfall On the first grass
127	1	With them the joyful tidings first begun
127	1	tidings first begun of God incarnate and the Virgin's Son
127	3	The first apostles of his infant fame
127	4	Till man's first heavenly state again takes place
141	T,1	The First Nowell, the angel did say
230	6	Through him the first fond prayers are said
259	2	Darkling our great forefathers went The first steps
259	2	The first steps of the way
325	T,1	Lord Christ, When First Thou cam'st to men
349	2	Where is the blessedness I knew When first I saw the Lord
371	1	His first avowed intent To be a pilgrim
388	2	martyr first, whose eagle eye Could pierce beyond the grave
391	3	Thou and thou only, first in my heart
403	1	Thus the first disciples found him
461	2	First the blade, and then the ear
490	4	Spirit of Christ, do thou Our first bright days inspire
501	1	And unto thee we dedicate The first fruits of the day

fish

484	2	Some fish in mighty rivers, Some hunt across the snow

fisher

340	1	Such happy, simple fisher-folk, Before the Lord came down

fishermen
340 2   Contented, peaceful fishermen, Before they ever knew ... God

fit
36 6   Only, O Lord, in thy dear love Fit us for perfect rest above
41 2   Monarch of all things, fit us for thy mansions
389 3   Give us each day our daily bread, And raiment fit provide
471 5   Fit him to follow thee through pain and loss
490 1   Our fervent gift receive, And fit us to fulfill

fitness
112 3   witness Which can shape the world to fitness

fix
228 1   Fix in us thy humble dwelling
477 2   Come, fix thy glorious presence here

fixed
360 1   To one fixed trust my spirit clings, I know that God is good

flag
496 1   Gave proof through the night that our flag was still there

flame
89 5   One holy light, one heavenly flame
232 5   My heart an altar, and thy love the flame
239 1   And kindle it, thy holy flame bestowing
240 1   Kindle a flame of sacred love In these cold hearts of ours
303 3   We see the beckoning vision flame
372 4   The flame shall not hurt thee
380 1   Who, thrust in prison or cast to flame
380 1   cast to flame, Still made their glory in thy name
388 3   And mocked the cross and flame
421 4   O'er hill and dale in saffron flame and red
422 2   Shooting out tongues of flame like leaping blood
450 1   race ... shall rise With flame of freedom in their souls
451 1   Yet thou, her child, whose head is crowned with flame
493 1-4   But only in his heart a flame
498 2   Make thou thy flame in us to glow

flames
89 1   Thy glory flames from sun and star
422 4   Flames out the sunshine of the great tomorrow

flaming
294 T,1   Eternal God, Whose Power Upholds Both flower & flaming star

flapping
340 3   Young John who trimmed the flapping sail

flaring
422 2   When through the night the furnace fires aflaring
443 2   I can read his righteous sentence by the dim & flaring lamps

flash

67	2	When lightnings flash and storm-winds blow ... is thy power
67	2	lightnings flash ... There is thy power, thy law is there

flashing

8	2	Flowery meadow, flashing sea ... call us to rejoice

flaw

440	2	America, America, God mend thine every flaw

fled

372	1	To you who for refuge to Jesus have fled

flee

37	1	When the bird waketh, and the shadows flee
37	4	morning, When the soul waketh and life's shadows flee
59	2	Let evil thoughts and spirits flee before us
91	2	To him for safety I will flee, My God ... my trust shall be
123	2	Doth entreat, Flee from woe and danger
128	2	Heaven and earth shall flee away When he comes to reign
209	1	When other helpers fail, and comforts flee
209	5	Heaven's morning breaks, and earth's vain shadows flee
284	4	when these failing lips grow dumb, And mind and memory flee
347	T,1	Lord, As to Thy Dear Cross we flee, And plead to be forgiven
370	3	E'en death's cold wave, I will not flee
371	3	Then fancies, flee away, I'll fear not what men say
576	3	Or whither from thy presence flee

fleecy

459	2	His hoary frost, his fleecy snow, Descend

fleeting

358	4	While I draw this fleeting breath

flesh

104	3	all flesh shall see the token That his word is never broken
107	T,1	Let All Mortal Flesh Keep Silence
120	2	Veiled in flesh the God-head see, Hail the incarnate Deity
132	4	Word of the Father, now in flesh appearing
148	3	And if Satan, vexing sore, Flesh or spirit should assail
169	1	take Frail flesh and die
253	3	Praise him for the Word made flesh
341	5	Let sense be dumb, let flesh retire
385	3	The arm of flesh will fail you, Ye dare not trust your own
445	4	Thy Word made flesh, and in a manger laid
468	1	From this our world of flesh set free, We know them living

flickering

399	2	I yield my flickering torch to thee
422	4	Toiling in twilight flickering and dim

flight

109	3	Traveler, darkness takes its flight
110	2	And death's dark shadows put to flight
117	1	Wing your flight o'er all the earth

fling

114	2	Fling wide the portals of your heart
129	4	peace shall over all the earth Its ancient splendors fling
296	T,1-4	Fling Out the Banner
311	1	Fling open wide the golden gates, And let the victors in

flinty

381	2	Whether beneath was flinty rock Or yielding grassy sod

float

296	1,3	let it float Sky-ward and sea-ward, high and wide

floateth

252	3	It floateth like a banner Before God's hosts unfurled

floating

61	4	Keep love's banner floating o'er you

floats

129	2	still their heavenly music floats O'er all the weary world

flock

265	1	Break every bar that holds Thy flock in diverse folds
327	2	Keep thy flock, from sin defend us

flocking

432	3	The eager peoples flocking to be free

flocks

117	2	Watching o'er your flocks by night
146	T,1	While Shepherds Watched Their Flocks by night
464	1	Flocks that whiten all the plain
488	1	While shepherds kept their watching O'er silent flocks
488	1	O'er silent flocks by night

flood

65	2	Creatures of the field and flood
360	1	When tossed by storm and flood
363	1	Our helper he amid the flood Of mortal ills prevailing

floods

130	2	While fields and floods, rocks, hills and plains Repeat
236	4	Hurling floods of tyrant wrong From the sacred limits back

floor

422	5	Sweeping the shavings from his workshop floor
463	3	He hath filled the garner floor

flourish

7	3	We blossom and flourish as leaves on the tree

flow

32	5	Praise God from whom all blessings flow
56	4	Praise God, from whom all blessings flow
67	1	Thy present life through all doth flow

79	2	Where streams of living water flow
93	2	fountain, Whence the healing stream doth flow
99	3	We read thee ... In the seas that swell & streams that flow
105	3	And righteousness, in fountains, From hill to valley flow
167	V-3	Where the healing waters flow, Hear us, holy Jesus
177	3	Sorrow and love flow mingled down
236	5	Flow still in the prophet's word And the people's liberty
305	3	Flow thou to every nation, Nor in thy richness stay
358	2	Could my zeal no respite know, Could my tears forever flow
399	1	that in thine ocean depths its flow May richer, fuller be
404	1	Let them flow in ceaseless praise
459	2	The liquid streams forbear to flow, In icy fetters bound
462	3	Source whence all our blessings flow
464	3	Source whence all our blessings flow
486	1	Through the earth and sky God's great mercies flow
514	1	Praise God from whom all blessings flow
515	1	Praise God from whom all blessings flow

flowed

94	2	From whom those comforts flowed
249	4	From thee have flowed, as from a pleasant river, Our plenty
358	1	Let the water & the blood, From thy riven side which flowed

flower

53	T,1	The Duteous Day Now Closeth, Each flower and tree reposeth
66	2	Hill & vale, and tree & flower, Sun & moon & stars of light
68	3	not a plant or flower below But makes thy glories known
95	2	Truth from the earth, like a flower, Shall bud and blossom
294	T,1	Eternal God, Whose Power Upholds Both flower & flaming star
316	1	Summoned forth its fruit and flower
366	1	Bring to bud her glorious flower
460	2	He paints the wayside flower, He lights the evening star
478	1	Each little flower that opens, Each little bird that sings
487	2	Praise him, field and flower, Praise his mighty power
492	3	grant us power That worthy thoughts in deeds may flower
492	3	flower In Christ-like lives, we pray

floweret

131	1	It came, a floweret bright, Amid the cold of winter

flowers

8	1	Hearts unfold like flowers before thee
66	5	Graces, human and divine, Flowers of earth & buds of heaven
105	3	love, joy, hope, like flowers, Spring from his path to birth
152	3	While birds and flowers and sky above are preaching
184	2	Bring flowers of song to strew his way
458	2	Starring all the land with flowers
486	1	Birds above me fly, Flowers bloom below

flowery

8	2	Flowery meadow, flashing sea ... call us to rejoice

floweth

14	2	His spirit floweth free, High surging where it will
79	5	O what transport of delight From thy pure chalice floweth

385	1	Till every foe is vanquished, And Christ is Lord indeed
395	5	And claim the kingdom of the earth For thee and not thy foe
429	4	shield in danger's hour From rock and tempest, fire and foe
489	2	I would be friend of all, the foe, the friendless

foes
16	3	Rescues us from all our foes
84	4	My table thou hast furnished In presence of my foes
163	1	By foes derided, by thine own rejected, O most afflicted
164	2	While soldiers scoff and foes deride
166	1	Craving pardon for thy foes, Hear us, holy Jesus
201	3	left the lonesome place of death, Despite the rage of foes
222	2	Foes who would molest me Cannot reach me here
231	3	Keep far our foes, give peace at home
258	2	When our foes are near us, Then thy word doth cheer us
267	1	Thou may'st smile at all thy foes
303	4	And still with haughty foes must cope
324	3	No foes, no evils need I fear
347	4	Should friends misjudge, or foes defame
354	1	Our shield from foes, our balm for woes
371	2	No foes shall stay his might, Though he with giants fight
372	5	I will not, I will not desert to his foes
385	2	Ye that are men now serve him Against unnumbered foes
490	3	The lovers of all holy things, The foes of all things wrong
558	1	And friends betrayed him to his foes
575	3	Keep far our foes, give peace at home

foes'
| 378 | 3 | Calm thy foes' raging |

foil
| 209 | 3 | What but thy grace can foil the tempter's power |

fold
9	2	He brought us to his fold again
42	1	Mists fold away, Gray wakes to green again
45	2	Gather us who seek thy face To the fold of thy embrace
61	1	With his sheep securely fold you
377	1	Soon again his arms will fold thee To his loving heart
377	4	Thou his people art, & surely He will fold his own securely
410	T,1	O Brother Man, Fold to the Heart thy brother
471	4	Tending with care the lambs within the fold
483	1	How he called little children as lambs to his fold

folded
| 183 | 1 | Kept the folded grave-clothes Where the body lay |
| 467 | 2 | And we grow quiet, folded in thy peace |

folds
265	1	Break every bar that holds Thy flock in diverse folds
296	1	The sun that lights its shining folds
327	1	For our use thy folds prepare

folk

4	2	We are his folk, he doth us feed
124	1	It is Jesus, good folk of the village
340	1	Such happy, simple fisher-folk, Before the Lord came down
435	2	Still the weary folk are pining for the hour
451	3	Earth shall be fair, and all her folk be one
476	2	And made our folk a nation
481	3	For the saints of God are just folk like me
487	2	God's care like a cloak Wraps us country folk

follow

84	5	Goodness and mercy all my life Shall surely follow me
96	1	And follow where he guideth
97	3	God of the coming years, through paths unknown we follow
108	1	We follow where thy voice shall call
141	3	And to follow the star wherever it went
152	5	Still as of old he calleth, Follow me
218	3	O Jesus, thou has promised To all who follow thee
218	3	O give me grace to follow, My master and my friend
220	2	Through ... thrust of driving trade We follow
220	2	We follow where the Master leads, Serene and unafraid
247	3	And the blessed martyrs follow
275	3	free To follow truth, and thus to follow thee
318	2	Joyful to follow thee Through paths unknown
322	1	Saying, Christian, follow me
324	4	Savior, where'er thy steps I see ... I follow thee
324	4	Dauntless, untired, I follow thee
339	3	Christ doth call One and all, Ye who follow shall not fall
341	2	Let us, like them, without a word, Rise up and follow thee
347	5	O may we lead the pilgrim's life, And follow thee to heaven
371	1	Let him in constancy Follow the Master
375	3	Lead on, O King eternal, We follow, not with fears
388	4	O God, to us may grace be given To follow in their train
403	1	who love and ... labor follow in the way of Christ
409	2	who tread the path of labor Follow where thy feet have trod
410	2	Follow with reverent steps the great example Of him
423	6	And follow where thy feet have trod
471	5	Fit him to follow thee through pain and loss

followed

481	2	And they followed the right, for Jesus' sake
481	2	followed ... The whole of their good lives long

follower

370	R	His faithful follower I would be For by his hand he leadeth

followest

399	2	O Light that followest all my way

following

143	1	Field and fountain, moor and mountain, Following yonder star
182	4	Following our exalted Head

follows

388	1,2	Who follows in his train

388	1	Who patient bears his cross below, He follows in his train
388	2	Who follows in his train
388	3	Who follows in their train

folly

| 376 | 2 | While passion stains and folly dims our youth |

fond

230	6	Through him the first fond prayers are said
367	2	When fond hopes fail and skies are dark before us
467	2	When fond hopes fail and skies are dark before us

food

33	2	Day by day provide us food
68	2	goodness of the Lord, That filled the earth with food
79	2	where the verdant pastures grow With food celestial feedeth
107	2	His own self for heavenly food
260	2	One holy name she blesses, Partakes one holy food
280	2	That living bread, that heavenly wine, Be our immortal food
281	1	For thou art our food indeed
289	1	Didst give man food for all his days
292	3	And by this food, so aweful and so sweet Deliver us
460	3	seed-time and the harvest, Our life, our health, our food
479	1	For rest and food and loving care
558	3	Receive and eat the living food

foolish

79	3	Perverse and foolish oft I strayed
265	2	Lord, set thy churches free From foolish rivalry
341	T,1	Dear Lord and Father of Mankind, Forgive our foolish ways
431	5	For frantic boast and foolish word, Thy mercy
451	T,1	Turn Back, O Man, Forswear Thy Foolish Ways

foot

85	2	Thy foot he'll not let slide
185	1	Led them with unmoistened foot Through the Red Sea waters
298	2	utmost east to utmost west, Where'er man's foot hath trod
299	1	Where'er the foot of man hath trod

footsteps

87	1	He plants his footsteps in the sea And rides upon the storm
95	1	His footsteps cannot err
252	1	A lantern to our footsteps, Shines on from age to age
258	T,1	Lord, Thy Word Abideth, And our footsteps guideth
308	4	In their footsteps will we tread
386	1	send thy light To set our footsteps in the homeward way
389	3	Our wandering footsteps guide
405	3	Some dews of mercy shed, Some wayward footsteps led

forbear

| 459 | 2 | The liquid streams forbear to flow, In icy fetters bound |

forbid

| 177 | 2 | Forbid it, Lord, that I should boast |

forbidden
374 2   With forbidden pleasures Would this vain world charm

forbids
182 3   Death in vain forbids him rise

force
356 1   Force me to render up my sword, And I shall conqueror be
381 2   They cared not, but with force unspent ... they onward went

fore'er
250 3   We all confess the Holy Ghost Who from both fore'er proceeds

forefather
568 6   To perform the oath which he sware to our forefather Abraham

forefathers
259 2   Darkling our great forefathers went The first steps
568 5   To perform the mercy promised to our forefathers
570 9   as he promised to our forefathers, Abraham and his seed

foreign
294 1   No alien race, no foreign shore, No child unsought, unknown
484 3   Till all the distant people In every foreign place

forest
8 2   Field and forest, vale and mountain ... call us to rejoice
126 3   Myrrh from the forest or gold from the mine
326 3   In the shade of the forest tree

forests
484 2   Some work in sultry forests Where apes swing to and fro

foretell
109 1   Watchman, does its beauteous ray ... joy or hope foretell
109 a   Aught of joy or hope foretell

foretold
131 2   Isaiah 'twas foretold it, The Rose I have in mind
448 3   Speed, speed the longed-for time Foretold by raptured seers

forever
2 2   we trust And give thee thanks forever
3 1   Praise his name forever
4 4   His mercy is forever sure
16 2   Praise him, still the same forever
16 2   same forever, Slow to chide and swift to bless
22 3   To thee, our great Redeemer, forever be praise
45 3   When forever from our sight Pass the stars ... day ... night
46 4   in the spirit's secret cell May hymn & prayer forever dwell
47 5   Thy kingdom stands, and grows forever
49 3   Thee ... The world doth glorify And shall exalt forever
50 2   Be my last thought how sweet to rest Forever on my Savior's
50 2   Forever on my Savior's breast
72 3   Forever singing as they shine

77	3	hour is hastening on When we shall be forever with the Lord
79	1	I nothing lack if I am his and he is mine forever
82	2	Forever firm thy justice stands
85	4	Henceforth thy going out and in God keep forever will
103	3	Born to reign in us forever, Now thy gracious kingdom bring
105	4	His name shall stand forever, That name to us is Love
143	2	King forever, ceasing never Over us all to reign
170	3	O make me thine forever, And should I fainting be
188	3	Thine own redeemed forever shield
208	1	Let thy clear light forever shine
218	1	Be thou forever near me, My master and my friend
230	T,1	Immortal Love, Forever Full, Forever flowing free
230	1	Forever shared, forever whole, A never-ebbing sea
242	4	Be my law, and I shall be Firmly bound, forever free
250	3	Blest and Holy Trinity, Praise forever be to thee
263	1	Holy Zion's help forever, And her confidence alone
263	3	What they gain from thee forever With the blessed to retain
265	2	Let all past bitterness Now and forever cease
268	3	Hallowed be thy name forever, Heal our differences of old
271	3	Unbroken be the golden chain, Keep on the song forever
276	4	Thy gospel light forever shine
306	1	Thy name, O Jesus, be forever blest
309	3	Forever and forever Are clad in robes of white
354	2	And guide our steps forever
358	2	Could my zeal no respite know, Could my tears forever flow
361	3	Have faith in God, my soul, His cross forever stands
363	4	His kingdom is forever
368	2	Not forever in green pastures Do we ask our way to be
368	3	Not forever by still waters Would we idly rest and stay
398	5	Thou art our Lord, Thou dost forever reign
441	1	choice goes by forever 'Twixt that darkness and that light
441	3	Truth forever on the scaffold, Wrong forever on the throne
461	4	There forever purified, In thy presence to abide
502	1	Forever ready at thy service stand
559	13	govern them and lift them up forever

forevermore

24	1	our song shall soar In praise to God forevermore
115	4	Whom with the Father we adore and Holy Ghost forevermore
156	3	And in that temple dwell forevermore
276	2	Large as thy love forevermore
387	3	Where the one almighty Father Reigns in love forevermore
472	5	O thou, who art the same Forevermore

forfeit

| 335 | 1 | O what peace we often forfeit |

forge

| 395 | 4 | Thine are the loom, the forge, the mart, The wealth of land |

forget

100	1	forget not All his mercies to proclaim
362	2	Forget the steps already trod, And onward urge thy way
425	2	with leathern hearts, forget That we owe mankind a debt
431	1,2	Lord God of hosts, be with us yet, Lest we forget

forlorn

42	2	So, o'er the hills of life, Stormy, forlorn
142	1	Came he to a world forlorn, the Lord of every nation

form

6	2	His chariots of wrath the deep thunder-clouds form
55	2	What if thy form we cannot see
150	1	God, the Son of God, should take Our mortal form
150	1	take out mortal form for mortals' sake
160	2	see The very dying form of one Who suffered there for me
330	4	So, Love itself in human form, For love of me he came
347	1	So let thy life our pattern be, & form our souls for heaven
445	1	Spirit of life, which moved ere form was made
482	1	See the fur to keep you warm, Snugly round your tiny form

formal

240	2	In vain we tune our formal songs, In vain we strive to rise

formed

9	2	Made us of clay and formed us men
68	2	He formed the creatures with his word
78	1	throne of him Who formed the earth and sky
267	1	He whose word cannot be broken Formed thee for his own abode
294	3	Till Christ is formed in all mankind And every land is thine
316	1	Thou who formed the earth's wide reaches

former

311	2	O joy, for all its former woes, A thousand-fold repaid
352	2	Above the level of the former years
402	3	Thy former mercies here renew

forms

129	3	ye, beneath life's crushing load Whose forms are bending low

forsake

22	2	When perils o'ertake us, thou wilt not forsake us
157	2	Never shall the cross forsake me
198	2	When Christ is throned as Lord, Men shall forsake their fear
335	3	Do thy friends despise, forsake thee
372	5	I'll never, no, never, no, never forsake

forsaken

174	3	Thou dost ask him -- can it be, Why has thou forsaken me
178	3	Yet he that hath in anguish knelt Is not forsaken
178	3	Is not forsaken by his God
377	4	Upward gaze and happy be, God hath not forsaken thee
446	2	earth hath forsaken Thy ways all holy, and slighted thy word

forsaketh

377	2	Never God his own forsaketh

forsook

83	3	God never yet forsook at need the soul that trusted him

forswear

451	T,1	Turn Back, O Man, Forswear Thy Foolish Ways

forth

forthwith

fortify

fortress

fortune

foundations

82	2	firm thy justice stands As mountains their foundations keep
264	2	We mark her goodly battlements, And her foundations strong
444	3	And finely build for days to come Foundations that endure
448	4	Till rise in ordered plan On firm foundations broad

founded

6	3	Almighty, thy power hath founded of old
267	1	On the Rock of Ages founded, What can shake thy sure repose
297	1	The shrines our fathers founded stand
339	T,1	All My Hope on God Is Founded, He doth still my trust renew
477	T,1	Founded on Thee, Our Only Lord
477	1	Founded ... On thee, the everlasting Rock

fount

3	3	O thou Fount of blessing, Purify my spirit
86	4	Thou hidden fount of love, Of Peace, and truth and beauty
180	3	Alleluia to the Spirit, Fount of love and sanctity
256	1	Stream from the fount of heavenly grace
290	1	Thou fount of life, thou light of men
471	4	Be in his heart, the fount of all his loving

fountain

8	2	Chanting bird & flowing fountain call us to rejoice in thee
73	3	Silver fountain, clearly gushing
82	4	Life, like a fountain rich and free Springs from ... my Lord
93	2	Open now the crystal fountain
93	2	fountain, Whence the healing stream doth flow
143	1	Field and fountain, moor and mountain, Following yonder star
210	3	Thou of life the fountain art, Freely let me take of thee
236	2	Thine is every time & place, Fountain sweet of heart & mind
328	1	And he shall for thy spirit be A fountain ever full
358	3	Foul, I to the fountain fly, Wash me, Savior, or I die
467	1	Thou art the fountain whence our healing flows

fountains

7	2	Thy clouds which are fountains of goodness and love
105	3	And righteousness, in fountains, From hill to valley flow
276	3	Here make the well-springs of thy grace Like fountains
276	3	Like fountains in the wilderness
368	3	But would smite the living fountains From the rocks

four

420	1	Within whose four-square walls shall come No night

fourfold

591	T	Fourfold Amen

fowler's

91	3	Preserve thee from the fowler's snare

foxes

326	3	The foxes found rest, and the birds their nest In the shade

fragile

492	2	for friends who stirred The fragile wills of youth

fragrant
| 487 | 1 | Pearly rice and corn, Fragrant autumn morn |

frail
6	5	Frail children of dust, and feeble as frail
169	1	O who am I, That for my sake My Lord should take Frail flesh
169	1	take Frail flesh and die

frame
9	3	We are his ... Our souls, and all our mortal frame
16	3	Well our feeble frame he knows
72	1	blue ethereal sky And spangled heavens, a shining frame
95	4	all shall frame To bow them low before thee, Lord
225	2	No voice can sing, no heart can frame
230	6	prayers ... Our lips of childhood frame
232	5	One holy passion filling all my frame
349	T,1	O For a Closer Walk With God, A calm and heavenly frame

frankincense
| 141 | 5 | Their gold and myrrh and frankincense |
| 143 | 3 | Frankincense to offer have I, Incense owns a deity nigh |

frantic
| 431 | 5 | For frantic boast and foolish word, Thy mercy |

fraternity
| 450 | 3 | The pulse of one fraternity |

fraught
| 370 | 1 | O words with heavenly comfort fraught |

fray
| 427 | 1 | Hark, the waking up of nations, Hosts advancing to the fray |

free
14	2	His spirit floweth free, High surging where it will
17	2	tell the story In accent strong, with voices free
21	3	Thy name be ever praised, O Lord, make us free
29	2	And free us from all ills In this world and the next
55	4	none, O Lord, have perfect rest, For none are wholly free
55	4	none are wholly free from sin
60	3	from harm and danger keep thy children free
73	4	Each glad soul its free course winging
73	4	Each blithe voice its free song singing
82	4	Life, like a fountain rich and free Springs from ... my Lord
89	5	Grant us thy truth to make us free
103	T,1	Come, Thou Long-Expected Jesus, Born to set thy people free
105	1	He comes to break oppression, to set the captive free
106	3	Lands of the East, awake, Soon shall your sons be free
106	5	City of God, the bond are free
113	2	Till thou, Redeemer, shouldest free Thine own
113	2	free Thine own in glorious liberty
115	4	Whose advent sets thy people free
119	3	So may we with holy joy Pure and free from sin's alloy
122	3	free all those who trust in him From Satan's power and might

452	5	And use the lives thy love sets free
453	5	Ring in the valiant man and free
461	4	Gather thou thy people in, Free from sorrow, free from sin
466	3	Who teachest us to find The love from self set free
468	1	From this our world of flesh set free, We know them living
472	3	witness of thy love, To all men free
484	3	God raise up more to help them To set the nations free
490	T,1	Now in the Days of Youth, When life flows fresh and free
491	4	Bearing his cross in service glad and free
496	1-2	O'er the land of the free and the home of the brave
496	2	O thus be it ever when free men shall stand
528	3	and uphold me with thy free spirit

freed

123	2	Brethren, come, from all doth grieve you You are freed
425	1	Are ye not base slaves indeed, Slaves unworthy to be freed
452	4	That from our bonds we might be freed

freedom

198	1	Freedom her bondage breaks, And night is turned to day
253	1	Bringing freedom, spreading truth
425	2	Is true freedom but to break Fetters for our own dear sake
425	2	No, true freedom is to share All the chains
437	1	From every mountain side Let freedom ring
438	3	Laws, freedom, truth, and faith in God Came with those
439	2	For the heritage of freedom
440	2	A thoroughfare for freedom beat Across the wilderness
446	4	Yet shall to freedom and truth be restored
450	1	race ... shall rise With flame of freedom in their souls

freedom's

308	2	Warriors wielding freedom's sword
437	3	And ring from all the trees Sweet freedom's song
437	4	Long may our land be bright With freedom's holy light

freely

66	5	For each perfect gift of thine Unto us so freely given
210	3	Thou of life the fountain art, Freely let me take of thee
239	2	O let it freely burn, Till earthly passions turn To dust
316	2	Naught withholding, freely yielding
356	2	It cannot freely move Till thou hast wrought its chain
413	2	Freely have thy gifts been granted
413	2	Freely may thy servants give
419	1	Whose life, like light, is freely poured On all
419	1	Whose life ... is freely poured On all beneath the sun

frees

| 442 | 3 | And, judging, pardons, frees, inspires |

freest

| 416 | 4 | Freest faith assailed in vain |

fresh

| 37 | 3 | A fresh and solemn splendor still is given |
| 38 | 1 | Praise for them, springing Fresh from the Word |

| 492 | 2 | for friends who stirred The fragile wills of youth |
| 558 | 1 | And friends betrayed him to his foes |

fro

| 484 | 2 | Some work in sultry forests Where apes swing to and fro |

from

1	1	Our shelter from the stormy blast, And our eternal home
1	3	From everlasting thou art God, To endless years the same
4	4	His truth ... shall from age to age endure
6	4	It streams from the hills, it descends to the plain
7	1	In light inaccessible hid from our eyes
11	T,1	From All That Dwell Below the Skies
11	2	Thy praise shall sound from shore to shore
12	T,1	From All That Dwell Below the Skies (No. 11 with alleluias)
15	4	Let the Amen Sound from his people again
16	3	Rescues us from all our foes
17	1	Praise him from morn till fall of night
21	1	The wicked oppressing now cease from distressing
21	2	So from the beginning the fight we were winning
23	2	And now, from sin released, Behold the Savior's face
28	1	word When it goes forth from heaven o'er all the earth
32	5	Praise God from whom all blessings flow
33	2	For from thee come all things good
33	2	Strength unto our souls afford From thy living Bread, O Lord
33	3	Lest from thee we stray abroad, Stay our wayward feet,O Lord
35	2	The night becomes as day, When from the heart we say
35	5	Let air, and sea, and sky From depth to height reply
38	1	Praise for them, springing Fresh from the Word
38	2	Sweet the rain's new fall Sunlit from heaven
43	1	Day-spring from on high be near, Day-star in my heart appear
45	3	When forever from our sight Pass the stars ... day ... night
50	1	no ... cloud arise To hide thee from thy servant's eyes
50	3	Abide with me from morn till eve
50	4	With blessings from thy boundless store
51	4	Those who plan some evil, From their sin restrain
53	2	splendor ...From myriad worlds unknown
55	4	none are wholly free from sin
55	6	No word from thee can fruitless fall
56	4	Praise God, from whom all blessings flow
59	2	In soul and body, thou from harm defend us
60	2	Guard thou the lips from sin, the hearts from shame
60	3	from harm and danger keep thy children free
63	3	when thy love shall call us, Savior, from the world away
66	1	For the love which from our birth Over and around us lies
68	3	clouds arise, and tempests blow, By order from thy throne
68	3	While all that borrows life from thee Is ever in thy care
69	3	From the north to southern pole Let the mighty chorus roll
72	1	The unwearied sun, from day to day ... power display
72	2	And spread the truth from pole to pole
73	3	From the mountain's deep vein poured
74	2	From thy ways so often turning, Yet thy love doth seek him
79	5	O what transport of delight From thy pure chalice floweth
82	4	Life, like a fountain rich and free Springs from ... my Lord
82	4	Springs from the presence of my Lord

85	1	My safety cometh from the Lord, Who heaven & earth hath made
85	4	he shall Preserve thee from all ill
86	2	Till truth from falsehood part, Our souls can find no rest
95	2	Truth from the earth, like a flower, Shall bud and blossom
95	2	justice, from her heavenly bower, Look down on mortal men
99	4	Sent by the Father from on high, Our life to live
100	1	Who redeems thee from destruction
100	2	Who redeems thee from destruction
100	3	Far as east from west is distant He hath put away our sin
103	1	From our fears and sins release us
105	3	love, joy, hope, like flowers, Spring from his path to birth
105	3	And righteousness, in fountains, From hill to valley flow
105	4	From age to age more glorious, All-blessing and all-blest
106	5	Lo, from the North we come, From East, and West, and South
107	3	the Light of light descendeth From the realms of endless day
115	1	Glad tidings from the King of kings
117	T,1	Angels, From the Realms of Glory
121	T,1	From Heaven Above to Earth I Come
122	1	To save us all from Satan's power When we were gone astray
122	3	free all those who trust in him From Satan's power and might
123	2	Hark, a voice from yonder manger, Soft and sweet
123	2	Brethren, come, from all doth grieve you You are freed
123	3	Hail the star That from far Bright with hope is burning
126	3	Myrrh from the forest or gold from the mine
127	1	mystery ...Which hosts of angels chanted from above
129	1	From angels bending near the earth
129	1	From heaven's all gracious King
131	T,1	Lo, How a Rose E'er Blooming From tender stem hath sprung
136	2	Ox and ass beside him From the cold would hide him
137	2	I love thee, Lord Jesus, look down from the sky
138	2	Glories stream from heaven afar
138	3	Radiant beams from thy holy face
141	3	Three wise men came from country far
144	2	From Jacob shall a star proceed
146	6	Good will henceforth from heaven to men Begin & never cease
148	2	Shall not we thy sorrow share, And from earthly joys abstain
149	2	know not how ... Calvary's cross A world from sin could free
150	5	For us he rose from death again
152	2	Light of the village life from day to day
157	3	From the cross the radiance streaming
158	1	Turn not from his griefs away
160	1	From the burning of the noon-tide heat
160	2	And from my smitten heart with tears Two wonders I confess
161	1	Across our restless living The light streams from his cross
165	2	from the cross on Calvary's height Gleams of eternity appear
168	3	Which thou didst take to save our souls from loss
169	2	He came from his blest throne, salvation to bestow
177	3	See, from his head, his hands, his feet, Sorrow and love
178	2	'Tis midnight, and from all removed
178	4	'Tis midnight, and from heavenly plains Is borne the song
180	1	Jesus Christ, the King of glory, Now is risen from the dead
180	2	Christ from death to life is born
181	3	He rises glorious from the dead
181	4	From death's dread sting thy servants free
185	1	God hath brought his Israel Into joy from sadness

295	4	The new-born souls, whose days Reclaimed from error's ways
296	2	distant lands Shall see from far the glorious sight
297	2	From out their tireless prayer and toil Emerge the gifts
299	2	Give power and unction from above
301	3	May her scattered children be From reproach of evil free
304	1	From age to age his righteous reign appears
304	1	From land to land the love of Christ is told
304	3	And from his waiting Church new hopes arise
305	1	Each breeze that sweeps the ocean Brings tidings from afar
306	T,1	For All the Saints who from their labors rest
309	3	There is the throne of David, And there, from care released
314	1	From earth-born passions set me free
318	3	Cleanse it from guilt and wrong, Teach it salvation's song
321	1	That I from thee no more may stray
321	1	No more from thee decline
322	2	Turned from home and toil and kindred
322	3	Jesus calls us from the worship of the vain world's
322	3	From each idol that would keep us
325	3	From old unfaith our souls release To seek the kingdom
327	2	Keep thy flock, from sin defend us
330	5	If there is aught of worth in me, It comes from thee alone
331	1	Nor should I aught withhold, Dear Lord, from thee
332	3	Hearts that far from thee were straying
332	4	From henceforth, the time redeeming, May we live to thee
332	5	Hearken from thy throne on high
333	3	Father of mercy, from thy watch & keeping No place can part
333	3	Give us thy good, and save us from our evil, Infinite Spirit
334	1,3	revealing Of trust and strength and calmness from above
336	2	We perish if we cease from prayer
339	3	Still from man to God eternal Sacrifice of praise be done
341	4	Take from our souls the strain and stress
345	4	From youth to age, by night and day, In gladness and in woe
348	1	Oh, let me from this day Be wholly thine
348	3	Nor let me every stray From thee aside
349	3	And drove thee from my breast
349	4	Help me to tear it from thy throne, And worship only thee
352	3	Till, sent from God, they mount to God again
354	1	Our shield from foes, our balm for woes
354	2	nor hell beneath, Our souls from thee shall sever
357	5	And yet we trust it comes from thee
357	6	Let knowledge grow from more to more
358	1	Let the water & the blood, From thy riven side which flowed
358	1	Be of sin the double cure, Cleanse me from its guilt & power
360	4	No harm from him can come to me On ocean or on shore
361	3	neither life nor death can pluck His children from his hands
362	3	'Tis God's all-animating voice That calls thee from on high
363	2	Lord Sabaoth his name, From age to age the same
365	3	And through the truth that comes from God Mankind ... free
366	2	From the fears that long have bound us Free our hearts
366	5	Save us from weak resignation to the evils we deplore
368	3	But would smite the living fountains From the rocks
368	3	From the rocks along our way
380	2	Heroic warriors, ne'er from Christ ... enticed
380	2	ne'er from Christ By any lure or guile enticed
384	3	From strength to strength go on, Wrestle and fight and pray

fruit
316	1	Summoned forth its fruit and flower
461	2	Fruit unto his praise to yield

fruited
75	3	Hill & vale & fruited land, All things living show his hand
440	1	For purple mountain majesties Above the fruited plain

fruitful
105	3	He shall come down like showers Upon the fruitful earth
461	3	But the fruitful ears to store In his garner evermore

fruition
413	4	grant our hope's fruition, Here on earth thy will be done
439	4	Till it find its full fruition In the brotherhood of man

fruitless
55	6	No word from thee can fruitless fall

fruits
63	2	May the fruits of thy salvation In our hearts & lives abound
462	2	All the fruits in full supply Ripened 'neath the summer sky
478	3	The ripe fruits in the garden, He made them every one
501	1	And unto thee we dedicate The first fruits of the day
579	1	For the valley's golden yield ... fruits of tree and field

fulfil
167	V-2	Thirst for us in mercy still, All thy holy work fulfil
361	1	God will fulfil in every part Each promise he has made
448	1	Fulfil of old thy word And make the nations one

fulfill
266	4	Fulfill thy task sublime
293	3	By feeblest agents may our God fulfill His righteous will
318	3	Till earth, as heaven, fulfill God's holy will
331	1	In love my soul would bow, My heart fulfill its vow
342	4	And thy rich promises In me fulfill
358	2	Not the labors of my hands Can fulfill thy law's demands
406	2	task thy wisdom hath assigned, O let me cheerfully fulfill
490	1	Our fervent gift receive, And fit us to fulfill

fulfilled
127	2	This day hath God fulfilled his promised word
135	1	Thy Father's will thou hast fulfilled
144	2	'Tis now fulfilled what God decreed

fulfilling
302	T,1	O Zion, Haste, Thy Mission High Fulfilling

fulfillment
310	2	Wish and fulfillment can severed be ne'er

full
45	R	Heaven and earth are full of thee
68	1	The moon shines full at his command, And all the stars obey
70	5	His full hand supplies their need

74	T,1	O How Glorious, Full of Wonder
74	1	full of wonder Is thy name o'er all the earth
74	2	Child of earth, yet full of yearning
82	1	Thy goodness in full glory shines
98	1	So full of splendor and of joy, Beauty and light
107	1	Our full homage to demand
141	5	Full reverently upon their knee
161	3	And make us brave and full of joy To answer to his call
162	5	Learning all the might that lies In a full self-sacrifice
224	2	To thee our full humanity, Its joys and pains belong
230	T,1	Immortal Love, Forever Full, Forever flowing free
265	1	Thy will from none withholds Full liberty
328	1	And he shall for thy spirit be A fountain ever full
345	3	With voice as full and strong As ocean's surging praise
352	4	Still shall those hearts respond, with full accord
362	2	A cloud of witnesses around Hold thee in full survey
439	4	Till it find its full fruition In the brotherhood of man
461	2	Then the full corn shall appear
462	2	All the fruits in full supply Ripened 'neath the summer sky
465	2	O perfect Life, be thou their full assurance
493	T,1	When Stephen, Full of Power and Grace
550	1	Heaven and earth are full of thy glory
551	1	Heaven and earth are full of thy glory
553	1	Heaven and earth are full of thy glory
559	3	heaven and earth are full of the majesty of thy glory

fuller
| 399 | 1 | that in thine ocean depths its flow May richer, fuller be |

fullest
| 263 | 2 | And thy fullest benediction Shed within its walls alway |

fullness
99	5	Still more in resurrection light We read the fullness
99	5	in resurrection light We read the fullness of thy might
397	4	fill me with thy fullness Lord, Until my very heart o'erflow

fully
199	2	No angel in the sky Can fully bear that sight
337	2	When fully he the work hath wrought that caused thy ... fear
361	2	God's mercy holds a wiser plan Than thou canst fully know

fulness
| 238 | 4 | Lead us to heaven that we may share Fulness of joy |
| 238 | 4 | Fulness of joy for ever there |

fur
| 482 | 1 | We will lend a coat of fur, We will rock you |
| 482 | 1 | See the fur to keep you warm, Snugly round your tiny form |

furnace
| 422 | 2 | When through the night the furnace fires aflaring |

furnish
| 36 | 5 | The trivial round, the common task, Will furnish all |
| 36 | 5 | the common task, Will furnish all we ought to ask |

furnished
| 84 | 4 | My table thou hast furnished In presence of my foes |
| 115 | 2 | And furnished for so great a guest |

furrows
| 467 | 4 | Yet shall thou praise him, when these darkened furrows |

fury
| 142 | 3 | All the little boys he killed At Bethlem in his fury |
| 377 | 2 | Though the sea his waves assemble And in fury fall on thee |

future
77	2	thy God doth undertake To guide the future as ... the past
111	1	And that future years shall see, Evermore and evermore
360	5	I know not what the future hath Of marvel or surprise
441	3	Yet that scaffold sways the future
454	3	The future, all to us unknown, We to thy guardian care commit

future's
| 418 | 4 | Far down the future's broadening way |

gaily
| 169 | 5 | In whose sweet praise I all my days Could gaily spend |

gain
125	3	Calls you one & calls you all, To gain his everlasting hall
160	3	Content to let the world go by, To know no gain nor loss
161	1	And by its clear, revealing beams We measure gain and loss
167	V-1	Thirsting more our love to gain, Hear us, holy Jesus
177	1	My richest gain I count but loss
224	3	Apart from thee all gain is loss, All labor vainly done
263	3	What they ask of thee to gain
263	3	What they gain from thee forever With the blessed to retain
297	1	And where the higher gain appears, We trace ... thy hand
308	3	Recked they not of their own gain
364	1	Christian, up and smite them, Counting gain but loss
388	T,1	The Son of God Goes Forth to War, A kingly crown to gain
413	3	Shame our selfish greed of gain
420	2	greed for gain In street and shop and tenement Wring gold
440	3	Till all success be nobleness, And every gain divine
452	3	What skill and science slowly gain Is soon ... betrayed

gaining
| 313 | 2 | Not with the hope of gaining aught, Not seeking a reward |

gales
| 249 | 3 | And calming passion's fierce and stormy gales |
| 459 | 3 | He calls the warmer gales to blow And bids the spring return |

Galilean
| 322 | 2 | As of old, Saint Andrew heart it By the Galilean lake |

Galilee
| 191 | 3 | Your Lord doth go to Galilee |
| 220 | 3 | The common hopes that makes us men Were his in Galilee |

| 503 | T,1 | Open Now Thy Gates of Beauty, Zion, let me enter there |
| 565 | 3 | O go your way into his gates with thanksgiving |

gather

2	3	And the lost sheep dost gather
21	T,1	We Gather Together to ask the Lord's blessing
45	2	Gather us who seek thy face To the fold of thy embrace
46	1	We gather in these hallowed walls
124	2	Silence, all, as you gather around
222	3	Though the storms may gather, Still have peace within
270	3	Now we may gather with our King E'en in the lowliest
301	5	Gather all the nations in
461	4	Gather thou thy people in, Free from sorrow, free from sin
509	1	We gather in these hallowed walls

gathered

128	3	Angels and archangels May have gathered there
134	2	For Christ is born of Mary, And gathered all above
152	3	With all the listening people gathered round
212	T,1	Blessed Jesus, at Thy Word, We are gathered all to hear thee
289	2	So from all lands thy Church be gathered Into thy kingdom
289	2	thy Church be gathered Into thy kingdom by thy Son
461	1	All is safely gathered in Ere the winter storms begin
462	1	All is safely gathered in Ere the winter storms begin

gathering

| 143 | 4 | Myrrh ... Breathes a life of gathering gloom |

gathers

| 157 | 1,5 | All the light of sacred story Gathers round its head sublime |

gave

34	3	To serve right gloriously The God who gave all worlds
34	3	The God who gave all worlds that are, And all that are to be
109	2	Gild the spot that gave them birth
136	1	Born on earth to save us, Him the Father gave us
136	4	Born on earth to save us, Peace and love he gave us
141	2	And to the earth it gave great light
150	4	For us gave up his dying breath
168	4	Thou lay the work he gave thee at his feet
169	4	He made the lame to run, He gave the blind their sight
220	3	The tasks he gives are those he gave Beside the restless sea
245	4	And whatever I can be Give to him who gave me thee
360	2	I can but give the gifts he gave, & plead his love for love
398	4	We render back the love thy mercy gave us
463	2	Praise him ... he gave the rain To mature the swelling grain
468	4	And bless thee for the love which gave Thy Son
468	4	gave Thy Son to fill a human grave
480	1	It gave him light to do his work, And smiled upon his play
496	1	Gave proof through the night that our flag was still there

gavest

47	T,1,	The Day Thou Gavest, Lord, Is Ended
48	T,1	The Day Thou Gavest, Lord, Is Ended (same words as No. 47)
331	T,1	Savior, Thy dying Love Thou gavest me
429	3	And gavest light, and life, and peace

gaze
68	2	If I survey the ground I tread or gaze upon the sky
377	4	Upward gaze and happy be, God hath not forsaken thee

Geburt
139	3	Christ, in deiner Geburt

gems
126	3	Gems of the mountain and pearls of the ocean
252	2	It is the golden casket Where gems of truth are stored

generation
271	1	We seek thee as thy saints have sought in every generation
476	2	Who graced their generation, Who helped the right
565	4	his truth endureth from generation to generation

generations
570	3	For behold, from henceforth all generations shall call me
570	3	all generations shall call me blessed
570	5	mercy is on them that fear him throughout all generations

Gentiles
431	4	Such boastings as the Gentiles use Or lesser breeds
572	4	To be a light to lighten the Gentiles

gentle
54	2	By gentle love thy cross proclaim
66	4	For all gentle thoughts and mild
76	T,1	How Gentle God's Commands, How kind his precepts are
98	2	So many gentle thoughts and deeds Circling us round
277	T,1	Jesus, Friend, So Kind and Gentle
346	3	faithful are the gentle hearts To whom the power is given
450	2	They shall be gentle, brave, and strong
542	1	O gentle Jesus, be our light

gentlemen
122	T,1	God Rest You Merry, Gentlemen, Let nothing you dismay

gentleness
188	2	O Jesus, King of gentleness
207	4	Thou hast the true and perfect gentleness
217	4	Lord of all gentleness, Lord of all calm

gently
15	2	Shelters thee under his wings, yea, so gently sustaineth
16	3	In his hands he gently bears us
50	2	My wearied eyelids gently steep
79	3	on his shoulder gently laid, And home rejoicing brought me
337	1	Through waves and clouds and storms He gently clears the way

Gethsemane
158	T,1	Go to Dark Gethsemane, Ye that feel the tempter's power
162	1	Then in thought I go to thee, Garden of Gethsemane
374	2	Bring to my remembrance Sad Gethsemane

93	3	songs of praises, I will ever give to thee
105	2	To give them songs for sighing, their darkness turn to light
107	2	He will give to all the faithful His own self
112	3	Thine, O God, to give the power
120	3	Born to raise the sons of earth ...to give them second birth
123	2	All you need I will surely give you
125	1	Give ye heed to what we say, Jesus Christ is born today
128	4	what can I give him, Poor as I am
128	4	Yet what I can I give him - Give my heart
152	5	Lord, we are thine, we give ourselves to thee
153	2	O give us strength in thee to fight, In thee to conquer sin
159	4	Give us compassion for thee, Lord
168	2	Yet give us strength to trust the sweet assurance
185	2	From his light, to whom we give Laud and praise undying
188	2	That we may give thee all our days the willing tribute
204	1	Rejoice, give thanks, and sing, And triumph evermore
206	4	Then let us adore and give him his right
207	3	And give us strength in every trying hour
207	5	Lord, give us peace, and make us calm and sure
214	4	Give us a pure and lowly heart, A temple meet for thee
217	1-4	and give us we pray, Your
218	3	O give me grace to follow, My master and my friend
231	3	Keep far our foes, give peace at home
245	4	And whatever I can be Give to him who gave me thee
246	2	Come, and thy people bless, And give thy word success
260	4	O happy ones and holy, Lord, give us grace that we
277	2	Give to all who teach and guide them Wisdom and humility
278	1	So give this child of thine, we pray Thy grace and blessing
281	2	'Tis thy wounds our healing give
289	1	Didst give man food for all his days
297	4	give us grace, through ampler years
297	4	give us grace ... To build the kingdom yet to be
298	2	Give ear to me, ye continents, Ye isles, give ear to me
299	2	Give tongues of fire and hearts of love
299	2	Give power and unction from above
300	1	Give heart and soul and mind and strength To serve
302	3	Give of thy sons to bear the message glorious
302	3	Give of thy wealth to speed them on their way
303	T,1	Creation's Lord, We Give Thee Thanks
315	T,1	Come Unto Me, Ye Weary, And I will give you rest
315	2	Come unto me, ye wanderers, And I will give you light
315	3	Come unto me, ye fainting, And I will give you life
316	3	We would give our lives to thee
318	2	In thee my strength renew, Give me thy work to do
322	5	Give our hearts to thine obedience
331	2	Give me a faithful heart, Guided by thee
333	3	Give us thy good, and save us from our evil, Infinite Spirit
336	3	Give, what thine eye delights to see, Truth
336	4	Give deep humility, the sense Of godly sorrow give
336	5	Give these, and then thy will be done
337	T,1	Give to the Winds Thy Fears, Hope and be undismayed
338	T,1	Give to the Winds Thy Fears (same words as no. 337 in 4 vs)
345	T,1	Rejoice, Ye Pure in Heart, Rejoice, give thanks and sing
345	R	Rejoice, rejoice, Rejoice, give thanks and sing
360	2	I can but give the gifts he gave, & plead his love for love
372	2	For I am thy God, and will still give thee aid

58	1	Who the day for toil hast given, For rest the night
65	1	Peace and blessing he has given
66	5	For each perfect gift of thine Unto us so freely given
74	3	Thou hast given man dominion o'er the wonders of thy hand
121	4	God ... Who unto men his son hath given
132	4	Jesus, to thee be all glory given
134	3	How silently, how silently The wondrous gift is given
159	3	Then let all praise be given thee Who livest evermore
173	3	The souls for whom Christ prays to Christ are given
182	5	Praise to thee by both be given
200	4	To them the cross, with all its shame ... is given
200	4	To them the cross ... With all its grace, is given
204	3	The keys of death and hell Are to our Jesus given
205	1	Christ, awhile to mortals given
219	3	Toil by the truth, life, way that thou hast given
223	3	Glory to God and praise and love Be ever, ever given
244	1	Where thou shinest life from heaven There is given
269	3	To her my cares and toils be given
269	5	Sure as thy truth shall last, To Zion shall be given
279	1	Let the little ones be given Unto me, of such is heaven
316	3	Thou hast given thy Son to save us
321	4	Let every thought, and work, and word To thee be ever given
346	3	faithful are the gentle hearts To whom the power is given
351	3	All that thou sendest me In mercy given
352	3	Lift every gift that thou thyself hast given
359	3	Thrice blest is he to whom is given The instinct
388	4	O God, to us may grace be given To follow in their train
398	2	Still let thy Spirit unto us be given
423	4	The cup of water given for thee Still holds the freshness
536	1	and of thine own have we given thee
577	R	Then to thy name be glory given

giver

8	1	Giver of immortal gladness, Fill us with the light of day
49	3	O Son of God, Life-giver
53	1	On God, Our Maker, calling ... the Giver good
73	4	Praise him ever, bounteous giver
249	4	O Holy Ghost, the Lord and Life-giver
267	2	Grace, which like the Lord, the Giver, Never fails
271	3	Bless the same boundless Giver
308	1	Source & giver of all good, Lord, we praise, we worship thee
339	2	Daily doth the almighty giver Bounteous gifts on us bestow

gives

23	3	Take what he gives And praise him still
78	4	He gives the conquest to the weak
220	3	The tasks he gives are those he gave Beside the restless sea
249	4	Thine is the quickening power that gives increase
267	3	Safe they feed upon the manna Which he gives them
267	3	Which he gives them when they pray
272	4	When we are called to part it gives us inward pain
298	4	Vainly we hope for the harvest-tide Till God gives life
298	4	Till God gives life to the seed
303	4	It gives us that for which to pray
412	3	O thou who didst the vision send And gives to each his task
460	2	Much more, to us his children, He gives our daily bread

491	4	Bearing his cross in service glad and free
504	1	Let heaven rejoice, let earth be glad
562	2	and show ourselves glad in him with psalms
577	R	Glad praise and adoration

gladly

15	4	Gladly for aye we adore him
22	3	And gladly our songs of true worship we raise
492	2	For prophet voices gladly heard, For daring dreams
506	2	Gladly hail the sun returning

gladness

8	1	Giver of immortal gladness, Fill us with the light of day
30	4	O friends, in gladness let us sing, Supernal anthems echoing
119	T,1	As With Gladness Men of Old Did the guiding star behold
145	2	Here in sadness Eye and heart long for thy gladness
180	1	Sing to God a hymn of gladness, Sing to God a hymn of praise
185	T,1	Come, Ye Faithful, Raise the Strain Of triumphant gladness
192	1	The Passover of gladness, the Passover of God
192	3	Let all things seen and unseen Their notes of gladness blend
193	2	Let his church with gladness Hymns of triumph sing
222	3	For the Lord of gladness, Jesus, enters in
244	1	To strength and gladness wake us
293	2	To young and old the gospel gladness bear
315	2	But morning brings us gladness, And songs the break of day
345	4	From youth to age, by night and day, In gladness and in woe
366	3	Shame our wanton, selfish gladness
375	3	For gladness breaks like morning Where'er thy face appears
387	3	One the gladness of rejoicing On the far eternal shore
486	2	Bright skies overhead, Gladness in my heart
565	!	serve the Lord with gladness

gladsome

20	3	Then all my gladsome way along, I sing aloud thy praises
49	T,1	O Gladsome Light, O grace of God the Father's face
70	T,1,6	Let Us With a Gladsome Mind
71	T,1	Let Us With a Gladsome Mind (same words as No. 70)
108	2	And gladsome join the advent song
274	3	With joy and gladsome cheer
377	1	Rise and be of gladsome heart

glance

39	2	O thou true Sun, on us thy glance Let fall
39	2	thy glance Let fall in royal radiance
55	5	Thy kind but searching glance can scan the very wounds

glanced

| 257 | 3 | So when thy truth began its race, It touched and glanced on |
| 257 | 2 | It touched and glanced on every land |

glare

| 496 | 1 | And the rockets' red glare, the bombs bursting in air |

glass

| 401 | 2 | A man that looks on glass On it may stay his eye |

glassy
251 2 Casting down their golden crowns around the glassy sea

gleam
36 4 Some soft'ning gleam of love and prayer Shall dawn
36 4 Some soft'ning gleam ... Shall dawn on every cross and care
64 1 Thou silver moon with softer gleam
261 3 How gleam thy watch-fires through the night
440 4 Thine alabaster cities gleam, Undimmed by human tears

gleaming
41 3 Thine is the glory, gleaming and resounding
41 3 glory, gleaming and resounding Through all creation
424 1 Only righteous men and women Dwell within its gleaming wall
494 2 O Master, lend us sight To see the towers gleaming
494 2 To see the towers gleaming in the light
496 1 What so proudly we hailed at the twilight's last gleaming

gleams
165 2 from the cross on Calvary's height Gleams of eternity appear
387 1 Clear before us through the darkness Gleams ... light
387 1 Gleams and burns the guiding light

glee
142 5 While the choir with peals of glee Doth rend the air asunder

glittering
455 2 And clothes the boughs with glittering wreaths

gloom
43 3 Pierce the gloom of sin and grief
108 2 She wakes, she rises from her gloom
143 4 Myrrh ... Breathes a life of gathering gloom
174 2 Left alone with human sin, Gloom around thee and within
174 4 Teach me by that bitter cry In the gloom to know thee nigh
189 1 And filled the gloom and darkness With resurrection light
193 2 Lovingly he greets thee, Scatters fear and gloom
209 5 Shine through the gloom, and point me to the skies
215 T,1 Lead, Kingly Light, amid the encircling gloom
387 2 Chasing far the gloom and terror

gloomy
110 2 Disperse the gloomy clouds of night
293 3 Away with gloomy doubts and faithless fear
405 2 Toilsome and gloomy ways Brightened with song

gloria
116 R Gloria in excelsis Deo
133 2 Gloria in Excelsis Deo
133 3 Jesu, tibi sit gloria
136 R Ideo ... Ideo gloria in excelsis Deo

glories
19 T,1 Praise the Lord, His Glories Show
68 3 not a plant or flower below But makes thy glories known
82 4 in thy light our souls shall see The glories promised

82	4	The glories promised in thy word
130	3	And makes the nations prove The glories of his righteousness
138	2	Glories stream from heaven afar
199	3	His glories now we sing Who died and rose on high
209	2	Earth's joys grow dim, its glories pass away
223	1	The glories of my God and King, The triumphs of his grace
269	5	brightest glories earth can yield & brighter bliss of heaven

glorified

| 199 | 2 | Rich wounds, yet visible above, In beauty glorified |

glorify

49	3	Thee ... O Most High, The world doth glorify
49	3	Thee ... The world doth glorify And shall exalt forever
95	4	And glorify thy name
299	4	The name of Jesus glorify Till every kindred call him Lord
472	4	Thy cross we lift on high This house to glorify
473	2	O Lord, and glorify thy name, For holy thou alone
490	2	But take as from thy hands our tasks And glorify them all
554	2	we glorify thee, we give thanks to thee for thy great glory

glorious

6	T,1	O Worship the King, All Glorious Above
7	1	Most blessed, most glorious, the Ancient of Days
13	2	Praise the Lord for he is glorious
16	2	Glorious in his faithfulness
18	4	The apostles glorious company ... Thy constant praise recite
24	1	All thy gates with pearl are glorious
25	4	Stand up and bless his glorious name Henceforth for evermore
30	2	O higher than the cherubim, More glorious than the seraphim
37	4	Shall rise the glorious thought, I am with thee
52	3	Hope and faith and love rise glorious
54	1	Our heavenly Sun, our glorious Light
69	2	Kings of knowledge and of law, To the glorious circle draw
72	3	And utter forth a glorious voice
74	T,1	O How Glorious, Full of Wonder
74	4	O how wondrous, O how glorious is thy name in every land
75	2	See the glorious orb of day Breaking through the clouds
98	1	So many glorious things are here, Noble and right
103	4	By ... all-sufficient merit Raise us to thy glorious throne
105	4	From age to age more glorious, All-blessing and all-blest
108	2	For her Lord comes down all glorious
108	3	In praises round thy glorious throne
113	2	free Thine own in glorious liberty
114	4	Thy Holy Spirit guide us on Until the glorious crown be won
129	T,1	It Came Upon the Midnight Clear, that glorious song of old
143	5	Glorious now behold him arise, King and God and Sacrifice
145	1	Thou art holy, Fair and glorious, all victorious
160	2	The wonders of his glorious love And my unworthiness
180	2	Glorious life, and life immortal On this holy Easter morn
181	3	He rises glorious from the dead
182	2	Lives again our glorious King
191	1	The King of heaven, the glorious King
193	3	No more we doubt thee, Glorious Prince of life
201	4	brighter than that glorious morn Shall this fair morning be
203	T,1	Look, Ye Saints, the Sight Is Glorious

41	3	Thine is the glory, gleaming and resounding
41	3	glory, gleaming and resounding Through all creation
43	T,1	Christ, Whose Glory Fills the Skies
52	2	Soon as dies the sunset glory, Stars of heaven shine out
65	T,1	Glory Be to God on High
65	3	Stars that have no voice to sing Give ... glory to our King
69	T,1	Let the Whole Creation Cry, Glory to the Lord on high
69	3	Holy, holy, holy One, Glory be to God alone
81	5	Be glory, as it was, is now, And shall be evermore
82	1	Thy goodness in full glory shines
89	1	Thy glory flames from sun and star
104	3	For the glory of the Lord Now o'er earth is shed abroad
108	3	No vision ever brought ... such great glory
108	3	No ear hath ever caught Such great glory
111	3	Honor, glory, and dominion, And eternal victory, Evermore
114	1	Behold the King of glory waits
117	T,1	Angels, From the Realms of Glory
119	4	need no star to guide, Where no clouds thy glory hide
120	T,1,R	Hark, The Herald Angels Sing, Glory to the new-born King
120	3	Mild he lays his glory by, Born that man no more may die
121	4	Glory to God in highest heaven
132	2	Glory to God, all glory in the highest
132	4	Jesus, to thee be all glory given
146	1	The angel of the Lord came down, And glory shone around
146	6	All glory be to God on high And to the earth be peace
147	1	Didst yield the glory that of right was thine
150	6	All glory to our Lord and God For love to deep
155	T,1,3	All Glory, Laud, and Honor To thee, Redeemer, King
157	T,1,5	In the Cross of Christ I Glory
160	3	My sinful self my only shame, My glory all the cross
177	1	cross On which the Prince of glory died
180	1	Jesus Christ, the King of glory, Now is risen from the dead
180	3	Alleluia, Alleluia, Glory be to God on high
181	3	All glory to our risen Head
183	2	Lives in glory now on high, Pleads for us and hears our cry
193	T,1,R	This Is the Glory, Risen, conquering Son
197	1	Every tongue confess him King of glory now
197	4	Filled it with the glory Of that perfect rest
200	1	Is crowned with glory now
201	2	But crowned with glory like the sun
205	2	Take the King of glory in
206	4	All glory and power, all wisdom and might
218	3	That where thou art in glory There shall thy servant be
223	3	Glory to God and praise and love Be ever, ever given
225	5	Jesus, be thou our glory now, And through eternity
227	1	Thee will I honor, Thou, my soul's glory, joy and crown
228	3	Glory in thy perfect love
228	4	Changed from glory into glory
246	4	His sovereign majesty May we in glory see
248	2	And in the coming glory Thou shalt be Sovereign Lord
249	T,1	Ancient of Days, Who Sittest Throned in Glory
251	3	Though the eye of sinful man thy glory may not see
253	2	story Of the Word, and showed his glory
257	T,1	The Heavens Declare Thy Glory, Lord
263	3	And hereafter in thy glory Evermore with thee to reign
263	4	One in might, and One in glory, While unending ages run

267	3	For a glory and a covering, Showing that the Lord is near
268	1	Glory, glory, thine the kingdom
268	2	Glory, glory, thine the power As in heaven thy will be done
268	3	Glory, glory, thine the glory Through the ages evermore
275	1	from the night profound Into the glory of the perfect day
296	3	Our glory only in the cross, Our only hope, the Crucified
298	1,4	When the earth shall be filled with the glory of God
298	2,3	That the earth may be filled with the glory of God
306	4	We feebly struggle, they in glory shine
309	1	What radiancy of glory, What bliss beyond compare
310	T,1	O What Their Joy and Their Glory Must Be
312	2	Thy saints are crowned with glory great
316	2	Purge our pride and our vain-glory
317	1	Of Jesus and his glory, Of Jesus and his love
317	R	I love to tell the story, 'Twill be my theme in glory
317	2	And when, in scenes of glory, I sing the new, new song
366	T,1	God of Grace and God of Glory On thy people pour thy power
366	5	Let the search for thy salvation Be our glory evermore
369	T,1	God's Glory Is a Wondrous Thing
369	1	God's Glory ... Most strange in all its ways
380	1	cast to flame, Still made their glory in thy name
382	4	Glory, laud and honor Unto Christ the King
383	2	Poets sung its glory, Heroes for it died
385	4	He with the King of glory Shall reign eternally
399	4	I lay in dust life's glory dead
407	4	All grace and glory be to thee From age to age eternally
413	1	Thou, our head, who, throned in glory
420	4	bids us seize the whole of life And build its glory there
421	4	We've seen thy glory like a mantle spread O'er hill and dale
422	5	Then will he come with meekness for his glory
433	4	And glory, laud, and praise be ever thine
435	3	Through the glory of the Lord
439	3	For the glory that illumines Patriot souls of deathless fame
443	T,1	Mine Eyes Have Seen the Glory of the coming of the Lord
443	R	Glory, glory, Hallelujah ... His truth is marching on
443	4	With a glory in his bosom that transfigures you and me
463	4	Glory to our bounteous King, Glory let creation sing
463	4	Glory to the Father, Son, And blest Spirit, Three in One
471	3	He sees the glory that shall end our night
472	5	Still may these courts proclaim the glory of thy name
475	T,1	O Lord of Hosts, Whose Glory Fills
475	1	glory fills The bounds of the eternal hills
476	1	praise the Lord, who now as then Reveals in man his glory
484	2	The truth that comes from Jesus, The glory of his Word
511	1	Glory be to the Father, and to the Son and to the Holy Ghost
512	1	Glory be to the Father, and to the Son, & to the Holy Ghost
513	1	Glory be to the Father, and to the Son, & to the Holy Ghost
525	1	Give we all, with one accord, Glory to our common Lord
546	T,1	Glory Be to Thee, O Lord
547	T,1	Glory Be to Thee, O Lord
550	1	Heaven and earth are full of thy glory
550	1	Glory be to thee, O Lord most high
551	1	Heaven and earth are full of thy glory
551	1	Glory be to thee, O Lord most high
553	1	Heaven and earth are full of thy glory
553	1	Glory be to thee, O Lord most high

67	4	The indwelling God, proclaimed of old
68	T,1	I Sing the Mighty Power of God That made the mountains rise
68	3	And everywhere that man can be, Thou, God, art present there
69	1	Heaven & earth, awake & sing, God is good and therefore King
69	1	Sun & moon, uplift your voice, Night & stars, in God rejoice
69	3	Holy, holy, holy One, Glory be to God alone
73	1-3	Praise ye, praise ye, God the Lord
74	4	Spirit in our spirit speaking, Make us sons of God indeed
77	1	Leave to thy God to order and provide
77	2	thy God doth undertake To guide the future as ... the past
81	1	The praises of my God shall still My heart and tongue employ
81	5	To Father, Son, and Holy Ghost, the God whom we adore
82	T,1	High in the Heavens, Eternal God
82	3	My God, how excellent thy grace
83	T,1	If Thou but Suffer God to Guide Thee
83	3	God never yet forsook at need the soul that trusted him
85	4	Henceforth thy going out and in God keep forever will
86	T,1	Our God, to Whom We Turn, When weary with illusion
87	T,1	God Moves in a Mysterious Way His wonders to perform
87	4	God is his own interpreter, And he will make it plain
88	T,1	God Moves in a Mysterious Way (same words as No. 87)
91	1	found abode Within the secret place of God
91	1	Shall with almighty God abide
91	2	I of the Lord my God will say, He is my refuge and my stay
91	2	To him for safety I will flee, My God ... my trust shall be
91	6	Because thy trust is God alone ... no evil shall ... come
94	T,1	When All Thy Mercies, O My God, My rising soul surveys
95	3	Rise, God, judge thou the earth in might
95	5	Thou in thy everlasting seat Remainest God alone
96	T,1-3	Whate'er My God Ordains Is Right
96	1	He is my God
97	T,1	God of Our Life, Through All the Circling Years
97	2	God of our past, our times are in thy hand, With us abide
97	3	God of the coming years, through paths unknown we follow
98	T,1	My God, I Thank Thee, Who Hast Made The earth so bright
99	T,1	O Love of God, How Strong and True, Eternal and yet ever new
99	2	O love of God, how deep and great, Far deeper than ... hate
99	2	love of God ... Far deeper than man's deepest hate
100	T,1	O My Soul, Bless God, the Father
101	2	love of God is broader Than the measure of man's mind (102-3)
104	1	Speak ye peace, thus saith our God
104	2	Oh, that warning cry obey, Now prepare for God a way
106	5	City of God, the bond are free
107	1	blessing in his hand, Christ our God to earth descendeth
109	3	Traveler, lo, the Prince of peace ... Son of God is come
110	1	mourns in lonely exile here Until the Son of God appear
111	2	And extol our God and King
111	3	Christ, to thee with God the Father, & O Holy Ghost to thee
112	3	Thine, O God, to give the power
117	2	God with man is now residing, Yonder shines the infant light
120	1	God and sinners reconciled
121	4	Glory to God in highest heaven
121	4	God ... Who unto men his son hath given
122	T,1	God Rest You Merry, Gentlemen, Let nothing you dismay
122	2	From God, our heavenly Father, A blessed angel came
122	2	How that in Bethlehem was born The Son of God by name

298	3	March we forth in the strength of God
298	4	All we can do is nothing worth Unless God blesses the deed
298	4	Vainly we hope for the harvest-tide Till God gives life
298	4	Till God gives life to the seed
299	T,1	Spirit of the Living God, In all thy plenitude of grace
299	3	prepare All the round earth her God to meet
300	T,1-3	Rise Up, O Men of God
300	4	As brothers of the Son of man Rise up, O men of God
302	1	To tell to all the world that God is light
302	2	Proclaim to every people, tongue & nation ... God ...is love
302	2	God, in whom they live and move, is love
305	2	See all the nations bending Before the God we love
309	4	Who art, with God the Father And Spirit, ever blest
310	1	God shall be all, and in all ever blest
312	2	They see God face to face
312	6	Jerusalem, Jerusalem, God grant that I may see ... joy
313	T,1	My God, I Love Thee
313	3	love ... Solely because thou art my God, And my eternal King
316	T,1	God of Earth and Sea and Heaven
319	1-4	O Lamb of God, I come
321	T,1	My God, Accept My Heart This Day, And make it always thine
324	3	No harm, while thou, my God, art near
326	3	O thou Son of God
328	2	The Lord is glorious and strong, Our God is very high
335	1	What a privilege to carry Everything to God in prayer
335	1	All because we do not carry Everything to God in prayer
336	T,1	O Thou by Whom we Come to God, The Life, the Truth, the Way
336	3	God of all grace, we come to thee With broken ... hearts
337	1	God hears thy sighs and counts thy tears
337	1	God shall lift up thy head
339	T,1	All My Hope on God Is Founded, He doth still my trust renew
339	1	God unknown, He alone Calls my heart to be his own
339	3	Still from man to God eternal Sacrifice of praise be done
340	2	Before they every knew The peace of God
340	2	peace of God that filled their hearts Brimful, & broke them
340	4	peace of God, it is no peace, But strife closed in the sod
343	1	But God is round about me, And can I be dismayed
344	1	Yet possessing every blessing, If our God our Father be
344	3	Spirit of our God, descending, Fill our hearts
345	6	The Father, Son, and Holy Ghost, One God for evermore
349	T,1	O For a Closer Walk With God, A calm and heavenly frame
349	5	So shall my walk be close with God, Calm and serene my frame
350	T,1	O for a Closer Walk With God (same words as no. 349)
351	T,1,R	Nearer, My God, to Thee, Nearer to thee
351	1	Still all my song would be, Nearer, my God, to thee
351	2	Yet in my dreams I'd be Nearer, my God, to thee
351	3	Angels to beckon me Nearer, my God, to thee
351	4	So by my woes to be Nearer, my God, to thee
351	5	Still all my song shall be, Nearer, my God, to thee
352	3	Till, sent from God, they mount to God again
354	T,1	Who Trusts in God, a Strong Abode
354	3	O God, renew with heavenly dew Our body, soul and spirit
355	T,1	Who Trusts in God, a Strong Abode (words same as no. 354)
357	T,1	Strong Son of God, Immortal Love
360	1	To one fixed trust my spirit clings, I know that God is good
361	T,1	Have Faith in God, my heart, Trust and be unafraid

361	1	God will fulfil in every part Each promise he has made
361	2	Have faith in God, my mind, Though oft thy light burns low
361	3	Have faith in God, my soul, His cross forever stands
363	T,1	A Mighty Fortress Is Our God, A bulwark never failing
363	3	We will not fear, for God hath willed His truth to triumph
365	3	And through the truth that comes from God Mankind ... free
366	T,1	God of Grace and God of Glory On thy people pour thy power
359	2	Workman of God, O lose not heart, But learn what God is like
359	2	The instinct that can tell That God is on the field
359	3	God is on the field when he Is most invisible
359	5	For right is right, since God is God
370	2	Content whatever lot I see, Since 'tis my God that leadeth
370	3	Since God through Jordan leadeth me
372	2	For I am thy God, and will still give thee aid
373	T,1	God Is My Strong Salvation, What foe have I to fear
373	2	What terror can confound me With God at my right hand
375	3	The crown awaits the conquest, Lead on, O God of might
377	2	Never God his own forsaketh
377	3	Though the hills & vales be riven God created with his hand
377	4	Upward gaze and happy be, God hath not forsaken thee
378	T,1	Lord of Our Life, and God of Our Salvation
378	1	Lord God almighty
379	T,1	Lord of Our Life, and God of Our Salvation (words of 378)
381	2	they bent Their zealous course to God
382	2	Like a mighty army Moves the Church of God
384	1	Strong in the strength that God supplies
384	1	God supplies Through his eternal Son
384	2	And take, to arm you for the fight, The panoply of God
387	2	One the hope our God inspires
387	3	One the conflict, one the peril, One the march in God begun
388	T,1	The Son of God Goes Forth to War, A kingly crown to gain
388	4	O God, to us may grace be given To follow in their train
389	T,1	O God of Bethel, by Whose Hand Thy people still are fed
389	2	God of our fathers, be the God Of their succeeding race
390	1	So longs my soul, O God, for thee, And thy refreshing grace
390	2	For thee, my God, the living God, My thirsty soul doth pine
390	3	praise of him who is thy God, Thy health's eternal spring
393	T,1	God Be in My Head, And in my understanding
393	1	God be in mine eyes, And in my looking
393	1	God be in my mouth, And in my speaking
393	1	God be in my heart, And in my thinking
393	1	God be in my heart, And in my thinking
393	1	God be at mine end, And at my departing
396	T,1	Fill Thou My Life, O Lord my God, In every part with praise
401	T,1	Teach Me, My God and King, In all things thee to see
401	5	that which God doth touch and own cannot for less be told
403	2	Where the many work together, they with God himself abide
409	2	They who work without complaining Do the holy will of God
410	1	Where pity dwells, the peace of God is there
411	T,1	Lord God of Hosts, Whose Purpose
411	2	Strong Son of God, whose work was his that sent thee
411	2	And make us one in thee with God the Lord
411	3	Light for the path of life, and God brought near
411	4	Lord God, whose grace has called us to thy service
413	T,1	Son of God, Eternal Savior, Source of life and truth & grace
417	2	True hearts will leap at the trumpet of God

461	1	God, our Maker, doth provide For our wants to be supplied
461	3	For the Lord our God shall come And shall take his harvest
462	1	God, our Maker, doth provide For our wants to be supplied
462	3	These to thee, our God, we owe
463	T,1	Praise, O Praise Our God and King, Hymns of adoration sing
464	T,1	Praise to God, Immortal Praise
464	3	All to thee, our God, we owe
468	T,1	God of the Living, in Whose eyes
469	4	O happy they in God who rest
470	T,1	God of the Prophets, bless the prophets' sons
473	T,1	O Lord, Almighty God, Thy Works Both great and wondrous be
474	T,1	O Lord, Almighty God, Thy Works (same words as no. 473)
477	3	Our God, our Strength, our King, our Tower
477	4	Accept, O God, this earthly shrine
478	R	All things wise and wonderful, The Lord God made them all
480	3	The same great God that hears my prayers, Heard his
481	T,1	I Sing a Song of the Saints of God
481	1	saints of God Patient and brave and true
481	1	They were all of them saints of God
481	1	saints ... and I mean, God helping, to be one too
481	3	For the saints of God are just folk like me
484	3	God bless the men and women Who serve him over-sea
484	3	God raise up more to help them To set the nations free
485	3	though the wrong seems oft so strong, God is the ruler yet
485	3	God reigns, let the earth be glad
487	T,1	Praise Our God Above For his boundless love
487	1	Though our work is hard, God gives us reward
488	3	And God sent us salvation That blessed Christmas morn
491	T,1	O God of Youth, Whose Spirit in our hearts is stirring
492	T,1	O Gracious God, Whose Constant Care
481	1	And I mean, God helping, to be one too
493	3	prayer That God, in sweet forgiveness' name ... spare
493	3	God, in sweet forgiveness' name, Should understand and spare
494	1	let thy plan Reveal the life that God would give to man
496	2	And this be our motto, In God is our trust
498	2	O God, thou star of dawning day
499	T,1,2	Lo, God Is Here
500	T,1	Lord God of Morning and of Night
500	2	Praise God, our Maker and our Friend
501	2	Let this day praise thee, O Lord God
502	2	All hail to him, the mighty God, for aye
503	2	Gracious God, I come before thee
506	2	God hath tended With his care thy helpless hours
509	3	O God, our Light, to thee we bow
514	1	Praise God from whom all blessings flow
515	1	Praise God from whom all blessings flow
528	T,1	Create in Me a Clean Heart, O God
529	T,1	The Sacrifices of God are a broken spirit
529	1	A broken and a contrite heart, O God, thou wilt not despise
530	T,1	O Thou by Whom We Come to God, The Life, the Truth, the Way
531	1	O God, make clean our hearts within us
532	1	Son of God, we beseech thee to hear us
533	1	O God, make clean our hearts within us
538	1	The rest, O God, is in thy hand
543	T,1	God Be in My Head, and in my understanding
543	1	God be in mine eyes and in my looking

God's

424	T,1	Hail the Glorious Golden City, Pictured by the seers of old
457	1	One more the glad earth yields Her golden wealth
457	1	golden wealth of ripening grain And breath of clover fields
467	4	Where now he ploweth, wave with golden grain
486	T,1	Golden Breaks the Dawn
492	1	whose constant care Supplies our golden days
579	1	For the valley's golden yield ... fruits of tree and field

gone

1	4	A thousand ages in thy sight Are like an evening gone
77	3	When disappointment, grief, and fear are gone
122	1	To save us all from Satan's power When we were gone astray
215	3	o'er crag and torrent, till The night is gone
259	3	And look down from supernal heights On all the by-gone time
287	4	The feast, though not the love is past and gone
351	2	Though like the wanderer, The sun gone down

good

4	4	For why, the Lord our God is good
23	3	praise him still Through good and ill, Who ever lives
33	2	For from thee come all things good
53	1	On God, Our Maker, calling ... the Giver good
65	2	Earth and sea cry, God is good
68	2	And then pronounced them good
69	1	Heaven & earth, awake & sing, God is good and therefore King
69	2	All who work & all who wait, Sing, The Lord is good & great
74	2	Mixture strange of good and ill
79	6	Good Shepherd may I sing thy praise Within thy house forever
92	3	Thy providence turns all to good
121	1	To bear good news to every home
124	1	It is Jesus, good folk of the village
125	T,1-3	Good Christian Men, Rejoice, With heart and soul and voice
127	2	Behold, I bring good tidings of a Savior's birth
129	1	Peace on the earth, good will to men
140	2	Good Christian, fear
146	6	Good will henceforth from heaven to men Begin & never cease
155	3	Who in all good delightest, Thou good and gracious King
171	3	He died that we may be forgiven, He died to make us good
184	T,1	Good Christian Men Rejoice and Sing
212	2	Thou must work all good within us
225	3	How good to those who seek
236	3	Freshening time with truth and good
245	4	Separate from sin, I would Choose & cherish all things good
276	2	And warm and bright and good to all
290	2	To them that seek thee, thou art good
294	3	Inspire thy heralds of good news To live thy life divine
297	2	Yields harvests rich in lasting good
308	1	Source & giver of all good, Lord, we praise, we worship thee
332	2	Good that we have left undone
333	2	Lead us, good Shepherd
333	3	Give us thy good, and save us from our evil, Infinite Spirit
339	1	Only good and only true
347	2	Help us, through good report & ill, Our daily cross to bear
367	T,1	Fight the Good Fight with all thy might
367	2	Run the straight race through God's good grace
371	2	He will make good his right To be a pilgrim

406	2	And prove thy good and perfect will
409	1	Thou has taught us toil is good
410	2	example Of him whose holy work was doing good
411	3	O Prince of peace, thou bringer of good tidings
411	4	How good thy thoughts toward us, how great their sum
412	3	Give us a conscience bold and good, Give us a purpose true
420	3	where the sun that shineth is God's grace for human good
432	4	For hearts aflame to serve thy destined good
436	2	From sleep and from damnation, Deliver us, good Lord
440	1,4	And crown thy good with brotherhood From sea to shining sea
441	1	decide In the strife of truth with falsehood, For the good
441	1	For the good or evil side
441	2	Time makes ancient good uncouth
449	3	Give us the peace of vision clear To see our brother's good
449	3	our brother's good our own
453	4	Ring in the common love of good
456	2	And clearer sounds the angel hymn, Good will to men on earth
457	2	We know who giveth all the good That doth our cup o'erbrim
460	T,1	We Plow the Fields and Scatter The good seed on the land
460	R	All good gifts around us Are sent from heaven above
460	3	We thank thee, then, O Father, For all things bright & good
479	2	To be to others kind and good
481	2	followed ... The whole of their good lives long
532	T,1	Have Mercy Upon Us, Good Lord, deliver us
532	1	Spare us, good Lord.
554	1	and on earth peace, good will towards men
565	3	be thankful unto him, and speak good of his name
570	8	He hath filled the hungry with good things

goodly

| 264 | 2 | We mark her goodly battlements, And her foundations strong |
| 559 | 4 | the goodly fellowship of the prophets praise thee |

goodness

2	1	O thank him for his goodness
7	2	Thy clouds which are fountains of goodness and love
15	3	Surely his goodness and mercy here daily attend thee
68	2	I sing the goodness of the Lord
68	2	goodness of the Lord, That filled the earth with food
76	4	His goodness stands approved Down to the present day
79	1	Whose goodness faileth never
79	6	so through all the length of days thy goodness faileth never
82	1	Thy goodness in full glory shines
84	5	Goodness and mercy all my life Shall surely follow me
161	2	The faith we keep in goodness
249	5	Praise we the goodness that doth crown our days
277	1	Now enfold them in thy goodness
433	3	Thy bounteous goodness nourish us in peace
454	4	Thy goodness all our hopes shall raise
467	3	Nought shall affright us, on thy goodness leaning

goods

| 363 | 4 | Let goods and kindred go, This mortal life also |

gory

| 388 | 3 | They met the tyrant's brandished steel, The lion's gory mane |

293	1	While all around him waves the golden grain
440	T,1	O Beautiful for Spacious Skies, For amber waves of grain
457	1	golden wealth of ripening grain And breath of clover fields
458	3	Feeding, day and night, the grain
460	1	he sends the snow in winter, The warmth to swell the grain
461	2	Lord of harvest, grant that we Wholesome grain & pure may be
464	2	Yellow sheaves of ripened grain
467	4	Where now he ploweth, wave with golden grain
487	1	Spring wind, summer rain, Then the harvest grain

grand
427	T,1	We Are Living, We Are Dwelling In a grand and aweful time

grandeur
67	3	Thy grandeur in the march of night

grant
51	3	Grant to little children Visions bright of thee
60	2	Grant us thy peace upon our homeward way
60	3	Grant us thy peace, Lord, through the coming night
60	4	Grant us thy peace throughout our earthly life
89	5	Grant us thy truth to make us free
148	3	Thou, his vanquisher before, Grant we may not faint nor fail
207	4	O grant to us the grace we find in thee
256	5	Lord, grant us all aright to learn The wisdom it imparts
277	1	Grant to them thy dearest blessing
277	3	Grant to us a deep compassion For thy children everywhere
292	3	And grant us nevermore to part with thee
312	6	Jerusalem, Jerusalem, God grant that I may see ... joy
336	2	O grant us power to pray
346	4	And grant us in thy love To sing the songs of victory
361	4	Grant me no resting place Until I rest ... The captive
366	1	Grant us wisdom ... courage, For the facing of his hour
366	2	Grant us wisdom ... courage For the living of these days
366	3	Grant us wisdom ... courage, Lest we miss thy kingdom's goal
366	4	Grant us wisdom ... courage, That we fail not man nor thee
366	5	Grant us wisdom ... courage, Serving thee whom we adore
374	3	Grant that I may never Fail thy hand to see
374	3	Grant that I may ever Cast my care on thee
378	2	Grant us thy peace, Lord
378	4	Grant us thy help til backward they are driven
378	4	Grant them thy truth, that they may be forgiven
378	4	Grant peace on earth
407	2	Above all boons, I pray, Grant me thy voice to hear
411	1	Grant us to march among thy faithful legions
413	4	grant our hope's fruition, Here on earth thy will be done
461	2	Lord of harvest, grant that we Wholesome grain & pure may be
465	3	Grant them the joy which brightens earthly sorrow
465	3	Grant them the peace which calms all earthly strife
475	2	Grant that all we, who here today ... this foundation lay
492	3	grant us power That worthy thoughts in deeds may flower
494	3	O grant enduring worth Until the heavenly kingdom comes
526	1	O grant us peace, almighty Lord
531	1	And grant us thy salvation
532	1	Grant us thy peace
533	1	O Lord, show thy mercy upon us, and grant us thy salvation

| 555 | 1 | grant us thy peace |
| 556 | 1 | grant us thy peace |

granted
15	2	Hast thou not seen How thy desires e'er have been Granted
15	2	desires ... Granted in what he ordaineth
413	2	Freely have thy gifts been granted

grants
| 200 | 3 | To whom he manifests his love, And grants his name to know |

grapes
| 443 | 1 | He is trampling out the vintage where the grapes of wrath |
| 443 | 1 | where the grapes of wrath are stored |

grasp
| 287 | 1 | Here grasp with firmer hand the eternal grace |
| 557 | 1 | Here grasp with firmer hand eternal grace |

grass
38	2	Like the first dewfall On the first grass
458	4	Praise him for his garden root, Meadow grass & orchard fruit
459	1	He makes the grass the mountains crown
485	2	In the rustling grass I hear him pass

grassy
| 381 | 2 | Whether beneath was flinty rock Or yielding grassy sod |

grateful
20	3	That men may hear the grateful song My voice unwearied raises
22	1	In grateful devotion our tribute we bring
66	R	Lord of all ... we raise This our hymn of grateful praise
75	1	Wake, my soul, awake & sing, Now thy grateful praises bring
316	3	Now in grateful dedication Our allegiance we would own
433	1	Our grateful songs before thy throne arise
454	3	With grateful hearts the past we own
462	3	And for these our souls shall raise Grateful vows
462	3	Grateful vows and solemn praise
464	2	Lord, for these, our souls shall raise Grateful vows
464	2	Grateful vows and solemn praise
469	3	Shall rise our psalm of grateful trust
505	1	And pay a grateful song of praise To heaven's almighty King
537	1	And hence with grateful hearts today

gratefully
| 6 | 1 | O gratefully sing his power and his love |
| 471 | T,1 | Lord of True Light, We Gratefully Adore Thee |

gratitude
| 305 | 2 | And thousand hearts ascending In gratitude above |
| 410 | 2 | Each loving life a psalm of gratitude |

grave
99	5	bless and save E'en in the darkness of the grave
125	3	Now ye need not fear the grave
182	2	Where thy victory, O grave

182	4	Ours the cross, the grave, the skies
183	3	He who slumbered in the grave Is exalted now to save
187	2	Who endured the cross and grave ... Sinners to redeem & save
189	2	The grave has lost its triumph And death has lost its sting
199	3	Crown him the Lord of life, Who triumphed o'er the grave
209	4	Where is death's sting, where, grave, thy victory
388	2	martyr first, whose eagle eye Could pierce beyond the grave
468	4	gave Thy Son to fill a human grave

graven

| 269 | 2 | Dear as the apple of thine eye, And graven on thy hand |

graves

| 438 | 3 | The God they trusted guards their graves |

gray

42	1	Black turns to gray, Bird-song the valley fills
42	1	Mists fold away, Gray wakes to green again
106	3	On your far hills, long cold and gray, Has dawned

great

3	3	in all, Great and small, Seek to do ... what thou lovest
7	1	Almighty, victorious, thy great name we praise
7	3	To all, life thou givest to both great and small
7	4	Great Father of glory, pure Father of light
22	3	To thee, our great Redeemer, forever be praise
34	2	See how the giant sun soars up, Great lord of years and days
69	2	All who work & all who wait, Sing, The Lord is good & great
72	1	heavens ... Their great Original proclaim
73	4	Praise the great and mighty Lord
75	4	Lord, great wonders workest thou
93	T,1	Guide Me, O Thou Great Jehovah
95	5	For great thou art
95	5	wonders great By thy strong hand are done
99	2	O love of God, how deep and great, Far deeper than ... hate
105	T,1	Hail to the Lord's Anointed, Great David's greater Son
106	2	And makes your wastes his great highway
108	1	Hallelujah, Lo, great and small, We answer all
108	3	No vision ever brought ... such great glory
108	3	No ear hath ever caught Such great glory
113	4	At thy great name exalted now All knees must bend
115	2	And furnished for so great a guest
115	3	thou art ... Our refuge and our great reward
117	3	Seek the great Desire of nations
121	1	Glad tidings of great joy I bring
123	3	Here let all, Great and small, Kneel in awe and wonder
134	4	We hear the Christmas angels The great glad tidings tell
141	2	And to the earth it gave great light
146	2	Glad tidings of great joy I bring To you and all mankind
161	2	Our will to dare great things for God
161	3	On us let now the healing Of his great Spirit fall
197	2	All the heavenly orders, In their great array
198	3	One Lord, in one great name Unite us all who own thee
206	2	The great congregation his triumph shall sing
219	T,1	O Thou Great Friend to all the sons of men
223	T,1	O for a Thousand Tongues to Sing My great Redeemer's praise

| 423 | 2 | From paths where hide the lures of greed |
| 426 | 1 | Whom shall I send to loosen The bonds of shame and greed |

green

42	1	Mists fold away, Gray wakes to green again
84	1	He makes me down to lie In pastures green
171	T,1	There Is a Green Hill Far Away, Without a city wall
172	T,1	There Is a Green Hill Far Away (same words as No. 171)
333	2	To pastures green beside the peaceful waters
343	3	Green pastures are before me, Which yet I have not seen
368	2	Not forever in green pastures Do we ask our way to be
458	2	Praise him for his budding green, April's resurrection scene
481	1	And one was a shepherdess on the green
487	2	He makes green things grow, Ripens what we sow

greet

104	2	And the hills bow down to greet him
132	4	Yea, Lord, we greet thee, born this happy morning
140	1	Whom angels greet with anthems sweet
156	2	And silently thy promised advent greet
182	5	Thee we greet triumphant now ... Hail, the Resurrection thou
207	T,1	I Greet Thee, Who My Sure Redeemer Art
304	2	and eager hearts awoke to greet the day

greets

| 193 | 2 | Lovingly he greets thee, Scatters fear and gloom |

grief

43	3	Pierce the gloom of sin and grief
77	1	Bear patiently the cross of grief or pain
77	3	When disappointment, grief, and fear are gone
169	5	Never was love, dear King, Never was grief like thine
170	1	With grief and shame weighed down
174	1	King of grief, I watch with thee
178	2	Heeds not his Master's grief and tears
275	3	One with the grief that trembleth into prayer
331	3	Ever in joy or grief, My Lord, for thee
347	2	Our brethren's grief to share
398	5	Who by this sign didst conquer grief and pain
423	3	From woman's grief, man's burdened toil
453	3	Ring out the grief that saps the mind

griefs

96	2	His hand can turn my griefs away
158	1	Turn not from his griefs away
335	1	All our sins and griefs to bear
348	3	While life's dark maze I tread, And griefs around me spread
351	4	Out of my stony griefs Bethel I'll raise
445	2	And sharing not our griefs, no joy can share

grieve

| 123 | 2 | Brethren, come, from all doth grieve you You are freed |

grieving

| 377 | 4 | Though in chains thou now art grieving |

grim
363   3   The prince of darkness grim, We tremble not for him

groan
113   2   travail ... That made the whole creation groan

groaning
427   1   Hark, what soundeth is creation's Groaning
427   1   Groaning for the latter day

groans
424   2   All our joys and all our groans Help to rear its shining

grope
53   3   And grope in faithless strife
376   2   Unhelped by thee, in error's maze we grope

groping
219   2   light Which guides the nations groping on their way

ground
68   2   If I survey the ground I tread or gaze upon the sky
146   1   All seated on the ground
364   T,1   Christian, Dost Thou See Them On the holy ground
399   4   from the ground ... blossoms red Life that shall endless be
402   1   And every place is hallowed ground
459   2   descend and clothe the ground
468   3   Not spilt like water on the ground

grow
74   3   Teach us more of human pity, That we in thine image grow
78   2   can an all-creating arm Grow weary or decay
79   2   where the verdant pastures grow With food celestial feedeth
167   VI-2   While we grow in holiness, Hear us, holy Jesus
209   2   Earth's joys grow dim, its glories pass away
259   2   'Twas but the dawning yet to grow Into the perfect day
259   2   And grow it shall, our glorious sun More fervid rays afford
284   4   when these failing lips grow dumb, And mind and memory flee
357   5   A beam in darkness, let it grow
357   6   Let knowledge grow from more to more
401   3   Which with this tincture, For thy sake, Will not grow bright
401   3   Will not grow bright and clean
432   4   Then, for thy grace to grow in brotherhood
459   1   And corn in valleys grow
466   2   And knowing thee may grow in grace
467   2   And we grow quiet, folded in thy peace
479   2   In all we do in work or play To grow more loving every day
487   2   He makes green things grow, Ripens what we sow

groweth
112   2   Like the sheltering tree that groweth, Comes the life

growing
78   6   With growing ardor onward move ... growing brightness shine

guests
286	1	Nay, let us be thy guests, the feast is thine

guidance
13	1	Laws which never shall be broken for their guidance
13	1	laws ... For their guidance he hath made
144	3	Let not our slothful hearts refuse The guidance of thy light
144	3	The guidance of thy light to use

guide
21	2	Beside us to guide us, our God with us joining
22	2	Through life's storm and tempest our guide hast thou been
29	2	And keep us in his grace, And guide us when perplexed
39	4	To guide whate'er we nobly do, With love all envy to subdue
61	1	By his counsels guide, uphold you
76	2	hand which bears all nature up Shall guide his children well
77	2	thy God doth undertake To guide the future as ... the past
79	4	Thy cross before to guide me
83	T,1	If Thou but Suffer God to Guide Thee
93	T,1	Guide Me, O Thou Great Jehovah
97	2	Be thou our guide
98	3	So that earth's bliss may be our guide, And not our chain
114	4	Thy Holy Spirit guide us on Until the glorious crown be won
119	4	need no star to guide, Where no clouds thy glory hide
126	1,5	Guide where our infant Redeemer is laid
143	R	Guide us to thy perfect light
150	5	For us he sent his Spirit here To guide,
150	5	To guide, to strengthen, and to cheer
208	1	To shame and guide this life of mine
209	3	Who like thyself my guide and stay can be
210	1	Safe into the haven guide, O receive my soul at last
218	1	Nor wander from the pathway If thou wilt be my guide
229	3	Be thou my counsellor, My pattern and my guide
231	3	Where thou art guide no ill can come
238	1	Be thou our guardian, thou our guide
256	2	Our guide & chart, wherein we read Of realms beyond the sky
275	1	Guide of the nations
276	3	dwell thou ... to guide and bless
277	2	Give to all who teach and guide them Wisdom and humility
301	1	Be her savior, lord, and guide
301	2	May she guide the poor and blind
333	2	Tenderest guide, in ways of cheerful duty, Lead us
343	2	Wherever he may guide me, No want shall turn me back
344	1	Guard us, guide us, keep us, feed us
348	3	Be thou my guide, Bid darkness turn to day
354	2	Thy rod and staff shall keep us safe, And guide our steps
354	2	And guide our steps forever
367	3	Cast care aside, lean on thy guide
368	4	In our wanderings be our guide
381	2	I have a guide, and in his steps When travelers have trod
389	3	Our wandering footsteps guide
418	2	And guide them in the homeward way
433	2	Be thou our ruler, guardian, guide, and stay
568	12	and to guide our feet into the way of peace
575	3	Where thou art guide no ill can come

had

127	3	ran To see the wonder God had wrought for man
128	1	Snow had fallen, snow on snow
146	2	Fear not, said he, for mighty dread had seized
146	2	mighty dread Had seized their troubled mind
171	2	We may not know, we cannot tell What pains he had to bear
204	2	When he had purged our stains, he took his seat above
315	2	Our hearts are filled with sadness, And we had lost our way
483	2	I wish that his hands had been placed on my head
483	2	That his arm had been thrown around me
493	2	He had no friend to plead his cause
493	3	had no curse nor vengeful cry For those who broke his bones

hadst

559	9	When thou hadst overcome the sharpness of death

hail

105	T,1	Hail to the Lord's Anointed, Great David's greater Son
105	1	Hail, in the time appointed, His reign on earth begun
120	2	Veiled in flesh the God-head see, Hail the incarnate Deity
120	3	Hail the heaven-born Prince of peace
120	3	Hail the Sun of righteousness
123	3	Hail the star That from far Bright with hope is burning
182	5	Hail the Lord of earth and heaven
182	5	Thee we greet triumphant now ... Hail, the Resurrection thou
192	2	His own, All hail, and, hearing, May raise the victor-strain
195	T,1	All Hail the Power of Jesus' Name, Let angels prostrate fall
195	3	Hail him who saves you by his grace
196	T,1	All Hail the Power of Jesus' Name (R differs from no. 195)
199	1	And hail him as thy matchless King Through all eternity
199	4	All hail, Redeemer, hail, For thou hast died for me
201	5	Hail, Christ the Lord, thy people pray
205	T,1	Hail the Day That Sees Him Rise
424	T,1	Hail the Glorious Golden City, Pictured by the seers of old
502	2	All hail to him, the mighty God, for aye
506	2	Gladly hail the sun returning
581	T,1	All Hail the Power of Jesus' Name (as no. 195 with descant)

hailed

119	1	As with joy they hailed its light
488	2	Rang out the angel chorus That hailed our Savior's birth
496	1	What so proudly we hailed at the twilight's last gleaming

half

131	1,2	When half spent was the night

hall

125	3	Calls you one & calls you all, To gain his everlasting hall
158	2	See him at the judgment hall

hallelujah

17	1	Be magnified eternally, Hallelujah, Hallelujah
17	1,2	Hallelujah, Hallelujah
108	1	Hallelujah, Lo, great and small, We answer all
108	2	Hallelujah, We haste along, An eager throng
443	R	Glory, glory, Hallelujah ... His truth is marching on

hallow

36	3	If on our daily course our mind Be set to hallow all we find
247	3	Lo, the apostolic train Joins thy sacred name to hallow
270	3	His truth doth hallow the temple
324	2	Hallow each thought, let all within Be clean

hallowed

46	1	We gather in these hallowed walls
252	1	We praise thee for the radiance That from the hallowed page
268	3	Hallowed be thy name forever, Heal our differences of old
402	1	And every place is hallowed ground
509	1	We gather in these hallowed walls

hallows

413	1	Son of man, whose birth incarnate Hallows all our human race

halls

309	2	They stand, those halls of Zion, All jubilant with song

hand

23	T,1	Ye Holy Angels Bright, Who wait at God's right hand
26	1	Raise your voice and rejoice In the bounty of his hand
26	2	Standing fast to the last, By his hand our lives are stayed
70	5	His full hand supplies their need
72	1	And publishes to every land the work of an almighty hand
72	3	singing ... The hand that made us is divine
74	2	Creature that thy hand hath made
74	3	Thou hast given man dominion o'er the wonders of thy hand
75	3	Hill & vale & fruited land, All things living show his hand
76	2	hand which bears all nature up Shall guide his children well
85	3	the Lord thy shade On thy right hand doth stay
92	4	Thy hand in all things I behold, and all things in thy hand
93	1	Hold me with thy powerful hand
95	5	wonders great By thy strong hand are done
96	2	His hand can turn my griefs away
97	1	In all the past ... our hopes & fears, Thy hand we see
97	2	God of our past, our times are in thy hand, With us abide
107	1	blessing in his hand, Christ our God to earth descendeth
154	3	Thy hand the victory won
209	4	I fear no foe, with thee at hand to bless
269	2	Dear as the apple of thine eye, And graven on thy hand
286	2	Faith still receives the cup as from thy hand
287	1	Here grasp with firmer hand the eternal grace
297	1	And where the higher gain appears, We trace ... thy hand
297	1	We trace the working of thy hand
308	3	strong in heart and hand and brain
312	3	There David stands with harp in hand As master of the choir
324	4	O let thy hand support me still
329	2	O Jesus, thou art knocking, And lo, that hand is scarred
337	2	How wise, how strong his hand
339	2	Love doth stand At his hand, Joy doth wait on his command
346	2	Who steadfast stand at God's right hand
354	3	Until we stand at thy right hand Through Jesus' saving merit
356	1	Imprison me within thine arms, And strong shall be my hand
358	3	Nothing in my hand I bring, Simply to thy cross I cling
362	3	'Tis his own hand presents the prize To thine aspiring eye

29	T,1	Now Thank We All Our God With heart and hands and voices
66	6	For thy Church that evermore Lifteth holy hands above
78	3	him thou canst not see, nor trace the working of his hands
82	2	Wise are the wonders of thy hands
168	4	And, to thy Father's hands thy soul commending
177	3	See, from his head, his hands, his feet, Sorrow and love
199	2	Crown him the Lord of love, Behold his hands and side
217	2	Whose strong hands were skilled at the plane and the lathe
217	3	Your hands swift to welcome your arms to embrace
264	4	A house not made with hands
270	2	Surely in temples made with hands, God ... is not dwelling
303	1	thanks ... That work awaits our hands and feet
325	4	O wounded hands of Jesus, build In us thy new creation
358	2	Not the labors of my hands Can fulfill thy law's demands
407	3	Clean hands in holy worship raise
404	2	Take my hands and let them move At the impulse of thy love
414	3	Join hands, then, brothers of the faith
424	3	Oft with bleeding hands and tears
475	1	To dwell in temples made with hands
477	4	Accept the work our hands have wrought
483	2	I wish that his hands had been placed on my head
490	2	But take as from thy hands our tasks And glorify them all
494	3	may our hands Ne'er falter when the dream is in our hearts
527	T,1	Enrich, Lord, Heart, Mouth, Hands in Me
538	T,1	Bless Thou the Gifts our hands have brought
562	5	and his hands prepared the dry land

hangs

164	2	Ah, look how patiently he hangs
210	2	Other refuge have I none, Hangs my helpless soul on thee

happy

8	3	Well-spring of the joy of living, Ocean depth of happy rest
8	4	Mortals, join the happy chorus Which the morning stars began
69	3	let children's happy hearts In this worship bear their parts
127	T,1	Christians, Awake, Salute the Happy Morn
132	4	Yea, Lord, we greet thee, born this happy morning
260	4	O happy ones and holy, Lord, give us grace that we
274	2	Happy, who in thy house reside, Where thee they ever praise
274	2	Happy, whose strength in thee doth hide
312	T,1	Jerusalem, My Happy Home, When shall I come to thee
312	2	Most happy is their case
340	1	Such happy, simple fisher-folk, Before the Lord came down
377	4	Upward gaze and happy be, God hath not forsaken thee
382	4	Onward, then, ye people, Join our happy throng
453	2	Ring, happy bells, across the snow
457	2	winging thoughts, and happy moods Of love and joy and prayer
458	5	Praise for happy dreams of birth Brooding in the quiet earth
469	4	O happy they in God who rest

harbinger

95	1	Before him righteousness shall go, His royal harbinger

hard

128	1	Earth stood hard as iron, Water like a stone
487	1	Though our work is hard, God gives us reward

hardens

494	2	upon the solid rock We set the dream that hardens into deed

hark

104	2	Hark, the voice of one that crieth in the desert far & near
106	1	River and mountain-spring, Hark to the advent voice
120	T,1,R	Hark, The Herald Angels Sing, Glory to the new-born King
123	2	Hark, a voice from yonder manger, Soft and sweet
174	3	Hark, that cry that peals aloud
175	1	Hark, all the tribes hosanna cry
183	1	Hark, the angels shout for joy, Singing evermore on high
199	1	Hark, how the heavenly anthem drowns All music but its own
203	4	Hark, those bursts of acclamation
203	4	Hark, those loud triumphant chords
247	2	Hark, the glad celestial hymn Angel choirs above are raising
427	1	Hark, the waking up of nations, Hosts advancing to the fray
427	1	Hark, what soundeth is creation's Groaning

harm

2	1	To us no harm shall now come nigh
59	2	In soul and body, thou from harm defend us
60	3	from harm and danger keep thy children free
91	5	No deadly shaft by day shall harm
177	2	All the vain things that charm me most
324	3	No harm, while thou, my God, art near
360	4	No harm from him can come to me On ocean or on shore
374	2	With forbidden pleasures Would this vain world charm
374	2	Or its sordid treasures Spread to work me harm

harmony

66	3	For the mystic harmony Linking sense to sound and sight
312	5	With blessed saints, whose harmony In every street doth ring

harp

108	3	With harp and cymbal's clearest tone
312	3	There David stands with harp in hand As master of the choir

harps

3	2	God himself is with us, Hear the harps resounding
24	1	Let harps and cymbals now unite
129	1	To touch their harps of gold
311	2	What ringing of a thousand harps Bespeaks the triumph nigh

harshness

207	4	No harshness hast thou and no bitterness

hart

390	T,1	As Pants the Hart for cooling streams

harvest

261	2	One working band, one harvest song, One King omnipotent
293	1	Who dares stand idle on the harvest plain
460	3	seed-time and the harvest, Our life, our health, our food
461	1	Raise the song of harvest home
461	1	Come to God's own temple, come, Raise the song of harvest

461	2	Lord of harvest, grant that we Wholesome grain & pure may be
461	3	For the Lord our God shall come And shall take his harvest
461	3	And shall take his harvest home
461	4	Even so, Lord, quickly come To thy final harvest home
461	4	Raise the glorious harvest home
462	1,3	Raise the song of harvest home
463	3	Praise him for our harvest store
487	1	Spring wind, summer rain, Then the harvest grain
487	2	Through him we are strong, Sing our harvest song
579	T,1	Summer Ended, Harvest O'er, Lord, to thee our song we pour
579	2	Seed-time, harvest, cold, and heat shall their yearly round

harvests

297	2	And seed laid deep in sacred soil Yields harvests
297	2	Yields harvests rich in lasting good
439	1	Not alone for bounteous harvests Lift we up our hearts

haste

76	3	Haste to your heavenly Father's throne
108	2	Hallelujah, We haste along, An eager throng
140	R	Haste, haste to bring him laud, The babe, the son of Mary
152	1	Haste, let us lay our gifts before the King
302	T,1	O Zion, Haste, Thy Mission High Fulfilling
423	5	O Master, from the mountain side, Make haste to heal
423	5	Make haste to heal these hearts of pain

hasten

123	3	Come, then, let us hasten yonder
218	2	O speak to reassure me, To hasten or control
406	4	And hasten to thy glorious day

hastening

77	3	hour is hastening on When we shall be forever with the Lord
129	4	For lo, the days are hastening, on By prophet bards foretold
446	4	Through the thick darkness thy kingdom is hastening

hastens

| 21 | 1 | He chastens and hastens his will to make known |

hate

99	2	O love of God, how deep and great, Far deeper than ... hate
99	2	love of God ... Far deeper than man's deepest hate
163	1	That man to judge thee hath in hate pretended
237	3	And cleanse them of their hate and strife
294	2	Till greed and hate shall cease
325	3	Till in the night of hate and war We perish as we lose thee
349	3	I hate the sins that made thee mourn And drove thee
363	1	And armed with cruel hate, On earth is not his equal
434	4	All truth to love, all wrong to hate
568	4	and from the hand of all that hate us

hatred

| 275 | 3 | We would be one in hatred of all wrong |
| 425 | 3 | They are slaves who will not choose Hatred, scoffing & abuse |

haughty
303   4   And still with haughty foes must cope

hauled
340   3   Peter, who hauled the teeming net, Head down was crucified

haunt
444   4   That war may haunt the earth no more And desolation cease

haunted
451   2   Would man but wake from out his haunted sleep

haunts
423   2   In haunts of wretchedness and need

haven
210   1   Safe into the haven guide, O receive my soul at last

having
292   1   And having with us him that pleads above
384   2   That, having all things done, And all your conflicts past

hay
137   1   The little Lord Jesus, asleep on the hay
152   1   There in a manger on the hay reclining

head
  84   4   My head thou dost with oil anoint, And my cup overflows
  87   2   clouds ... shall break In blessings on your head
126   2   Low lies his head with the beasts of the stall
136   3   God's bright star, o'er his head, Wise men three to him led
137   1   The little Lord Jesus laid down his sweet head
157   1,5   All the light of sacred story Gathers round its head sublime
170   T,1   O Sacred Head, Now Wounded
175   4   Bow thy meek head to mortal pain
177   3   See, from his head, his hands, his feet, Sorrow and love
181   3   All glory to our risen Head
182   4   Following our exalted Head
200   T,1   The Head That Once Was Crowned With Thorns
202   2   And praises throng to crown his head
210   2   Cover my defenseless head With the shadow of thy wing
263   1   Christ the head and cornerstone
286   4   one in thee, Who art one Savior and one living Head
337   1   God shall lift up thy head
340   3   Peter, who hauled the teeming net, Head down was crucified
377   T,1   Lift Thy Head, O Zion, Weeping, Still the Lord thy Father is
392   +2   O Motherland, we pledge to thee Head, heart, and hand
392   +2   Head, heart, and hand through the years to be
393   T,1   God Be in My Head, And in my understanding
399   4   O Cross that liftest up my head
413   1   Thou, our head, who, throned in glory
451   1   Yet thou, her child, whose head is crowned with flame
472   4   O Christ, the Church's head, Who for us all has bled
483   2   I wish that his hands had been placed on my head
543   T,1   God Be in My Head, and in my understanding

headed
478   2   The purple-headed mountain, The river running by

headland
431   3   On dune and headland sinks the fire

heads
114   T,1   Lift Up Your Heads, Ye Mighty Gates
205   2   Lift your heads, eternal gates

heal
55   6   And in thy mercy heal us all
198   3   To heal its ancient wrong, Come, Prince of peace, and reign
245   1   with words that help and heal Would thy life in mine reveal
268   3   Hallowed be thy name forever, Heal our differences of old
295   1   Sinsick and sorrow-worn, Whom Christ doth heal
328   2   Thy sicknesses to heal
398   2   To heal earth's wounds and end her bitter strife
413   1   Heal our wrongs, and help our need
423   5   O Master, from the mountain side, Make haste to heal
423   5   Make haste to heal these hearts of pain
442   2   And judge, that thou may'st heal us

healed
16   1   Ransomed, healed, restored, forgiven

healing
20   1   With healing balm my soul he fills
93   2   fountain, Whence the healing stream doth flow
120   3   Risen with healing in his wings
152   4   We would see Jesus, in his work of healing
161   3   On us let now the healing Of his great Spirit fall
167   V-3   Where the healing waters flow, Hear us, holy Jesus
210   3   Let the healing streams abound, Make and keep me pure within
230   5   The healing of his seamless dress Is by our beds of pain
281   2   'Tis thy wounds our healing give
319   3   Sight, riches, healing of the mind
435   1   Solace all its wide dominion With the healing of thy wings
467   1   Thou art the fountain whence our healing flows

heals
221   1   It soothes his sorrows, heals his wounds

health
15   1   O my soul, praise him, for he is thy health and salvation
41   2   Banish our weakness, health and wholeness sending
314   2   In all my pain and misery Be thou my health and life
460   3   seed-time and the harvest, Our life, our health, our food

health's
390   3   praise of him who is thy God, Thy health's eternal spring

healthily
328   2   thou shalt surely feel His wind, that bloweth healthily

heaps

417	1	The nations sleep starving on heaps of gold

hear

2	3	hear our cry, Have mercy on us, Jesus
3	2	God himself is with us, Hear the harps resounding
3	2	Holy, holy, holy, Hear the hymn ascending
3	2	Hear, O Christ the praises That thy Church how raises
15	1	All ye who hear, Now to his temple draw near
20	3	That men may hear the grateful song My voice unwearied raises
42	3	Hear we no beat of drums, Fanfare nor cry
55	6	Hear, in this solemn evening hour
64	3	Make music for thy Lord to hear, Alleluia, Alleluia
67	3	when the morning breaks in power, We hear thy word
67	3	we hear thy word, Let there be light
113	1	We pray thee, hear us when we call
118	1	But hear the angel's warning
123	1	As I hear, Far and near, Sweetest angel voices
125	2	Now ye hear of endless bliss, Jesus Christ was born for this
129	1	The world in solemn stillness lay To hear the angels sing
129	3	O rest beside the weary road, And hear the angels sing
134	3	No ear may hear his coming, But in this world of sin
134	4	We hear the Christmas angels The great glad tidings tell
158	3	It is finished, hear him cry, Learn of Jesus Christ to die
166	1	Craving pardon for thy foes, Hear us, holy Jesus
166	2	For we know not what we do, Hear us, holy Jesus
166	3	When with wrong our spirits bleed, Hear us, holy Jesus
167	II-1	Promising him paradise, Hear us, holy Jesus
167	II-2	Calling humbly on thy name, Hear us, holy Jesus
167	II-3	Cheer our souls with hope divine, Hear us, holy Jesus
167	III-1	And thy dearest human friend, Hear us, holy Jesus
167	III-2	And enjoy thy tender care, Hear us, holy Jesus
167	III-3	Loving all for the love of thee, Hear us, holy Jesus
167	IV-1	While no light from heaven is shown, Hear us, holy Jesus
167	IV-2	In the darkness be our stay, Hear us, holy Jesus
167	IV-3	Though no Father seems to hear .. no light our spirits cheer
167	IV-3	Tell our faith that God is near, Hear us, holy Jesus
167	V-1	Thirsting more our love to gain, Hear us, holy Jesus
167	V-2	Satisfy thy loving will, Hear us, holy Jesus
167	V-3	Where the healing waters flow, Hear us, holy Jesus
167	VI-1	By thy sufferings perfect made, Hear us, holy Jesus
167	VI-2	While we grow in holiness, Hear us, holy Jesus
167	VI-3	Till we pass to perfect day, Hear us, holy Jesus
167	VII-1	Yielding up thy soul at last, Hear us, holy Jesus
167	VII-2	Keep us in that trial hour, Hear us, holy Jesus
167	VII-3	Grace to reach the home on high, Hear us, holy Jesus
192	2	And, listening to his accents, May hear so calm and plain
212	T,1	Blessed Jesus, at Thy Word, We are gathered all to hear thee
212	3	Hear the cry thy people raises
212	3	Hear, and bless our prayers and praises
213	3	May I hear thee say to me, Fear not, I will pilot thee
218	1	Be thou forever hear me, My master and my friend
218	2	O Let me hear thee speaking In accents clear and still
220	4	o'er the centuries still we hear The Master's winsome call
224	1	We own thy sway, we hear thy call
224	4	We faintly hear, we dimly see, In differing phrase we pray

249	5	Pray we that thou wilt hear us, still imploring Thy love
263	2	With thy wonted loving-kindness Hear thy people as they pray
264	2	We hear within the solemn voice Of her unending song
301	1-5	We beseech thee, hear us
312	3	Ten thousand times that man were blest ... this music hear
312	3	That might this music hear
317	2	Seem hungering and thirsting To hear it, like the rest
322	5	Jesus calls us, by thy mercies, Savior, may we hear thy call
327	2	Blessed Jesus, Hear thy children when they pray
332	5	Loving Savior, Holy Spirit, Hear and heed our humble cry
333	1	Hear thou our prayer, the spoken and unspoken
333	1	Hear us, our Father
336	4	A strong, desiring confidence To hear thy voice and live
348	1	Savior divine, Now hear me while I pray
364	3	Christian, dost thou hear them, How they speak thee fair
365	1	Whene'er we hear that glorious word
368	T,1	Father, Hear the Prayer We Offer
378	1	Hear and receive thy Church's supplication,
400	1	Hear thou the prayer I make On bended knee
407	2	Above all boons, I pray, Grant me thy voice to hear
423	1	We hear thy voice, O Son of man
426	2	I hear my people crying In cot and mine and slum
429	1-3	O hear us when we cry to thee, For those in peril on the sea
432	4	God of thy people, hear us cry to thee
436	T,1	O God of Earth and Altar, Bow down and hear our cry
451	1	Still wilt not hear thine inner God proclaim
472	2	shrine Where thy pure light may shine, O hear our call
485	2	In the rustling grass I hear him pass
520	T,1	Almighty Father, Hear Our Prayer
532	1	Son of God, we beseech thee to hear us
532	1	We beseech thee to hear us, O Lord
579	3	Have mercy, now, upon my soul, Hear this my humble prayer

heard

24	1	No mortal eye hath seen, No mortal ear hath heard such
24	1	No mortal ear hath heard such wondrous things
47	4	And hour by hour fresh lips are making ... heard
47	4	lips are making Thy wondrous doings heard on high
78	T,1	Hast Thou Not Known, hast thou not heard
116	T,1	Angels We Have Heard on High Sweetly singing o'er the plains
127	2	Who heard the angelic herald's voice
259	3	Upward we press, the air is clear, & the sphere-music heard
262	3	A sweeter song shall then be heard
299	2	Whene'er thy joyful sound is heard
341	2	In simple trust like theirs who heard, Beside the Syrian sea
429	2	The winds and waves submissive heard
480	3	The same great God that hears my prayers, Heard his
480	3	Heard his, when Jesus knelt to pray
484	2	Remember all God's children Who yet have never heard
492	2	For prophet voices gladly heard, For daring dreams

heard'st

438	2	Thou heard'st well pleased, the song, the prayer

hearest

526	T,1	O Thou Who Hearest Prayer, Give ear unto our cry

hearing

192	2	His own, All hail, and, hearing, May raise the victor-strain

hearken

115	1	Come then and hearken, for he brings Glad tidings
332	5	Hearken from thy throne on high

hears

108	2	Zion hears the watchmen singing
183	2	Lives in glory now on high, Pleads for us and hears our cry
337	1	God hears thy sighs and counts thy tears
480	3	The same great God that hears my prayers, Heard his

heart

14	2	law ... Deep writ upon the human heart, On sea, or land
20	3	Be joyful in the Lord, my heart
23	4	And with a well-tuned heart Sing thou the songs of love
25	1	Stand up & bless the Lord your God with heart & soul & voice
28	3	And all rejoice with Christian heart and voice
29	T,1	Now Thank We All Our God With heart and hands and voices
31	2	High on his heart he will bear it for thee
32	2	Wake and lift up thyself, my heart
35	T,1	When Morning Gilds the Skies, My heart awakening cries
35	2	The night becomes as day, When from the heart we say
43	1	Day-spring from on high be near, Day-star in my heart appear
64	4	And all ye men of tender heart
66	3	For the joy of ear and eye, For the heart and mind's delight
75	4	Write thou deeply in my heart What I am, and what thou art
78	4	He ... Supports the fainting heart
81	1	The praises of my God shall still My heart and tongue employ
83	2	with heart content To take whate'er thy Father's pleasure
86	4	May thy fresh light arise Within each clouded heart
89	1	Yet to each loving heart how near
92	2	But let me only think of thee And then new heart springs up
94	2	Before my infant heart conceived From whom those comforts
94	3	Nor in the least a cheerful heart that tastes those gifts
101	2	heart of the Eternal Is most wonderfully kind (102-3)
103	2	Dear desire of every nation, Joy of every longing heart
108	2	Her heart with deep delight is springing
110	4	Desire of nations, bind All peoples in one heart and mind
114	2	Fling wide the portals of your heart
114	3	Redeemer, come, I open wide My heart to thee
121	3	Make thee a bed, soft, undefiled Within my heart
121	3	heart, that it may be A quiet chamber kept for thee
123	T,1	All My Heart This Night Rejoices
125	T,1-3	Good Christian Men, Rejoice, With heart and soul and voice
128	4	Yet what I can I give him - Give my heart
130	1	Let every heart prepare him room
145	1	thou hast won My heart to serve thee solely
145	2	O deep within my heart now shine
145	2	Here in sadness Eye and heart long for thy gladness
160	2	And from my smitten heart with tears Two wonders I confess
166	3	O may we, who mercy need, Be like thee in heart and deed
167	III-1	Jesus, loving to the end Her whose heart thy sorrows rend
168	2	assurance That thou, O Lord, art greater than our heart
204	R	Lift up your heart, lift up your voice

207	1	My only trust and savior of my heart
210	3	Spring thou up within my heart, Rise to all eternity
212	3	Open thou our ears and heart
214	T,1	Blest Are the Pure in Heart For they shall see our God
214	3	for his dwelliing and his throne Chooseth the pure in heart
214	4	Give us a pure and lowly heart, A temple meet for thee
221	4	Weak is the effort of my heart, And cold my warmest thought
222	1	Long my heart hath panted, Till it well-nigh fainted
222	2	Though the earth be shaking, Every heart be quaking
225	2	No voice can sing, no heart can frame
225	3	O hope of every contrite heart, O joy of all the meek
227	2	Jesus is purer, Who makes the woeful heart to sing
228	1	Visit us with thy salvation, Enter every trembling heart
232	T,1	Spirit of God, Descend Upon My Heart
232	3	All, all thine own, soul, heart, and strength, and mind
232	3	I see thy cross -- there teach my heart to cling
232	5	My heart an altar, and thy love the flame
233	2	Until my heart is pure
235	3	And call him Father from the heart
236	2	Thine is every time & place, Fountain sweet of heart & mind
238	2	Plant holy fear in every heart
239	1	O Comforter, draw near, Within my heart appear
242	2	Holy Spirit, Love divine, Glow within this heart of mine
246	3	Thou who almighty art, Now rule in every heart
249	5	O Triune God, with heart and voice adoring
255	2	With joy they fill the heart
255	4	The thoughts within my heart, Accept, O Lord
268	1	Joining heart to heart with others
272	4	But we shall still be joined in heart
280	1	Savior, abide with us, and spread Thy table in our heart
282	1	Look on the heart by sorrow broken
300	1	Give heart and soul and mind and strength To serve
308	3	strong in heart and hand and brain
309	1	Beneath thy contemplation Sink heart and voice oppressed
321	T,1	My God, Accept My Heart This Day, And make it always thine
322	2	As of old, Saint Andrew heart it By the Galilean lake
324	1	Search, prove my heart, it longs for thee
326	1-4	O come to my heart, Lord Jesus
326	1-4	There is room in my heart for thee
326	5	my heart shall rejoice, Lord Jesus, When thou comest
331	1	In love my soul would bow, My heart fulfill its vow
331	2	Give me a faithful heart, Guided by thee
339	1	God unknown, He alone Calls my heart to be his own
343	T,1	In Heavenly Love Abiding, No change my heart shall fear
343	1	The storm may roar without me, My heart may low be laid
345	T,1	Rejoice, Ye Pure in Heart, Rejoice, give thanks and sing
346	1	One brotherhood in heart are we, And one our Lord and King
348	2	May thy rich grace impart Strength to my fainting heart
352	3	Low lie the bounding heart, the teeming brain
353	R,1-4	In my heart
354	1	No fear his heart oppresses
356	2	My heart is weak and poor Until it master find
361	T,1	Have Faith in God, my heart, Trust and be unafraid
361	4	Until I rest, heart, mind and soul, The captive of thy grace
365	2	Were still in heart and conscience free
359	2	Workman of God, O lose not heart, But learn what God is like

19	2	Earth to heaven, and heaven to earth ...tell his wonders
28	1	word When it goes forth from heaven o'er all the earth
29	3	The Son, and him who reigns With them in highest heaven
29	3	The one eternal God, Whom earth and heaven adore
36	2	New thoughts of God, new hopes of heaven
36	4	lovelier be, As more of heaven in each we see
37	3	Breathe each day nearness unto thee and heaven
38	2	Sweet the rain's new fall Sunlit from heaven
41	2	Bring us to heaven, where thy saints united Joy
45	T,1	Day is Dying in the West, Heaven is touching earth with rest
45	R	Heaven and earth are full of thee
45	R	Heaven and earth are praising thee, O Lord most high
50	5	Till in the ocean of thy love we lose ourselves in heaven
50	5	We lose ourselves in heaven above
52	2	Soon as dies the sunset glory, Stars of heaven shine out
58	T,1	God That Madest Earth and Heaven, Darkness and light
64	2	Ye clouds that sail in heaven along
65	1	Earth repeat the songs of heaven
66	5	Graces, human and divine, Flowers of earth & buds of heaven
69	1	Heaven & earth, awake & sing, God is good and therefore King
74	2	When we see thy lights of heaven
75	T,1	Heaven and Earth, and Sea and Air
85	1	My safety cometh from the Lord, Who heaven & earth hath made
93	1	Bread of heaven, Feed me till I want no more
101	1	where earth's sorrows...more felt than up in heaven (102-2)
107	3	Rank on rank the host of heaven Spreads its vanguard
111	2	O ye heights of heaven adore him
112	2	For e'en now the reign of heaven Spreads throughout
112	.2	heaven Spreads throughout the world like leaven
119	2	There to bend the knee before Him who heaven and earth adore
120	2	Christ, by highest heaven adored
121	T,1	From Heaven Above to Earth I Come
121	4	Glory to God in highest heaven
128	2	Our God, heaven cannot hold him, Nor earth sustain
128	2	Heaven and earth shall flee away When he comes to reign
130	1	And heaven and nature sing
132	2	Sing, all ye citizens of heaven above
134	3	So God imparts to human hearts The blessings of his heaven
138	2	Glories stream from heaven afar
144	2	And lo, the eastern sages stand to read in heaven
144	2	To read in heaven the Lord's command
146	6	Good will henceforth from heaven to men Begin & never cease
165	3	And sons of earth hold heaven in fee
167	IV-1	While no light from heaven is shown, Hear us, holy Jesus
171	3	we might go at last to heaven, Saved by his precious blood
173	3	O word of hope, to raise us nearer heaven
180	T,1	Alleluia, Alleluia, Hearts to Heaven and voices raise
182	5	Hail the Lord of earth and heaven
191	1	The King of heaven, the glorious King
200	2	The highest place that heaven affords Is his ... by right
200	4	Their name an everlasting name, Their joy the joy of heaven
203	2	While the vault of heaven rings
204	3	His kingdom cannot fail, He rules o'er earth and heaven
205	1	Enters now the highest heaven
205	3	See, the heaven its Lord receives
219	3	The holiest know - Light, Life, and Way of heaven

| 577 | R | Creator of the earth and heaven, Thou bringer of salvation |
| 579 | 2 | For the promise ever sure that, while heaven & earth endure |

heaven's

35	5	In heaven's eternal bliss The loveliest strain is this
110	4	Fill the whole world with heaven's peace
114	2	set apart From earthly use for heaven's employ
129	1	From heaven's all gracious King
136	4	Praising Christ, heaven's King
200	2	King of kings, and Lord of lords, And heaven's eternal light
209	5	Heaven's morning breaks, and earth's vain shadows flee
326	2	Heaven's arches rang when the angels sang
377	4	Zion, if thou die believing, Heaven's path shall open lie
391	4	May I reach heaven's joys, O bright heaven's Sun
499	2	Heaven's hosts their noblest praises bring
500	2	Thro' heaven's great day of evermore
501	2	O let heaven's eternal day Be thine eternal praise
505	1	And pay a grateful song of praise To heaven's almighty King

heavenly

18	3	O holy, holy, holy Lord, Whom heavenly hosts obey
23	3	Ye saints who toil below, Adore your heavenly King
32	5	Praise him above, ye heavenly host
33	5	Praise we, with the heavenly host, Father, Son & Holy Ghost
53	2	all the heavenly splendor Breaks forth in starlight tender
54	1	Our heavenly Sun, our glorious Light
56	4	Praise him above, ye heavenly host
76	3	Haste to your heavenly Father's throne
77	1	thy best, thy heavenly friend Through thorny ways leads
78	4	And courage in the evil hour His heavenly aids impart
89	5	One holy light, one heavenly flame
95	2	justice, from her heavenly bower, Look down on mortal men
107	2	His own self for heavenly food
116	2	Say what may the tidings be Which inspire your heavenly song
118	T,1	Break Forth, O Beauteous Heavenly Light
119	3	treasures bring, Christ, to thee, our heavenly King
122	2	From God, our heavenly Father, A blessed angel came
125	2	He hath oped the heavenly door, And man is blessed evermore
127	4	Till man's first heavenly state again takes place
129	2	still their heavenly music floats O'er all the weary world
135	1	For thou hast left thy heavenly throne
138	1	Holy infant so tender and mild, Sleep in heavenly peace
138	2	Heavenly hosts sing alleluia, Christ the Savior is born
144	4	To God the Father, heavenly Light
145	2	Thou heavenly Brightness, Light divine
146	4	The heavenly babe you there shall find
165	2	Lo, a more heavenly lamp shines here
178	4	'Tis midnight, and from heavenly plains Is borne the song
187	2	Unto Christ, our heavenly King
187	4	Praise him, all ye heavenly host, Father .. Son & Holy Ghost
197	2	All the heavenly orders, In their great array
199	1	Hark, how the heavenly anthem drowns All music but its own
230	3	We may not climb the heavenly steeps
238	T,1	Come, Gracious Spirit, Heavenly Dove
240	T,1,3	Come, Holy Spirit, Heavenly Dove
248	2	High in the heavenly Zion Thou reignest God adored

250	1	Ever-present help in need, Praised by all the heavenly host
256	1	Stream from the fount of heavenly grace
256	5	to its heavenly teaching turn With simple, child-like hearts
269	4	Beyond my highest joy I prize her heavenly ways
280	2	That living bread, that heavenly wine, Be our immortal food
287	3	This is the heavenly table spread for me
291	T,1	Lord, Enthroned in Heavenly Splendor
314	3	Through darkness and perplexity Point thou the heavenly way
321	3	Anoint me with thy heavenly grace, Adopt me for thine own
330	3	Ah, did not he the heavenly throne A little thing esteem
332	5	Heavenly Father, bless thy children
343	T,1	In Heavenly Love Abiding, No change my heart shall fear
344	T,1	Lead Us, Heavenly Father, Lead Us
344	3	Fill our hearts with heavenly joy
349	T,1	O For a Closer Walk With God, A calm and heavenly frame
354	3	O God, renew with heavenly dew Our body, soul and spirit
362	1	A heavenly race demands thy zeal, And an immortal crown
370	1	O words with heavenly comfort fraught
375	2	But deeds of love and mercy, The heavenly kingdom comes
376	4	Lead us, O Father, to thy heavenly rest
395	5	Then let us prove our heavenly birth In all we do and know
490	1	Our heavenly Father's will
494	3	O grant enduring worth Until the heavenly kingdom comes
494	3	Until the heavenly kingdom comes on earth
514	1	Praise him above, ye heavenly host
515	1	Praise him above, ye heavenly host
554	3	O Lord God, heavenly King, God the Father almighty

heavens

9	4	High as the heavens our voices raise
13	T.1	Praise the Lord, Ye Heavens, Adore Him
26	2	By his might the heavens ring, In his love we live and move
72	1	blue ethereal sky And spangled heavens, a shining frame
72	1	heavens ... Their great Original proclaim
82	T,1	High in the Heavens, Eternal God
108	3	Now let all the heavens adore thee
182	1	Sing, ye heavens, and earth reply, Alleluia
192	3	Now let the heavens be joyful, Let earth her song begin
214	2	The Lord, who left the heavens Our life and peace to bring
247	2	Fill the heavens with sweet accord, Holy, holy, holy Lord
257	T,1	The Heavens Declare Thy Glory, Lord
270	2	Yet he whom heavens cannot contain Chose to abide on earth
311	3	Show in the heavens thy promised sign
326	5	When the heavens shall ring & the angels sing At thy coming
455	1	snow Has left the heavens all coldly clear
459	1	Over the heavens he spreads his clouds
485	3	The Lord is king, let the heavens ring
488	1	Behold throughout the heavens There shone a holy light
559	2	To thee all angels cry aloud, the heavens and all the powers

heavenward

| 167 | VI-3 | Brighten all our heavenward way With an ever holier ray |

heaviest

| 222 | 2 | Sin and hell ... With their heaviest storms assail us |

heavy

335	3	Are we weak and heavy laden, Cumbered with a load of care
467	4	Patient, O heart, though heavy be thy sorrows

Hebrews

155	1	The people of the Hebrews With palms before thee went

heed

125	1	Give ye heed to what we say, Jesus Christ is born today
332	5	Loving Savior, Holy Spirit, Hear and heed our humble cry
391	3	Riches I heed not, nor man's empty praise
419	2	One in the patient company Of those who heed thy will
426	3	We heed, O Lord, thy summons, And answer, Here are we

heeds

178	2	E'en that disciple whom he loved Heeds not
178	2	Heeds not his Master's grief and tears

height

13	1	Praise him, angels, in the height
35	5	Let air, and sea, and sky From depth to height reply
109	1	Traveler, o'er yon mountain's height See
165	2	from the cross on Calvary's height Gleams of eternity appear
197	4	Through all ranks of creatures, To the central height
412	2	Build us a tower of Christ-like height
497	T,1	Praise to the Holiest in the Height
499	2	To him, enthroned above all height ... praises bring
576	2	Unfathomed depth, unmeasured height

heights

108	1	The watchmen on the heights are crying
111	2	O ye heights of heaven adore him
259	3	And look down from supernal heights On all the by-gone time
421	1	lead To blazoned heights and down the slopes of need

heirs

308	4	Heirs of their great heritage

held

92	4	Enfolded deep in thy dear love, Held in thy law, I stand
413	2	We but stewards of thy bounty, Held in solemn trust for thee
421	3	And, 'neath the burdens there, thy sovereignty Has held
421	3	Has held our hearts enthralled while serving thee

hell

107	3	powers of hell may vanish As the darkness clears away
204	3	The keys of death and hell Are to our Jesus given
222	2	Sin and hell in conflict fell
222	2	Sin and hell ... With their heaviest storms assail us
229	2	joyful news ... Of hell subdued and peace with heaven
354	2	Nor shades of death, nor hell beneath, Our souls ... sever
372	5	That soul, though all hell should endeavor to shake
378	2	Lord, o'er thy rock nor death nor hell prevaileth
382	3	Gates of hell can never 'Gainst that Church prevail
558	1	When powers of earth and hell arose

hell's

93	3	Death of death, and hell's destruction land me safe

help

1	T,1,6	Our God Our Help In Ages Past, our hope for years to come
7	4	All praise we would render, O help us to see
7	4	help us to see 'Tis only the splendor of light hideth thee
16	4	Angels, help us to adore him, Ye behold him face to face
22	2	And with thy help, O Lord, life's battles we win
36	6	help us, this and every day, To live more nearly as we pray
105	2	To help the poor and needy, And bid the weak be strong
135	2	Help us to do as thou hast willed
167	VI-2	Save us in our soul's distress, Be our help to cheer & bless
208	2	Help me, oppressed by things undone
209	1	Help of the helpless, O abide with me
210	2	All my trust on thee is stayed ... my help from thee I bring
212	3	Help us by thy Spirit's pleading
230	4	But warm, sweet, tender, even yet A present help is he
245	1	with words that help and heal Would thy life in mine reveal
246	1	Help us thy name to sing, Help us to praise
250	1	Ever-present help in need, Praised by all the heavenly host
263	1	Holy Zion's help forever, And her confidence alone
287	5	I have no help but thine, nor do I need Another arm
294	2	Help us to spread thy gracious reign
297	3	Help us to pass it on unspent Until the dawn lights up
316	1	Help us know thy grace and power
344	1	For we have no help but thee
347	2	Help us, through good report & ill, Our daily cross to bear
349	4	Help me to tear it from thy throne, And worship only thee
372	2	I'll strengthen thee, help thee, and cause thee to stand
373	1	In darkness and temptation My light, my help is near
378	2	Lord, thou canst help when earthly armor faileth
378	4	Grant us thy help til backward they are driven
392	1	O help thy children when they call
409	3	Jesus, thou divine companion, Help us all to work our best
413	1	Heal our wrongs, and help our need
416	2	Thou canst help their load to bear
418	1	Tell me thy secret, help be bear The strain of toil
418	2	Help me the slow of heart to move
424	2	All our joys and all our groans Help to rear its shining
424	2	Help to rear its shining ramparts
472	1	As we thy help have sought, With labor long have wrought
479	2	Help us to do the things we should
484	3	God raise up more to help them To set the nations free
519	1	Save thy servant that hath none Help nor hope but thee alone
557	3	I have no help but thine, nor do I need Another arm
559	11	we therefore pray thee, help thy servants
583	T,1	Our God, Our Help in Ages Past (as no. 1 with descant)

helped

376	2	Unhelped by thee, in error's maze we grope
476	2	Who graced their generation, Who helped the right
476	2	Who helped the right and fought the wrong

helper

| 363 | 1 | Our helper he amid the flood Of mortal ills prevailing |
| 377 | 3 | Yet, O Zion, have no fear, Ever is thy helper near |

helper

| 209 | 1 | When other helpers fail, and comforts flee |

helping

| 481 | 1 | saints ... and I mean, God helping, to be one too |
| 481 | 1 | And I mean, God helping, to be one too |

helpless

209	1	Help of the helpless, O abide with me
210	2	Other refuge have I none, Hangs my helpless soul on thee
358	3	Helpless, look to thee for grace
506	2	God hath tended With his care thy helpless hours

helplessness

| 423 | 3 | From tender childhood's helplessness |

hem

| 291 | 3 | Touch we now thy garment's hem |

hence

222	3	Hence, all thoughts of sadness
246	4	To the great One in Three Eternal praises be Hence evermore
537	1	And hence with grateful hearts today

henceforth

25	4	Stand up and bless his glorious name Henceforth for evermore
85	4	Henceforth thy going out and in God keep forever will
146	6	Good will henceforth from heaven to men Begin & never cease
331	2	That each departing day Henceforth may see Some work of love
332	4	From henceforth, the time redeeming, May we live to thee
375	1	Henceforth in fields of conquest Thy tents shall be our home
570	3	For behold, from henceforth all generations shall call me

herald

42	3	When Christ the herald comes Quietly nigh
105	3	Before him on the mountains Shall peace, the herald, go
120	T,1,R	Hark, The Herald Angels Sing, Glory to the new-born King

herald's

| 127 | 2 | Who heard the angelic herald's voice |

heralds

| 294 | 3 | Inspire thy heralds of good news To live thy life divine |
| 470 | 5 | Make them apostles, Heralds of thy cross |

here

3	2	Bow thine ear To us here
15	3	Surely his goodness and mercy here daily attend thee
32	5	Praise him, all creatures here below
46	2	May struggling hearts that seek release Here find the rest
46	2	strengthened here by hymn and prayer
55	2	We know and feel that thou art here

56	4	Praise him, all creatures here below
59	1	And 'neath his shadow here to rest we yield us
96	3	Here shall my stand be taken
98	1	So many glorious things are here, Noble and right
104	2	Bidding all men to repentance Since the kingdom now is here
110	1	mourns in lonely exile here Until the Son of God appear
110	2	cheer Our spirits by thine advent here
112	2	Comes the life eternal here
114	1	The Savior of the world is here
114	3	here, Lord, abide. Let me thy inner presence feel
123	3	Here let all, Great and small, Kneel in awe and wonder
127	3	Here Son, the Savior, in a manger laid
140	2	for sinners here The silent Word is pleading
145	2	Here in sadness Eye and heart long for thy gladness
150	5	For us he sent his Spirit here To guide,
156	3	for here Thou hast a temple, too, as Zion dear
165	2	Lo, a more heavenly lamp shines here
165	3	Here in o'erwhelming final strife the Lord ... hath victory
168	2	our weak endurance Make us unworthy here to take our part
169	5	Here might I stay and sing, No story so divine
170	2	Lo, here I fall, my Savior, 'Tis I deserve thy place
222	2	Foes who would molest me Cannot reach me here
222	3	Yea, whate'er we here must bear
263	3	Here vouchsafe to all thy servants What they ask of thee
276	3	Here make the well-springs of thy grace Like fountains
276	4	May thy whole truth be spoken here
278	1	As thou wast once an infant here
279	T,1	Blessed Jesus, Here Are We, Thy beloved word obeying
287	T,1	Here, O My Lord, I See Thee Face to Face
287	1	Here would I touch and handle things unseen
287	1	Here grasp with firmer hand the eternal grace
287	2	Here would I feed upon the bread of God
287	2	Here drink with thee the royal wine of heaven
287	2	Here would I lay aside each earthly load
287	2	Here taste afresh the calm of sin forgiven
287	3	Here let me feast, and, feasting, still prolong
287	4	The bread and wine remove, but thou art here
287	4	thou art here, Nearer than ever, still my shield and sun
291	2	Here our humblest homage pay we
291	2	Here in loving reverence bow
291	2	Here for faith's discernment pray we
291	2	Thou art here, we ask not how
292	1	We here present, we here spread forth to thee
293	3	No arm so weak but may do service here
294	1	To whom there is no here nor there, No time, no near nor far
343	1	And safe is such confiding, For nothing changes here
352	1	Here at thy feet none other may we see
402	3	Great Shepherd of thy chosen few ... mercies here renew
402	3	Thy former mercies here renew
402	3	Here to our waiting hearts proclaim The sweetness
402	4	Here may we prove the power of prayer To strengthen faith
413	4	grant our hope's fruition, Here on earth thy will be done
416	4	Born in heaven and radiant here
417	2	Who would ... While the Lord of all ages is here
426	3	We heed, O Lord, thy summons, And answer, Here are we

432	1	Through whose deep purpose stranger thousands stand Here
432	1	stand Here in the borders of our promised land
438	4	And here thy name, O God of love ... children shall adore
453	3	For those that here we see no more
469	2	All souls are thine, and here or there They rest
471	2	We praise thee, Lord, that now the light is falling Here
471	2	Here on thy servant in this solemn hour
475	2	Grant that all we, who here today ... this foundation lay
477	2	Come, fix thy glorious presence here
477	3	Here plant thy throne, and here abide
483	1	When Jesus was here among men
499	T,1,2	Lo, God Is Here
509	2	May struggling hearts that seek release Here find the rest
509	2	Here find the rest of God's own peace
509	2	And strengthened here by hymn and prayer
514	1	Praise him, all creatures here below
515	1	Praise him, all creatures here below
557	T,1	Here, O My Lord, I See Thee face to face
557	1	Here would I touch and handle things unseen
557	1	Here grasp with firmer hand eternal grace
557	2	Here would I feed upon the bread of God
557	2	Here drink with thee the royal wine of heaven
557	2	Here would I lay aside each earthly load
557	2	Here taste afresh the calm of sin forgiven

hereafter
| 263 | 3 | And hereafter in thy glory Evermore with thee to reign |

heritage
308	4	Heirs of their great heritage
392	1	That they may build from age to age An undefiled heritage
439	2	For the heritage of freedom
559	13	O Lord, save thy people and bless thine heritage

hero's
| 236 | 3 | Pulsing in the hero's blood |
| 253 | 1 | Statesman's, teacher's, hero's treasure |

Herod
| 142 | 3 | Herod then with fear was filled |

heroes
383	2	Poets sung its glory, Heroes for it died
439	3	For all heroes of the spirit, Give we thanks to thee, O Lord
440	3	O beautiful for heroes proved In liberating strife

heroic
| 380 | 2 | Heroic warriors, ne'er from Christ ... enticed |

hid
| 7 | 1 | In light inaccessible hid from our eyes |

hidden
86	4	Thou hidden fount of love, Of Peace, and truth and beauty
397	3	And wing my words, that they may reach The hidden depths
397	3	The hidden depths of many a heart

| 445 | 4 | How shall we love thee, holy, hidden Being, If we love not |
| 468 | 2 | With thee is hidden still their life |

hide

50	1	Oh, may no earth-born cloud arise To hide thee
50	1	no ... cloud arise To hide thee from thy servant's eyes
55	5	The very wounds that shame would hide
61	2	'Neath his wings protecting hide you
91	1	And in his shadow safely hide
91	4	His outspread pinions shall thee hide
119	4	need no star to guide, Where no clouds thy glory hide
136	2	Ox and ass beside him From the cold would hide him
210	1	Hide me, O my Savior, hide, Till the storm of life is past
222	1	I will suffer nought to hide thee
251	3	Holy, holy, holy, though the darkness hide thee
274	2	Happy, whose strength in thee doth hide
358	T,1,4	Rock of Ages, Cleft for me, Let me hide myself in thee
423	2	From paths where hide the lures of greed
452	2	Our faces from each other hide
576	2	My words from thee I cannot hide

hides

| 87 | 3 | Behind a frowning providence He hides a smiling face |

hideth

| 7 | 4 | help us to see 'Tis only the splendor of light hideth thee |
| 576 | 5 | The darkness hideth not from thee |

hiding

| 213 | 1 | Hiding rock and treacherous shoal |

hie

| 109 | 3 | Hie thee to thy quiet home |

high

2	T,1	All Glory Be to God on High Who hath our race befriended
2	3	Thou Lamb of God, enthroned on high Behold our need
7	2	Thy justice like mountains high soaring above
9	4	High as the heavens our voices raise
13	2	Hosts on high, his power proclaim
14	2	His spirit floweth free, High surging where it will
18	2	To thee, the powers on high ... Continually do cry
23	1	Assist our song, For else the theme Too high doth seem
23	1	Too high doth seem For mortal tongue
25	2	Though high above all praise, Above all blessing high
28	2	Upon a mountain builded high
28	4	nations ... raise on high the victory song
31	2	High on his heart he will bear it for thee
32	2	sing High praise to the eternal King
35	4	To God, the Word, on high, The hosts of angels cry
42	T,1	High O'er the Lonely Hills
43	1	Day-spring from on high be near, Day-star in my heart appear
45	R	Heaven and earth are praising thee, O Lord most high
47	4	lips are making Thy wondrous doings heard on high
49	3	Thee ... O Most High, The world doth glorify
65	T,1	Glory Be to God on High

413	4	host advancing, High and lowly, great and small
414	2	In him shall true hearts ... Their high communion find
414	2	true hearts everywhere Their high communion find
446	1	Show forth thy pity on high where thou reignest
452	2	High walls of ignorance around
471	2	Confirm in him his high and holy calling
472	4	Thy cross we lift on high This house to glorify
508	1	Shall speak thy praises, Lord most high
526	1	O let thy children share thy blessing from on high
550	1	Glory be to thee, O Lord most high
551	1	Glory be to thee, O Lord most high
553	1	Glory be to thee, O Lord most high
554	T,1	Glory Be to God on High
554	9	Thou only, O Christ, with the Holy Ghost, art most high
554	9	most high in the glory of God the Father
568	11	whereby the Dayspring from on high hath visited us
577	R	To thee we sing, O Lord most high

higher

30	2	O higher than the cherubim, More glorious than the seraphim
67	4	But higher far, and far more clear Thee in man's spirit
109	2	Higher yet that star ascends
259	3	Our souls would higher climb
297	1	And where the higher gain appears, We trace ... thy hand
495	2	Every round goes higher, higher

highest

29	3	The Son, and him who reigns With them in highest heaven
91	6	Thy dwelling-place the highest One
120	2	Christ, by highest heaven adored
121	4	Glory to God in highest heaven
132	2	Glory to God, all glory in the highest
200	2	The highest place that heaven affords Is his ... by right
203	4	Jesus takes the highest station
205	1	Enters now the highest heaven
269	4	Beyond my highest joy I prize her heavenly ways
357	3	The highest, holiest manhood, thou
398	2	God's gift from highest heaven
412	3	That it may be our highest joy Our Father's work to do
504	2	Hosanna in the highest strains The Church on earth can raise
504	2	The highest heaven, in which he reigns
504	2	The highest heaven ... Shall give him nobler praise
568	9	And thou, child, shalt be called the prophet of the Highest

highland

73	2	Rock and highland, wood and island

highway

106	2	And makes your wastes his great highway

highways

398	3	afoot on dusty highways

hilariter

194	R	Hilariter, Hilariter ... Alleluia, Alleluia

hill

42	4	What though the hill be steep, Strength's in the sun
66	2	Hill & vale, and tree & flower, Sun & moon & stars of light
75	3	Hill & vale & fruited land, All things living show his hand
105	3	And righteousness, in fountains, From hill to valley flow
162	3	Hill of Calvary, I go To thy scenes of fear and woe
171	T,1	There Is a Green Hill Far Away, Without a city wall
172	T,1	There Is a Green Hill Far Away (same words as No. 171)
308	4	High above the restless tides Stands their city on the hill
324	4	and lead me to thy holy hill
421	4	We've seen thy glory like a mantle spread O'er hill and dale
421	4	O'er hill and dale in saffron flame and red
456	1	And laid a silent loveliness On hill and wood and field

hills

1	3	Before the hills in order stood, Or earth received her frame
6	4	It streams from the hills, it descends to the plain
42	T,1	High O'er the Lonely Hills
42	2	So, o'er the hills of life, Stormy, forlorn
85	T,1	I to the Hills Will Lift Mine Eyes
104	2	And the hills bow down to greet him
106	T,1	Hills of the North, Rejoice
106	3	On your far hills, long cold and gray, Has dawned
130	2	While fields and floods, rocks, hills and plains Repeat
201	1	When beauty gilds the eastern hills And life to joy awakes
264	4	Unshaken as eternal hills, Immovable she stands
340	T,1	They Cast Their Nets in Galilee Just off the hills of brown
341	3	O sabbath rest by Galilee, O calm of hills above
377	3	Though the hills & vales be riven God created with his hand
437	2	I love ... Thy woods and templed hills
438	4	Till these eternal hills remove
458	4	Praise for hills and valleys broad
475	1	glory fills The bounds of the eternal hills
488	T,R	Go, Tell It on the Mountain, Over the hills and everywhere
562	4	and the strength of the hills is his also

hillsides

289	2	As grain, once scattered on the hillsides

himmlischer

139	1	Schlaf in himmlischer Ruh

himself

3	T,1	God Himself is With Us
3	2	God himself is with us, Hear the harps resounding
150	3	Still seeking not himself but us
214	3	Still to the lowly soul He doth himself impart
403	2	Where the many work together, they with God himself abide

hinder

198	3	Cast out our pride and shame That hinder to enthrone thee

hints

86	3	Hints of the music vast Of thine eternal hymn

Hirten

139	2	Hirten erst kundgemacht

hoary

456	1	Hath sent the hoary frost of heaven
459	2	His hoary frost, his fleecy snow, Descend

hochheilige

139	1	Nur das traute, hochheilige Paar

hold

93	1	Hold me with thy powerful hand
128	2	Our God, heaven cannot hold him, Nor earth sustain
161	2	The hopes that lead us onward, The fears that hold us back
165	3	And sons of earth hold heaven in fee
174	1	None can tell what pangs unknown Hold thee silent and alone
185	4	Nor the watchers, nor the seal Hold thee as a mortal
209	5	Hold thou thy cross before my closing eyes
290	3	Blest when our faith can hold thee fast
321	2	Before the cross of him who died, Behold, I prostrate fall
362	2	A cloud of witnesses around Hold thee in full survey
367	1	Lay hold on life, & it shall be Thy joy and crown eternally
377	1	To his loving heart and hold thee
408	2	'Twas not so much that I on thee took hold, As thou
431	1	Beneath whose awful hand we hold Dominion over palm and pine
578	2	'Twas not so much that I on thee took hold As thou

holder

139	1	Holder Knabe im lockigen Haar

holding

422	3	Holding his pick more splendid than the sword
458	3	Praise him for his tiny seed, Holding all his world ... need

holds

96	1	Though dark my road, He holds me that I shall not fall
96	3	He holds me that I shall not fall
265	1	Break every bar that holds Thy flock in diverse folds
361	2	God's mercy holds a wiser plan Than thou canst fully know
423	4	The cup of water given for thee Still holds the freshness
423	4	Still holds the freshness of thy grace

holier

167	VI-3	Brighten all our heavenward way With an ever holier ray

holiest

219	3	The holiest know - Light, Life, and Way of heaven
357	3	The highest, holiest manhood, thou
497	T,1	Praise to the Holiest in the Height

holiness

31	T,1	Worship the Lord in the Beauty of Holiness
167	VI-2	While we grow in holiness, Hear us, holy Jesus
238	3	Lead us to holiness
238	4	holiness, the road That we must take to dwell with God

145	1	Thou art holy, Fair and glorious, all victorious
150	2	for us he bore His holy fast, and hungered sore
152	2	We would see Jesus, Mary's son most holy
154	T,1	O thou Who Through This Holy Week Didst suffer for us all
163	T,1	Ah, Holy Jesus, How Hast Thou Offended
166	1	Craving pardon for thy foes, Hear us, holy Jesus
166	2	For we know not what we do, Hear us, holy Jesus
166	3	When with wrong our spirits bleed, Hear us, holy Jesus
167	II-1	Promising him paradise, Hear us, holy Jesus
167	II-2	Calling humbly on thy name, Hear us, holy Jesus
167	II-3	Cheer our souls with hope divine, Hear us, holy Jesus
167	III-1	And thy dearest human friend, Hear us, holy Jesus
167	III-2	And enjoy thy tender care, Hear us, holy Jesus
167	III-3	May we all thy loved ones be, All one holy family
167	III-3	Loving all for the love of thee, Hear us, holy Jesus
167	IV-1	While no light from heaven is shown, Hear us, holy Jesus
167	IV-2	In the darkness be our stay, Hear us, holy Jesus
167	IV-3	Tell our faith that God is near, Hear us, holy Jesus
167	V-1	Thirsting more our love to gain, Hear us, holy Jesus
167	V-2	Thirst for us in mercy still, All thy holy work fulfil
167	V-2	Satisfy thy loving will, Hear us, holy Jesus
167	V-3	Where the healing waters flow, Hear us, holy Jesus
167	VI-1	By thy sufferings perfect made, Hear us, holy Jesus
167	VI-2	While we grow in holiness, Hear us, holy Jesus
167	VI-3	Till we pass to perfect day, Hear us, holy Jesus
167	VII-1	Yielding up thy soul at last, Hear us, holy Jesus
167	VII-2	Keep us in that trial hour, Hear us, holy Jesus
167	VII-3	Grace to reach the home on high, Hear us, holy Jesus
168	T,1	Lord, Through This Holy Week of our salvation
180	2	Glorious life, and life immortal On this holy Easter morn
181	2	Let shouts of holy joy outburst
187	1	Our triumphant holy day
187	4	Praise him, all ye heavenly host, Father .. Son & Holy Ghost
191	5	On the most holy day of days, Our hearts and voices, Lord
194	4	He, Father, Son, and Holy Ghost
197	5	All that is not holy, All that is not true
212	1	By thy teachings sweet and holy
231	T,1	Come, Holy Ghost, Our Souls Inspire
232	5	One holy passion filling all my frame
235	T,1	Come, Holy Spirit, God and Lord
235	3	Thou strong Defense, thou holy Light
236	4	Consecrating art and song, Holy book and pilgrim track
238	2	Plant holy fear in every heart
239	1	And kindle it, thy holy flame bestowing
239	3	the place Wherein the Holy Spirit makes his dwelling
240	T,1,3	Come, Holy Spirit, Heavenly Dove
242	T,1	Holy Spirit, Truth Divine, dawn upon this soul of mine
242	2	Holy Spirit, Love divine, Glow within this heart of mine
242	3	Holy Spirit, Power divine, Fill and nerve this will of mine
242	4	Holy Spirit, Right divine, King within my conscience reign
243	T,1	Holy Spirit, Truth Divine (words same as no. 242)
244	T,1	O Holy Spirit, Enter In, Among these hearts thy work begin
244	2	In thy pure love & holy faith From thee true wisdom learning
245	4	Holy Spirit, dwell with me, I myself would holy be
246	3	Come, holy Comforter
247	T,1	Holy God, We Praise Thy Name

247	2	Fill the heavens with sweet accord, Holy, holy, holy Lord
247	4	Holy Father, holy Son, Holy Spirit, Three we name thee
248	3	In name of God the Father, And Son, and Holy Ghost
249	2	O holy Father, who hast led thy children In all the ages
249	3	O holy Jesus, Prince of peace and Savior
249	4	O Holy Ghost, the Lord and Life-giver
250	T,1	We All Believe in One True God, Father, Son, and Holy Ghost
250	3	We all confess the Holy Ghost Who from both fore'er proceeds
250	3	Blest and Holy Trinity, Praise forever be to thee
251	T,1,4	Holy, Holy, Holy, Lord God Almighty
251	1,4	Holy, holy, holy, merciful and mighty
251	2	Holy, holy, holy, all the saints adore thee
251	3	Holy, holy, holy, though the darkness hide thee
251	3	Only thou art holy, there is none beside thee Perfect
258	6	O, that we discerning Its most holy learning
260	1	From heaven he came and sought her To be his holy bride
260	2	One holy name she blesses, Partakes one holy food
260	4	O happy ones and holy, Lord, give us grace that we
261	2	One holy Church, one army strong, One steadfast high intent
263	1	Holy Zion's help forever, And her confidence alone
264	3	For not like kingdoms of the world Thy holy Church, O God
266	T,1	One Holy Church of God Appears Through every age and race
275	2	Descend, O Holy Spirit, like a dove Into our hearts
289	1	planted Thy holy name within our hearts
290	4	Shed o'er the world thy holy light
301	5	May she holy triumphs win, Overthrow the hosts of sin
305	3	Stay not till all the holy Proclaim, The Lord is come
318	3	Till earth, as heaven, fulfill God's holy will
324	4	and lead me to thy holy hill
326	1	no room For thy holy nativity
332	5	Loving Savior, Holy Spirit, Hear and heed our humble cry
345	6	The Father, Son, and Holy Ghost, One God for evermore
349	3	Return, O holy Dove, return, Sweet messenger of rest
353	3	Lord I want to be more holy
364	T,1	Christian, Dost Thou See Them On the holy ground
364	1	In the strength that cometh By the holy cross
365	R	Faith of our fathers, holy faith, We will be true to thee
380	2	taught To fear no ill, to fight The holy fight they fought
380	4	Not long the conflict, soon The holy war shall cease
395	1	And met within thy holy place To rest awhile with thee
407	3	Clean hands in holy worship raise
409	2	They who work without complaining Do the holy will of God
410	2	example Of him whose holy work was doing good
419	2	One in the holy fellowship Of those who challenge wrong
420	T,1	O Holy City, Seen of John
420	1	O holy city ... Where Christ, the Lamb, doth reign
426	4	Take us, and make us holy, Teach us thy will and way
429	3	O Holy Spirit, who didst brood Upon the chaos dark and rude
437	4	Long may our land be bright With freedom's holy light
438	2	onward through all ages bear The memory of that holy hour
443	4	As he died to make men holy, let us die to make men free
445	4	How shall we love thee, holy, hidden Being, If we love not
446	2	earth hath forsaken Thy ways all holy, and slighted thy word
471	2	Confirm in him his high and holy calling
472	2	Come, thou, O Lord divine, Make this thy holy shrine
473	2	O Lord, and glorify thy name, For holy thou alone

488	1	Behold throughout the heavens There shone a holy light
490	3	The lovers of all holy things, The foes of all things wrong
508	2	O Light all clear, O Truth most holy
509	1	vesper hymn and vesper prayer Rise mingling on the holy air
511	1	Glory be to the Father, and to the Son and to the Holy Ghost
512	1	Glory be to the Father, and to the Son, & to the Holy Ghost
513	1	Glory be to the Father, and to the Son, & to the Holy Ghost
514	1	Praise Father, Son, and Holy Ghost
515	1	Praise Father, Son, and Holy Ghost
528	2	and take not thy Holy Spirit from me
531	1	And take not thy Holy Spirit from us
533	1	And take not thy Holy Spirit from us
539	1	With the Holy Spirit's favor Rest upon us from above
548	T,1	Thanks Be to Thee, O Christ, for this thy holy gospel
549	T,1	Holy, Holy, Holy, Lord God of hosts
551	T,1	Holy, Holy, Holy, Lord God of hosts
553	T,1	Holy, Holy, Holy, Lord God of hosts
554	8	For thou only art holy, thou only art the Lord
554	9	Thou only, O Christ, with the Holy Ghost, art most high
559	3	Holy, holy, holy, Lord God of Sabaoth
559	5	holy Church throughout all the world doth acknowledge thee
559	6	also the Holy Ghost, the Comforter
562	R	Glory be to the Father and to the Son and to the Holy Ghost
565	R	Glory be to the Father and to the Son and to the Holy Ghost
568	3	As he spake by the mouth of his holy prophets
568	5	and to remember his holy covenant
568	R	Glory be to the Father and to the Son and to the Holy Ghost
570	4	For he that is mighty hath magnified me and holy is his name
575	T,1	Come, Holy Ghost, Our Souls Inspire
575	R	Praise to thy eternal merit, Father, Son and Holy Spirit

homage

107	1	Our full homage to demand
291	2	Here our humblest homage pay we
407	3	That, cleansed from stain of sin, I may meet homage give

home

1	1	Our shelter from the stormy blast, And our eternal home
1	6	Be thou our guard while troubles last, and our eternal home
45	2	Lord of life, beneath the dome Of the universe, thy home
79	3	on his shoulder gently laid, And home rejoicing brought me
91	6	Nor plague approach thy guarded home
97	3	Our heart's true home when all our years have sped
106	5	Shout, while ye journey home, Songs be in evry mouth
109	3	Hie thee to thy quiet home
121	1	To bear good news to every home
160	1	A home within the wilderness, A rest upon the way
167	VII-3	Grace to reach the home on high, Hear us, holy Jesus
193	3	Bring us safe through Jordan To thy home above
215	1	The night is dark and I am far from home, Lead thou me on
231	3	Keep far our foes, give peace at home
241	1	And make this house thy home
241	4	And make this world thy home
276	1	And pray that this may be our home Until we touch eternity

276	2	The common home of rich and poor, Of bond and free
276	2	common home of ... great and small
305	3	Stay not till all the lowly Triumphant reach their home
309	4	O sweet and blessed country, The home of God's elect
311	3	Appear, Desire of nations, Thine exiles long for home
312	T,1	Jerusalem, My Happy Home, When shall I come to thee
322	2	Turned from home and toil and kindred
326	1	But in Bethlehem's home there was found no room
326	5	Let thy voice call me home, saying, Yet there is room
346	3	Of every hearth to make a home, Of every home a heaven
380	4	Faith's warfare ended, won The home of endless peace
402	2	And going take thee to their home
430	2	Yea, love with thee shall make his home
439	2	For the home, the church, the school
454	2	By day, by night, at home abroad, Still we are guarded
455	3	Home closer draws her circle now
461	1	Raise the song of harvest home
461	3	And shall take his harvest home
461	4	Even so, Lord, quickly come To thy final harvest home
461	4	Raise the glorious harvest home
462	1,3	Raise the song of harvest home
466	2	O Christ, thyself a child Within an earthly home
466	3	In all our hearts such love increase, That every home
466	3	That every home ... May be the dwelling place of peace
466	3	every home, by this release, May be the dwelling place
490	4	And for the life ineffable Within the Father's home
496	1-2	O'er the land of the free and the home of the brave
575	3	Keep far our foes, give peace at home

homeless

340	3	Young John ... Homeless, in Patmos died

homeliest

395	3	On homeliest work thy blessing falls

homes

449	4	That useful labor yet may build Its homes with love
449	4	homes with love and laughter filled
466	1	guarding well ... The homes in which thy people dwell
476	4	men of skill Who builded homes of beauty
496	2	stand Between their loved homes and the war's desolation

homesteads

435	2	homesteads & the woodlands Plead in silence for their peace

homeward

60	2	Grant us thy peace upon our homeward way
386	1	send thy light To set our footsteps in the homeward way
418	2	And guide them in the homeward way

homing

217	3	Be there at our homing

honey

309	T,1	Jerusalem the Golden, with milk and honey blest

horned

| 70 | 4 | The horned moon to shine by night |

hosanna

155	3	Hosanna, welcome to our hearts
175	1	Hark, all the tribes hosanna cry
504	2	Hosanna in the highest strains The Church on earth can raise

hosannas

155	1,3	To whom the lips of children Made sweet hosannas ring
169	3	Resounding all the day Hosannas to their king
240	2	Hosannas languish on our tongues, And our devotion dies

host

32	5	Praise him above, ye heavenly host
33	5	Praise we, with the heavenly host, Father, Son & Holy Ghost
56	4	Praise him above, ye heavenly host
107	3	Rank on rank the host of heaven Spreads its vanguard
120	1	With the angelic host proclaim, Christ is born in Bethlehem
227	3	And all the twinkling starry host, Jesus shines brighter
250	1	Ever-present help in need, Praised by all the heavenly host
413	4	See the Christ-like host advancing
413	4	host advancing, High and lowly, great and small
432	2	Thou wast the shield for Israel's marching host
514	1	Praise him above, ye heavenly host
515	1	Praise him above, ye heavenly host

hosts

13	2	Hosts on high, his power proclaim
18	3	O holy, holy, holy Lord, Whom heavenly hosts obey
35	4	To God, the Word, on high, The hosts of angels cry
45	R	Holy, holy, holy, Lord God of Hosts
69	1	Praise him, all ye hosts above, Ever bright and fair in love
111	2	Angel hosts, his praises sing
127	1	mystery ...Which hosts of angels chanted from above
138	2	Heavenly hosts sing alleluia, Christ the Savior is born
197	2	All the angel faces, All the hosts of light
228	3	Serve thee as thy hosts above
248	1	From whom all hosts of angels Have life and power received
252	3	It floateth like a banner Before God's hosts unfurled
263	2	To this temple, where we call thee, Come, O Lord of hosts
263	2	Come, O Lord of hosts, today
274	T,1	How Lovely Are Thy Dwellings Fair, O Lord of hosts
274	4	Lord God of hosts that reignest on high
301	5	May she holy triumphs win, Overthrow the hosts of sin
346	4	O Lord of hosts, our faith renew
366	2	hosts of evil round us Scorn thy Christ assail his ways
373	2	Though hosts encamp around me, Firm in the fight I stand
384	1	Strong in the Lord of hosts, And in his mighty power
411	T,1	Lord God of Hosts, Whose Purpose
427	1	Hark, the waking up of nations, Hosts advancing to the fray
431	1,2	Lord God of hosts, be with us yet, Lest we forget
431	4	Lord God of hosts, be with us yet, Lest we forget
449	T,1	Let There Be Light, Lord God of Hosts
475	T,1	O Lord of Hosts, Whose Glory Fills
499	2	Heaven's hosts their noblest praises bring

549	T,1	Holy, Holy, Holy, Lord God of hosts
551	T,1	Holy, Holy, Holy, Lord God of hosts
553	T,1	Holy, Holy, Holy, Lord God of hosts

hour

37	4	O in that hour, fairer than daylight dawning
47	4	And hour by hour fresh lips are making ... heard
55	6	Hear, in this solemn evening hour
66	2	For the beauty of each hour Of the day and of the night
67	3	We feel thy calm at evening's hour
77	3	hour is hastening on When we shall be forever with the Lord
78	4	And courage in the evil hour His heavenly aids impart
108	1	Midnight's solemn hour is tolling
112	3	Comes the Lord when strikes the hour
158	1	Watch with him one bitter hour
159	3	This is earth's darkest hour
159	4	That, as we share this hour, Thy cross may bring us ... joy
167	VII-2	Keep us in that trial hour, Hear us, holy Jesus
173	1	Breathed in the hour of loneliness and pain
197	5	Crown him as your captain In temptation's hour
207	3	And give us strength in every trying hour
209	3	I need thy presence every passing hour
246	3	Thy sacred witness bear In this glad hour
287	3	This is the hour of banquet and of song
287	3	prolong The brief, bright hour of fellowship with thee
304	3	Rejoice, O people, in this living hour
333	3	No place can part, nor hour of time remove us
342	T,1	I Need Thee Every Hour, Most gracious Lord
342	R	I need thee, oh, I need thee, Every hour I need thee
342	2	I need thee every hour, Stay thou near by
342	3	I need thee every hour In joy or pain
342	4	I need thee every hour, Teach me thy will
354	3	Temptation's hour shall lose its power
366	1	Grant us wisdom ... courage, For the facing of his hour
374	T,1	In the Hour of Trial, Jesus, plead for me
395	2	And scarcely can we turn aside For one brief hour of prayer
426	3	Our strength is dust and ashes, Our years a passing hour
427	2	Thou hast but an hour to fight
429	4	shield in danger's hour From rock and tempest, fire and foe
435	2	Still the weary folk are pining for the hour
435	2	For the hour that brings release
438	2	onward through all ages bear The memory of that holy hour
444	1	Come with thy ... judgment now To match our present hour
451	3	Nor till that hour shall God's whole will be done
452	5	To bring at last the glorious hour
452	5	glorious hour When all men find thy liberty
471	2	Here on thy servant in this solemn hour
490	3	And let us not for one short hour An evil thought endure
492	3	Companion of this sacred hour, Renew
577	1	delivered us ... In many an evil hour

hours

98	3	That shadows fall on brightest hours, That thorns remain
129	3	Look now, for glad and golden hours Come swiftly on the wing
164	3	And all three hours his silence cried for mercy on the souls
174	2	Silent through those three dread hours

293	2	Redeem the time, its hours too swiftly fly
322	4	In our joys and in our sorrows, Days of toil & hours of ease
328	3	And he shall be to thee a rest When evening hours arrive
368	4	Be our strength in hours of weakness
413	3	By thy patient years of toiling, By thy silent hours of pain
458	2	Praise him for his shining hours
472	5	Lord, though these hours of praise ... soon be o'er
504	1	He calls the hours his own
506	2	God hath tended With his care thy helpless hours

house

60	2	That in this house have called upon thy name
79	6	Good Shepherd may I sing thy praise Within thy house forever
84	5	And in God's house for evermore My dwelling place shall be
241	1	And make this house thy home
264	4	A house not made with hands
269	T,1	I Love Thy Kingdom, Lord, The house of thine abode
274	2	Happy, who in thy house reside, Where thee they ever praise
472	1	Building for thine employ This house of prayer
472	4	Thy cross we lift on high This house to glorify
477	2	For thee this house of praise we rear
568	2	in the house of his servant David

hover

| 36 | 2 | New mercies, each returning day Hover around us |
| 36 | 2 | New mercies ... Hover around us while we pray |

hovering

| 129 | 2 | Above its sad and lowly plains They bend on hovering wing |
| 267 | 3 | Round each habitation hovering, See the cloud & fire appear |

how

6	5	Thy mercies how tender, how firm to the end
8	3	Teach us how to love each other
15	2	Hast thou not seen How thy desires e'er have been Granted
19	T,1	Praise the Lord, His Glories Show
34	2	See how the giant sun soars up, Great lord of years and days
50	2	Be my last thought how sweet to rest Forever on my Savior's
68	2	Lord, how thy wonders are displayed, Where'er I turn my eye
74	T,1	O How Glorious, Full of Wonder
74	4	O how wondrous, O how glorious is thy name in every land
75	3	See how he hath everywhere Made this earth so rich and fair
76	T,1	How Gentle God's Commands, How kind his precepts are
81	3	How blest are they, and only they, Who in his truth confide
82	3	My God, how excellent thy grace
89	1	Yet to each loving heart how near
99	T,1	O Love of God, How Strong and True, Eternal and yet ever new
99	2	O love of God, how deep and great, Far deeper than ... hate
122	2	How that in Bethlehem was born The Son of God by name
124	2	Hush, hush, see how fast he slumbers
124	2	Hush, hush, see how fast he sleeps
124	3	Look and see how charming is Jesus
124	3	How he is white, his cheeks are rosy
124	3	Hush, hush, see how the child is sleeping
124	3	Hush, hush, see how he smiles in dreams

74	3	Teach us more of human pity, That we in thine image grow
74	4	Conscious of our human need
78	5	Mere human power shall fast decay, And youthful vigor cease
107	2	Lord of lords, in human vesture, In the body and the blood
134	3	So God imparts to human hearts The blessings of his heaven
146	4	babe ... To human view displayed
152	4	Divine and human, in his deep revealing
167	III-1	And thy dearest human friend, Hear us, holy Jesus
174	2	Left alone with human sin, Gloom around thee and within
185	4	That thy peace which evermore Passeth human knowing
197	4	Bore it up triumphant, With its human light
239	3	Shall far outpass the power of human telling
276	4	And human life become divine
277	3	May we see our human family Free from sorrow and despair
294	2	O God of love, whose spirit wakes In every human breast
294	2	kindness dwell in human hearts And all the earth find peace
304	3	Low lies man's pride and human wisdom dies
330	4	So, Love itself in human form, For love of me he came
357	3	Thou seemest human and divine
409	1	By thy lowly human birth Thou hast come to join the workers
413	1	Son of man, whose birth incarnate Hallows all our human race
420	2	Wring gold from human pain
420	3	where the sun that shineth is God's grace for human good
440	4	Thine alabaster cities gleam, Undimmed by human tears
465	T,1	O Perfect Love, all human thought transcending
468	4	gave Thy Son to fill a human grave
470	2	their hearts awake To human need
494	1	And hearts creative bridge the human rift

humanity

224	2	To thee our full humanity, Its joys and pains belong
262	2	One Church for all humanity
449	1	Let broad humanity have birth

humble

104	3	Let your hearts be true and humble
104	3	true and humble, As befits his holy reign
113	3	not in splendor bright As monarch, but the humble child
175	1	Thy humble beast pursues his road
228	1	Fix in us thy humble dwelling
332	5	Loving Savior, Holy Spirit, Hear and heed our humble cry
402	2	thou, within no walls confined, Inhabitest the humble mind
416	3	Give him thanks in humble zeal
424	2	Whether humble or exalted, All are called to task divine
431	2	An humble and a contrite heart
460	3	And, what thou most desirest, Our humble, thankful hearts
488	3	Down in a lowly manger The humble Christ was born
489	2	I would be humble, for I know my weakness
501	1	Our humble thanks we pay
519	T,1	To My Humble Supplication, Lord give ear and acceptation
559	8	Thou didst humble thyself to be born of a virgin
570	7	and hath exalted the humble and meek
579	3	Have mercy, now, upon my soul, Hear this my humble prayer

humbled

| 197 | 3 | Humbled for a season, To receive a name |

humbleness
64   5   And worship him in humbleness

humblest
219   1   Who once appeared in humblest guise below
291   2   Here our humblest homage pay we

humbling
147   3   Humbling thyself to death on Calvary

humbly
26   1   Sons of every land, Humbly now before him stand
74   1   Humbly now we bow before thee
161   3   Yet humbly, in our striving, O God, we face its test
167   II-2   Calling humbly on thy name, Hear us, holy Jesus
291   3   For when humbly, in thy name, Two or three are met together
332   1   Our misdeeds to thee confessing, On thy name we humbly call
407   4   Thy grace, O Father, give, I humbly thee implore

humility
277   2   Give to all who teach and guide them Wisdom and humility
284   T,1   According to Thy Gracious Word, In meek humility
326   2   And in great humility
336   4   Give deep humility, the sense Of godly sorrow give

humming
422   T,1   When Through the Whirl of Wheels, and engines humming

hundred
443   2   have seen him in the watchfires of a hundred circling camps

hundreds
481   3   There are hundreds of thousands still

hung
171   2   But we believe it was for us He hung and suffered there

hunger
266   4   With Bread of life earth's hunger feed

hungered
150   2   for us he bore His holy fast, and hungered sore

hungering
317   2   Seem hungering and thirsting To hear it, like the rest

hungry
221   2   'Tis manna to the hungry soul, And to the weary, rest
398   2   Bringing to hungry souls the bread of life
432   3   Thy hand has led across the hungry sea The eager peoples
435   3   Feed the faint and hungry peoples with the richness
570   8   He hath filled the hungry with good things

hunt
484   2   Some fish in mighty rivers, Some hunt across the snow

hurling

236	4	Hurling floods of tyrant wrong From the sacred limits back

hurt

372	4	The flame shall not hurt thee
392	5	Teach us the strength that cannot seek ... to hurt the weak
392	5	cannot seek By deed or thought, to hurt the weak

hush

37	2	The solemn hush of nature newly born
124	2	Hush, hush, see how fast he slumbers
124	2	Hush, hush, see how fast he sleeps
124	3	Hush, hush, see how the child is sleeping
124	3	Hush, hush, see how he smiles in dreams
213	2	As a mother stills her child, Thou canst hush the ocean wild
413	3	Hush the storm of strife and passion

hymn

3	2	Holy, holy, holy, Hear the hymn ascending
46	1	vesper hymn and vesper prayer rise mingling on the holy air
46	2	strengthened here by hymn and prayer
46	4	in the spirit's secret cell May hymn & prayer forever dwell
49	2	Our wonted hymn outpouring
52	1	Let our vesper hymn be blending With the holy calm around
60	1	With one accord our parting hymn of praise
66	R	Lord of all ... we raise This our hymn of grateful praise
86	3	Hints of the music vast Of thine eternal hymn
111	3	Hymn & chant and high thanksgiving And unwearied praises be
180	1	Sing to God a hymn of gladness, Sing to God a hymn of praise
247	2	Hark, the glad celestial hymn Angel choirs above are raising
410	1	Each smile a hymn, each kindly deed a prayer
456	2	And clearer sounds the angel hymn, Good will to men on earth
509	1	vesper hymn and vesper prayer Rise mingling on the holy air
509	2	And strengthened here by hymn and prayer

hymns

35	4	Let mortals, too, upraise, Their voice in hymns of praise
47	1	To thee our morning hymns ascended
108	3	Therefore will we, eternally, Sing hymns of joy and praise
155	2	To thee, before thy passion, They sang their hymns of praise
187	2	Hymns of praise then let us sing
192	1	Our Christ hath brought us over With hymns of victory
193	2	Let his church with gladness Hymns of triumph sing
269	4	Her sweet communion, solemn vows, Her hymns of love & praise
345	3	Send forth the hymns our fathers loved
429	4	Thus evermore shall rise to thee Glad hymns of praise
429	4	Glad hymns of praise from land and sea
463	T,1	Praise, O Praise Our God and King, Hymns of adoration sing
508	1	Once more to thee our hymns ascending
525	T,1	Come, & Let Us Sweetly Join Christ to praise in hymns divine

icy

459	2	The liquid streams forbear to flow, In icy fetters bound

ideo

136	R	Ideo ... Ideo gloria in excelsis Deo

idle
293   1   Who dares stand idle on the harvest plain

idly
368   3   Not forever by still waters Would we idly rest and stay

idol
  20   4   Cast each false idol from his throne
322   3   From each idol that would keep us
349   4   The dearest idol I have known, Whate'er that idol be

if
  15   3   If with his love he befriend thee
  36   3   If on our daily course our mind Be set to hallow all we find
  50   1   It is not night if thou be near
  55   2   What if thy form we cannot see
  68   2   If I survey the ground I tread or gaze upon the sky
  79   1   I nothing lack if I am his and he is mine forever
  83   T,1   If Thou but Suffer God to Guide Thee
101   2   If our love were but more simple   (102-4)
128   4   If I were a shepherd, I would bring a lamb
128   4   If I were a wiseman, I would do my part
148   3   And if Satan, vexing sore, Flesh or spirit should assail
209   4   I triumph still if thou abide with me
218   1   I shall not fear the battle If thou art by my side
218   1   Now wander from the pathway If thou wilt be my guide
324   3   If in this darksome wild I stray
330   5   If there is aught of worth in me, It comes from thee alone
336   2   We perish if we cease from prayer
344   1   Yet possessing every blessing, If our God our Father be
351   5   Or if on joyful wing Cleaving the sky
356   3   If it would reach a monarch's throne It must ... resign
365   2   And blest would be their children's fate If they ... die for
365   2   If they, like them, should die for thee
377   4   Zion, if thou die believing, Heaven's path shall open lie
392   3   That we may bring, if need arise, no ... worthless sacrifice
395   6   Work shall be prayer, if all be wrought As thou wouldst
401   2   Or if he pleaseth through it pass, And then the heaven espy
425   1   If there breathe on earth a slave, Are ye truly free & brave
425   1   If ye do not feel the chain when it works a brother's pain
428   2   If not I'll smite your first-born dead
431   4   If drunk with sight of power, we loose Wild tongues
442   1   Convict us now, if we rebel, Our nation judge, and shame it
445   4   How shall we love thee, holy, hidden Being, If we love not
445   4   If we love not the world which thou hast made
470   3   Ah, if with them the world might pass astray
495   4   If you love him, why not serve him
576   4   If I the wings of morning take
576   5   If deepest darkness cover me

ignorance
452   2   High walls of ignorance around

ignorantly
386   3   To all the gods we ignorantly make And worship

ill

23	3	praise him still Through good and ill, Who ever lives
39	4	To make ill-fortune turn to fair
56	2	Forgive me, Lord, for thy dear Son, The ill that I this day
56	2	The ill that I this day have done
74	2	Mixture strange of good and ill
79	4	In death's dark vale I fear no ill
79	4	I fear no ill With thee, dear Lord, beside me
84	3	Yet will I fear no ill, For thou art with me
85	4	he shall Preserve thee from all ill
231	3	Where thou art guide no ill can come
292	3	Deliver us from every touch of ill
347	2	Help us, through good report & ill, Our daily cross to bear
380	2	taught To fear no ill, to fight The holy fight they fought
575	3	Where thou art guide no ill can come

ills

29	2	And free us from all ills In this world and the next
55	2	we, Oppressed with various ills, draw near
209	4	Ills have no weight, and tears no bitterness
363	1	Our helper he amid the flood Of mortal ills prevailing

illumines

| 439 | 3 | For the glory that illumines Patriot souls of deathless fame |

illuming

| 239 | 2 | And clothe me round, the while my path illuming |

illumining

| 39 | 1 | O Day, all days illumining |

illusion

| 86 | T,1 | Our God, to Whom We Turn, When weary with illusion |

image

| 67 | 4 | Thine image and thyself are there, The indwelling God |
| 74 | 3 | Teach us more of human pity, That we in thine image grow |

imagination

| 570 | 6 | scattered the proud in the imagination of their hearts |

immortal

7	T,1	Immortal, Invisible, God only Wise
8	1	Giver of immortal gladness, Fill us with the light of day
108	3	Where we shall join the choirs immortal
180	2	Glorious life, and life immortal On this holy Easter morn
230	T,1	Immortal Love, Forever Full, Forever flowing free
280	2	That living bread, that heavenly wine, Be our immortal food
289	1	Knowledge and faith and life immortal Jesus ... imparts
292	1	The one true, pure, immortal sacrifice
357	T,1	Strong Son of God, Immortal Love
362	1	A heavenly race demands thy zeal, And an immortal crown
464	T,1	Praise to God, Immortal Praise

immortality

| 149 | 3 | I only know a living Christ, Our immortality |

immovable

264	4	Unshaken as eternal hills, Immovable she stands

impart

33	4	While we daily search thy Word, Wisdom true impart, O Lord
43	2	Till they inward light impart Glad my eyes and warm my heart
78	4	And courage in the evil hour His heavenly aids impart
212	3	Glorious Lord, thyself impart
214	3	Still to the lowly soul He doth himself impart
231	1	Who dost thy seven-fold gifts impart
235	3	The Word of life and truth impart
262	2	Thy grace impart
348	2	May thy rich grace impart Strength to my fainting heart
381	3	Thy spirit, Lord, to me impart, O make me what thou ever art
397	3	The precious things thou dost impart
575	1	Who dost thy seven-fold gifts impart

imparted

258	4	By the word imparted To the simple hearted

imparts

134	3	So God imparts to human hearts The blessings of his heaven
256	5	Lord, grant us all aright to learn The wisdom it imparts
289	1	Knowledge and faith and life immortal Jesus ... imparts
289	1	Jesus thy Son to us imparts
290	1	From the best bliss that earth imparts, We turn unfilled
460	3	Accept the gifts we offer, For all thy love imparts

impassioned

440	2	pilgrim feet, Whose stern, impassioned stress

impels

144	3	O Jesus, while the star of grace Impels us
144	3	Impels us on to seek thy face

implanted

14	3	He hath eternal life Implanted in the soul

implore

39	3	The Father, too, our prayers implore
244	1	We before thee For that precious gift implore thee
268	3	Make us one we now implore
407	4	Thy grace, O Father, give, I humbly thee implore
472	3	May all who seek this door, And saving grace implore

imploring

249	5	Pray we that thou wilt hear us, still imploring Thy love

imprison

356	1	Imprison me within thine arms, And strong shall be my hand

impulse

404	2	Take my hands and let them move At the impulse of thy love

inaccessible

7	1	In light inaccessible hid from our eyes

inarmed

450	3	Nation with nation, land with land, Inarmed shall live
450	3	Inarmed shall live as comrades free

incarnate

49	2	Thee, his incarnate Son, And Holy Spirit adoring
120	2	Veiled in flesh the God-head see, Hail the incarnate Deity
127	1	tidings first begun of God incarnate and the Virgin's Son
246	2	Come, thou incarnate Word
252	T,1	O Word of God Incarnate, O Wisdom from on high
413	1	Son of man, whose birth incarnate Hallows all our human race

incarnation

163	3	For me, Kind Jesus, was thy incarnation

incense

31	1	With gold of obedience and incense of lowliness
140	3	So bring him incense, gold, and myrrh
141	5	Their gold and myrrh and frankincense
143	3	Frankincense to offer have I, Incense owns a deity nigh
405	1	Yet may love's incense rise, Sweeter than sacrifice
506	2	Ready burning Be the incense of thy powers

incessant

454	2	By his incessant bounty fed, By his unerring counsel led

incline

544	1	and incline our hearts to keep this law

incomplete

303	1	thanks That this thy world is incomplete

increase

249	4	Thine is the quickening power that gives increase
259	4	O Father, Son, and Spirit, send Us increase from above
373	4	His love thy joy increase
376	1	And doubts appall, and sorrows still increase
433	3	Thy true religion in our hearts increase
466	3	In all our hearts such love increase, That every home
467	2	When the vain cares that vex our life increase
521	2	Make strong our faith, increase our light

indeed

4	2	The Lord, ye know, is God indeed
74	4	Spirit in our spirit speaking, Make us sons of God indeed
83	3	The soul that trusted him indeed
169	2	But O, my friend, My friend indeed
281	1	For thou art our food indeed
287	5	It is enough, my Lord, enough indeed
365	3	Mankind shall then indeed be free
385	1	Till every foe is vanquished, And Christ is Lord indeed
425	1	Are ye not base slaves indeed, Slaves unworthy to be freed
439	4	Make our nation free indeed
557	3	It is enough, my Lord, enough indeed

indwelling
67	4	Thine image and thyself are there, The indwelling God
67	4	The indwelling God, proclaimed of old

ineffable
248	2	Ineffable in loving, Unthinkable in might
490	4	And for the life ineffable Within the Father's home

ineffably
199	4	Creator of the rolling spheres, Ineffably sublime

infancy
118	1	This child, now weak in infancy, Our confidence ... shall be

infant
94	2	Before my infant heart conceived From whom those comforts
117	2	God with man is now residing, Yonder shines the infant light
126	1,5	Guide where our infant Redeemer is laid
127	3	The first apostles of his infant fame
138	1	Holy infant so tender and mild, Sleep in heavenly peace
202	3	And infant voices shall proclaim their early blessings
278	1	As thou wast once an infant here

infants'
50	4	Be every mourner's sleep tonight Like infants' slumbers
50	4	Like infants' slumbers, pure and light

infinite
99	2	Changeless, eternal, infinite
173	2	O infinite compassion, still revealing ... forgiveness
173	2	revealing The infinite forgiveness won for man
206	4	And thanks never ceasing and infinite love
247	1	Infinite thy vast domain, Everlasting is thy reign
333	3	Give us thy good, and save us from our evil, Infinite Spirit
559	6	The Father, of an infinite majesty

inflicts
224	2	The wrong of man to man on thee Inflicts a deeper wrong

inhabitest
402	2	thou, within no walls confined, Inhabitest the humble mind

inherit
228	2	Let us all in thee inherit, Let us find thy promised rest
371	3	We know we at the end Shall life inherit

inheritance
391	3	Thou mine inheritance, now and always

injuries
169	4	Sweet injuries

inly
44	2	Did not their spirits inly yearn

inmost

| 83 | 2 | Nor doubt our inmost wants are known To him |
| 406 | 3 | Thee ... Whose eyes my inmost substance see |

inner

| 114 | 3 | here, Lord, abide. Let me thy inner presence feel |
| 451 | 1 | Still wilt not hear thine inner God proclaim |

inprison

| 380 | 1 | Who, thrust inprison or cast to flame |

inspire

86	4	Inspire us from above With joy and strength for duty
116	2	Say what may the tidings be Which inspire your heavenly song
231	T,1	Come, Holy Ghost, Our Souls Inspire
294	3	Inspire thy heralds of good news To live thy life divine
348	2	My zeal inspire
490	4	Spirit of Christ, do thou Our first bright days inspire
575	T,1	Come, Holy Ghost, Our Souls Inspire

inspired

253	3	Praise we God, who hath inspired Those whose wisdom
295	4	Inspired with hope and praise, To Christ belong
395	6	prayer, by thee inspired and taught, Itself with work be one
470	5	Inspired of thee, may they count all but loss

inspires

| 387 | 2 | One the hope our God inspires |
| 442 | 3 | And, judging, pardons, frees, inspires |

inspiring

| 416 | 2 | Thou canst bring inspiring light |

instead

| 449 | 1 | Let there be deeds, instead of boasts |

instil

| 542 | 1 | Thy word into our minds instil |

instill

| 449 | 2 | Within our passioned hearts instill The calm |

instinct

44	1	Love's blind instinct made them bold to crave thy presence
359	3	Thrice blest is he to whom is given The instinct
359	3	The instinct that can tell That God is on the field

intent

| 141 | 3 | To seek for a king was their intent |
| 371 | 1 | His first avowed intent To be a pilgrim |

interceding

| 173 | 1 | O voice, which, through the ages interceding |

intercessor
173 4 O Intercessor, who art ever living To plead for ... souls

intercessors
470 3 Anoint them priests, Strong intercessors they For pardon

interpreted
341 3 The silence of eternity, Interpreted by love

interpreter
87 4 God is his own interpreter, And he will make it plain

into
47 2 While earth rolls onward into light
60 3 Turn thou for us its darkness into light
92 4 Thou ... turnest my mourning into praise
97 2 And faith's fair vision changes into sight
185 1 God hath brought his Israel Into joy from sadness
210 1 Safe into the haven guide, O receive my soul at last
228 2 O breathe thy loving Spirit Into every troubled breast
228 4 Changed from glory into glory
259 2 'Twas but the dawning yet to grow Into the perfect day
275 1 from the night profound Into the glory of the perfect day
275 2 Descend, O Holy Spirit, like a dove Into our hearts
275 3 One with the joy that breaketh into song
275 3 One with the grief that trembleth into prayer
289 2 So from all lands thy Church be gathered Into thy kingdom
289 2 thy Church be gathered Into thy kingdom by thy Son
318 1 Breathe into every wish Thy will divine
364 2 Striving, tempting, luring, Goading into sin
382 1 Forward into battle, See his banners go
424 3 It will pass into the splendors Of the city of the light
470 3 pass astray Into the dear Christ's life of sacrifice
484 3 Shall understand his kingdom And come into his grace
494 2 upon the solid rock We set the dream that hardens into deed
542 1 Thy word into our minds instil
565 3 O go your way into his gates with thanksgiving
565 3 and into his courts with praise
568 12 and to guide our feet into the way of peace

introduced
362 4 Blest Savior, introduced by thee, Have I my race begun

invisible
7 T,1 Immortal, Invisible, God only Wise
359 3 God is on the field when he Is most invisible

involved
376 3 Involved in shadows of a mortal night

inward
43 2 Till they inward light impart Glad my eyes and warm my heart
242 1 Word of God, and inward light
262 3 Confessing, in a world's accord, The inward Christ
262 3 The inward Christ, the living Word

| 272 | 4 | When we are called to part It gives us inward pain |
| 336 | 3 | Truth in the inward parts |

ire
| 436 | 3 | In ire and exultation Aflame with faith and free |

iron
128	1	Earth stood hard as iron, Water like a stone
180	2	Now the iron bars are broken
417	2	Each old age of gold was an iron age too
431	5	In reeking tube and iron shard
452	2	Our souls are bound In iron chains of fear and pride

Isabella
| 124 | 1 | Bring a Torch, Jeannette, Isabella |

Isaiah
| 131 | 2 | Isaiah 'twas foretold it, The Rose I have in mind |

island
| 47 | 3 | As o'er each continent and island The dawn leads on |
| 73 | 2 | Rock and highland, wood and island |

islands
| 360 | 3 | I know not where his islands lift Their fronded palms in air |

isles
| 106 | 2 | Isles of the southern seas, Deep in your coral caves |
| 298 | 2 | Give ear to me, ye continents, Ye isles, give ear to me |

Israel
85	2	Behold, he that keeps Israel, He slumbers not, nor sleeps
109	1	traveler, yes, it brings the day, Promised day of Israel
110	T,1	O Come, O Come Emmanuel, And ransom captive Israel
110	R	Rejoice, Rejoice, Emmanuel Shall come to thee, O Israel
141	R	Nowell, Nowell, Nowell, Nowell, Born is the King of Israel
155	2	Thou art the King of Israel, Thou David's royal son
185	1	God hath brought his Israel Into joy from sadness
428	T,1	When Israel Was in Egypt's Land
568	T,1	Blessed Be the Lord God of Israel
570	9	He, remembering his mercy, hath holpen his servant Israel
572	4	and to be the glory of thy people Israel

Israel's
103	2	Israel's strength and consolation
195	3	Ye seed of Israel's chosen race, Ye ransomed from the fall
432	2	Thou wast the shield for Israel's marching host

jacket
| 422 | 5 | God in a workman's jacket as before |

Jacob
| 144 | 2 | From Jacob shall a star proceed |

Jacob's
| 185 | 1 | Loosed from Pharaoh's bitter yoke Jacob's sons and daughters |

495 T,1 We Are Climbing Jacob's Ladder

jealousies
445 3 In wrath and fear, by jealousies surrounded

Jeannette
124 1 Bring a Torch, Jeannette, Isabella

Jehovah
93 T,1 Guide Me, O Thou Great Jehovah

Jehovah's
9 T,1 Before Jehovah's Aweful Throne
10 T,1 Before Jehovah's Aweful Throne (same as Hymn No. 9)
427 2 Up, it is Jehovah's rally, God's own arm hath need of thine

Jerusalem
104 1 Speak ye to Jerusalem Of the peace that waits for them
108 1 Awake, Jerusalem, arise
156 T,1 Draw Nigh to Thy Jerusalem, O Lord
185 3 Comes to glad Jerusalem Who with true affection
309 T,1 Jerusalem the Golden, with milk and honey blest
310 2 Truly Jerusalem name we that shore
312 T,1 Jerusalem, My Happy Home, When shall I come to thee
312 6 Jerusalem, Jerusalem, God grant that I may see ... joy

Jesse
145 1 Thou Root of Jesse, David's Son, My Lord and Master

Jesse's
131 1 Of Jesse's lineage coming As men of old have sung
195 2 Extol the stem of Jesse's rod

Jesu
133 3 Jesu, tibi sit gloria
135 T,1,2 O Jesu Sweet, O Jesu Mild

Jesus
2 3 O Jesus Christ, our God and Lord, Begotten of the Father
2 3 hear our cry, Have mercy on us, Jesus
34 2 So let the love of Jesus come And set thy soul ablaze
35 1-6 May Jesus Christ be praised
35 1 Alike at work and prayer, To Jesus I repair
44 T,1 Lord Jesus, in the Days of Old
49 1 Our Savior Jesus Christ, Joyful in thine appearing
51 2 Jesus, give the weary Calm and sweet repose
54 T,1 Now Cheer Our Hearts This Eventide, Lord Jesus Christ
103 T,1 Come, Thou Long-Expected Jesus, Born to set thy people free
106 4 High raise the note, that Jesus died, Yet lives and reigns
119 4 Holy Jesus, every day Keep us in the narrow way
120 2 Pleased as man with men to dwell, Jesus our Emmanuel
121 3 Ah, dearest Jesus, holy child, Make thee a bed
124 1 It is Jesus, good folk of the village
124 2 Lest your noise should waken Jesus

joined
145 2   Thy member, ever joined to thee In love that cannot falter
272 4   But we shall still be joined in heart

joining
21 2   Beside us to guide us, our God with us joining
268 1   Joining heart to heart with others

joins
247 3   Lo, the apostolic train Joins thy sacred name to hallow

Jordan
93 3   When I tread the verge of Jordan
193 3   Bring us safe through Jordan To thy home above
370 3   Since God through Jordan leadeth me

Jordan's
115 T,1   On Jordan's Bank the Baptist's Cry

Joseph
127 3   And found, with Joseph and the blessed maid, Her Son

Joseph's
149 3   know not how that Joseph's tomb Could solve death's mystery

journey
93 2   Let the fire & cloudy pillar Lead me all my journey through
106 5   Shout, while ye journey home, Songs be in every mouth
274 3   They journey on from strength to strength
375 3   Thy cross is lifted o'er us, We journey in its light
376 3   Only with thee we journey safely on
387 2   One the object of our journey

journeys
202 1   sun Doth his successive journeys run
421 1   And he who journeys in them walks with thee

joy
4 3   Approach with joy his courts unto
8 2   All thy works with joy surround thee
8 3   Well-spring of the joy of living, Ocean depth of happy rest
8 3   Lift us to the joy divine
9 1   Ye nations bow with sacred joy
24 1   Therefore with joy our song shall soar In praise to God
41 2   Bring us to heaven, where thy saints united Joy
41 2   Joy without ending
53 2   For joy of beauty not his own
55 1   O in what diverse pains they met ... what joy they went away
63 1   Fill our hearts with joy and peace
66 3   For the joy of ear and eye, For the heart and mind's delight
66 4   For the joy of human love, Brother, sister, parent, child
81 1   In trouble and in joy
86 4   Inspire us from above With joy and strength for duty
94 3   That tastes those gifts with joy
98 1   So full of splendor and of joy, Beauty and light
98 2   I thank thee, too, that thou hast made Joy to abound

312	6	see Thine endless joy, and of the same Partaker ever be
314	4	I may the eternal brightness see, And share thy joy at last
315	1	Of joy that hath no ending, Of love which cannot cease
331	3	Ever in joy or grief, My Lord, for thee
339	2	Love doth stand At his hand, Joy doth wait on his command
342	3	I need thee every hour In joy or pain
344	3	Fill our hearts with heavenly joy
365	1	O how our hearts beat high with joy
367	1	Lay hold on life, & it shall be Thy joy and crown eternally
373	4	His love thy joy increase
376	4	Through joy or sorrow, as thou deemest best
399	3	O Joy that seekest me through pain
400	2	Once earthly joy I craved, Sought peace and rest
412	3	That it may be our highest joy Our Father's work to do
416	3	Let thine alms be hope and joy
430	2	With joy and peace thou shalt abound
445	2	And sharing not our griefs, no joy can share
449	3	To joy and suffer not alone
451	3	Peals forth in joy man's old undaunted cry
454	4	In scenes exalted or depressed, Thou art our joy & ... rest
457	2	winging thoughts, and happy moods Of love and joy and prayer
457	2	For summer joy in field and wood We lift our song to him
461	2	Wheat and tares together sown, Unto joy or sorrow grown
464	1	Bounteous source of every joy
465	3	Grant them the joy which brightens earthly sorrow
467	1	Dark though the night, joy cometh with the morrow
470	5	And stand at last with joy before thy face
472	T,1	Lord, Thou Hast Known Our Joy
505	1	And joy to see the cheerful light That riseth in the east
528	3	Restore to me the joy of thy salvation
577	R	to thee, the source of all our joy, To thee we sing

joyful

8	T,1	Joyful, Joyful, We Adore Thee, God of glory, Lord of love
8	4	Joyful music leads us sunward, In the triumph song of life
20	3	Be joyful in the Lord, my heart
23	3	And onward as ye go Some joyful anthem sing
26	T,1	O Be Joyful in the Lord, Sing before him, all the earth
27	T,1	O Be Joyful in the Lord (words the same as No. 26)
29	2	With ever joyful hearts And blessed peace to cheer us
32	1	joyful rise To pay thy morning sacrifice
49	1	Our Savior Jesus Christ, Joyful in thine appearing
63	2	Thanks we give and adoration For thy Gospel's joyful sound
77	1	Through thorny ways leads to a joyful end
94	4	Through all eternity to thee A joyful song I'll raise
119	2	As with joyful steps they sped To that lowly manger-bed
120	1	Joyful, all ye nations rise, Join the triumph of the skies
127	1	With them the joyful tidings first begun
132	T,1	O Come, All Ye Faithful, joyful and triumphant
146	5	angels ... who thus Addressed their joyful song
188	3	O Lord of all, with us abide In this our joyful Eastertide
189	2	Now let the earth be joyful In spring-time's bright array
192	3	Now let the heavens be joyful, Let earth her song begin
229	2	By thee the joyful news Of our salvation came
229	2	The joyful news of sins forgiven
229	2	joyful news ... Of hell subdued and peace with heaven

295	4	With joyful song
299	2	Whene'er thy joyful sound is heard
318	2	Joyful to follow thee Through paths unknown
351	5	Or if on joyful wing Cleaving the sky
503	1	Where my soul in joyful duty Waits for him who answers
565	T,1	O Be Joyful in the Lord all ye lands

joyless

43	2	Joyless is the day's return Till thy mercy's beams I see

joyous

35	3	Let all the earth around Ring joyous with the sound
116	1	And the mountains in reply Echo back their joyous strains
116	2	Shepherds, why this jubilee, Why your joyous strains prolong
337	1	Soon end in joyous day
455	4	As well as summer's joyous rays
481	3	The world is bright with the joyous saints
492	1	Whose joyous fellowship we share At work, at rest

joys

77	3	Sorrow forgot, love's purest joys restored
142	4	Lead us all with hearts aflame Unto the joys above us
148	2	Shall not we thy sorrow share, And from earthly joys abstain
157	4	Joys that through all time abide
182	1	Raise your joys and triumphs high
209	2	Earth's joys grow dim, its glories pass away
224	2	To thee our full humanity, Its joys and pains belong
309	1	I know not, O I know not, What joys await us there
312	1	Thy joys, when shall I see
322	4	In our joys and in our sorrows, Days of toil & hours of ease
391	4	May I reach heaven's joys, O bright heaven's Sun
424	2	All our joys and all our groans Help to rear its shining
539	2	possess in sweet communion Joys which earth cannot afford

jubilant

304	1	Lift up your hearts in jubilant accord
309	2	They stand, those halls of Zion, All jubilant with song
443	3	O be swift, my soul, to answer him, be jubilant, my feet

jubilate

52	R	Jubilate, Jubilate, Jubilate, Amen

jubilee

116	2	Shepherds, why this jubilee, Why your joyous strains prolong
191	5	we raise To thee, in jubilee and praise

judge

87	3	Judge not the Lord by feeble sense
95	3	Rise, God, judge thou the earth in might
163	1	That man to judge thee hath in hate pretended
248	1	The righteous Judge of judges, The almighty King of kings
392	4	On thee for judge and not our friends
431	3	Judge of the nations, spare us yet, Lest we forget
435	T,1	Judge Eternal, Throned in Splendor
442	T,1	Thou Judge by Whom Each Empire Fell

442	1	Convict us now, if we rebel, Our nation judge, and shame it
442	2	And judge, that thou may'st heal us
559	11	We believe that thou shalt come to be our judge
562	9	For he cometh, for he cometh to judge the earth
562	9	with righteousness to judge the world
562	9	judge ... the peoples with his truth

judged

| 161 | T,1 | Before the Cross of Jesus Our lives are judged today |

judges

| 248 | 1 | The righteous Judge of judges, The almighty King of kings |

judging

| 442 | 3 | And, judging, pardons, frees, inspires |

judgment

101	1	no place ... earth's failing Have such kindly judgment given
106	1	He judgment brings and victory
158	2	See him at the judgment hall
161	2	On all, the judgment of the cross Falls steady, clear & sure
358	4	See thee on thy judgment throne
435	1	With thy living fire of judgment Purge this land
442	2	The present be our judgment day
443	3	He is sifting out the hearts of men before his judgment seat
444	1	Come with thy ... judgment now To match our present hour
444	1	Come with thy timeless judgment now

judgments

82	2	Thy judgments are a mighty deep
444	5	Let there be light again, and set thy judgments in the earth
473	2	For judgments thine are known

just

2	2	O Father, that thy rule is just And wise, and changes never
20	2	Within the kingdom of his might, Lo, all is just ... right
319	T,1	Just As I Am, Without One Plea
319	2	Just as I am, though tossed about
319	3	Just as I am, poor, wretched, blind
319	4	Just as I am, thou wilt receive
320	T,1	Just as I Am, Without One Plea (same words as no. 319)
340	T,1	They Cast Their Nets in Galilee Just off the hills of brown
357	2	And thou hast made him thou art just
468	4	Thy word is true, thy will is just
469	3	Thy word is true, thy ways are just
473	1	Just, King of saints, and true thy ways
481	3	For the saints of God are just folk like me
496	2	Then conquer we must, when our cause it is just

justice

7	2	Thy justice like mountains high soaring above
82	2	Forever firm thy justice stands
82	2	firm thy justice stands As mountains their foundations keep
95	2	justice, from her heavenly bower, Look down on mortal men
101	1	There's a kindness in his justice (102-1)
257	2	But the blest volume thou hast writ Reveals thy justice

257	2	Reveals thy justice and thy grace
424	1	Justice reigns supreme o'er all
439	4	God of justice, save the people From the war of race & creed
442	3	Though selfish, mean, & base we be, Thy justice is unbounded
444	3	Bring justice to our land, That all may dwell secure

keen

381	3	My faith, it is a trusty sword, May falsehood find it keen
455	2	His life within the keen air breathes
455	3	And skies are chill, and frosts are keen

keenest

| 344 | 2 | Thou didst feel its keenest woe |
| 380 | 3 | In keenest strife, Lord, may we stand, Upheld |

keep

3	1	God is in his temple, All within keep silence
29	2	And keep us in his grace, And guide us when perplexed
56	1	O keep me, King of kings Beneath thine own almighty wings
60	3	from harm and danger keep thy children free
61	4	Keep love's banner floating o'er you
82	2	firm thy justice stands As mountains their foundations keep
83	3	Sing, pray, and keep his ways unswerving
85	4	The Lord shall keep thy soul
85	4	Henceforth thy going out and in God keep forever will
100	5	Unto such as keep his covenant And are steadfast in his way
107	T,1	Let All Mortal Flesh Keep Silence
119	4	Holy Jesus, every day Keep us in the narrow way
127	4	O may we keep and ponder in our mind God's wondrous love
134	2	While mortals sleep, the angels keep Their watch
148	4	Keep, O keep us, Savior dear, Ever constant by thy side
161	2	The faith we keep in goodness
167	VII-2	Keep us in that trial hour, Hear us, holy Jesus
192	3	The round world keep high triumph, And all that is therein
210	3	Let the healing streams abound, Make and keep me pure within
215	1	Keep thou my feet
229	3	And through this desert land, Still keep me near thy side
231	3	Keep far our foes, give peace at home
271	3	Unbroken be the golden chain, Keep on the song forever
277	1	From all danger keep them free
277	2	Vision true to keep them noble
322	3	From each idol that would keep us
327	2	Keep thy flock, from sin defend us
329	1	O shame, thrice shame upon us To keep his standing there
330	5	Then keep me safe, for so, O Lord Thou keepest but thine own
344	1	Guard us, guide us, keep us, feed us
354	2	Thy rod and staff shall keep us safe, And guide our steps
429	1	Who bidd'st the mighty ocean deep Its ... limits keep
429	1	Its own appointed limits keep
430	3	And keep his truth for evermore
439	4	Keep her faith in simple manhood
441	2	Thy must upward still and onward Who would keep ... truth
441	2	Who would keep abreast of truth
455	4	And keep us through life's wintry days
480	3	He is my Father, who will keep His child through every day
482	1	See the fur to keep you warm, Snugly round your tiny form

491	1	Keep us, we pray thee, steadfast and unerring
494	3	O keep us building Master
517	1	teach me ... the way ... And I shall keep it unto the end
541	T,1	Thou Wilt Keep him in Perfect Peace
544	1	and incline our hearts to keep this law
559	15	Vouchsafe, O Lord, to keep us this day without sin
575	3	Keep far our foes, give peace at home

keeper

| 507 | 1 | thou Wouldst be our guard and keeper now |

keepest

| 330 | 5 | Then keep me safe, for so, O Lord Thou keepest but thine own |

keepeth

| 20 | 2 | What God's almighty power hath made, His ... mercy keepeth |
| 20 | 2 | His gracious mercy keepeth |

keeping

47	2	Through all the world her watch is keeping
140	1	While shepherds watch are keeping
141	1	In fields where they lay keeping their sheep
268	1	Keeping faith with us and thee
333	3	Father of mercy, from thy watch & keeping No place can part
377	1	Thou art daily in his keeping, And thine every care is his
441	3	God within the shadow Keeping watch above his own

keeps

85	2	nor will He slumber that thee keeps
85	2	Behold, he that keeps Israel, He slumbers not, nor sleeps
85	3	The Lord thee keeps
418	3	In work that keeps faith sweet and strong

ken

| 248 | 2 | Beyond our ken thou shinest, The everlasting Light |

kept

98	4	I thank thee, Lord, that thou hast kept The best in store
121	3	heart, that it may be A quiet chamber kept for thee
183	1	Kept the folded grave-clothes Where the body lay
249	5	Thy love and favor, kept to us always
347	5	Kept peaceful in the midst of strife, Forgiving and forgiven
488	1	While shepherds kept their watching O'er silent flocks

keys

| 204 | 3 | The keys of death and hell Are to our Jesus given |

kill

| 363 | 4 | The body they may kill, God's truth abideth still |
| 449 | 2 | Purge us from lusts that curse and kill |

killed

| 142 | 3 | All the little boys he killed At Bethlem in his fury |

kin

| 414 | 3 | Who serves my Father as a son Is surely kin to me |

kind

26	4	For the Lord our God is kind, And his love shall constant be
55	5	Thy kind but searching glance can scan the very wounds
70	1,6	Praise the Lord, for he is kind
76	T,1	How Gentle God's Commands, How kind his precepts are
101	2	heart of the Eternal Is most wonderfully kind (102-3)
131	2	With Mary we behold it, The Virgin Mother kind
163	3	For me, Kind Jesus, was thy incarnation
163	4	Therefore, kind Jesus, since I cannot pay thee
225	3	To those who fall, how kind thou art
245	2	with wisdom kind and clear Let thy life in mine appear
277	T,1	Jesus, Friend, So Kind and Gentle
328	T,1	The Lord Is Rich and Merciful, The Lord is very kind
471	4	Make him a shepherd, kind to young and old
479	2	To be to others kind and good
483	2	and that I might have seen his kind look when he said

kindle

239	1	And kindle it, thy holy flame bestowing
240	1	Kindle a flame of sacred love In these cold hearts of ours
240	3	Come, shed abroad a Savior's love, & that shall kindle ours
242	2	Kindle every high desire, Perish self in thy pure fire

kindled

99	2	Self-fed, self-kindled like the light

kindlier

453	5	The larger heart, the kindlier hand

kindliness

217	3	Lord of all kindliness, Lord of all grace

kindling

89	5	And kindling hearts that burn for thee
334	1	Fain would our souls feel all thy kindling love
334	3	Our spirits yearn to feel thy kindling love
397	4	heart o'erflow In kindling thought and glowing word

kindly

50	2	When the soft dews of kindly sleep
100	2	Who with thee so kindly deals
101	1	no place ... earth's failing Have such kindly judgment given
215	T,1	Lead Kindly Light amid the encircling gloom
216	T,1	Lead Kindly Light (same words as no. 215)
365	4	And preach thee, too, as love knows how, By kindly words
365	4	By kindly words and virtuous life
410	1	Each smile a hymn, each kindly deed a prayer

kindness

101	1	There's a kindness in his justice (102-1)
101	1	kindness ... Which is more than liberty (102-1)
263	2	With thy wonted loving-kindness Hear thy people as they pray
294	2	kindness dwell in human hearts And all the earth find peace
330	1	Thou of thy love hast named a friend, O kindness wonderful
331	2	Some work of love begun, Some deed of kindness done
347	3	And kindness in our bosoms dwell As free and true as thine

405	2	Some deeds of kindness done, Some souls by patience won
409	3	Every deed of love and kindness Done to man is done to thee
498	T,1	Each Morning Brings us fresh outpoured The loving-kindness
498	1	The loving-kindness of the Lord

kindred

195	4	Let every kindred, every tribe, On this terrestrial ball
272	1	The fellowship of kindred minds Is like to that above
299	4	The name of Jesus glorify Till every kindred call him Lord
322	2	Turned from home and toil and kindred
363	4	Let goods and kindred go, This mortal life also

king

6	T,1	O Worship the King, All Glorious Above
15	T,1	Praise to the Lord, the Almighty, the King of creation
16	T,1	Praise, My Soul, the King of Heaven
16	1	Praise the everlasting King
23	3	Ye saints who toil below, Adore your heavenly King
26	2	Know ye ... the Lord is King, All his works his wisdom prove
32	2	sing High praise to the eternal King
56	1	O keep me, King of kings Beneath thine own almighty wings
64	T,1	All Creatures of Our God and King
65	3	Stars that have no voice to sing Give ... glory to our King
79	T,1	The King of Love My Shepherd Is
80	T,1	The King of Love My Shepherd Is (words the same as No. 79)
103	3	Born thy people to deliver, Born a child, and yet a king
107	2	King of kings, yet born of Mary, As of old on earth he stood
111	2	And extol our God and King
114	1	Behold the King of glory waits
114	1	The King of kings is drawing near
115	1	Glad tidings from the King of kings
117	R	Come and worship, Worship Christ, the new-born King
119	3	treasures bring, Christ, to thee, our heavenly King
120	T,1,R	Hark, The Herald Angels Sing, Glory to the new-born King
129	1	From heaven's all gracious King
130	1	Let earth receive her King
132	1	Come and behold him, born the King of angels
134	2	And praises sing to God the King, And peace to men on earth
136	1	With the song children sing To the Lord, Christ our King
136	4	Praising Christ, heaven's King
140	R	This, this is Christ the King
140	3	Come peasant, king, to own him
140	3	The King of kings salvation brings
141	R	Nowell, Nowell, Nowell, Nowell, Born is the King of Israel
141	3	To seek for a king was their intent
142	T,1	Unto Us a Boy Is Born, The King of all creation
143	2	Born a king on Bethlehem's plain
143	2	King forever, ceasing never Over us all to reign
143	5	Glorious now behold him arise, King and God and Sacrifice
144	1	'Tis sent to announce a new-born king
147	T,1	All Praise to Thee, for Thou, O King Divine
152	1	Haste, let us lay our gifts before the King
155	T,1,3	All Glory, Laud, and Honor To thee, Redeemer, King
155	2	Thou art the King of Israel, Thou David's royal son
155	2	Who in the Lord's name cometh, The King and blessed One
155	3	Who in all good delightest, Thou good and gracious King

kingdoms

264	3	For not like kingdoms of the world Thy holy Church, O God
382	3	Crowns and thrones may perish, Kingdoms rise and wane
491	4	When all its kingdoms shall his kingdom be

kingly

326	T,1	Thou Didst Leave Thy Throne and thy kingly crown
388	T,1	The Son of God Goes Forth to War, A kingly crown to gain
470	4	Anoint them kings, Aye, kingly kings, O Lord

kings

56	1	O keep me, King of kings Beneath thine own almighty wings
69	2	Kings of knowledge and of law, To the glorious circle draw
107	2	King of kings, yet born of Mary, As of old on earth he stood
114	1	The King of kings is drawing near
115	1	Glad tidings from the King of kings
140	3	The King of kings salvation brings
143	T,1	We Thee Kings of Orient Are, Bearing gifts we traverse afar
183	3	through Christendom it rings That the Lamb is King of kings
200	2	King of kings, and Lord of lords, And heaven's eternal light
201	5	Come quickly, King of kings
203	2	Crown the Savior King of kings
203	4	crown him King of kings, and Lord of lords
248	1	The righteous Judge of judges, The almighty King of kings
264	T,1	O Where Are Kings and Empires Now Of old that went and came
300	1	To serve the King of kings
431	2	The captains and the kings depart
435	1	Lord of lords and King of kings
470	4	Anoint them kings, Aye, kingly kings, O Lord

kingship

325	1	And mocked thy saving kingship then

kiss

128	3	his mother ... Worshipped the beloved With a kiss

Knabe

139	1	Holder Knabe im lockigen Haar

knee

116	3	Come adore on bended knee Christ the Lord, the new-born King
119	2	There to bend the knee before Him who heaven and earth adore
141	5	Full reverently upon their knee
197	T,1	At the Name of Jesus Every knee shall bow
203	1	Every knee to him shall bow
247	4	And adoring bend the knee While we sing our praise to thee
332	3	While in prayer we bowed the knee
386	3	Lighten our darkness when we bow the knee To all the gods
400	1	Hear thou the prayer I make On bended knee

kneel

22	1	We lay it before thee, we kneel and adore thee
31	1	Kneel and adore him, the Lord is his name
123	3	Here let all, Great and small, Kneel in awe and wonder
465	1	Lowly we kneel in prayer before thy throne
562	6	and kneel before the Lord our maker

kneeling

60	1	Then, lowly kneeling, wait thy word of peace
136	3	Kneeling low by his bed, Lay their gifts before him
334	T,1	Father, in Thy Mysterious Presence kneeling
334	3	Now, Father, now, in thy dear presence kneeling

knees

113	4	At thy great name exalted now All knees must bend
113	4	All knees must bend, all hearts must bow
249	1	To thee all knees are bent, all voices pray
288	T,1	Let us Break Bread Together on our knees
288	R	When I fall on my knees with my face to the rising sun
288	2	Let us drink wine together on our knees
288	3	Let us praise God together on our knees

knelt

178	3	Yet he that hath in anguish knelt Is not forsaken
341	3	Where Jesus knelt to share with thee The silence of eternity
480	3	Heard his, when Jesus knelt to pray

knew

150	2	For us temptations sharp he knew
229	1	That mortals ever knew, That angels ever bore
340	2	Contented, peaceful fishermen, Before they ever knew ... God
340	2	Before they every knew The peace of God
349	2	Where is the blessedness I knew When first I saw the Lord
388	3	Twelve valiant saints, their hope they knew
407	T,1	O Light That Knew No Dawn, that shines to endless day
408	T,1	I sought the Lord, and afterward I knew
481	1	For the Lord they loved and knew
578	T,1	I Sought the Lord, and Afterward I Knew

knight

493	4	Let me, O Lord, thy cause defend, A knight without a sword

knocking

329	2	O Jesus, thou art knocking, And lo, that hand is scarred

know

4	2	The Lord, ye know, is God indeed
9	1	Know that the Lord is God alone
26	2	Know ye ... the Lord is King, All his works his wisdom prove
26	3	In the sacred silence wait, As we seek to know his will
44	2	And though their Lord they failed to know
44	2	Much more must we who know thee pray
55	2	We know and feel that thou art here
77	2	the waves and winds still know his voice
96	2	I know he will not leave me
112	3	Not for us ... to know the times and seasons
149	T,1	I Know Not How That Bethlehem's Babe Could in the Godhead b
149	1	I only know the manger child Has brought God's life to me
149	2	know not how ... Calvary's cross A world from sin could free
149	2	I only know its matchless love Has brought God's love to me
149	3	know not how that Joseph's tomb Could solve death's mystery
149	3	I only know a living Christ, Our immortality
154	2	O Lamb of God, we only know That all our hopes are there

knowest

knoweth

knowing

185	4	That thy peace which evermore Passeth human knowing
466	2	And knowing thee may grow in grace

knowledge

69	2	Kings of knowledge and of law, To the glorious circle draw
99	1	Beyond all knowledge and all thought
110	3	To us the path of knowledge show
110	3	knowledge show, And cause us in her ways to go
212	2	All our knowledge, sense and sight Lie in deepest darkness
253	3	Light of knowledge, ever burning, Shed on us
289	1	Knowledge and faith and life immortal Jesus ... imparts
329	2	O love that passeth knowledge, So patiently to wait
357	5	For knowledge is of the things we see
357	6	Let knowledge grow from more to more
409	2	Thou the peace that passeth knowledge Dwellest in the daily
450	1	And light of knowledge in their eyes
568	10	To give knowledge of salvation unto his people
576	2	O wondrous knowledge, awful might

known

21	1	He chastens and hastens his will to make known
68	3	not a plant or flower below But makes thy glories known
78	T,1	Hast Thou Not Known, hast thou not heard
83	2	Nor doubt our inmost wants are known To him
83	2	known To him who chose us for his own
98	4	A yearning for a deeper peace Not known before
113	2	To thee the travail deep was known
280	T,1	Be Known to Us in Breaking Bread, But do not then depart
286	4	Be known to us in breaking of the bread
318	2	Through me thy truth be shown, Thy love made known
349	4	The dearest idol I have known, Whate'er that idol be
423	3	Thy heart has never known recoil
431	T,1	God of Our Fathers, Known of Old
450	1	a loftier race Than e'er the world hath known shall rise
472	T,1	Lord, Thou Hast Known Our Joy
473	2	For judgments thine are known

knows

16	3	Well our feeble frame he knows
157	4	Peace is there that knows no measure
335	2	Jesus knows our every weakness
343	2	He knows the way he taketh, And I will walk with him
357	2	Thou madest man, he knows not why
365	4	And preach thee, too, as love knows how, By kindly words
465	1	That theirs may be the love which knows no ending

kundgemacht

139	2	Hirten erst kundgemacht

labor

58	2	May we, born anew like morning, To labor rise
167	VII-1	Jesus, all thy labor vast, All thy woe and conflict past
224	3	Apart from thee all gain is loss, All labor vainly done
293	T,1-4	Come, Labor On
371	3	I'll labor night and day to be a pilgrim

383	2	For it we must labor, Till our faith is sight
403	T,1	Those Who Love and Those Who Labor
403	1	who love and ... labor follow in the way of Christ
406	T,1	Forth in Thy Name, O Lord, I Go, My daily labor to pursue
406	3	And labor on at thy command, And offer all my works to thee
409	2	who tread the path of labor Follow where thy feet have trod
409	3	Bless us in our daily labor, Lead us to our sabbath rest
422	4	When on the sweat of labor and its sorrow
449	4	That useful labor yet may build Its homes with love
472	1	As we thy help have sought, With labor long have wrought

labors

217	2	Be there at our labors
306	T,1	For All the Saints who from their labors rest
358	2	Not the labors of my hands Can fulfill thy law's demands
405	4	And when earth's labors cease, Bid us depart in peace

lacht

| 139 | 3 | Gottes Sohn, o wie lacht |

lack

79	1	I nothing lack if I am his and he is mine forever
161	2	The courage that we lack
343	2	My shepherd is beside me, And nothing can I lack
442	2	When all our lack thou dost survey
498	2	That we no lack of grace may know

ladder

| 495 | T,1 | We Are Climbing Jacob's Ladder |

laden

| 335 | 3 | Are we weak and heavy laden, Cumbered with a load of care |

laeti

| 133 | 1 | Laeti triumphantes, Venite, venite in Bethlehem |

laid

79	3	on his shoulder gently laid, And home rejoicing brought me
126	1,5	Guide where our infant Redeemer is laid
127	3	Here Son, the Savior, in a manger laid
137	1	The little Lord Jesus laid down his sweet head
140	T,1	What Child Is This, Who, Laid to Rest
146	4	All meanly wrapped in swathing bands, And in a manger laid
179	3	Were you there when they laid him in the tomb
184	4	The life laid down, the life restored
297	2	And seed laid deep in sacred soil Yields harvests
343	1	The storm may roar without me, My heart may low be laid
372	1	foundation ... Is laid for your faith in his excellent word
445	4	Thy Word made flesh, and in a manger laid
456	1	And laid a silent loveliness On hill and wood and field

lake

| 322 | 2 | As of old, Saint Andrew heart it By the Galilean lake |

lamb

| 2 | 3 | Thou Lamb of God, enthroned on high Behold our need |

128	4	If I were a shepherd, I would bring a lamb
154	2	O Lamb of God, we only know That all our hopes are there
174	2	Till the appointed time is nigh ... the Lamb of God may die
183	3	through Christendom it rings That the Lamb is King of kings
199	T,1	Crown Him With Many Crowns, The Lamb upon his throne
206	3	Fall down on their faces and worship the Lamb
222	1	Thirsting after thee, Thine I am, O spotless Lamb
311	3	Bring near thy great salvation, Thou Lamb for sinners slain
319	1-4	O Lamb of God, I come
348	T,1	My Faith Looks Up to Thee, Thou Lamb of Calvary
349	1	A light to shine upon the road That leads me to the Lamb
420	1	O holy city ... Where Christ, the Lamb, doth reign
554	4	O Lord God, Lamb of God, Son of the Father
555	T,1	O Lamb of God, that takest away the sins of the world
556	T,1	O Christ, Thou Lamb of God
558	5	The marriage supper of the Lamb

lambs

| 471 | 4 | Tending with care the lambs within the fold |
| 483 | 1 | How he called little children as lambs to his fold |

lame

| 169 | 4 | He made the lame to run, He gave the blind their sight |

lament

| 580 | 2 | A gate which opens wide to those That do lament their sin |

lamenting

| 580 | 1 | Lamenting all their sinful lives, Before thy mercy gate |

lamp

165	2	Lo, a more heavenly lamp shines here
252	4	O make thy Church, dear Savior, A lamp of burnished gold
256	T,1	Lamp of Our Feet, Whereby We Trace Our path
516	1	Thy word is a lamp unto my feet And a light unto my path

lamps

| 45 | 1 | Wait and worship while the night sets her evening lamps |
| 45 | 1 | night Sets her evening lamps alight Through all the sky |

land

11	1	Let the Redeemer's name be sung through every land
11	1	sung Through every land, by every tongue
14	2	law ... Deep writ upon the human heart, On sea, or land
26	1	Sons of every land, Humbly now before him stand
28	3	Through her shall every land proclaim the sacred might
52	T,1	Now on Land and Sea Descending
72	1	And publishes to every land the work of an almighty hand
74	3	Made him fly with eagle pinion, Master over sea and land
74	4	O how wondrous, O how glorious is thy name in every land
75	3	Hill & vale & fruited land, All things living show his hand
93	1	Pilgrim through this barren land
93	3	Death of death, and hell's destruction land me safe
93	3	Land me safe on Canaan's side
97	2	Lead us by faith to hope's true promised land
160	1	The shadow of a mighty rock Within a weary land

229	3	And through this desert land, Still keep me near thy side
235	2	Thou in the faith dost men unite of every land ... tongue
257	2	It touched and glanced on every land
270	1	Crumbled have spires in every land
294	3	Till Christ is formed in all mankind And every land is thine
304	1	From land to land the love of Christ is told
308	3	Valiantly o'er sea and land Trod they the untrodden way
309	4	Jesus, in mercy bring us To that dear land of rest
387	1	Singing songs of expectation, Marching to the promised land
392	+1	Land of our birth, we pledge to thee Our love and toil
392	+2	Land of our birth, our faith, our pride
392	+2	Land of our birth ... For whose dear sake our fathers died
395	4	Thine are the loom, the forge, the mart, The wealth of land
395	4	Thine are ... the wealth of land and sea
412	2	Build us a tower ... That we the land may view
413	2	Thine the wealth of land and sea
421	1	They reach thy throne, encompass land and sea
428	T,1	When Israel Was in Egypt's Land
428	R	Go down, Moses, 'Way down in Egypt's land
429	4	Glad hymns of praise from land and sea
430	T,1	Rejoice, O Land, in God Thy Might
430	1	Fear not, O land, in God rejoice
432	1	stand Here in the borders of our promised land
433	2	In this free land by thee our lot is cast
435	1	With thy living fire of judgment Purge this land
435	1	Purge this land of bitter things
437	1	Sweet land of liberty, Of thee I sing
437	1	Land where my fathers died, Land of the pilgrim's pride
437	2	My native country, thee, Land of the noble free
437	4	Long may our land be bright With freedom's holy light
439	1	Stretching far o'er land and sea
439	2	For the open door to manhood, In a land the people rule
444	3	Bring justice to our land, That all may dwell secure
450	3	Nation with nation, land with land, Inarmed shall live
453	5	Ring out the darkness of the land
458	2	Starring all the land with flowers
460	T,1	We Plow the Fields and Scatter The good seed on the land
462	2	Scatters o'er the smiling land
464	3	Scatters o'er the smiling land
493	1	When Stephen ... Went forth throughout the land
496	1-2	O'er the land of the free and the home of the brave
496	2	Blest with victory and peace, may the heaven-rescued land
502	1	All things that live and move, by sea and land
562	5	and his hands prepared the dry land

lands

106	3	Lands of the East, awake, Soon shall your sons be free
289	2	So from all lands thy Church be gathered Into thy kingdom
294	1	send us forth ... prophets true, To make all lands thine own
296	2	distant lands Shall see from far the glorious sight
475	1	And yet vouchsafes in Christian lands To dwell in temples
484	T,1	Remember All the People, Who live in far-off lands
565	T,1	O Be Joyful in the Lord all ye lands

lanes

| 481 | 3 | You can meet them in school, or in lanes, or at sea |

461	3	Give his angels charge at last In the fire the tares to cast
470	1	Make each one nobler, stronger than the last
470	5	And stand at last with joy before thy face
491	4	Winning the world to that last consummation
496	1	What so proudly we hailed at the twilight's last gleaming
498	1	But gives us strength while life shall last
508	2	With one last prayer thy children fall

lasting

9	3	What lasting honors shall we rear ... to thy name
9	3	What lasting honors ...Almighty Maker, to thy name
297	2	Yields harvests rich in lasting good

lasts

| 100 | 4 | As it was without beginning, So it lasts without an end |

late

| 51 | 4 | Comfort every sufferer Watching late in pain |
| 120 | 2 | Late in time behold him come, Offspring of the Virgin's womb |

lately

| 178 | 1 | The star is dimmed that lately shone |

latest

| 400 | 3 | Then shall my latest breath Whisper thy praise |

lathe

| 217 | 2 | Whose strong hands were skilled at the plane and the lathe |

latter

| 427 | 1 | Groaning for the latter day |

laud

4	3	Praise, laud, and bless his name always
13	2	Heaven and earth and all creation Laud and magnify his name
17	2	servants of the Triune God, Father and Son and Spirit laud
25	2	Who would not fear his holy name, And laud and magnify
140	R	Haste, haste to bring him laud, The babe, the son of Mary
155	T,1,3	All Glory, Laud, and Honor To thee, Redeemer, King
185	2	From his light, to whom we give Laud and praise undying
263	4	Laud and honor to the Father, Laud and honor to the Son
263	4	Laud and honor to the Spirit, Ever Three and ever One
382	4	Glory, laud and honor Unto Christ the King
433	4	And glory, laud, and praise be ever thine

laugh

| 489 | 2 | I would look up, and laugh, and love, and lift |

laughter

| 449 | 4 | homes with love and laughter filled |

laut

| 139 | 2 | Tont es laut von fern und nah, Christ der Retter ist da |

law

| 14 | 2 | Established is his law, And changeless it shall stand |

14	2	law ... Deep writ upon the human heart, On sea, or land
26	4	Yea, his law is sure, In his light we walk secure
67	2	lightnings flash ... There is thy power, thy law is there
69	2	Kings of knowledge and of law, To the glorious circle draw
92	4	Enfolded deep in thy dear love, Held in thy law, I stand
242	4	Be my law, and I shall be Firmly bound, forever free
255	T,1	Most Perfect Is the Law of God, Restoring those that stray
412	2	Who shapest man to God's own law, Thyself the fair design
416	4	Come then, law divine, and reign
431	4	Or lesser breeds without the law
433	2	Thy word our law, thy paths our chosen way
440	2	Confirm thy soul in self control, Thy liberty in law
456	3	O thou from whose unfathomed law The year in beauty flows
544	1	and incline our hearts to keep this law

law's

358	2	Not the labors of my hands Can fulfill thy law's demands

laws

13	1	Laws which never shall be broken for their guidance
13	1	laws ... For their guidance he hath made
401	4	Who sweeps a room, as for thy laws
420	3	city that hath stood Too long a dream, whose laws are love
434	1	But to live out the laws of Christ In every thought
434	2	Until the laws of Christ become The laws and habits of
434	2	laws and habits of the state
438	3	Laws, freedom, truth, and faith in God Came with those
493	2	Stephen preached against the laws & by those laws was tried
544	1	and write all these thy laws in our hearts, we beseech thee

lay

22	1	We lay it before thee, we kneel and adore thee
31	2	Low at his feet lay the burden of carefulness
31	3	truth ... love ... are the offerings to lay on his shrine
46	2	Lay down the burden and the care
55	1	The sick, O Lord, around thee lay
129	1	The world in solemn stillness lay To hear the angels sing
136	3	Kneeling low by his bed, Lay their gifts before him
137	1	The stars in the sky looked down where he lay
141	1	Was to certain poor shepherds in fields as they lay
141	1	In fields where they lay keeping their sheep
141	4	stop and stay, Right over the place where Jesus lay
152	1	Haste, let us lay our gifts before the King
156	1	behold we lay Our passions, lusts, & proud wills in thy way
168	4	Thou lay the work he gave thee at his feet
191	2	their way To seek the tomb where Jesus lay
183	1	Kept the folded grave-clothes Where the body lay
287	2	Here would I lay aside each earthly load
362	4	crowned with victory, at thy feet I'll lay my honors down
367	1	Lay hold on life, & it shall be Thy joy and crown eternally
386	4	And in the midnight lay us down to die
399	4	I lay in dust life's glory dead
405	1	May we, like Magdelene, Lay at thy feet
475	2	Grant that all we, who here today ... this foundation lay

475	2	Rejoicing this foundation lay
509	2	Lay down the burden and the care
537	1	Thine own before thy feet we lay
557	2	Here would I lay aside each earthly load

lays

| 120 | 3 | Mild he lays his glory by, Born that man no more may die |

lead

30	2	Lead their praises, Alleluia
93	2	Let the fire & cloudy pillar Lead me all my journey through
97	2	Lead us by faith to hope's true promised land
142	4	Lead us all with hearts aflame Unto the joys above us
161	2	The hopes that lead us onward, The fears that hold us back
167	V-3	May we thirst thy love to know, Lead us in our sin and woe
215	T,1	Lead, Kindly Light, amid the encircling gloom
215	1	The night is dark and I am far from home, Lead thou me on
215	2	nor prayed that thou Shouldst lead me on
215	2	I loved to choose and see my path, but now Lead thou me on
215	3	sure it still Will lead me on O'er moor and fen
216	T,1	Lead, Kindly Light (same words as no. 215)
238	3	Lead us to Christ, the living Way
238	3	Lead us to holiness
238	4	Lead us to heaven that we may share Fulness of joy
238	4	Lead us to God, our final rest
318	2	Lead forth my soul, O Christ, One with thine own
324	4	and lead me to thy holy hill
327	T,1	Savior, Like a Shepherd Lead Us
333	2	Tenderest guide, in ways of cheerful duty, Lead us
333	2	Lead us, good Shepherd
344	T,1	Lead Us, Heavenly Father, Lead Us
344	1	lead us O'er the world's tempestuous sea
347	5	O may we lead the pilgrim's life, And follow thee to heaven
375	T,1	Lead On, O King Eternal, The day of march has come
375	2	Lead on, O King eternal, Till sin's fierce war shall cease
375	3	Lead on, O King eternal, We follow, not with fears
375	3	The crown awaits the conquest, Lead on, O God of might
376	T,1	Lead Us, O Father, in the paths of peace
376	1	Lead us through Christ, the true and living Way
376	2	Lead us, O Father, in the paths of truth
376	3	Lead us, O Father, in the paths of right
376	4	Lead us, O Father, to thy heavenly rest
385	1	From victory unto victory His army shall he lead
409	3	Bless us in our daily labor, Lead us to our sabbath rest
411	4	We work with thee, we go where thou wilt lead us
421	1	lead To blazoned heights and down the slopes of need
433	4	Lead us from night to never-ending day
524	T,1	Lead Me, Lord, lead me in thy righteousness

leader

21	3	We all do extol thee, thou leader triumphant
33	3	Be our guard in sin and strife, Be the leader of our life
309	3	And they, who with their leader, Have conquered in the fight

leaders

| 439 | 3 | For the people's prophet leaders, Loyal to the living Word |

leadest

| 92 | 4 | Thou leadest me by unsought ways |

leadeth

79	2	My ransomed soul he leadeth
84	1	he leadeth me The quiet waters by
370	T,1	He Leadeth Me, O Blessed Thought
370	1	Still 'tis God's hand that leadeth me
370	R	He leadeth me, he leadeth me, By his own hand he leadeth me
370	R	His faithful follower I would be For by his hand he leadeth
370	2	Content whatever lot I see, Since 'tis my God that leadeth
370	3	Since God through Jordan leadeth me
576	4	The hand that leadeth me is thine

leading

119	1	Leading onward, beaming bright
143	R	Westward leading, still proceeding
168	3	Along that sacred way where thou art leading

leads

8	4	Joyful music leads us sunward, In the triumph song of life
47	3	As o'er each continent and island The dawn leads on
47	3	The dawn leads on another day
77	1	thy best, thy heavenly friend Through thorny ways leads
77	1	Through thorny ways leads to a joyful end
96	2	He never will deceive me, He leads me by the proper path
220	2	We follow where the Master leads, Serene and unafraid
339	2	Pleasure leads us where we go
349	1	A light to shine upon the road That leads me to the Lamb
349	5	So purer light shall mark the road That leads me to the Lamb
382	1	Christ the royal Master Leads against the foe
411	1	purpose never swerving Leads toward the day of Jesus Christ
411	1	Leads to the day of Jesus Christ thy Son
433	1	almighty hand Leads forth in beauty all the starry band

leafless

| 455 | 1 | Through leafless boughs the sharp winds blow |

lean

287	1	And all my weariness upon thee lean
287	5	Another arm save thine to lean upon
367	3	Cast care aside, lean on thy guide
381	3	My faith, it is an oaken staff, O let me on it lean
557	1	And all my weariness upon thee lean
557	3	Another arm save thine to lean upon

leaned

| 372 | 5 | The soul that on Jesus hath leaned for repose |

leaning

| 213 | 3 | Then, while leaning on thy breast |
| 467 | 3 | Nought shall affright us, on thy goodness leaning |

leant

356	3	When on thy bosom it has leant And found in thee its life

leap

417	2	True hearts will leap at the trumpet of God

leaping

422	2	Shooting out tongues of flame like leaping blood

leaps

202	4	The prisoner leaps to lose his chains

learn

158	1	Learn of Jesus Christ to pray
158	2	Learn of Christ to bear the cross
158	3	It is finished, hear him cry, Learn of Jesus Christ to die
256	5	Lord, grant us all aright to learn The wisdom it imparts
328	3	O learn of him, learn now of him, Then with thee it is well
359	2	Workman of God, O lose not heart, But learn what God is like
423	6	Till sons of men shall learn thy love
434	3	mind equipped His will to learn, his work to do
467	3	Chastened by pain we learn life's deeper meaning

learning

162	5	Then to life I turn again, Learning all the worth of pain
162	5	Learning all the might that lies In a full self-sacrifice
253	3	Shed on us thy deathless learning
258	6	O, that we discerning Its most holy learning
416	3	Learning all his will to feel

learns

471	5	He learns at length the triumph of the cross

least

94	3	Nor in the least a cheerful heart that tastes those gifts
369	1	of all things on earth least like What men agree to praise
427	3	O for Christ at least be men
481	2	there's not any reason, no, not the least

leathern

425	2	with leathern hearts, forget That we owe mankind a debt

leave

44	1,2	O leave us not at close of day
59	4	But thy dear presence will not leave them lonely
59	4	will not leave them lonely Who seek thee only
77	1	Leave to thy God to order and provide
96	1	Wherefore to him I leave it all
96	2	I know he will not leave me
96	3	And so to him I leave it all
97	3	When we are strong, Lord, leave us not alone, Our refuge be
117	3	Sages, leave your contemplations
168	2	We would not leave thee, though our weak endurance
210	2	Leave, ah, leave me not alone, Still support and comfort me
228	3	Suddenly return, and never, Nevermore thy temples leave
326	T,1	Thou Didst Leave Thy Throne and thy kingly crown

329	3	Dear Savior, enter, enter, And leave us nevermore
337	2	Leave to this sovereign sway To choose and to command
357	2	Thou wilt not leave us in the dust
384	3	Leave no unguarded place, No weakness of the soul
454	3	And, peaceful, leave before thy feet
468	4	To thee we leave them, Lord, in trust

leaven

| 112 | 2 | heaven Spreads throughout the world like leaven |

leaves

| 7 | 3 | We blossom and flourish as leaves on the tree |
| 205 | 3 | Yet he loves the earth he leaves |

leaving

| 322 | 2 | Leaving all for his dear sake |

led

119	1	So most gracious Lord, may we Evermore be led to thee
136	3	God's bright star, o'er his head, Wise men three to him led
182	4	Soar we now where Christ has led
185	1	Led them with unmoistened foot Through the Red Sea waters
249	2	O holy Father, who hast led thy children In all the ages
249	2	led ... with the fire and cloud
308	4	Lord and light of every age, By thy same sure counsel led
405	3	Some dews of mercy shed, Some wayward footsteps led
432	1	from dawn of days Hast led thy people in their widening ways
432	3	Thy hand has led across the hungry sea The eager peoples
433	2	Thy love divine hath led us in the past
454	2	By his incessant bounty fed, By his unerring counsel led

left

42	4	Now shall you find at last Night's left behind at last
135	1	For thou hast left thy heavenly throne
167	IV-1	Jesus, whelmed in fears unknown With our evil left alone
174	2	Left alone with human sin, Gloom around thee and within
174	4	That thine own might ne'er be left
201	3	left the lonesome place of death, Despite the rage of foes
214	2	The Lord, who left the heavens Our life and peace to bring
312	5	There Magdalen hath left her moan And cheerfully doth sing
325	2	Till not a stone was left on stone
332	2	Good that we have left undone
439	3	Lives that passed and left no name
455	1	snow Has left the heavens all coldly clear
468	3	Not left to lie like fallen tree, Not dead, but living

legions

| 181 | 2 | But Christ their legions hath dispersed |
| 411 | 1 | Grant us to march among thy faithful legions |

leisure

| 83 | 2 | Only be still, and wait his leisure in cheerful hope |

lend

| 126 | 1,5 | Dawn on our darkness, and lend us thine aid |
| 482 | 1 | We will lend a coat of fur, We will rock you |

494 2   O Master, lend us sight To see the towers gleaming

lendeth
271 2   The Spirit who in them did sing To us his music lendeth

length
79 6   so through all the length of days thy goodness faileth never
274 3   Till all before our God at length In Zion do appear
380 4   Look up, the victor's crown at length
471 5   He learns at length the triumph of the cross

lengthen
373 4   Mercy thy days shall lengthen, The Lord will give thee peace

lent
297 3   The torch of their devotion lent, Lightens the dark

less
401 5   that which God doth touch and own cannot for less be told

lesser
237 3   Send down thy love, thy life, Our lesser lives to crown
300 1   Have done with lesser things
431 4   Such boastings as the Gentiles use Or lesser breeds
431 4   Or lesser breeds without the law

lest
33 3   Lest from thee we stray abroad, Stay our wayward feet,O Lord
124 2   Lest your noise should waken Jesus
291 2   pray we Lest we fail to know thee now
366 3   Grant us wisdom ... courage, Lest we miss thy kingdom's goal
374 1   Lest by base denial I depart from thee
398 3   Walk thou beside us lest the tempting byways Lure us away
431 1,2   Lord God of hosts, be with us yet, Lest we forget
431 3   Judge of the nations, spare us yet, Lest we forget
431 4   Lord God of hosts, be with us yet, Lest we forget

let
3 1   Let us now adore him, And with awe appear before him
11 1   Let the Creator's praise arise
11 1   Let the Redeemer's name be sung through every land
15 4   O let all that is in me adore him
15 4   Let the Amen Sound from his people again
21 3   Let thy congregation escape tribulation
23 4   Let all thy days Till life shall end ... filled with praise
24 T,1   Now Let Every Tongue Adore Thee
24 1   Let men with angels sing before thee
24 1   Let harps and cymbals now unite
26 3   Enter now his holy gate, Let our burdened hearts be still
26 3   Let our lives express Our abundant thankfulness
30 4   O friends, in gladness let us sing, Supernal anthems echoing
34 2   Come, let thy voice be one with theirs
34 2   So let the love of Jesus come And set thy soul ablaze
35 3   Let all the earth around Ring joyous with the sound
35 4   Let mortals, too, upraise, Their voice in hymns of praise
35 5   Let air, and sea, and sky From depth to height reply

39	2	O thou true Sun, on us thy glance Let fall
39	2	thy glance Let fall in royal radiance
44	2	They could not let the Stranger go
45	3	Lord of angels, on our eyes Let eternal morning rise
52	1	Let our vesper hymn be blending With the holy calm around
53	1	Let us, as night is falling ... Give thanks to him
58	2	Let not ease and self enthrall us
59	2	Let evil thoughts and spirits flee before us
59	3	Let our last thoughts be thine when sleep o'ertakes us
59	3	Let us serve thee, in all that we are doing
63	1	Let us each, thy love possessing Triumph
64	5	Let all things their creator bless
65	1	Let the whole creation cry
67	3	we hear thy word, Let there be light
69	T,1	Let the Whole Creation Cry, Glory to the Lord on high
69	3	let children's happy hearts In this worship bear their parts
69	3	From the north to southern pole Let the mighty chorus roll
70	T,1,6	Let Us With a Gladsome Mind
71	T,1	Let Us With a Gladsome Mind (same words as No. 70)
76	2	While providence supports, Let saints securely dwell
77	2	Thy hope, thy confidence let nothing shake
85	2	Thy foot he'll not let slide
92	2	But let me only think of thee And then new heart springs up
93	2	Let the fire & cloudy pillar Lead me all my journey through
103	1	Let us find our rest in thee
104	2	Let the valleys rise to meet him
104	3	Let your hearts be true and humble
107	T,1	Let All Mortal Flesh Keep Silence
108	3	Now let all the heavens adore thee
109	3	Watchman, let thy wanderings cease
111	2	Let no tongue on earth be silent
114	3	here, Lord, abide. Let me thy inner presence feel
114	4	Let new and nobler life begin
115	2	let us each our hearts prepare For Christ to come and enter
122	T,1	God Rest You Merry, Gentlemen, Let nothing you dismay
122	3	Fear not, then, said the angel, Let nothing you affright
123	3	Come, then, let us hasten yonder
123	3	Here let all, Great and small, Kneel in awe and wonder
130	1	Let earth receive her King
130	1	Let every heart prepare him room
130	2	Let men their songs employ
132	R	O come, let us adore him ... Christ the Lord
140	3	Let loving hearts enthrone him
142	5	Alpha and Omega be, Let the organ thunder
144	3	Let not our slothful hearts refuse The guidance of thy light
147	3	Let this mind be in us which was in thee
147	4	Let every tongue confess with one accord
152	1	Haste, let us lay our gifts before the King
152	5	Let us arise, all meaner service scorning
159	3	Then let all praise be given thee Who livest evermore
160	3	Content to let the world go by, To know no gain nor loss
161	3	On us let now the healing Of his great Spirit fall
164	1	O come, together let us mourn
168	3	Let us go also, till we see thee pleading
170	3	Lord, let me never, never, Outlive my love to thee
181	2	Let shouts of holy joy outburst

453	1	Ring out, wild bells, and let him die
453	2	The year is going, let him go
463	4	Glory to our bounteous King, Glory let creation sing
464	1	Let thy praise our tongues employ
483	2	Let the little ones come unto me
485	3	Oh, let me ne'er forget That though the wrong seems oft
485	3	The Lord is king, let the heavens ring
485	3	God reigns, let the earth be glad
486	2	Simple wants provide, Evil let he shun
490	3	And let us not for one short hour An evil thought endure
493	4	Let me, O Lord, thy cause defend, A knight without a sword
494	1	let thy plan Reveal the life that God would give to man
499	1	Let us adore And own how solemn is this place
499	1	Let all within us feel his power
501	2	Let this day praise thee, O Lord God
501	2	And so let all our days
501	2	O let heaven's eternal day Be thine eternal praise
503	T,1	Open Now Thy Gates of Beauty, Zion, let me enter there
503	2	To my heart O enter thou, Let it be thy temple now
504	1	Let heaven rejoice, let earth be glad
518	T,1	Let Thy Word Abide in Us, O Lord
521	1	And let thy truth within us shine
522	T,1	Let the Words of My Mouth, and the meditation of my heart
525	T,1	Come, & Let Us Sweetly Join Christ to praise in hymns divine
526	1	O let thy children share thy blessing from on high
531	1	Let us pray
533	T,1	The Lord Be With You, And with thy spirit. Let us pray
552	1	Let us give thanks unto the Lord our God
559	16	O Lord, let thy mercy be upon us, as our trust is in thee
559	16	O Lord, in thee have I trusted, let me never be confounded
562	T,1	O Come, Let Us Sing unto the Lord
562	1	let us heartily rejoice in the strength of our salvation
562	2	Let us come before his presence with thanksgiving
562	6	O come, let us worship and fall down
562	8	let the whole earth stand in awe of him
580	2	Shut not that gate against me, Lord, But let me enter in
580	3	For mercy, Lord, is all my suit, O let thy mercy spare

lettest

572	T,1	Lord, Now Lettest Thou Thy Servant Depart in peace

level

352	2	Above the level of the former years

liberal

462	2	All that liberal autumn pours From her rich ... stores
464	3	All that liberal autumn pours From her rich ... stores

liberating

440	3	O beautiful for heroes proved In liberating strife
452	1	We wait thy liberating deed To signal hope and set us free

liberty

26	4	In his will our peace we find, In his service, liberty
101	1	kindness ... Which is more than liberty (102-1)
106	3	The sleep of ages break, And rise to liberty

113	2	free Thine own in glorious liberty
228	2	Set our hearts at liberty
236	1	Flowing in the prophet's word And the people's liberty
236	5	Flow still in the prophet's word And the people's liberty
265	1	Thy will from none withholds Full liberty
437	1	Sweet land of liberty, Of thee I sing
437	4	Our father's God, to thee Author of Liberty, To thee we sing
440	2	Confirm thy soul in self control, Thy liberty in law
452	5	glorious hour When all men find thy liberty

lids

50	2	My wearied eyelids gently steep
51	2	With thy tenderest blessing May our eyelids close
56	3	And with sweet sleep mine eye-lids close
510	2	With thy tenderest blessing May our eyelids close

lie

3	1	Prostrate lie with deepest reverence
84	1	He makes me down to lie In pastures green
134	T,1	O Little Town of Bethlehem, How still we see thee lie
212	2	All our knowledge, sense and sight Lie in deepest darkness
212	2	Lie in deepest darkness shrouded
293	4	Till the long shadows o'er our pathway lie
352	3	Low lie the bounding heart, the teeming brain
359	4	Blest too is he who can divine Where real right doth lie
372	4	When through fiery trials thy pathway shall lie
377	4	Zion, if thou die believing, Heaven's path shall open lie
468	3	Not left to lie like fallen tree, Not dead, but living
580	T,1	O Lord, Turn Not Thy Face From Them, Who lie in woeful state

lieb'

| 139 | 3 | Lieb' aus deinem gottlichen Mund |

lies

66	1	For the love which from our birth Over and around us lies
126	2	Low lies his head with the beasts of the stall
140	2	Why lies he in such mean estate Where ox and ass are feeding
162	5	Learning all the might that lies In a full self-sacrifice
222	3	Still in thee lies purest pleasure, Jesus priceless treasure
297	3	Lightens the dark that round us lies
304	3	Low lies man's pride and human wisdom dies
352	3	Low lies the best till lifted up to heaven
367	2	Life with its way before us lies
380	3	'Gainst lies and lusts & wrongs, Let courage rule our souls
436	2	From all that terror teaches, From lies of tongue and pen
455	1	And all the earth lies dead and drear
468	1	in whose eyes Unveiled thy whole creation lies

life

7	3	To all, life thou givest to both great and small
7	3	In all life thou livest, the true life of all
8	4	Joyful music leads us sunward, In the triumph song of life
14	3	He hath eternal life Implanted in the soul
15	4	All ... life and breath, come now with praises before him
17	1	While o'er my life his strong arm he raises I shall sing
17	1	thanks to God, my light, Who life and soul hath given me

490	4	And for the life ineffable Within the Father's home
491	2	To right the wrongs that shame this mortal life
494	1	let thy plan Reveal the life that God would give to man
498	1	But gives us strength while life shall last
530	T,1	O Thou by Whom We Come to God, The Life, the Truth, the Way
568	8	all the days of our life
575	2	blessed unction from above Is comfort, life and fire of love

life's

22	2	Through life's storm and tempest our guide hast thou been
22	2	And with thy help, O Lord, life's battles we win
37	4	morning, When the soul waketh and life's shadows flee
46	4	Life's tumult we must meet again
53	3	when life's day is over Shall death's fair night discover
61	3	When life's perils thick confound you
129	3	ye, beneath life's crushing load Whose forms are bending low
163	3	For me ... thy mortal sorrow, and thy life's oblation
209	2	Swift to its close ebbs out life's little day
213	T,1	Jesus, Savior, Pilot Me Over life's tempestuous sea
230	5	touch him in life's throng and press, And we are whole again
252	3	It is the chart and compass That o'er life's surging sea
322	1	tumult Of our life's wild, restless sea
345	4	Yes, on through life's long path, Still chanting as ye go
348	3	While life's dark maze I tread, And griefs around me spread
348	4	When ends life's transient dream
356	1	I sink in life's alarms When by myself I stand
386	T,1	Lighten the Darkness of our life's long night
399	4	I lay in dust life's glory dead
455	4	And keep us through life's wintry days
465	3	And to life's day the glorious unknown morrow that dawns
467	3	Chastened by pain we learn life's deeper meaning
491	3	And through life's darkness, danger, and disaster
542	1	Through life's long day and death's dark night

lift

2	4	Do thou our troubled souls uplift Against the foe prevailing
8	3	Lift us to the joy divine
32	2	Wake and lift up thyself, my heart
33	1	So to thee with one accord Lift we up our Hearts, O Lord
64	1	Lift up your voice and with us sing Alleluia, Alleluia
69	1	Sun & moon, uplift your voice, Night & stars, in God rejoice
85	T,1	I to the Hills Will Lift Mine Eyes
108	1	He comes, O Church, lift up thine eyes
114	T,1	Lift Up Your Heads, Ye Mighty Gates
189	T,1	Lift Up Your Hearts, Ye People, In songs of glad accord
204	R	Lift up your heart, lift up your voice
205	2	Lift your heads, eternal gates
300	4	Lift high the cross of Christ Tread where his feet have trod
304	1	Lift up your hearts in jubilant accord
318	3	Lift thou thy world, O Christ, Closer to thee
337	1	God shall lift up thy head
345	5	Still lift your standard high, Still march in firm array
352	T,1	Lift Up Your Hearts, We lift them, Lord, to thee
352	1	Lift up your hearts, E'en so, with one accord
352	1,4,	We lift them up, we lift them to the Lord
352	2	O Lord of light, lift all our hearts today

352	3	Lift every gift that thou thyself hast given
352	4	Lift up your hearts, rings pealing in our ears
360	3	I know not where his islands lift Their fronded palms in air
367	2	Lift up thine eyes, and seek his face
371	T,1	Lift Up Your Hearts, Ye People (same words as no. 189)
375	1	And now, O King eternal, We lift our battle song
377	T,1	Lift Thy Head, O Zion, Weeping, Still the Lord thy Father is
385	1	Lift high his royal banner, It must not suffer loss
387	3	One the strain that lips of thousands Lift as from the heart
419	1	To thee we lift our hearts
419	2	And lift the spirit's sword
430	1	For thee the saints uplift their voice
436	3	Lift up a living nation, A single sword to thee
439	1	Not alone for bounteous harvests Lift we up our hearts
439	1	Lift we up our hearts to thee
452	1	in bitter need Thy children lift their cry to thee
457	2	For summer joy in field and wood We lift our song to him
472	4	Thy cross we lift on high This house to glorify
489	2	I would look up, and laugh, and love, and lift
494	1	O'er crumbling walls their crosses scarcely lift
505	1	Now lift your hearts, your voices raise
552	T,1	Lift Up Your Hearts. We lift them up unto the Lord
559	13	govern them and lift them up forever

lifted

86	3	The line of lifted sea, Where spreading moonlight quivers
184	3	And sing with hearts uplifted high
332	3	Lips that, while thy praises sounding, Lifted not the soul
332	3	Lifted not the soul to thee
352	3	Low lies the best till lifted up to heaven
375	3	Thy cross is lifted o'er us, We journey in its light
476	3	Whose music like a mighty wind The souls of men uplifted

liftest

291	1	Thou alone, our strong defender Liftest up thy people's head
399	4	O Cross that liftest up my head

lifteth

66	6	For thy Church that evermore Lifteth holy hands above
252	2	And still that light she lifteth O'er all the earth to shine

lifting

74	1	Lifting up our hearts in praise

lifts

97	1	With each new day, when morning lifts the veil

light

6	2	Whose robe is the light, whose canopy space
6	4	It breathes in the air, it shines in the light
7	1	In light inaccessible hid from our eyes
7	2	Unresting, unhasting, and silent as light
7	4	Great Father of glory, pure Father of light
7	4	help us to see 'Tis only the splendor of light hideth thee
8	1	Giver of immortal gladness, Fill us with the light of day
13	1	Praise him, all ye stars of light

17	1	thanks to God, my light, Who life and soul hath given me
18	4	prophets crowned with light, with all the martyrs noble host
23	1	Or through the realms of light Fly at your Lord's command
23	2	God's praises sound, As in his light ... ye do abound
24	1	partake ... With angels round thy throne of light
26	4	Yea, his law is sure, In his light we walk secure
38	3	Born of the one light Eden saw play
39	1	O thou that bringest light from light
39	1	O Light of light, light's living spring
42	2	Swift grows the light for us, Ended is night for us
42	3	Suddenly breaks on earth Light from the sky
43	1	Christ, the true, the only Light
43	2	Till they inward light impart Glad my eyes and warm my heart
44	1	Two walked with thee in waning light
46	3	O God, our Light, to thee we bow
47	2	While earth rolls onward into light
49	T,1	O Gladsome Light, O grace of God the Father's face
49	2	Now, ere day fadeth quite, We see the evening light
50	4	Like infants' slumbers, pure and light
54	1	Our heavenly Sun, our glorious Light
56	1	All praise to thee ... For all the blessings of the light
58	T,1	God That Madest Earth and Heaven, Darkness and light
59	1	The light and darkness are of his disposing
60	3	Turn thou for us its darkness into light
60	3	For dark and light are both alike to thee
64	3	That givest man both warmth and light
65	2	Saints in light the strain prolong
66	2	Hill & vale, and tree & flower, Sun & moon & stars of light
67	3	we hear thy word, Let there be light
70	2	Filled the new-made world with light
75	2	Moon and stars with silvery light Praise him
82	4	in thy light our souls shall see The glories promised
86	4	May thy fresh light arise Within each clouded heart
89	2	Star of our hope, thy softened light Cheers
89	4	Whose light is truth, whose warmth is love
89	5	Till all thy living altars claim One holy light
89	5	One holy light, one heavenly flame
91	5	Nor plagues that waste in noonday light
97	2	With thee to bless, the darkness shines as light
98	1	So full of splendor and of joy, Beauty and light
99	2	Self-fed, self-kindled like the light
99	5	Still more in resurrection light We read the fullness
99	5	in resurrection light We read the fullness of thy might
107	3	the Light of light descendeth From the realms of endless day
108	2	Her star is risen, her light is come
109	2	Traveler, blessedness and light ... its course portends
113	1	Thy People's Everlasting light
118	T,1	Break Forth, O Beauteous Heavenly Light
119	1	As with joy they hailed its light
120	3	Light and life to all he brings
134	1	Yet in thy dark streets shineth The everlasting Light
138	3	Son of God, love's pure light
141	2	And to the earth it gave great light
141	3	And by the light of that same star Three wise men came
143	R	Guide us to thy perfect light
144	1	More lovely than the noon-day light

144	3	The guidance of thy light to use
144	4	To God the Father, heavenly Light
145	1	Thou beamest forth in truth and light
145	2	Thou heavenly Brightness, Light divine
152	2	Light of the village life from day to day
157	1,5	All the light of sacred story Gathers round its head sublime
157	3	When the sun of bliss is beaming Light and love upon my way
159	3	but thou Dost light and life restore
161	1	Across our restless living The light streams from his cross
165	2	E'en though the sun witholds its light
167	IV-1	While no light from heaven is shown, Hear us, holy Jesus
167	IV-3	Though no Father seems to hear .. no light our spirits cheer
185	2	From his light, to whom we give Laud and praise undying
189	1	And filled the gloom and darkness With resurrection light
192	2	The Lord in rays eternal Of resurrection light
197	2	All the angel faces, All the hosts of light
197	4	Bore it up triumphant, With its human light
197	5	Let his will enfold you In its light and power
198	T,1	Christ Is the World's True Light, Its captain of salvation
201	1	And light triumphant breaks
201	5	morning dawns, And light and beauty brings
207	2	Shine on us with the light of thy pure day
208	1	Let thy clear light forever shine
212	3	Light of life, from God proceeding
215	T,1	Lead, Kingly Light, amid the encircling gloom
216	T,1	Lead, Kingly Light (same words as no. 215)
219	2	Thee would I sing, thy truth is still the light
219	2	light Which guides the nations groping on their way
219	3	The holiest know - Light, Life, and Way of heaven
224	4	But dim or clear, we own in thee The light ... truth ... way
231	2	Enable with perpetual light The dullness of... blinded sight
235	2	Lord, by the brightness of thy light ... men unite
235	3	Thou strong Defense, thou holy Light
238	1	With light and comfort from above
238	2	The light of truth to us display
239	2	And let thy glorious light Shine ever on my sight
242	1	Word of God, and inward light
244	1	Sun of the soul, thou Light divine
248	2	Beyond our ken thou shinest, The everlasting Light
249	1	blessed ... With light and life since Eden's dawning day
252	1	O Truth unchanged, unchanging, O Light of our dark sky
252	2	And still that light she lifteth O'er all the earth to shine
252	4	To bear among the nations Thy true light as of old
253	1	Shedding light that none can measure
253	3	Light of knowledge, ever burning, Shed on us
255	2	The Lord's commandments all are pure & clearest light impart
257	2	The rolling sun, the changing light, And nights and days
257	4	That see the light or feel the sun
258	1	Who its truth believeth Light and joy receiveth
258	3	Then its light directeth, And our way protecteth
259	R	The Lord hath yet more light and truth To break forth
267	3	deriving from their banner Light by night and shade by day
276	4	Thy gospel light forever shine
290	1	Thou fount of life, thou light of men
290	4	Shed o'er the world thy holy light
296	2	Baptize their spirits in its light

488	1	Behold throughout the heavens There shone a holy light
491	1	With light and love divine our souls endue
493	2	And in his eyes a light ... God's daybreak to proclaim
494	2	To see the towers gleaming in the light
496	1	O say can you see by the dawn's early light
498	2	Give us that light for which we pray
500	1	We thank thee for thy gift of light
502	1	We praise thee with the glowing light of day
503	1	place, Filled with solace, light, and grace
505	1	And joy to see the cheerful light That riseth in the east
508	2	O Light all clear, O Truth most holy
509	3	O God, our Light, to thee we bow
516	1	Thy word is a lamp unto my feet And a light unto my path
521	2	Make strong our faith, increase our light
542	1	O gentle Jesus, be our light
568	12	To give light to them that sit in darkness
572	4	To be a light to lighten the Gentiles
575	2	Enable with perpetual light The dullness
576	5	The darkness shineth as the light

light's

39	1	O Light of light, light's living spring

lighten

231	1	And lighten with celestial fire
386	T,1	Lighten the Darkness of our life's long night
386	2	Lighten our darkness of our self-conceit
386	3	Lighten our darkness when we bow the knee To all the gods
386	4	Lighten our darkness when we fail at last
572	4	To be a light to lighten the Gentiles
575	1	And lighten with celestial fire

lightens

297	3	The torch of their devotion lent, Lightens the dark
297	3	Lightens the dark that round us lies

lightning

443	1	He hath loosed the fateful lightning of his ... swift sword
443	1	lightning of his terrible swift sword
446	1	Thunder thy clarion, the lightning thy sword

lightnings

67	2	When lightnings flash and storm-winds blow ... is thy power
67	2	lightnings flash ... There is thy power, thy law is there

lights

64	2	Ye lights of evening, find a voice
74	2	When we see thy lights of heaven
201	2	like the sun That lights the morning sky
296	1	The sun that lights its shining folds
297	3	Help us to pass it on unspent Until the dawn lights up
297	3	Until the dawn lights up the skies
357	4	They are but broken lights of thee
460	2	He paints the wayside flower, He lights the evening star

like

1	4	A thousand ages in thy sight Are like an evening gone
1	5	Time, like an ever-rolling stream, Bears all its sons away
3	3	Like the holy angels Who behold thy glory ... adore thee
6	3	And round it hath cast, like a mantle, the sea
7	2	Thy justice like mountains high soaring above
8	1	Hearts unfold like flowers before thee
9	2	And when, like wandering sheep we strayed, He brought us
16	1	Who, like me, his praise should sing
16	3	Father-like he tends and spares us
35	1	Alike at work and prayer, To Jesus I repair
38	T,1	Morning Has Broken, Like the first morning
38	1	Blackbird has spoken Like the first bird
38	2	Like the first dewfall On the first grass
47	5	Like earth's proud empires, pass away
50	4	Be every mourner's sleep tonight Like infants' slumbers
50	4	Like infants' slumbers, pure and light
58	2	May we, born anew like morning, To labor rise
60	3	For dark and light are both alike to thee
82	4	Life, like a fountain rich and free Springs from ... my Lord
95	2	Truth from the earth, like a flower, Shall bud and blossom
99	2	Self-fed, self-kindled like the light
100	3	Like the pity of a father Hath the Lord's compassion been
101	1	God's mercy, Like the wideness of the sea (102-1)
105	3	He shall come down like showers Upon the fruitful earth
105	3	love, joy, hope, like flowers, Spring from his path to birth
112	2	heaven Spreads throughout the world like leaven
112	2	Unobserved, and very near, Like the seed when no man knoweth
112	2	Like the sheltering tree that groweth, Comes the life
128	1	Earth stood hard as iron, Water like a stone
166	3	O may we, who mercy need, Be like thee in heart and deed
169	5	Never was love, dear King, Never was grief like thine
182	4	Made like him, like him we rise
201	2	But crowned with glory like the sun
201	2	like the sun That lights the morning sky
202	2	His name like sweet perfume shall rise With every morning
209	3	Who like thyself my guide and stay can be
217	1	Whose trust, ever child-like, no cares could destroy
241	2	Come as the fire and purge our hearts Like sacrificial flame
252	3	It floateth like a banner Before God's hosts unfurled
252	3	It shineth like a beacon Above the darkling world
256	5	to its heavenly teaching turn With simple, child-like hearts
260	4	Like them, the meek and lowly, On high may dwell with thee
264	3	For not like kingdoms of the world Thy holy Church, O God
267	2	Grace, which like the Lord, the Giver, Never fails
272	1	The fellowship of kindred minds Is like to that above
275	2	Descend, O Holy Spirit, like a dove Into our hearts
276	3	Here make the well-springs of thy grace Like fountains
276	3	Like fountains in the wilderness
297	4	Fill thou our hearts with faith like theirs
297	4	faith like theirs Who served the days they could not see
299	3	Breathe thou abroad like morning air Till hearts ... beat
317	2	Seem hungering and thirsting To hear it, like the rest
327	T,1	Savior, Like a Shepherd Lead Us
328	1	Like flowing waters cool
328	2	He shall be to thee like the sea

341	2	In simple trust like theirs who heard, Beside the Syrian sea
341	2	Let us, like them, without a word, Rise up and follow thee
342	1	No tender voice like thine Can peace afford
347	2	Like thee, to do our Father's will
347	4	Then, like thine own, be all our aim To conquer them by love
351	2	Though like the wanderer, The sun gone down
353	4	Lord I want to be like Jesus
365	2	If they, like them, should die for thee
366	4	Armored with all Christ-like graces in the fight
369	1	of all things on earth least like What men agree to praise
375	3	For gladness breaks like morning Where'er thy face appears
380	1	Like those strong men of old
382	2	Like a mighty army Moves the Church of God
388	2	Like him, with pardon on his tongue, In midst of mortal pain
405	1	May we, like Magdelene, Lay at thy feet
412	2	Build us a tower of Christ-like height
412	2	And see like thee our noblest work Our Father's work to do
413	4	See the Christ-like host advancing
419	1	Whose life, like light, is freely poured On all
421	4	We've seen thy glory like a mantle spread O'er hill and dale
422	1	Peals like a trumpet promise of his coming
422	2	Shooting out tongues of flame like leaping blood
424	2	All must aid alike to carry Forward one sublime design
437	2	My heart with rapture thrills Like that above
465	2	With child-like trust that fears nor pain nor death
468	3	Not spilt like water on the ground
468	3	Not left to lie like fallen tree, Not dead, but living
469	2	One providence alike they share
476	3	Whose music like a mighty wind The souls of men uplifted
481	3	For the saints of God are just folk like me
483	1	I should like to have been with him then
486	1	Comes the eastern sun Like a man of brawn
486	1	Like a man of brawn Set his course to run
487	2	God's care like a cloak Wraps us country folk
492	3	flower In Christ-like lives, we pray

liked

413	4	Liked in bonds of common service For the common Lord of all

lilies

443	4	In the beauty of the lilies Christ was born across the sea

lily

485	2	morning light, the lily white, Declare their Maker's praise

limit

259	T,1	We Limit Not the Truth of God To our poor reach of mind

limits

236	4	Hurling floods of tyrant wrong From the sacred limits back
429	1	Who bidd'st the mighty ocean deep Its ... limits keep
429	1	Its own appointed limits keep

line

86	3	The line of lifted sea, Where spreading moonlight quivers
146	3	To you, in David's town, this day Is born of David's line

little

51	3	Grant to little children Visions bright of thee
121	2	This little child, of lowly birth, Shall be the joy
124	3	Softly to the little stable, Softly for a moment come
134	T,1	O Little Town of Bethlehem, How still we see thee lie
137	1	The little Lord Jesus laid down his sweet head
137	1	The little Lord Jesus, asleep on the hay
137	2	But little Lord Jesus, no crying he makes
142	3	All the little boys he killed At Bethlem in his fury
201	2	Not as of old a little child To bear, and fight, and die
209	2	Swift to its close ebbs out life's little day
277	1	Little ones we bring to thee
279	1	Let the little ones be given Unto me, of such is heaven
330	3	Ah, did not he the heavenly throne A little thing esteem
357	4	Our little systems have their day
363	3	One little word shall fell him
395	T,1	Behold Us, Lord, a Little Space From daily tasks set free
478	1	Each little flower that opens, Each little bird that sings
482	T,1	Little Jesus, Sweetly Sleep, do not stir
482	2	Mary's little baby, sleep, sweetly sleep
482	2	We will serve you all we can, Darling, darling little man
483	1	How he called little children as lambs to his fold
483	2	Let the little ones come unto me

live

8	3	All who live in love are thine
26	2	By his might the heavens ring, In his love we live and move
36	6	help us, this and every day, To live more nearly as we pray
50	3	For without thee I cannot live
99	4	Sent by the Father from on high, Our life to live
99	4	Our life to live, our death to die
106	5	We come to live and reign in thee
167	VII-3	May thy life and death supply Grace to live and grace to die
173	4	To plead for dying souls that they may live
181	4	That we may live and sing to thee
207	3	Thou art the life, by which alone we live
233	4	But live with thee the perfect life Of thine eternity
242	3	By thee may I strongly live, Bravely bear, and nobly strive
281	2	To thy cross we look and live
294	3	Inspire thy heralds of good news To live thy life divine
302	2	God, in whom they live and move, is love
302	2	And died on earth that man might live above
332	4	From henceforth, the time redeeming, May we live to thee
332	4	May we live to thee alone
336	4	A strong, desiring confidence To hear thy voice and live
368	1	But for strength that we may ever Live ... courageously
368	1	Live our lives courageously
392	2	The truth whereby the nations live
407	3	And, pure in heart, behold Thy beauty while I live
413	2	Lord, as thou hast lived for others, So may we ... live
418	4	With thee, O Master, let me live
424	3	It will live and shine transfigured In the final reign
434	1	But to live out the laws of Christ In every thought
450	3	Nation with nation, land with land, Inarmed shall live
450	3	Inarmed shall live as comrades free
472	4	bled That we might live

484	T,1	Remember All the People, Who live in far-off lands
490	2	Teach us where'er we live, To act as in thy sight
490	4	That we may live the life of love And loftiest desire
502	1	All things that live and move, by sea and land

lived

308	4	Evermore their life abides Who have lived to do thy will
413	2	Lord, as thou hast lived for others, So may we ... live
481	1	Who toiled and fought and lived and died for the Lord
481	3	They lived not only in ages past

lives

23	3	praise him still Through good and ill, Who ever lives
26	1	Praise him with a glad accord & with lives of noblest worth
26	2	Standing fast to the last, By his hand our lives are stayed
26	3	Let our lives express Our abundant thankfulness
63	2	May the fruits of thy salvation In our hearts & lives abound
67	1	Creation lives and moves in thee
101	2	And our lives would be all sunshine (102-4)
106	4	High raise the note, that Jesus died, Yet lives and reigns
106	4	Yet lives and reigns, the Crucified
161	T,1	Before the Cross of Jesus Our lives are judged today
182	2	Lives again our glorious King
183	2	Lives in glory now on high, Pleads for us and hears our cry
199	3	Who died, eternal life to bring, & lives that death may die
224	1	We test our lives by thine
237	3	Send down thy love, thy life, Our lesser lives to crown
316	1	Man, created in thine image, Lives nor breathes without
316	1	Lives nor breathes without thine aid
316	3	We would give our lives to thee
341	1	In purer lives thy service find
341	4	And let our ordered lives confess The beauty of thy peace
366	4	Gird our lives that they may be Armored
368	1	Live our lives courageously
376	4	Until our lives are perfected in thee
398	4	Take thou our lives and use them as thou wilt
405	2	Daily our lives would show Weakness made strong
424	2	All our lives are building stones
433	4	Fill all our lives with love and grace divine
436	3	Bind all our lives together, Smite us and save us all
439	3	Lives that passed and left no name
452	5	And use the lives thy love sets free
481	2	followed ... The whole of their good lives long
490	1	Lord of all our hearts and lives, We give ourselves to thee
491	1	Hope and desire for noble lives and true
492	3	flower In Christ-like lives, we pray
580	1	Lamenting all their sinful lives, Before thy mercy gate

livest

7	3	In all life thou livest, the true life of all
159	3	Then let all praise be given thee Who livest evermore

liveth

193	2	For her Lord now liveth, Death hath lost its sting

living

8	3	Well-spring of the joy of living, Ocean depth of happy rest
14	3	Praise to the living God, All praised be his name
33	2	Strength unto our souls afford From thy living Bread, O Lord
39	1	O Light of light, light's living spring
70	5	All things living he doth feed
73	1	Earth and sky, all living nature ... praise
75	3	Hill & vale & fruited land, All things living show his hand
79	2	Where streams of living water flow
89	5	Till all thy living altars claim One holy light
149	3	I only know a living Christ, Our immortality
161	1	Across our restless living The light streams from his cross
173	4	O Intercessor, who art ever living To plead for ... souls
194	3	And all you living things make praise
237	3	Thy living love send down
238	3	Lead us to Christ, the living Way
252	2	It is the heaven-drawn picture of Christ, the living Word
254	1	My spirit pants for thee, O living Word
256	4	Word of the ever-living God, Will of his glorious Son
258	5	Word of mercy, giving Succor to the living
262	3	The inward Christ, the living Word
266	4	O living Church, thine errand speed
267	2	See ... streams of living waters Springing from eternal love
280	2	That living bread, that heavenly wine, Be our immortal food
281	1	Ever may our souls be fed With this true and living bread
286	4	one in thee, Who art one Savior and one living Head
291	1	Jesus, true and living Bread
299	T,1	Spirit of the Living God, In all thy plenitude of grace
304	3	Rejoice, O people, in this living hour
308	2	Long forgotten, living still
326	4	Thou camest, O Lord, with the living word
326	4	living word That should set thy people free
348	2	Pure, warm, and changeless be, A living fire
365	1	living still In spite of dungeon, fire, and sword
366	2	Grant us wisdom ... courage For the living of these days
368	3	But would smite the living fountains From the rocks
376	1	Lead us through Christ, the true and living Way
383	3	Bound by God's far purpose In one living whole
390	2	For thee, my God, the living God, My thirsty soul doth pine
397	1	speak In living echoes of thy tone
422	5	Living again the eternal gospel story
427	T,1	We Are Living, We Are Dwelling In a grand and aweful time
427	1	In an age on ages telling, To be living is sublime
435	1	With thy living fire of judgment Purge this land
436	3	Tie in a living tether The prince and priest and thrall
436	3	Lift up a living nation, A single sword to thee
439	1	Standing in the living present, Memory and hope between
439	3	For the people's prophet leaders, Loyal to the living Word
468	T,1	God of the Living, in Whose eyes
468	1	From this our world of flesh set free, We know them living
468	1	We know them living unto thee
468	2	well we know where'er they be, Our dead are living unto thee
468	3	Not left to lie like fallen tree, Not dead, but living
468	3	Not dead, but living unto thee
468	4	That none might fear that world to see Where all are living
468	4	Where all are living unto thee

lofty

68	1	spread the flowing seas abroad, And built the lofty skies
366	4	Set our feet on lofty places
434	2	His lofty precepts to translate
492	3	Renew in us each day Our lofty purpose

lone

178	2	The Savior wrestles lone with fears
344	2	Lone and dreary, faint and weary, Through the desert
397	1	Thy erring children lost and lone

loneliness

173	1	Breathed in the hour of loneliness and pain

lonely

42	T,1	High O'er the Lonely Hills
59	4	But thy dear presence will not leave them lonely
59	4	will not leave them lonely Who seek thee only
110	1	mourns in lonely exile here Until the Son of God appear
189	2	Let hearts downcast and lonely Rejoice this Easter day
403	2	But the lonely worker also finds him ever at his side

lonesome

201	3	left the lonesome place of death, Despite the rage of foes

long

32	2	angels ... Who all night long, unwearied, sing
35	6	Be this the eternal song Through all the ages long
58	1	Holy dreams and hopes attend us, This live-long night
64	4	Ye who long pain and sorrow bear, Praise God
89	2	Cheers the long watches of the night
98	4	We have enough, yet not too much To long for more
104	3	Make ye straight what long was crooked
106	1	Though absent long, your Lord is nigh
106	3	On your far hills, long cold and gray, Has dawned
106	4	Shores of the utmost West, Ye that have waited long
117	4	Watching long in hope and fear
128	1	In the bleak midwinter, Long ago
142	4	Now may Mary's son, who came So long ago to love us
145	2	Here in sadness Eye and heart long for thy gladness
185	2	All the winter of our sins, Long and dark, is flying
198	3	The world has waited long, Has travailed long in pain
215	3	So long thy power hath blest me
215	3	faces smile Which I have loved long since, and lost awhile
222	1	Long my heart hath panted, Till it well-nigh fainted
237	T,1	Send Down Thy Truth, O God, Too long the shadows frown
237	1	Too long the darkened way we've trod
239	3	And so the yearning strong With which the soul will long
293	4	Till the long shadows o'er our pathway lie
300	2	His kingdom tarries long
303	4	What though the kingdom long delay
306	5	And when the strife is fierce, the warfare long
308	1	Brotherhood and sisterhood Of earth's age-long chivalry
308	2	Long forgotten, living still
311	3	Appear, Desire of nations, Thine exiles long for home
315	3	The foe is stern and eager, The fight is fierce and long

317	2	'Twill be the old, old story That I have loved so long
345	4	Yes, on through life's long path, Still chanting as ye go
366	2	From the fears that long have bound us Free our hearts
380	4	Not long the conflict, soon The holy war shall cease
385	4	Stand up, stand up for Jesus, The strife will not be long
386	T,1	Lighten the Darkness of our life's long night
408	3	For thou wert long beforehand with my soul
419	3	One in the love that suffers long To seek, & serve & save
420	3	city that hath stood Too long a dream, whose laws are love
423	4	Yet long these multitudes to see The sweet compassion
437	4	Long may our land be bright With freedom's holy light
472	1	As we thy help have sought, With labor long have wrought
481	2	followed ... The whole of their good lives long
491	2	never Falter or fail however long the strife
542	1	Through life's long day and death's dark night
578	3	For thou wert long before-hand with my soul

longed

| 169 | 2 | and none The longed-for Christ would know |
| 445 | 3 | speed the longed-for time Foretold by raptured sears |

longer

| 404 | 3 | Take my will, and make it thine, It shall be no longer mine |
| 459 | 3 | The fields no longer mourn |

longing

103	2	Dear desire of every nation, Joy of every longing heart
145	2	Toward thee longing Doth possess me, turn and bless me
156	2	with longing expectation seem to wait The consecration
188	1	When to their longing eyes restored
260	3	Till with the vision glorious, Her longing eyes are blest
270	1	above all the soul distressed, Longing for rest everlasting
477	2	To thee with longing hearts we turn

longings

| 317 | 1 | It satisfies my longings As nothing else would do |

longs

| 324 | 1 | Search, prove my heart, it longs for thee |
| 390 | 1 | So longs my soul, O God, for thee, And thy refreshing grace |

look

92	T,1	I Look to Thee in Every Need And never look in vain
95	2	justice, from her heavenly bower, Look down on mortal men
112	1	Look not back, the past regretting
124	3	Look and see how charming is Jesus
129	3	Look now, for glad and golden hours Come swiftly on the wing
137	2	I love thee, Lord Jesus, look down from the sky
164	2	Ah, look how patiently he hangs
170	2	Look on me with thy favor, Vouch-safe to me thy grace
175	3	The winged squadrons of the sky Look down
175	3	Look down with sad and wondering eye To see
203	T,1	Look, Ye Saints, the Sight Is Glorious
259	3	And look down from supernal heights On all the by-gone time
281	2	To thy cross we look and live
282	1	Look on the heart by sorrow broken

282	1	Look on the tears by sinners shed
292	2	Look, Father, look on his anointed face
292	2	And only look on us as found in him
292	2	Look not on our misusings of thy grace
330	4	I cannot look upon his face For shame, for bitter shame
358	3	Helpless, look to thee for grace
374	1	When thou seest me waver, With a look recall
380	4	Look up, the victor's crown at length
392	4	Teach us to look in all our ends On thee
406	4	And still to things eternal look
467	T,1	Father, to Thee We Look in All Our Sorrow
483	2	and that I might have seen his kind look when he said
489	2	I would look up, and laugh, and love, and lift

looked

| 137 | 1 | The stars in the sky looked down where he lay |
| 141 | 2 | They looked up and saw a star Shining in the east |

looking

167	II-3	O remember us who pine, Looking from our cross to thine
387	2	One the earnest looking forward
393	1	God be in mine eyes, And in my looking
543	1	God be in mine eyes and in my looking

looks

348	T,1	My Faith Looks Up to Thee, Thou Lamb of Calvary
354	1	Who looks in love to Christ above No fear
401	2	A man that looks on glass On it may stay his eye
422	4	When all the world looks up because of him

loom

| 395 | 4 | Thine are the loom, the forge, the mart, The wealth of land |

loose

| 431 | 4 | If drunk with sight of power, we loose Wild tongues |

loosed

| 185 | 1 | Loosed from Pharaoh's bitter yoke Jacob's sons and daughters |
| 443 | 1 | He hath loosed the fateful lightning of his ... swift sword |

loosen

| 426 | 1 | Whom shall I send to loosen The bonds of shame and greed |

Lord

2	3	O Jesus Christ, our God and Lord, Begotten of the Father
4	1	Sing to the Lord with cheerful voice
4	2	The Lord, ye know, is God indeed
4	4	For why, the Lord our God is good
8	T,1	Joyful, Joyful, We Adore Thee, God of glory, Lord of love
9	1	Know that the Lord is God alone
11	2	Eternal are thy mercies, Lord
13	T.1	Praise the Lord, Ye Heavens, Adore Him
13	1	Praise the Lord, for he hath spoken
13	2	Praise the Lord for he is glorious
15	T,1	Praise to the Lord, the Almighty, the King of creation
15	1-4	Praise to the Lord

15	2	Lord, who o'er all things so wondrously reigneth
15	3	Lord, who doth prosper thy work and defend thee
17	T,1	Praise Thou the Lord, O My Soul, Sing Praises
18	1	That thou the only Lord And everlasting Father art
18	3	O holy, holy, holy Lord, Whom heavenly hosts obey
18	5	The holy Church throughout the world, O Lord, confesses thee
19	T,1	Praise the Lord, His Glories Show
19	3	Praise the Lord, his mercies trace
19	4	All that breathe, your Lord adore ... praise him evermore
20	3	Be joyful in the Lord, my heart
20	4	The Lord is God, and he alone
21	2	Thou, Lord, wast at our side, all glory be thine
21	3	Thy name be ever praised, O Lord, make us free
22	2	And with thy help, O Lord, life's battles we win
25	T,1	Stand Up and Bless the Lord, Ye people of his choice
25	1	Stand up & bless the Lord your God with heart & soul & voice
25	4	Stand up and bless the Lord, The Lord your God adore
26	T,1	O Be Joyful in the Lord, Sing before him, all the earth
26	2	Know ye ... the Lord is King, All his works his wisdom prove
26	4	For the Lord our God is kind, And his love shall constant be
27	T,1	O Be Joyful in the Lord (words the same as No. 26)
28	T,1	We Worship Thee, Almighty Lord
30	2	bearer of the eternal Word, Most gracious, magnify the Lord
31	T,1	Worship the Lord in the Beauty of Holiness
31	1	Kneel and adore him, the Lord is his name
32	3	Lord, I my vows to thee renew
33	1	So to thee with one accord Lift we up our Hearts, O Lord
33	4	While we daily search thy Word, Wisdom true impart, O Lord
33	5	Thee would we with one accord Praise and magnify, O Lord
34	1	Their blessings on the Lord of life, As he goes meekly by
34	2	See how the giant sun soars up, Great lord of years and days
36	6	Only, O Lord, in thy dear love Fit us for perfect rest above
44	T,1	Lord Jesus, in the Days of Old
44	2	And though their Lord they failed to know
45	R	Holy, holy, holy, Lord God of Hosts
45	R	Heaven and earth are praising thee, O Lord most high
45	2	Lord of life, beneath the dome Of the universe, thy home
45	3	Lord of angels, on our eyes Let eternal morning rise
47	T,1	The Day Thou Gavest, Lord, Is Ended
47	5	So be it, Lord, thy throne shall never ... pass away
48	T,1	The Day Thou Gavest, Lord, Is Ended (same words as No. 47)
54	T,1	Now Cheer Our Hearts This Eventide, Lord Jesus Christ
55	1	The sick, O Lord, around thee lay
55	4	none, O Lord, have perfect rest, For none are wholly free
56	2	Forgive me, Lord, for thy dear Son, The ill that I this day
60	3	Grant us thy peace, Lord, through the coming night
60	4	Call us, O Lord, to thine eternal peace
63	T,1	Lord, Dismiss Us With Thy Blessing
64	3	Make music for thy Lord to hear, Alleluia, Alleluia
66	R	Lord of all ... we raise This our hymn of grateful praise
68	2	I sing the goodness of the Lord
68	2	goodness of the Lord, That filled the earth with food
68	2	Lord, how thy wonders are displayed, Where'er I turn my eye
69	T,1	Let the Whole Creation Cry, Glory to the Lord on high
69	2	Warriors fighting for the Lord
69	2	All who work & all who wait, Sing, The Lord is good & great

558	4	Meet at my table and record The love of your departed Lord
559	T,1	We Praise Thee, O God, we acknowledge thee to be the Lord
559	3	Holy, holy, holy, Lord God of Sabaoth
559	13	O Lord, save thy people and bless thine heritage
559	15	Vouchsafe, O Lord, to keep us this day without sin
559	14	O Lord, have mercy upon us
559	16	O Lord, let thy mercy be upon us, as our trust is in thee
559	16	O Lord, in thee have I trusted, let me never be confounded
562	T,1	O Come, Let Us Sing unto the Lord
562	3	For the Lord is a great God and a great King above all gods
562	6	and kneel before the Lord our maker
562	7	For he is the Lord our God
562	8	O worship the Lord in the beauty of holiness
565	T,1	O Be Joyful in the Lord all ye lands
565	!	serve the Lord with gladness
565	2	Be ye sure that the Lord he is God
565	4	For the Lord is gracious, his mercy is everlasting
568	T,1	Blessed Be the Lord God of Israel
568	9	shalt go before the face of the Lord to prepare his ways
569	T,1	Blessed Art Thou, O Lord, God of our fathers
570	T,1	My Soul Doth Magnify the Lord
572	T,1	Lord, Now Lettest Thou Thy Servant Depart in peace
576	T,1	Lord, Thou Hast Searched Me and dost know Where'er I rest
577	R	To thee we sing, O Lord most high
578	T,1	I Sought the Lord, and Afterward I Knew
578	2	not so much that I ... As thou, dear Lord, on me
578	3	the whole Of love is but my answer, Lord, to thee
579	T,1	Summer Ended, Harvest O'er, Lord, to thee our song we pour
580	T,1	O Lord, Turn Not Thy Face From Them, Who lie in woeful state
580	2	Shut not that gate against me, Lord, But let me enter in
580	3	For mercy, Lord, is all my suit, O let thy mercy spare
582	T,1	Christ the Lord Is Risen Today (as no. 182 with descant)

Lord's

21	T,1	We Gather Together to ask the Lord's blessing
23	1	Or through the realms of light Fly at your Lord's command
84	T,1	The Lord's My Shepherd, I'll not want
100	3	Like the pity of a father Hath the Lord's compassion been
105	T,1	Hail to the Lord's Anointed, Great David's greater Son
112	1	Rise, and join the Lord's command
144	2	To read in heaven the Lord's command
155	2	Who in the Lord's name cometh, The King and blessed One
245	2	And with actions brotherly Speak my Lord's sincerity
255	2	The Lord's commandments all are pure & clearest light impart
534	1	Praise ye the Lord. The Lord's name be praised

lords

107	2	Lord of lords, in human vesture, In the body and the blood
200	2	King of kings, and Lord of lords, And heaven's eternal light
203	4	crown him King of kings, and Lord of lords
435	1	Lord of lords and King of kings

lordship

450	2	dare All that may plant man's lordship firm On earth

lose

50	5	Till in the ocean of thy love we lose ourselves in heaven
50	5	We lose ourselves in heaven above
202	4	The prisoner leaps to lose his chains
325	3	Till in the night of hate and war We perish as we lose thee
342	2	Temptations lose their power When thou art nigh
354	3	Temptation's hour shall lose its power
359	2	Workman of God, O lose not heart, But learn what God is like
383	3	In each loss or triumph Lose or triumph all

losing

363	2	Our striving would be losing

loss

127	4	trace we the babe, Who hath retrieved our loss
158	2	Shun not suffering, shame, or loss
160	3	Content to let the world go by, To know no gain nor loss
161	1	And by its clear, revealing beams We measure gain and loss
168	3	Which thou didst take to save our souls from loss
177	1	My richest gain I count but loss
183	2	He who bore all pain and loss Comfortless upon the cross
187	1	Who did once upon the cross ... Suffer to redeem our loss
224	3	Apart from thee all gain is loss, All labor vainly done
325	4	O love that triumphs over loss, we bring our hearts
364	1	Christian, up and smite them, Counting gain but loss
383	3	In each loss or triumph Lose or triumph all
385	1	Lift high his royal banner, It must not suffer loss
470	5	Inspired of thee, may they count all but loss
471	5	Fit him to follow thee through pain and loss

lost

2	3	And the lost sheep dost gather
94	1	Transported with the view, I'm lost in wonder, love & praise
127	4	God's wondrous love in saving lost mankind
154	1	sick to cure, the lost to seek, To raise up them that fall
189	2	The grave has lost its triumph And death has lost its sting
193	2	For her Lord now liveth, Death hath lost its sting
215	3	faces smile Which I have loved long since, and lost awhile
228	4	Lost in wonder, love and praise
295	2	The wayward and the lost, By restless passions tossed
301	2	Seek the lost until she find
302	1	One soul should perish, lost in shades of night
302	2	Tell how he stooped to save his lost creation
313	1	Nor yet because who love thee not Are lost eternally
315	2	Our hearts are filled with sadness, And we had lost our way
397	1	Thy erring children lost and lone
417	2	Who would sit down and sigh for a lost age of gold

lot

290	3	Where'er our changeful lot is cast
370	2	Content whatever lot I see, Since 'tis my God that leadeth
433	2	In this free land by thee our lot is cast

loud

124	2	It is wrong to talk so loud
202	5	And earth repeat the loud Amen

love

177	3	See, from his head, his hands, his feet, Sorrow and love
177	3	Sorrow and love flow mingled down
177	3	Did e'er such love and sorrow meet
177	4	Love so amazing, so divine, Demands my soul, my life, my all
180	3	Alleluia to the Spirit, Fount of love and sanctity
184	3	Praise we in songs of victory That love
184	3	That love, that life which cannot die
187	4	Sing we to our God above ... Praise eternal as his love
193	3	Make us more than conquerors, Through thy deathless love
199	2	Crown him the Lord of love, Behold his hands and side
200	3	To whom he manifests his love, And grants his name to know
202	3	People and realms of every tongue Dwell on his love
202	3	Dwell on his love with sweetest song
204	2	The Lord, our Savior, reigns, The God of truth and love
206	4	And thanks never ceasing and infinite love
212	1	Now to seek and love and fear thee
212	1	Drawn from earth to love thee solely
217	3	Your love in our hearts, Lord, at the eve of the day
222	3	Those who love the Father ... Still have peace within
223	3	Glory to God and praise and love Be ever, ever given
225	4	The love of Jesus, what it is None but his loved ones know
228	T,1	Love Divine, All Loves Excelling
228	1	Pure, unbounded love thou art
228	2	Take away the love of sinning
228	3	Glory in thy perfect love
228	4	Lost in wonder, love and praise
229	T,1	Join All the Glorious Names Of wisdom, love, and power
230	T,1	Immortal Love, Forever Full, Forever flowing free
230	2	Love only knoweth whence it came, And comprehendeth love
230	4	And faith has still its Olivet, And love its Galilee
232	1	And make me love thee as I ought to love
232	3	Hast thou not bid us love thee, God and King
232	5	Teach me to love thee as thine angels love
232	5	My heart an altar, and thy love the flame
233	1	Fill me with life anew, That I may love what thou dost love
235	4	That we may love not doctrines strange
236	T,1,5	Life of Ages, Richly Poured, Love of God unspent and free
237	3	Send down thy love, thy life, Our lesser lives to crown
237	3	Thy living love send down
239	T,1	Come Down, O Love divine, Seek thou this soul of mine
240	1	Kindle a flame of sacred love In these cold hearts of ours
240	3	Come, shed abroad a Savior's love, & that shall kindle ours
241	3	The wings of peaceful love
242	2	Holy Spirit, Love divine, Glow within this heart of mine
244	2	In thy pure love & holy faith From thee true wisdom learning
246	4	And to eternity, Love and adore
249	1	Thy love has blessed the wide world's wondrous story
249	2	To thee in reverent love, our hearts are bowed
249	5	Pray we that thou wilt hear us, still imploring Thy love
249	5	Thy love and favor, kept to us always
251	3	Perfect in power, in love and purity
258	6	Lord, may love and fear thee, Evermore be near thee
259	4	Enlarge, expand all Christian souls To comprehend thy love
262	4	One hope, one faith, one love restore The seamless robe
269	T,1	I Love Thy Kingdom, Lord, The house of thine abode
269	2	I love thy Church, O God, Her walls before they stand

334	3	Our spirits yearn to feel thy kindling love
339	2	Love doth stand At his hand, Joy doth wait on his command
341	3	The silence of eternity, Interpreted by love
343	T,1	In Heavenly Love Abiding, No change my heart shall fear
344	3	Love with every passion blending
346	2	Faithful are all who love the truth
346	4	And grant us in thy love To sing the songs of victory
348	2	As thou hast died for me, Oh, may my love to thee
348	2	O may my love to thee Pure, warm and changeless be
348	4	Blest Savior, then, in love, Fear and distrust remove
354	1	Who looks in love to Christ above No fear
356	2	Enslave it with thy matchless love
357	T,1	Strong Son of God, Immortal Love
360	2	I can but give the gifts he gave, & plead his love for love
360	3	I only know I cannot drift Beyond his love and care
365	4	Faith of our fathers, we will love Both friend and foe
365	4	love Both friend and foe in all our strife
365	4	And preach thee, too, as love knows how, By kindly words
367	3	Christ is its life, and Christ its love
373	4	His love thy joy increase
375	2	But deeds of love and mercy, The heavenly kingdom comes
383	2	Wider grows the kingdom, Reign of love and light
386	2	The subtle darkness that we love so well
387	3	Where the one almighty Father Reigns in love forevermore
392	6	And love to all men 'neath the sun
392	+1	Land of our birth, we pledge to thee Our love and toil
392	+1	Our love and toil in the years to be
394	1	are dependent on thy will and love alone
396	3	Let all my being speak Of thee and of thy love, O Lord
397	4	Thy love to tell, thy praise to show
398	4	We render back the love thy mercy gave us
399	T,1	O Love That Wilt Not Let Me Go
400	T,1,R	More Love to Thee, O Christ, More love to thee
400	1	This is my earnest plea, More love, O Christ, to thee
400	2	This all my prayer shall be, More love, O Christ, to thee
400	3	This still its prayer shall be, More Love, O Christ, to thee
403	T,1	Those Who Love and Those Who Labor
403	1	who love and ... labor follow in the way of Christ
403	1	thus the gift of love sufficed
404	4	Take my love, my Lord I pour At thy feet its treasure store
408	3	I find, I walk, I love, but oh, the whole Of Love
408	3	the whole Of love is but my answer, Lord, to thee
409	3	Every deed of love and kindness Done to man is done to thee
410	1	To worship rightly is to love each other
410	3	Love shall tread out the baleful fire of anger
404	2	Take my hands and let them move At the impulse of thy love
413	1	Fill us with thy love and pity
413	3	King of love and Prince of peace
414	1	But one great fellowship of love
414	1	fellowship of love Throughout the whole wide earth
416	4	Perfect love bereft of fear
418	2	move By some clear, winning word of love
419	3	One in the love that suffers long To seek, & serve & save
420	3	city that hath stood Too long a dream, whose laws are love
421	3	Abound with love and solace for the day
422	2	Speak to the heart of love, alive and daring

495	3	Brother, do you love my Jesus
495	4	If you love him, why not serve him
499	1	Serve him with awe, with reverence, love
508	1	In perfect love and faultless tone
508	2	Thine ear discerns, thy love rejoices When hearts rise up
539	1	And the Father's boundless love
542	1	And make our luke-warm hearts to glow With lowly love
542	1	With lowly love and fervent will
558	2	What love through all his actions ran
558	2	What wondrous words of love he spake
558	4	Meet at my table and record The love of your departed Lord
577	1	delivered us By thy great love and mighty power
577	1	power supreme, thy love sublime
577	1	That love that never faileth
578	3	I find, I walk, I love, but O the whole Of love is
578	3	the whole Of love is but my answer, Lord, to thee

love's

44	1	love's blind instinct made them bold to crave thy presence
61	4	Keep love's banner floating o'er you
77	3	Sorrow forgot, love's purest joys restored
138	3	Son of God, love's pure light
159	2	Till through our pity & our shame Love answers love's appeal
182	3	Love's redeeming work is done
304	4	Shall ring love's gracious song of victory
352	2	The mist of doubt, the blight of love's decay
405	1	Yet may love's incense rise, Sweeter than sacrifice

loved

55	3	And some have never loved thee well
167	III-3	May we all thy loved ones be, All one holy family
178	2	E'en that disciple whom he loved Heeds not
215	2	I loved to choose and see my path, but now Lead thou me on
215	2	I loved the garish day
215	3	faces smile Which I have loved long since, and lost awhile
225	4	The love of Jesus, what it is None but his loved ones know
313	2	But as thyself hast loved me, O everloving Lord
317	2	'Twill be the old, old story That I have loved so long
327	3	Blessed Jesus, Thou hast loved us, love us still
345	3	Send forth the hymns our fathers loved
381	1	faith ... The traveler's well-loved aid
389	4	And at our Father's loved abode Our souls arrive in peace
440	3	Who more than self their country loved
481	1	For the Lord they loved and knew
481	2	They loved their Lord so dear, so dear
496	2	stand Between their loved homes and the war's desolation

lovedst

| 408 | 3 | Always thou lovedst me |
| 578 | 3 | Always thou lovedst me |

loveless

| 169 | 1 | Love to the loveless show, That they might lovely be |

lovelier

| 36 | 4 | Old friends, old scenes, will lovelier be |
| 36 | 4 | lovelier be, As more of heaven in each we see |

37	1	Fairer than morning, lovelier than daylight
37	1	lovelier ... Dawns the sweet consciousness, I am with thee

loveliest
35	5	In heaven's eternal bliss The loveliest strain is this

loveliness
456	1	And laid a silent loveliness On hill and wood and field

lovely
144	1	More lovely than the noon-day light
169	1	Love to the loveless show, That they might lovely be
274	T,1	How Lovely Are Thy Dwellings Fair, O Lord of hosts
484	1	In strange and lovely cities, Or roam the desert sands

lover
210	T,1	Jesus, Lover of My Soul, Let me to thy bosom fly
211	T,1	Jesus, Lover of My Soul (same words as no. 210)

lovers
490	3	The lovers of all holy things, The foes of all things wrong

loves
205	3	Yet he loves the earth he leaves
228	T,1	Love Divine, All Loves Excelling

lovest
3	3	in all, Great and small, Seek to do ... what thou lovest
3	3	Seek to do most nearly What thou lovest dearly
392	T,1	Father in Heaven, Who Lovest All

loving
89	1	Yet to each loving heart how near
132	3	Who would not love thee, loving us so dearly
140	3	Let loving hearts enthrone him
152	4	Of God and man in loving service met
167	III-1	Jesus, loving to the end Her whose heart thy sorrows rend
167	III-3	Loving all for the love of thee, Hear us, holy Jesus
167	V-2	Satisfy thy loving will, Hear us, holy Jesus
228	2	O breathe thy loving Spirit Into every troubled breast
248	2	Ineffable in loving, Unthinkable in might
290	T,1	Jesus, Thou Joy of Loving Hearts
291	2	Here in loving reverence bow
295	1	With loving zeal
313	2	But as thyself hast loved me, O everloving Lord
315	2	O loving voice of Jesus, Which comes to cheer the night
332	5	Loving Savior, Holy Spirit, Hear and heed our humble cry
353	2	Lord, I want to be more loving
377	1	Soon again his arms will fold thee To his loving heart
377	1	To his loving heart and hold thee
397	2	and strong in thee, I may stretch out a loving hand
397	2	a loving hand To wrestlers with the troubled sea
410	2	Each loving life a psalm of gratitude
457	2	God's praises in their loving strain Unconsciously they sing
471	4	Be in his heart, the fount of all his loving
479	1	For rest and food and loving care

479 2   In all we do in work or play To grow more loving every day

lovingkindness
53   3   Awhile his mortal blindness May miss God's lovingkindness

lovingly
193 2   Lovingly he greets thee, Scatters fear and gloom

low
31   2   Low at his feet lay the burden of carefulness
95   4   all shall frame To bow them low before thee, Lord
126 2   Low lies his head with the beasts of the stall
136 3   Kneeling low by his bed, Lay their gifts before him
161 2   Our love, as low or pure
230 6   The last low whispers of our dead Are burdened with his name
304 3   Low lies man's pride and human wisdom dies
310 4   Low before him with our praises we fall
318 1   Raised my low self above, Won by thy deathless love
329 3   O Jesus, thou art pleading In accents meek and low
332 1   Low before thy throne we fall
343 1   The storm may roar without me, My heart may low be laid
352 3   Low lies the best till lifted up to heaven
352 3   Low lie the bounding heart, the teeming brain
361 2   Have faith in God, my mind, Though oft thy light burns low
467 3   Low in the heart faith singeth still her song

lower
167 VII-2 When the death shades round us lower

lowest
230 3   In vain we search the lowest deeps

lowing
137 2   cattle are lowing, the baby awakes

lowland
106 1   Valley and lowland, sing

lowliest
270 3   Now we may gather with our King E'en in the lowliest
270 3   E'en in the lowliest dwelling

lowliness
31   1   With gold of obedience and incense of lowliness
147 2   Thou cam'st to us in lowliness of thought
214 2   To dwell in lowliness with men, their pattern and their King
570 2   For he hath regarded the lowliness of his hand-maiden

lowly
60   1   Then, lowly kneeling, wait thy word of peace
73   T,1   Angels Holy, High and Lowly, Sing the praises of the Lord
119 2   As with joyful steps they sped To that lowly manger-bed
121 2   This little child, of lowly birth, Shall be the joy
129 2   Above its sad and lowly plains They bend on hovering wing
135 1   Our lowly state to make thine own
152 2   Shining revealed through every task most lowly

175	2	In lowly pomp ride on to die
214	3	Still to the lowly soul He doth himself impart
214	4	Give us a pure and lowly heart, A temple meet for thee
248	3	Thou to the meek and lowly Thy secrets dost unfold
260	4	Like them, the meek and lowly, On high may dwell with thee
305	3	Stay not till all the lowly Triumphant reach their home
326	2	But in lowly birth didst thou come to earth
329	1	In lowly patience waiting To pass the threshold o'er
409	1	By thy lowly human birth Thou hast come to join the workers
413	4	host advancing, High and lowly, great and small
418	1	In lowly paths of service free
465	1	Lowly we kneel in prayer before thy throne
488	3	Down in a lowly manger The humble Christ was born
508	2	Before thy feet, abashed and lowly
542	1	And make our luke-warm hearts to glow With lowly love
542	1	With lowly love and fervent will

loyal

439	3	For the people's prophet leaders, Loyal to the living Word

luke

542	1	make our luke-warm hearts to glow With lowly love

lulled

106	2	Pent be each warring breeze, Lulled be your restless waves

lulls

386	2	darkness ... lulls our spirits with its baneful spell

lure

380	2	ne'er from Christ By any lure or guile enticed
398	3	Walk thou beside us lest the tempting byways Lure us away
398	3	Lure us away from thee to endless night

lures

423	2	From paths where hide the lures of greed

luring

364	2	Striving, tempting, luring, Goading into sin

lust

420	2	O shame to us who rest content While lust and greed for gain

luster

89	4	Before thy ever-blazing throne We ask no luster of our own
157	3	Adds more luster to the day

lustered

407	1	All things in earth and heaven Are lustered by thy ray

lusts

156	1	behold we lay Our passions, lusts, & proud wills in thy way
380	3	'Gainst lies and lusts & wrongs, Let courage rule our souls
449	2	Purge us from lusts that curse and kill

maddening

made

maimed

392	3	No maimed or worthless sacrifice

maintaining

21	2	Ordaining, maintaining his kingdom divine

majestic

18	3	The world is with the glory filled Of thy majestic sway

majesties

440	1	For purple mountain majesties Above the fruited plain

majesty

18	5	That thou eternal Father art, Of boundless majesty
175	T,1-4	Ride on, Ride on in Majesty
176	T,1	Ride on, Ride on in Majesty (same words as no. 175)
180	3	Alleluia, Alleluia, To the Triune Majesty
195	4	To him all majesty ascribe
246	4	His sovereign majesty May we in glory see
390	2	O when shall I behold thy face, Thou majesty divine
559	3	heaven and earth are full of the majesty of thy glory
559	6	The Father, of an infinite majesty
569	2	Blessed art thou for the name of thy majesty

make

4	2	Without our aid he did us make
21	1	He chastens and hastens his will to make known
21	3	Thy name be ever praised, O Lord, make us free
39	4	To make ill-fortune turn to fair
56	3	Sleep that may me more vigorous make To serve my God
64	3	Make music for thy Lord to hear, Alleluia, Alleluia
74	4	Spirit in our spirit speaking, Make us sons of God indeed
81	3	Oh make but trial of his love, Experience will decide
81	4	Make you his service your delight
81	4	He'll make your wants his care
84	2	me to walk doth make Within the paths of righteousness
87	4	God is his own interpreter, And he will make it plain
89	5	Grant us thy truth to make us free
104	3	Make ye straight what long was crooked
104	3	Make the rougher places plain
114	2	Make it a temple set apart From earthly use
121	3	Ah, dearest Jesus, holy child, Make thee a bed
121	3	Make thee a bed, soft, undefiled Within my heart
135	1	Our lowly state to make thine own
145	2	And make thee there an altar
159	2	Make us thy sorrow feel
161	3	And make us brave and full of joy To answer to his call
165	1	For God doth make his world anew
168	2	our weak endurance Make us unworthy here to take our part
170	3	O make me thine forever, And should I fainting be
171	3	He died that we may be forgiven, He died to make us good
193	3	Make us more than conquerors, Through thy deathless love
194	3	And all you living things make praise
207	5	Lord, give us peace, and make us calm and sure
210	3	Let the healing streams abound, Make and keep me pure within
218	2	O speak, and make me listen, Thou guardian of my soul

232	1	And make me love thee as I ought to love
235	1	On ... mind and soul, To strengthen, save, and make us whole
238	2	And make us know and choose thy way
241	1	And make this house thy home
241	4	And make this world thy home
244	1	Thy temple deign to make us
252	4	O make thy Church, dear Savior, A lamp of burnished gold
259	4	And make us to go on, to know With nobler powers conferred
266	3	And feet on mercy's errands swift Do make her pilgrimage
268	3	For thy kingdom make us bold
268	3	Make us one we now implore
271	1	The eternal arms, their dear abode, We make our habitation
276	3	Here make the well-springs of thy grace Like fountains
286	1	Thyself at thine own board make manifest in ...our sacrament
289	1	Thou, Lord, didst make all for thy pleasure
290	4	Make all our moments calm and bright
292	3	In thine own service make us glad and free
294	1	send us forth ... prophets true, To make all lands thine own
300	3	Her strength unequal to her task, Rise up and make her great
314	1	And make me pure within
321	T,1	My God, Accept My Heart This Day, And make it always thine
334	3	Now make us strong, we need thy deep revealing
346	3	Of every hearth to make a home, Of every home a heaven
356	T,1	Make Me a Captive, Lord, And then I shall be free
357	3	Our wills are ours to make them thine
357	6	That mind and soul, according well, May make one music
357	6	May make one music as before
361	4	Lord Jesus, make me whole
364	4	But that toil shall make thee Some day all mine own
371	1	There's no discouragement Shall make him once relent
371	2	He will make good his right To be a pilgrim
381	3	Thy spirit, Lord, to me impart, O make me what thou ever art
386	3	To all the gods we ignorantly make And worship
400	1	Hear thou the prayer I make On bended knee
404	3	Take my will, and make it thine, It shall be no longer mine
411	2	One make us all, true comrades in thy service
411	2	And make us one in thee with God the Lord
419	1	and pray That thou wilt make us one
423	5	O Master, from the mountain side, Make haste to heal
423	5	Make haste to heal these hearts of pain
425	2	And, with heart and hand, to be Earnest to make others free
426	4	Take us, and make us holy, Teach us thy will and way
430	2	Yea, love with thee shall make his home
439	4	From the strife of class and faction Make our nation free
439	4	Make our nation free indeed
443	4	As he died to make men holy, let us die to make men free
447	1	Make wars throughout the world to cease
448	1	Fulfil of old thy word And make the nations one
449	2	Make us thy ministers of life
467	3	And in our weakness thou dost make us strong
470	1	Make each one nobler, stronger than the last
470	2	Make their ears attent To thy divinest speech
470	2	their lips make eloquent To assure the right
470	5	Make them apostles, Heralds of thy cross
471	4	Make him a shepherd, kind to young and old
472	2	Come, thou, O Lord divine, Make this thy holy shrine

475	3	The gold and silver, make them thine
498	2	Make thou thy flame in us to glow
521	2	Make strong our faith, increase our light
524	1	make thy way plain before my face
531	1	O God, make clean our hearts within us
533	1	O God, make clean our hearts within us
542	1	And make our luke-warm hearts to glow With lowly love
559	12	Make them ... numbered with thy saints in glory everlasting
576	4	And far away my dwelling make
577	1	Make manifest in this dread time Thy power supreme

maker

6	5	Our Maker, Defender, Redeemer and Friend
9	3	What lasting honors ...Almighty Maker, to thy name
53	1	On God, Our Maker, calling ... the Giver good
67	T,1	God of Earth, the Sky, the Sea, Maker of all above, below
126	2	Maker, and Monarch, and Savior of all
248	1	O God, thou art the Maker Of all created things
460	2	He only is the maker Of all things near and far
461	1	God, our Maker, doth provide For our wants to be supplied
462	1	God, our Maker, doth provide For our wants to be supplied
500	2	Praise God, our Maker and our Friend
562	6	and kneel before the Lord our maker

maker's

75	1	All their maker's praise declare
303	2	As friends who share the Maker's plan
485	2	morning light, the lily white, Declare their Maker's praise

makes

42	3	Splendor he makes on earth, Color awakes on earth
68	3	not a plant or flower below But makes thy glories known
84	1	He makes me down to lie In pastures green
106	2	And makes your wastes his great highway
130	3	And makes the nations prove The glories of his righteousness
137	2	But little Lord Jesus, no crying he makes
169	4	Why, what hath my Lord done, What makes this rage and spite
220	1	Beside us walks our brother Christ, & makes our task his own
220	3	The common hopes that makes us men Were his in Galilee
221	2	It makes the wounded spirit whole
227	2	Jesus is purer, Who makes the woeful heart to sing
239	3	the place Wherein the Holy Spirit makes his dwelling
275	3	One in the power that makes the children free
401	4	A servant with this clause Makes drudgery divine
401	4	Who sweeps a room ... Makes that and the action fine
419	3	One in the truth that makes men free
419	3	The faith that makes men brave
441	2	Time makes ancient good uncouth
459	1	He makes the grass the mountains crown
479	1	And all that makes the day so fair
487	2	He makes green things grow, Ripens what we sow

makest

| 524 | 1 | For it is thou, Lord, thou, Lord only, that makest me dwell |
| 524 | 1 | thou, Lord, only, that makest me dwell in safety |

man's

manger

manhood

466 2   With heart still undefiled, Thou didst to manhood come

manifest
286 1   Thyself at thine own board make manifest in ...our sacrament
577 1   Make manifest in this dread time Thy power supreme

manifests
200 3   To whom he manifests his love, And grants his name to know

manifold
69 3   Men and women, young and old, Raise the anthem manifold
383 1   Manifold the service, One the sure reward

mankind
35 3   Ye nations of mankind, In this your concord find
42 4   And for mankind at last Day has begun
127 4   God's wondrous love in saving lost mankind
146 2   Glad tidings of great joy I bring To you and all mankind
184 2   Let all mankind rejoice and say
205 3   Still he calls mankind his own
225 2   O Savior of mankind
294 3   Till Christ is formed in all mankind And every land is thine
341 T,1   Dear Lord and Father of Mankind, Forgive our foolish ways
365 3   And through the truth that comes from God Mankind ... free
365 3   Mankind shall then indeed be free
414 2   His service is the golden cord Close-binding all mankind
425 2   with leathern hearts, forget That we owe mankind a debt
453 3   ring in redress to all mankind

manna
61 2   Daily manna still provide you
221 2   'Tis manna to the hungry soul, And to the weary, rest
256 2   True manna from on high
267 3   Safe they feed upon the manna Which he gives them

mansions
41 2   Monarch of all things, fit us for thy mansions

mantle
6 3   And round it hath cast, like a mantle, the sea
421 4   We've seen thy glory like a mantle spread O'er hill and dale
470 1   Elijah's mantle o'er Elisha cast

many
98 1   So many glorious things are here, Noble and right
98 2   So many gentle thoughts and deeds Circling us round
199 T,1   Crown Him With Many Crowns, The Lamb upon his throne
253 2   Many diverse scrolls completing
268 2   Many tongues of many nations Sing the greater unity
298 2   By the mouth of many messengers Goes forth the voice of God
309 2   And bright with many an angel, And all the martyr throng
319 2   With many a conflict, many a doubt
397 3   The hidden depths of many a heart
403 2   Where the many work together, they with God himself abide
577 1   delivered us ... In many an evil hour

mar
| 262 | 1 | The wrangling tongues that mar thy praise |

march
8	4	Ever singing march we onward, Victors in the midst of strife
67	3	Thy grandeur in the march of night
298	3	March we forth in the strength of God
298	3	March we forth ... With the banner of Christ unfurled
345	5	Still lift your standard high, Still march in firm array
375	T,1	Lead On, O King Eternal, The day of march has come
380	T,1	March on, O Soul, With Strength
380	3	March on, O soul, with strength, As strong the battle rolls
380	4	March on, O soul, march on with strength
387	3	One the conflict, one the peril, One the march in God begun
411	1	Grant us to march among thy faithful legions
456	T,1	All Beautiful the March of Days, As seasons come and go

marching
382	T,1,R	Onward, Christian Soldiers, Marching as to war
387	1	Singing songs of expectation, Marching to the promised land
432	2	Thou wast the shield for Israel's marching host
443	1	His truth is marching on
443	R	Glory, glory, Hallelujah ... His truth is marching on
443	2	His day is marching on
443	3	Our God is marching on
443	4	While God is marching on

mark
158	3	Mark that miracle of time, God's own sacrifice complete
264	2	We mark her goodly battlements, And her foundations strong
349	5	So purer light shall mark the road That leads me to the Lamb

market
220	2	Through din of market, whirl of wheels
403	2	Lo, the Prince of common welfare dwells within the market
403	2	dwells within the market strife

marred
| 329 | 2 | tears thy face have marred |

marriage
| 558 | 5 | Till thou return and we shall eat The marriage supper |
| 558 | 5 | The marriage supper of the Lamb |

marshaled
| 303 | 1 | thanks ... That battle calls our marshaled ranks |

mart
| 395 | 4 | Thine are the loom, the forge, the mart, The wealth of land |
| 426 | 2 | No field or mart is silent, No city street is dumb |

martyr
304	2	Till saint and martyr sped the venture bold
309	2	And bright with many an angel, And all the martyr throng
388	2	martyr first, whose eagle eye Could pierce beyond the grave

388	2	Who saw his Master in the sky, And called on him to save
405	T,1	Master, No Offering Costly and Sweet
412	T,1	O Master Workman of the Race, Thou Man of Galilee
418	T,1	O Master, Let Me Walk With Thee
418	4	With thee, O Master, let me live
423	5	O Master, from the mountain side, Make haste to heal
491	3	Teach us to know the way of Jesus Christ, our Master
494	1	We would be building, Master,
494	2	O Master, lend us sight To see the towers gleaming
494	3	O keep us building Master
584	T,1	Ye Servants of God, Your Master Proclaim (206 with descant)

master's
| 178 | 2 | Heeds not his Master's grief and tears |
| 220 | 4 | o'er the centuries still we hear The Master's winsome call |

masterful
| 64 | 3 | Thou fire so masterful and bright |

match
| 444 | 1 | Come with thy ... judgment now To match our present hour |

matchless
149	2	I only know its matchless love Has brought God's love to me
199	1	And hail him as thy matchless King Through all eternity
356	2	Enslave it with thy matchless love

matron
| 388 | 4 | A noble army, men and boys, The matron and the maid |

mature
| 463 | 2 | Praise him ... he gave the rain To mature the swelling grain |

may
3	3	May I ceaselessly adore thee
20	3	That men may hear the grateful song My voice unwearied raises
29	2	O may this bounteous God Through all our life be near us
31	2	Guiding thy steps as may best for thee be
32	4	my powers, with all their might, In thy sole glory may unite
35	1-6	May Jesus Christ be praised
46	2	May struggling hearts that seek release Here find the rest
46	4	in the spirit's secret cell May hymn & prayer forever dwell
50	1	Oh, may no earth-born cloud arise To hide thee
51	2	With thy tenderest blessing May our eyelids close
53	3	Awhile his mortal blindness May miss God's lovingkindness
54	2	May we and all who bear thy name ...thy cross proclaim
56	2	That with the world, myself and thee, I ... at peace may be
56	2	That ... I, ere I sleep, at peace may be
56	3	O may my soul on thee repose
56	3	Sleep that may me more vigorous make To serve my God
58	1	May thine angel-guards defend us
58	2	May we, born anew like morning, To labor rise
63	2	May the fruits of thy salvation In our hearts & lives abound
63	2	Ever faithful To the truth may we be found
63	3	may we ever Reign with thee in endless day
79	6	Good Shepherd may I sing thy praise Within thy house forever

86	4	May thy fresh light arise Within each clouded heart
98	3	So that earth's bliss may be our guide, And not our chain
107	3	powers of hell may vanish As the darkness clears away
116	2	Say what may the tidings be Which inspire your heavenly song
119	1	So most gracious Lord, may we Evermore be led to thee
119	2	So may we with willing feet Ever seek thy mercy seat
119	3	So may we with holy joy Pure and free from sin's alloy
120	3	Mild he lays his glory by, Born that man no more may die
121	3	heart, that it may be A quiet chamber kept for thee
127	4	O may we keep and ponder in our mind God's wondrous love
128	3	Angels and archangels May have gathered there
134	3	No ear may hear his coming, But in this world of sin
135	2	O may we ever faithful be
142	4	Now may Mary's son, who came So long ago to love us
148	3	Thou, his vanquisher before, Grant we may not faint nor fail
148	4	That with thee we may appear At the eternal Eastertide
153	4	An Easter of unending joy We may attain at last
159	4	That, as we share this hour, Thy cross may bring us ... joy
159	4	Thy cross may bring us to thy joy And resurrection power
166	3	O may we, who mercy need, Be like thee in heart and deed
167	II-2	May we, in our guilt and shame Still thy love & mercy claim
167	III-2	May we in thy sorrows share, And for thee all perils dare
167	III-3	May we all thy loved ones be, All one holy family
167	V-3	May we thirst thy love to know, Lead us in our sin and woe
167	VII-3	May thy life and death supply Grace to live and grace to die
171	2	We may not know, we cannot tell What pains he had to bear
171	3	He died that we may be forgiven, He died to make us good
173	4	To plead for dying souls that they may live
174	2	Till the appointed time is nigh ... the Lamb of God may die
181	4	That we may live and sing to thee
188	2	That we may give thee all our days the willing tribute
192	2	Our hearts be pure from evil, That we may see aright
192	2	And, listening to his accents, May hear so calm and plain
192	2	His own, All hail, and, hearing, May raise the victor-strain
195	5	O that, with yonder sacred throng, We at his feet may fall
199	3	Who died, eternal life to bring, & lives that death may die
207	4	That we may dwell in perfect unity
213	3	May I hear thee say to me, Fear not, I will pilot thee
214	4	May ours this blessing be
222	3	Though the storms may gather, Still have peace within
230	3	We may not climb the heavenly steeps
233	1	Fill me with life anew, That I may love what thou dost love
235	4	That we may love not doctrines strange
238	2	That we from thee may ne'er depart
238	4	Lead us to heaven that we may share Fulness of joy
242	3	By thee may I strongly live, Bravely bear, and nobly strive
246	4	His sovereign majesty May we in glory see
251	3	Though the eye of sinful man thy glory may not see
258	6	Lord, may love and fear thee, Evermore be near thee
260	4	Like them, the meek and lowly, On high may dwell with thee
270	3	Now we may gather with our King E'en in the lowliest
270	3	Praises to him we there may bring
275	1	Rule in our hearts, that we may ever be Guided
275	2	Descend ... that we may be as one
276	1	And pray that this may be our home Until we touch eternity
276	4	May thy whole truth be spoken here

277	3	May we see our human family Free from sorrow and despair
281	1	Ever may our souls be fed With this true and living bread
286	4	Then open thou our eyes, that we may see
293	3	No arm so weak but may do service here
293	3	By feeblest agents may our God fulfill His righteous will
298	2,3	That the earth may be filled with the glory of God
298	3	That the light of the glorious gospel of truth May shine
298	3	May shine throughout the world
301	2	May she guide the poor and blind
301	3	May her scattered children be From reproach of evil free
301	4	May she one in doctrine be, One in truth and charity
301	5	May she holy triumphs win, Overthrow the hosts of sin
306	3	O may thy soldiers, faithful, true and bold Fight
312	6	Jerusalem, Jerusalem, God grant that I may see ... joy
314	4	I may the eternal brightness see, And share thy joy at last
316	2	May we offer for thy service All our wealth & all our days
316	3	That all men thy love may see
318	3	Not for myself alone May my prayer be
321	1	That I from thee no more may stray
321	3	That I may see thy glorious face, And worship at thy throne
322	5	Jesus calls us, by thy mercies, Savior, may we hear thy call
325	1	And still our wrongs may weave thee now New thorns
331	2	That each departing day Henceforth may see Some work of love
332	4	From henceforth, the time redeeming, May we live to thee
332	4	May we live to thee alone
343	1	The storm may roar without me, My heart may low be laid
343	2	Wherever he may guide me, No want shall turn me back
347	5	O may we lead the pilgrim's life, And follow thee to heaven
348	2	May thy rich grace impart Strength to my fainting heart
348	2	As thou hast died for me, Oh, may my love to thee
348	2	O may my love to thee Pure, warm and changeless be
352	1	Here at thy feet none other may we see
357	6	That mind and soul, according well, May make one music
357	6	May make one music as before
363	2	Dost ask who that may be, Christ Jesus, it is he
363	4	The body they may kill, God's truth abideth still
366	4	Gird our lives that they may be Armored
368	1	But for strength that we may ever Live ... courageously
368	2	But the steep and rugged pathway May we tread rejoicingly
374	3	Grant that I may never Fail thy hand to see
374	3	Grant that I may ever Cast my care on thee
376	4	However rough and steep the path may be
378	4	Grant them thy truth, that they may be forgiven
380	3	In keenest strife, Lord, may we stand, Upheld
381	3	My faith, it is a trusty sword, May falsehood find it keen
382	3	Crowns and thrones may perish, Kingdoms rise and wane
384	2	Ye may o'ercome through Christ alone & stand entire at last
388	4	O God, to us may grace be given To follow in their train
391	4	May I reach heaven's joys, O bright heaven's Sun
392	1	That they may build from age to age An undefiled heritage
392	2	That in our time, thy grace may give the truth
392	3	That we may bring, if need arise, no ... worthless sacrifice
392	4	That we, with thee, may walk uncowed By fear
392	5	That, under thee, we may possess Man's strength to comfort
396	1	That my whole being may proclaim Thy being and thy ways
397	T,1	Lord, Speak to Me, That I May Speak

397	2	and strong in thee, I may stretch out a loving hand
397	3	O teach me, Lord, that I may teach the precious things
397	3	And wing my words, that they may reach The hidden depths
399	1	that in thine ocean depths its flow May richer, fuller be
399	2	That in thy sunshine's blaze its day May brighter, fairer be
401	2	A man that looks on glass On it may stay his eye
401	3	All may of thee partake, Nothing can be so mean
402	4	Here may we prove the power of prayer To strengthen faith
405	1	May we, like Magdelene, Lay at thy feet
405	1	Yet may love's incense rise, Sweeter than sacrifice
405	4	Till eventide Closes the day of life, May we abide
406	3	Thee may I set at my right hand
407	2	Thy grace, O Father, give, That I may serve with fear
407	3	That, cleansed from stain of sin, I may meet homage give
412	2	Build us a tower ... That we the land may view
412	3	That it may be our highest joy Our Father's work to do
413	2	Lord, as thou hast lived for others, So may we ... live
413	2	Freely may thy servants give
414	3	Whate'er your race may be
417	2	And the meekest of saints may find stern work to do
437	4	Long may our land be bright With freedom's holy light
440	3	America, America, May God thy gold refine
444	3	Bring justice to our land, That all may dwell secure
444	4	That war may haunt the earth no more And desolation cease
449	4	That useful labor yet may build Its homes with love
450	2	dare All that may plant man's lordship firm On earth
450	4	Though pain and passion may not die
451	1	Old now is earth, and none may count her days
461	2	Lord of harvest, grant that we Wholesome grain & pure may be
465	1	That theirs may be the love which knows no ending
466	2	That they may all behold thy face
466	2	And knowing thee may grow in grace
466	3	That every home ... May be the dwelling place of peace
466	3	every home, by this release, May be the dwelling place
470	1	Each age its solemn task may claim but once
470	5	Forth may they go to tell all realms thy grace
470	5	Inspired of thee, may they count all but loss
472	2	shrine Where thy pure light may shine, O hear our call
472	3	May this new temple prove True witness of thy love
472	3	May all who seek this door, And saving grace implore
472	5	Still may these courts proclaim the glory of thy name
475	2	May be in very deed thine own
490	4	That we may live the life of love And loftiest desire
491	3	Oh, may we never from his side depart
491	4	May we be true to him, our Captain of salvation
492	3	grant us power That worthy thoughts in deeds may flower
493	4	that the stones of earthly shame A jewelled crown may seem
494	3	may our hands Ne'er falter when the dream is in our hearts
496	2	Blest with victory and peace, may the heaven-rescued land
498	2	That we no lack of grace may know
499	2	To him may all our thoughts arise In never-ceasing sacrifice
502	2	O may we echo on the song afar
509	2	May struggling hearts that seek release Here find the rest
510	2	With thy tenderest blessing May our eyelids close
521	2	That we may know thy name aright
523	T,1	May the Words of Our Mouths & the meditations of our hearts

527	1	That I may run, rise, rest with thee
535	T,1	We Give Thee But Thine Own, Whate'er the gift may be
539	T,1	May the Grace of Christ our Savior
539	2	Thus may we abide in union with each other and the Lord
575	4	That through the ages all along This may be our endless song

may'st

267	1	With salvation's walls surrounded, Thou may'st smile
267	1	Thou may'st smile at all thy foes
442	2	And judge, that thou may'st heal us

mayst

| 395 | 3 | those are not the only walls Wherein thou mayst be sought |

maze

348	3	While life's dark maze I tread, And griefs around me spread
360	T,1	Within the Maddening Maze of Things
376	2	Unhelped by thee, in error's maze we grope

meadow

| 8 | 2 | Flowery meadow, flashing sea ... call us to rejoice |
| 458 | 4 | Praise him for his garden root, Meadow grass & orchard fruit |

meadows

| 227 | 2 | Fair are the meadows, Fairer still the woodlands |

mean

140	2	Why lies he in such mean estate Where ox and ass are feeding
229	1	All are too mean to speak his worth
229	1	Too mean to set my Savior forth
396	2	Praise in each duty and each deed, However small or mean
401	3	All may of thee partake, Nothing can be so mean
442	3	Though selfish, mean, & base we be, Thy justice is unbounded
481	1	saints ... and I mean, God helping, to be one too
481	3	And I mean to be one too
481	1	And I mean, God helping, to be one too

meaner

| 152 | 5 | Let us arise, all meaner service scorning |

meaning

| 161 | 1 | The meaning of our eager strife Is tested by his Way |
| 467 | 3 | Chastened by pain we learn life's deeper meaning |

meanly

| 146 | 4 | All meanly wrapped in swathing bands, And in a manger laid |

measure

101	2	love of God is broader Than the measure of man's mind (102-3
157	4	Peace is there that knows no measure
161	1	And by its clear, revealing beams We measure gain and loss
253	1	Shedding light that none can measure
343	3	My hope I cannot measure, The path to life is free
383	1	Gifts in differing measure, Hearts of one accord

meditation
41	1	Singing, we offer prayer and meditation, Thus we adore thee
522	T,1	Let the Words of My Mouth, and the meditation of my heart

meditations
523	T,1	May the Words of Our Mouths & the meditations of our hearts

meek
134	3	Where meek souls will receive him ... Christ enters in
175	4	Bow thy meek head to mortal pain
225	3	O hope of every contrite heart, O joy of all the meek
245	1	with actions bold and meek Would for Christ my Savior speak
248	3	Thou to the meek and lowly Thy secrets dost unfold
260	4	Like them, the meek and lowly, On high may dwell with thee
284	T,1	According to Thy Gracious Word, In meek humility
329	3	O Jesus, thou art pleading In accents meek and low
345	2	Strong men and maidens meek
570	7	and hath exalted the humble and meek

meekest
417	2	And the meekest of saints may find stern work to do

meekly
34	1	Their blessings on the Lord of life, As he goes meekly by
158	2	See him meekly bearing all

meekness
422	5	Then will he come with meekness for his glory

meet
46	4	Life's tumult we must meet again
61	T,1	God Be With You Till We Meet Again
61	1-4	God be with you till we meet again
62	T,1	God Be With You Till We Meet Again (same words as No. 61)
77	3	All safe and blessed we shall meet at last
104	2	Let the valleys rise to meet him
108	1	Rise up, with willing feet Go forth, the Bridegroom meet
177	3	Did e'er such love and sorrow meet
198	2	In Christ all races meet, Their ancient feuds forgetting
214	4	Give us a pure and lowly heart, A temple meet for thee
261	3	How rise thy towers, serene & bright To meet the dawning day
272	4	And hope to meet again
286	2	We meet, as in that upper room they met
299	3	prepare All the round earth her God to meet
336	2	And, when to meet thee we prepare, Lord, meet us by the way
402	T,1	Jesus, Where'er Thy People Meet
407	3	That, cleansed from stain of sin, I may meet homage give
414	4	In Christ now meet both East and West
414	4	In him meet South and North
481	3	You can meet them in school, or in lanes, or at sea
552	1	It is meet and right so to do
558	4	Meet at my table and record The love of your departed Lord

meets
193	2	Lo, Jesus meets thee, risen from the tomb

melody

| 155 | 2 | To thee, now high exalted, Our melody we raise |

melt

| 8 | 1 | Melt the clouds of sin and sadness |
| 431 | 3 | Far-called, our navies melt away |

melts

| 459 | 3 | He sends his word and melts the snow |

member

| 145 | 2 | Fill me with joy and strength to be Thy member |
| 145 | 2 | Thy member, ever joined to thee In love that cannot falter |

memory

225	2	Nor can the memory find A sweeter sound than thy blest name
284	4	when these failing lips grow dumb, And mind and memory flee
438	2	onward through all ages bear The memory of that holy hour
439	1	Standing in the living present, Memory and hope between
558	4	In memory of your dying friend

men

2	1	God showeth his good-will to men
9	2	Made us of clay and formed us men
20	3	That men may hear the grateful song My voice unwearied raises
24	1	Let men with angels sing before thee
64	4	And all ye men of tender heart
69	3	Men and women, young and old, Raise the anthem manifold
95	2	justice, from her heavenly bower, Look down on mortal men
104	2	Bidding all men to repentance Since the kingdom now is here
108	3	And men and angels sing before thee
119	T,1	As With Gladness Men of Old Did the guiding star behold
120	2	Pleased as man with men to dwell, Jesus our Emmanuel
121	4	God ... Who unto men his son hath given
125	T,1-3	Good Christian Men, Rejoice, With heart and soul and voice
129	1	Peace on the earth, good will to men
130	2	Let men their songs employ
131	1	Of Jesse's lineage coming As men of old have sung
131	2	To show God's love aright She bore to men a Savior
134	2	And praises sing to God the King, And peace to men on earth
136	3	God's bright star, o'er his head, Wise men three to him led
141	3	And by the light of that same star Three wise men came
141	4	Three wise men came from country far
141	5	Then entered in those wise men three
142	2	But the very beasts could see that he all men surpasses
143	3	Prayer & praising, all men raising, Worship him, God on high
146	6	Good will henceforth from heaven to men Begin & never cease
150	4	For us to wicked men betrayed
164	3	mercy on the souls of men
169	2	But men made strange
182	1	Sons of men and angels say, Alleluia
184	T,1	Good Christian Men Rejoice and Sing
198	1	New life, new hope awakes Where'er men own his sway
198	2	When Christ is throned as Lord, Men shall forsake their fear
214	2	To dwell in lowliness with men, their pattern and their King
219	T,1	O Thou Great Friend to all the sons of men

220	3	The common hopes that makes us men Were his in Galilee
235	2	Lord, by the brightness of thy light ... men unite
235	2	Thou in the faith dost men unite of every land ... tongue
261	1	The true thy chartered free-men are, Of every age and clime
265	1	All men have equal right To worship thee
270	2	to abide on earth with men, Built in our bodies his temple
290	1	Thou fount of life, thou light of men
300	T,1-3	Rise Up, O Men of God
300	4	As brothers of the Son of man Rise up, O men of God
316	3	That all men thy love may see
325	T,1	Lord Christ, When First Thou cam'st to men
345	2	Strong men and maidens meek
366	4	In the fight to set men free
369	1	of all things on earth least like What men agree to praise
371	3	Then fancies, flee away, I'll fear not what men say
380	1	Like those strong men of old
382	4	This through countless ages Men and angels sing
385	2	Ye that are men now serve him Against unnumbered foes
388	4	A noble army, men and boys, The matron and the maid
392	6	And love to all men 'neath the sun
392	+1	When we are grown and take our place As men and women
392	+1	As men and women with our race
419	3	One in the truth that makes men free
419	3	The faith that makes men brave
421	4	But in the eyes of men, redeemed and free
422	1	Patiently powerful for the sons of men
423	6	Till sons of men shall learn thy love
424	1	Only righteous men and women Dwell within its gleaming wall
425	T,1	Men, Whose Boast It Is that ye Come of fathers brave & free
426	T,1	The Voice of God Is Calling Its summons unto men
427	3	O for Christ at least be men
434	T,1	God Send Us Men Whose Aim 'Twill Be
434	2	God send us men alert and quick ... precepts to translate
434	3	God send us men of steadfast will, Patient, courageous
434	4	God send us men with hearts ablaze
436	2	From all the easy speeches That comfort cruel men
443	3	He is sifting out the hearts of men before his judgment seat
443	4	As he died to make men holy, let us die to make men free
451	2	Earth might be fair and all men glad and wise
452	5	glorious hour When all men find thy liberty
456	2	And clearer sounds the angel hymn, Good will to men on earth
472	3	witness of thy love, To all men free
476	T,1	Now Praise We Great and Famous Men
476	3	Whose music like a mighty wind The souls of men uplifted
476	4	Praise we the peaceful men of skill
476	4	men of skill Who builded homes of beauty
483	1	When Jesus was here among men
484	3	God bless the men and women Who serve him over-sea
493	1	overcame The foe-men of the Lord
496	2	O thus be it ever when free men shall stand
554	1	and on earth peace, good will towards men

men's

249	3	Stilling the rude wills of men's wild behavior

mend

| 440 | 2 | America, America, God mend thine every flaw |

mercies

6	5	Thy mercies how tender, how firm to the end
11	2	Eternal are thy mercies, Lord
19	3	Praise the Lord, his mercies trace
36	2	New mercies, each returning day Hover around us
36	2	New mercies ... Hover around us while we pray
70	R	For his mercies aye endure, Ever faithful, ever sure
94	T,1	When All Thy Mercies, O My God, My rising soul surveys
97	1	We own thy mercies, Lord, which never fail
100	1	forget not All his mercies to proclaim
228	1	All thy faithful mercies crown
322	5	Jesus calls us, by thy mercies, Savior, may we hear thy call
402	3	Great Shepherd of thy chosen few ... mercies here renew
402	3	Thy former mercies here renew
463	1-3	For his mercies still endure, Ever faithful, ever sure
486	1	Through the earth and sky God's great mercies flow
501	T,1	Lord, for the Mercies of the Night

merciful

251	1,4	Holy, holy, holy, merciful and mighty
328	T,1	The Lord Is Rich and Merciful, The Lord is very kind
446	2	God the All-merciful

mercy

2	3	hear our cry, Have mercy on us, Jesus
4	4	His mercy is forever sure
15	3	Surely his goodness and mercy here daily attend thee
16	3	praise him Widely as his mercy flows
20	2	What God's almighty power hath made, His ... mercy keepeth
20	2	His gracious mercy keepeth
55	6	And in thy mercy heal us all
58	1	Slumber sweet thy mercy send us
84	5	Goodness and mercy all my life Shall surely follow me
87	2	The clouds ye so much dread Are big with mercy
101	T,1	There's a Wideness in God's Mercy (102-T,1)
101	1	God's mercy, Like the wideness of the sea (102-1)
102	T,1	There's a Wideness in God's Mercy (same as No. 101 in 4 vs.)
119	2	So may we with willing feet Ever seek thy mercy seat
120	1	Peace on earth, and mercy mild
164	3	And all three hours his silence cried for mercy on the souls
164	3	mercy on the souls of men
166	3	O may we, who mercy need, Be like thee in heart and deed
167	II-2	May we, in our guilt and shame Still thy love & mercy claim
167	V-2	Thirst for us in mercy still, All thy holy work fulfil
207	2	Thou art the King of mercy and of grace
258	5	Word of mercy, giving Succor to the living
270	3	His wondrous mercy forth telling
282	T,1	Bread of the World in Mercy Broken
282	1	Wine of the soul, in mercy shed
283	T,1	Bread of the World, in Mercy Broken (like 282 in 2 verses)
288	R	O Lord, have mercy on me
289	2	Watch o'er thy Church, O Lord, in mercy
309	4	Jesus, in mercy bring us To that dear land of rest

316	3	Offering talents, time and treasure, For the mercy
316	3	For the mercy thou hast shown
332	T,1	Lord, Thy Mercy Now Entreating
332	4	Lord, thy mercy still entreating
333	3	Father of mercy, from thy watch & keeping No place can part
351	3	All that thou sendest me In mercy given
360	5	Assured alone that life and death His mercy underlies
361	2	God's mercy holds a wiser plan Than thou canst fully know
367	3	His boundless mercy will provide
373	4	Mercy thy days shall lengthen, The Lord will give thee peace
374	3	Should thy mercy send me Sorrow, toil, or woe
375	2	But deeds of love and mercy, The heavenly kingdom comes
398	4	We render back the love thy mercy gave us
405	3	Some dews of mercy shed, Some wayward footsteps led
407	2	From sin thy child in mercy free
407	4	And let thy mercy bless Thy servant more and more
431	5	For frantic boast and foolish word, Thy mercy
431	5	Thy mercy on thy people, Lord
440	3	And mercy more than life
454	1	The opening year thy mercy shows
454	1	That mercy crowns it till it close
508	2	O boundless Mercy pardoning all
531	1	O Lord, show thy mercy upon us
532	T,1	Have Mercy Upon Us, Good Lord, deliver us
533	1	O Lord, show thy mercy upon us, and grant us thy salvation
544	1	Lord, have mercy upon us
545	T,1	Lord, Have Mercy Upon Us, Christ have mercy upon us
554	5	That takest away the sins of the world, have mercy upon us
554	7	Have mercy upon us
555	1	Have mercy upon us
556	1	have mercy upon us
559	14	O Lord, have mercy upon us
559	16	O Lord, let thy mercy be upon us, as our trust is in thee
565	4	For the Lord is gracious, his mercy is everlasting
568	5	To perform the mercy promised to our forefathers
568	11	Through the tender mercy of our God
570	5	mercy is on them that fear him throughout all generations
570	9	He, remembering his mercy, hath holpen his servant Israel
580	1	Lamenting all their sinful lives, Before thy mercy gate
579	3	Have mercy, now, upon my soul, Hear this my humble prayer
580	3	For mercy, Lord, is all my suit, O let thy mercy spare

mercy's

43	2	Joyless is the day's return Till thy mercy's beams I see
89	3	Our rainbow arch, thy mercy's sign
266	3	And feet on mercy's errands swift Do make her pilgrimage

mere

| 78 | 5 | Mere human power shall fast decay, And youthful vigor cease |

merit

3	3	Trusting only in thy merit
103	4	By ... all-sufficient merit Raise us to thy glorious throne
296	4	Nor skill, nor might, nor merit ours
575	R	Praise to thy eternal merit, Father, Son and Holy Spirit

merry
  122 T,1 God Rest You Merry, Gentlemen, Let nothing you dismay

message
  258 2 Word of consolation, Message of salvation
  302 3 Give of thy sons to bear the message glorious

messenger
  349 3 Return, O holy Dove, return, Sweet messenger of rest

messengers
  298 2 By the mouth of many messengers Goes forth the voice of God
  304 2 Rejoice in God's glad messengers of peace
  304 2 messengers ... Who bore the Savior's gospel of release

Messiah
  441 1 Some great cause, God's new messiah
  441 1 God's new messiah, Offering each the bloom or blight

Messiah's
  117 1 Ye who sang creation's story Now proclaim Messiah's birth

met
  55 1 O in what diverse pains they met ... what joy they went away
  134 1 The hopes and fears of all the years Are met in thee tonight
  152 4 Of God and man in loving service met
  286 2 We meet, as in that upper room they met
  291 3 For when humbly, in thy name, Two or three are met together
  388 3 They met the tyrant's brandished steel, The lion's gory mane
  395 1 And met within thy holy place To rest awhile with thee

midnight
  89 3 Our midnight is thy smile withdrawn
  129 T,1 It Came Upon the Midnight Clear, that glorious song of old
  178 T,1 'Tis Midnight, and on Olive's Brow
  178 1 'Tis midnight, in the garden now The suffering Savior
  178 2 'Tis midnight, and from all removed
  178 3 'Tis midnight, and, for others' guilt
  178 4 'Tis midnight, and from heavenly plains Is borne the song
  386 4 And in the midnight lay us down to die

midnight's
  108 1 Midnight's solemn hour is tolling

midst
  8 4 Ever singing march we onward, Victors in the midst of strife
  291 3 Thou art in the midst of them
  347 5 Kept peaceful in the midst of strife, Forgiving and forgiven
  388 2 Like him, with pardon on his tongue, In midst of mortal pain

midwinter
  128 T,1 In the bleak Midwinter, Frosty wind made moan
  128 1 In the bleak midwinter, Long ago
  128 2 In the bleak midwinter A stable place sufficed

might

6	2	O tell of his might, O sing of his grace
7	2	Nor wanting, nor wasting, thou rulest in might
20	2	Within the kingdom of his might, Lo, all is just ... right
26	2	By his might the heavens ring, In his love we live and move
28	3	Through her shall every land proclaim the sacred might
28	3	-proclaim The sacred might of Jesus' name
32	4	my powers, with all their might, In thy sole glory may unite
39	3	The Father of all grace and might
49	2	Father of might unknown
70	2	He, with all commanding might, Filled the new-made earth
95	3	Rise, God, judge thou the earth in might
99	5	in resurrection light We read the fullness of thy might
145	1	Rich in blessing, Rule and might o'er all possessing
147	1	That in our darkened hearts thy grace might shine
147	3	Who wast a servant that we might be free
162	5	Learning all the might that lies In a full self-sacrifice
169	1	Love to the loveless show, That they might lovely be
169	5	Here might I stay and sing, No story so divine
171	3	we might go at last to heaven, Saved by his precious blood
174	4	That thine own might ne'er be left
185	4	Neither might the gates of death, Nor the tomb's dark portal
194	2	To him who rose that we might rise
206	4	All glory and power, all wisdom and might
248	2	Ineffable in loving, Unthinkable in might
263	4	One in might, and One in glory, While unending ages run
287	5	My strength is in thy might, thy might alone
296	4	Nor skill, nor might, nor merit ours
302	2	And died on earth that man might live above
306	2	Thou wast their rock, their fortress, and their might
312	3	That might this music hear
336	5	Thus strengthened with all might
367	T,1	Fight the Good Fight with all thy might
371	2	No foes shall stay his might, Though he with giants fight
373	4	His might thy heart shall strengthen
375	3	The crown awaits the conquest, Lead on, O God of might
384	2	Stand, then, in his great might
430	T,1	Rejoice, O Land, in God Thy Might
432	2	Thine ancient might destroyed the Pharaoh's boast
437	4	Protect us by thy might, Great God, our King
451	2	Earth might be fair and all men glad and wise
452	4	That from our bonds we might be freed
468	4	That none might fear that world to see Where all are living
470	3	Ah, if with them the world might pass astray
472	4	bled That we might live
483	2	and that I might have seen his kind look when he said
557	3	My strength is in my might, thy might alone
568	7	might serve him without fear
576	2	O wondrous knowledge, awful might

mightier

92	1	The thought of thee is mightier far than sin and pain
92	1	mightier far than sin and pain and sorrow are

mighty

13	1	Worlds his mighty voice obeyed

mind

mind's

minded

mindful

minds

mine

85	T,1	I to the Hills Will Lift Mine Eyes
85	1	From whence doth come mine aid
96	3	Though sorrow, need, or death be mine, Yet am I not forsaken
126	3	Myrrh from the forest or gold from the mine
143	4	Myrrh is mine, its bitter perfume
160	2	Upon that cross of Jesus Mine eye at times can see
170	2	Mine, mine was the transgression, But thine the deadly pain
177	4	Were the whole realm of nature mine
208	1	To shame and guide this life of mine
239	T,1	Come Down, O Love divine, Seek thou this soul of mine
242	T,1	Holy Spirit, Truth Divine, dawn upon this soul of mine
242	2	Holy Spirit, Love divine, Glow within this heart of mine
242	3	Holy Spirit, Power divine, Fill and nerve this will of mine
245	1	with words that help and heal Would thy life in mine reveal
245	2	with wisdom kind and clear Let thy life in mine appear
308	2	Toilers in the mine and mill
318	1	Ever, O Christ, through mine Let thy life shine
358	4	When mine eyes shall close in death
364	4	But that toil shall make thee Some day all mine own
370	2	Lord, I would clasp thy hand in mine
391	3	Thou mine inheritance, now and always
393	1	God be in mine eyes, And in my looking
393	1	God be at mine end, And at my departing
404	3	Take my will, and make it thine, It shall be no longer mine
408	2	Thou didst reach forth thy hand and mine enfold
426	2	I hear my people crying In cot and mine and slum
443	T,1	Mine Eyes Have Seen the Glory of the coming of the Lord
543	1	God be in mine eyes and in my looking
543	1	God be at mine end, and at my departing
572	2	For mine eyes have seen thy salvation
578	2	Thou didst reach forth thy hand and mine enfold

miner
| 422 | 3 | When in the depths the patient miner striving |

mingled
| 177 | 3 | Sorrow and love flow mingled down |

mingling
| 46 | 1 | vesper hymn and vesper prayer rise mingling on the holy air |
| 509 | 1 | vesper hymn and vesper prayer Rise mingling on the holy air |

ministers
| 449 | 2 | Make us thy ministers of life |

miracle
| 158 | 3 | Mark that miracle of time, God's own sacrifice complete |

mire
| 352 | 2 | The mire of sin, the weight of guilty fears |

mirth
4	1	Him serve with mirth, his praise forth tell
121	4	While angels sing with pious mirth
136	2	His the doom, ours the mirth When he came down to earth

392 6   Teach us delight in simple things And mirth
392 6   And mirth that has no bitter springs

misdeeds
332 1   Our misdeeds to thee confessing, On thy name we humbly call

misery
250 2   By whose cross and death are we Rescued from all misery
314 2   In all my pain and misery Be thou my health and life

misjudge
347 4   Should friends misjudge, or foes defame

mislead
386 1   Shadows mislead us

miss
53 3   Awhile his mortal blindness May miss God's lovingkindness
366 3   Grant us wisdom ... courage, Lest we miss thy kingdom's goal

mission
302 T,1   O Zion, Haste, Thy Mission High Fulfilling

mist
352 2   The mist of doubt, the blight of love's decay

mists
42 1   Mists fold away, Gray wakes to green again
252 3   'Mid mists, and rocks, and quicksands Still guides

misusings
292 2   Look not on our misusings of thy grace

mixture
74 2   Mixture strange of good and ill

moan
128 T,1   In the bleak Midwinter, Frosty wind made moan
312 5   There Magdalen hath left her moan And cheerfully doth sing

mock
494 2   Ribbed with the steel that time and change doth mock

mocked
150 4   Scourged, mocked, in purple robe arrayed
325 1   And mocked thy saving kingship then
388 3   And mocked the cross and flame
445 2   By wars and tumults love is mocked, derided

mocking
203 3   Mocking thus the Savior's claim
326 4   But with mocking scorn and with crown of thorn they bore

molest
222 2   Foes who would molest me Cannot reach me here

moment
124	3	Softly to the little stable, Softly for a moment come
406	4	And every moment watch and pray
441	T,1	Once to Every Man and Nation Comes the moment to decide

moments
| 290 | 4 | Make all our moments calm and bright |
| 404 | 1 | Take my moments and my days |

monarch
41	2	Monarch of all things, fit us for thy mansions
113	3	not in splendor bright As monarch, but the humble child
126	2	Maker, and Monarch, and Savior of all

monarch's
| 356 | 3 | If it would reach a monarch's throne It must ... resign |

moods
| 457 | 2 | winging thoughts, and happy moods Of love and joy and prayer |

moon
13	1	Sun and moon, rejoice before him
16	4	Sun and moon, bow down before him
16	4	Sun and moon ... Dwellers in all time and space
64	1	Thou silver moon with softer gleam
66	2	Hill & vale, and tree & flower, Sun & moon & stars of light
68	1	The moon shines full at his command, And all the stars obey
69	1	Sun & moon, uplift your voice, Night & stars, in God rejoice
70	4	The horned moon to shine by night
70	4	moon to shine by night 'Mid her spangled sisters bright
72	2	Soon as the evening shades prevail The moon takes up .. tale
72	2	The moon takes up the wondrous tale
74	2	Moon and stars, thy power displayed
75	2	Moon and stars with silvery light Praise him
85	3	moon by night thee shall not smite, Nor yet the sun by day
257	3	Sun, moon, and stars convey thy praise Round the whole earth
351	5	sun, moon, and stars forgot, Upward I fly
480	2	The same white moon, with silver face ... He used to see
480	2	moon ... That sails across the sky at night

moonlight
| 86 | 3 | The line of lifted sea, Where spreading moonlight quivers |
| 227 | 3 | Fair is the sunshine, Fairer still the moonlight |

moons
| 202 | 1 | Till moons shall wax and wane no more |

moor
| 143 | 1 | Field and fountain, moor and mountain, Following yonder star |
| 215 | 3 | sure it still Will lead me on O'er moor and fen |

more
| 11 | 2 | Till suns shall rise and set no more |
| 19 | 4 | All that breathe, your Lord adore ... praise him evermore |

30	2	O higher than the cherubim, More glorious than the seraphim
36	4	lovelier be, As more of heaven in each we see
36	6	help us, this and every day, To live more nearly as we pray
43	3	More and more thyself display, Shining to the perfect day
44	2	Much more must we who know thee pray
55	2	Once more 'tis eventide, and we ... draw near
56	3	Sleep that may me more vigorous make To serve my God
67	4	But higher far, and far more clear Thee in man's spirit
74	3	Teach us more of human pity, That we in thine image grow
93	1	Bread of heaven, Feed me till I want no more
98	3	I thank thee more that all our joy Is touched with pain
98	4	We have enough, yet not too much To long for more
99	5	Still more in resurrection light We read the fullness
101	1	kindness ... Which is more than liberty (102-1)
101	1	There is no place where earth's sorrows are more felt (102-1
101	1	where earth's sorrows Are more felt than up in heaven (102-2
101	2	If our love were but more simple (102-4)
105	4	From age to age more glorious, All-blessing and all-blest
115	3	Once more upon thy people shine
120	3	Mild he lays his glory by, Born that man no more may die
144	1	More lovely than the noon-day light
157	3	Adds more luster to the day
165	2	Lo, a more heavenly lamp shines here
167	V-1	Thirsting more our love to gain, Hear us, holy Jesus
193	3	No more we doubt thee, Glorious Prince of life
193	3	Make us more than conquerors, Through thy deathless love
202	1	Till moons shall wax and wane no more
259	R	The Lord hath yet more light and truth To break forth
259	2	And grow it shall, our glorious sun More fervid rays afford
321	1	That I from thee no more may stray
321	1	No more from thee decline
322	3	Saying, Christian, love me more
322	4	Christian, love me more than these
353	2	Lord, I want to be more loving
353	3	Lord I want to be more holy
357	4	And thou, O Lord, art more than they
357	6	Let knowledge grow from more to more
357	6	But more of reverence in us dwell
371	2	Do but themselves confound, His strength the more is.
372	1	What more can he say than to you he hath said
384	1	Who in the strength of Jesus trusts Is more than conqueror
400	T,1,R	More Love to Thee, O Christ, More love to thee
400	1	This is my earnest plea, More love, O Christ, to thee
400	2	This all my prayer shall be, More love, O Christ, to thee
400	3	This still its prayer shall be, More Love, O Christ, to thee
407	4	And let thy mercy bless Thy servant more and more
422	3	Holding his pick more splendid than the sword
428	3	No more in bondage shall they toil
438	4	And spring adorns the earth no more
440	3	Who more than self their country loved
440	3	And mercy more than life
444	4	That war may haunt the earth no more And desolation cease
450	4	There shall be no more sin, nor shame
451	3	Now, even now, once more from earth to sky Peals forth
453	3	For those that here we see no more

457	1	One more the glad earth yields Her golden wealth
460	2	Much more, to us his children, He gives our daily bread
469	4	No more by fear and doubt oppressed
472	3	Love one another more As they seek thee
479	2	In all we do in work or play To grow more loving every day
484	3	God raise up more to help them To set the nations free
500	1	We seem to find thee now more nigh
508	1	Once more to thee our hymns ascending

morn

17	1	Praise him from morn till fall of night
37	2	In the calm dew and freshness of the morn
42	2	Soundless and bright for us Breaketh God's morn
43	2	Dark and cheerless is the morn Unaccompanied by thee
50	3	Abide with me from morn till eve
64	2	Thou rising morn, in praise rejoice
127	T,1	Christians, Awake, Salute the Happy Morn
127	1	morn Whereon the Savior of the world was born
170	1	How does that visage languish Which once was bright as morn
180	2	Glorious life, and life immortal On this holy Easter morn
191	2	That Easter morn at break of day, The faithful women went
201	3	O brighter than the rising morn When he, victorious, rose
201	4	brighter than that glorious morn Shall this fair morning be
215	3	And with the morn those angels faces smile
247	3	from morn to set of sun Through the Church the song goes on
399	3	And feel the promise is not vain that morn shall tearless be
417	1	The night is darkest before the morn
487	1	Pearly rice and corn, Fragrant autumn morn
488	3	And God sent us salvation That blessed Christmas morn

morning

8	4	Mortals, join the happy chorus Which the morning stars began
20	2	By morning glow or evening shade His ... eye ne'er sleepeth
32	1	joyful rise To pay thy morning sacrifice
32	3	Disperse my sins as morning dew
33	T,1	As the Sun Doth Daily Rise Bright'ning all the morning skies
35	T,1	When Morning Gilds the Skies, My heart awakening cries
36	T,1	New Every Morning Is the Love Our wakening & uprising prove
37	T,1	Still, Still With Thee, when purple morning breaketh
37	1	Fairer than morning, lovelier than daylight
37	3	Still, still with thee, As to each new-born morning
37	4	So shall it be at last, in that bright morning
37	4	morning, When the soul waketh and life's shadows flee
38	T,1	Morning Has Broken, Like the first morning
38	1	Praise for the singing, Praise for the morning
38	3	Mine is the sunlight, Mine is the morning
38	3	Praise with elation, Praise every morning
45	3	Lord of angels, on our eyes Let eternal morning rise
47	1	To thee our morning hymns ascended
58	2	May we, born anew like morning, To labor rise
59	2	The morning cometh, watch, Protector, o'er us
59	3	Our earliest thoughts be thine when morning wakes us
67	3	when the morning breaks in power, We hear thy word
97	1	With each new day, when morning lifts the veil
109	3	For the morning seems to dawn
118	1	And usher in the morning

126	T,1,5	Brightest and Best of the Sons of the Morning
132	4	Yea, Lord, we greet thee, born this happy morning
134	2	O morning stars, together Proclaim the holy birth
137	2	And stay by my cradle till morning is nigh
145	T,1	O Morning Star, How Fair and Bright
152	5	We would see Jesus in the early morning
201	T,1	The King Shall Come When Morning Dawns
201	2	like the sun That lights the morning sky
201	4	brighter than that glorious morn Shall this fair morning be
201	5	The King shall come when morning dawns
201	5	morning dawns, And light and beauty brings
202	2	His name like sweet perfume shall rise With every morning
202	2	With every morning sacrifice
209	5	Heaven's morning breaks, and earth's vain shadows flee
251	1	Early in the morning our song shall rise to thee
299	3	Breathe thou abroad like morning air Till hearts ... beat
305	T,1	The Morning Light Is Breaking, The darkness disappears
315	2	But morning brings us gladness, And songs the break of day
375	3	For gladness breaks like morning Where'er thy face appears
386	4	And daylight breaks across the morning sky
478	2	The sunset, and the morning That brightens up the sky
479	1	And for the pleasant morning light
485	2	morning light, the lily white, Declare their Maker's praise
498	T,1	Each Morning Brings us fresh outpoured The loving-kindness
500	T,1	Lord God of Morning and of Night
502	T,1	We Praise Thee, Lord, with earliest morning ray
505	1	Your morning tribute bring
576	4	If I the wings of morning take

morns

| 456 | 2 | O'er white expanses sparkling pure The radiant morns unfold |

morrow

334	2	And we will ever trust each unknown morrow
465	3	And to life's day the glorious unknown morrow that dawns
465	3	morrow That dawns upon eternal love and life
467	1	Dark though the night, joy cometh with the morrow

mortal

9	3	We are his ... Our souls, and all our mortal frame
23	1	Too high doth seem For mortal tongue
24	1	No mortal eye hath seen, No mortal ear hath heard such
24	1	No mortal ear hath heard such wondrous things
53	3	Awhile his mortal blindness May miss God's lovingkindness
95	2	justice, from her heavenly bower, Look down on mortal men
107	T,1	Let All Mortal Flesh Keep Silence
150	1	God, the Son of God, should take Our mortal form
150	1	take out mortal form for mortals' sake
163	3	For me ... thy mortal sorrow, and thy life's oblation
175	4	Bow thy meek head to mortal pain
185	4	Nor the watchers, nor the seal Hold thee as a mortal
330	3	And not unworthy for my sake A mortal body deem
354	3	In all the strife of mortal life Our feet shall stand
363	1	Our helper he amid the flood Of mortal ills prevailing
363	4	Let goods and kindred go, This mortal life also

376	3	Involved in shadows of a mortal night
388	2	Like him, with pardon on his tongue, In midst of mortal pain
437	3	Let mortal tongues awake, Let all that breathe partake
491	2	To right the wrongs that shame this mortal life

mortals

8	4	Mortals, join the happy chorus Which the morning stars began
35	4	Let mortals, too, upraise, Their voice in hymns of praise
134	2	While mortals sleep, the angels keep Their watch
178	4	Unheard by mortals are the strains That sweetly soothe
205	1	Christ, awhile to mortals given
229	1	That mortals ever knew, That angels ever bore

mortals'

| 150 | 1 | take out mortal form for mortals' sake |

Moses

| 428 | R | Go down, Moses, 'Way down in Egypt's land |
| 428 | 2 | Thus saith the Lord, bold Moses said |

most

3	3	Seek to do most nearly What thou lovest dearly
7	1	Most blessed, most glorious, the Ancient of Days
30	2	bearer of the eternal Word, Most gracious, magnify the Lord
45	R	Heaven and earth are praising thee, O Lord most high
49	3	Thee ... O Most High, The world doth glorify
55	4	they who fain would serve thee best Are conscious most
55	4	who serve thee best .... Are conscious most of wrong within
58	2	Strong through thee whate'er befall us, O God most wise
107	4	Alleluia, Alleluia, Alleluia, Lord Most High
119	1	So most gracious Lord, may we Evermore be led to thee
119	3	As they offered gifts most rare, At the manger rude and bare
152	2	We would see Jesus, Mary's son most holy
152	2	Shining revealed through every task most lowly
163	1	By foes derided, by thine own rejected, O most afflicted
177	2	All the vain things that charm me most
191	5	On the most holy day of days, Our hearts and voices, Lord
194	4	Our God most high, our joy and boast
255	T,1	Most Perfect Is the Law of God, Restoring those that stray
255	1	His testimony is most sure, Proclaiming wisdom's way
255	3	And righteousness most pure
258	6	O, that we discerning Its most holy learning
270	2	God, the Most High, is not dwelling
278	T,1	Lord Jesus Christ, Our Lord Most Dear
292	3	Most patient Savior who canst love us still
312	2	Most happy is their case
342	T,1	I Need Thee Every Hour, Most gracious Lord
369	1	God's Glory ... Most strange in all its ways
359	3	God is on the field when he Is most invisible
439	1	Lord, we would with deep thanksgiving Praise thee most for
439	1	Praise thee most for things unseen
460	3	And, what thou most desirest, Our humble, thankful hearts
468	2	All thine, and yet most truly ours
497	1	In all his words most wonderful, Most sure in all his ways
508	1	Shall speak thy praises, Lord most high

508	2	O Light all clear, O Truth most holy
550	1	Glory be to thee, O Lord most high
551	1	Glory be to thee, O Lord most high
553	1	Glory be to thee, O Lord most high
554	9	Thou only, O Christ, with the Holy Ghost, art most high
554	9	most high in the glory of God the Father
577	R	To thee we sing, O Lord most high

mother

113	3	child Of Mary, blameless mother mild
121	2	a child Of Mary, chosen mother mild
124	1	Ah, ah, beautiful is the mother
128	3	But his mother only, In her maiden bliss
128	3	his mother ... Worshipped the beloved With a kiss
131	2	With Mary we behold it, The Virgin Mother kind
138	1	All is calm, all is bright Round yon virgin mother and child
213	2	As a mother stills her child, Thou canst hush the ocean wild

motherland

| 392 | +2 | O Motherland, we pledge to thee Head, heart, and hand |

mothers'

| 29 | 1 | Who, from our mothers' arms, Hath blessed us on our way |

motto

| 496 | 2 | And this be our motto, In God is our trust |

mount

| 352 | 3 | Till, sent from God, they mount to God again |

mountain

8	2	Field and forest, vale and mountain ... call us to rejoice
28	2	Upon a mountain builded high
126	3	Gems of the mountain and pearls of the ocean
143	1	Field and fountain, moor and mountain, Following yonder star
152	3	We would see Jesus, on the mountain teaching
158	3	Calvary's mournful mountain climb
264	4	A mountain that shall fill the earth
423	5	O Master, from the mountain side, Make haste to heal
437	1	From every mountain side Let freedom ring
440	1	For purple mountain majesties Above the fruited plain
478	2	The purple-headed mountain, The river running by
484	1	Or farm the mountain pastures, Or till the endless plains
488	T,R	Go, Tell It on the Mountain, Over the hills and everywhere
488	R	Go, tell it on the mountain That Jesus Christ is born

mountain's

| 73 | 3 | From the mountain's deep vein poured |
| 109 | 1 | Traveler, o'er yon mountain's height See |

mountains

7	2	Thy justice like mountains high soaring above
68	T,1	I Sing the Mighty Power of God That made the mountains rise
73	2	Mighty mountains, purple breasted
82	2	firm thy justice stands As mountains their foundations keep
86	3	All beauty speaks of thee, The mountains and the rivers

105	3	Before him on the mountains Shall peace, the herald, go
116	1	And the mountains in reply Echo back their joyous strains
459	1	He makes the grass the mountains crown

mounting
| 304 | T,1 | Rejoice, O People, in the Mounting Years |

mounts
| 456 | 2 | Life mounts in every throbbing vein |

mourn
153	1	Teach us ... to mourn our sins, And close by thee to stay
164	T,1	O Come and Mourn with Me Awhile
164	1	O come, together let us mourn
295	1	The poor, and them that mourn, The faint and overborne
349	3	I hate the sins that made thee mourn And drove thee
459	3	The fields no longer mourn

mourner's
| 50 | 4 | Be every mourner's sleep tonight Like infants' slumbers |

mournful
| 158 | 3 | Calvary's mournful mountain climb |
| 558 | 2 | Before the mournful scene began, He took the bread |

mourning
| 92 | 4 | Thou ... turnest my mourning into praise |
| 104 | 1 | Mourning 'neath their sorrows' load |

mourns
| 110 | 1 | mourns in lonely exile here Until the Son of God appear |

mouth
106	5	Shout, while ye journey home, Songs be in every mouth
255	4	The words which from my mouth proceed
298	2	By the mouth of many messengers Goes forth the voice of God
393	1	God be in my mouth, And in my speaking
522	T,1	Let the Words of My Mouth, and the meditation of my heart
527	T,1	Enrich, Lord, Heart, Mouth, Hands in Me
534	1	And our mouth shall show forth thy praise
543	1	God be in my mouth, and in my speaking
568	3	As he spake by the mouth of his holy prophets

mouths
| 523 | T,1 | May the Words of Our Mouths & the meditations of our hearts |

move
9	5	thy truth must stand When rolling years shall cease to move
26	2	By his might the heavens ring, In his love we live and move
72	3	What though, in solemn silence, all Move
72	3	Move round the dark terrestrial ball
78	6	With growing ardor onward move ... growing brightness shine
83	1	Builds on the rock that nought can move
232	1	Wean it from earth, through all its pulses move
302	2	God, in whom they live and move, is love
356	2	It cannot freely move Till thou hast wrought its chain

199	1	Hark, how the heavenly anthem drowns All music but its own
259	3	Upward we press, the air is clear, & the sphere-music heard
271	2	The Spirit who in them did sing To us his music lendeth
312	3	Ten thousand times that man were blest ... this music hear
312	3	That might this music hear
357	6	That mind and soul, according well, May make one music
357	6	May make one music as before
410	3	clangor Of wild war music o'er the earth shall cease
437	3	Let music swell the breeze
476	3	Whose music like a mighty wind The souls of men uplifted
485	1	and round me rings The music of the spheres

must

9	5	Firm as a rock thy truth must stand
9	5	thy truth must stand When rolling years shall cease to move
44	2	Much more must we who know thee pray
46	4	Life's tumult we must meet again
113	4	At thy great name exalted now All knees must bend
113	4	All knees must bend, all hearts must bow
171	4	O dearly, dearly has he love, And we must love him too
212	2	Thou must work all good within us
222	3	Yea, whate'er we here must bear
238	4	holiness, the road That we must take to dwell with God
245	3	Mighty so as to prevail Where unaided man must fail
303	4	And still with haughty foes must cope
310	T,1	O What Their Joy and Their Glory Must Be
325	2	doomed to death must bring to doom The power which crucified
356	3	If it would reach a monarch's throne It must ... resign
356	3	It must its crown resign
358	2	All for sin could not atone, Thou must save and thou alone
363	2	And he must win the battle
359	5	And right the day must win
383	2	For it we must labor, Till our faith is sight
385	1	Lift high his royal banner, It must not suffer loss
424	2	All must aid alike to carry Forward one sublime design
425	3	shrink From the truth they needs must think
441	2	Thy must upward still and onward Who would keep ... truth
468	1	we must not say that those are dead who pass away
496	2	Then conquer we must, when our cause it is just
503	2	There a heaven on earth must be
506	T,1	Come, My Soul, Thou Must Be Waking

myriad

53	2	splendor ...From myriad worlds unknown

myrrh

126	3	Myrrh from the forest or gold from the mine
140	3	So bring him incense, gold, and myrrh
141	5	offered there, in his presence, Their gold and myrrh
141	5	Their gold and myrrh and frankincense
143	4	Myrrh is mine, its bitter perfume
143	4	Myrrh ... Breathes a life of gathering gloom

myself

56	2	That with the world, myself and thee, I ... at peace may be
245	T,1	Gracious Spirit, Dwell With Me, I myself would gracious be

245	2	Truthful Spirit, dwell with me, I myself would truthful be
245	3	Mighty Spirit, dwell with me, I myself would mighty be
245	4	Holy Spirit, dwell with me, I myself would holy be
318	3	Not for myself alone May my prayer be
356	1	I sink in life's alarms When by myself I stand
358	T,1,4	Rock of Ages, Cleft for me, Let me hide myself in thee
394	2	Sinful, I commit myself to thee
404	4	Take myself, and I will be Ever, only, all for thee

mysteries
| 199 | 2 | But downward bends his burning eye At mysteries so bright |

mysterious
77	2	All now mysterious shall be bright at last
87	T,1	God Moves in a Mysterious Way His wonders to perform
88	T,1	God Moves in a Mysterious Way (same words as No. 87)
334	T,1	Father, in Thy Mysterious Presence kneeling

mystery
127	1	Rise to adore the mystery of love
127	1	mystery ...Which hosts of angels chanted from above
149	3	know not how that Joseph's tomb Could solve death's mystery

mystic
37	2	Alone with thee, amid the mystic shadows
66	3	For the mystic harmony Linking sense to sound and sight
74	1	Marveling at thy mystic ways
260	4	And mystic sweet communion With those whose rest is won

Nacht
| 139 | T,1-3 | Stille Nacht, Heilige Nacht |

nah
| 139 | 2 | Tont es laut von fern und nah, Christ der Retter ist da |

nail
| 324 | 2 | Nail my affections to the cross |

nailed
| 179 | 2 | Were you there when they nailed him to the tree |

naked
| 358 | 3 | Naked, come to thee for dress |

name
3	1	Praise his name forever
4	3	Praise, laud, and bless his name always
7	1	Almighty, victorious, thy great name we praise
9	3	What lasting honors shall we rear ... to thy name
9	3	What lasting honors ...Almighty Maker, to thy name
11	1	Let the Redeemer's name be sung through every land
13	2	Heaven and earth and all creation Laud and magnify his name
14	T,1,	The God of Abraham Praise, All praised be his name
14	3	Praise to the living God, All praised be his name
20	4	ye who name Christ's holy name, Give God all praise & glory
21	1	Sing praises to his name, he forgets not his own

21	3	Thy name be ever praised, O Lord, make us free
22	1	We bless thy holy name, glad praises we sing
25	2	Who would not fear his holy name, And laud and magnify
25	4	Stand up and bless his glorious name Henceforth for evermore
28	3	proclaim The sacred might of Jesus' name
31	1	Kneel and adore him, the Lord is his name
54	2	May we and all who bear thy name ...thy cross proclaim
60	T,1	Savior, Again to Thy Dear Name we raise
60	2	That in this house have called upon thy name
74	1	full of wonder Is thy name o'er all the earth
74	4	O how wondrous, O how glorious is thy name in every land
81	2	Oh magnify the Lord with me, With me exalt his name
95	4	And glorify thy name
100	1	All within me bless his name
105	4	His name shall stand forever, That name to us is Love
113	4	At thy great name exalted now All knees must bend
122	2	How that in Bethlehem was born The Son of God by name
155	2	Who in the Lord's name cometh, The King and blessed One
167	II-2	Calling humbly on thy name, Hear us, holy Jesus
184	4	Thy name we bless, O risen Lord
195	T,1	All Hail the Power of Jesus' Name, Let angels prostrate fall
196	T,1	All Hail the Power of Jesus' Name (R differs from no. 195)
197	T,1	At the Name of Jesus Every knee shall bow
197	3	Humbled for a season, To receive a name
198	3	One Lord, in one great name Unite us all who own thee
200	3	To whom he manifests his love, And grants his name to know
200	4	Their name an everlasting name, Their joy the joy of heaven
202	2	His name like sweet perfume shall rise With every morning
202	3	Their early blessings on his name
203	3	Own his title, praise his name
206	1	And publish abroad his wonderful name
206	1	The name, all victorious, of Jesus extol
221	T,1	How Sweet the Name of Jesus Sounds In a believer's ear
223	2	spread through all the earth abroad The honors of thy name
224	T,1	O Lord and Master of Us All Whate'er our name or sign
225	2	Nor can the memory find A sweeter sound than thy blest name
229	2	Great Prophet of my God, My tongue would bless thy name
230	2	Our outward lips confess the Name All other names above
241	2	Let our whole soul an offering be To our Redeemer's name
246	1	Help us thy name to sing, Help us to praise
247	T,1	Holy God, We Praise Thy Name
247	3	Lo, the apostolic train Joins thy sacred name to hallow
247	4	Holy Father, holy Son, Holy Spirit, Three we name thee
248	3	In name of God the Father, And Son, and Holy Ghost
251	4	All thy works shall praise thy name in earth and sky and sea
257	1	But when our eyes behold thy Word, We read thy name
257	1	We read thy name in fairer lines
260	2	One holy name she blesses, Partakes one holy food
268	3	Hallowed be thy name forever, Heal our differences of old
286	3	One name we bear, one bread of life we break
289	1	planted Thy holy name within our hearts
291	3	For when humbly, in thy name, Two or three are met together
299	4	The name of Jesus glorify Till every kindred call him Lord
306	1	Thy name, O Jesus, be forever blest
310	2	Truly Jerusalem name we that shore
329	1	Shame on us, Christian brothers, His name and sign who bear

nativity
326	1	no room For thy holy nativity

nature
37	2	The solemn hush of nature newly born
73	1	Earth and sky, all living nature ... praise
76	2	hand which bears all nature up Shall guide his children well
130	1	And heaven and nature sing
177	4	Were the whole realm of nature mine
227	T,1	Fairest Lord Jesus, Ruler of all nature
485	1	And to my listening ears, All nature sings

nature's
458	5	Snow that falls on nature's breast
458	6	Praise and love to nature's King

natus
133	3	Ergo qui natus Die hodierna

naught
7	3	And wither and perish, but naught changeth thee
159	1	Is this thy sorrow naught to us Who pass unheeding by
316	3	Naught withholding, freely yielding

navies
431	3	Far-called, our navies melt away

nay
286	1	Nay, let us be thy guests, the feast is thine

Nazareth
409	1	Thou, the carpenter of Nazareth, Toiling for thy daily bread
412	2	O Carpenter of Nazareth, Builder of life divine

ne'er
20	2	By morning glow or evening shade His ... eye ne'er sleepeth
20	2	His watchful eye ne'er sleepeth
174	4	That thine own might ne'er be left
229	3	O let my feet ne'er run astray
238	2	That we from thee may ne'er depart
246	3	And ne'er from us depart, Spirit of power
310	2	Wish and fulfillment can severed be ne'er
380	2	Heroic warriors, ne'er from Christ ... enticed
380	2	ne'er from Christ By any lure or guile enticed
485	3	Oh, let me ne'er forget That though the wrong seems oft
494	3	may our hands Ne'er falter when the dream is in our hearts

near
15	1	All ye who hear, Now to his temple draw near
29	2	O may this bounteous God Through all our life be near us
43	1	Day-spring from on high be near, Day-star in my heart appear
50	1	It is not night if thou be near
50	5	Come near and bless us when we wake
55	2	Once more 'tis eventide, and we ... draw near
55	2	we, Oppressed with various ills, draw near

89	1	Yet to each loving heart how near
104	2	Hark, the voice of one that crieth in the desert far & near
112	2	Unobserved, and very near, Like the seed when no man knoweth
114	1	The King of kings is drawing near
123	1	As I hear, Far and near, Sweetest angel voices
129	1	From angels bending near the earth
167	II-1	Jesus, pitying the sighs Of the thief, who near thee dies
167	IV-3	Tell our faith that God is near, Hear us, holy Jesus
213	3	When at last I near the shore And the fearful breakers roar
218	1	Be thou forever near me, My Master and my friend
229	3	And through this desert land, Still keep me near thy side
239	1	O Comforter, draw near, Within my heart appear
258	2	When our foes are near us, Then thy word doth cheer us
258	6	Lord, may love and fear thee, Evermore be near thee
267	3	For a glory and a covering, Showing that the Lord is near
274	1	Where thou dost dwell so near
294	1	To whom there is no here nor there, No time, no near nor far
304	4	To east and west his kingdom bringing near
311	3	Bring near thy great salvation, Thou Lamb for sinners slain
316	2	In our hearts thou'rt ever near
324	3	No harm, while thou, my God, art near
342	2	I need thee every hour, Stay thou near by
354	2	While thou art near we will not fear
364	4	And the end of sorrow Shall be near my throne
367	4	Faint not nor fear, his arms are near
372	3	For I will be near thee, thy troubles to bless
373	1	In darkness and temptation My light, my help is near
377	3	Yet, O Zion, have no fear, Ever is thy helper near
411	3	Light for the path of life, and God brought near
460	2	He only is the maker Of all things near and far
508	T,1	Before the Day Draws Near Its Ending

nearer

36	5	Room to deny ourselves - a road To bring us daily nearer God
108	1	His chariot wheels are nearer rolling
173	3	O word of hope, to raise us nearer heaven
210	1	While the nearer waters roll ... the tempest still is high
287	4	thou art here, Nearer than ever, still my shield and sun
298	1,4	Nearer & nearer draws the time ... time that shall surely be
351	T,1,R	Nearer, My God, to Thee, Nearer to thee
351	1	Still all my song would be, Nearer, my God, to thee
351	2	Yet in my dreams I'd be Nearer, my God, to thee
351	3	Angels to beckon me Nearer, my god, to thee
351	4	So by my woes to be Nearer, my god, to thee
351	5	Still all my song shall be, Nearer, my God, to thee

nearly

3	3	Seek to do most nearly What thou lovest dearly
36	6	help us, this and every day, To live more nearly as we pray

nearness

37	3	Breathe each day nearness unto thee and heaven

necessity

450	4	For man shall be at one with God in bonds of firm necessity

necks

388	3	They bowed their necks the death to feel

need

2	3	Thou Lamb of God, enthroned on high Behold our need
70	5	His full hand supplies their need
74	4	Conscious of our human need
83	3	God never yet forsook at need the soul that trusted him
92	T,1	I Look to Thee in Every Need And never look in vain
96	3	Though sorrow, need, or death be mine, Yet am I not forsaken
119	4	Bring our ransomed souls at last Where they need no star
119	4	need no star to guide, Where no clouds thy glory hide
123	2	All you need I will surely give you
125	3	Now ye need not fear the grave
166	3	O may we, who mercy need, Be like thee in heart and deed
169	2	Who at my need His life did spend
209	3	I need thy presence every passing hour
250	1	Ever-present help in need, Praised by all the heavenly host
287	5	I have no help but thine, nor do I need Another arm
319	3	Yea, all I need in thee to find
324	3	No foes, no evils need I fear
327	1	Much we need thy tender care
334	1	For we are weak, and need some deep revealing
334	3	Now make us strong, we need thy deep revealing
342	T,1	I Need Thee Every Hour, Most gracious Lord
342	R	I need thee, oh, I need thee, Every hour I need thee
342	2	I need thee every hour, Stay thou near by
342	3	I need thee every hour In joy or pain
342	4	I need thee every hour, Teach me thy will
392	3	That we may bring, if need arise, no ... worthless sacrifice
413	1	Heal our wrongs, and help our need
420	1	No night, nor need, nor pain
421	1	lead To blazoned heights and down the slopes of need
423	2	In haunts of wretchedness and need
426	1	Whom shall I send to succor My people in their need
427	2	Up, it is Jehovah's rally, God's own arm hath need of thine
434	4	These are the patriots nations need
452	1	in bitter need Thy children lift their cry to thee
452	4	but thou hast send The Savior whom we sorely need
470	2	their hearts awake To human need
557	3	I have no help but thine, nor do I need Another arm

needless

335	1	Oh, what needless pain we bear
337	2	That caused thy needless fear

needs

173	4	Teach us to know our sin which needs forgiving
250	3	Who upholds and comforts us in all trials, fears, and needs
425	3	shrink From the truth they needs must think

needy

105	2	To help the poor and needy, And bid the weak be strong

neither

185	4	Neither might the gates of death, Nor the tomb's dark portal

361	3	neither life nor death can pluck His children from his hands

nerve

92	3	Around me flows thy quickening life, To nerve my ... will
92	3	To nerve my faltering will
242	3	Holy Spirit, Power divine, Fill and nerve this will of mine
362	T,1	Awake, My Soul, Stretch Every nerve
427	3	Strike, let every nerve and sinew Tell on ages, tell for God

nerving

236	3	Nerving simplest thought and deed

nest

326	3	The foxes found rest, and the birds their nest In the shade

net

340	3	Peter, who hauled the teeming net, Head down was crucified

nets

340	T,1	They Cast Their Nets in Galilee Just off the hills of brown

never

2	2	O Father, that thy rule is just And wise, and changes never
13	1	Laws which never shall be broken for their guidance
13	2	Never shall his promise fail
47	3	The voice of prayer is never silent
47	5	So be it, Lord, thy throne shall never ... pass away
54	1	with us bide, Thou that canst never set in night
55	3	And some have never loved thee well
79	1	Whose goodness faileth never
83	3	God never yet forsook at need the soul that trusted him
92	T,1	I Look to Thee in Every Need And never look in vain
96	2	He never will deceive me, He leads me by the proper path
97	1	We own thy mercies, Lord, which never fail
104	3	all flesh shall see the token That his word is never broken
105	4	The tide of time shall never His covenant remove
143	2	King forever, ceasing never Over us all to reign
146	6	Good will henceforth from heaven to men Begin & never cease
157	2	Never shall the cross forsake me
169	5	Never was love, dear King, Never was grief like thine
170	3	Lord, let me never, never, Outlive my love to thee
199	4	Thy praise shall never, never fail Throughout eternity
206	4	And thanks never ceasing and infinite love
228	3	Suddenly return, and never, Nevermore thy temples leave
233	4	So shall I never die
236	2	Never was to chosen race That unstinted tide confined
257	3	Round the whole earth and never stand
261	3	watchfires ... With never fainting ray
267	2	Grace, which like the Lord, the Giver, Never fails
267	2	Never fails from age to age
271	2	We raise it high, we send it on, The song that never endeth
335	2	We should never be discouraged
343	2	His wisdom ever waketh, His sight is never dim
344	3	Pleasure that can never cloy
354	2	Thy strength shall never fail us
363	T,1	A Mighty Fortress Is Our God, A bulwark never failing

Nineveh
431 3   Lo, all our pomp of yesterday Is one with Nineveh and Tyre

noble
18 4   prophets crowned with light, with all the martyrs noble host
98 1   So many glorious things are here, Noble and right
277 2   Vision true to keep them noble
388 4   A noble army, men and boys, The matron and the maid
437 2   My native country, thee, Land of the noble free
491 1   Hope and desire for noble lives and true
559 5   The noble army of martyrs praise thee

nobleness
440 3   Till all success be nobleness, And every gain divine

nobler
114 4   Let new and nobler life begin
259 4   And make us to go on, to know With nobler powers conferred
470 1   Make each one nobler, stronger than the last
504 2   The highest heaven ... Shall give him nobler praise

noblest
26 1   Praise him with a glad accord and with lives of noblest worth
412 2   And see like thee our noblest work Our Father's work to do
494 2   The unfailing purpose of our noblest creed
499 2   Heaven's hosts their noblest praises bring

nobly
39 4   To guide whate'er we nobly do, With love all envy to subdue
242 3   By thee may I strongly live, Bravely bear, and nobly strive
306 3   Fight as the saints who nobly fought of old

noise
124 2   Lest your noise should waken Jesus
385 4   This day the noise of battle, The next the victor's song
423 1   Where sounds the cries of race and clan Above the noise
423 1   Above the noise of selfish strife

none
55 4   none, O Lord, have perfect rest, For none are wholly free
55 4   none are wholly free from sin
59 4   We have no refuge, none on earth to aid us
169 2   and none The longed-for Christ would know
174 1   None its lines of woe can trace
174 1   None can tell what pangs unknown Hold thee silent and alone
210 2   Other refuge have I none, Hangs my helpless soul on thee
225 4   The love of Jesus, what it is None but his loved ones know
239 3   For none can guess its grace, Till he become the place
251 3   Only thou art holy, there is none beside thee Perfect
253 1   Shedding light that none can measure
265 1   Thy will from none withholds Full liberty
352 1   Here at thy feet none other may we see
447 3   None ever called on thee in vain
451 1   Old now is earth, and none may count her days
468 4   That none might fear that world to see Where all are living
519 1   Save thy servant that hath none Help nor hope but thee alone

noon

noonday

nor

378	2	Lord, o'er thy rock nor death nor hell prevaileth
391	3	Riches I heed not, nor man's empty praise
407	1	Nor mind thy brightness comprehend
420	1	No night, nor need, nor pain
450	4	There shall be no more sin, nor shame
451	3	Nor till that hour shall God's whole will be done
465	2	With child-like trust that fears nor pain nor death
477	1	Nor fear the storm, nor dread the shock
490	2	Not choosing what is great, Nor spurning what is small
493	3	had no curse nor vengeful cry For those who broke his bones
519	1	Save thy servant that hath none Help nor hope but thee alone
557	3	I have no help but thine, nor do I need Another arm

north

69	3	From the north to southern pole Let the mighty chorus roll
106	T,1	Hills of the North, Rejoice
106	5	Lo, from the North we come, From East, and West, and South
414	4	In him meet South and North

northwest

| 141 | 4 | This star drew nigh to the northwest |

not

13	2	Sin and death shall not prevail
15	2	Hast thou not seen How thy desires e'er have been Granted
21	1	Sing praises to his name, he forgets not his own
22	2	When perils o'ertake us, thou wilt not forsake us
25	2	Who would not fear his holy name, And laud and magnify
31	3	Fear not to enter his courts in the slenderness of the poor
44	1,2	O leave us not at close of day
44	2	Did not their hearts within them burn
44	2	Did not their spirits inly yearn
44	2	They could not let the Stranger go
47	2	And rests not now by day or night
50	1	It is not night if thou be near
50	3	For without thee I dare not die
53	2	For joy of beauty not his own
58	2	Let not ease and self enthrall us
59	4	But thy dear presence will not leave them lonely
59	4	will not leave them lonely Who seek thee only
63	3	Fear of death shall not appall us
68	3	not a plant or flower below But makes thy glories known
78	T,1	Hast Thou Not Known, hast thou not heard
78	3	him thou canst not see, nor trace the working of his hands
84	T,1	The Lord's My Shepherd, I'll not want
85	2	Thy foot he'll not let slide
85	2	Behold, he that keeps Israel, He slumbers not, nor sleeps
85	3	moon by night thee shall not smite, Nor yet the sun by day
87	3	Judge not the Lord by feeble sense
95	T,1	The Lord Will Come and Not Be Slow
96	1	Though dark my road, He holds me that I shall not fall
96	2	I know he will not leave me
96	3	Though sorrow, need, or death be mine, Yet am I not forsaken
96	3	He holds me that I shall not fall
97	3	When we are strong, Lord, leave us not alone, Our refuge be
98	3	So that earth's bliss may be our guide, And not our chain

98	4	We have enough, yet not too much To long for more
98	4	A yearning for a deeper peace Not known before
100	1	forget not All his mercies to proclaim
112	T,1	Ah! Think Not the Lord Delayeth
112	1	Do you yet not understand
112	1	Look not back, the past regretting
112	3	Not for us to find the reasons
112	3	Not for us ... to know the times and seasons
113	3	not in splendor bright As monarch, but the humble child
118	1	Ye shepherds, shrink not with affright
122	3	Fear not, then, said the angel, Let nothing you affright
125	3	Now ye need not fear the grave
132	3	Who would not love thee, loving us so dearly
144	3	Let not our slothful hearts refuse The guidance of thy light
146	2	Fear not, said he, for mighty dread had seized
148	2	Shall not we thy sorrow share, And from earthly joys abstain
148	3	Thou, his vanquisher before, Grant we may not faint nor fail
149	T,1	I Know Not How That Bethlehem's Babe Could in the Godhead be
149	2	know not how ... Calvary's cross A world from sin could free
149	3	know not how that Joseph's tomb Could solve death's mystery
150	3	Still seeking not himself but us
158	1	Turn not from his griefs away
158	2	Shun not suffering, shame, or loss
159	2	Our sins, not thine, thou bearest, Lord
163	4	Think on thy pity and thy love unswerving, Not my deserving
166	2	For we know not what we do, Hear us, holy Jesus
168	2	We would not leave thee, though our weak endurance
178	2	E'en that disciple whom he loved Heeds not
178	2	Heeds not his Master's grief and tears
178	3	Yet he that hath in anguish knelt Is not forsaken
178	3	Is not forsaken by his God
191	4	How blest are they who have not seen
197	5	All that is not holy, All that is not true
201	2	Not as of old a little child To bear, and fight, and die
209	2	O thou who changest not, abide with me
210	2	Leave, ah, leave me not alone, Still support and comfort me
213	3	May I hear thee say to me, Fear not, I will pilot thee
215	1	I do not ask to see The distant scene
215	2	I was not ever thus
215	2	remember not past years
218	1	I shall not fear the battle If thou art by my side
220	T,1	We Bear the Strain of Earthly Care, But bear it not alone
222	2	Jesus will not fail us
230	3	We may not climb the heavenly steeps
232	3	Hast thou not bid us love thee, God and King
235	4	That we may love not doctrines strange
251	3	Though the eye of sinful man thy glory may not see
259	T,1	We Limit Not the Truth of God To our poor reach of mind
264	3	For not like kingdoms of the world Thy holy Church, O God
264	4	A house not made with hands
270	2	Surely in temples made with hands, God ... is not dwelling
270	2	God, the Most High, is not dwelling
280	T,1	Be Known to Us in Breaking Bread, But do not then depart
287	4	The feast, though not the love is past and gone
291	2	Thou art here, we ask not how
292	2	Look not on our misusings of thy grace

297	4	faith like theirs Who served the days they could not see
302	1	he who made all nations is not willing One soul ... perish
303	2	thou hast not yet finished man ...we are in the making still
305	3	Stay not till all the lowly Triumphant reach their home
305	3	Stay not till all the holy Proclaim, The Lord is come
308	3	Recked they not of their own gain
309	1	I know not, O I know not, What joys await us there
313	1	not because I hope for heaven thereby
313	1	Nor yet because who love thee not Are lost eternally
313	2	Not with the hope of gaining aught, Not seeking a reward
315	4	And whosoever cometh I will not cast him out
318	3	Not for myself alone May my prayer be
325	2	Till not a stone was left on stone
330	3	Ah, did not he the heavenly throne A little thing esteem
330	3	And not unworthy for my sake A mortal body deem
332	3	Lips that, while thy praises sounding, Lifted not the soul
332	3	Lifted not the soul to thee
335	1	All because we do not carry Everything to God in prayer
339	3	Christ doth call One and all, Ye who follow shall not fall
343	3	Green pastures are before me, Which yet I have not seen
354	2	While thou art near we will not fear
356	3	My will is not my own Till thou hast made it thine
357	1	Whom we, that have not seen thy face, By faith ... embrace
357	2	Thou wilt not leave us in the dust
357	2	Thou madest man, he knows not why
357	2	He thinks he was not made to die
357	3	Our wills are ours, we know not how
358	2	Not the labors of my hands Can fulfill thy law's demands
358	2	All for sin could not atone, Thou must save and thou alone
360	3	I know not where his islands lift Their fronded palms in air
360	5	I know not what the future hath Of marvel or surprise
363	1	And armed with cruel hate, On earth is not his equal
363	2	Were not the right man on our side
363	3	We will not fear, for God hath willed His truth to triumph
363	3	The prince of darkness grim, We tremble not for him
366	4	Grant us wisdom ... courage, That we fail not man nor thee
367	4	Faint not nor fear, his arms are near
367	4	He changeth not, and thou art dear
368	1	Not for ease that prayer shall be
368	2	Not forever in green pastures Do we ask our way to be
368	3	Not forever by still waters Would we idly rest and stay
359	2	Workman of God, O lose not heart, But learn what God is like
370	3	E'en death's cold wave, I will not flee
371	3	Then fancies, flee away, I'll fear not what men say
372	2	Fear not, I am with thee, oh, be not dismayed
372	3	The rivers of woe shall not thee overflow
372	4	The flame shall not hurt thee
372	5	I will not, I will not desert to his foes
375	2	not with swords' loud clashing Nor roll of stirring drums
375	3	Lead on, O King eternal, We follow, not with fears
377	4	Upward gaze and happy be, God hath not forsaken thee
380	4	Not long the conflict, soon The holy war shall cease
381	2	They cared not, but with force unspent ... they onward went
382	2	We are not divided, All one body we
383	3	Not alone we conquer, Not alone we fall
385	1	Lift high his royal banner, It must not suffer loss

385	3	The arm of flesh will fail you, Ye dare not trust your own
385	4	Stand up, stand up for Jesus, The strife will not be long
391	3	Riches I heed not, nor man's empty praise
392	4	On thee for judge and not our friends
395	3	those are not the only walls Wherein thou mayst be sought
395	5	And claim the kingdom of the earth For thee and not thy foe
399	T,1	O Love That Wilt Not Let Me Go
399	3	And feel the promise is not vain that morn shall tearless be
399	4	I dare not ask to fly from thee
401	3	Which with this tincture, For thy sake, Will not grow bright
401	3	Will not grow bright and clean
408	1	It was not I that found, O Savior true
408	2	I walked and sank not on the storm-vexed sea
408	2	'Twas not so much that I on thee took hold, As thou
412	1	Did ye not know it is my work My Father's work to do
420	1	And where the tears are wiped from eyes That shall not weep
420	1	That shall not weep again
424	3	Will not perish with our years
425	1	If ye do not feel the chain when it works a brother's pain
425	1	Are ye not base slaves indeed, Slaves unworthy to be freed
425	3	They are slaves who will not choose Hatred, scoffing & abuse
425	3	slaves who dare not be In the right with two or three
428	2	If not I'll smite your first-born dead
430	1	Fear not, O land, in God rejoice
431	4	Wild tongues that have not thee in awe
431	5	And guarding, calls not thee to guard
434	1	aim ... Not to defend some ancient creed
436	1	Take not thy thunder from us, But take away our pride
439	T,1	Not Alone for Mighty Empire
439	1	Not alone for bounteous harvests Lift we up our hearts
439	2	Not for battleship and fortress ... conquests of the sword
441	2	With the cross that turns not back
445	2	And sharing not our griefs, no joy can share
445	3	Building proud towers which shall not reach to heaven
445	4	How shall we love thee, holy, hidden Being, If we love not
445	4	If we love not the world which thou hast made
446	2	Bid not thy wrath in its terrors awaken
446	3	Falsehood and wrong shall not tarry beside thee
447	2	Remember not our sin's dark stain
449	3	To joy and suffer not alone
450	4	Though pain and passion may not die
451	1	Still wilt not hear thine inner God proclaim
455	2	And yet God's love is not withdrawn
467	4	Be not cast down, disquieted in vain
468	1	we must not say that those are dead who pass away
468	3	Not spilt like water on the ground
468	3	Not wrapped in dreamless sleep profound
468	3	Not wandering in unknown despair Beyond thy voice
468	3	Not left to lie like fallen tree, Not dead, but living
468	3	Not dead, but living unto thee
470	4	Theirs not a jeweled crown, a blood-stained sword
473	1	Who shall not reverence thee
481	2	there's not any reason, no, not the least
481	2	not any reason ... Why I shouldn't be one too
481	3	They lived not only in ages past
482	T,1	Little Jesus, Sweetly Sleep, do not stir

now

2	1	To us no harm shall now come nigh
3	1	Let us now adore him, And with awe appear before him
3	2	Hear, O Christ the praises That thy Church now raises
14	1	The one eternal God, Ere aught that now appears
15	1	All ye who hear, Now to his temple draw near
15	4	All ... life and breath, come now with praises before him
21	1	The wicked oppressing now cease from distressing
22	3	Our sins now confessing, we pray for thy blessing
23	2	And now, from sin released, Behold the Savior's face
24	T,1	Now Let Every Tongue Adore Thee
24	1	Let harps and cymbals now unite
26	1	Sons of every land, Humbly now before him stand
26	3	Enter now his holy gate, Let our burdened hearts be still
29	T,1	Now Thank We All Our God With heart and hands and voices
29	3	All praise and thanks to God The Father now be given
29	3	For thus it was, is now, And shall be evermore
41	T,1,	Father, We Praise Thee, Now the Night Is Over
42	4	Now shall you find at last Night's left behind at last
47	2	And rests not now by day or night
49	2	Now, ere day fadeth quite, We see the evening light
51	T,1	Now the Day Is Over, Night is drawing nigh
52	T,1	Now on Land and Sea Descending
52	1	Now ... Brings the night its peace profound
53	T,1	The Duteous Day Now Closeth, Each flower and tree reposeth
54	T,1	Now Cheer Our Hearts This Eventide, Lord Jesus Christ
59	T,1	Now God Be With Us, for the night is closing
74	1	Humbly now we bow before thee
75	1	Wake, my soul, awake & sing, Now thy grateful praises bring
77	2	All now mysterious shall be bright at last
81	5	Be glory, as it was, is now, And shall be evermore
93	2	Open now the crystal fountain
103	3	Born to reign in us forever, Now thy gracious kingdom bring
104	1	Tell her that her sins I cover, And her warfare now is over
104	2	Bidding all men to repentance Since the kingdom now is here
104	2	Oh, that warning cry obey, Now prepare for God a way
104	3	For the glory of the Lord Now o'er earth is shed abroad
108	3	Now let all the heavens adore thee
112	2	For e'en now the reign of heaven Spreads throughout
113	4	At thy great name exalted now All knees must bend
117	1	Ye who sang creation's story Now proclaim Messiah's birth
117	2	God with man is now residing, Yonder shines the infant light
118	1	This child, now weak in infancy, Our confidence ... shall be
121	1	joy I bring, Whereof I now will say and sing
122	4	Now to the Lord sing praises, All you within this place
122	4	And with true love and brotherhood Each other now embrace
123	1	Till the air Everywhere Now with joy is ringing
125	1	Ox and ass before him bow, And he is in the manger now
125	2	Now ye hear of endless bliss, Jesus Christ was born for this
125	3	Now ye need not fear the grave
129	3	Look now, for glad and golden hours Come swiftly on the wing
129	4	the whole world send back the song Which now the angels sing
132	4	Word of the Father, now in flesh appearing
142	4	Now may Mary's son, who came So long ago to love us
143	5	Glorious now behold him arise, King and God and Sacrifice
144	2	'Tis now fulfilled what God decreed

329	1	In lowly patience waiting To pass the threshold o'er
343	3	Bright skies will soon be o'er me
344	1	lead us O'er the world's tempestuous sea
344	2	Savior, breathe forgiveness o'er us
375	3	Thy cross is lifted o'er us, We journey in its light
378	2	Lord, o'er thy rock nor death nor hell prevaileth
387	2	light ... O'er his ransomed people shed
394	2	He can give me victory o'er all that threatens me
398	5	O Christ, o'er death victorious
410	3	clangor Of wild war music o'er the earth shall cease
421	4	We've seen thy glory like a mantle spread O'er hill and dale
421	4	O'er hill and dale in saffron flame and red
424	1	Everlasting light shines o'er it
424	1	Justice reigns supreme o'er all
438	3	Came with those exiles o'er the waves
439	1	Stretching far o'er land and sea
456	2	O'er white expanses sparkling pure The radiant morns unfold
462	2	Scatters o'er the smiling land
464	3	Scatters o'er the smiling land
467	2	Comes with its calm the thought that thou art o'er us
470	1	Elijah's mantle o'er Elisha cast
472	5	Lord, though these hours of praise ... soon be o'er
472	5	though ... all our earthly days Will soon be o'er
488	1	While shepherds kept their watching O'er silent flocks
488	1	O'er silent flocks by night
494	1	O'er crumbling walls their crosses scarcely lift
496	1	O'er the ramparts we watched were so gallantly streaming
496	1-2	O'er the land of the free and the home of the brave
506	1	Now is breaking O'er the earth another day
508	1	And evening steals o'er earth and sky
579	T,1	Summer Ended, Harvest O'er, Lord, to thee our song we pour

o'erbrim

457	2	We know who giveth all the good That doth our cup o'erbrim

o'ercame

442	1	empire fell ... When pride of power o'ercame it

o'ercome

384	2	Ye may o'ercome through Christ alone & stand entire at last

o'erflow

397	4	heart o'erflow In kindling thought and glowing word

o'erflowing

462	2	From her rich o'erflowing stores
464	3	From her rich o'erflowing stores

o'ertake

22	2	When perils o'ertake us, thou wilt not forsake us
157	2	When the woes of life o'ertake me

o'ertakes

59	3	Let our last thoughts be thine when sleep o'ertakes us

o'erthrown
325 2 a nation's pride o'erthrown, Went down to dust beside thee

o'erwhelm
256 3 When waves o'erwhelm our tossing bark

o'erwhelming
165 3 Here in o'erwhelming final strife the Lord ... hath victory

oak
475 3 The beauty of the oak and pine

oaken
381 T,1 My Faith, It Is an Oaken Staff
381 3 My faith, it is an oaken staff, O let me on it lean

oar
360 4 And so beside the silent sea I wait the muffled oar

oath
568 6 To perform the oath which he sware to our forefather Abraham

obedience
31 1 With gold of obedience and incense of lowliness
322 5 Give our hearts to thine obedience

obey
18 3 O holy, holy, holy Lord, Whom heavenly hosts obey
63 3 Glad thy summons to obey
68 1 The moon shines full at his command, And all the stars obey
100 5 Unto those who still remember His commandments and obey
104 2 Oh, that warning cry obey, Now prepare for God a way
213 2 Boisterous waves obey thy will
305 2 While sinners, now confessing, The gospel call obey
308 3 True and faithful to command, Swift and fearless to obey
385 2 Stand Up, stand up for Jesus, The trumpet call obey
426 4 Speak, and behold, we answer, Command, and we obey
430 1 His will obey, him serve aright
459 3 The changing wind, the flying cloud, Obey his mighty word
460 2 The winds and waves obey him, By him the birds are fed

obeyed
13 1 Worlds his mighty voice obeyed
167 VI-1 Jesus, all our ranson paid, All thy Father's will obeyed
444 2 The quiet of a steadfast faith, Calm of a call obeyed

obeying
279 T,1 Blessed Jesus, Here Are We, Thy beloved word obeying

object
387 2 One the object of our journey

oblation
126 4 Vainly we offer each ample oblation
163 3 For me ... thy mortal sorrow, and thy life's oblation

occasions
| 441 | 2 | New occasions teach new duties |

ocean
8	3	Well-spring of the joy of living, Ocean depth of happy rest
50	5	Till in the ocean of thy love we lose ourselves in heaven
126	3	Gems of the mountain and pearls of the ocean
213	2	As a mother stills her child, Thou canst hush the ocean wild
237	4	Earth's bitter voices drown In one deep ocean of accord
305	1	Each breeze that sweeps the ocean Brings tidings from afar
360	4	No harm from him can come to me On ocean or on shore
399	1	that in thine ocean depths its flow May richer, fuller be
429	1	Who bidd'st the mighty ocean deep Its ... limits keep

ocean's
| 345 | 3 | With voice as full and strong As ocean's surging praise |

odors
| 126 | 3 | Odors of Edom and offerings divine |

off
32	1	Shake off dull sloth
340	T,1	They Cast Their Nets in Galilee Just off the hills of brown
421	2	But often in some far off Galilee Beheld thee fairer
484	T,1	Remember All the People, Who live in far-off lands

offended
| 163 | T,1 | Ah, Holy Jesus, How Hast Thou Offended |

offenses
| 461 | 3 | From his field shall in that day All offenses purge away |

offer
22	3	With voices united our praises we offer
41	1	Singing, we offer prayer and meditation, Thus we adore thee
126	4	Vainly we offer each ample oblation
143	3	Frankincense to offer have I, Incense owns a deity nigh
316	2	May we offer for thy service All our wealth & all our days
368	T,1	Father, Hear the Prayer We Offer
394	T,1,2	Heart and Mind, Possessions, Lord, I offer unto thee
406	3	And labor on at thy command, And offer all my works to thee
460	3	Accept the gifts we offer, For all thy love imparts
537	1	no gift have we, Lord of all gifts, to offer thee

offered
119	3	As they offered gifts most rare, At the manger rude and bare
141	5	offered there, in his presence, Their gold and myrrh
331	3	My ransomed soul ... Through all eternity Offered to thee

offering
66	6	Offering up on every shore Her pure sacrifice of love
241	2	Let our whole soul an offering be To our Redeemer's name
292	1	That only offering perfect in thine eyes
316	3	Offering talents, time and treasure, For the mercy
331	1	Some offering bring thee now, Something for thee
360	2	No offering of my own I have, Nor works my faith to prove

oldest

Olive's

Olivet

Omega

omnipotent

once

one

14	1	The one eternal God, Ere aught that now appears
29	3	The one eternal God, Whom earth and heaven adore
30	4	To God the Father, God the Son ... the Spirit Three in One
33	1	So to thee with one accord Lift we up our Hearts, O Lord
33	5	Thee would we with one accord Praise and magnify, O Lord
34	2	Come, let thy voice be one with theirs
38	3	Born of the one light Eden saw play
60	1	With one accord our parting hymn of praise
64	5	And praise the Spirit, three in One
69	3	Holy, holy, holy One, Glory be to God alone
89	5	Till all thy living altars claim One holy light
89	5	One holy light, one heavenly flame
91	6	Thy dwelling-place the highest One
104	2	Hark, the voice of one that crieth in the desert far & near
108	2	Ah, come thou blessed One, God's own beloved Son
108	3	Of one pearl each shining portal
110	4	Desire of nations, bind All peoples in one heart and mind
125	3	Calls you one & calls you all, To gain his everlasting hall
147	4	Let every tongue confess with one accord
155	2	Who in the Lord's name cometh, The King and blessed One
156	1	Draw nigh ... Thy faithful people cry with one accord
158	1	Watch with him one bitter hour
160	2	see The very dying form of one Who suffered there for me
167	III-3	May we all thy loved ones be, All one holy family
174	3	Thou, the Father's only Son, Thou, his own anointed one
184	4	And sing today with one accord
198	3	One Lord, in one great name Unite us all who own thee
208	2	O thou whose deeds and dreams were one
215	1	one step enough for me
232	5	One holy passion filling all my frame
233	2	Until with thee I will one will To do and to endure
237	2	Till wilderness and town One temple for thy worship be
237	4	Earth's bitter voices drown In one deep ocean of accord
246	4	To the great One in Three Eternal praises be Hence evermore
247	4	While in essence only One, Undivided God we claim thee
250	T,1	We All Believe in One True God, Father, Son, and Holy Ghost
260	T,1	The Church's One Foundation Is Jesus Christ her Lord
260	2	Elect from every nation, Yet one o'er all the earth
260	2	Her charter of salvation, One Lord, one faith, one birth
260	2	One holy name she blesses, Partakes one holy food
260	2	And to one hope she presses, With every grace endued
260	4	Yet she on earth hath union With God, the Three in One
261	2	One holy Church, one army strong, One steadfast high intent
261	2	One working band, one harvest song, One King omnipotent
262	2	in time to be Shall one great temple rise to thee
262	2	One Church for all humanity
262	4	One hope, one faith, one love restore The seamless robe
263	1	Binding all the Church in one
263	4	Laud and honor to the Spirit, Ever Three and ever One
263	4	One in might, and One in glory, While unending ages run
266	T,1	One Holy Church of God Appears Through every age and race
266	2	One unseen Presence she adores, With silence, or with psalm
268	1	Let us sing with one great voice
268	2	When our song is raised as one
268	3	One our Christ and one our gospel

493	1-4	But only in his heart a flame
524	1	For it is thou, Lord, thou, Lord only, that makest me dwell
524	1	thou, Lord, only, that makest me dwell in safety
554	4	O Lord, the only begotten Son, Jesus Christ
554	8	For thou only art holy, thou only art the Lord
554	9	Thou only, O Christ, with the Holy Ghost, art most high
559	6	thine adorable, true and only Son

onward

8	4	Ever singing march we onward, Victors in the midst of strife
23	3	And onward as ye go Some joyful anthem sing
47	2	While earth rolls onward into light
78	6	With growing ardor onward move ... growing brightness shine
119	1	Leading onward, beaming bright
161	2	The hopes that lead us onward, The fears that hold us back
305	3	Blest river of salvation, Pursue thy onward way
334	2	And thou hast made each step an onward one
362	2	Forget the steps already trod, And onward urge thy way
381	2	They cared not, but with force unspent ... they onward went
381	2	Unmoved by pain, they onward went
382	T,1,R	Onward, Christian Soldiers, Marching as to war
382	4	Onward, then, ye people, Join our happy throng
387	1	Onward goes the pilgrim band
427	2	On, right onward for the right
438	2	Thy blessing came, and still its power Shall onward
438	2	onward through all ages bear The memory of that holy hour
441	2	Thy must upward still and onward Who would keep ... truth

oped

125	2	He hath oped the heavenly door, And man is blessed evermore
302	2	Tell how he stooped to save his lost creation

open

86	4	And give us open eyes To see thee as thou art
93	2	Open now the crystal fountain
114	3	Redeemer, come, I open wide My heart to thee
212	3	Open thou our ears and heart
286	4	Then open thou our eyes, that we may see
311	1	Fling open wide the golden gates, And let the victors in
329	3	O Lord, with shame and sorrow We open now the door
377	4	Zion, if thou die believing, Heaven's path shall open lie
439	2	For the open door to manhood, In a land the people rule
503	T,1	Open Now Thy Gates of Beauty, Zion, let me enter there
534	T,1	O Lord, Open Thou Our Lips
559	9	Thou didst open the kingdom of heaven to all believers

opened

182	3	Christ has opened Paradise

opening

1	5	They fly, forgotten, as a dream Dies at the opening day
8	1	Opening to the sun above
232	2	No angel visitant, no opening skies
454	1	The opening year thy mercy shows

opens
478 1 Each little flower that opens, Each little bird that sings
580 2 A gate which opens wide to those That do lament their sin

oppose
385 2 Let courage rise with danger, & strength to strength oppose

oppressed
55 2 we, Oppressed with various ills, draw near
208 2 Help me, oppressed by things undone
309 1 Beneath thy contemplation Sink heart and voice oppressed
315 1 O blessed voice of Jesus, Which comes to hearts oppressed
469 4 No more by fear and doubt oppressed

oppresses
354 1 No fear his heart oppresses

oppressing
21 1 The wicked oppressing now cease from distressing

oppression
105 1 He comes to break oppression, to set the captive free

orb
75 2 See the glorious orb of day Breaking through the clouds

orbs
72 3 no real voice nor sound Amidst their radiant orbs be found

orchard
458 4 Praise him for his garden root, Meadow grass & orchard fruit

ordained
68 1 I sing the wisdom that ordained The sun to rule the day

ordainest
446 T,1 God the Omnipotent, King, who ordainest

ordaineth
15 2 desires ... Granted in what he ordaineth

ordaining
21 2 Ordaining, maintaining his kingdom divine

ordains
2 2 Thou dost whate'er thy will ordains
96 T,1-3 Whate'er My God Ordains Is Right

order
1 3 Before the hills in order stood, Or earth received her frame
68 3 clouds arise, and tempests blow, By order from thy throne
77 1 Leave to thy God to order and provide
86 1 Thine is the mighty plan, The steadfast order sure
110 3 And order all things, far and nigh

ordered

341	4	And let our ordered lives confess The beauty of thy peace
448	4	Till rise in ordered plan On firm foundations broad

orders

197	2	All the heavenly orders, In their great array

organ

86	3	The deep-toned organ blast That rolls through arches dim
142	5	Alpha and Omega be, Let the organ thunder

orient

143	T,1	We Thee Kings of Orient Are, Bearing gifts we traverse afar

original

72	1	heavens ... Their great Original proclaim

other

8	3	Teach us how to love each other
122	4	And with true love and brotherhood Each other now embrace
160	3	I ask no other sunshine than The sunshine of his face
207	5	Our hope is in no other save in thee
209	1	When other helpers fail, and comforts flee
210	2	Other refuge have I none, Hangs my helpless soul on thee
230	2	Our outward lips confess the Name All other names above
235	4	Nor e'er to other teachers range
272	3	And often for each other flows The sympathizing tear
286	4	One with each other, Lord, for one in thee
352	1	Here at thy feet none other may we see
410	1	To worship rightly is to love each other
452	2	Our faces from each other hide
539	2	Thus may we abide in union with each other and the Lord

other's

272	3	We share each other's woes, Each other's burdens bear

others

64	4	Forgiving others, take your part, O sing ye, Alleluia
268	1	Joining heart to heart with others
413	2	Lord, as thou hast lived for others, So may we ... live
425	2	And, with heart and hand, to be Earnest to make others free
479	2	To be to others kind and good

others'

178	3	'Tis midnight, and, for others' guilt

ought

36	5	the common task, Will furnish all we ought to ask
232	1	And make me love thee as I ought to love

ourselves

36	5	Room to deny ourselves - a road To bring us daily nearer God
50	5	Till in the ocean of thy love we lose ourselves in heaven
50	5	We lose ourselves in heaven above
152	5	Lord, we are thine, we give ourselves to thee
392	3	Teach us to rule ourselves alway

442	2	Show us ourselves and save us
452	3	we strive in vain To save ourselves without thine aid
490	1	Lord of all our hearts and lives, We give ourselves to thee
562	2	and show ourselves glad in him with psalms
565	2	it is he that hath made us, and not we ourselves

out

30	1	Cry out, dominion, princedoms, powers
30	1	Cry out ... Virtues, archangels, angels' choirs, Alleluia
42	2	Out of the cloud and strife Sunrise is born
52	2	Soon as dies the sunset glory, Stars of heaven shine out
52	2	Stars ... shine out above, Telling still the ancient story
85	4	Henceforth thy going out and in God keep forever will
134	4	Cast out our sin and enter in, Be born in us today
150	1	take out mortal form for mortals' sake
188	1	The sun shone out with fair array
192	T,1	The Day of Resurrection, Earth, tell it out abroad
198	3	Cast out our pride and shame That hinder to enthrone thee
209	2	Swift to its close ebbs out life's little day
276	4	Thy perfect love cast out all fear
296	T,1-4	Fling Out the Banner
297	2	From out their tireless prayer and toil Emerge the gifts
298	T,1	God Is Working His Purpose Out, As year succeeds to year
298	1	God is working his purpose out, And the time is drawing near
302	3	Pour out thy soul for them in prayer victorious
315	4	And whosoever cometh I will not cast him out
324	2	Wash out its stains, refine its dross
351	4	Out of my stony griefs Bethel I'll raise
396	2	Praise in the common things of life, Its goings out and in
397	2	and strong in thee, I may stretch out a loving hand
410	3	Love shall tread out the baleful fire of anger
422	2	Shooting out tongues of flame like leaping blood
422	4	Flames out the sunshine of the great tomorrow
428	3	Let them come out with Egypt's spoil
434	1	But to live out the laws of Christ In every thought
443	1	He is trampling out the vintage where the grapes of wrath
443	3	He is sifting out the hearts of men before his judgment seat
449	3	The love that casteth out all fear
451	2	Would man but wake from out his haunted sleep
453	T,1	Ring Out, Wild Bells, to the wild sky
453	1	Ring out, wild bells, and let him die
453	2	Ring out the old, ring in the new
453	2	Ring out the false, ring in the true
453	3	Ring out the grief that saps the mind
453	3	Ring out the feud of rich and poor
453	4	Ring out false pride in place and blood
453	5	Ring out the darkness of the land
488	2	Rang out the angel chorus That hailed our Savior's birth
568	7	That we being delivered out of the hand our enemies

outburst

| 181 | 2 | Let shouts of holy joy outburst |

outcast

| 147 | 2 | By thee the outcast and the poor were sought |

outlive
170　3　　Lord, let me never, never, Outlive my love to thee

outpass
239　3　　Shall far outpass the power of human telling

outpoured
235　1　　Be all thy graces now outpoured On the believer's mind
498　T,1　Each Morning Brings us fresh outpoured The loving-kindness

outpouring
49　2　　Our wonted hymn outpouring

outside
329　T,1　O Jesus, Thou Art Standing Outside the fast-closed door

outspread
91　4　　His outspread pinions shall thee hide
261　T,1　City of God, How Broad and Far Outspread thy walls sublime

outward
230　2　　Our outward lips confess the Name All other names above

over
41　T,1,　Father, We Praise Thee, Now the Night Is Over
51　T,1　Now the Day Is Over, Night is drawing nigh
53　3　　when life's day is over Shall death's fair night discover
66　1　　For the love which from our birth Over and around us lies
74　3　　Made him fly with eagle pinion, Master over sea and land
129　4　　peace shall over all the earth Its ancient splendors fling
141　4　　stop and stay, Right over the place where Jesus lay
143　2　　King forever, ceasing never Over us all to reign
192　1　　Our Christ hath brought us over With hymns of victory
206　1　　His kingdom is glorious, he rules over all
213　T,1　Jesus, Savior, Pilot Me Over life's tempestuous sea
246　1　　Come, and reign over us, Ancient of Days
325　4　　O love that triumphs over loss, we bring our hearts
351　2　　Darkness be over me, My rest a stone
388　1　　Who best can drink the cup of woe, Triumphant over pain
418　3　　In trust that triumphs over wrong
431　1　　Beneath whose awful hand we hold Dominion over palm and pine
459　1　　Over the heavens he spreads his clouds
488　T,R　Go, Tell It on the Mountain, Over the hills and everywhere
510　T,1　Now the Day Is Over, Night is drawing nigh

overborne
295　1　　The poor, and them that mourn, The faint and overborne

overcame
493　1　　And on his lips a sword Wherewith he smote and overcame
493　1　　overcame The foe-men of the Lord

overcome
559　9　　When thou hadst overcome the sharpness of death

overcometh
385 4   To him that overcometh A crown of life shall be

overflow
372 3   The rivers of woe shall not thee overflow

overflows
84 4   My head thou dost with oil anoint, And my cup overflows

overhead
486 2   Bright skies overhead, Gladness in my heart

overpast
153 4   Abide with us, that so, this life Of suffering overpast

overthrew
150 2   For us the tempter overthrew

overthrow
301 5   May she holy triumphs win, Overthrow the hosts of sin

owe
249 3   To thee we owe the peace that still prevails
253 1   All the best we have we owe thee
399 1   I give thee back the life I owe
425 2   with leathern hearts, forget That we owe mankind a debt
462 3   These to thee, our God, we owe
464 3   All to thee, our God, we owe

own
3 1   Him alone God we own, Him, our God and Savior
20 4   All ye who own his power, proclaim Aloud the wondrous story
21 1   Sing praises to his name, he forgets not his own
46 2   the rest of God's own peace
47 5   grows ... Till all thy creatures own thy sway
53 2   For joy of beauty not his own
56 1   O keep me, King of kings Beneath thine own almighty wings
59 4   Save thee, O Father, who thine own hast made us
83 3   So do thine own part faithfully, And trust his word
84 2   E'en for his own name's sake
87 4   God is his own interpreter, And he will make it plain
89 4   Before thy ever-blazing throne We ask no luster of our own
97 1   We own thy mercies, Lord, which never fail
103 4   By thine own eternal Spirit Rule in all our hearts alone
107 2   He will give to all the faithful His own self
107 2   His own self for heavenly food
108 2   Ah, come thou blessed One, God's own beloved Son
109 2   Traveler, ages are its own, See it bursts o'er all the earth
113 2   Till thou, Redeemer, shouldest free Thine own
113 2   free Thine own in glorious liberty
113 4   things celestial thee shall own ...terrestrial, Lord alone
135 1   Our lowly state to make thine own
140 3   Come peasant, king, to own him
158 3   Mark that miracle of time, God's own sacrifice complete
163 1   By foes derided, by thine own rejected, O most afflicted
174 3   Thou, the Father's only Son, Thou, his own anointed one

381	2	Unmoved by pain, they onward went
388	1	Who best can drink the cup of woe, Triumphant over pain
388	4	They climbed ... Through peril, toil, and pain
398	5	Who by this sign didst conquer grief and pain
399	3	O Joy that seekest me through pain
417	1	When the pain is sorest the child is born
420	1	No night, nor need, nor pain
420	2	Wring gold from human pain
423	5	Make haste to heal these hearts of pain
425	1	If ye do not feel the chain when it works a brother's pain
450	4	Though pain and passion may not die
465	2	With child-like trust that fears nor pain nor death
467	3	Chastened by pain we learn life's deeper meaning
471	5	Fit him to follow thee through pain and loss

painful

129	3	Who toil along the climbing way With painful steps and slow

pains

55	1	O in what diverse pains they met ... what joy they went away
171	2	We may not know, we cannot tell What pains he had to bear
187	3	the pains which he endured ... Our salvation have procured
224	2	To thee our full humanity, Its joys and pains belong
284	3	Remember thee, and all thy pains, And all thy love to me

paints

455	2	His beauty paints the crimson dawn
460	2	He paints the wayside flower, He lights the evening star

pale

170	1	How art thou pale with anguish

palm

266	2	Beneath the pine or palm
431	1	Beneath whose awful hand we hold Dominion over palm and pine

palms

155	1	The people of the Hebrews With palms before thee went
175	1	With palms and scattered garments strowed
360	3	I know not where his islands lift Their fronded palms in air

pangs

166	2	Savior, for our pardon sue, When our sins thy pangs renew
174	1	None can tell what pangs unknown Hold thee silent and alone

panoply

384	2	And take, to arm you for the fight, The panoply of God

panted

222	1	Long my heart hath panted, Till it well-nigh fainted

pants

254	1	My spirit pants for thee, O living Word
390	T,1	As Pants the Hart for cooling streams

| 401 | 3 | All may of thee partake, Nothing can be so mean |
| 437 | 3 | Let mortal tongues awake, Let all that breathe partake |

partaker

| 312 | 6 | see Thine endless joy, and of the same Partaker ever be |

partakes

| 260 | 2 | One holy name she blesses, Partakes one holy food |

partial

| 259 | 1 | By notions of our day and sect, Crude, partial and confined |

parting

| 60 | 1 | With one accord our parting hymn of praise |
| 400 | 3 | This be the parting cry My heart shall raise |

parts

19	4	Strings and voices, hands and hearts ... bear your parts
19	4	In the concert bear your parts
336	3	Truth in the inward parts

pass

38	2	Sprung in completeness Where his feet pass
45	3	When forever from our sight Pass the stars ... day ... night
47	5	So be it, Lord, thy throne shall never ... pass away
47	5	Like earth's proud empires, pass away
159	1	Is this thy sorrow naught to us Who pass unheeding by
167	VI-3	Till we pass to perfect day, Hear us, holy Jesus
209	2	Earth's joys grow dim, its glories pass away
297	3	Help us to pass it on unspent Until the dawn lights up
329	1	In lowly patience waiting To pass the threshold o'er
401	2	Or if he pleaseth through it pass, And then the heaven espy
403	1	Jesus says to those who seek him, I will never pass thee by
424	3	It will pass into the splendors Of the city of the light
468	1	we must not say that those are dead who pass away
470	3	Ah, if with them the world might pass astray
470	3	pass astray Into the dear Christ's life of sacrifice
485	2	In the rustling grass I hear him pass

passed

197	3	Brought it back victorious, When from death he passed
259	3	The valleys passed, ascending still
439	3	Lives that passed and left no name

passeth

185	4	That thy peace which evermore Passeth human knowing
329	2	O love that passeth knowledge, So patiently to wait
409	2	Thou the peace that passeth knowledge Dwellest in the daily

passing

150	1	How passing thought and fantasy
209	3	I need thy presence every passing hour
426	3	Our strength is dust and ashes, Our years a passing hour
456	3	Thyself the vision passing by In crystal and in rose

passion

155	2	To thee, before thy passion, They sang their hymns of praise
163	3	Thy death of anguish and thy bitter passion For my salvation
218	2	Above the storms of passion, the murmurs of self-will
232	5	One holy passion filling all my frame
292	2	lo, between our sins and their reward, We set the passion
292	2	We set the passion of thy Son, our Lord
344	3	Love with every passion blending
376	2	While passion stains and folly dims our youth
398	1	Save us, thy people, from consuming passion
413	3	Hush the storm of strife and passion
450	4	Though pain and passion may not die

passion's

249	3	And calming passion's fierce and stormy gales

passioned

449	2	Within our passioned hearts instill The calm

passions

156	1	behold we lay Our passions, lusts, & proud wills in thy way
239	2	O let it freely burn, Till earthly passions turn To dust
295	2	The wayward and the lost, By restless passions tossed
314	1	From earth-born passions set me free

Passover

192	1	The Passover of gladness, the Passover of God

past

1	T,1,6	Our God Our Help In Ages Past, our hope for years to come
36	2	New perils past, new sins forgiven
77	2	thy God doth undertake To guide the future as ... the past
77	3	when change and tears are past
97	1	In all the past ... our hopes & fears, Thy hand we see
97	2	God of our past, our times are in thy hand, With us abide
112	1	Look not back, the past regretting
119	4	And when earthly things are past
167	VII-1	Jesus, all thy labor vast, All thy woe and conflict past
210	1	Hide me, O my Savior, hide, Till the storm of life is past
215	2	remember not past years
265	2	Let all past bitterness Now and forever cease
287	4	The feast, though not the love is past and gone
314	4	That when this life is past ... the eternal brightness see
384	2	That, having all things done, And all your conflicts past
386	4	We trust to find thee when the night is past
432	2	And, all the ages through, past crumbling throne
432	2	past crumbling throne And broken fetter, thou hast brought
433	2	Thy love divine hath led us in the past
454	3	With grateful hearts the past we own
481	3	They lived not only in ages past
498	1	It ends not as the day goes past
583	T,1	Our God, Our Help in Ages Past (as no. 1 with descant)

pasture

562	7	we are the people of his pasture, and the sheep of his hand
565	2	we are his people and the sheep of his pasture

pastures

79	2	where the verdant pastures grow With food celestial feedeth
84	1	He makes me down to lie In pastures green
309	2	The pastures of the blessed Are decked in glorious sheen
327	1	In thy pleasant pastures feed us
333	2	To pastures green beside the peaceful waters
343	3	Green pastures are before me, Which yet I have not seen
368	2	Not forever in green pastures Do we ask our way to be
484	1	Or farm the mountain pastures, Or till the endless plains

path

6	2	And dark is his path on the wings of the storm
78	6	They with unwearied feet shall tread the path of life divine
89	2	Sheds on our path the glow of day
96	2	He never will deceive me, He leads me by the proper path
105	3	love, joy, hope, like flowers, Spring from his path to birth
110	3	To us the path of knowledge show
154	3	Thy feet the path of suffering trod
215	2	I loved to choose and see my path, but now Lead thou me on
239	2	And clothe me round, the while my path illuming
252	4	O teach thy wandering pilgrims By this their path to trace
256	T,1	Lamp of Our Feet, Whereby We Trace Our path
256	1	Our path when wont to stray
336	1	The path of prayer thyself hast trod
343	3	My hope I cannot measure, The path to life is free
345	4	Yes, on through life's long path, Still chanting as ye go
354	2	Though Satan's wrath beset our path
367	2	Christ is the path, and Christ the prize
374	3	Or should pain attend me On my path below
376	4	However rough and steep the path may be
377	4	Zion, if thou die believing, Heaven's path shall open lie
386	2	darkness ... Which shrouds the path of wisdom from our feet
387	2	Brightening all the path we tread
389	3	Through each perplexing path of life
398	3	Showing to wandering souls the path of light
409	2	who tread the path of labor Follow where thy feet have trod
411	3	Light for the path of life, and God brought near
516	1	Thy word is a lamp unto my feet And a light unto my path
530	1	path of prayer thyself hast trod, Lord, teach us how to pray

paths

84	2	me to walk doth make Within the paths of righteousness
97	3	God of the coming years, through paths unknown we follow
156	2	Thy road is ready, and thy paths made straight
318	2	Joyful to follow thee Through paths unknown
376	T,1	Lead Us, O Father, in the paths of peace
376	2	Lead us, O Father, in the paths of truth
376	3	Lead us, O Father, in the paths of right
418	1	In lowly paths of service free
421	T,1	We Thank Thee, Lord, Thy Paths of Service
423	2	From paths where hide the lures of greed
433	2	Thy word our law, thy paths our chosen way

pathway

218	1	Nor wander from the pathway If thou wilt be my guide
293	4	Till the long shadows o'er our pathway lie

| 368 | 2 | But the steep and rugged pathway May we tread rejoicingly |
| 372 | 4 | When through fiery trials thy pathway shall lie |

patience

232	4	Teach me the patience of unanswered prayer
329	1	In lowly patience waiting To pass the threshold o'er
395	3	In truth and patience wrought
405	2	Some deeds of kindness done, Some souls by patience won
409	1	By thy patience and thy courage, Thou hast taught us
418	3	Teach me thy patience, still with thee In closer

patient

292	3	Most patient Savior who canst love us still
381	3	Of patient & courageous heart, As all true saints have been
388	1	Who patient bears his cross below, He follows in his train
413	3	By thy patient years of toiling, By thy silent hours of pain
419	2	One in the patient company Of those who heed thy will
422	3	When in the depths the patient miner striving
434	3	God send us men of steadfast will, Patient, courageous
465	2	Of patient hope, and quiet, brave endurance
467	4	Patient, O heart, though heavy be thy sorrows
471	4	Patient and watchful when thy sheep are roving
481	1	saints of God Patient and brave and true

patiently

77	1	Bear patiently the cross of grief or pain
96	2	And patiently I wait his day
164	2	Ah, look how patiently he hangs
329	2	O love that passeth knowledge, So patiently to wait
422	1	Patiently powerful for the sons of men

Patmos

| 340 | 3 | Young John ... Homeless, in Patmos died |

patriarchs

| 30 | 3 | Respond ... Ye patriarchs and prophets blest, Alleluia |

patriot

| 439 | 3 | For the glory that illumines Patriot souls of deathless fame |
| 440 | 4 | O beautiful for patriot dream That sees beyond the years |

patriots

| 434 | 4 | These are the patriots nations need |

Patris

| 133 | 3 | Patris aeterni Verbum caro factum |

pattern

214	2	To dwell in lowliness with men, their pattern and their King
229	3	Be thou my counsellor, My pattern and my guide
347	1	So let thy life our pattern be, & form our souls for heaven

pavilioned

| 6 | 1 | Pavilioned in splendor, and girded with praise |

pay

32	1	joyful rise To pay thy morning sacrifice
163	4	Therefore, kind Jesus, since I cannot pay thee
291	2	Here our humblest homage pay we
501	1	Our humble thanks we pay
505	1	And pay a grateful song of praise To heaven's almighty King
506	1	See thou render All thy feeble strength can pay

peace

2	1	And peace shall reign on earth again
2	3	O thou who hast our peace restored
26	4	In his will our peace we find, In his service, liberty
29	2	With ever joyful hearts And blessed peace to cheer us
46	2	the rest of God's own peace
52	1	Now ... Brings the night its peace profound
54	2	Thy gift of peace on earth secure
56	2	That with the world, myself and thee, I ... at peace may be
56	2	That ... I, ere I sleep, at peace may be
60	1	Then, lowly kneeling, wait thy word of peace
60	2	Grant us thy peace upon our homeward way
60	3	Grant us thy peace, Lord, through the coming night
60	4	Grant us thy peace throughout our earthly life
60	4	Call us, O Lord, to thine eternal peace
63	1	Fill our hearts with joy and peace
65	1	Peace and blessing he has given
86	4	Thou hidden fount of love, Of Peace, and truth and beauty
98	4	A yearning for a deeper peace Not known before
104	1	Speak ye peace, thus saith our God
104	1	Speak ye to Jerusalem Of the peace that waits for them
105	3	Before him on the mountains Shall peace, the herald, go
109	2	Peace and truth its course portends
109	3	Traveler, lo, the Prince of peace ... Son of God is come
110	4	Fill the whole world with heaven's peace
118	1	The power of Satan breaking, Our peace eternal making
120	1	Peace on earth, and mercy mild
120	3	Hail the heaven-born Prince of peace
129	1	Peace on the earth, good will to men
129	4	peace shall over all the earth Its ancient splendors fling
134	2	And praises sing to God the King, And peace to men on earth
136	4	Born on earth to save us, Peace and love he gave us
138	1	Holy infant so tender and mild, Sleep in heavenly peace
146	6	All glory be to God on high And to the earth be peace
157	2	Lo, it glows with peace and joy
157	4	Peace is there that knows no measure
185	4	That thy peace which evermore Passeth human knowing
198	3	To heal its ancient wrong, Come, Prince of peace, and reign
207	5	Lord, give us peace, and make us calm and sure
214	2	The Lord, who left the heavens Our life and peace to bring
217	4	Your peace in our hearts, Lord, at the end of the day
222	3	Those who love the Father ... Still have peace within
222	3	Though the storms may gather, Still have peace within
229	2	joyful news ... Of hell subdued and peace with heaven
231	3	Keep far our foes, give peace at home
237	4	Send down thy peace, O Lord
237	4	Thy peace, O God, send down
249	3	O holy Jesus, Prince of peace and Savior

526	1	O grant us peace, almighty Lord
532	1	Grant us thy peace
540	T,1	Father, Give Thy Benediction, Give thy peace before we part
541	T,1	Thou Wilt Keep him in Perfect Peace
554	1	and on earth peace, good will towards men
555	1	grant us thy peace
556	1	grant us thy peace
568	12	and to guide our feet into the way of peace
572	T,1	Lord, Now Lettest Thou Thy Servant Depart in peace
575	3	Keep far our foes, give peace at home

peaceful

129	2	With peaceful wings unfurled
213	3	'Twixt me and the peaceful rest
241	3	The wings of peaceful love
333	2	To pastures green beside the peaceful waters
340	2	Contented, peaceful fishermen, Before they ever knew ... God
347	5	Kept peaceful in the midst of strife, Forgiving and forgiven
454	3	And, peaceful, leave before thy feet
476	4	Praise we the peaceful men of skill

peaks

73	2	Peaks cloud-cleaving snowy crested

pealing

352	4	Lift up your hearts, rings pealing in our ears

peals

142	5	While the choir with peals of glee Doth rend the air asunder
174	3	Hark, that cry that peals aloud
174	3	peals aloud Upward through the whelming cloud
422	1	Peals like a trumpet promise of his coming
451	3	Now, even now, once more from earth to sky Peals forth
451	3	Peals forth in joy man's old undaunted cry

pearl

24	1	All thy gates with pearl are glorious
108	3	Of one pearl each shining portal

pearls

126	3	Gems of the mountain and pearls of the ocean

pearly

487	1	Pearly rice and corn, Fragrant autumn morn

peasant

140	3	Come peasant, king, to own him
308	2	Prince and peasant, bond and free

peculiar

202	5	Let every creature rise & bring Peculiar honors to our King

pen

225	4	Ah, this Nor tongue nor pen can show
436	2	From all that terror teaches, From lies of tongue and pen

penitence
| 153 | 3 | through these days of penitence, & through thy passion-tide |

penitential
| 305 | 1 | The sons of earth are waking To penitential tears |

pent
| 106 | 2 | Pent be each warring breeze, Lulled be your restless waves |

people
4	T,1	All People That on Earth Do Dwell
5	T,1	All People That on Earth Do Dwell (same as No. 4)
9	3	We are his people, we his care
15	4	Let the Amen Sound from his people again
25	T,1	Stand Up and Bless the Lord, Ye people of his choice
103	T,1	Come, Thou Long-Expected Jesus, Born to set thy people free
103	3	Born thy people to deliver, Born a child, and yet a king
104	T,1	Comfort, Comfort Ye My People
115	3	Once more upon thy people shine
115	4	Whose advent sets thy people free
152	3	With all the listening people gathered round
155	1	The people of the Hebrews With palms before thee went
156	1	Draw nigh ... Thy faithful people cry with one accord
189	T,1	Lift Up Your Hearts, Ye People, In songs of glad accord
190	T,1	Lift Up Your Hearts, Ye People (same words as no. 189)
201	5	Hail, Christ the Lord, thy people pray
202	3	People and realms of every tongue Dwell on his love
212	3	Hear the cry thy people raises
246	2	Come, and thy people bless, And give thy word success
263	2	With thy wonted loving-kindness Hear thy people as they pray
302	2	Proclaim to every people, tongue & nation ... God ...is love
304	T,1	Rejoice, O People, in the Mounting Years
304	1	Rejoice, O people, in your glorious Lord
304	2	Rejoice, O people, in the years of old
304	3	Rejoice, O people, in this living hour
304	4	Rejoice, O people, in the days to be
310	3	Thy blessed people shall evermore raise
326	4	living word That should set thy people free
366	T,1	God of Grace and God of Glory On thy people pour thy power
377	4	Thou his people art, & surely He will fold his own securely
382	4	Onward, then, ye people, Join our happy throng
387	2	light ... O'er his ransomed people shed
389	T,1	O God of Bethel, by Whose Hand Thy people still are fed
398	1	Save us, thy people, from consuming passion
402	T,1	Jesus, Where'er Thy People Meet
413	4	thou who willest That thy people should be one
426	1	Whom shall I send to succor My people in their need
426	2	I hear my people crying In cot and mine and slum
426	2	I see my people falling In darkness and despair
428	R	Let my people go
428	R	Tell old Pharaoh, To let my people go
431	5	Thy mercy on thy people, Lord
432	1	from dawn of days Hast led thy people in their widening ways
432	4	God of thy people, hear us cry to thee
433	4	Refresh thy people on their toilsome way
436	1	Our earthly rulers falter, Our people drift and die

439	2	For the open door to manhood, In a land the people rule
439	4	God of justice, save the people From the war of race & creed
451	3	Earth shall be fair, and all her people one
461	T,1	Come, Ye Thankful People, Come
461	4	Gather thou thy people in, Free from sorrow, free from sin
462	T,1	Come, Ye Thankful People Come (different vs. 2-3)
462	3	Come, then, thankful people, come, Raise the song of harvest
466	1	guarding well ... The homes in which thy people dwell
484	T,1	Remember All the People, Who live in far-off lands
484	3	Till all the distant people In every foreign place
502	2	Thy people, Lord, are singing night and day
559	13	O Lord, save thy people and bless thine heritage
562	7	we are the people of his pasture, and the sheep of his hand
565	2	we are his people and the sheep of his pasture
568	1	for he hath visited and redeemed his people
568	10	To give knowledge of salvation unto his people
572	3	Which thou hast prepared before the face of all people
572	4	and to be the glory of thy people Israel

people's

113	1	Thy People's Everlasting light
236	1	Flowing in the prophet's word And the people's liberty
236	5	Flow still in the prophet's word And the people's liberty
253	T,1	Book of Books, Our People's Strength
291	1	Thou alone, our strong defender Liftest up thy people's head
439	3	For the people's prophet leaders, Loyal to the living Word

peoples

110	4	Desire of nations, bind All peoples in one heart and mind
432	3	Thy hand has led across the hungry sea The eager peoples
432	3	The eager peoples flocking to be free
435	3	Feed the faint and hungry peoples with the richness
445	2	Races and peoples, lo, we stand divided
475	3	Endue all peoples with thy grace
475	3	all peoples ... That shall adorn thy dwelling place
562	9	judge ... the peoples with his truth

perfect

36	6	Only, O Lord, in thy dear love Fit us for perfect rest above
43	3	More and more thyself display, Shining to the perfect day
55	4	none, O Lord, have perfect rest, For none are wholly free
66	5	For each perfect gift of thine Unto us so freely given
143	R	Guide us to thy perfect light
167	VI-1	By thy sufferings perfect made, Hear us, holy Jesus
167	VI-3	Till we pass to perfect day, Hear us, holy Jesus
197	4	Filled it with the glory Of that perfect rest
207	4	Thou hast the true and perfect gentleness
207	4	That we may dwell in perfect unity
219	2	Yet hoping ever for the perfect day
228	3	Glory in thy perfect love
233	4	But live with thee the perfect life Of thine eternity
251	3	Only thou art holy, there is none beside thee Perfect
251	3	Perfect in power, in love and purity
255	T,1	Most Perfect Is the Law of God, Restoring those that stray
259	2	'Twas but the dawning yet to grow Into the perfect day
275	1	from the night profound Into the glory of the perfect day

276	4	Thy perfect love cast out all fear
289	2	Perfect it in thy love, unite it
292	1	That only offering perfect in thine eyes
406	2	And prove thy good and perfect will
416	4	Perfect love bereft of fear
465	T,1	O Perfect Love, all human thought transcending
465	2	O perfect Life, be thou their full assurance
508	1	In perfect love and faultless tone
541	T,1	Thou Wilt Keep him in Perfect Peace

perfected
| 376 | 4 | Until our lives are perfected in thee |

perfectly
| 228 | 4 | Let us see thy great salvation Perfectly restored in thee |

perform
87	T,1	God Moves in a Mysterious Way His wonders to perform
416	1	Seek the right, perform the true
568	5	To perform the mercy promised to our forefathers
568	6	To perform the oath which he sware to our forefather Abraham

perfume
| 143 | 4 | Myrrh is mine, its bitter perfume |
| 202 | 2 | His name like sweet perfume shall rise With every morning |

peril
387	3	One the conflict, one the peril, One the march in God begun
388	4	They climbed ... Through peril, toil, and pain
429	1-3	O hear us when we cry to thee, For those in peril on the sea

perilous
| 496 | 1 | Whose broad stripes & bright stars through the perilous fight |

perils
22	2	When perils o'ertake us, thou wilt not forsake us
36	2	New perils past, new sins forgiven
61	3	When life's perils thick confound you
167	III-2	May we in thy sorrows share, And for thee all perils dare
381	1	By all my perils undeterred, A soldier-pilgrim staid

perish
7	3	And wither and perish, but naught changeth thee
242	2	Kindle every high desire, Perish self in thy pure fire
302	1	he who made all nations is not willing One soul ... perish
302	1	One soul should perish, lost in shades of night
325	3	Till in the night of hate and war We perish as we lose thee
336	2	We perish if we cease from prayer
382	3	Crowns and thrones may perish, Kingdoms rise and wane
424	3	Will not perish with our years

perpetual
| 231 | 2 | Enable with perpetual light The dullness of... blinded sight |
| 575 | 2 | Enable with perpetual light The dullness |

perplexed
  29   2   And keep us in his grace, And guide us when perplexed

perplexing
  389   3   Through each perplexing path of life

perplexity
  314   3   Through darkness and perplexity Point thou the heavenly way

persons
  251   1,4   God in three persons, blessed Trinity

perverse
  79   3   Perverse and foolish oft I strayed

pestilence
  91   5   Nor pestilence that walks by night
  433   3   From war's alarms, from deadly pestilence

Peter
  340   3   Peter, who hauled the teeming net, Head down was crucified

Pharaoh
  428   R   Tell old Pharaoh, To let my people go

Pharaoh's
  185   1   Loosed from Pharaoh's bitter yoke Jacob's sons and daughters
  432   2   Thine ancient might destroyed the Pharaoh's boast

phrase
  224   4   We faintly hear, we dimly see, In differing phrase we pray

pick
  422   3   Holding his pick more splendid than the sword

picture
  252   2   It is the heaven-drawn picture of Christ, the living Word

pictured
  424   T,1   Hail the Glorious Golden City, Pictured by the seers of old

piece
  385   3   Put on the gospel armor, Each piece put on with prayer

pierce
  43   3   Pierce the gloom of sin and grief
  325   1   New thorns to pierce that steady brow
  388   2   martyr first, whose eagle eye Could pierce beyond the grave

pilgrim
  93   1   Pilgrim through this barren land
  236   4   Consecrating art and song, Holy book and pilgrim track
  371   1   His first avowed intent To be a pilgrim
  371   2   He will make good his right To be a pilgrim
  371   3   I'll labor night and day to be a pilgrim

381	1	By all my perils undeterred, A soldier-pilgrim staid
387	1	Onward goes the pilgrim band
438	3	And where their pilgrim feet have trod, The God they trusted
440	2	O beautiful for pilgrim feet
440	2	pilgrim feet, Whose stern, impassioned stress

pilgrim's

| 347 | 5 | O may we lead the pilgrim's life, And follow thee to heaven |
| 437 | 1 | Land where my fathers died, Land of the pilgrim's pride |

pilgrimage

| 266 | 3 | And feet on mercy's errands swift Do make her pilgrimage |
| 389 | 1 | Who through this earthly pilgrimage Hast all our fathers led |

pilgrims

| 65 | 2 | Toiling pilgrims raise the song |
| 252 | 4 | O teach thy wandering pilgrims By this their path to trace |

pillar

| 93 | 2 | Let the fire & cloudy pillar Lead me all my journey through |
| 256 | 3 | Pillar of fire through watches dark, & radiant cloud by day |

pilot

213	T,1	Jesus, Savior, Pilot Me Over life's tempestuous sea
213	1	Chart and compass come from thee, Jesus, Savior, pilot me
213	2	Wondrous Sovereign of the Sea, Jesus, Savior, pilot me
213	3	May I hear thee say to me, Fear not, I will pilot thee

pine

167	II-3	O remember us who pine, Looking from our cross to thine
266	2	Beneath the pine or palm
390	2	For thee, my God, the living God, My thirsty soul doth pine
475	3	The beauty of the oak and pine

pining

| 435 | 2 | Still the weary folk are pining for the hour |

pinion

| 74 | 3 | Made him fly with eagle pinion, Master over sea and land |

pinions

| 91 | 4 | His outspread pinions shall thee hide |

pious

| 121 | 4 | While angels sing with pious mirth |

pity

74	3	Teach us more of human pity, That we in thine image grow
100	3	Like the pity of a father Hath the Lord's compassion been
159	2	Till through our pity & our shame Love answers love's appeal
163	4	Think on thy pity and thy love unswerving, Not my deserving
170	3	For this thy dying sorrow, Thy pity without end
173	T,1	O Word of Pity, for Our Pardon Pleading
410	1	Where pity dwells, the peace of God is there
413	1	Fill us with thy love and pity
446	1	Show forth thy pity on high where thou reignest

pitying
  167 II-1   Jesus, pitying the sighs Of the thief, who near thee dies

place
84	5	And in God's house for evermore My dwelling place shall be
91	1	found abode Within the secret place of God
91	6	Thy dwelling-place the highest One
101	1	There is no place where earth's sorrows are more felt (102-1
101	1	no place ... earth's failing Have such kindly judgment given
122	4	Now to the Lord sing praises, All you within this place
127	4	Till man's first heavenly state again takes place
128	2	In the bleak midwinter A stable place sufficed
128	2	A stable place sufficed The Lord God almighty, Jesus Christ
141	4	stop and stay, Right over the place where Jesus lay
160	3	I take, O cross, thy shadow For my abiding place
170	2	Lo, here I fall, my Savior, 'Tis I deserve thy place
200	2	The highest place that heaven affords Is his ... by right
201	3	left the lonesome place of death, Despite the rage of foes
207	2	Reigning omnipotent in every place
228	4	Till in heaven we take our place
236	2	Thine is every time & place, Fountain sweet of heart & mind
239	3	For none can guess its grace, Till he become the place
239	3	the place Wherein the Holy Spirit makes his dwelling
266	1	Unwasted by the lapse of years, Unchanged by changing place
271	3	Safe in the same dear dwelling place
276	3	And dwell thou with us in this place, Thou and thy Christ
308	1	Whose forgotten resting place Rolling years have buried deep
333	3	Father of mercy, from thy watch & keeping No place can part
333	3	No place can part, nor hour of time remove us
361	4	Grant me no resting place Until I rest ... The captive
373	3	Place on the Lord reliance, My soul, with courage wait
384	3	Leave no unguarded place, No weakness of the soul
392	+1	When we are grown and take our place As men and women
395	1	And met within thy holy place To rest awhile with thee
402	1	And every place is hallowed ground
421	2	We've sought and found thee in the secret place
426	4	From ease and plenty save us, From pride of place absolve
453	4	Ring out false pride in place and blood
466	2	Our children bless, in every place
466	3	That every home ... May be the dwelling place of peace
466	3	every home, by this release, May be the dwelling place
475	3	all peoples ... That shall adorn thy dwelling place
484	3	Till all the distant people In every foreign place
499	1	Let us adore And own how solemn is this place
503	1	O how blessed is this place
503	1	place, Filled with solace, light, and grace

placed
  483 2   I wish that his hands had been placed on my head

places
  104 3   Make the rougher places plain
  366 4   Set our feet on lofty places

lague
  91 6   Nor plague approach thy guarded home

plagues

91	3	When fearful plagues around prevail, No fatal stroke shall
91	5	Nor plagues that waste in noonday light

plain

6	4	It streams from the hills, it descends to the plain
87	4	God is his own interpreter, And he will make it plain
104	3	Make the rougher places plain
143	2	Born a king on Bethlehem's plain
192	2	And, listening to his accents, May hear so calm and plain
293	1	Who dares stand idle on the harvest plain
440	1	For purple mountain majesties Above the fruited plain
464	2	Flocks that whiten all the plain
524	1	make thy way plain before my face

plains

129	2	Above its sad and lowly plains They bend on hovering wing
130	2	While fields and floods, rocks, hills and plains Repeat
178	4	'Tis midnight, and from heavenly plains Is borne the song
459	1	He sends his showers of blessing down To cheer the plains
459	1	To cheer the plains below
484	1	Or farm the mountain pastures, Or till the endless plains

plan

51	4	Those who plan some evil, From their sin restrain
86	1	Thine is the mighty plan, The steadfast order sure
86	1	plan ... in which the world began, Endures, and shall endure
303	2	As friends who share the Maker's plan
361	2	God's mercy holds a wiser plan Than thou canst fully know
448	4	Till rise in ordered plan On firm foundations broad
494	1	let thy plan Reveal the life that God would give to man

plane

217	2	Whose strong hands were skilled at the plane and the lathe

planets

72	2	And all the planets in their turn, Confirm the tidings
275	T,1	Eternal Ruler of the Ceaseless Round Of circling planets
275	1	round Of circling planets singing on their way

planned

74	4	Toward the goal that thou hast planned
538	1	Bless thou the work our hearts have planned
576	1	Thou knowest all that I have planned

plans

394	1	Plans and my thoughts and everything I ever do are dependent

plant

68	3	not a plant or flower below But makes thy glories known
238	2	Plant holy fear in every heart
410	3	And in its ashes plant the tree of peace
450	2	dare All that may plant man's lordship firm On earth
477	3	Here plant thy throne, and here abide

planted
| 289 | T,1 | Father, We Thank Thee Who Hast Planted |
| 289 | 1 | planted Thy holy name within our hearts |

plants
| 87 | 1 | He plants his footsteps in the sea And rides upon the storm |

play
38	3	Born of the one light Eden saw play
377	1	And with courage play thy part
427	2	Will ye play then, will ye dally Far behind the battle line
479	2	In all we do in work or play To grow more loving every day
480	1	It gave him light to do his work, And smiled upon his play
492	1	At work, at rest, in play and prayer

plea
| 319 | T,1 | Just As I Am, Without One Plea (same words No. 320) |
| 400 | 1 | This is my earnest plea, More love, O Christ, to thee |

plead
173	4	O Intercessor, who art ever living To plead for ... souls
173	4	To plead for dying souls that they may live
347	T,1	Lord, As to Thy Dear Cross we flee, And plead to be forgiven
360	2	I can but give the gifts he gave, & plead his love for love
374	T,1	In the Hour of Trial, Jesus, plead for me
413	1	For thine own dost ever plead
435	2	homesteads & the woodlands Plead in silence for their peace
493	2	He had no friend to plead his cause
526	1	We plead the promise of thy word

pleading
140	2	for sinners here The silent Word is pleading
168	3	Let us go also, till we see thee pleading
173	T,1	O Word of Pity, for Our Pardon Pleading
212	3	Help us by thy Spirit's pleading
329	3	O Jesus, thou art pleading In accents meek and low

pleads
| 183 | 2 | Lives in glory now on high, Pleads for us and hears our cry |
| 292 | 1 | And having with us him that pleads above |

pleasant
249	4	From thee have flowed, as from a pleasant river, Our plenty
274	1	how dear The pleasant tabernacles are Where thou dost dwell
327	1	In thy pleasant pastures feed us
478	3	The cold wind in the winter, The pleasant summer sun
479	1	And for the pleasant morning light

pleased
120	2	Pleased as man with men to dwell, Jesus our Emmanuel
154	2	We cannot understand the woe Thy love was pleased to bear
438	2	Thou heard'st well pleased, the song, the prayer

pleaseth
| 401 | 2 | Or if he pleaseth through it pass, And then the heaven espy |

pleasure

83	2	with heart content To take whate'er thy Father's pleasure
157	4	Bane and blessing, pain and pleasure ... are sanctified
157	4	pain and pleasure, By the cross are sanctified
197	1	'Tis the Father's pleasure We should call him Lord
222	T,1	Jesus, Priceless Treasure, Source of purest pleasure
222	3	Still in thee lies purest pleasure, Jesus priceless treasure
258	4	Who can tell the pleasure, Who recount the treasure
289	1	Thou, Lord, didst make all for thy pleasure
339	2	Pleasure leads us where we go
344	3	Pleasure that can never cloy
413	3	Quench our fevered thirst of pleasure

pleasures

322	4	Still he calls in cares and pleasures
374	2	With forbidden pleasures Would this vain world charm
381	2	Unstayed by pleasures, still they bent Their zealous course

pledge

392	+1	Land of our birth, we pledge to thee Our love and toil
392	+2	O Motherland, we pledge to thee Head, heart, and hand

pledged

422	1	Who in the clouds is pledged to come again

plenitude

299	T,1	Spirit of the Living God, In all thy plenitude of grace

plenteous

210	3	Plenteous grace with thee is found

plenty

249	4	From thee have flowed, as from a pleasant river, Our plenty
249	4	Our plenty, wealth, prosperity, and peace
426	4	From ease and plenty save us, From pride of place absolve

plough

198	2	To plough-share beat the sword, To pruning-hook the spear

plow

460	T,1	We Plow the Fields and Scatter The good seed on the land

ploweth

467	4	Where now he ploweth, wave with golden grain

pluck

361	3	neither life nor death can pluck His children from his hands

poets

253	2	Poets, prophets, scholars, saints
383	2	Poets sung its glory, Heroes for it died

point

209	5	Shine through the gloom, and point me to the skies
314	3	Through darkness and perplexity Point thou the heavenly way

pole

69	3	From the north to southern pole Let the mighty chorus roll
72	2	And spread the truth from pole to pole
419	T,1	Thou God of All, Whose Spirit Moves From pole to silent pole

pomp

175	2	In lowly pomp ride on to die
431	3	Lo, all our pomp of yesterday Is one with Nineveh and Tyre

ponder

15	3	Ponder anew What the Almighty can do
107	1	Ponder nothing earthly-minded
127	4	O may we keep and ponder in our mind God's wondrous love

poor

31	3	Fear not to enter his courts in the slenderness of the poor
31	3	slenderness Of the poor wealth thou wouldst reckon as thine
50	4	Watch by the sick, enrich the poor with blessings
105	2	To help the poor and needy, And bid the weak be strong
126	4	Dearer to God are the prayers of the poor
127	4	Trace we the babe ... his poor manger to his bitter cross
128	4	what can I give him, Poor as I am
132	3	Child, for us sinners poor and in the manger
141	1	Was to certain poor shepherds in fields as they lay
147	2	By thee the outcast and the poor were sought
207	1	Who pain didst undergo for my poor sake
259	T,1	We Limit Not the Truth of God To our poor reach of mind
276	2	The common home of rich and poor, Of bond and free
295	1	The poor, and them that mourn, The faint and overborne
301	2	May she guide the poor and blind
319	3	Just as I am, poor, wretched, blind
356	2	My heart is weak and poor Until it master find
366	3	Rich in things and poor in soul
396	3	Poor though I be and weak
453	3	Ring out the feud of rich and poor

portal

108	3	Of one pearl each shining portal

portals

114	2	Fling wide the portals of your heart

portends

109	2	Traveler, blessedness and light ... its course portends
109	2	Peace and truth its course portends

possess

95	3	For thou art he who shalt by right The nations all possess
145	2	Toward thee longing Doth possess me, turn and bless me
188	2	Do thou thyself our hearts possess
265	2	And all our souls possess Thy charity
392	5	That, under thee, we may possess Man's strength to comfort
539	2	possess in sweet communion Joys which earth cannot afford

possesses

354	1	strong abode In heaven and earth possesses

possessing

possessions

potentate

pour

poured

pours

power

496	2	Praise the power that hath made and preserved us a nation
499	1	Let all within us feel his power
499	1	Who know his power, his grace who prove, Serve him
576	2	I feel thy power on every side
576	4	And my support thy power divine
577	1	delivered us By thy great love and mighty power
577	1	Make manifest in this dread time Thy power supreme
577	1	power supreme, thy love sublime
581	T,1	All Hail the Power of Jesus' Name (as no. 195 with descant)

powerful

| 93 | 1 | Hold me with thy powerful hand |
| 422 | 1 | Patiently powerful for the sons of men |

powers

18	2	To thee, the powers on high ... Continually do cry
25	3	his love in Christ proclaimed with all our ransomed powers
30	1	Cry out, dominion, princedoms, powers
32	4	my powers, with all their might, In thy sole glory may unite
35	2	The powers of darkness fear, When this sweet chant they hear
65	3	Silent powers and angels' song ... All unto our God belong
107	3	powers of hell may vanish As the darkness clears away
111	2	Powers, dominions, bow before him
174	2	Wrestling with the evil powers
181	2	The powers of death have done their worst
240	1,3	Spirit ... With all thy quickening powers
241	1,4	Descend with all thy gracious powers
259	4	And make us to go on, to know With nobler powers conferred
363	4	That word above all earthly powers ... abideth
364	1	How the powers of darkness Compass thee around
384	3	Tread all the powers of darkness down
468	2	Thine are their thoughts, their works, their powers
506	2	Ready burning Be the incense of thy powers
558	1	When powers of earth and hell arose

praise

2	2	We praise, we worship thee, we trust and give thee thanks
3	1	Praise his name forever
4	1	Him serve with mirth, his praise forth tell
4	3	O enter then his gates with praise
4	3	Praise, laud, and bless his name always
4	3	Praise ... for it is seemly so to do
6	1	Pavilioned in splendor, and girded with praise
7	1	Almighty, victorious, thy great name we praise
7	4	All praise we would render, O help us to see
9	4	Shall fill thy courts with sounding praise
11	1	Let the Creator's praise arise
11	2	Thy praise shall sound from shore to shore
13	T,1	Praise the Lord, Ye Heavens, Adore Him
13	1	Praise him, angels, in the height
13	1	Praise him, all ye stars of light
13	1	Praise the Lord, for he hath spoken
13	2	Praise the Lord for he is glorious
13	2	Praise the God of our salvation
14	T,1	The God of Abraham Praise, All praised be his name
14	3	Praise to the living God, All praised be his name

15	T,1	Praise to the Lord, the Almighty, the King of creation
15	1	O my soul, praise him, for he is thy health and salvation
15	1-4	Praise to the Lord
16	T,1	Praise, My Soul, the King of Heaven
16	1	Who, like me, his praise should sing
16	1-4	Praise him, praise him, Praise him, praise him
16	1	Praise the everlasting King
16	2	Praise him for this grace and favor To our fathers
16	2	Praise him, still the same forever
16	3	praise him Widely as his mercy flows
16	4	Praise with us the God of grace
17	T,1	Praise Thou the Lord, O My Soul, Sing Praises
17	1	Praise him from morn till fall of night
18	T,1	O God, We Praise Thee,and Confess
18	4	The apostles glorious company ... Thy constant praise recite
19	T,1	Praise the Lord, His Glories Show
19	2	Age to age and shore to shore ... praise him evermore
19	3	Praise the Lord, his mercies trace
19	3	Praise his providence and grace
19	4	All that breathe, your Lord adore ... praise him evermore
20	T,1	Sing Praise to God Who Reigns Above
20	1-4	To God all praise and glory
20	4	ye who name Christ's holy name, Give God all praise & glory
22	T,1	We Praise Thee, O God, our Redeemer, Creator
22	3	To thee, our great Redeemer, forever be praise
23	3	Take what he gives And praise him still
23	3	praise him still Through good and ill, Who ever lives
23	4	Let all thy days Till life shall end ... filled with praise
24	1	Therefore with joy our song shall soar In praise to God
24	1	our song shall soar In praise to God forevermore
25	2	Though high above all praise, Above all blessing high
26	1	Praise him with a glad accord and with lives of noblest worth
29	3	All praise and thanks to God The Father now be given
32	2	sing High praise to the eternal King
32	5	Praise God from whom all blessings flow
32	5	Praise him, all creatures here below
32	5	Praise him above, ye heavenly host
32	5	Praise Father, Son, and Holy Ghost
33	5	Praise we, with the heavenly host, Father, Son & Holy Ghost
33	5	Thee would we with one accord Praise and magnify, O Lord
34	2	Shout with their shout of praise
35	4	Let mortals, too, upraise, Their voice in hymns of praise
38	1	Praise for the singing, Praise for the morning
38	1	Praise for them, springing Fresh from the Word
38	2	Praise for the sweetness Of the wet garden
38	3	Praise with elation, Praise every morning
41	T,1,	Father, We Praise Thee, Now the Night Is Over
47	1	Thy praise shall sanctify our rest
47	3	Nor dies the strain of praise away
49	3	To thee of right belongs All praise of holy songs
56	T,1	All Praise to Thee, My God, this night
56	1	All praise to thee ... For all the blessings of the light
56	4	Praise God, from whom all blessings flow
56	4	Praise him, all creatures here below
56	4	Praise him above, ye heavenly host
56	4	Praise Father, Son, and Holy Ghost

57	T,1	All Praise to Thee, My God (same words as 56)
59	3	Thy praise pursuing
60	1	With one accord our parting hymn of praise
64	R	O praise him, O praise him, Alleluia, Alleluia, Alleluia
64	2,5	O praise him, Alleluia
64	2	Thou rising morn, in praise rejoice
64	4	Ye who long pain and sorrow bear, Praise God
64	4	Praise God and on him cast your care
64	5	Praise, praise the Father, praise the Son
64	5	And praise the Spirit, three in One
66	R	Lord of all ... we raise This our hymn of grateful praise
69	1	Praise him, all ye hosts above, Ever bright and fair in love
70	1,6	Praise the Lord, for he is kind
73	1	Earth and sky, all living nature ... praise
73	1	Man, the stamp of thy Creator, Praise ye
73	1-3	Praise ye, praise ye, God the Lord
73	3	Rolling river, praise him ever
73	4	Praise him ever, bounteous giver
73	4	Praise him, Father, Friend, and Lord
73	4	Praise the great and mighty Lord
74	1	Lifting up our hearts in praise
75	1	All their maker's praise declare
75	2	Moon and stars with silvery light Praise him
75	2	Praise him through the silent night
79	6	Good Shepherd may I sing thy praise Within thy house forever
92	4	Thou ... turnest my mourning into praise
94	4	For, oh, eternity's too short To utter all thy praise
108	3	Therefore will we, eternally, Sing hymns of joy and praise
115	4	All praise, eternal Son, to thee
136	3	Praise him and adore him
144	4	And endless song of thankful praise
147	T,1	All Praise to Thee, for Thou, O King Divine
155	1	Our praise and prayer and anthems Before thee we present
159	3	Then let all praise be given thee Who livest evermore
169	5	In whose sweet praise I all my days Could gaily spend
182	5	Praise to thee by both be given
184	3	Praise we in songs of victory That love
185	2	From his light, to whom we give Laud and praise undying
187	2	Hymns of praise then let us sing
187	4	Sing we to our God above ... Praise eternal as his love
187	4	Praise him, all ye heavenly host, Father .. Son & Holy Ghost
188	2	The willing tribute of our praise
189	1	And in your adoration Praise Christ, your risen Lord
191	5	we raise To thee, in jubilee and praise
194	3	And all you living things make praise
199	4	Thy praise shall never, never fail Throughout eternity
203	3	Own his title, praise his name
221	3	My Lord, my Life, my Way, my End, Accept the praise I bring
221	4	But when I see thee as thou art, I'll praise thee as I ought
223	T,1	O for a Thousand Tongues to Sing My great Redeemer's praise
223	3	Glory to God and praise and love Be ever, ever given
228	3	Pray and praise thee without ceasing
228	4	Lost in wonder, love and praise
235	2	This to thy praise, O Lord, be sung
246	1	Help us thy name to sing, Help us to praise
247	T,1	Holy God, We Praise Thy Name

459	3	With songs and honors sounding loud, Praise ye
459	3	Praise ye the sovereign Lord
461	2	Fruit unto his praise to yield
462	3	Grateful vows and solemn praise
463	T,1	Praise, O Praise Our God and King, Hymns of adoration sing
463	2	Praise him ... he gave the rain To mature the swelling grain
463	3	Praise him for our harvest store
464	T,1	Praise to God, Immortal Praise
464	1	praise For the love that crowns our days
464	1	Let thy praise our tongues employ
464	2	Grateful vows and solemn praise
467	4	Yet shall thou praise him, when these darkened furrows
471	2	We praise thee, Lord, that now the light is falling Here
472	5	Lord, though these hours of praise ... soon be o'er
476	T,1	Now Praise We Great and Famous Men
476	1	praise the Lord, who now as then Reveals in man his glory
476	2	Praise we the wise and brave and strong
476	3	Praise we the great of heart and mind
476	4	Praise we the peaceful men of skill
477	2	For thee this house of praise we rear
485	2	morning light, the lily white, Declare their Maker's praise
487	T,1	Praise Our God Above For his boundless love
487	2	Praise him, field and flower, Praise his mighty power
492	1	Accept our heartfelt praise
496	2	Praise the power that hath made and preserved us a nation
497	T,1	Praise to the Holiest in the Height
497	1	And in the depth be praise
500	2	Praise God, our Maker and our Friend
500	2	Praise him through time, till time shall end
501	2	Let this day praise thee, O Lord God
501	2	O let heaven's eternal day Be thine eternal praise
502	T,1	We Praise Thee, Lord, with earliest morning ray
502	1	We praise thee with the glowing light of day
504	1	And praise surround the throne
504	2	The highest heaven ... Shall give him nobler praise
505	1	And pay a grateful song of praise To heaven's almighty King
514	1	Praise God from whom all blessings flow
514	1	Praise him, all creatures here below
514	1	Praise him above, ye heavenly host
514	1	Praise Father, Son, and Holy Ghost
515	1	Praise God from whom all blessings flow
515	1	Praise him, all creatures here below
515	1	Praise him above, ye heavenly host
515	1	Praise Father, Son, and Holy Ghost
521	2	Unseal our lips to sing thy praise
525	T,1	Come, & Let Us Sweetly Join Christ to praise in hymns divine
534	1	And our mouth shall show forth thy praise
534	1	Praise ye the Lord. The Lord's name be praised
548	T,1	Praise Be to Thee, O Christ
554	2	We praise thee, we bless thee, we worship thee
559	T,1	We Praise Thee, O God, we acknowledge thee to be the Lord
559	4	The glorious company of the apostles praise thee
559	4	the goodly fellowship of the prophets praise thee
559	5	The noble army of martyrs praise thee
565	3	and into his courts with praise

pray

21	3	And pray that thou still our defender wilt be
22	3	Our sins now confessing, we pray for thy blessing
36	2	New mercies ... Hover around us while we pray
36	6	help us, this and every day, To live more nearly as we pray
44	1	As night descends, we too would pray
44	2	Much more must we who know thee pray
83	3	Sing, pray, and keep his ways unswerving
113	1	We pray thee, hear us when we call
134	4	O holy Child of Bethlehem, Descend to us, we pray
153	T,1	For us didst fast and pray
158	1	Learn of Jesus Christ to pray
163	4	I do adore thee, and will ever pray thee
167	IV-2	When we vainly seem to pray, And our hope seems far away
201	5	Hail, Christ the Lord, thy people pray
207	1	I pray thee from our hearts all cares to take
217	1-4	and give us we pray, Your
219	3	And they who dearest hope and deepest pray Toil
224	4	We faintly hear, we dimly see, In differing phrase we pray
228	3	Pray and praise thee without ceasing
249	1	To thee all knees are bent, all voices pray
249	5	Pray we that thou wilt hear us, still imploring Thy love
267	3	Which he gives them when they pray
276	1	And pray that this may be our home Until we touch eternity
278	1	So give this child of thine, we pray Thy grace and blessing
291	2	Here for faith's discernment pray we
291	2	pray we Lest we fail to know thee now
303	4	It gives us that for which to pray
327	2	Blessed Jesus, Hear thy children when they pray
336	1	Lord, teach us how to pray
336	2	O grant us power to pray
336	5	We by thy Spirit, and thy Son, Shall pray, and pray aright
340	4	brothers, pray for but one thing, The marvelous peace of God
348	1	Savior divine, Now hear me while I pray
364	2	Gird thee for the battle, Watch and pray and fast
384	3	From strength to strength go on, Wrestle and fight and pray
406	4	And every moment watch and pray
407	2	Above all boons, I pray, Grant me thy voice to hear
419	1	and pray That thou wilt make us one
480	3	Heard his, when Jesus knelt to pray
491	1	Keep us, we pray thee, steadfast and unerring
492	3	flower In Christ-like lives, we pray
498	2	Give us that light for which we pray
507	1	Creator of the world, we pray That, with thy wonted favor
531	1	Let us pray
533	T,1	The Lord Be With You, And with thy spirit. Let us pray
559	11	we therefore pray thee, help thy servants

prayed

150	3	For us he prayed, for us he taught
215	2	nor prayed that thou Shouldst lead me on
310	2	Nor the thing prayed for come short of the prayer
388	2	He prayed for them that did the wrong

prayedst

413	4	Thou who prayedst

530 1   path of prayer thyself hast trod, Lord, teach us how to pray
554 6   that takest away the sins of the world, receive our prayer
579 3   Have mercy, now, upon my soul, Hear this my humble prayer

prayerfulness
31 2   Comfort thy sorrows and answer thy prayerfulness

prayers
39 3   The Father, too, our prayers implore
126 4   Dearer to God are the prayers of the poor
155 3   Thou didst accept their praises, Accept the prayers we bring
212 3   Hear, and bless our prayers and praises
230 6   Through him the first fond prayers are said
230 6   prayers ... Our lips of childhood frame
241 T,1,4 Spirit Divine, Attend our Prayers
269 3   For her my tears shall fall, For her my prayers ascend
272 2   Before our Father's throne We pour our ardent prayers
389 2   Our vows, our prayers, we now present Before thy throne
480 3   The same great God that hears my prayers, Heard his

praying
162 2   See that suffering friendless one Weeping, praying ... alone
264 1   Lord, thy Church is praying yet, A thousand years the same

prays
173 3   The souls for whom Christ prays to Christ are given
178 1   The suffering Savior prays alone

preach
299 2   To preach the reconciling word
365 4   And preach thee, too, as love knows how, By kindly words

preached
493 2   Stephen preached against the laws & by those laws was tried

preaching
152 3   While birds and flowers and sky above are preaching

precepts
76 T,1   How Gentle God's Commands, How kind his precepts are
238 3   Nor let us from his precepts stray
255 2   The precepts of the Lord are right
434 2   God send us men alert and quick ... precepts to translate
434 2   His lofty precepts to translate

precious
2 4   O Holy Spirit, precious Gift, Thou Comforter unfailing
94 3   Ten thousand precious gifts My daily thanks employ
105 2   Whose souls, condemned and dying, Were precious in his sight
171 3   we might go at last to heaven, Saved by his precious blood
244 1   We before thee For that precious gift implore thee
263 1   Chosen of the Lord and precious
269 1   Church our blest Redeemer saved With his own precious blood
335 3   Precious Savior, still our refuge
397 3   O teach me, Lord, that I may teach the precious things
397 3   The precious things thou dost impart

68	3	And everywhere that man can be, Thou, God, art present there
76	4	His goodness stands approved Down to the present day
155	1	Our praise and prayer and anthems Before thee we present
177	4	That were a present far too small
230	4	But warm, sweet, tender, even yet A present help is he
250	1	Ever-present help in need, Praised by all the heavenly host
292	1	We here present, we here spread forth to thee
303	3	Beyond the present sin and shame
389	2	Our vows, our prayers, we now present Before thy throne
439	1	Standing in the living present, Memory and hope between
442	2	The present be our judgment day
444	1	Come with thy ... judgment now To match our present hour
475	4	when we bring them to thy throne, We but present thee
475	4	We but present thee with thine own
521	T,1	Lord Jesus Christ, Be Present Now

presents
362	3	'Tis his own hand presents the prize To thine aspiring eye

preserve
85	4	he shall Preserve thee from all ill
91	3	He shall with all protecting care Preserve thee
91	3	Preserve thee from the fowler's snare

preserved
496	2	Praise the power that hath made and preserved us a nation

preside
238	1	O'er every thought and step preside

press
76	3	Why should this anxious load Press down your weary mind
230	5	touch him in life's throng and press, And we are whole again
259	3	Upward we press, the air is clear, & the sphere-music heard
362	1	And press with vigor on

presses
260	2	And to one hope she presses, With every grace endued
354	1	No fear his heart oppresses

pressing
21	1	The wicked oppressing now cease from distressing
245	3	Ever by a mighty hope, Pressing on and bearing up

pretended
163	1	That man to judge thee hath in hate pretended

prevail
13	2	Sin and death shall not prevail
72	2	Soon as the evening shades prevail The moon takes up .. tale
91	3	When fearful plagues around prevail, No fatal stroke shall
245	3	Mighty so as to prevail Where unaided man must fail
382	3	Gates of hell can never 'Gainst that Church prevail

prevaileth
378	2	Lord, o'er thy rock nor death nor hell prevaileth

prevailing
168	3	In all-prevailing prayer upon thy cross
363	1	Our helper he amid the flood Of mortal ills prevailing

prevails
249	3	To thee we owe the peace that still prevails

price
36	3	New treasures still, of countless price, God will provide

priceless
222	T,1	Jesus, Priceless Treasure, Source of purest pleasure
222	3	Still in thee lies purest pleasure, Jesus priceless treasure

pride
73	2	Crag where eagle's pride hath soared
177	1	And pour contempt on all my pride
198	3	Cast out our pride and shame That hinder to enthrone thee
215	2	and, spite of fears, Pride ruled my will
304	3	Low lies man's pride and human wisdom dies
316	2	Purge our pride and our vain-glory
325	2	a nation's pride o'erthrown, Went down to dust beside thee
325	4	Our pride is dust, our vaunt is stilled
366	3	Bend our pride to thy control
392	+2	Land of our birth, our faith, our pride
426	4	From ease and plenty save us, From pride of place absolve
436	1	Take not thy thunder from us, But take away our pride
437	1	Land where my fathers died, Land of the pilgrim's pride
442	1	empire fell ... When pride of power o'ercame it
452	2	Our souls are bound In iron chains of fear and pride
453	4	Ring out false pride in place and blood
494	3	And all the pride of sinful will departs

priest
221	3	My Prophet, Priest, and King
436	3	Tie in a living tether The prince and priest and thrall
481	2	And one was a soldier, and one was a priest

priests
470	3	Anoint them priests, Strong intercessors they For pardon

prince
109	3	Traveler, lo, the Prince of peace ... Son of God is come
120	3	Hail the heaven-born Prince of peace
142	3	A prince, he said, in Jewry
177	1	cross On which the Prince of glory died
193	3	No more we doubt thee, Glorious Prince of life
198	3	To heal its ancient wrong, Come, Prince of peace, and reign
249	3	O holy Jesus, Prince of peace and Savior
308	2	Prince and peasant, bond and free
309	2	The Prince is ever in them, The daylight is serene
311	3	Thou Prince and Savior, come
363	3	The prince of darkness grim, We tremble not for him
403	2	Lo, the Prince of common welfare dwells within the market
411	3	O Prince of peace, thou bringer of good tidings
413	3	King of love and Prince of peace

436　3　　Tie in a living tether The prince and priest and thrall

princedoms
30　1　　Cry out, dominion, princedoms, powers

prison
185　2　　'Tis the spring of souls today, Christ hath burst his prison
380　1　　Who, thrust in prison or cast to flame

prisoner
202　4　　The prisoner leaps to lose his chains

prisons
365　2　　Our fathers, chained in prisons dark, Were still ... free

privilege
335　1　　What a privilege to carry Everything to God in prayer

prize
225　5　　Jesus, our only joy be thou, As thou our prize wilt be
269　4　　Beyond my highest joy I prize her heavenly ways
362　3　　'Tis his own hand presents the prize To thine aspiring eye
367　2　　Christ is the path, and Christ the prize

proceed
144　2　　From Jacob shall a star proceed
255　4　　The words which from my mouth proceed

proceeding
143　R　　Westward leading, still proceeding
212　3　　Light of life, from God proceeding

proceeds
250　3　　We all confess the Holy Ghost Who from both fore'er proceeds

proclaim
13　2　　Hosts on high, his power proclaim
20　4　　All ye who own his power, proclaim Aloud the wondrous story
28　3　　Through her shall every land proclaim the sacred might
28　3　　proclaim The sacred might of Jesus' name
31　1　　Bow down before him, his glory proclaim
54　2　　May we and all who bear thy name ...thy cross proclaim
54　2　　By gentle love thy cross proclaim
72　1　　heavens ... Their great Original proclaim
100　1　　forget not All his mercies to proclaim
117　1　　Ye who sang creation's story Now proclaim Messiah's birth
120　1　　With the angelic host proclaim, Christ is born in Bethlehem
127　3　　Amazed, the wondrous story they proclaim
134　2　　O morning stars, together Proclaim the holy birth
202　3　　And infant voices shall proclaim their early blessings
206　T,1　Ye Servants of God, Your Master Proclaim
206　3　　The praises of Jesus the angels proclaim
223　2　　My gracious Master and my God, Assist me to proclaim
302　2　　Proclaim to every people, tongue & nation ... God ...is love
305　3　　Stay not till all the holy Proclaim, The Lord is come
396　1　　That my whole being may proclaim Thy being and thy ways

402	3	Here to our waiting hearts proclaim The sweetness
451	1	Still wilt not hear thine inner God proclaim
456	3	Day unto day doth utter speech, And night to night proclaim
466	1	Who dost in love proclaim Each family thine own
472	5	Still may these courts proclaim the glory of thy name
493	2	And in his eyes a light ... God's daybreak to proclaim
493	2	God's daybreak to proclaim And rend the veils of night
584	T,1	Ye Servants of God, Your Master Proclaim (206 with descant)

proclaimed

25	3	Then be his love in Christ proclaimed
25	3	his love in Christ proclaimed with all our ransomed powers
67	4	The indwelling God, proclaimed of old
383	2	Prophets have proclaimed it, Martyrs testified

proclaiming

| 255 | 1 | His testimony is most sure, Proclaiming wisdom's way |
| 326 | 2 | angels sang Proclaiming thy royal degree |

procured

| 187 | 3 | the pains which he endured ... Our salvation have procured |

profanation

| 436 | 2 | From sale and profanation Of honor and the sword |

profound

52	1	Now ... Brings the night its peace profound
275	1	from the night profound Into the glory of the perfect day
468	3	Not wrapped in dreamless sleep profound

prolong

65	2	Saints in light the strain prolong
287	3	Here let me feast, and, feasting, still prolong
287	3	prolong The brief, bright hour of fellowship with thee
437	3	Let rocks their silence break, The sound prolong

promise

13	2	Never shall his promise fail
109	1	of the night, What its signs of promise are
207	5	Our faith is built upon thy promise free
319	4	Because thy promise I believe
361	1	God will fulfil in every part Each promise he has made
382	3	We have Christ's own promise, And that cannot fail
399	3	And feel the promise is not vain that morn shall tearless be
422	1	Peals like a trumpet promise of his coming
526	1	We plead the promise of thy word
579	2	For the promise ever sure that, while heaven & earth endure

promised

82	4	in thy light our souls shall see The glories promised
82	4	The glories promised in thy word
97	2	Lead us by faith to hope's true promised land
109	1	traveler, yes, it brings the day, Promised day of Israel
127	2	This day hath God fulfilled his promised word
156	2	And silently thy promised advent greet
218	T,1	O Jesus, I Have Promised, To serve thee to the end

218	3	O Jesus, thou has promised To all who follow thee
218	3	And, Jesus, I have promised, To serve thee to the end
228	2	Let us all in thee inherit, Let us find thy promised rest
311	3	Show in the heavens thy promised sign
387	1	Singing songs of expectation, Marching to the promised land
432	1	stand Here in the borders of our promised land
568	5	To perform the mercy promised to our forefathers
570	9	as he promised to our forefathers, Abraham and his seed

promises

342	4	And thy rich promises In me fulfill

promising

167	II-1	Promising him paradise, Hear us, holy Jesus

pronounced

68	2	And then pronounced them good

proof

496	1	Gave proof through the night that our flag was still there

proper

96	2	He never will deceive me, He leads me by the proper path

prophecy

448	3	The prophecy sublime, The hope of all the years

prophet

129	4	For lo, the days are hastening, on By prophet bards foretold
221	3	My Prophet, Priest, and King
229	2	Great Prophet of my God, My tongue would bless thy name
232	2	I ask no dreams, no prophet ecstasies
439	3	For the people's prophet leaders, Loyal to the living Word
492	2	For prophet voices gladly heard, For daring dreams
568	9	And thou, child, shalt be called the prophet of the Highest

prophet's

14	2	In prophet's words he spoke of old He speaketh still
236	1	Flowing in the prophet's word And the people's liberty
236	5	Flow still in the prophet's word And the people's liberty

prophetic

266	3	The truth is her prophetic gift

prophets

18	4	prophets crowned with light, with all the martyrs noble host
30	3	Respond ... Ye patriarchs and prophets blest, Alleluia
69	2	Prophets burning with his word
247	3	Prophets swell the glad refrain
253	2	Poets, prophets, scholars, saints
294	1	send us forth ... prophets true, To make all lands thine own
383	2	Prophets have proclaimed it, Martyrs testified
470	T,1	God of the Prophets, bless the prophets' sons
470	2	Anoint them prophets
559	4	the goodly fellowship of the prophets praise thee
568	3	As he spake by the mouth of his holy prophets

proved

297	2	Emerge the gifts that time has proved
440	3	O beautiful for heroes proved In liberating strife

provide

33	2	Day by day provide us food
36	3	New treasures still, of countless price, God will provide
36	3	New treasures still ... God will provide for sacrifice
61	2	Daily manna still provide you
77	1	Leave to thy God to order and provide
367	3	His boundless mercy will provide
389	3	Give us each day our daily bread, And raiment fit provide
461	1	God, our Maker, doth provide For our wants to be supplied
462	1	God, our Maker, doth provide For our wants to be supplied
486	2	Simple wants provide, Evil let he shun

provided

344	3	provided, pardoned, guided, Nothing can our peace destroy

providence

19	3	Praise his providence and grace
76	2	While providence supports, Let saints securely dwell
87	3	Behind a frowning providence He hides a smiling face
92	3	Thy providence turns all to good
469	2	One providence alike they share

provident

446	4	God the All-provident

pruning

198	2	to plough-share beat the sword, To pruning-hook the spear

psalm

266	2	One unseen Presence she adores, With silence, or with psalm
268	2	Sweet the psalm and sweet the carol When our song is raised
410	2	Each loving life a psalm of gratitude
438	1	With prayer and psalm they worshiped thee
469	3	Above the requiem, Dust to dust, Shall rise our psalm
469	3	Shall rise our psalm of grateful trust
500	2	Till psalm and song his name adore

psalms

345	3	The psalms of ancient days
562	2	and show ourselves glad in him with psalms

publish

206	1	And publish abroad his wonderful name
302	R	Publish glad tidings, Tidings of peace

publishes

72	1	And publishes to every land the work of an almighty hand

pulse

284	3	Yea, while a breath, a pulse remains, Will I remember thee
450	3	In every heart and brain shall throb the pulse of one
450	3	The pulse of one fraternity

pulses

232	1	Wean it from earth, through all its pulses move
341	5	Breathe through the pulses of desire Thy coolness & thy balm

pulsing

236	3	Pulsing in the hero's blood

pure

7	4	Great Father of glory, pure Father of light
50	4	Like infants' slumbers, pure and light
64	3	Thou flowing water, pure and clear
66	6	Offering up on every shore Her pure sacrifice of love
79	5	O what transport of delight From thy pure chalice floweth
119	3	So may we with holy joy Pure and free from sin's alloy
122	3	This day is born a Savior, Of a pure virgin bright
138	3	Son of God, love's pure light
161	2	Our love, as low or pure
192	2	Our hearts be pure from evil, That we may see aright
207	2	Shine on us with the light of thy pure day
210	3	Let the healing streams abound, Make and keep me pure within
214	T,1	Blest Are the Pure in Heart For they shall see our God
214	3	for his dwelling and his throne Chooseth the pure in heart
214	4	Give us a pure and lowly heart, A temple meet for thee
228	1	Pure, unbounded love thou art
228	4	Pure and spotless let us be
233	2	Until my heart is pure
242	2	Kindle every high desire, Perish self in thy pure fire
244	2	In thy pure love & holy faith From thee true wisdom learning
255	2	The Lord's commandments all are pure & clearest light impart
255	3	statutes of the Lord are truth And righteousness ... pure
255	3	And righteousness most pure
292	1	The one true, pure, immortal sacrifice
314	1	And make me pure within
345	T,1	Rejoice, Ye Pure in Heart, Rejoice, give thanks and sing
348	2	O may my love to thee Pure, warm and changeless be
348	2	Pure, warm, and changeless be, A living fire
407	3	And, pure in heart, behold Thy beauty while I live
456	2	O'er white expanses sparkling pure The radiant morns unfold
461	2	Lord of harvest, grant that we Wholesome grain & pure may be
472	2	shrine Where thy pure light may shine, O hear our call
489	1	I would be pure, for there are those who care
490	3	Teach us to love the true, The beautiful and pure

purer

227	2	Jesus is fairer, Jesus is purer
227	2	Jesus is purer, Who makes the woeful heart to sing
227	3	Jesus shines purer Than all the angels heaven can boast
341	1	In purer lives thy service find
349	5	So purer light shall mark the road That leads me to the Lamb

purest

77	3	Sorrow forgot, love's purest joys restored
222	T,1	Jesus, Priceless Treasure, Source of purest pleasure
222	3	Still in thee lies purest pleasure, Jesus priceless treasure

purge

241	2	Come as the fire and purge our hearts Like sacrificial flame
314	1	And purge away my sin
316	2	Purge our pride and our vain-glory
435	1	With thy living fire of judgment Purge this land
435	1	Purge this land of bitter things
449	2	Purge us from lusts that curse and kill
461	3	From his field shall in that day All offenses purge away

purged

204	2	When he had purged our stains, he took his seat above

purified

461	4	There forever purified, In thy presence to abide

purify

3	3	O thou Fount of blessing, Purify my spirit

purity

251	3	Perfect in power, in love and purity

purple

37	T,1	Still, Still With Thee, when purple morning breaketh
73	2	Mighty mountains, purple breasted
150	4	Scourged, mocked, in purple robe arrayed
440	1	For purple mountain majesties Above the fruited plain

purpose

74	4	Thou whose purpose moves before us Toward the goal
298	T,1	God Is Working His Purpose Out, As year succeeds to year
298	1	God is working his purpose out, And the time is drawing near
383	3	Bound by God's far purpose In one living whole
411	T,1	Lord God of Hosts, Whose Purpose
411	1	purpose never swerving Leads toward the day of Jesus Christ
412	3	Give us a conscience bold and good, Give us a purpose true
419	1	Whose purpose binds the starry spheres
432	1	Through whose deep purpose stranger thousands stand Here
492	3	Renew in us each day Our lofty purpose
494	2	The unfailing purpose of our noblest creed

purposes

304	1	years Wherein God's mighty purposes unfold

pursue

305	3	Blest river of salvation, Pursue thy onward way
406	T,1	Forth in Thy Name, O Lord, I Go, My daily labor to pursue
419	2	And steadfastly pursue the way Of thy commandments still

pursues

175	1	Thy humble beast pursues his road

pursuing

59	3	Thy praise pursuing

put

61	3	Put his arms unfailing round you

100	3	Far as east from west is distant He hath put away our sin
110	2	And death's dark shadows put to flight
235	4	But Jesus for our Master own, And put our trust in him alone
384	T,1	Soldiers of Christ, Arise And put your armor on
385	3	Put on the gospel armor, Each piece put on with prayer
570	7	He hath put down the mighty from their seat

puts
| 431 | 5 | For heathen heart that puts her trust In reeking tube |

quake
| 138 | 2 | Shepherds quake at the sight |
| 264 | 3 | Though earth-quake shocks are threatening her |

quaketh
| 377 | 2 | Zion, calm the breast that quaketh |

quaking
| 222 | 2 | Though the earth be shaking, Every heart be quaking |

quarrels
| 110 | 4 | Bid envy, strife and quarrels cease |

queen
| 185 | 3 | Now the queen of seasons, bright With the day of splendor |
| 481 | 1 | And one was a doctor, and one was a queen |

quench
| 413 | 3 | Quench our fevered thirst of pleasure |

quest
| 86 | 2 | It is because thou art We're driven to the quest |

qui
| 133 | 3 | Ergo qui natus Die hodierna |

quick
| 434 | 2 | God send us men alert and quick ... precepts to translate |

quickened
| 33 | 4 | Quickened by the Spirit's grace All thy holy will to trace |

quickening
67	2	Thy life is in the quickening air
89	2	Sun of our life, thy quickening ray Sheds
92	3	Around me flows thy quickening life, To nerve my ... will
240	1,3	Spirit ... With all thy quickening powers
249	4	Thine is the quickening power that gives increase

quickly
181	3	The three sad days are quickly sped
201	5	Come quickly, King of kings
342	3	Come quickly, and abide Or life is vain
461	4	Even so, Lord, quickly come To thy final harvest home

quicksands

252	3	'Mid mists, and rocks, and quicksands Still guides

quiet

84	1	he leadeth me The quiet waters by
109	3	Hie thee to thy quiet home
121	3	heart, that it may be A quiet chamber kept for thee
444	2	The quiet of a steadfast faith, Calm of a call obeyed
458	5	Praise for happy dreams of birth Brooding in the quiet earth
465	2	Of patient hope, and quiet, brave endurance
467	2	And we grow quiet, folded in thy peace
505	T,1	You That Have Spent the Silent Night In sleep and quiet rest

quietly

42	3	When Christ the herald comes Quietly nigh

quietness

341	4	Drop thy still dews of quietness, Till ... strivings cease

quite

49	2	Now, ere day fadeth quite, We see the evening light

quivers

86	3	The line of lifted sea, Where spreading moonlight quivers

race

2	T,1	All Glory Be to God on High Who hath our race befriended
23	2	Ye blessed souls at rest, Who ran this earthly race
195	3	Ye seed of Israel's chosen race, Ye ransomed from the fall
236	2	Never was to chosen race That unstinted tide confined
257	3	So when thy truth began its race, It touched and glanced on
266	T,1	One Holy Church of God Appears Through every age and race
294	1	No alien race, no foreign shore, No child unsought, unknown
299	1	Descend on our apostate race
308	T,1	For the Brave of Every Race
362	1	A heavenly race demands thy zeal, And an immortal crown
362	4	Blest Savior, introduced by thee, Have I my race begun
367	2	Run the straight race through God's good grace
389	2	God of our fathers, be the God Of their succeeding race
392	+1	As men and women with our race
412	T,1	O Master Workman of the Race, Thou Man of Galilee
414	3	Whate'er your race may be
423	1	Where sounds the cries of race and clan Above the noise
439	4	God of justice, save the people From the war of race & creed
450	1	a loftier race Than e'er the world hath known shall rise
450	1	race ... shall rise With flame of freedom in their souls
459	2	he bids the sun cut short his race, And wintry days appear
471	1	For all thy gifts bestowed upon our race

races

198	2	In Christ all races meet, Their ancient feuds forgetting
445	2	Races and peoples, lo, we stand divided

racing

194	2	Then shout beneath the racing skies

radiance

39	2	thy glance Let fall in royal radiance
157	3	From the cross the radiance streaming
252	1	We praise thee for the radiance That from the hallowed page
421	2	And marveled at the radiance of thy face

radiancy

43	3	Fill me, Radiancy divine, Scatter all my unbelief
309	1	What radiancy of glory, What bliss beyond compare

radiant

72	3	no real voice nor sound Amidst their radiant orbs be found
138	3	Radiant beams from thy holy face
256	3	Pillar of fire through watches dark, & radiant cloud by day
416	4	Born in heaven and radiant here
456	2	O'er white expanses sparkling pure The radiant morns unfold
490	2	And do what thou wouldst have us do With radiant delight

rage

169	4	Why, what hath my Lord done, What makes this rage and spite
201	3	left the lonesome place of death, Despite the rage of foes
363	3	His rage we can endure, For lo, his doom is sure
429	2	And calm amid its rage didst sleep

raging

378	3	Calm thy foes' raging

raiment

193	1	Angels in bright raiment Rolled the stone away
311	T,1	Ten Thousand Times Ten Thousand, In sparkling raiment bright
389	3	Give us each day our daily bread, And raiment fit provide

rain

6	4	And sweetly distills in the dew and the rain
399	3	I trace the rainbow through the rain
458	3	Praise him for his summer rain
460	1	The breezes and the sunshine, And soft, refreshing rain
463	2	Praise him ... he gave the rain To mature the swelling grain
487	1	Spring wind, summer rain, Then the harvest grain

rain's

38	2	Sweet the rain's new fall Sunlit from heaven

rainbow

89	3	Our rainbow arch, thy mercy's sign
399	3	I trace the rainbow through the rain

raise

9	4	High as the heavens our voices raise
22	3	And gladly our songs of true worship we raise
26	1	Raise your voice and rejoice In the bounty of his hand
28	4	nations ... raise on high the victory song
30	1	Bright seraphs, cherubim and thrones, Raise the glad strain
30	1	Raise the glad strain, Alleluia
30	3	Ye holy twelve, ye martyrs strong ... raise the song
30	3	All saints triumphant raise the song, Alleluia

60	T,1	Savior, Again to Thy Dear Name we raise
60	1	raise ... our parting hymn of praise
65	2	Toiling pilgrims raise the song
66	R	Lord of all ... we raise This our hymn of grateful praise
69	3	Men and women, young and old, Raise the anthem manifold
94	4	Through all eternity to thee A joyful song I'll raise
103	4	By ... all-sufficient merit Raise us to thy glorious throne
106	4	High raise the note, that Jesus died, Yet lives and reigns
120	3	Born to raise the sons of earth ...to give them second birth
144	4	To God the Holy Ghost we raise An endless song
154	1	sick to cure, the lost to seek, To raise up them that fall
155	2	To thee, now high exalted, Our melody we raise
173	3	O word of hope, to raise us nearer heaven
180	T,1	Alleluia, Alleluia, Hearts to Heaven and voices raise
182	1	Raise your joys and triumphs high
185	T,1	Come, Ye Faithful, Raise the Strain Of triumphant gladness
186	T,1	Come, Ye Faithful, Raise the Strain (same words as no. 185)
191	5	we raise To thee, in jubilee and praise
192	2	His own, All hail, and, hearing, May raise the victor-strain
262	1	The rival altars that we raise
271	2	We raise it high, we send it on, The song that never endeth
310	3	praise ...Thy blessed people shall evermore raise
345	2	Raise high your free, exulting song
351	4	Out of my stony griefs Bethel I'll raise
400	3	This be the parting cry My heart shall raise
403	1	Raise the stone and thou shalt find me
407	3	Clean hands in holy worship raise
416	1	Raise thy work and life anew
454	4	Thy goodness all our hopes shall raise
461	1	Raise the song of harvest home
461	1	Come to God's own temple, come, Raise the song of harvest
461	4	Raise the glorious harvest home
462	1,3	Raise the song of harvest home
462	3	And for these our souls shall raise Grateful vows
462	3	Come, then, thankful people, come, Raise the song of harvest
464	2	Lord, for these, our souls shall raise Grateful vows
484	3	God raise up more to help them To set the nations free
485	2	The birds their carols raise
494	1	waiting till love can raise the broken stone
505	1	Now lift your hearts, your voices raise
521	2	Our souls to thee in worship raise

raised

268	2	Sweet the psalm and sweet the carol When our song is raised
268	2	When our song is raised as one
318	1	Raised my low self above, Won by thy deathless love

raises

17	1	While o'er my life his strong arm he raises I shall sing
20	3	grateful song My voice unwearied raises
212	3	Hear the cry thy people raises

raiseth

| 351 | 1 | E'en though it be a cross That raiseth me |

raising

143	3	Prayer & praising, all men raising, Worship him, God on high
247	2	celestial hymn, Angel choirs above are raising

rally

427	2	Up, it is Jehovah's rally, God's own arm hath need of thine

ramparts

424	2	Help to rear its shining ramparts
496	1	O'er the ramparts we watched were so gallantly streaming

ran

23	2	Ye blessed souls at rest, Who ran this earthly race
127	3	To Bethlehem straight the enlightened shepherds ran
127	3	ran To see the wonder God had wrought for man
558	2	What love through all his actions ran

rang

326	2	Heaven's arches rang when the angels sang
488	2	Rang out the angel chorus That hailed our Savior's birth

range

235	4	Nor e'er to other teachers range

rank

107	3	Rank on rank the host of heaven Spreads its vanguard

ranks

197	4	Through all ranks of creatures, To the central height
303	1	thanks ... That battle calls our marshaled ranks

ransom

110	T,1	O Come, O Come Emmanuel, And ransom captive Israel

ransomed

16	1	Ransomed, healed, restored, forgiven
25	3	his love in Christ proclaimed with all our ransomed powers
79	2	My ransomed soul he leadeth
119	4	Bring our ransomed souls at last Where they need no star
167	VI-1	Jesus, all our ransom paid, All thy Father's will obeyed
195	3	Ye seed of Israel's chosen race, Ye ransomed from the fall
304	4	Church ... binds the ransomed nations 'neath the sun
311	1	armies of the ransomed saints throng up the steeps of light
331	3	and when thy face I see, My ransomed soul shall be
331	3	My ransomed soul ... Through all eternity Offered to thee
348	4	Oh, bear me safe above, a ransomed soul
387	2	light ... O'er his ransomed people shed

rapt

74	1	Rapt in reverence we adore thee

rapture

437	2	My heart with rapture thrills Like that above

raptured

448	3	Speed, speed the longed-for time Foretold by raptured seers

rare

119	3	As they offered gifts most rare, At the manger rude and bare

rather

425	3	Rather than in silence shrink From the truth

ray

89	2	Sun of our life, thy quickening ray Sheds
109	1	Watchman, does its beauteous ray ... joy or hope foretell
167	VI-3	Brighten all our heavenward way With an ever holier ray
261	3	watchfires ... With never fainting ray
399	2	My heart restores its borrowed ray
407	1	All things in earth and heaven Are lustered by thy ray
418	4	In hope that sends a shining ray Far down
502	T,1	We Praise Thee, Lord, with earliest morning ray

rays

8	2	Earth and heaven reflect thy rays
192	2	The Lord in rays eternal Of resurrection light
259	2	And grow it shall, our glorious sun More fervid rays afford
455	4	As well as summer's joyous rays

reach

167	VII-3	Grace to reach the home on high, Hear us, holy Jesus
222	2	Foes who would molest me Cannot reach me here
259	T,1	We Limit Not the Truth of God To our poor reach of mind
305	3	Stay not till all the lowly Triumphant reach their home
356	3	If it would reach a monarch's throne It must ... resign
391	4	May I reach heaven's joys, O bright heaven's Sun
397	3	And wing my words, that they may reach The hidden depths
408	2	Thou didst reach forth thy hand and mine enfold
421	1	They reach thy throne, encompass land and sea
445	3	Building proud towers which shall not reach to heaven
578	2	Thou didst reach forth thy hand and mine enfold

reaches

316	1	Thou who formed the earth's wide reaches

reaching

471	3	Till, from the shadows to thy presence reaching, He sees

read

99	3	wide-embracing, wondrous love, We read thee in the sky above
99	3	We read thee in the earth below
99	3	We read thee ... In the seas that swell & streams that flow
99	4	We read thee best in him who came To bear for us the cross
99	5	We read thy power to bless and save
99	5	Still more in resurrection light We read the fullness
99	5	in resurrection light We read the fullness of thy might
144	2	And lo, the eastern sages stand to read in heaven
144	2	To read in heaven the Lord's command
256	2	Our guide & chart, wherein we read Of realms beyond the sky
257	1	But when our eyes behold thy Word, We read thy name

257	1	We read thy name in fairer lines
443	2	I can read his righteous sentence by the dim & flaring lamps
483	T,1	I Think When I Read That Sweet Story of old

ready
156	2	Thy road is ready, and thy paths made straight
502	1	Forever ready at thy service stand
506	2	Ready burning Be the incense of thy powers

real
72	3	What though no real voice nor sound ... be found
72	3	no real voice nor sound Amidst their radiant orbs be found
359	4	Blest too is he who can divine Where real right doth lie

realm
| 177 | 4 | Were the whole realm of nature mine |

realms
23	1	Or through the realms of light Fly at your Lord's command
107	3	the Light of light descendeth From the realms of endless day
117	T,1	Angels, From the Realms of Glory
202	3	People and realms of every tongue Dwell on his love
256	2	Our guide & chart, wherein we read Of realms beyond the sky
470	5	Forth may they go to tell all realms thy grace

rear
9	3	What lasting honors shall we rear ... to thy name
424	2	All our joys and all our groans Help to rear its shining
424	2	Help to rear its shining ramparts
477	2	For thee this house of praise we rear

reason
| 481 | 2 | there's not any reason, no, not the least |
| 481 | 2 | not any reason ... Why I shouldn't be one too |

reason's
| 72 | 3 | In reason's ear they all rejoice |

reasons
| 112 | 3 | Not for us to find the reasons |

reassure
| 218 | 2 | O speak to reassure me, To hasten or control |

rebel
| 232 | 4 | To check the rising doubt, the rebel sigh |
| 442 | 1 | Convict us now, if we rebel, Our nation judge, and shame it |

rebuke
| 219 | 1 | Sin to rebuke, to break the captive's chain |

recall
| 374 | 1 | When thou seest me waver, With a look recall |

receive
| 130 | 1 | Let earth receive her King |

134	3	Where meek souls will receive him ... Christ enters in
197	3	Humbled for a season, To receive a name
207	3	And all our substance and our strength receive
210	1	Safe into the haven guide, O receive my soul at last
228	3	Come, almighty to deliver, Let us all thy life receive
277	2	Thou didst receive the children to thyself so tenderly
319	4	Just as I am, thou wilt receive
378	1	Hear and receive thy Church's supplication,
490	1	Our fervent gift receive, And fit us to fulfill
554	6	that takest away the sins of the world, receive our prayer
558	3	Receive and eat the living food

received

1	3	Before the hills in order stood, Or earth received her frame
248	1	From whom all hosts of angels 'Have life and power received
252	2	The Church from her dear Master Received the gift divine

receives

| 205 | 3 | See, the heaven its Lord receives |
| 286 | 2 | Faith still receives the cup as from thy hand |

receiveth

| 258 | 1 | Who its truth believeth Light and joy receiveth |

recite

| 6 | 4 | Thy bountiful care, what tongue can recite |

recked

| 308 | 3 | Recked they not of their own gain |

reckon

| 31 | 3 | slenderness Of the poor wealth thou wouldst reckon as thine |

reclaimed

| 295 | 4 | The new-born souls, whose days Reclaimed from error's ways |

reclining

| 126 | 2 | Angels adore him, in slumber reclining |
| 152 | 1 | There in a manger on the hay reclining |

reclothe

| 341 | 1 | Reclothe us in our rightful mind |

recoil

| 423 | 3 | Thy heart has never known recoil |

reconciled

| 120 | 1 | God and sinners reconciled |

reconciling

| 299 | 2 | To preach the reconciling word |

record

| 299 | 4 | The triumphs of the cross record |
| 558 | 4 | Meet at my table and record The love of your departed Lord |

recount

258	4	Who can tell the pleasure, Who recount the treasure

red

185	1	Led them with unmoistened foot Through the Red Sea waters
388	1	His blood-red banner streams afar
399	4	from the ground ... blossoms red Life that shall endless be
421	4	O'er hill and dale in saffron flame and red
496	1	And the rockets' red glare, the bombs bursting in air

redeem

187	1	Who did once upon the cross ... Suffer to redeem our loss
187	2	Who endured the cross and grave ... Sinners to redeem & save
266	4	Redeem the evil time
293	2	Redeem the time, its hours too swiftly fly

redeemed

168	4	The world redeemed, the will of God complete
188	3	Thine own redeemed forever shield
295	2	Redeemed at countless cost From dark despair
421	4	But in the eyes of men, redeemed and free
559	11	servants whom thou hast redeemed with thy precious blood
568	1	for he hath visited and redeemed his people

redeemer

6	5	Our Maker, Defender, Redeemer and Friend
22	T,1	We Praise Thee, O God, our Redeemer, Creator
22	3	To thee, our great Redeemer, forever be praise
113	2	Till thou, Redeemer, shouldest free Thine own
114	3	Redeemer, come, I open wide My heart to thee
126	1,5	Guide where our infant Redeemer is laid
155	T,1,3	All Glory, Laud, and Honor To thee, Redeemer, King
199	4	All hail, Redeemer, hail, For thou hast died for me
207	T,1	I Greet Thee, Who My Sure Redeemer Art
255	4	Accept, O Lord, for thou my Rock And my Redeemer art
269	1	Church our blest Redeemer saved With his own precious blood
522	1	O Lord, my strength and my redeemer
523	1	O Lord, our strength and our redeemer

redeemer's

11	1	Let the Redeemer's name be sung through every land
158	1	Your Redeemer's conflict see
165	1	On the Redeemer's thorn-crowned brow ... that dawn we view
223	T,1	O for a Thousand Tongues to Sing My great Redeemer's praise
241	2	Let our whole soul an offering be To our Redeemer's name

redeeming

63	1	Triumph in redeeming grace
122	4	This holy tide of Christmas Doth bring redeeming grace
138	3	With the dawn of redeeming grace, Jesus, Lord, at thy birth
171	4	And trust in his redeeming blood, And try his works to do
182	3	Love's redeeming work is done
332	4	From henceforth, the time redeeming, May we live to thee

redeems

100	1	Who redeems thee from destruction

100 2   Who redeems thee from destruction

redemption
302 R   Tidings of Jesus, Redemption and release

redress
95 3   This wicked earth redress
453 3   ring in redress to all mankind

reeking
431 5   For heathen heart that puts her trust In reeking tube
431 5   In reeking tube and iron shard

refine
324 2   Wash out its stains, refine its dross
347 3   Let grace our selfishness expel, Our earthliness refine
372 4   I only design Thy dross to consume and thy gold to refine
440 3   America, America, May God thy gold refine

reflect
8 2   Earth and heaven reflect thy rays

refrain
247 3   Prophets swell the glad refrain

refresh
63 1   O refresh us, Traveling through this wilderness
433 4   Refresh thy people on their toilsome way

refreshing
349 2   Where is the soul-refreshing view Of Jesus and his word
390 1   So longs my soul, O God, for thee, And thy refreshing grace
460 1   The breezes and the sunshine, And soft, refreshing rain

refreshment
76 3   And sweet refreshment find

refuge
59 4   We have no refuge, none on earth to aid us
59 4   We have no refuge ... Save thee, O Father
91 2   I of the Lord my God will say, He is my refuge and my stay
97 3   When we are strong, Lord, leave us not alone, Our refuge be
115 3   thou art ... Our refuge and our great reward
210 2   Other refuge have I none, Hangs my helpless soul on thee
335 3   Precious Savior, still our refuge
372 1   To you who for refuge to Jesus have fled

refuse
144 3   Let not our slothful hearts refuse The guidance of thy light
325 3   Shall we again refuse thee

regarded
570 2   For he hath regarded the lowliness of his hand-maiden

Regem
133 1   Natum videte Regem angelorum

regretting
112 1 Look not back, the past regretting

reign
2 1 And peace shall reign on earth again
63 3 may we ever Reign with thee in endless day
103 3 Born to reign in us forever, Now thy gracious kingdom bring
104 3 true and humble, As befits his holy reign
105 1 Hail, in the time appointed, His reign on earth begun
106 2 He comes to reign with boundless sway
106 5 We come to live and reign in thee
112 2 For e'en now the reign of heaven Spreads throughout
128 2 Heaven and earth shall flee away When he comes to reign
143 2 King forever, ceasing never Over us all to reign
150 5 For us he went on high to reign
175 4 Then take, O Christ, thy power, and reign
198 3 To heal its ancient wrong, Come, Prince of peace, and reign
202 T,1 Jesus Shall Reign Where'er the Sun
242 4 Holy Spirit, Right divine, King within my conscience reign
246 1 Come, and reign over us, Ancient of Days
247 1 Infinite thy vast domain, Everlasting is thy reign
263 3 And hereafter in thy glory Evermore with thee to reign
294 2 Help us to spread thy gracious reign
304 1 From age to age his righteous reign appears
356 2 Enslave it ... And deathless it shall reign
383 2 Wider grows the kingdom, Reign of love and light
385 4 He with the King of glory Shall reign eternally
398 5 Thou art our Lord, Thou dost forever reign
413 3 Come, O Christ, and reign above us
416 4 Come then, law divine, and reign
420 1 O holy city ... Where Christ, the Lamb, doth reign
424 3 It will live and shine transfigured In the final reign
424 3 In the final reign of right
484 3 Till all the distant people In every foreign place

reignest
248 2 High in the heavenly Zion Thou reignest God adored
274 4 Lord God of hosts that reignest on high
446 1 Show forth thy pity on high where thou reignest

reigneth
15 2 Lord, who o'er all things so wondrously reigneth

reigning
8 4 Father love is reigning o'er us
207 2 Reigning omnipotent in every place
229 4 Thy scepter and thy sword, Thy reigning grace I sing

reigns
2 2 Thy boundless power o'er all things reigns
20 T,1 Sing Praise to God Who Reigns Above
29 3 The Son, and him who reigns With them in highest heaven
106 4 High raise the note, that Jesus died, Yet lives and reigns
106 4 Yet lives and reigns, the Crucified
130 2 Joy to the earth, the Savior reigns
202 4 Blessings abound where'er he reigns

204	2	The Lord, our Savior, reigns, The God of truth and love
345	6	Praise him who reigns on high, The Lord whom we adore
387	3	Where the one almighty Father Reigns in love forevermore
424	1	Justice reigns supreme o'er all
485	3	God reigns, let the earth be glad
504	2	The highest heaven, in which he reigns

rejected

| 163 | 1 | By foes derided, by thine own rejected, O most afflicted |

rejoice

4	1	Come ye before him and rejoice
8	2	Field and forest, vale and mountain ... call us to rejoice
8	2	Flowery meadow, flashing sea ... call us to rejoice
8	2	Chanting bird & flowing fountain call us to rejoice in thee
13	1	Sun and moon, rejoice before him
26	1	Raise your voice and rejoice In the bounty of his hand
28	3	And all rejoice with Christian heart and voice
64	2	Thou rising morn, in praise rejoice
72	3	In reason's ear they all rejoice
106	T,1	Hills of the North, Rejoice
110	R	Rejoice, Rejoice, Emmanuel Shall come to thee, O Israel
125	T,1-3	Good Christian Men, Rejoice, With heart and soul and voice
184	T,1	Good Christian Men Rejoice and Sing
184	2	Let all mankind rejoice and say
189	2	Let hearts downcast and lonely Rejoice this Easter day
204	T,1	Rejoice, the Lord Is King, Your Lord and King adore
204	1	Rejoice, give thanks, and sing, And triumph evermore
204	R	Rejoice, again I say, rejoice
268	1	Churches in thy Church rejoice
304	T,1	Rejoice, O People, in the Mounting Years
304	1	Rejoice, O people, in your glorious Lord
304	2	Rejoice, O people, in the years of old
304	2	Rejoice in God's glad messengers of peace
304	3	Rejoice, O people, in this living hour
304	3	Rejoice that while the sin of man divides
304	4	Rejoice, O people, in the days to be
304	4	Rejoice, rejoice, his Church on earth is one
312	2	They triumph still, they still rejoice
326	5	my heart shall rejoice, Lord Jesus, When thou comest
345	T,1	Rejoice, Ye Pure in Heart, Rejoice, give thanks and sing
345	R	Rejoice, rejoice, Rejoice, give thanks and sing
388	4	Around the Savior's throne rejoice In robes of light arrayed
430	T,1	Rejoice, O Land, in God Thy Might
430	1	Fear not, O land, in God rejoice
504	1	Let heaven rejoice, let earth be glad
562	1	let us heartily rejoice in the strength of our salvation

rejoiced

| 570 | 1 | And my spirit hath rejoiced in God my Savior |

rejoices

29	1	Who wondrous things hath done, In whom his world rejoices
123	T,1	All My Heart This Night Rejoices
194	T,1	The Whole Bright World Rejoices Now
508	2	Thine ear discerns, thy love rejoices When hearts rise up

rejoicing

79	3	on his shoulder gently laid, And home rejoicing brought me
387	3	One the gladness of rejoicing On the far eternal shore
475	2	Rejoicing this foundation lay

rejoicingly

368	2	But the steep and rugged pathway May we tread rejoicingly

release

46	2	May struggling hearts that seek release Here find the rest
103	1	From our fears and sins release us
302	R	Tidings of Jesus, Redemption and release
304	2	messengers ... Who bore the Savior's gospel of release
325	3	From old unfaith our souls release To seek the kingdom
435	2	For the hour that brings release
466	3	every home, by this release, May be the dwelling place
509	2	May struggling hearts that seek release Here find the rest

released

23	2	And now, from sin released, Behold the Savior's face
309	3	There is the throne of David, And there, from care released
468	2	Released from earthly toil and strife

relent

371	1	There's no discouragement Shall make him once relent

reliance

373	3	Place on the Lord reliance, My soul, with courage wait

relieve

319	4	Wilt welcome, pardon, cleanse, relieve

religion

433	3	Thy true religion in our hearts increase

rely

28	2	Thy Church doth in thy strength rely
274	4	That man is truly blest Who only on thee doth rely
472	4	On thee our hearts rely Thy power to give

remain

46	4	We cannot at the shrine remain
77	1	In every change he faithful will remain
98	3	That shadows fall on brightest hours, That thorns remain
382	3	But the Church of Jesus Constant will remain

remainest

95	5	Thou in thy everlasting seat Remainest God alone

remains

78	1	firm remains on high The everlasting throne of him
164	4	And victory remains with love, For he, our Lord is crucified
284	3	Yea, while a breath, a pulse remains, Will I remember thee

remember

100	5	Unto those who still remember His commandments and obey

122	1	Remember Christ, our Savior, Was born on Christmas Day
167	II-3	O remember us who pine, Looking from our cross to thine
215	2	remember not past years
284	1	This will I do, my dying Lord, I will remember thee
284	2	Thy testamental cup I take, And thus remember thee
284	3	Remember thee, and all thy pains, And all thy love to me
284	3	Yea, while a breath, a pulse remains, Will I remember thee
284	4	When thou shalt in thy kingdom come, Jesus, remember me
430	3	Remember thou his love of old
447	2	Remember, Lord, thy works of old
447	2	Remember not our sin's dark stain
484	T,1	Remember All the People, Who live in far-off lands
484	2	Remember all God's children Who yet have never heard
568	5	and to remember his holy covenant

remembering
570	9	He, remembering his mercy, hath holpen his servant Israel

remembrance
374	2	Bring to my remembrance Sad Gethsemane

remission
568	10	by the remission of their sins

remove
105	4	The tide of time shall never His covenant remove
267	2	And all fear of want remove
287	4	The bread and wine remove, but thou art here
333	3	No place can part, nor hour of time remove us
348	4	Blest Savior, then, in love, Fear and distrust remove
438	4	Till these eternal hills remove

removed
178	2	'Tis midnight, and from all removed

rend
142	5	While the choir with peals of glee Doth rend the air asunder
167	III-1	Jesus, loving to the end Her whose heart thy sorrows rend
493	2	God's daybreak to proclaim And rend the veils of night

render
7	4	All praise we would render, O help us to see
154	3	What shall we render to our God For all that he hath done
185	3	With the royal feast of feasts, Comes its joy to render
356	1	Force me to render up my sword, And I shall conqueror be
398	4	We render back the love thy mercy gave us
506	1	See thou render All thy feeble strength can pay

rending
232	2	No sudden rending of the veil of clay

renew
32	3	Lord, I my vows to thee renew
166	2	Savior, for our pardon sue, When our sins thy pangs renew
318	2	In thee my strength renew, Give me thy work to do
339	T,1	All My Hope on God Is Founded, He doth still my trust renew

reposeth
  53 T,1   The Duteous Day Now Closeth, Each flower and tree reposeth

reproach
  295 3   With us the work to share, With us reproach to dare
  301 3   May her scattered children be From reproach of evil free

requiem
  469 3   Above the requiem, Dust to dust, Shall rise our psalm

requires
  442 3   So large, it nought but love requires

rescue
  81 2   When in distress to him I called, He to my rescue came

rescued
  250 2   By whose cross and death are we Rescued from all misery
  496 2   Blest with victory and peace, may the heaven-rescued land

rescues
  16 3   Rescues us from all our foes

reside
  274 2   Happy, who in thy house reside, Where thee they ever praise

residing
  117 2   God with man is now residing, Yonder shines the infant light

resign
  356 3   If it would reach a monarch's throne It must ... resign
  356 3   It must its crown resign

resignation
  366 5   Save us from weak resignation to the evils we deplore

resolved
  406 1   only thee resolved to know In all I think or speak or do

resounding
  3 2   God himself is with us, Hear the harps resounding
  41 3   Thine is the glory, gleaming and resounding
  41 3   glory, gleaming and resounding Through all creation
  169 3   Resounding all the day Hosannas to their king

respite
  358 2   Could my zeal no respite know, Could my tears forever flow

respond
  30 3   Respond, ye souls in endless rest
  30 3   Respond ... Ye patriarchs and prophets blest, Alleluia
  352 4   Still shall those hearts respond, with full accord

rest
  8 3   Well-spring of the joy of living, Ocean depth of happy rest
  23 2   Ye blessed souls at rest, Who ran this earthly race

454	4	In scenes exalted or depressed, Thou art our joy & ... rest
458	5	Praise him for the winter's rest
467	1	Safely they rest who on thy love repose
469	2	All souls are thine, and here or there They rest
469	2	They rest within thy sheltering care
469	4	O happy they in God who rest
479	1	For rest and food and loving care
485	1	I rest me in the thought Of rocks and trees, of skies & seas
492	1	Whose joyous fellowship we share At work, at rest
492	1	At work, at rest, in play and prayer
509	2	May struggling hearts that seek release Here find the rest
509	2	Here find the rest of God's own peace
527	1	That I may run, rise, rest with thee
538	1	The rest, O God, is in thy hand
539	1	With the Holy Spirit's favor Rest upon us from above
576	T,1	Lord, Thou Hast Searched Me and dost know Where'er I rest
576	1	Where'er I rest, where'er I go

resting

| 308 | 1 | Whose forgotten resting place Rolling years have buried deep |
| 361 | 4 | Grant me no resting place Until I rest ... The captive |

restless

106	2	Pent be each warring breeze, Lulled be your restless waves
161	1	Across our restless living The light streams from his cross
220	3	The tasks he gives are those he gave Beside the restless sea
290	3	Our restless spirits yearn for thee
295	2	The wayward and the lost, By restless passions tossed
308	4	High above the restless tides Stands their city on the hill
322	1	tumult Of our life's wild, restless sea
390	3	Why restless, why cast down, my soul
423	5	Among these restless throngs abide
429	1	Whose arm doth bind the restless wave

restlessness

| 92 | 3 | Thy calmness bends serene above, My restlessness to still |

restore

84	2	My soul he doth restore again
159	3	but thou Dost light and life restore
262	4	One hope, one faith, one love restore The seamless robe
528	3	Restore to me the joy of thy salvation

restored

2	3	O thou who hast our peace restored
16	1	Ransomed, healed, restored, forgiven
36	1	Restored to life and power and thought
77	3	Sorrow forgot, love's purest joys restored
184	4	The life laid down, the life restored
188	1	When to their longing eyes restored
228	4	Let us see thy great salvation Perfectly restored in thee
446	4	earth by thy chastening Yet shall ... be restored
446	4	Yet shall to freedom and truth be restored

restores

| 399 | 2 | My heart restores its borrowed ray |

restoring
255   T,1   Most Perfect Is the Law of   God, Restoring those that stray

restrain
51   4   Those who plan some evil, From their sin restrain
447   1   The wrath of sinful man restrain

rests
47   2   And rests not now by day or night
220   4   Our brotherhood still rests in him, The brother of us all

resurrection
99   5   Still more in resurrection light We read the fullness
99   5   in resurrection light We read the fullness of thy might
159   4   Thy cross may bring us to thy joy And resurrection power
180   2   We with him to life eternal By his resurrection rise
182   5   Thee we greet triumphant now ... Hail, the Resurrection thou
185   3   Welcomes in unwearied strains Jesus' resurrection
189   1   And filled the gloom and darkness With resurrection light
192   T,1   The Day of Resurrection, Earth, tell it out abroad
192   2   The Lord in rays eternal Of resurrection light
458   2   Praise him for his budding green, April's resurrection scene

retain
263   3   What they gain from thee forever With the blessed to retain

retire
341   5   Let sense be dumb, let flesh retire

retreat
443   3   trumpet that shall never call retreat

retrieved
127   4   trace we the babe, Who hath retrieved our loss

rettende
139   3   Da uns schlagt die rettende Stund'

Retter
139   2   Tont es laut von fern und nah, Christ der Retter ist da

return
43   2   Joyless is the day's return Till thy mercy's beams I see
228   3   Suddenly return, and never, Nevermore thy temples leave
349   3   Return, O holy Dove, return, Sweet messenger of rest
558   5   Till thou return and we shall eat The marriage supper

returned
203   1   From the fight returned victorious

returning
36   2   New mercies, each returning day Hover around us
58   2   When the constant sun returning Unseals our eyes
205   3   Though returning to his throne
506   2   Gladly hail the sun returning

reveal

114	3	Thy grace and love in me reveal
245	1	with words that help and heal Would thy life in mine reveal
294	3	Whose life and death reveal thy face
442	2	In best and worst reveal us
494	1	let thy plan Reveal the life that God would give to man

revealed

144	4	To Christ, revealed in earthly night
152	2	Shining revealed through every task most lowly
395	4	The worlds of science and of art, Revealed and ruled by thee

revealing

152	4	Divine and human, in his deep revealing
161	1	And by its clear, revealing beams We measure gain and loss
173	2	O infinite compassion, still revealing ... forgiveness
173	2	revealing The infinite forgiveness won for man
334	1	For we are weak, and need some deep revealing
334	1,3	revealing Of trust and strength and calmness from above
334	3	Now make us strong, we need thy deep revealing
492	2	Each thought-revealing truth

reveals

257	2	But the blest volume thou hast writ Reveals thy justice
257	2	Reveals thy justice and thy grace
304	3	But on the cross God's love reveals his power
476	1	praise the Lord, who now as then Reveals in man his glory

revelation

325	4	We wait thy revelation

revere

28	1	Our hearts revere thy gracious word

reverence

3	1	Prostrate lie with deepest reverence
74	1	Rapt in reverence we adore thee
291	2	Here in loving reverence bow
341	1	In deeper reverence, praise
357	6	But more of reverence in us dwell
473	1	Who shall not reverence thee
499	1	Serve him with awe, with reverence, love

reverent

249	2	To thee in reverent love, our hearts are bowed
410	2	Follow with reverent steps the great example Of him

reverently

141	5	Full reverently upon their knee

reviled

158	2	Beaten, bound, reviled, arraigned

reward

115	3	thou art ... Our refuge and our great reward
292	2	lo, between our sins and their reward, We set the passion

313	2	Not with the hope of gaining aught, Not seeking a reward
383	1	Manifold the service, One the sure reward
487	1	Though our work is hard, God gives us reward

ribbed

| 494 | 2 | Ribbed with the steel that time and change doth mock |

rice

484	1	Where children wade through rice fields
484	1	wade through rice fields And watch the camel trains
487	1	Pearly rice and corn, Fragrant autumn morn

rich

75	3	See how he hath everywhere Made this earth so rich and fair
82	4	Life, like a fountain rich and free Springs from ... my Lord
145	1	Rich in blessing, Rule and might o'er all possessing
177	3	Or thorns compose so rich a crown
199	2	Rich wounds, yet visible above, In beauty glorified
203	2	Rich the trophies Jesus brings
271	3	Rich with the same eternal grace
276	2	The common home of rich and poor, Of bond and free
297	2	Yields harvests rich in lasting good
328	T,1	The Lord Is Rich and Merciful, The Lord is very kind
342	4	And thy rich promises In me fulfill
348	2	May thy rich grace impart Strength to my fainting heart
366	3	Rich in things and poor in soul
453	3	Ring out the feud of rich and poor
462	2	All that liberal autumn pours From her rich ... stores
462	2	From her rich o'erflowing stores
464	3	All that liberal autumn pours From her rich ... stores
464	3	From her rich o'erflowing stores
476	4	rich in art, made richer still The brotherhood of duty
570	8	and the rich he hath sent empty away

richer

126	4	Richer by far is the heart's adoration
399	1	that in thine ocean depths its flow May richer, fuller be
476	4	rich in art, made richer still The brotherhood of duty

riches

| 319 | 3 | Sight, riches, healing of the mind |
| 391 | 3 | Riches I heed not, nor man's empty praise |

richest

| 177 | 1 | My richest gain I count but loss |

richly

| 236 | T,1,5 | Life of Ages, Richly Poured, Love of God unspent and free |

richness

305	3	Flow thou to every nation, Nor in thy richness stay
435	3	Feed the faint and hungry peoples with the richness
435	3	With the richness of thy Word

ride

| 156 | 1 | Ride on in triumph, Lord |

| 175 | T,1-4 | Ride on, Ride on in Majesty (same words in No. 176) |
| 175 | 2 | In lowly pomp ride on to die |

rides

| 87 | 1 | He plants his footsteps in the sea And rides upon the storm |

rift

| 494 | 1 | And hearts creative bridge the human rift |

right

20	2	Within the kingdom of his might, Lo, all is just ... right
23	T,1	Ye Holy Angels Bright, Who wait at God's right hand
34	3	To serve right gloriously The God who gave all worlds
49	3	To thee of right belongs All praise of holy songs
85	3	the Lord thy shade On thy right hand doth stay
95	3	For thou art he who shalt by right The nations all possess
96	T,1-3	Whate'er My God Ordains Is Right
98	1	So many glorious things are here, Noble and right
141	4	stop and stay, Right over the place where Jesus lay
147	1	Didst yield the glory that of right was thine
200	2	The highest place that heaven affords Is his ... by right
206	4	Then let us adore and give him his right
242	4	Holy Spirit, Right divine, King within my conscience reign
255	2	The precepts of the Lord are right
265	1	All men have equal right To worship thee
303	3	The blessed kingdom of the right
346	2	Who steadfast stand at God's right hand
354	3	Until we stand at thy right hand Through Jesus' saving merit
363	2	Were not the right man on our side
367	1	Christ is thy strength, and Christ thy right
359	4	Blest too is he who can divine Where real right doth lie
359	5	For right is right, since God is God
359	5	And right the day must win
371	2	He will make good his right To be a pilgrim
373	2	What terror can confound me With God at my right hand
376	3	Lead us, O Father, in the paths of right
406	3	Thee may I set at my right hand
416	1	Seek the right, perform the true
424	3	In the final reign of right
425	3	slaves who dare not be In the right with two or three
427	2	On, right onward for the right
453	4	Ring in the love of truth and right
470	2	their lips make eloquent To assure the right
476	2	Who graced their generation, Who helped the right
476	2	Who helped the right and fought the wrong
481	2	And they followed the right, for Jesus' sake
491	2	To right the wrongs that shame this mortal life
528	1	And renew a right spirit within me
552	1	It is meet and right so to do
554	7	Thou that sittest at the right hand of God the Father
559	10	sittest at the right hand of God in the glory of the Father

righteous

248	1	The righteous Judge of judges, The almighty King of kings
293	3	By feeblest agents may our God fulfill His righteous will
304	1	From age to age his righteous reign appears

372	2	Upheld by my righteous, omnipotent hand
424	1	Only righteous men and women Dwell within its gleaming wall
443	2	I can read his righteous sentence by the dim & flaring lamps
446	3	God the all-righteous One

righteousness

43	1	Sun of righteousness arise, Triumph o'er the shades of night
84	2	me to walk doth make Within the paths of righteousness
95	1	Before him righteousness shall go, His royal harbinger
100	4	To ... children's children ever ... his righteousness extend
105	3	And righteousness, in fountains, From hill to valley flow
120	3	Hail the Sun of righteousness
255	3	statutes of the Lord are truth And righteousness ... pure
255	3	And righteousness most pure
294	3	O God of righteousness and grace, Seen in the Christ thy Son
448	2	The service glad and free Of truth and righteousness
524	T,1	Lead Me, Lord, lead me in thy righteousness
562	9	with righteousness to judge the world
568	8	In holiness and righteousness before him

rightful

| 341 | 1 | Reclothe us in our rightful mind |

rightly

| 410 | 1 | To worship rightly is to love each other |

rills

| 437 | 2 | Thy name I love, I love thy rocks and rills |

ring

26	2	By his might the heavens ring, In his love we live and move
35	3	Let all the earth around Ring joyous with the sound
111	2	Every voice in concert ring, Evermore and evermore
136	T,1	On This Day Earth Shall Ring
136	4	With their song earth shall ring
155	1,3	To whom the lips of children Made sweet hosannas ring
304	4	When o'er the strife of nations sounding clear Shall ring
304	4	Shall ring love's gracious song of victory
326	5	When the heavens shall ring & the angels sing At thy coming
437	1	From every mountain side Let freedom ring
437	3	And ring from all the trees Sweet freedom's song
453	T,1	Ring Out, Wild Bells, to the wild sky
453	1	Ring out, wild bells, and let him die
453	2	Ring out the old, ring in the new
453	2	Ring, happy bells, across the snow
453	2	Ring out the false, ring in the true
453	3	Ring out the grief that saps the mind
453	3	Ring out the feud of rich and poor
453	3	ring in redress to all mankind
453	4	Ring out false pride in place and blood
453	4	Ring in the love of truth and right
453	4	Ring in the common love of good
453	5	Ring in the valiant man and free
453	5	Ring out the darkness of the land
453	5	Ring in the Christ that is to be
485	3	The Lord is king, let the heavens ring

ringing

123	1	Till the air Everywhere Now with joy is ringing
311	2	What ringing of a thousand harps Bespeaks the triumph nigh

rings

183	3	through Christendom it rings That the Lamb is King of kings
203	2	While the vault of heaven rings
352	4	Lift up your hearts, rings pealing in our ears
485	1	and round me rings The music of the spheres

ripe

478	3	The ripe fruits in the garden, He made them every one

ripened

462	2	All the fruits in full supply Ripened 'neath the summer sky
464	2	Yellow sheaves of ripened grain

ripening

457	1	golden wealth of ripening grain And breath of clover fields

ripens

487	2	He makes green things grow, Ripens what we sow

rise

11	2	Till suns shall rise and set no more
32	1	joyful rise To pay thy morning sacrifice
33	T,1	As the Sun Doth Daily Rise Bright'ning all the morning skies
37	4	Shall rise the glorious thought, I am with thee
42	4	Bid then farewell to sleep Rise up and run
45	3	Lord of angels, on our eyes Let eternal morning rise
46	1	vesper hymn and vesper prayer rise mingling on the holy air
52	3	Hope and faith and love rise glorious
58	2	May we, born anew like morning, To labor rise
68	T,1	I Sing the Mighty Power of God That made the mountains rise
95	3	Rise, God, judge thou the earth in might
104	2	Let the valleys rise to meet him
106	3	The sleep of ages break, And rise to liberty
108	1	Rise up, with willing feet Go forth, the Bridegroom meet
112	1	Rise, and join the Lord's command
120	1	Joyful, all ye nations rise, Join the triumph of the skies
127	1	Rise to adore the mystery of love
180	2	We with him to life eternal By his resurrection rise
182	3	Death in vain forbids him rise
182	4	Made like him, like him we rise
194	2	To him who rose that we might rise
202	2	His name like sweet perfume shall rise With every morning
202	5	Let every creature rise & bring Peculiar honors to our King
205	T,1	Hail the Day That Sees Him Rise
210	3	Spring thou up within my heart, Rise to all eternity
240	2	In vain we tune our formal songs, In vain we strive to rise
251	1	Early in the morning our song shall rise to thee
261	3	How rise thy towers, serene & bright To meet the dawning day
262	2	in time to be Shall one great temple rise to thee
287	4	Too soon we rise, the symbols disappear
300	T,1-3	Rise Up, O Men of God
300	3	Her strength unequal to her task, Rise up and make her great

300	4	As brothers of the Son of man Rise up, O men of God
332	2	Sinful thoughts & words unloving Rise against us one by one
341	2	Let us, like them, without a word, Rise up and follow thee
377	1	Rise and be of gladsome heart
382	3	Crowns and thrones may perish, Kingdoms rise and wane
385	2	Let courage rise with danger, & strength to strength oppose
402	4	To teach our faint desires to rise
405	1	Yet may love's incense rise, Sweeter than sacrifice
416	T,1	Christian, Rise and Act Thy Creed
429	4	Thus evermore shall rise to thee Glad hymns of praise
448	4	Till rise in ordered plan On firm foundations broad
450	1	a loftier race Than e'er the world hath known shall rise
450	1	race ... shall rise With flame of freedom in their souls
451	2	Age after age their tragic empires rise
469	3	Above the requiem, Dust to dust, Shall rise our psalm
469	3	Shall rise our psalm of grateful trust
508	2	Thine ear discerns, thy love rejoices When hearts rise up
508	2	When hearts rise up to thee in truth
509	1	vesper hymn and vesper prayer Rise mingling on the holy air
527	1	That I may run, rise, rest with thee

risen

108	2	Her star is risen, her light is come
120	3	Risen with healing in his wings
180	1	Jesus Christ, the King of glory, Now is risen from the dead
181	3	All glory to our risen Head
182	T,1	Christ the Lord Is Risen Today
183	T,1	Christ the Lord Is Risen Again
184	2	The Lord of life is risen for aye
184	4	Thy name we bless, O risen Lord
185	2	And from three days' sleep in death As a sun hath risen
187	T,1	Jesus Christ Is Risen Today, Alleluia
188	1	The Apostles saw their risen Lord
189	1	And in your adoration Praise Christ, your risen Lord
189	2	O, sing in exultation To Christ, your risen King
192	3	For Christ the Lord is risen, Our joy that hath no end
193	T,1,R	Thine Is the Glory, Risen, conquering Son
193	2	Lo, Jesus meets thee, risen from the tomb
286	T,1	Come, Risen Lord, and deign to be our guest
582	T,1	Christ the Lord Is Risen Today (as no. 182 with descant)

rises

108	2	She wakes, she rises from her gloom
181	3	He rises glorious from the dead

riseth

420	4	Already in the mind of God That city riseth fair
505	1	And joy to see the cheerful light That riseth in the east

rising

1	4	Short as the watch that ends the night Before the rising sun
64	2	Thou rising morn, in praise rejoice
94	T,1	When All Thy Mercies, O My God, My rising soul surveys
201	3	O brighter than the rising morn When he, victorious, rose
232	4	To check the rising doubt, the rebel sigh
288	R	When I fall on my knees with my face to the rising sun

rival

262	1	The rival altars that we raise

rivalry

265	2	Lord, set thy churches free From foolish rivalry

riven

358	1	Let the water & the blood, From thy riven side which flowed
377	3	Though the hills & vales be riven God created with his hand

river

73	3	Rolling river, praise him ever
106	1	River and mountain-spring, Hark to the advent voice
249	4	From thee have flowed, as from a pleasant river, Our plenty
267	2	Who can faint, while such a river Ever flows
305	3	Blest river of salvation, Pursue thy onward way
478	2	The purple-headed mountain, The river running by

rivers

86	3	All beauty speaks of thee, The mountains and the rivers
372	3	The rivers of woe shall not thee overflow
484	2	Some fish in mighty rivers, Some hunt across the snow

road

36	5	Room to deny ourselves - a road To bring us daily nearer God
92	2	Shamed by its failures or its fears, I sink beside the road
96	1	Though dark my road, He holds me that I shall not fall
129	3	O rest beside the weary road, And hear the angels sing
156	2	Thy road is ready, and thy paths made straight
175	1	Thy humble beast pursues his road
238	4	holiness, the road That we must take to dwell with God
349	1	A light to shine upon the road That leads me to the Lamb
349	5	So purer light shall mark the road That leads me to the Lamb

roam

484	1	In strange and lovely cities, Or roam the desert sands

roar

213	3	When at last I near the shore And the fearful breakers roar
343	1	The storm may roar without me, My heart may low be laid

robe

6	2	Whose robe is the light, whose canopy space
150	4	Scourged, mocked, in purple robe arrayed
262	4	One hope, one faith, one love restore The seamless robe
262	4	The seamless robe that Jesus wore
325	1	And robe of sorrow round thee

robed

227	2	woodlands Robed in the blooming garb of spring

robes

309	3	Forever and forever Are clad in robes of white
388	4	Around the Savior's throne rejoice In robes of light arrayed

rock

9	5	Firm as a rock thy truth must stand
73	2	Rock and highland, wood and island
78	3	Supreme in wisdom as in power The Rock of ages stands
83	1	Who trusts in God's unchanging love Builds on the rock
83	1	Builds on the rock that nought can move
160	1	The shadow of a mighty rock Within a weary land
213	1	Hiding rock and treacherous shoal
244	2	O mighty Rock, O Source of life
255	4	Accept, O Lord, for thou my Rock And my Redeemer art
261	4	Unharmed upon the eternal rock The eternal city stands
267	1	On the Rock of Ages founded, What can shake thy sure repose
270	T,1	Built on the Rock the Church doth stand
271	T,1	We Come Unto Our Father's God, Their Rock is our salvation
306	2	Thou wast their rock, their fortress, and their might
358	T,1,4	Rock of Ages, Cleft for me, Let me hide myself in thee
359	T,1,4	Rock of Ages (same words as no. 358)
378	2	Lord, o'er thy rock nor death nor hell prevaileth
381	2	Whether beneath was flinty rock Or yielding grassy sod
397	2	O strengthen me, that while I stand firm on the rock
429	4	shield in danger's hour From rock and tempest, fire and foe
477	1	Founded ... On thee, the everlasting Rock
477	4	Be thou our rock, our life, our thought
482	1	We will lend a coat of fur, We will rock you
482	2	Sleep in comfort, slumber deep, We will rock you
494	2	upon the solid rock We set the dream that hardens into deed

rockets'

496	1	And the rockets' red glare, the bombs bursting in air

rocks

130	2	While fields and floods, rocks, hills and plains Repeat
252	3	'Mid mists, and rocks, and quicksands Still guides
368	3	But would smite the living fountains From the rocks
368	3	From the rocks along our way
437	2	Thy name I love, I love thy rocks and rills
437	3	Let rocks their silence break, The sound prolong
485	1	I rest me in the thought Of rocks and trees, of skies & seas

rod

79	4	Thy rod and staff my comfort still
84	3	thy rod And staff me comfort still
195	2	Extol the stem of Jesse's rod
354	2	Thy rod and staff shall keep us safe, And guide our steps

roll

14	3	His love shall be our strength and stay, While ages roll
69	3	From the north to southern pole Let the mighty chorus roll
72	2	Confirm the tidings as they roll
174	4	Lord, should fear & anguish roll Darkly o'er my sinful soul
210	1	While the nearer waters roll ... the tempest still is high
213	1	Unknown waves before me roll
311	3	Fill up the roll of thine elect, Then take thy power & reign
348	4	When death's cold, sullen stream Shall e'er me roll
375	2	not with swords' loud clashing Nor roll of stirring drums
417	T,1	The Day of the Lord Is at Hand, Its storms roll up the sky

rolled

193	1	Angels in bright raiment Rolled the stone away
392	3	Controlled and cleanly night and day

rolling

1	5	Time, like an ever-rolling stream, Bears all its sons away
9	5	thy truth must stand When rolling years shall cease to move
73	3	Rolling river, praise him ever
108	1	His chariot wheels are nearer rolling
199	4	Creator of the rolling spheres, Ineffably sublime
257	2	The rolling sun, the changing light, And nights and days
308	1	Whose forgotten resting place Rolling years have buried deep

rolls

47	2	While earth rolls onward into light
86	3	The deep-toned organ blast That rolls through arches dim
380	3	March on, O soul, with strength, As strong the battle rolls
395	2	Around us rolls the ceaseless tide Of business, toil, & care

room

36	5	Room to deny ourselves - a road To bring us daily nearer God
130	1	Let every heart prepare him room
286	2	We meet, as in that upper room they met
325	2	aweful love ... found no room In life where sin denied thee
326	1	But in Bethlehem's home there was found no room
326	1	no room For thy holy nativity
326	1-4	There is room in my heart for thee
326	5	Let thy voice call me home, saying, Yet there is room
326	5	There is room at my side for thee
401	4	Who sweeps a room, as for thy laws
401	4	Who sweeps a room ... Makes that and the action fine

root

145	1	Thou Root of Jesse, David's Son, My Lord and Master
458	4	Praise him for his garden root, Meadow grass & orchard fruit

rooted

281	2	Thou our life, O let us be Rooted, grafted, built on thee

rose

131	T,1	Lo, How a Rose E'er Blooming From tender stem hath sprung
131	2	Isaiah 'twas foretold it, The Rose I have in mind
150	5	For us he rose from death again
191	1	O'er death today rose triumphing
194	2	To him who rose that we might rise
199	3	And rose victorious in the strife For those he came to save
199	3	His glories now we sing Who died and rose on high
201	3	O brighter than the rising morn When he, victorious, rose
456	1	The hand that shaped the rose hath wrought The ... snow
456	3	Thyself the vision passing by In crystal and in rose

rosy

124	3	How he is white, his cheeks are rosy

rough

376	4	However rough and steep the path may be

rougher

104	3	Make the rougher places plain

round

6	3	And round it hath cast, like a mantle, the sea
19	1	Angels round his throne above
24	1	partake ... With angels round thy throne of light
36	5	The trivial round, the common task, Will furnish all
61	3	Put his arms unfailing round you
72	2	Whilst all the stars that round her burn ... confirm
72	3	Move round the dark terrestrial ball
96	3	My Father's care Is round me there
98	2	So many gentle thoughts and deeds Circling us round
108	3	In praises round thy glorious throne
129	4	with the ever-circling years Comes round the age of gold
138	1	All is calm, all is bright Round yon virgin mother and child
152	3	With all the listening people gathered round
157	1,5	All the light of sacred story Gathers round its head sublime
167	VII-2	When the death shades round us lower
192	3	The round world keep high triumph, And all that is therein
198	2	the whole round world complete, From sunrise to its setting
239	2	And clothe me round, the while my path illuming
257	3	Sun, moon, and stars convey thy praise Round the whole earth
257	3	Round the whole earth and never stand
267	3	Round each habitation hovering, See the cloud & fire appear
275	T,1	Eternal Ruler of the Ceaseless Round Of circling planets
275	1	round Of circling planets singing on their way
297	3	Lightens the dark that round us lies
299	3	O Spirit of the Lord, prepare All the round earth
299	3	prepare All the round earth her God to meet
325	1	And robe of sorrow round thee
343	1	But God is round about me, And can I be dismayed
366	2	hosts of evil round us Scorn thy Christ assail his ways
371	2	Who so beset him round With dismal stories
456	2	Love deepens round the hearth
482	1	See the fur to keep you warm, Snugly round your tiny form
485	1	and round me rings The music of the spheres
495	2	Every round goes higher, higher
579	2	Seed-time, harvest, cold, and heat shall their yearly round
579	2	Shall their yearly round complete

rove

229	3	Nor rove, nor seek the crooked way

roving

471	4	Patient and watchful when thy sheep are roving

royal

39	2	thy glance Let fall in royal radiance
95	1	Before him righteousness shall go, His royal harbinger
143	R	star of wonder, star of night, Star with royal beauty bright
155	2	Thou art the King of Israel, Thou David's royal son
185	3	With the royal feast of feasts, Comes its joy to render
195	1	Bring forth the royal diadem
200	1	A royal diadem adorns The mighty victor's brow

287	2	Here drink with thee the royal wine of heaven
326	2	angels sang Proclaiming thy royal degree
382	1	Christ the royal Master Leads against the foe
385	1	Lift high his royal banner, It must not suffer loss
404	3	Take my heart, it is thine own, It shall be thy royal throne
557	2	Here drink with thee the royal wine of heaven

rude
119	3	As they offered gifts most rare, At the manger rude and bare
249	3	Stilling the rude wills of men's wild behavior
429	3	O Holy Spirit, who didst brood Upon the chaos dark and rude

rugged
| 368 | 2 | But the steep and rugged pathway May we tread rejoicingly |

Ruh
| 139 | 1 | Schlaf in himmlischer Ruh |

ruined
| 74 | 3 | Soaring spire and ruined city ... our hopes & failures show |

rule
2	2	O Father, that thy rule is just And wise, and changes never
68	1	I sing the wisdom that ordained The sun to rule the day
103	4	By thine own eternal Spirit Rule in all our hearts alone
105	1	To take away transgression, And rule in equity
145	1	Rich in blessing, Rule and might o'er all possessing
246	3	Thou who almighty art, Now rule in every heart
275	1	Rule in our hearts, that we may ever be Guided
380	3	'Gainst lies and lusts & wrongs, Let courage rule our souls
392	3	Teach us to rule ourselves alway
439	2	For the open door to manhood, In a land the people rule

ruled
77	2	His voice who ruled them while he dwelt below
215	2	and, spite of fears, Pride ruled my will
395	4	The worlds of science and of art, Revealed and ruled by thee

ruler
2	2	'Tis well thou art our ruler
227	T,1	Fairest Lord Jesus, Ruler of all nature
275	T,1	Eternal Ruler of the Ceaseless Round Of circling planets
391	4	Still be my vision, O Ruler of all
433	2	Be thou our ruler, guardian, guide, and stay
445	T,1	Father Eternal, Ruler of Creation
485	3	though the wrong seems oft so strong, God is the ruler yet

rulers
| 436 | 1 | Our earthly rulers falter, Our people drift and die |

rules
130	3	He rules the world with truth and grace
204	3	His kingdom cannot fail, He rules o'er earth and heaven
206	1	His kingdom is glorious, he rules over all

rulest

7	2	Nor wanting, nor wasting, thou rulest in might

ruleth

206	2	God ruleth on high, almighty to save

run

32	1	Thy daily stage of duty run
42	4	Bid then farewell to sleep Rise up and run
70	3	He the golden-tressed sun Caused all day his course to run
124	1	Bring a torch, to the cradle run
169	4	He made the lame to run, He gave the blind their sight
202	1	sun Doth his successive journeys run
229	3	O let my feet ne'er run astray
257	4	Till through the world thy truth has run
263	4	One in might, and One in glory, While unending ages run
367	2	Run the straight race through God's good grace
486	1	Like a man of brawn Set his course to run
527	1	That I may run, rise, rest with thee

running

478	2	The purple-headed mountain, The river running by

rush

311	2	What rush of alleluias Fills all the earth and sky

rushing

64	2	Thou rushing wind that art so strong
73	3	Troubled torrent, madly rushing

rustling

485	2	In the rustling grass I hear him pass

Sabaoth

363	2	Lord Sabaoth his name, From age to age the same
559	3	Holy, holy, holy, Lord God of Sabaoth

sabbath

341	3	O sabbath rest by Galilee, O calm of hills above
409	3	Bless us in our daily labor, Lead us to our sabbath rest

sabbaths

310	1	Those endless sabbaths the blessed ones see

sacrament

286	1	In this our sacrament of bread and wine
403	2	Lo, the Bread of heaven is broken in the sacrament of life
409	2	Thou, the Bread of heaven, art broken In the sacrament
409	2	In the sacrament of life

sacred

9	1	Ye nations bow with sacred joy
26	3	In the sacred silence wait, As we seek to know his will
28	3	Through her shall every land proclaim the sacred might
28	3	proclaim The sacred might of Jesus' name
157	1,5	All the light of sacred story Gathers round its head sublime

saint

304	2	Till saint and martyr sped the venture bold
316	2	Shown thyself in saint and seer
322	2	As of old, Saint Andrew heart it By the Galilean lake

saints

1	2	Under the shadow of thy throne Thy saints have dwelt secure
3	2	Angels, saints, their voices blending
13	2	God hath made his saints victorious
19	1	Saints within his courts below
23	3	Ye saints who toil below, Adore your heavenly King
30	3	All saints triumphant raise the song, Alleluia
41	2	Bring us to heaven, where thy saints united Joy
65	2	Saints in light the strain prolong
76	2	While providence supports, Let saints securely dwell
81	4	Fear him, ye saints, and ... then Have nothing else to fear
87	2	Ye fearful saints, fresh courage take
117	4	Saints before the altar bending
203	T,1	Look, Ye Saints, the Sight Is Glorious
203	3	Saints and angels throng around him
223	3	By saints below and saints above
251	2	Holy, holy, holy, all the saints adore thee
253	2	Poets, prophets, scholars, saints
271	1	We seek thee as thy saints have sought in every generation
271	3	Ye saints to come, take up the strain
286	3	With all thy saints on earth and saints at rest
306	T,1	For All the Saints who from their labors rest
306	3	Fight as the saints who nobly fought of old
307	T,1	For All the Saints (same words as no. 306)
311	1	armies of the ransomed saints throng up the steeps of light
312	2	Thy saints are crowned with glory great
312	5	With blessed saints, whose harmony In every street doth ring
372	T,1	How Firm a Foundation, ye saints of the Lord
381	3	Of patient & courageous heart, As all true saints have been
382	2	Brothers, we are treading Where the saints have trod
388	3	Twelve valiant saints, their hope they knew
417	2	And the meekest of saints may find stern work to do
430	1	For thee the saints uplift their voice
471	1	For saints of old, who made their vows before thee
473	1	Just, King of saints, and true thy ways
481	T,1	I Sing a Song of the Saints of God
481	1	saints of God Patient and brave and true
481	1	They were all of them saints of God
481	1	saints ... and I mean, God helping, to be one too
481	3	The world is bright with the joyous saints
481	3	saints Who love to do Jesus' will
481	3	For the saints of God are just folk like me
559	12	Make them ... numbered with thy saints in glory everlasting

saith

104	1	Speak ye peace, thus saith our God
428	2	Thus saith the Lord, bold Moses said

sake

84	2	E'en for his own name's sake

150	1	take out mortal form for mortals' sake
169	1	O who am I, That for my sake My Lord should take Frail flesh
207	1	Who pain didst undergo for my poor sake
284	2	Thy body, broken for my sake, My bread from heaven shall be
322	2	Leaving all for his dear sake
330	3	And not unworthy for my sake A mortal body deem
392	+2	Land of our birth ... For whose dear sake our fathers died
401	3	Which with this tincture, For thy sake, Will not grow bright
425	2	Is true freedom but to break Fetters for our own dear sake
427	3	O let all the soul within you For the truth's sake go abroad
481	2	And they followed the right, for Jesus' sake

sale

436	2	From sale and profanation Of honor and the sword

salute

127	T,1	Christians, Awake, Salute the Happy Morn

salvation

13	2	Praise the God of our salvation
15	1	O my soul, praise him, for he is thy health and salvation
20	1	The God of power, the God of love, The God of our salvation
25	3	God is our strength and song, And his salvation ours
41	3	send us thy salvation
63	2	May the fruits of thy salvation In our hearts & lives abound
115	3	For thou art our salvation, Lord
140	3	The King of kings salvation brings
147	2	And by thy death was God's salvation wrought
168	T,1	Lord, Through This Holy Week of our salvation
168	1	salvation Which thou has won for us who went astray
169	2	He came from his blest throne, salvation to bestow
180	1	He who on the cross as Savior For the world's salvation bled
187	3	the pains which he endured ... Our salvation have procured
198	T,1	Christ Is the World's True Light, Its captain of salvation
206	2	Ascribing salvation to Jesus, our King
206	3	Salvation to God who sits on the throne
228	1	Visit us with thy salvation, Enter every trembling heart
228	4	Let us see thy great salvation Perfectly restored in thee
229	2	By thee the joyful news Of our salvation came
250	2	Who descended from his throne And for us salvation won
258	2	Word of consolation, Message of salvation
260	2	Her charter of salvation, One Lord, one faith, one birth
271	T,1	We Come Unto Our Father's God, Their Rock is our salvation
305	3	Blest river of salvation, Pursue thy onward way
311	3	Bring near thy great salvation, Thou Lamb for sinners slain
354	1	Our great and sure salvation
366	5	Let the search for thy salvation Be our glory evermore
373	T,1	God Is My Strong Salvation, What foe have I to fear
378	T,1	Lord of Our Life, and God of Our Salvation
379	T,1	Lord of Our Life, and God of Our Salvation (words of 378)
488	3	And God sent us salvation That blessed Christmas morn
491	4	May we be true to him, our Captain of salvation
528	3	Restore to me the joy of thy salvation
531	1	And grant us thy salvation
533	1	O Lord, show thy mercy upon us, and grant us thy salvation
562	1	let us heartily rejoice in the strength of our salvation

568	2	And hath raised up a mighty salvation for us
568	10	To give knowledge of salvation unto his people
572	2	For mine eyes have seen thy salvation
577	R	Creator of the earth and heaven, Thou bringer of salvation

salvation's

| 267 | 1 | With salvation's walls surrounded, Thou may'st smile |
| 318 | 3 | Cleanse it from guilt and wrong, Teach it salvation's song |

same

1	3	From everlasting thou art God, To endless years the same
14	1,3	Who was, and is, and is to be, For aye the same
16	2	Praise him, still the same forever
16	2	same forever, Slow to chide and swift to bless
122	2	And unto certain shepherds Brought tidings of the same
141	3	And by the light of that same star Three wise men came
264	1	Lord, thy Church is praying yet, A thousand years the same
271	3	The same sweet theme endeavor
271	3	Safe in the same dear dwelling place
271	3	Rich with the same eternal grace
271	3	Bless the same boundless Giver
308	4	Lord and light of every age, By thy same sure counsel led
312	6	see Thine endless joy, and of the same Partaker ever be
363	2	Lord Sabaoth his name, From age to age the same
472	5	O thou, who art the same Forevermore
480	1	Jesus saw The same bright sun that shines today
480	2	The same white moon, with silver face ... He used to see
480	3	The same great God that hears my prayers, Heard his

sanctified

| 157 | 4 | Bane and blessing, pain and pleasure ... are sanctified |
| 157 | 4 | pain and pleasure, By the cross are sanctified |

sanctify

| 47 | 1 | Thy praise shall sanctify our rest |
| 372 | 3 | And sanctify to thee thy deepest distress |

sanctifying

| 39 | 2 | The Spirit's sanctifying beam Upon our earthly senses stream |

sanctity

| 180 | 3 | Alleluia to the Spirit, Fount of love and sanctity |

sands

| 261 | 4 | In vain the surge's angry shock, In vain the drifting sands |
| 484 | 1 | In strange and lovely cities, Or roam the desert sands |

sang

117	1	Ye who sang creation's story Now proclaim Messiah's birth
155	2	To thee, before thy passion, They sang their hymns of praise
326	2	Heaven's arches rang when the angels sang
326	2	angels sang Proclaiming thy royal degree

sank

| 408 | 2 | I walked and sank not on the storm-vexed sea |
| 578 | 2 | I walked and sank not on the storm-vexed sea |

saps

453	3	Ring out the grief that saps the mind

sat

191	3	angel clad in white they see, Who sat & spake unto the three

Satan

118	1	The power of Satan breaking, Our peace eternal making
148	3	And if Satan, vexing sore, Flesh or spirit should assail
153	2	As thou with Satan didst contend, And didst the victory win

Satan's

122	1	To save us all from Satan's power When we were gone astray
122	3	free all those who trust in him From Satan's power and might
354	2	Though Satan's wrath beset our path

satisfies

317	1	It satisfies my longings As nothing else would do

satisfy

167	V-2	Satisfy thy loving will, Hear us, holy Jesus

save

59	4	We have no refuge ... Save thee, O Father
59	4	Save thee, O Father, who thine own hast made us
89	3	All, save the clouds of sin, are thine
99	5	We read thy power to bless and save
99	5	bless and save E'en in the darkness of the grave
122	1	To save us all from Satan's power When we were gone astray
125	3	Jesus Christ was born to save
125	3	Christ was born to save
136	1	Born on earth to save us, Him the Father gave us
136	4	Born on earth to save us, Peace and love he gave us
167	VI-2	Save us in our soul's distress, Be our help to cheer & bless
168	3	Which thou didst take to save our souls from loss
171	1	Where the dear Lord was crucified, Who died to save us all
177	2	Save in the death of Christ, my God
182	2	Dying once, ye all doth save
183	3	He who slumbered in the grave Is exalted now to save
199	3	And rose victorious in the strife For those he came to save
206	2	God ruleth on high, almighty to save
207	5	Our hope is in no other save in thee
235	1	On ... mind and soul, To strengthen, save, and make us whole
287	5	Another arm save thine to lean upon
289	2	Save it from evil, guard it still
302	2	Tell how he stooped to save his lost creation
316	3	Thou hast given thy Son to save us
333	3	Give us thy good, and save us from our evil, Infinite Spirit
358	2	All for sin could not atone, Thou must save and thou alone
366	5	Save us from weak resignation to the evils we deplore
378	2	Lord, thou canst save when sin itself assaileth
388	2	Who saw his Master in the sky, And called on him to save
391	1	Nought be all else to me save that thou art
398	1	Save us, thy people, from consuming passion
398	4	who by thy cross didst save us
398	4	save us From death and dark despair, from sin and guilt

419	3	One in the love that suffers long To seek, & serve & save
426	4	From ease and plenty save us, From pride of place absolve
429	T,1	Eternal Father, Strong to Save
436	3	Bind all our lives together, Smite us and save us all
439	4	God of justice, save the people From the war of race & creed
442	2	Show us ourselves and save us
452	T,1-4	Lord, Save Thy World
452	3	we strive in vain To save ourselves without thine aid
452	5	Then save us now, by Jesus' power
519	1	Save thy servant that hath none Help nor hope but thee alone
557	3	Another arm save thine to lean upon
559	13	O Lord, save thy people and bless thine heritage

saved
171	3	we might go at last to heaven, Saved by his precious blood
269	1	Church our blest Redeemer saved With his own precious blood
568	4	That we should be saved from our enemies

saves
| 195 | 3 | Hail him who saves you by his grace |

savest
| 290 | 2 | Thou savest those that on thee call |

saving
127	4	God's wondrous love in saving lost mankind
325	1	And mocked thy saving kingship then
354	3	Until we stand at thy right hand Through Jesus' saving merit
402	3	The sweetness of thy saving name
472	3	May all who seek this door, And saving grace implore

Savior
3	1	Him alone God we own, Him, our God and Savior
49	1	Our Savior Jesus Christ, Joyful in thine appearing
50	T,1	Sun of My Soul, Thou Savior Dear
55	3	A Savior Christ, our woes dispel
55	5	O Savior Christ, thou too art man
60	T,1	Savior, Again to Thy Dear Name we raise
63	3	when thy love shall call us, Savior, from the world away
113	1	O Christ, thou Savior of us all
114	1	The Savior of the world is here
122	1	Remember Christ, our Savior, Was born on Christmas Day
122	3	This day is born a Savior, Of a pure virgin bright
126	2	Maker, and Monarch, and Savior of all
127	1	morn Whereon the Savior of the world was born
127	2	This day is born a Savior, Christ the Lord
127	3	Here Son, the Savior, in a manger laid
130	2	Joy to the earth, the Savior reigns
131	2	To show God's love aright She bore to men a Savior
138	2	Heavenly hosts sing alleluia, Christ the Savior is born
146	3	The Savior, who is Christ the Lord
148	4	Keep, O keep us, Savior dear, Ever constant by thy side
166	2	Savior, for our pardon sue, When our sins thy pangs renew
170	2	Lo, here I fall, my Savior, 'Tis I deserve thy place
178	1	'Tis midnight, in the garden now The suffering Savior
178	1	The suffering Savior prays alone

178	4	That sweetly soothe the Savior's woe
203	3	Mocking thus the Savior's claim
240	3	Come, shed abroad a Savior's love, & that shall kindle ours
304	2	messengers ... Who bore the Savior's gospel of release
305	2	And seek the Savior's blessing, A nation in a day
388	4	Around the Savior's throne rejoice In robes of light arrayed
488	2	Rang out the angel chorus That hailed our Savior's birth

saw

38	3	Born of the one light Eden saw play
136	2	Bethlehem saw his birth
141	2	They looked up and saw a star Shining in the east
188	1	The Apostles saw their risen Lord
349	2	Where is the blessedness I knew When first I saw the Lord
388	2	Who saw his Master in the sky, And called on him to save
480	T,1	I Love to Think That Jesus Saw
480	1	Jesus saw The same bright sun that shines today

say

35	2	The night becomes as day, When from the heart we say
91	2	I of the Lord my God will say, He is my refuge and my stay
116	2	Say what may the tidings be Which inspire your heavenly song
121	1	joy I bring, Whereof I now will say and sing
125	1	Give ye heed to what we say, Jesus Christ is born today
126	3	Say, shall we yield him, in costly devotion
141	T,1	The First Nowell, the angel did say
182	1	Sons of men and angels say, Alleluia
184	2	Let all mankind rejoice and say
204	R	Rejoice, again I say, rejoice
213	3	May I hear thee say to me, Fear not, I will pilot thee
293	1	And to each servant does the Master say, Go work today
371	3	Then fancies, flee away, I'll fear not what men say
372	1	What more can he say than to you he hath said
468	1	we must not say that those are dead who pass away
496	1	O say can you see by the dawn's early light
496	1	O say does that star-spangled banner yet wave

sayest

| 213 | 2 | When thou sayest to them, Be still |

sayeth

| 112 | 1 | I am with you, still he sayeth |

saying

279	1	As thou biddest in thy saying
322	1	Saying, Christian, follow me
322	3	Saying, Christian, love me more
326	5	Let thy voice call me home, saying, Yet there is room

says

| 403 | 1 | Jesus says to those who seek him, I will never pass thee by |

scaffold

| 441 | 3 | Truth forever on the scaffold, Wrong forever on the throne |
| 441 | 3 | Yet that scaffold sways the future |

scan

55	5	Thy kind but searching glance can scan the very wounds
87	4	Blind unbelief is sure to err And scan his work in vain

scarcely

395	2	And scarcely can we turn aside For one brief hour of prayer
494	1	O'er crumbling walls their crosses scarcely lift

scarred

329	2	O Jesus, thou art knocking, And lo, that hand is scarred

scatter

43	3	Fill me, Radiancy divine, Scatter all my unbelief
460	T,1	We Plow the Fields and Scatter The good seed on the land

scattered

175	1	With palms and scattered garments strowed
289	2	As grain, once scattered on the hillsides
301	3	May her scattered children be From reproach of evil free
570	6	scattered the proud in the imagination of their hearts

scatters

193	2	Lovingly he greets thee, Scatters fear and gloom
462	2	All that spring with bounteous hand Scatters
462	2	Scatters o'er the smiling land
464	3	All that spring with bounteous hand Scatters
464	3	Scatters o'er the smiling land

scene

215	1	I do not ask to see The distant scene
558	2	Before the mournful scene began, He took the bread

scenes

36	4	Old friends, old scenes, will lovelier be
81	T,1	Through All the Changing Scenes of life
162	3	Hill of Calvary, I go To thy scenes of fear and woe
317	2	And when, in scenes of glory, I sing the new, new song
454	4	In scenes exalted or depressed, Thou art our joy & ... rest

scepter

229	4	Thy scepter and thy sword, Thy reigning grace I sing
247	1	All on earth thy scepter claim

schlaf

139	1	Schlaf in himmlischer Ruh

schlaft

139	1	Alles schlaft, eisam wacht

schlagt

139	3	Da uns schlagt die rettende Stund'

scholar

330	T,1	One Who Is All Unfit to Count As scholar in thy school

scholars
253	2	Poets, prophets, scholars, saints

school
330	T,1	One Who Is All Unfit to Count As scholar in thy school
439	2	For the home, the church, the school
481	3	You can meet them in school, or in lanes, or at sea

science
395	4	The worlds of science and of art, Revealed and ruled by thee
452	3	What skill and science slowly gain Is soon ... betrayed

scoff
164	2	While soldiers scoff and foes deride

scoffing
425	3	They are slaves who will not choose Hatred, scoffing & abuse

scorching
303	3	Beyond ... Wrong's bitter, cruel, scorching blight

scorn
170	1	With sore abuse and scorn
326	4	But with mocking scorn and with crown of thorn they bore
354	2	And worldly scorn assail us
366	2	hosts of evil round us Scorn thy Christ assail his ways
436	1	The walls of gold entomb us, The swords of scorn divide

scorned
308	3	Their own safety scorned to seek

scornfully
170	1	Now scornfully surrounded With thorns thy only crown

scorning
152	5	Let us arise, all meaner service scorning

scourged
150	4	Scourged, mocked, in purple robe arrayed

scrolls
253	2	Many diverse scrolls completing

sea
6	3	And round it hath cast, like a mantle, the sea
8	2	Flowery meadow, flashing sea ... call us to rejoice
14	2	law ... Deep writ upon the human heart, On sea, or land
35	5	Let air, and sea, and sky From depth to height reply
51	3	Guard the sailors tossing On the deep blue sea
52	T,1	Now on Land and Sea Descending
65	2	Earth and sea cry, God is good
67	T,1	God of Earth, the Sky, the Sea, Maker of all above, below
74	3	Made him fly with eagle pinion, Master over sea and land
75	T,1	Heaven and Earth, and Sea and Air
86	3	The line of lifted sea, Where spreading moonlight quivers
87	1	He plants his footsteps in the sea And rides upon the storm

searched
576 T,1 Lord, Thou Hast Searched Me and dost know Where'er I rest

searching
55 5 Thy kind but searching glance can scan the very wounds
324 T,1 O Thou to Whose All-Searching Sight

seas
68 1 spread the flowing seas abroad, And built the lofty skies
99 3 We read thee ... In the seas that swell & streams that flow
106 2 Isles of the southern seas, Deep in your coral caves
249 2 Through seas dry-shod, through weary wastes bewildering

season
197 3 Humbled for a season, To receive a name

seasons
112 3 Not for us ... to know the times and seasons
185 3 Now the queen of seasons, bright With the day of splendor
456 T,1 All Beautiful the March of Days, As seasons come and go

seat
95 5 Thou in thy everlasting seat Remainest God alone
119 2 So may we with willing feet Ever seek thy mercy seat
203 2 In the seat of power enthrone him
204 2 When he had purged our stains, he took his seat above
402 1 There they behold thy mercy-seat
570 7 He hath put down the mighty from their seat

seated
146 1 All seated on the ground

second
120 3 Born to raise the sons of earth ...to give them second birth

secret
46 4 in the spirit's secret cell May hymn & prayer forever dwell
91 1 found abode Within the secret place of God
214 1 The secret of the Lord is theirs
418 1 Tell me thy secret, help be bear The strain of toil
421 2 We've sought and found thee in the secret place

secrets
248 3 Thou to the meek and lowly Thy secrets dost unfold

sect
259 1 By notions of our day and sect, Crude, partial and confined

secure
1 2 Under the shadow of thy throne Thy saints have dwelt secure
26 4 Yea, his law is sure, In his light we walk secure
54 2 Thy gift of peace on earth secure
126 4 Vainly with gifts would his favor secure
248 3 I walk secure and blessed In every clime or coast
444 3 Bring justice to our land, That all may dwell secure

securely

61	1	With his sheep securely fold you
76	2	While providence supports, Let saints securely dwell
354	3	Our feet shall stand securely
377	4	Thou his people art, & surely He will fold his own securely

security

328	2	O trust in him, trust now in him, And have security

see

3	2	See the crowds the throne surrounding
7	4	All praise we would render, O help us to see
7	4	help us to see 'Tis only the splendor of light hideth thee
19	1	All that see and share his love
34	2	See how the giant sun soars up, Great lord of years and days
36	4	lovelier be, As more of heaven in each we see
43	2	Joyless is the day's return Till thy mercy's beams I see
49	2	Now, ere day fadeth quite, We see the evening light
55	2	What if thy form we cannot see
74	2	When we see thy lights of heaven
75	2	See the glorious orb of day Breaking through the clouds
75	3	See how he hath everywhere Made this earth so rich and fair
78	3	him thou canst not see, nor trace the working of his hands
82	4	in thy light our souls shall see The glories promised
86	4	And give us open eyes To see thee as thou art
97	1	In all the past ... our hopes & fears, Thy hand we see
104	3	all flesh shall see the token That his word is never broken
109	1	Traveler, o'er yon mountain's height See
109	1	See that glory-beaming star
109	2	Traveler, ages are its own, See it bursts o'er all the earth
111	1	And that future years shall see, Evermore and evermore
116	3	Come to Bethlehem and see Him whose birth the angels sing
120	2	Veiled in flesh the God-head see, Hail the incarnate Deity
124	2	Hush, hush, see how fast he slumbers
124	2	Hush, hush, see how fast he sleeps
124	3	Look and see how charming is Jesus
124	3	Hush, hush, see how the child is sleeping
124	3	Hush, hush, see how he smiles in dreams
127	3	ran To see the wonder God had wrought for man
134	T,1	O Little Town of Bethlehem, How still we see thee lie
142	2	But the very beasts could see that he all men surpasses
152	T,1	We Would See Jesus, Lo, His Star Is Shining
152	2	We would see Jesus, Mary's son most holy
152	3	We would see Jesus, on the mountain teaching
152	4	We would see Jesus, in his work of healing
152	5	We would see Jesus in the early morning
158	1	Your Redeemer's conflict see
158	2	See him at the judgment hall
158	2	See him meekly bearing all
160	2	Upon that cross of Jesus Mine eye at times can see
160	2	see The very dying form of one Who suffered there for me
162	2	See that suffering friendless one Weeping, praying ... alone
162	4	See his anguish ... faith, Love triumphant still in death
168	3	Let us go also, till we see thee pleading
168	4	Until thou see thy bitter travail's ending
175	3	Look down with sad and wondering eye To see

175	3	To see the approaching sacrifice
177	3	See, from his head, his hands, his feet, Sorrow and love
191	3	angel clad in white they see, Who sat & spake unto the three
192	2	Our hearts be pure from evil, That we may see aright
203	1	See the Man of Sorrows now
205	3	See, the heaven its Lord receives
208	T,1	Dear Master, In Whose Life I See
209	2	Change and decay in all around I see
214	T,1	Blest Are the Pure in Heart For they shall see our God
215	1	I do not ask to see The distant scene
215	2	I loved to choose and see my path, but now Lead thou me on
221	4	But when I see thee as thou art, I'll praise thee as I ought
224	4	We faintly hear, we dimly see, In differing phrase we pray
225	1	But sweeter far thy face to see, And in thy presence rest
228	4	Let us see thy great salvation Perfectly restored in thee
232	3	I see thy cross -- there teach my heart to cling
246	4	His sovereign majesty May we in glory see
251	3	Though the eye of sinful man thy glory may not see
252	4	Till, clouds and darkness ended, They see thee face to face
257	4	That see the light or feel the sun
267	2	See ... streams of living waters Springing from eternal love
267	3	Round each habitation hovering, See the cloud & fire appear
277	3	May we see our human family Free from sorrow and despair
286	4	Then open thou our eyes, that we may see
287	T,1	Here, O My Lord, I See Thee Face to Face
290	3	Glad when thy gracious smile we see
296	2	distant lands Shall see from far the glorious sight
297	4	faith like theirs Who served the days they could not see
303	3	We see the beckoning vision flame
305	2	See all the nations bending Before the God we love
310	1	Those endless sabbaths the blessed ones see
312	1	Thy joys, when shall I see
312	2	They see God face to face
312	6	Jerusalem, Jerusalem, God grant that I may see ... joy
312	6	see Thine endless joy, and of the same Partaker ever be
314	4	That when this life is past ... the eternal brightness see
314	4	I may the eternal brightness see, And share thy joy at last
316	3	That all men thy love may see
321	3	That I may see thy glorious face, And worship at thy throne
324	4	Savior, where'er thy steps I see ... I follow thee
331	2	That each departing day Henceforth may see Some work of lov◄
331	3	and when thy face I see, My ransomed soul shall be
336	3	Give, what thine eye delights to see, Truth
352	1	Here at thy feet none other may we see
357	5	For knowledge is of the things we see
358	4	See thee on thy judgment throne
364	T,1	Christian, Dost Thou See Them On the holy ground
367	4	Only believe, and thou shalt see That Christ is all in all
370	2	Content whatever lot I see, Since 'tis my God that leadeth
374	3	Grant that I may never Fail thy hand to see
382	1	Forward into battle, See his banners go
401	T,1	Teach Me, My God and King, In all things thee to see
406	3	Thee ... Whose eyes my inmost substance see
412	1	Who with the eyes of early youth Eternal things did see
412	2	And see like thee our noblest work Our Father's work to do
413	4	See the Christ-like host advancing

423	4	Yet long these multitudes to see The sweet compassion
426	2	I see my people falling In darkness and despair
430	2	Until thou see God's kingdom come
432	4	For faith, and will to win what faith shall see
449	3	Give us the peace of vision clear To see our brother's good
453	3	For those that here we see no more
468	4	That none might fear that world to see Where all are living
480	2	The same white moon, with silver face ... He used to see
480	2	He used to see in Galilee, And watch it with delight
482	1	See the fur to keep you warm, Snugly round your tiny form
494	2	O Master, lend us sight To see the towers gleaming
494	2	To see the towers gleaming in the light
496	1	O say can you see by the dawn's early light
505	1	And joy to see the cheerful light That riseth in the east
506	1	See thou render All thy feeble strength can pay
557	T,1	Here, O My Lord, I See Thee face to face

seed

112	2	Unobserved, and very near, Like the seed when no man knoweth
195	3	Ye seed of Israel's chosen race, Ye ransomed from the fall
297	2	And seed laid deep in sacred soil Yields harvests
298	4	Till God gives life to the seed
458	3	Praise him for his tiny seed, Holding all his world ... need
460	T,1	We Plow the Fields and Scatter The good seed on the land
570	9	as he promised to our forefathers, Abraham and his seed

seeing

| 53 | 2 | man, the marvel seeing, Forgets his selfish being |
| 445 | 4 | O give us brother love for better seeing Thy Word made flesh |

seek

3	3	in all, Great and small, Seek to do ... what thou lovest
3	3	Seek to do most nearly What thou lovest dearly
26	3	In the sacred silence wait, As we seek to know his will
45	2	Gather us who seek thy face To the fold of thy embrace
46	2	May struggling hearts that seek release Here find the rest
59	4	will not leave them lonely Who seek thee only
74	2	From thy ways so often turning, Yet thy love doth seek him
74	2	Yet thy love doth seek him still
117	3	Seek the great Desire of nations
119	2	So may we with willing feet Ever seek thy mercy seat
141	3	To seek for a king was their intent
144	3	Impels us on to seek thy face
154	1	sick to cure, the lost to seek, To raise up them that fall
162	1	When for deeper faith I seek
162	3	When for stronger faith I seek
191	2	their way To seek the tomb where Jesus lay
212	1	Now to seek and love and fear thee
214	4	Lord, we thy presence seek
225	3	How good to those who seek
229	3	Nor rove, nor seek the crooked way
232	3	O let me seek thee, and O let me find
239	T,1	Come Down, O Love divine, Seek thou this soul of mine
254	1	Beyond the sacred page I seek thee, Lord
271	1	We seek thee as thy saints have sought in every generation
290	2	To them that seek thee, thou art good

301	2	Seek the lost until she find
305	2	And seek the Savior's blessing, A nation in a day
308	3	Their own safety scorned to seek
325	3	From old unfaith our souls release To seek the kingdom
325	3	seek the kingdom of thy peace, By which alone we choose thee
327	2	Seek us when we go astray
327	3	Early let us seek thy favor, Early let us do thy will
333	2	Shepherd of souls who bringest all who seek thee To pastures
363	1	For still our ancient foe Doth seek to work us woe
367	2	Lift up thine eyes, and seek his face
392	5	Teach us the strength that cannot seek ... to hurt the weak
392	5	cannot seek By deed or thought, to hurt the weak
397	1	As thou hast sought, so let me seek Thy erring children
400	2	Now thee alone I seek, Give what is best
402	1	Where'er they seek thee, thou art found
403	1	Jesus says to those who seek him, I will never pass thee by
408	1	He moved my soul to seek him, seeking me
416	1	Seek the right, perform the true
419	3	One in the love that suffers long To seek, & serve & save
472	3	May all who seek this door, And saving grace implore
472	3	Love one another more As they seek thee
509	2	May struggling hearts that seek release Here find the rest
578	1	He moved my soul to seek him, seeking me

seekest
399	3	O Joy that seekest me through pain

seeking
74	4	'Tis thy will our hearts are seeking
150	3	By words and signs and actions, thus Still seeking
150	3	Still seeking not himself but us
313	2	Not with the hope of gaining aught, Not seeking a reward
408	1	He moved my soul to seek him, seeking me
578	1	He moved my soul to seek him, seeking me

seem
23	1	Assist our song, For else the theme Too high doth seem
23	1	Too high doth seem For mortal tongue
156	2	with longing expectation seem to wait The consecration
167	IV-2	When we vainly seem to pray, And our hope seems far away
317	2	Seem hungering and thirsting To hear it, like the rest
410	2	So shall the wide earth seem our Father's temple
493	4	that the stones of earthly shame A jewelled crown may seem
500	1	As in the dawn the shadows fly, We seem to find the now
500	1	We seem to find thee now more nigh

seemest
357	3	Thou seemest human and divine

seemly
4	3	Praise ... for it is seemly so to do

seems
109	3	For the morning seems to dawn
167	IV-2	When we vainly seem to pray, And our hope seems far away
167	IV-3	Though no Father seems to hear .. no light our spirits cheer

359	4	dares to take the side that seems Wrong to man's ... eye
359	4	seems Wrong to man's blindfold eye
485	3	Oh, let me ne'er forget That though the wrong seems oft
485	3	though the wrong seems oft so strong, God is the ruler yet

seen

15	2	Hast thou not seen How thy desires e'er have been Granted
24	1	No mortal eye hath seen, No mortal ear hath heard such
42	1	Beauty is seen again
117	3	Ye have seen his natal star
191	4	How blest are they who have not seen
192	3	Let all things seen and unseen Their notes of gladness blend
294	3	O God of righteousness and grace, Seen in the Christ thy Son
343	3	Green pastures are before me, Which yet I have not seen
357	1	Whom we, that have not seen thy face, By faith ... embrace
420	T,1	O Holy City, Seen of John
421	4	We've seen thy glory like a mantle spread O'er hill and dale
443	T,1	Mine Eyes Have Seen the Glory of the coming of the Lord
443	2	have seen him in the watchfires of a hundred circling camps
483	2	and that I might have seen his kind look when he said
557	1	Here would I touch and handle things unseen
572	2	For mine eyes have seen thy salvation

seer

| 316 | 2 | Shown thyself in saint and seer |

seers

| 424 | T,1 | Hail the Glorious Golden City, Pictured by the seers of old |
| 448 | 3 | Speed, speed the longed-for time Foretold by raptured seers |

sees

205	T,1	Hail the Day That Sees Him Rise
440	4	O beautiful for patriot dream That sees beyond the years
471	3	Till, from the shadows to thy presence reaching, He sees
471	3	He sees the glory that shall end our night

seest

| 374 | 1 | When thou seest me waver, With a look recall |

seize

| 420 | 4 | bids us seize the whole of life And build its glory there |

seized

| 146 | 2 | Fear not, said he, for mighty dread had seized |
| 146 | 2 | mighty dread Had seized their troubled mind |

self

58	2	Let not ease and self enthrall us
107	2	He will give to all the faithful His own self
107	2	His own self for heavenly food
160	3	My sinful self my only shame, My glory all the cross
242	2	Kindle every high desire, Perish self in thy pure fire
318	1	Raised my low self above, Won by thy deathless love
440	2	Confirm thy soul in self control, Thy liberty in law
440	3	Who more than self their country loved
466	3	Who teachest us to find The love from self set free

471   5   Be in his will, his strength for self denial

selfish
53	2	man, the marvel seeing, Forgets his selfish being
366	3	Shame our wanton, selfish gladness
413	3	Shame our selfish greed of gain
423	1	Above the noise of selfish strife
442	3	Though selfish, mean, & base we be, Thy justice is unbounded

selfishness
347	3	Let grace our selfishness expel, Our earthliness refine

semblance
374	2	Or, in darker semblance, Cross-crowned Calvary

send
23	4	Till life shall end, Whate'er he send, Be filled with praise
41	3	send us thy salvation
58	1	Slumber sweet thy mercy send us
59	2	Thine angels send us
129	4	the whole world send back the song Which now the angels sing
237	T,1	Send Down Thy Truth, O God, Too long the shadows frown
237	1	Thy truth, O Lord, send down
237	2	Send down thy Spirit free
237	2	Thy Spirit, O send down
237	3	Send down thy love, thy life, Our lesser lives to crown
237	3	Thy living love send down
237	4	Send down thy peace, O Lord
237	4	Thy peace, O God, send down
259	4	O Father, Son, and Spirit, send Us increase from above
271	2	We raise it high, we send it on, The song that never endeth
294	1	send us forth ... prophets true, To make all lands thine own
345	3	Send forth the hymns our fathers loved
374	3	Should thy mercy send me Sorrow, toil, or woe
386	1	Father, send thy light
386	1	send thy light To set our footsteps in the homeward way
412	3	O thou who didst the vision send And gives to each his task
426	1	Whom shall I send to succor My people in their need
426	1	Whom shall I send to loosen The bonds of shame and greed
426	2	Whom shall I send to shatter The fetters which they bear
426	3	Send us upon thine errand, Let us thy servants be
434	T,1	God Send Us Men Whose Aim 'Twill Be
434	2	God send us men alert and quick ... precepts to translate
434	3	God send us men of steadfast will, Patient, courageous
434	4	God send us men with hearts ablaze
452	4	but thou hast send The Savior whom we sorely need
521	1	Thy Spirit send with grace divine

sendest
351	3	All that thou sendest me In mercy given

sending
41	2	Banish our weakness, health and wholeness sending

sends
19	3	All that he for man hath done ... sends us through his Son

418	4	In hope that sends a shining ray Far down
459	1	He sends his showers of blessing down To cheer the plains
459	3	He sends his word and melts the snow
460	1	he sends the snow in winter, The warmth to swell the grain

sense

66	3	For the mystic harmony Linking sense to sound and sight
87	3	Judge not the Lord by feeble sense
212	2	All our knowledge, sense and sight Lie in deepest darkness
336	4	Give deep humility, the sense Of godly sorrow give
341	5	Let sense be dumb, let flesh retire

senses

| 39 | 2 | The Spirit's sanctifying beam Upon our earthly senses stream |

sent

83	2	whate'er thy Father's ... and all deserving love have sent
96	2	And take, content, What he hath sent
99	4	Sent by the Father from on high, Our life to live
144	1	'Tis sent to announce a new-born king
150	5	For us he sent his Spirit here To guide,
352	3	Till, sent from God, they mount to God again
411	2	Strong Son of God, whose work was his that sent thee
456	1	Hath sent the hoary frost of heaven
460	R	All good gifts around us Are sent from heaven above
488	3	And God sent us salvation That blessed Christmas morn
570	8	and the rich he hath sent empty away

sentence

| 443 | 2 | I can read his righteous sentence by the dim & flaring lamps |

sentinel

| 466 | 1 | With constant love as sentinel |

separate

| 245 | 4 | Separate from sin, I would Choose & cherish all things good |

seraph

| 107 | 4 | At his feet the six-winged seraph |
| 146 | 5 | spake the seraph, and forthwith Appeared a shining throng |

seraphim

18	2	Both cherubim and seraphim, Continually do cry
28	4	while cherubim reply to seraphim
30	2	O higher than the cherubim, More glorious than the seraphim
128	3	Cherubim and seraphim Thronged the air
247	2	Cherubim and seraphim In unceasing chorus praising
251	2	Cherubim and seraphim falling down before thee
559	2	To thee cherubim and seraphim continually do cry

seraphs

| 30 | 1 | Bright seraphs, cherubim and thrones, Raise the glad strain |

serene

| 42 | 1 | Gold and serene again Dawneth the day |
| 92 | 3 | Thy calmness bends serene above, My restlessness to still |

220	2	We follow where the Master leads, Serene and unafraid
261	3	How rise thy towers, serene & bright To meet the dawning day
309	2	The Prince is ever in them, The daylight is serene
349	5	So shall my walk be close with God, Calm and serene my frame

serenely

| 86 | 1 | Whose stars serenely burn Above this earth's confusion |

servant

147	3	Who wast a servant that we might be free
218	3	That where thou art in glory There shall thy servant be
293	1	And to each servant does the Master say, Go work today
401	4	A servant with this clause Makes drudgery divine
407	4	And let thy mercy bless Thy servant more and more
471	2	Here on thy servant in this solemn hour
519	1	Save thy servant that hath none Help nor hope but thee alone
568	2	in the house of his servant David
570	9	He, remembering his mercy, hath holpen his servant Israel
572	T,1	Lord, Now Lettest Thou Thy Servant Depart in peace

servant's

| 50 | 1 | no ... cloud arise To hide thee from thy servant's eyes |

servants

17	2	servants of the Triune God, Father and Son and Spirit laud
181	4	From death's dread sting thy servants free
206	T,1	Ye Servants of God, Your Master Proclaim
263	3	Here vouchsafe to all thy servants What they ask of thee
308	2	All thy servants tell thy praise
413	2	Freely may thy servants give
426	3	Send us upon thine errand, Let us thy servants be
559	11	we therefore pray thee, help thy servants
559	11	servants whom thou hast redeemed with thy precious blood
584	T,1	Ye Servants of God, Your Master Proclaim (206 with descant)

serve

4	1	Him serve with mirth, his praise forth tell
34	3	To serve right gloriously The God who gave all worlds
55	4	they who fain would serve thee best Are conscious most
55	4	who serve thee best .... Are conscious most of wrong within
56	3	Sleep that may me more vigorous make To serve my God
56	3	To serve my God when I awake
59	3	Let us serve thee, in all that we are doing
145	1	thou hast won My heart to serve thee solely
218	T,1	O Jesus, I Have Promised, To serve thee to the end
218	3	And, Jesus, I have promised, To serve thee to the end
228	3	Serve thee as thy hosts above
277	2	Love to serve them faithfully
300	1	Give heart and soul and mind and strength To serve
300	1	To serve the King of kings
322	5	Serve and love thee best of all
346	2	And strive to serve him well
385	2	Ye that are men now serve him Against unnumbered foes
407	2	Thy grace, O Father, give, That I may serve with fear
419	3	One in the love that suffers long To seek, & serve & save
430	1	His will obey, him serve aright

432	4	For hearts aflame to serve thy destined good
442	1	To serve thee by repentance
482	2	We will serve you all we can, Darling, darling little man
484	3	God bless the men and women Who serve him over-sea
495	4	If you love him, why not serve him
499	1	Who know his power, his grace who prove, Serve him
499	1	Serve him with awe, with reverence, love
565	1	serve the Lord with gladness
568	7	might serve him without fear

served

| 297 | 4 | faith like theirs Who served the days they could not see |
| 308 | 1 | All who served and fell on sleep |

serves

| 414 | 3 | Who serves my Father as a son Is surely kin to me |

service

26	4	In his will our peace we find, In his service, liberty
81	4	Make you his service your delight
152	4	Of God and man in loving service met
152	5	Let us arise, all meaner service scorning
292	3	In thine own service make us glad and free
293	3	No arm so weak but may do service here
316	2	May we offer for thy service All our wealth & all our days
321	4	Then life shall be thy service, Lord
341	1	In purer lives thy service find
383	1	Manifold the service, One the sure reward
405	4	Thus, in thy service, Lord, Till eventide Closes the day
411	2	One make us all, true comrades in thy service
411	4	Lord God, whose grace has called us to thy service
413	4	Liked in bonds of common service For the common Lord of all
414	2	His service is the golden cord Close-binding all mankind
418	1	In lowly paths of service free
421	T,1	We Thank Thee, Lord, Thy Paths of Service
448	2	The service glad and free Of truth and righteousness
491	4	Bearing his cross in service glad and free
502	1	Forever ready at thy service stand
508	1	Whose duteous service never slumbers

serving

83	2	whate'er thy Father's ... and all deserving love have sent
83	3	though undeserving, Thou yet shalt find it true for thee
163	4	Think on thy pity and thy love unswerving, Not my deserving
366	5	Grant us wisdom ... courage, Serving thee whom we adore
421	2	Beheld thee fairer yet while serving thee
421	3	Has held our hearts enthralled while serving thee
421	4	A splendor greater yet while serving thee
471	5	Serving the world, until through every trial

set

11	2	Till suns shall rise and set no more
34	2	So let the love of Jesus come And set thy soul ablaze
36	3	If on our daily course our mind Be set to hallow all we find
54	1	with us bide, Thou that canst never set in night
55	T,1	At Even, Ere the Sun Was Set

103	T,1	Come, Thou Long-Expected Jesus, Born to set thy people free
105	1	He comes to break oppression, to set the captive free
114	2	Make it a temple set apart From earthly use
114	2	set apart From earthly use for heaven's employ
152	4	At even-tide before the sun was set
228	2	Set our hearts at liberty
229	1	Too mean to set my Savior forth
247	3	from morn to set of sun Through the Church the song goes on
265	2	Lord, set thy churches free From foolish rivalry
265	2	Lord, set us free
292	2	lo, between our sins and their reward, We set the passion
292	2	We set the passion of thy Son, our Lord
298	3	To set their captives free
314	1	From earth-born passions set me free
324	1	O burst these bonds, and set it free
326	4	living word That should set thy people free
366	4	Set our feet on lofty places
366	4	In the fight to set men free
386	1	send thy light To set our footsteps in the homeward way
395	T,1	Behold Us, Lord, a Little Space From daily tasks set free
406	3	Thee may I set at my right hand
444	5	Let there be light again, and set Thy judgments in the earth
452	1	We wait thy liberating deed To signal hope and set us free
466	3	Who teachest us to find The love from self set free
468	1	From this our world of flesh set free, We know them living
484	3	God raise up more to help them To set the nations free
486	1	Like a man of brawn Set his course to run
494	2	upon the solid rock We set the dream that hardens into deed

sets

45	1	Wait and worship while the night sets her evening lamps
45	1	night Sets her evening lamps alight Through all the sky
115	4	Whose advent sets thy people free
409	3	Every task, however simple, Sets the soul that does it free
452	5	And use the lives thy love sets free

setting

112	1	On the dawn your hearts be setting
198	2	the whole round world complete, From sunrise to its setting
293	4	glad sound comes with the setting sun, Well done, well done

seven

| 164 | 3 | Seven times he spake, seven words of love |

sever

| 354 | 2 | Nor shades of death, nor hell beneath, Our souls ... sever |
| 354 | 2 | nor hell beneath, Our souls from thee shall sever |

severed

| 310 | 2 | Wish and fulfillment can severed be ne'er |

severing

| 262 | T,1 | Forgive, O Lord, Our Severing Ways |

shackles

| 410 | 3 | Then shall all shackles fall, the stormy clangor Of ... war |

shaft

91	5	No deadly shaft by day shall harm

shake

32	1	Shake off dull sloth
77	2	Thy hope, thy confidence let nothing shake
267	1	On the Rock of Ages founded, What can shake thy sure repose
372	5	That soul, though all hell should endeavor to shake

shaking

222	2	Though the earth be shaking, Every heart be quaking

shall

2	1	To us no harm shall now come nigh
2	1	And peace shall reign on earth again
4	4	His truth ... shall from age to age endure
9	3	What lasting honors shall we rear ... to thy name
9	4	earth, with her ten thousand tongues Shall fill thy courts
9	4	Shall fill thy courts with sounding praise
9	5	thy truth must stand When rolling years shall cease to move
11	2	Thy praise shall sound from shore to shore
11	2	Till suns shall rise and set no more
13	1	Laws which never shall be broken for their guidance
13	2	Never shall his promise fail
13	2	Sin and death shall not prevail
14	2	Established is his law, And changeless it shall stand
14	3	His love shall be our strength and stay, While ages roll
17	1	While o'er my life his strong arm he raises I shall sing
23	4	Let all thy days Till life shall end ... filled with praise
23	4	Till life shall end, Whate'er he send, Be filled with praise
24	1	Therefore with joy our song shall soar In praise to God
24	1	our song shall soar In praise to God forevermore
26	3	All our days, all our ways, shall our Father's love confess
26	4	For the Lord our God is kind, And his love shall constant be
26	4	Evermore, as of yore, Shall his changeless truth endure
28	3	Through her shall every land proclaim the sacred might
28	4	All nations to thy throne shall throng
29	3	For thus it was, is now, And shall be evermore
36	4	Some soft'ning gleam of love and prayer Shall dawn
36	4	Some soft'ning gleam ... Shall dawn on every cross and care
37	4	So shall it be at last, in that bright morning
37	4	Shall rise the glorious thought, I am with thee
42	4	Now shall you find at last Night's left behind at last
47	1	Thy praise shall sanctify our rest
47	5	So be it, Lord, thy throne shall never ... pass away
49	3	Thee ... The world doth glorify And shall exalt forever
53	3	when life's day is over Shall death's fair night discover
60	2	With thee began, with thee shall end the day
60	4	Then, when thy voice shall bid our conflict cease
63	3	when thy love shall call us, Savior, from the world away
63	3	Fear of death shall not appall us
76	2	hand which bears all nature up Shall guide his children well
77	2	All now mysterious shall be bright at last
77	3	hour is hastening on When we shall be forever with the Lord
77	3	All safe and blessed we shall meet at last
78	2	afraid his power shall fail When comes thy evil day

148	2	Shall not we thy sorrow share, And from earthly joys abstain
154	3	What shall we render to our God For all that he hath done
157	2	Never shall the cross forsake me
170	3	What language shall I borrow To thank thee, dearest friend
191	4	For they eternal life shall win
197	T,1	At the Name of Jesus Every knee shall bow
198	2	When Christ is throned as Lord, Men shall forsake their fear
199	4	Thy praise shall never, never fail Throughout eternity
201	T,1	The King Shall Come When Morning Dawns
201	4	brighter than that glorious morn Shall this fair morning be
201	4	Christ, our King, in beauty comes, And we his face shall see
201	5	The King shall come when morning dawns
202	T,1	Jesus Shall Reign Where'er the Sun
202	1	Till moons shall wax and wane no more
202	2	For him shall endless prayer be made
202	2	His name like sweet perfume shall rise With every morning
202	3	And infant voices shall proclaim their early blessings
203	1	Every knee to him shall bow
206	2	The great congregation his triumph shall sing
214	T,1	Blest Are the Pure in Heart For they shall see our God
218	1	I shall not fear the battle If thou art by my side
218	3	That where thou art in glory There shall thy servant be
233	4	So shall I never die
239	3	Shall far outpass the power of human telling
240	3	Come, shed abroad a Savior's love, & that shall kindle ours
242	4	Be my law, and I shall be Firmly bound, forever free
251	1	Early in the morning our song shall rise to thee
251	4	All thy works shall praise thy name in earth and sky and sea
254	2	Then shall all bondage cease, All fetters fall
254	2	And I shall find my peace, My all in all
255	3	The fear of God is undefiled And ever shall endure
257	4	Nor shall thy spreading gospel rest
259	2	And grow it shall, our glorious sun More fervid rays afford
260	3	And the great Church victorious Shall be the Church at rest
262	2	in time to be Shall one great temple rise to thee
262	3	A sweeter song shall then be heard
262	4	That song shall swell from shore to shore
264	4	A mountain that shall fill the earth
269	3	For her my tears shall fall, For her my prayers ascend
269	3	Till toils and cares shall end
269	5	Sure as thy truth shall last, To Zion shall be given
272	4	But we shall still be joined in heart
284	2	Thy body, broken for my sake, My bread from heaven shall be
294	2	Till greed and hate shall cease
296	2	distant lands Shall see from far the glorious sight
298	1,4	Nearer & nearer draws the time ... time that shall surely be
298	1,4	When the earth shall be filled with the glory of God
304	4	When o'er the strife of nations sounding clear Shall ring
304	4	Shall ring love's gracious song of victory
310	1	God shall be all, and in all ever blest
310	3	Safely the anthems of Zion shall sing
310	3	Thy blessed people shall evermore raise
312	T,1	Jerusalem, My Happy Home, When shall I come to thee
312	1	When shall my sorrows have an end
312	1	Thy joys, when shall I see
321	4	Then life shall be thy service, Lord

325	3	Shall we again refuse thee
326	5	When the heavens shall ring & the angels sing At thy coming
326	5	my heart shall rejoice, Lord Jesus, When thou comest
328	1	His comforts, they shall strengthen thee
328	1	And he shall for thy spirit be A fountain ever full
328	2	He shall be to thee like the sea
328	3	And he shall be to thee a rest When evening hours arrive
331	3	and when thy face I see, My ransomed soul shall be
336	5	We by thy Spirit, and thy Son, Shall pray, and pray aright
337	1	God shall lift up thy head
337	1	Wait thou his time, so shall this night Soon end
337	2	Far, far above thy thought His counsel shall appear
339	3	Christ doth call One and all, Ye who follow shall not fall
343	T,1	In Heavenly Love Abiding, No change my heart shall fear
343	2	Wherever he may guide me, No want shall turn me back
348	4	When death's cold, sullen stream Shall e'er me roll
349	5	So shall my walk be close with God, Calm and serene my frame
349	5	So purer light shall mark the road That leads me to the Lamb
351	5	Still all my song shall be, Nearer, my God, to thee
352	4	Still shall those hearts respond, with full accord
354	2	Thy strength shall never fail us
354	2	Thy rod and staff shall keep us safe, And guide our steps
354	2	nor hell beneath, Our souls from thee shall sever
354	3	In all the strife of mortal life Our feet shall stand
354	3	Our feet shall stand securely
354	3	Temptation's hour shall lose its power
356	T,1	Make Me a Captive, Lord, And then I shall be free
356	1	Force me to render up my sword, And I shall conqueror be
356	1	Imprison me within thine arms, And strong shall be my hand
356	2	Enslave it ... And deathless it shall reign
358	4	When mine eyes shall close in death
363	3	One little word shall fell him
364	4	But that toil shall make thee Some day all mine own
364	4	And the end of sorrow Shall be near my throne
365	3	Faith of our fathers, God's great power shall win
365	3	Shall will all nations unto thee
365	3	Mankind shall then indeed be free
367	1	Lay hold on life, & it shall be Thy joy and crown eternally
367	3	Trust, and thy trusting soul shall prove Christ is its life
368	1	Not for ease that prayer shall be
371	1	There's no discouragement Shall make him once relent
371	2	No foes shall stay his might, Though he with giants fight
371	3	We know we at the end Shall life inherit
372	3	The rivers of woe shall not thee overflow
372	4	When through fiery trials thy pathway shall lie
372	4	My grace, all-sufficient, shall be thy supply
372	4	The flame shall not hurt thee
373	4	His might thy heart shall strengthen
373	4	Mercy thy days shall lengthen, The Lord will give thee peace
375	1	Henceforth in fields of conquest Thy tents shall be our home
375	2	Lead on, O King eternal, Till sin's fierce war shall cease
375	2	And holiness shall whisper The sweet amen of peace
377	4	Zion, if thou die believing, Heaven's path shall open lie
380	4	Not long the conflict, soon The holy war shall cease
385	1	From victory unto victory His army shall he lead
385	4	To him that overcometh A crown of life shall be

385	4	He with the King of glory Shall reign eternally
390	2	O when shall I behold thy face, Thou majesty divine
395	6	Work shall be prayer, if all be wrought As thou wouldst
396	4	So shall no part of day or night From sacredness be free
399	3	And feel the promise is not vain that morn shall tearless be
399	4	from the ground ... blossoms red Life that shall endless be
400	2	This all my prayer shall be, More love, O Christ, to thee
400	3	Then shall my latest breath Whisper thy praise
400	3	This be the parting cry My heart shall raise
400	3	This still its prayer shall be, More Love, O Christ, to thee
404	3	Take my will, and make it thine, It shall be no longer mine
404	3	Take my heart, it is thine own, It shall be thy royal throne
410	2	So shall the wide earth seem our Father's temple
410	3	Then shall all shackles fall, the stormy clangor Of ... war
410	3	clangor Of wild war music o'er the earth shall cease
410	3	Love shall tread out the baleful fire of anger
414	2	In him shall true hearts ... Their high communion find
420	1	Within whose four-square walls shall come No night
420	1	And where the tears are wiped from eyes That shall not weep
420	1	That shall not weep again
423	6	Till sons of men shall learn thy love
423	6	Till glorious from thy heaven above Shall come the city
423	6	Shall come the city of our God
426	1	Whom shall I send to succor My people in their need
426	1	Whom shall I send to loosen The bonds of shame and greed
426	2	Whom shall I send to shatter The fetters which they bear
428	3	No more in bondage shall they toil
429	4	Thus evermore shall rise to thee Glad hymns of praise
430	2	Yea, love with thee shall make his home
430	3	He shall forgive thy sins untold
432	4	For faith, and will to win what faith shall see
438	2	Thy blessing came, and still its power Shall onward
438	4	And here thy name, O God of love ... children shall adore
438	4	thy name ... Their children's children shall adore
443	3	trumpet that shall never call retreat
445	3	Building proud towers which shall not reach to heaven
445	4	How shall we love thee, holy, hidden Being, If we love not
446	3	Falsehood and wrong shall not tarry beside thee
446	4	earth by thy chastening Yet shall ... be restored
446	4	Yet shall to freedom and truth be restored
447	3	Whom shall we trust but thee, O Lord
450	T,1	These Things Shall Be
450	1	a loftier race Than e'er the world hath known shall rise
450	1	race ... shall rise With flame of freedom in their souls
450	2	They shall be gentle, brave, and strong
450	3	Nation with nation, land with land, Inarmed shall live
450	3	Inarmed shall live as comrades free
450	3	In every heart and brain shall throb the pulse of one
450	4	There shall be no more sin, nor shame
450	4	For man shall be at one with God in bonds of firm necessity
451	3	Earth shall be fair, and all her people one
451	3	Nor till that hour shall God's whole will be done
451	3	Earth shall be fair, and all her folk be one
454	4	Thy goodness all our hopes shall raise
461	2	Then the full corn shall appear
461	3	For the Lord our God shall come And shall take his harvest

461	3	And shall take his harvest home
461	3	From his field shall in that day All offenses purge away
462	3	And for these our souls shall raise Grateful vows
464	2	Lord, for these, our souls shall raise Grateful vows
467	3	Nought shall affright us, on thy goodness leaning
467	4	Yet shall thou praise him, when these darkened furrows
469	3	Above the requiem, Dust to dust, Shall rise our psalm
469	3	Shall rise our psalm of grateful trust
471	3	He sees the glory that shall end our night
473	1	Who shall not reverence thee
473	2	For nations all shall worship thee
475	3	all peoples ... That shall adorn thy dwelling place
477	1	Thy Church shall stand as stands thy word
484	3	Shall understand his kingdom And come into his grace
491	2	Give us the valiant spirit that shall never Falter
491	4	When all its kingdoms shall his kingdom be
496	2	O thus be it ever when free men shall stand
496	2	And the star-spangled banner in triumph shall wave
498	1	But gives us strength while life shall last
500	2	Praise him through time, till time shall end
504	2	The highest heaven ... Shall give him nobler praise
508	1	Shall speak thy praises, Lord most high
511	1	As it was in the beginning, is now, and ever shall be
512	1	As it was in the beginning, is now, and ever shall be
512	1	As it was in the beginning, is now, and ever shall be
517	1	teach me ... the way ... And I shall keep it unto the end
534	1	And our mouth shall show forth thy praise
558	4	Do this, he cried, till time shall end
558	5	Till thou return and we shall eat The marriage supper
562	R	As it was in the beginning, is now, and ever shall be
565	R	As it was in the beginning, is now, and ever shall be
568	R	As it was in the beginning, is now, and ever shall be
570	3	For behold, from henceforth all generations shall call me
570	3	all generations shall call me blessed
579	2	Seed-time, harvest, cold, and heat shall their yearly round
579	2	Shall their yearly round complete

shalt

83	3	though undeserving, Thou yet shalt find it true for thee
91	4	Beneath his wings shalt thou confide
95	3	For thou art he who shalt by right The nations all possess
248	2	And in the coming glory Thou shalt be Sovereign Lord
251	2	thee Which wert and art and evermore shalt be
284	4	When thou shalt in thy kingdom come, Jesus, remember me
328	2	thou shalt surely feel His wind, that bloweth healthily
328	3	with his light thou shalt be blest, Therein to work and live
337	2	So shalt thou, wondering, own his way
354	3	For thou shalt guard us surely
367	4	Only believe, and thou shalt see That Christ is all in all
359	2	in the darkest battlefield Thou shalt know where to strike
390	3	Hope still, and thou shalt sing The praise of him
403	1	Raise the stone and thou shalt find me
419	3	When thou shalt be the God of all, And all be one in thee
430	2	Glad shalt thou be, with blessing crowned
430	2	With joy and peace thou shalt abound
559	11	We believe that thou shalt come to be our judge

| 568 | 9 | And thou, child, shalt be called the prophet of the Highest |
| 568 | 9 | shalt go before the face of the Lord to prepare his ways |

shame

55	5	The very wounds that shame would hide
60	2	Guard thou the lips from sin, the hearts from shame
99	4	To bear for us the cross of shame
158	2	Shun not suffering, shame, or loss
159	2	Till through our pity & our shame Love answers love's appeal
160	3	My sinful self my only shame, My glory all the cross
167	II-2	May we, in our guilt and shame Still thy love & mercy claim
170	1	With grief and shame weighed down
198	3	Cast out our pride and shame That hinder to enthrone thee
200	4	To them the cross, with all its shame ... is given
208	1	To shame and guide this life of mine
303	3	Beyond the present sin and shame
329	1	Shame on us, Christian brothers, His name and sign who bear
329	1	O shame, thrice shame upon us To keep his standing there
329	3	O Lord, with shame and sorrow We open now the door
330	2	Thou dwellest in unshadowed light, All sin and shame above
330	2	That thou shouldst bear our sin and shame, How can I tell
330	4	I cannot look upon his face For shame, for bitter shame
332	4	We with shame our sins would own
366	3	Shame our wanton, selfish gladness
413	3	Shame our selfish greed of gain
420	2	O shame to us who rest content While lust and greed for gain
426	1	Whom shall I send to loosen The bonds of shame and greed
442	1	Convict us now, if we rebel, Our nation judge, and shame it
450	4	There shall be no more sin, nor shame
491	2	To right the wrongs that shame this mortal life
493	4	that the stones of earthly shame A jewelled crown may seem

shamed

| 92 | 2 | Shamed by its failures or its fears, I sink beside the road |

shameful

| 150 | 4 | He bore the shameful cross and death |

shape

| 112 | 3 | witness Which can shape the world to fitness |

shaped

| 456 | 1 | The hand that shaped the rose hath wrought The ... snow |

shapest

| 412 | 2 | Who shapest man to God's own law, Thyself the fair design |

shard

| 431 | 5 | In reeking tube and iron shard |

share

19	1	All that see and share his love
148	2	Shall not we thy sorrow share, And from earthly joys abstain
159	4	That, as we share this hour, Thy cross may bring us ... joy
167	III-2	May we in thy sorrows share, And for thee all perils dare
198	2	To plough-share beat the sword, To pruning-hook the spear

238	4	Lead us to heaven that we may share Fulness of joy
272	3	We share each other's woes, Each other's burdens bear
293	2	Claim the high calling angels cannot share
295	3	With us the work to share, With us reproach to dare
303	2	As friends who share the Maker's plan
314	4	I may the eternal brightness see, And share thy joy at last
335	2	Who will all our sorrows share
341	3	Where Jesus knelt to share with thee The silence of eternity
347	2	Our brethren's grief to share
425	2	No, true freedom is to share All the chains
425	2	share All the chains our brothers wear
445	2	And sharing not our griefs, no joy can share
469	2	One providence alike they share
472	1	Our willing offerings brought This work to share
492	1	Whose joyous fellowship we share At work, at rest
526	1	O let thy children share thy blessing from on high

shared
230	1	Forever shared, forever whole, A never-ebbing sea

sharing
445	2	And sharing not our griefs, no joy can share

sharp
150	2	For us temptations sharp he knew
442	1	In each sharp crisis, Lord, appear
455	1	Through leafless boughs the sharp winds blow
455	3	And though abroad the sharp winds blow

sharpness
559	9	When thou hadst overcome the sharpness of death

shatter
426	2	Whom shall I send to shatter The fetters which they bear

shavings
422	5	Sweeping the shavings from his workshop floor

sheaves
464	2	Yellow sheaves of ripened grain

shed
2	4	For us the Savior's blood was shed
104	3	For the glory of the Lord Now o'er earth is shed abroad
164	2	Have we no tears to shed for him
240	3	Come, shed abroad a Savior's love, & that shall kindle ours
253	3	Light of knowledge, ever burning, Shed on us
253	3	Shed on us thy deathless learning
263	2	And thy fullest benediction Shed within its walls alway
282	1	Wine of the soul, in mercy shed
282	1	Look on the tears by sinners shed
290	4	Shed o'er the world thy holy light
319	1	But that thy blood was shed for me
387	2	light ... O'er his ransomed people shed
405	3	Some dews of mercy shed, Some wayward footsteps led
440	1	America, America, God shed his grace on thee

| 440 | 4 | America, America, God shed his grace on thee |
| 442 | 2 | Shed on our souls a blaze of light |

shedding

| 253 | 1 | Shedding light that none can measure |

sheds

| 89 | 2 | Sun of our life, thy quickening ray Sheds |
| 89 | 2 | Sheds on our path the glow of day |

sheen

| 309 | 2 | The pastures of the blessed Are decked in glorious sheen |

sheep

2	3	And the lost sheep dost gather
4	2	And for his sheep he doth us take
9	2	And when, like wandering sheep we strayed, He brought us
61	1	With his sheep securely fold you
141	1	In fields where they lay keeping their sheep
471	4	Patient and watchful when thy sheep are roving
562	7	we are the people of his pasture, and the sheep of his hand
565	2	we are his people and the sheep of his pasture

shelter

| 1 | 1 | Our shelter from the stormy blast, And our eternal home |

sheltering

| 112 | 2 | Like the sheltering tree that groweth, Comes the life |
| 469 | 2 | They rest within thy sheltering care |

shelters

| 15 | 2 | Shelters thee under his wings, yea, so gently sustaineth |

shepherd

79	T,1	The King of Love My Shepherd Is
79	6	Good Shepherd may I sing thy praise Within thy house forever
80	T,1	The King of Love My Shepherd Is (words the same as No. 79)
84	T,1	The Lord's My Shepherd, I'll not want
128	4	If I were a shepherd, I would bring a lamb
221	3	Jesus, my Savior, Shepherd, Friend
327	T,1	Savior, Like a Shepherd Lead Us
333	2	Shepherd of souls who bringest all who seek thee To pastures
333	2	Lead us, good Shepherd
343	2	My shepherd is beside me, And nothing can I lack
402	3	Great Shepherd of thy chosen few ... mercies here renew
471	4	Make him a shepherd, kind to young and old

shepherdess

| 481 | 1 | And one was a shepherdess on the green |

shepherds

116	2	Shepherds, why this jubilee, Why your joyous strains prolong
117	2	Shepherds in the fields abiding
118	1	Ye shepherds, shrink not with affright
122	2	And unto certain shepherds Brought tidings of the same
127	2	Then to the watchful shepherds it was told

shield

shine

shines

82	1	Thy goodness in full glory shines
97	2	With thee to bless, the darkness shines as light
117	2	God with man is now residing, Yonder shines the infant light
165	2	Lo, a more heavenly lamp shines here
227	3	And all the twinkling starry host, Jesus shines brighter
227	3	Jesus shines purer Than all the angels heaven can boast
252	1	A lantern to our footsteps, Shines on from age to age
257	1	In every star thy wisdom shines
407	T,1	O Light That Knew No Dawn, that shines to endless day
424	1	Everlasting light shines o'er it
480	1	Jesus saw The same bright sun that shines today
485	2	He shines in all that's fair

shinest
| 244 | 1 | Where thou shinest life from heaven There is given |
| 248 | 2 | Beyond our ken thou shinest, The everlasting Light |

shineth
134	1	Yet in thy dark streets shineth The everlasting Light
252	3	It shineth like a beacon Above the darkling world
324	1	The darkness shineth as the light
420	3	where the sun that shineth is God's grace for human good
576	5	The darkness shineth as the light

shining
43	3	More and more thyself display, Shining to the perfect day
52	3	Hope and ... Shining in the spirit's skies
72	1	blue ethereal sky And spangled heavens, a shining frame
108	3	Of one pearl each shining portal
126	2	Cold on his cradle the dew-drops are shining
141	2	They looked up and saw a star Shining in the east
141	2	Shining in the east, beyond them far
146	5	spake the seraph, and forthwith Appeared a shining throng
152	T,1	We Would See Jesus, Lo, His Star Is Shining
152	2	Shining revealed through every task most lowly
296	1	The sun that lights its shining folds
383	3	Move we on together to the shining goal
418	4	In hope that sends a shining ray Far down
424	2	All our joys and all our groans Help to rear its shining
424	2	Help to rear its shining ramparts
433	1	starry band Of shining worlds in splendor through the skies
440	1,4	And crown thy good with brotherhood From sea to shining sea
458	2	Praise him for his shining hours

shoal
| 213 | 1 | Hiding rock and treacherous shoal |

shock
| 261 | 4 | In vain the surge's angry shock, In vain the drifting sands |
| 477 | 1 | Nor fear the storm, nor dread the shock |

shocks
| 264 | 3 | Though earth-quake shocks are threatening her |

shod
| 249 | 2 | Through seas dry-shod, through weary wastes bewildering |

shone

146	1	The angel of the Lord came down, And glory shone around
178	1	The star is dimmed that lately shone
188	1	The sun shone out with fair array
412	1	boyhood faith That shone thy whole life through
488	1	Behold throughout the heavens There shone a holy light

shooting

422	2	Shooting out tongues of flame like leaping blood

shop

420	2	greed for gain In street and shop and tenement Wring gold
422	5	Sweeping the shavings from his workshop floor

shops

481	3	In church, or in trains, or in shops, or at tea

shore

11	2	Thy praise shall sound from shore to shore
19	2	Age to age and shore to shore ... praise him evermore
66	6	Offering up on every shore Her pure sacrifice of love
202	1	His kingdom stretch from shore to shore
213	3	When at last I near the shore And the fearful breakers roar
262	4	That song shall swell from shore to shore
294	1	No alien race, no foreign shore, No child unsought, unknown
310	2	Truly Jerusalem name we that shore
360	4	No harm from him can come to me On ocean or on shore
387	3	One the gladness of rejoicing On the far eternal shore

shores

106	4	Shores of the utmost West, Ye that have waited long
266	2	From oldest time, on farthest shores

short

1	4	Short as the watch that ends the night Before the rising sun
94	4	For, oh, eternity's too short To utter all thy praise
310	2	Nor the thing prayed for come short of the prayer
459	2	he bids the sun cut short his race, And wintry days appear
490	3	And let us not for one short hour An evil thought endure

should

16	1	Who, like me, his praise should sing
76	3	Why should this anxious load Press down your weary mind
101	2	We should take him at his word (102-4)
124	2	Lest your noise should waken Jesus
148	3	And if Satan, vexing sore, Flesh or spirit should assail
150	1	God, the Son of God, should take Our mortal form
169	1	O who am I, That for my sake My Lord should take Frail flesh
170	3	O make me thine forever, And should I fainting be
174	4	Lord, should fear & anguish roll Darkly o'er my sinful soul
177	2	Forbid it, Lord, that I should boast
197	1	'Tis the Father's pleasure We should call him Lord
302	1	One soul should perish, lost in shades of night
326	4	living word That should set thy people free
331	1	Nor should I aught withhold, Dear Lord, from thee
335	2	We should never be discouraged

347	4	Should friends misjudge, or foes defame
363	3	though this world ... Should threaten to undo us
365	2	If they, like them, should die for thee
372	5	That soul, though all hell should endeavor to shake
374	3	Should thy mercy send me Sorrow, toil, or woe
374	3	Or should pain attend me On my path below
413	4	thou who willest That thy people should be one
479	2	Help us to do the things we should
483	1	I should like to have been with him then
485	3	Why should my heart be sad
493	3	God, in sweet forgiveness' name, Should understand and spare
568	4	That we should be saved from our enemies

shoulder

79	3	on his shoulder gently laid, And home rejoicing brought me

shouldest

113	2	Till thou, Redeemer, shouldest free Thine own

shouldn't

481	2	not any reason ... Why I shouldn't be one too

shouldst

74	2	What is man that thou shouldst love him
215	2	nor prayed that thou Shouldst lead me on
330	2	That thou shouldst bear our sin and shame, How can I tell

shout

34	2	Shout with their shout of praise
106	5	Shout, while ye journey home, Songs be in every mouth
183	1	Hark, the angels shout for joy, Singing evermore on high
194	2	Then shout beneath the racing skies
309	3	The shout of them that triumph, The song of them that feast

shouting

431	2	The tumult and the shouting dies

shouts

181	2	Let shouts of holy joy outburst

show

19	T,1	Praise the Lord, His Glories Show
74	3	Soaring spire and ruined city ... our hopes & failures show
75	3	Hill & vale & fruited land, All things living show his hand
110	3	To us the path of knowledge show
110	3	knowledge show, And cause us in her ways to go
131	2	To show God's love aright She bore to men a Savior
169	1	Love to the loveless show, That they might lovely be
225	4	Ah, this Nor tongue nor pen can show
311	3	Show in the heavens thy promised sign
397	4	Thy love to tell, thy praise to show
405	2	Daily our lives would show Weakness made strong
412	3	with the task sufficient strength, Show us thy will, we ask
442	1	Forgive, and show our duty clear
442	2	Show us ourselves and save us
446	1	Show forth thy pity on high where thou reignest

531	1	O Lord, show thy mercy upon us
533	1	O Lord, show thy mercy upon us, and grant us thy salvation
534	1	And our mouth shall show forth thy praise
558	5	We show thy death, we sing thy name
562	2	and show ourselves glad in him with psalms

showed

| 253 | 2 | story Of the Word, and showed his glory |
| 570 | 6 | He hath showed strength with his arm |

shower

| 244 | 2 | Lord, thy graces on us shower |

showers

| 105 | 3 | He shall come down like showers Upon the fruitful earth |
| 459 | 1 | He sends his showers of blessing down To cheer the plains |

showeth

| 2 | 1 | God showeth his good-will to men |

showing

| 267 | 3 | For a glory and a covering, Showing that the Lord is near |
| 398 | 3 | Showing to wandering souls the path of light |

shown

167	IV-1	While no light from heaven is shown, Hear us, holy Jesus
316	2	Shown thyself in saint and seer
316	3	For the mercy thou hast shown
318	2	Through me thy truth be shown, Thy love made known

shows

| 454 | 1 | The opening year thy mercy shows |

shrine

31	3	truth ... love ... are the offerings to lay on his shrine
46	4	We cannot at the shrine remain
472	2	Come, thou, O Lord divine, Make this thy holy shrine
472	2	shrine Where thy pure light may shine, O hear our call
477	4	Accept, O God, this earthly shrine

shrines

| 297 | 1 | The shrines our fathers founded stand |

shrink

118	1	Ye shepherds, shrink not with affright
425	3	Rather than in silence shrink From the truth
425	3	shrink From the truth they needs must think

shrouded

| 212 | 2 | Lie in deepest darkness shrouded |

shrouds

| 386 | 2 | darkness ... Which shrouds the path of wisdom from our feet |

shun

158	2	Shun not suffering, shame, or loss
486	2	Simple wants provide, Evil let he shun

shut

580	2	Shut not that gate against me, Lord, But let me enter in

sick

50	4	Watch by the sick, enrich the poor with blessings
55	1	The sick, O Lord, around thee lay
55	3	For some are sick, and some are sad
154	1	sick to cure, the lost to seek, To raise up them that fall
295	1	Sinsick and sorrow-worn, Whom Christ doth heal

sicknesses

328	2	Thy sicknesses to heal

side

21	2	Thou, Lord, wast at our side, all glory be thine
77	T,1	Be Still, My Soul, the Lord is on thy side
93	3	Land me safe on Canaan's side
148	4	Keep, O keep us, Savior dear, Ever constant by thy side
164	1	O come ye to the Savior's side
199	2	Crown him the Lord of love, Behold his hands and side
218	1	I shall not fear the battle If thou art by my side
229	3	And through this desert land, Still keep me near thy side
268	2	God be praise for congregations Coming side by side to thee
326	5	There is room at my side for thee
358	1	Let the water & the blood, From thy riven side which flowed
363	2	Were not the right man on our side
359	4	dares to take the side that seems Wrong to man's ... eye
403	2	But the lonely worker also finds him ever at his side
423	5	O Master, from the mountain side, Make haste to heal
437	1	From every mountain side Let freedom ring
441	1	For the good or evil side
486	2	Jesus at my side Till the day is done
491	3	Oh, may we never from his side depart
493	2	No spokesman at his side
576	2	I feel thy power on every side

sideth

363	4	Through him who with us sideth

sifting

443	3	He is sifting out the hearts of men before his judgment seat

sigh

232	4	To check the rising doubt, the rebel sigh
417	1	All dreamers toss and sigh
417	2	Who would sit down and sigh for a lost age of gold

sighing

105	2	To give them songs for sighing, their darkness turn to light
143	4	Sorrowing, sighing, bleeding, dying

124	2	Silence, all, as you gather around
164	3	And all three hours his silence cried for mercy on the souls
173	2	O word of comfort, through the silence stealing
266	2	One unseen Presence she adores, With silence, or with psalm
341	3	Where Jesus knelt to share with thee The silence of eternity
341	3	The silence of eternity, Interpreted by love
425	3	Rather than in silence shrink From the truth
435	2	homesteads & the woodlands Plead in silence for their peace
437	3	Let rocks their silence break, The sound prolong

silent

7	2	Unresting, unhasting, and silent as light
47	3	The voice of prayer is never silent
65	3	Silent powers and angels' song ... All unto our God belong
75	2	Praise him through the silent night
111	2	Let no tongue on earth be silent
134	1	Above thy deep and dreamless sleep The silent stars go by
138	T,1-3	Silent Night, Holy Night
140	2	for sinners here The silent Word is pleading
174	1	None can tell what pangs unknown Hold thee silent and alone
174	2	Silent through those three dread hours
360	4	And so beside the silent sea I wait the muffled oar
381	1	I'll travel on, and still be stirred by silent thought
381	1	stirred By silent thought or social word
413	3	By thy patient years of toiling, By thy silent hours of pain
419	T,1	Thou God of All, Whose Spirit Moves From pole to silent pole
426	2	No field or mart is silent, No city street is dumb
432	3	from the breeds of earth thy silent sway Fashions the nation
456	1	And laid a silent loveliness On hill and wood and field
488	1	While shepherds kept their watching O'er silent flocks
488	1	O'er silent flocks by night
499	1	And silent bow before his face
505	T,1	You That Have Spent the Silent Night In sleep and quiet rest

silently

134	3	How silently, how silently The wondrous gift is given
156	2	And silently thy promised advent greet

silver

64	1	Thou silver moon with softer gleam
73	3	Silver fountain, clearly gushing
413	2	Thine the gold and thine the silver
475	3	The gold and silver, make them thine
480	2	The same white moon, with silver face ... He used to see

silvery

75	2	Moon and stars with silvery light Praise him

simple

101	2	If our love were but more simple (102-4)
152	3	The blessedness which simple trust has found
256	5	to its heavenly teaching turn With simple, child-like hearts
258	4	By the word imparted To the simple hearted
340	1	Such happy, simple fisher-folk, Before the Lord came down
341	2	In simple trust like theirs who heard, Beside the Syrian sea
392	6	Teach us delight in simple things And mirth

358	2	All for sin could not atone, Thou must save and thou alone
364	2	Striving, tempting, luring, Goading into sin
359	5	To doubt would be disloyalty, To falter would be sin
378	2	Lord, thou canst save when sin itself assaileth
398	4	save us From death and dark despair, from sin and guilt
407	2	From sin thy child in mercy free
407	3	That, cleansed from stain of sin, I may meet homage give
435	2	And the city's crowded clangor Cries aloud for sin to cease
450	4	There shall be no more sin, nor shame
461	4	Gather thou thy people in, Free from sorrow, free from sin
557	2	Here taste afresh the calm of sin forgiven
558	3	'This is my body, broke for sin
559	15	Vouchsafe, O Lord, to keep us this day without sin
580	2	A gate which opens wide to those That do lament their sin

sin's
119	3	So may we with holy joy Pure and free from sin's alloy
375	2	Lead on, O King eternal, Till sin's fierce war shall cease
447	2	Remember not our sin's dark stain

since
104	2	Bidding all men to repentance Since the kingdom now is here
163	4	Therefore, kind Jesus, since I cannot pay thee
215	3	faces smile Which I have loved long since, and lost awhile
249	1	blessed ... With light and life since Eden's dawning day
359	5	For right is right, since God is God
370	2	Content whatever lot I see, Since 'tis my God that leadeth
370	3	Since God through Jordan leadeth me
371	3	Since, Lord, thou dost defend Us with thy Spirit
568	3	which have been since the world began

sincerity
245	2	And with actions brotherly Speak my Lord's sincerity

sinew
427	3	Strike, let every nerve and sinew Tell on ages, tell for God

sinful
160	3	My sinful self my only shame, My glory all the cross
174	4	Lord, should fear & anguish roll Darkly o'er my sinful soul
251	3	Though the eye of sinful man thy glory may not see
332	2	Sinful thoughts & words unloving Rise against us one by one
394	2	Sinful, I commit myself to thee
447	1	The wrath of sinful man restrain
494	3	And all the pride of sinful will departs
580	1	Lamenting all their sinful lives, Before thy mercy gate

sing
4	1	Sing to the Lord with cheerful voice
6	1	O gratefully sing his power and his love
6	2	O tell of his might, O sing of his grace
8	2	Stars and angels sing around thee, Center of unbroken praise
16	1	Who, like me, his praise should sing
17	T,1	Praise Thou the Lord, O My Soul, Sing Praises
17	1	While o'er my life his strong arm he raises I shall sing
17	2	Sing, all ye nations, exalt the glory Of him whose arm

19	2	Tell his wonders, sing his worth
20	T,1	Sing Praise to God Who Reigns Above
20	3	Then all my gladsome way along, I sing aloud thy praises
21	1	Sing praises to his name, he forgets not his own
22	1	We bless thy holy name, glad praises we sing
23	3	And onward as ye go Some joyful anthem sing
23	4	And with a well-tuned heart Sing thou the songs of love
24	1	Let men with angels sing before thee
26	T,1	O Be Joyful in the Lord, Sing before him, all the earth
30	4	O friends, in gladness let us sing, Supernal anthems echoing
32	2	angels ... Who all night long, unwearied, sing
32	2	sing High praise to the eternal King
46	3	Give sweeter songs than lips can sing
64	1	Lift up your voice and with us sing Alleluia, Alleluia
64	4	Forgiving others, take your part, O sing ye, Alleluia
65	3	Stars that have no voice to sing Give ... glory to our King
68	T,1	I Sing the Mighty Power of God That made the mountains rise
68	1	I sing the wisdom that ordained The sun to rule the day
68	2	I sing the goodness of the Lord
69	1	Heaven & earth, awake & sing, God is good and therefore King
69	2	All who work & all who wait, Sing, The Lord is good & great
73	T,1	Angels Holy, High and Lowly, Sing the praises of the Lord
75	1	Wake, my soul, awake & sing, Now thy grateful praises bring
79	6	Good Shepherd may I sing thy praise Within thy house forever
83	3	Sing, pray, and keep his ways unswerving
106	1	Valley and lowland, sing
108	3	And men and angels sing before thee
108	3	Therefore will we, eternally, Sing hymns of joy and praise
111	2	Angel hosts, his praises sing
116	3	Come to Bethlehem and see Him whose birth the angels sing
120	T,1,R	Hark, The Herald Angels Sing, Glory to the new-born King
121	1	joy I bring, Whereof I now will say and sing
121	4	While angels sing with pious mirth
122	4	Now to the Lord sing praises, All you within this place
129	1	The world in solemn stillness lay To hear the angels sing
129	2	And ever o'er its Babel sounds The blessed angels sing
129	3	O rest beside the weary road, And hear the angels sing
130	1	And heaven and nature sing
132	2	Sing, choirs of angels, sing in exultation
132	2	Sing, all ye citizens of heaven above
134	2	And praises sing to God the King, And peace to men on earth
136	1	With the song children sing To the Lord, Christ our King
136	4	On this day angels sing
138	2	Heavenly hosts sing alleluia, Christ the Savior is born
140	R	Whom shepherds guard and angels sing
152	1	Above the stable while the angels sing
169	3	Sometimes they strew his way, And his sweet praises sing
169	5	Here might I stay and sing, No story so divine
180	1	Sing to God a hymn of gladness, Sing to God a hymn of praise
181	4	That we may live and sing to thee
182	1	Sing, ye heavens, and earth reply, Alleluia
184	T,1	Good Christian Men Rejoice and Sing
184	3	And sing with hearts uplifted high
184	4	And sing today with one accord
187	2	Hymns of praise then let us sing
187	3	Now above the sky he's King ... Where the angels ever sing

187	4	Sing we to our God above ... Praise eternal as his love
189	2	O, sing in exultation To Christ, your risen King
191	T,1	O Sons and Daughters, Let Us Sing
193	2	Let his church with gladness Hymns of triumph sing
194	1	The birds do sing on every bough
199	1	Awake, my soul, and sing Of him who died for thee
199	3	His glories now we sing Who died and rose on high
204	1	Rejoice, give thanks, and sing, And triumph evermore
206	2	The great congregation his triumph shall sing
219	2	Thee would I sing, thy truth is still the light
223	T,1	O for a Thousand Tongues to Sing My great Redeemer's praise
225	2	No voice can sing, no heart can frame
227	2	Jesus is purer, Who makes the woeful heart to sing
229	4	Thy scepter and thy sword, Thy reigning grace I sing
246	1	Help us thy name to sing, Help us to praise
247	4	And adoring bend the knee While we sing our praise to thee
268	1	With the cross our only standard Let us sing
268	1	Let us sing with one great voice
268	2	Many tongues of many nations Sing the greater unity
271	2	The Spirit who in them did sing To us his music lendeth
295	T,1-4	Christ for the World We Sing, The world to Christ we bring
310	3	Safely the anthems of Zion shall sing
312	5	There Magdalen hath left her moan And cheerfully doth sing
313	3	And in thy praise will sing
317	2	And when, in scenes of glory, I sing the new, new song
326	5	When the heavens shall ring & the angels sing At thy coming
326	5	angels sing At thy coming to victory
345	T,1	Rejoice, Ye Pure in Heart, Rejoice, give thanks and sing
345	R	Rejoice, rejoice, Rejoice, give thanks and sing
346	1	Our song of faith to sing
346	4	And grant us in thy love To sing the songs of victory
346	4	To sing the songs of victory With faithful souls above
382	4	This through countless ages Men and angels sing
390	3	Hope still, and thou shalt sing The praise of him
422	2	Sing of the boundless energy of God
437	1	Sweet land of liberty, Of thee I sing
454	T,1	Great God, We Sing That Mighty Hand
458	1	Hearts, bow down, & voices, sing Praises to the glorious One
458	6	Hearts, bow down and voices, sing Praise and love
463	T,1	Praise, O Praise Our God and King, Hymns of adoration sing
463	4	Glory to our bounteous King, Glory let creation sing
481	T,1	I Sing a Song of the Saints of God
487	2	Through him we are strong, Sing our harvest song
499	2	Him day and night The united choirs of angels sing
509	3	Give sweeter songs than lips can sing
521	2	Unseal our lips to sing thy praise
558	5	We show thy death, we sing thy name
562	T,1	O Come, Let Us Sing unto the Lord
577	R	to thee, the source of all our joy, To thee we sing
577	R	To thee we sing, O Lord most high

singers

476	3	The singers sweetly gifted

singeth

467	3	Low in the heart faith singeth still her song

singing

8	4	Ever singing march we onward, Victors in the midst of strife
38	1	Praise for the singing, Praise for the morning
41	1	Singing, we offer prayer and meditation, Thus we adore thee
72	3	Forever singing as they shine
72	3	singing ... The hand that made us is divine
73	4	Each blithe voice its free song singing
108	2	Zion hears the watchmen singing
116	T,1	Angels We Have Heard on High Sweetly singing o'er the plains
123	1	Christ is born, their choirs are singing
183	1	Hark, the angels shout for joy, Singing evermore on high
275	1	round Of circling planets singing on their way
387	1	Singing songs of expectation, Marching to the promised land
464	1	Singing thus through all our days
502	2	Thy people, Lord, are singing night and day

single

436	3	Lift up a living nation, A single sword to thee

sings

312	4	There Mary sings Magnificat With tune surpassing sweet
478	1	Each little flower that opens, Each little bird that sings
485	1	And to my listening ears, All nature sings

sink

92	2	Shamed by its failures or its fears, I sink beside the road
309	1	Beneath thy contemplation Sink heart and voice oppressed
356	1	I sink in life's alarms When by myself I stand
416	2	Hearts around thee sink with care

sinks

431	3	On dune and headland sinks the fire

sinner's

170	2	What thou, my Lord, hast suffered, Was all for sinner's gain

sinners

120	1	God and sinners reconciled
132	3	Child, for us sinners poor and in the manger
140	2	for sinners here The silent Word is pleading
187	2	Who endured the cross and grave ... Sinners to redeem & save
197	3	From the lips of sinners, Unto whom he came
203	3	Sinners in derision crowned him
282	1	Look on the tears by sinners shed
305	2	While sinners, now confessing, The gospel call obey
311	3	Bring near thy great salvation, Thou Lamb for sinners slain
315	4	Which calls us, very sinners, Unworthy though we be

sinning

228	2	Take away the love of sinning

sins

22	3	Our sins now confessing, we pray for thy blessing
32	3	Disperse my sins as morning dew
36	2	New perils past, new sins forgiven
103	1	From our fears and sins release us

104	1	Tell her that her sins I cover, And her warfare now is over
153	1	Teach us ... to mourn our sins, And close by thee to stay
159	2	Our sins, not thine, thou bearest, Lord
166	2	Savior, for our pardon sue, When our sins thy pangs renew
185	2	All the winter of our sins, Long and dark, is flying
229	2	The joyful news of sins forgiven
282	1	And in whose death our sins are dead
292	2	lo, between our sins and their reward, We set the passion
332	4	We with shame our sins would own
335	1	All our sins and griefs to bear
349	3	I hate the sins that made thee mourn And drove thee
430	3	He shall forgive thy sins untold
554	5	That takest away the sins of the world, have mercy upon us
554	6	that takest away the sins of the world, receive our prayer
555	T,1	O Lamb of God, that takest away the sins of the world
556	1	that takest away the sins of the world
568	10	by the remission of their sins

sinsick

| 295 | 1 | Sinsick and sorrow-worn, Whom Christ doth heal |

sister

| 66 | 4 | For the joy of human love, Brother, sister, parent, child |

sisterhood

| 308 | 1 | Brotherhood and sisterhood Of earth's age-long chivalry |

sisters

| 70 | 4 | moon to shine by night 'Mid her spangled sisters bright |

sit

104	1	Comfort those who sit in darkness
133	3	Jesu, tibi sit gloria
229	4	behold I sit In willing bonds before thy feet
417	2	Who would sit down and sigh for a lost age of gold
568	12	To give light to them that sit in darkness

sits

| 206 | 3 | Salvation to God who sits on the throne |

sittest

249	T,1	Ancient of Days, Who Sittest Throned in Glory
554	7	Thou that sittest at the right hand of God the Father
559	10	sittest at the right hand of God in the glory of the Father

sitting

| 312 | 4 | And all the virgins bear their part, Sitting about her feet |

six

| 107 | 4 | at his feet the six-winged seraph ... veiled their faces |

skies

11	T,1	From All That Dwell Below the Skies
12	T,1	From All That Dwell Below the Skies (No. 11 with alleluias)
35	T,1	When Morning Gilds the Skies, My heart awakening cries
43	T,1	Christ, Whose Glory Fills the Skies

52	3	Hope and ... Shining in the spirit's skies
66	T,1	For the Beauty of the Earth, For the beauty of the skies
68	1	spread the flowing seas abroad, And built the lofty skies
120	1	Joyful, all ye nations rise, Join the triumph of the skies
129	2	Still through the cloven skies they come
143	5	Alleluia, alleluia, Sounds through the earth and skies
182	4	Ours the cross, the grave, the skies
194	2	Then shout beneath the racing skies
205	1	Glorious to his native skies
209	5	Shine through the gloom, and point me to the skies
232	2	No angel visitant, no opening skies
297	3	Until the dawn lights up the skies
343	3	Bright skies will soon be o'er me
343	3	Bright skies ... Where the dark clouds have been
433	1	starry band Of shining worlds in splendor through the skies
440	T,1	O Beautiful for Spacious Skies, For amber waves of grain
455	3	And skies are chill, and frosts are keen
367	2	When fond hopes fail and skies are dark before us
485	1	I rest me in the thought Of rocks and trees, of skies & seas
486	2	Bright skies overhead, Gladness in my heart
467	2	When fond hopes fail and skies are dark before us

skill

296	4	Nor skill, nor might, nor merit ours
452	3	What skill and science slowly gain Is soon ... betrayed
476	4	Praise we the peaceful men of skill
476	4	men of skill Who builded homes of beauty

skilled

217	2	Whose strong hands were skilled at the plane and the lathe

sky

34	T,1	Awake, Awake to Love and Work, The lark is in the sky
35	5	Let air, and sea, and sky From depth to height reply
42	3	Suddenly breaks on earth Light from the sky
45	1	night Sets her evening lamps alight Through all the sky
47	4	Our brethren 'neath the western sky
51	1	Shadows of the evening Steal across the sky
67	T,1	God of Earth, the Sky, the Sea, Maker of all above, below
68	2	If I survey the ground I tread or gaze upon the sky
72	1	blue ethereal sky And spangled heavens, a shining frame
73	1	Earth and sky, all living nature ... praise
78	1	throne of him Who formed the earth and sky
99	3	wide-embracing, wondrous love, We read thee in the sky above
137	1	The stars in the sky looked down where he lay
137	2	I love thee, Lord Jesus, look down from the sky
152	3	While birds and flowers and sky above are preaching
175	3	The winged squadrons of the sky Look down
187	3	Now above the sky he's King ... Where the angels ever sing
192	1	From death to life eternal, From earth unto the sky
199	2	No angel in the sky Can fully bear that sight
201	2	like the sun That lights the morning sky
251	4	All thy works shall praise thy name in earth and sky and sea
252	1	O Truth unchanged, unchanging, O Light of our dark sky
256	2	Our guide & chart, wherein we read Of realms beyond the sky
293	4	No time for rest, till glows the western sky

311	2	What rush of alleluias Fills all the earth and sky
351	5	Or if on joyful wing Cleaving the sky
386	4	And daylight breaks across the morning sky
388	2	Who saw his Master in the sky, And called on him to save
417	T,1	The Day of the Lord Is at Hand, Its storms roll up the sky
451	3	Now, even now, once more from earth to sky Peals forth
453	T,1	Ring Out, Wild Bells, to the wild sky
459	1	And waters veil the sky
462	2	All the fruits in full supply Ripened 'neath the summer sky
478	2	The sunset, and the morning That brightens up the sky
480	2	moon ... That sails across the sky at night
486	1	Through the earth and sky God's great mercies flow
508	1	And evening steals o'er earth and sky
510	1	Shadows of the evening Steal across the sky

slain
165	3	And sin is slain, and death brings life
311	3	Bring near thy great salvation, Thou Lamb for sinners slain
481	2	And one was slain by a fierce wild beast

slander
453	4	The civic slander and the spite

slave
377	4	Though a tortured slave thou die
425	1	If there breathe on earth a slave, Are ye truly free & brave

slaves
425	1	Are ye not base slaves indeed, Slaves unworthy to be freed
425	3	They are slaves who fear to speak For the fallen & the weak
425	3	They are slaves who will not choose Hatred, scoffing & abuse
425	3	slaves who dare not be In the right with two or three

sleep
36	1	Through sleep and darkness safely brought
42	4	Bid then farewell to sleep Rise up and run
50	2	When the soft dews of kindly sleep
50	4	Be every mourner's sleep tonight Like infants' slumbers
56	2	That ... I, ere I sleep, at peace may be
56	3	And with sweet sleep mine eye-lids close
56	3	Sleep that may me more vigorous make To serve my God
59	3	Let our last thoughts be thine when sleep o'ertakes us
106	3	The sleep of ages break, And rise to liberty
134	1	Above thy deep and dreamless sleep The silent stars go by
134	2	While mortals sleep, the angels keep Their watch
138	1	Holy infant so tender and mild, Sleep in heavenly peace
185	2	And from three days' sleep in death As a sun hath risen
308	1	All who served and fell on sleep
377	2	Though untroubled still he sleep Who thy hope is on the deep
417	1	The nations sleep starving on heaps of gold
429	2	And calm amid its rage didst sleep
436	2	From sleep and from damnation, Deliver us, good Lord
451	2	Would man but wake from out his haunted sleep
468	3	Not wrapped in dreamless sleep profound
482	T,1	Little Jesus, Sweetly Sleep, do not stir
482	2	Mary's little baby, sleep, sweetly sleep

| 482 | 2 | Sleep in comfort, slumber deep, We will rock you |
| 505 | T,1 | You That Have Spent the Silent Night In sleep and quiet rest |

sleepeth

| 20 | 2 | By morning glow or evening shade His ... eye ne'er sleepeth |
| 20 | 2 | His watchful eye ne'er sleepeth |

sleeping

47	2	We thank thee that thy Church, unsleeping
124	2	It is wrong when the child is sleeping
124	3	Hush, hush, see how the child is sleeping
140	1	On Mary's lap is sleeping
217	4	Be there at our sleeping
391	1	Waking or sleeping, thy presence my light

sleepless

| 107 | 4 | Cherubim, with sleepless eye |

sleeply

| 142 | 2 | Cradled in a stall was he with sleeply cows and asses |

sleeps

| 85 | 2 | Behold, he that keeps Israel, He slumbers not, nor sleeps |
| 124 | 2 | Hush, hush, see how fast he sleeps |

slenderness

| 31 | 3 | Fear not to enter his courts in the slenderness of the poor |
| 31 | 3 | slenderness Of the poor wealth thou wouldst reckon as thine |

slide

| 85 | 2 | Thy foot he'll not let slide |

slighted

| 446 | 2 | earth hath forsaken Thy ways all holy, and slighted thy word |

slopes

| 421 | 1 | lead To blazoned heights and down the slopes of need |

sloth

| 32 | 1 | Shake off dull sloth |

slothful

| 144 | 3 | Let not our slothful hearts refuse The guidance of thy light |

slow

16	2	same forever, Slow to chide and swift to bless
95	T,1	The Lord Will Come and Not Be Slow
129	3	Who toil along the climbing way With painful steps and slow
418	2	Help me the slow of heart to move

slowly

| 452 | 3 | What skill and science slowly gain Is soon ... betrayed |

slum

| 426 | 2 | I hear my people crying In cot and mine and slum |

slumber

58	1	Slumber sweet thy mercy send us
85	2	nor will He slumber that thee keeps
126	2	Angels adore him, in slumber reclining
482	2	Sleep in comfort, slumber deep, We will rock you

slumbered

183	3	He who slumbered in the grave Is exalted now to save

slumbering

386	3	Till clearer light our slumbering souls awake

slumbers

50	4	Be every mourner's sleep tonight Like infants' slumbers
50	4	Like infants' slumbers, pure and light
85	2	Behold, he that keeps Israel, He slumbers not, nor sleeps
124	2	Hush, hush, see how fast he slumbers
508	1	Whose duteous service never slumbers

small

3	3	in all, Great and small, Seek to do ... what thou lovest
7	3	To all, life thou givest to both great and small
108	1	Hallelujah, Lo, great and small, We answer all
123	3	Here let all, Great and small, Kneel in awe and wonder
177	4	That were a present far too small
276	2	common home of ... great and small
341	5	O still, small voice of calm
396	2	Praise in each duty and each deed, However small or mean
413	4	host advancing, High and lowly, great and small
490	2	Not choosing what is great, Nor spurning what is small

smile

89	3	Our midnight is thy smile withdrawn
215	3	And with the morn those angels faces smile
215	3	faces smile Which I have loved long since, and lost awhile
267	1	With salvation's walls surrounded, Thou may'st smile
267	1	Thou may'st smile at all thy foes
290	3	Glad when thy gracious smile we see
410	1	Each smile a hymn, each kindly deed a prayer

smiled

480	1	It gave him light to do his work, And smiled upon his play

smiles

124	3	Hush, hush, see how he smiles in dreams

smiling

87	3	Behind a frowning providence He hides a smiling face
462	2	Scatters o'er the smiling land
464	3	Scatters o'er the smiling land

smite

61	4	Smite death's threatening wave before you
85	3	moon by night thee shall not smite, Nor yet the sun by day
364	1	Christian, up and smite them, Counting gain but loss
368	3	But would smite the living fountains From the rocks

428	2	If not I'll smite your first-born dead
436	3	Bind all our lives together, Smite us and save us all

smitten

160	2	And from my smitten heart with tears Two wonders I confess

smote

493	1	And on his lips a sword Wherewith he smote and overcame

snare

91	3	Preserve thee from the fowler's snare

snow

128	1	Snow had fallen, snow on snow
453	2	Ring, happy bells, across the snow
455	T,1	'Tis Winter Now, the Fallen Snow
455	1	snow Has left the heavens all coldly clear
456	1	The hand that shaped the rose hath wrought The ... snow
456	1	The crystal of the snow
458	5	Snow that falls on nature's breast
459	2	His hoary frost, his fleecy snow, Descend
459	3	He sends his word and melts the snow
460	1	he sends the snow in winter, The warmth to swell the grain
484	2	Some fish in mighty rivers, Some hunt across the snow

snowy

73	2	Peaks cloud-cleaving snowy crested

snugly

482	1	See the fur to keep you warm, Snugly round your tiny form

soar

24	1	Therefore with joy our song shall soar In praise to God
24	1	our song shall soar In praise to God forevermore
182	4	Soar we now where Christ has led
358	4	When I soar to worlds unknown

soared

73	2	Crag where eagle's pride hath soared

soaring

7	2	Thy justice like mountains high soaring above
74	3	Soaring spire and ruined city ... our hopes & failures show

soars

34	2	See how the giant sun soars up, Great lord of years and days

social

381	1	stirred By silent thought or social word

sod

326	3	But thy couch was the sod ... In the deserts of Galilee
340	4	peace of God, it is no peace, But strife closed in the sod
381	2	Whether beneath was flinty rock Or yielding grassy sod

soft
50	2	When the soft dews of kindly sleep
121	3	Make thee a bed, soft, undefiled Within my heart
123	2	Hark, a voice from yonder manger, Soft and sweet
460	1	The breezes and the sunshine, And soft, refreshing rain

soft'ning
36	4	Some soft'ning gleam of love and prayer Shall dawn
36	4	Some soft'ning gleam ... Shall dawn on every cross and care

softened
89	2	Star of our hope, thy softened light Cheers

softer
64	1	Thou silver moon with softer gleam

softly
124	3	Softly to the little stable, Softly for a moment come

Sohn
139	3	Gottes Sohn, o wie lacht

soil
297	2	And seed laid deep in sacred soil Yields harvests

soiled
231	3	Anoint and cheer our soiled face With ... thy grace
575	3	Anoint and cheer our soiled face with the abundance

solace
335	3	Thou wilt find a solace there
421	3	Abound with love and solace for the day
435	1	Solace all its wide dominion With the healing of thy wings
503	1	place, Filled with solace, light, and grace

soldier
481	2	And one was a soldier, and one was a priest

soldier's
381	1	My faith, it is a weapon stout, The soldier's trusty blade

soldiers
164	2	While soldiers scoff and foes deride
306	3	O may thy soldiers, faithful, true and bold Fight
382	T,1,R	Onward, Christian Soldiers, Marching as to war
384	T,1	Soldiers of Christ, Arise And put your armor on
385	T,1	Stand Up, Stand Up for Jesus, Ye soldiers of the cross
427	3	Sworn to be Christ's soldiers ever
495	1-4	Soldiers of the cross

sole
32	4	my powers, with all their might, In thy sole glory may unite

solely
145	1	thou hast won My heart to serve thee solely
212	1	Drawn from earth to love thee solely

313 3 love ... Solely because thou art my God, And my eternal King

solemn

37 2 The solemn hush of nature newly born
37 3 A fresh and solemn splendor still is given
55 6 Hear, in this solemn evening hour
72 3 What though, in solemn silence, all Move
108 1 Midnight's solemn hour is tolling
129 1 The world in solemn stillness lay To hear the angels sing
224 3 The solemn shadow of thy cross Is better than the sun
264 2 We hear within the solemn voice Of her unending song
269 4 Her sweet communion, solemn vows, Her hymns of love & praise
413 2 We but stewards of thy bounty, Held in solemn trust for thee
456 2 The solemn splendors of the night Burn brighter
462 3 Grateful vows and solemn praise
464 2 Grateful vows and solemn praise
470 1 Each age its solemn task may claim but once
471 2 Here on thy servant in this solemn hour
499 1 Let us adore And own how solemn is this place

solid

494 2 upon the solid rock We set the dream that hardens into deed

solitude

92 3 Thy presence fills my solitude

solve

149 3 know not how that Joseph's tomb Could solve death's mystery

some

23 3 And onward as ye go Some joyful anthem sing
36 4 Some soft'ning gleam of love and prayer Shall dawn
36 4 Some soft'ning gleam ... Shall dawn on every cross and care
51 4 Those who plan some evil, From their sin restrain
55 3 For some are sick, and some are sad
55 3 And some have never loved thee well
98 2 That in the darkest spot of earth Some love is found
331 1 Some offering bring thee now, Something for thee
331 2 That each departing day Henceforth may see Some work of love
331 2 Some work of love begun, Some deed of kindness done
331 2 Some wanderer sought and won, Something for thee
334 1 For we are weak, and need some deep revealing
364 4 But that toil shall make thee Some day all mine own
405 2 Some deeds of kindness done, Some souls by patience won
405 3 Some word of hope for hearts Burdened with fears
405 3 Some balm of peace for eyes Blinded with tears
405 3 Some dews of mercy shed, Some wayward footsteps led
418 2 move By some clear, winning word of love
421 2 But often in some far off Galilee Beheld thee fairer
434 1 aim ... Not to defend some ancient creed
441 1 Some great cause, God's new messiah
484 2 Some work in sultry forests Where apes swing to and fro
484 2 Some fish in mighty rivers, Some hunt across the snow

something

331 1 Some offering bring thee now, Something for thee

| 331 | 2 | Some wanderer sought and won, Something for thee |

310	4	Of whom, the Father, and in whom, the Son
316	3	Thou hast given thy Son to save us
326	3	O thou Son of God
336	5	We by thy Spirit, and thy Son, Shall pray, and pray aright
339	3	For the gift of Christ his Son
345	6	The Father, Son, and Holy Ghost, One God for evermore
357	T,1	Strong Son of God, Immortal Love
384	1	God supplies Through his eternal Son
388	T,1	The Son of God Goes Forth to War, A kingly crown to gain
391	2	Thou my great Father, I thy true son
411	1	Leads to the day of Jesus Christ thy Son
411	2	Strong Son of God, whose work was his that sent thee
413	T,1	Son of God, Eternal Savior, Source of life and truth & grace
413	1	Son of man, whose birth incarnate Hallows all our human race
414	3	Who serves my Father as a son Is surely kin to me
423	1	We hear thy voice, O Son of man
463	4	Glory to the Father, Son, And blest Spirit, Three in One
468	4	And bless thee for the love which gave Thy Son
468	4	gave Thy Son to fill a human grave
470	4	Anoint them with the Spirit of thy Son
511	1	Glory be to the Father, and to the Son and to the Holy Ghost
512	1	Glory be to the Father, and to the Son, & to the Holy Ghost
513	1	Glory be to the Father, and to the Son, & to the Holy Ghost
514	1	Praise Father, Son, and Holy Ghost
515	1	Praise Father, Son, and Holy Ghost
532	1	Son of God, we beseech thee to hear us
554	4	O Lord, the only begotten Son, Jesus Christ
554	4	O Lord God, Lamb of God, Son of the Father
558	1	arose Against the Son of God's delight
559	6	thine adorable, true and only Son
559	7	Thou art the everlasting Son of the Father
562	R	Glory be to the Father and to the Son and to the Holy Ghost
565	R	Glory be to the Father and to the Son and to the Holy Ghost
568	R	Glory be to the Father and to the Son and to the Holy Ghost
575	R	Praise to thy eternal merit, Father, Son and Holy Spirit
575	4	Teach us to know the Father, Son, And thee, of both to be

song

8	4	Joyful music leads us sunward, In the triumph song of life
20	3	That men may hear the grateful song My voice unwearied raises
23	1	Assist our song, For else the theme Too high doth seem
24	1	Therefore with joy our song shall soar In praise to God
24	1	our song shall soar In praise to God forevermore
25	3	God is our strength and song, And his salvation ours
28	4	nations ... raise on high the victory song
30	3	Ye holy twelve, ye martyrs strong ... raise the song
30	3	All saints triumphant raise the song, Alleluia
35	6	Be this the eternal song Through all the ages long
42	1	Black turns to gray, Bird-song the valley fills
65	2	Toiling pilgrims raise the song
65	3	Silent powers and angels' song ... All unto our God belong
69	2	Those to whom the arts belong Add their voices to the song
73	4	Each blithe voice its free song singing
76	4	I'll drop my burden at his feet, And bear a song away
94	4	Through all eternity to thee A joyful song I'll raise

106	4	Unvisited, unblest, Break forth to swelling song
108	2	And gladsome join the advent song
129	T,1	It Came Upon the Midnight Clear, that glorious song of old
129	4	the whole world send back the song Which now the angels sing
136	1	With the song children sing To the Lord, Christ our King
136	4	With their song earth shall ring
144	4	To God the Holy Ghost we raise An endless song
144	4	And endless song of thankful praise
146	5	angels ... who thus Addressed their joyful song
169	T,1	My Song Is Love Unknown, My Savior's love to me
178	4	'Tis midnight, and from heavenly plains Is borne the song
178	4	Is borne the song that angels know
181	1	The victory of life is won, The song of triumph has begun
184	2	Bring flowers of song to strew his way
192	3	Now let the heavens be joyful, Let earth her song begin
195	5	We'll join the everlasting song
202	3	Dwell on his love with sweetest song
236	4	Consecrating art and song, Holy book and pilgrim track
247	3	from morn to set of sun Through the Church the song goes on
251	1	Early in the morning our song shall rise to thee
261	2	One working band, one harvest song, One King omnipotent
262	3	A sweeter song shall then be heard
262	4	That song shall swell from shore to shore
264	2	We hear within the solemn voice Of her unending song
268	2	Sweet the psalm and sweet the carol When our song is raised
268	2	When our song is raised as one
271	2	Their song to us descendeth
271	2	His song in them, in us, is one
271	2	We raise it high, we send it on, The song that never endeth
271	3	Unbroken be the golden chain, Keep on the song forever
275	3	One with the joy that breaketh into song
287	3	This is the hour of banquet and of song
295	4	With joyful song
304	4	Shall ring love's gracious song of victory
306	5	Steals on the ear the distant triumph song
309	2	They stand, those halls of Zion, All jubilant with song
309	3	The shout of them that triumph, The song of them that feast
317	2	And when, in scenes of glory, I sing the new, new song
318	3	Cleanse it from guilt and wrong, Teach it salvation's song
345	3	Raise high your free, exulting song
346	1	Our song of faith to sing
351	1	Still all my song would be, Nearer, my God, to thee
351	5	Still all my song shall be, Nearer, my God, to thee
375	1	And now, O King eternal, We lift our battle song
382	4	Blend with ours your voices In the triumph song
385	4	This day the noise of battle, The next the victor's song
405	2	Toilsome and gloomy ways Brightened with song
437	3	And ring from all the trees Sweet freedom's song
438	2	Thou heard'st well pleased, the song, the prayer
457	2	For summer joy in field and wood We lift our song to him
461	1	Raise the song of harvest home
461	1	Come to God's own temple, come, Raise the song of harvest
462	1,3	Raise the song of harvest home
462	3	Come, then, thankful people, come, Raise the song of harvest
467	3	Low in the heart faith singeth still her song
481	T,1	I Sing a Song of the Saints of God

487	2	Through him we are strong, Sing our harvest song
500	2	Till psalm and song his name adore
502	2	O may we echo on the song afar
505	1	And pay a grateful song of praise To heaven's almighty King
565	1	and come before his presence with a song
579	T,1	Summer Ended, Harvest O'er, Lord, to thee our song we pour

songs

9	4	We'll crowd thy gates with thankful songs
22	3	And gladly our songs of true worship we raise
23	4	And with a well-tuned heart Sing thou the songs of love
46	3	Give sweeter songs than lips can sing
49	3	To thee of right belongs All praise of holy songs
65	1	Earth repeat the songs of heaven
93	3	songs of praises, I will ever give to thee
105	2	To give them songs for sighing, their darkness turn to light
106	5	Shout, while ye journey home, Songs be in every mouth
130	2	Let men their songs employ
184	3	Praise we in songs of victory That love
189	T,1	Lift Up Your Hearts, Ye People, In songs of glad accord
202	5	Angels descend with songs again
240	2	In vain we tune our formal songs, In vain we strive to rise
315	2	But morning brings us gladness, And songs the break of day
346	4	And grant us in thy love To sing the songs of victory
346	4	To sing the songs of victory With faithful souls above
387	1	Singing songs of expectation, Marching to the promised land
433	1	Our grateful songs before thy throne arise
459	T,1	With Songs and Honors Sounding Loud Address the Lord on high
459	3	With songs and honors sounding loud, Praise ye
509	3	Give sweeter songs than lips can sing

sons

1	5	Time, like an ever-rolling stream, Bears all its sons away
26	1	Sons of every land, Humbly now before him stand
74	4	Spirit in our spirit speaking, Make us sons of God indeed
82	3	The sons of Adam in distress Fly to the shadow of thy wing
106	3	Lands of the East, awake, Soon shall your sons be free
120	3	Born to raise the sons of earth ...to give them second birth
126	T,1,5	Brightest and Best of the Sons of the Morning
165	3	And sons of earth hold heaven in fee
182	1	Sons of men and angels say, Alleluia
185	1	Loosed from Pharaoh's bitter yoke Jacob's sons and daughters
191	T,1	O Sons and Daughters, Let Us Sing
202	4	The weary find eternal rest & all the sons of want are blest
219	T,1	O Thou Great Friend to all the sons of men
267	2	Well supply thy sons and daughters
302	3	Give of thy sons to bear the message glorious
303	2	As sons who know the Father's will
305	1	The sons of earth are waking To penitential tears
380	2	The sons of fathers we By whom our faith is taught
422	1	Patiently powerful for the sons of men
423	6	Till sons of men shall learn thy love
470	T,1	God of the Prophets, bless the prophets' sons

soon

| 52 | 2 | Soon as dies the sunset glory, Stars of heaven shine out |

72	2	Soon as the evening shades prevail The moon takes up .. tale
106	3	Lands of the East, awake, Soon shall your sons be free
287	4	Too soon we rise, the symbols disappear
337	1	Wait thou his time, so shall this night Soon end
337	1	Soon end in joyous day
343	3	Bright skies will soon be o'er me
377	1	Soon again his arms will fold thee To his loving heart
380	4	Not long the conflict, soon The holy war shall cease
452	3	What skill and science slowly gain Is soon ... betrayed
452	3	Is soon to evil ends betrayed
472	5	Lord, though these hours of praise ... soon be o'er
472	5	though ... all our earthly days Will soon be o'er

soothe
178	4	Unheard by mortals are the strains That sweetly soothe
178	4	That sweetly soothe the Savior's woe

soothes
221	1	It soothes his sorrows, heals his wounds

sordid
374	2	Or its sordid treasures Spread to work me harm

sore
148	3	And if Satan, vexing sore, Flesh or spirit should assail
150	2	for us he bore His holy fast, and hungered sore
168	1	In all the conflict of thy sore temptation
170	1	With sore abuse and scorn

sorely
452	4	but thou hast send The Savior whom we sorely need

sorest
417	1	When the pain is sorest the child is born

sorrow
60	4	Our balm in sorrow, and our stay in strife
64	4	Ye who long pain and sorrow bear, Praise God
77	3	Sorrow forgot, love's purest joys restored
92	1	mightier far than sin and pain and sorrow are
96	3	Though sorrow, need, or death be mine, Yet am I not forsaken
148	2	Shall not we thy sorrow share, And from earthly joys abstain
159	1	Is this thy sorrow naught to us Who pass unheeding by
159	2	Make us thy sorrow feel
163	3	For me ... thy mortal sorrow, and thy life's oblation
170	3	For this thy dying sorrow, Thy pity without end
177	3	See, from his head, his hands, his feet, Sorrow and love
177	3	Sorrow and love flow mingled down
177	3	Did e'er such love and sorrow meet
277	3	May we see our human family Free from sorrow and despair
282	1	Look on the heart by sorrow broken
298	3	Fight we the fight with sorrow and sin
325	1	And robe of sorrow round thee
329	3	O Lord, with shame and sorrow We open now the door
334	2	Lord, we have wandered forth through doubt and sorrow
336	4	Give deep humility, the sense Of godly sorrow give

318	T,1	Draw Thou My Soul, O Christ, Closer to thine
318	2	Lead forth my soul, O Christ, One with thine own
331	1	In love my soul would bow, My heart fulfill its vow
331	3	and when thy face I see, My ransomed soul shall be
331	3	My ransomed soul ... Through all eternity Offered to thee
332	3	Lips that, while thy praises sounding, Lifted not the soul
332	3	Lifted not the soul to thee
339	2	His desire our soul delighteth
348	4	Oh, bear me safe above, a ransomed soul
354	3	O God, renew with heavenly dew Our body, soul and spirit
357	6	That mind and soul, according well, May make one music
361	3	Have faith in God, my soul, His cross forever stands
361	4	Until I rest, heart, mind and soul, The captive of thy grace
362	T,1	Awake, My Soul, Stretch Every nerve
366	3	Rich in things and poor in soul
367	3	Trust, and thy trusting soul shall prove Christ is its life
373	3	Place on the Lord reliance, My soul, with courage wait
372	5	The soul that on Jesus hath leaned for repose
372	5	That soul, though all hell should endeavor to shake
380	T,1	March on, O Soul, With Strength
380	3	March on, O soul, with strength, As strong the battle rolls
380	4	March on, O soul, march on with strength
384	3	Leave no unguarded place, No weakness of the soul
390	1	So longs my soul, O God, for thee, And thy refreshing grace
390	2	For thee, my God, the living God, My thirsty soul doth pine
390	3	Why restless, why cast down, my soul
399	1	I rest my weary soul in thee
408	1	He moved my soul to seek him, seeking me
408	3	For thou wert long beforehand with my soul
409	3	Every task, however simple, Sets the soul that does it free
411	3	Rest for the soul, and strength for all man's striving
427	3	O let all the soul within you For the truth's sake go abroad
440	2	Confirm thy soul in self control, Thy liberty in law
443	3	O be swift, my soul, to answer him, be jubilant, my feet
493	4	And in my soul a dream
503	1	Where my soul in joyful duty Waits for him who answers
506	T,1	Come, My Soul, Thou Must Be Waking
570	T,1	My Soul Doth Magnify the Lord
578	1	He moved my soul to seek him, seeking me
578	3	For thou wert long before-hand with my soul
579	3	Have mercy, now, upon my soul, Hear this my humble prayer

soul's

167	VI-2	Save us in our soul's distress, Be our help to cheer & bless
227	1	Thee will I honor, Thou, my soul's glory, joy and crown

souls

2	4	Do thou our troubled souls uplift Against the foe prevailing
9	3	We are his ... Our souls, and all our mortal frame
23	2	Ye blessed souls at rest, Who ran this earthly race
30	3	Respond, ye souls in endless rest
33	2	Strength unto our souls afford From thy living Bread, O Lord
82	4	in thy light our souls shall see The glories promised
86	2	Till truth from falsehood part, Our souls can find no rest
105	2	Whose souls, condemned and dying, Were precious in his sight
119	4	Bring our ransomed souls at last Where they need no star

66	3	For the mystic harmony Linking sense to sound and sight
72	3	What though no real voice nor sound ... be found
72	3	no real voice nor sound Amidst their radiant orbs be found
225	2	Nor can the memory find A sweeter sound than thy blest name
293	4	glad sound comes with the setting sun, Well done, well done
299	2	Whene'er thy joyful sound is heard
437	3	Let rocks their silence break, The sound prolong

sounded

443	3	He has sounded forth the trumpet

soundeth

322	1	Day by day his sweet voice soundeth
427	1	Hark, what soundeth is creation's Groaning

sounding

9	4	Shall fill thy courts with sounding praise
130	2	Repeat the sounding joy
304	4	When o'er the strife of nations sounding clear Shall ring
332	3	Lips that, while thy praises sounding, Lifted not the soul
459	T,1	With Songs and Honors Sounding Loud Address the Lord on high
459	3	With songs and honors sounding loud, Praise ye

soundless

42	2	Soundless and bright for us Breaketh God's morn

sounds

129	2	And ever o'er its Babel sounds The blessed angels sing
143	5	Alleluia, alleluia, Sounds through the earth and skies
221	T,1	How Sweet the Name of Jesus Sounds In a believer's ear
423	1	Where sounds the cries of race and clan Above the noise
456	2	And clearer sounds the angel hymn, Good will to men on earth

source

111	1	He is Alpha and Omega, He the source, the ending he
222	T,1	Jesus, Priceless Treasure, Source of purest pleasure
244	2	O mighty Rock, O Source of life
308	1	Source & giver of all good, Lord, we praise, we worship thee
413	T,1	Son of God, Eternal Savior, Source of life and truth & grace
462	3	Source whence all our blessings flow
464	1	Bounteous source of every joy
464	3	Source whence all our blessings flow
577	R	to thee, the source of all our joy, To thee we sing

south

106	5	Lo, from the North we come, From East, and West, and South
414	T,1	In Christ There Is No East or West, In him no South or North
414	4	In him meet South and North

southern

69	3	From the north to southern pole Let the mighty chorus roll
106	2	Isles of the southern seas, Deep in your coral caves

sovereign

9	2	His sovereign power without our aid Made us of clay
114	4	So come, my Sovereign, enter in

213	2	Wondrous Sovereign of the Sea, Jesus, Savior, pilot me
246	4	His sovereign majesty May we in glory see
248	2	And in the coming glory Thou shalt be Sovereign Lord
337	2	Leave to this sovereign sway To choose and to command
444	4	Bring to our world of strife Thy sovereign word of peace
459	3	Praise ye the sovereign Lord

sovereignty

| 421 | 3 | And, 'neath the burdens there, thy sovereignty Has held |

sow

| 487 | 2 | He makes green things grow, Ripens what we sow |

sown

| 461 | 2 | Wheat and tares together sown, Unto joy or sorrow grown |

space

6	2	Whose robe is the light, whose canopy space
16	4	Sun and moon ... Dwellers in all time and space
395	T,1	Behold Us, Lord, a Little Space From daily tasks set free

spacious

| 72 | T,1 | The Spacious Firmament on High |
| 440 | T,1 | O Beautiful for Spacious Skies, For amber waves of grain |

spake

146	5	spake the seraph, and forthwith Appeared a shining throng
164	3	Seven times he spake, seven words of love
191	3	angel clad in white they see, Who sat & spake unto the three
426	1	As once he spake in Zion, So now he speaks again
558	2	What wondrous words of love he spake
568	3	As he spake by the mouth of his holy prophets

spangled

70	4	moon to shine by night 'Mid her spangled sisters bright
72	1	blue ethereal sky And spangled heavens, a shining frame
496	1	O say does that star-spangled banner yet wave
496	2	And the star-spangled banner in triumph shall wave

spare

431	3	Judge of the nations, spare us yet, Lest we forget
493	3	prayer That God, in sweet forgiveness' name ... spare
532	1	Spare us, good Lord.
580	3	For mercy, Lord, is all my suit, O let thy mercy spare

spares

| 16 | 3 | Father-like he tends and spares us |

sparkling

| 311 | T,1 | Ten Thousand Times Ten Thousand, In sparkling raiment bright |
| 456 | 2 | O'er white expanses sparkling pure The radiant morns unfold |

speak

104	1	Speak ye peace, thus saith our God
104	1	Speak ye to Jerusalem Of the peace that waits for them
218	2	O speak to reassure me, To hasten or control

218	2	O speak, and make me listen, Thou guardian of my soul
229	1	All are too mean to speak his worth
245	1	with actions bold and meek Would for Christ my Savior speak
245	2	And with actions brotherly Speak my Lord's sincerity
341	5	Speak through the earthquake, wind and fire
345	2	God's wondrous praises speak
364	3	Christian, dost thou hear them, How they speak thee fair
396	3	Let all my being speak Of thee and of thy love, O Lord
397	T,1	Lord, Speak to Me, That I May Speak
397	1	speak In living echoes of thy tone
398	1	Speak to our fearful hearts by conflict rent
406	1	only thee resolved to know In all I think or speak or do
411	3	Teach us to speak thy word of hope and cheer
422	2	Speak to the heart of love, alive and daring
425	3	They are slaves who fear to speak For the fallen & the weak
426	4	Speak, and behold, we answer, Command, and we obey
508	1	Shall speak thy praises, Lord most high
565	3	be thankful unto him, and speak good of his name

speaketh

| 14 | 2 | In prophet's words he spoke of old He speaketh still |

speaking

74	4	Spirit in our spirit speaking, Make us sons of God indeed
218	2	O Let me hear thee speaking In accents clear and still
393	1	God be in my mouth, And in my speaking
543	1	God be in my mouth, and in my speaking

speaks

86	3	All beauty speaks of thee, The mountains and the rivers
426	1	As once he spake in Zion, So now he speaks again
485	2	He speaks to me everywhere

spear

| 198 | 2 | To plough-share beat the sword, To pruning-hook the spear |

sped

97	3	Our heart's true home when all our years have sped
119	2	As with joyful steps they sped To that lowly manger-bed
181	3	The three sad days are quickly sped
304	2	Till saint and martyr sped the venture bold

speech

| 456 | 3 | Day unto day doth utter speech, And night to night proclaim |
| 470 | 2 | Make their ears attent To thy divinest speech |

speeches

| 436 | 2 | From all the easy speeches That comfort cruel men |

speed

266	4	O living Church, thine errand speed
302	3	Give of thy wealth to speed them on their way
448	3	Speed, speed the longed-for time Foretold by raptured seers

speedy

| 105 | 2 | He comes with succor speedy To those who suffer wrong |

spell

386	2	darkness ... lulls our spirits with its baneful spell

spend

34	3	To spend thyself nor count the cost
169	2	Who at my need His life did spend
169	5	In whose sweet praise I all my days Could gaily spend

spendest

302	3	And all thou spendest Jesus will repay

spent

131	1,2	When half spent was the night
398	1	Who by our own false hopes and aims are spent
452	4	For us his tears and blood were spent
505	T,1	You That Have Spent the Silent Night In sleep and quiet rest

sphere

89	1	Center and soul of every sphere

spheres

199	4	Creator of the rolling spheres, Ineffably sublime
419	1	Whose purpose binds the starry spheres
419	1	binds the starry spheres In one stupendous whole
485	1	and round me rings The music of the spheres

spill

450	2	strong To spill no drop of blood

spilt

468	3	Not spilt like water on the ground

spire

74	3	Soaring spire and ruined city ... our hopes & failures show

spires

270	1	Crumbled have spires in every land

Spirit

2	4	O Holy Spirit, precious Gift, Thou Comforter unfailing
3	3	O thou Fount of blessing, Purify my spirit
14	2	His spirit floweth free, High surging where it will
17	2	servants of the Triune God, Father and Son and Spirit laud
30	4	To God the Father, God the Son ... the Spirit Three in One
32	3	And with thyself my spirit fill
41	3	All holy Father, Son and equal Spirit, Trinity blessed
49	2	Thee, his incarnate Son, And Holy Spirit adoring
64	5	And praise the Spirit, three in One
67	4	But higher far, and far more clear Thee in man's spirit
67	4	Thee in man's spirit we behold
74	4	Spirit in our spirit speaking, Make us sons of God indeed
103	4	By thine own eternal Spirit Rule in all our hearts alone
114	4	Thy Holy Spirit guide us on Until the glorious crown be won
148	3	And if Satan, vexing sore, Flesh or spirit should assail
150	5	For us he sent his Spirit here To guide,
161	3	On us let now the healing Of his great Spirit fall

439	3	For all heroes of the spirit, Give we thanks to thee, O Lord
445	1	Spirit of life, which moved ere form was made
463	4	Glory to the Father, Son, And blest Spirit, Three in One
466	3	O spirit, who dost bind Our hearts in unity
470	4	Anoint them with the Spirit of thy Son
477	3	Come, with thy Spirit and thy power
490	4	Spirit of Christ, do thou Our first bright days inspire
491	T,1	O God of Youth, Whose Spirit in our hearts is stirring
491	2	Give us the valiant spirit that shall never Falter
521	1	Thy Spirit send with grace divine
528	1	And renew a right spirit within me
528	2	and take not thy Holy Spirit from me
528	3	and uphold me with thy free spirit
529	T,1	The Sacrifices of God are a broken spirit
531	T,1	The Lord Be With You, And with thy spirit
531	1	And take not thy Holy Spirit from us
533	1	And take not thy Holy Spirit from us
570	1	And my spirit hath rejoiced in God my Savior
575	1	Thou the anointing spirit art
575	R	Praise to thy eternal merit, Father, Son and Holy Spirit

spirit's

33	4	Quickened by the Spirit's grace All thy holy will to trace
39	2	The Spirit's sanctifying beam Upon our earthly senses stream
46	4	in the spirit's secret cell May hymn & prayer forever dwell
52	3	Hope and ... Shining in the spirit's skies
212	3	Help us by thy Spirit's pleading
291	3	Draw us in the Spirit's tether
419	2	And lift the spirit's sword
419	2	spirit's sword to shield The weak against the strong
539	1	With the Holy Spirit's favor Rest upon us from above

spirits

44	2	Did not their spirits inly yearn
59	2	Let evil thoughts and spirits flee before us
110	2	O Come, thou Day-spring, come and cheer Our spirits
110	2	cheer Our spirits by thine advent here
166	3	When with wrong our spirits bleed, Hear us, holy Jesus
167	IV-3	Though no Father seems to hear .. no light our spirits cheer
290	3	Our restless spirits yearn for thee
296	2	And nations, crowding to be born, Baptize their spirits
296	2	Baptize their spirits in its light
334	3	Our spirits yearn to feel thy kindling love
383	1-3	In unbroken line Move the faithful spirits
386	2	darkness ... lulls our spirits with its baneful spell
442	2	Search, Lord, our spirits in thy sight
477	2	For thee our waiting spirits yearn

spite

169	4	Why, what hath my Lord done, What makes this rage and spite
215	2	and, spite of fears, Pride ruled my will
365	1	living still In spite of dungeon, fire, and sword
453	4	The civic slander and the spite

splendid

422	3	Holding his pick more splendid than the sword

splendor

6	1	Pavilioned in splendor, and girded with praise
7	4	help us to see 'Tis only the splendor of light hideth thee
37	3	A fresh and solemn splendor still is given
39	T,1	O Splendor of God's Glory Bright
40	T,1	O Splendor of God's Glory Bright (same words as No. 39)
42	3	Splendor he makes on earth, Color awakes on earth
49	1	The eternal splendor wearing, Celestial, holy, blest
53	2	all the heavenly splendor Breaks forth in starlight tender
53	2	splendor ...From myriad worlds unknown
74	1	Thou who wrought creation's splendor
98	1	So full of splendor and of joy, Beauty and light
113	3	not in splendor bright As monarch, but the humble child
185	3	Now the queen of seasons, bright With the day of splendor
291	T,1	Lord, Enthroned in Heavenly Splendor
420	4	Lo, how its splendor challenges The souls that greatly dare
421	4	A splendor greater yet while serving thee
433	1	starry band Of shining worlds in splendor through the skies
435	T,1	Judge Eternal, Throned in Splendor
506	1	Come to him who made this splendor

splendors

129	4	peace shall over all the earth Its ancient splendors fling
424	3	It will pass into the splendors Of the city of the light
456	2	The solemn splendors of the night Burn brighter

spoil

428	3	Let them come out with Egypt's spoil

spoke

14	2	In prophet's words he spoke of old He speaketh still

spoken

13	1	Praise the Lord, for he hath spoken
38	1	Blackbird has spoken Like the first bird
267	T,1	Glorious Things of Thee Are Spoken, Zion, city of our God
276	4	May thy whole truth be spoken here
282	1	By whom the words of life were spoken
333	1	Hear thou our prayer, the spoken and unspoken

spokesman

493	2	No spokesman at his side

spot

98	2	That in the darkest spot of earth Some love is found
109	2	Watchman, will its beams alone Gild the spot
109	2	Gild the spot that gave them birth

spotless

197	3	Faithfully he bore it, Spotless to the last
222	1	Thirsting after thee, Thine I am, O spotless Lamb
228	4	Pure and spotless let us be

sprang

197	2	At his voice creation Sprang at once to sight

spread

68	1	spread the flowing seas abroad, And built the lofty skies
72	2	And spread the truth from pole to pole
203	3	Spread abroad the victor's fame
223	2	spread through all the earth abroad The honors of thy name
241	3	Come as the dove, and spread thy wings
280	1	Savior, abide with us, and spread Thy table in our heart
287	3	This is the heavenly table spread for me
292	1	We here present, we here spread forth to thee
294	2	Help us to spread thy gracious reign
348	3	While life's dark maze I tread, And griefs around me spread
374	2	Or its sordid treasures Spread to work me harm
389	4	Oh, spread thy covering wings around
421	4	We've seen thy glory like a mantle spread O'er hill and dale

spread'st

79	5	Thou spread'st a table in my sight

spreading

86	3	The line of lifted sea, Where spreading moonlight quivers
253	1	Bringing freedom, spreading truth
257	4	Nor shall thy spreading gospel rest

spreads

107	3	Rank on rank the host of heaven Spreads its vanguard
107	3	Spreads its vanguard on the way
112	2	For e'en now the reign of heaven Spreads throughout
112	2	heaven Spreads throughout the world like leaven
459	1	Over the heavens he spreads his clouds

spring

8	3	Well-spring of the joy of living, Ocean depth of happy rest
39	1	O Light of light, light's living spring
43	1	Day-spring from on high be near, Day-star in my heart appear
82	3	grace Whence all our hope and comfort spring
105	3	love, joy, hope, like flowers, Spring from his path to birth
106	1	River and mountain-spring, Hark to the advent voice
110	2	O Come, thou Day-spring, come and cheer Our spirits
185	2	'Tis the spring of souls today, Christ hath burst his prison
210	3	Spring thou up within my heart, Rise to all eternity
227	2	woodlands Robed in the blooming garb of spring
356	2	It has no spring of action sure, It varies with the wind
390	3	praise of him who is thy God, Thy health's eternal spring
438	4	And spring adorns the earth no more
459	3	He calls the warmer gales to blow And bids the spring return
462	2	All that spring with bounteous hand Scatters
464	3	All that spring with bounteous hand Scatters
487	1	Spring wind, summer rain, Then the harvest grain
568	11	whereby the Dayspring from on high hath visited us

springing

38	1	Praise for them, springing Fresh from the Word
108	2	Her heart with deep delight is springing
267	2	See ... streams of living waters Springing from eternal love

springs

32	3	Guard my first springs of thought and will
82	4	Life, like a fountain rich and free Springs from ... my Lord
82	4	Springs from the presence of my Lord
92	2	But let me only think of thee And then new heart springs up
276	3	Here make the well-springs of thy grace Like fountains
392	6	And mirth that has no bitter springs

sprung

38	2	Sprung in completeness Where his feet pass
131	T,1	Lo, How a Rose E'er Blooming From tender stem hath sprung

spurning

490	2	Not choosing what is great, Nor spurning what is small

squadrons

175	3	The winged squadrons of the sky Look down

square

420	1	Within whose four-square walls shall come No night

stable

124	3	Softly to the little stable, Softly for a moment come
128	2	In the bleak midwinter A stable place sufficed
128	2	A stable place sufficed The Lord God almighty, Jesus Christ
152	1	Above the stable while the angels sing

stablished

6	3	Hath stablished it fast by a changeless decree

staff

79	4	Thy rod and staff my comfort still
84	3	thy rod And staff me comfort still
354	2	Thy rod and staff shall keep us safe, And guide our steps
381	T,1	My Faith, It Is an Oaken Staff
381	3	My faith, it is an oaken staff, O let me on it lean

stage

32	1	Thy daily stage of duty run

staid

381	1	By all my perils undeterred, A soldier-pilgrim staid

stain

407	3	That, cleansed from stain of sin, I may meet homage give
447	2	Remember not our sin's dark stain

tained

470	4	Theirs not a jeweled crown, a blood-stained sword

tains

204	2	When he had purged our stains, he took his seat above
324	2	Wash out its stains, refine its dross
376	2	While passion stains and folly dims our youth

stall

126	2	Low lies his head with the beasts of the stall
142	2	Cradled in a stall was he with sleeply cows and asses

stamp

73	1	Man, the stamp of thy Creator, Praise ye

stand

9	5	Firm as a rock thy truth must stand
9	5	thy truth must stand When rolling years shall cease to move
14	2	Established is his law, And changeless it shall stand
25	T,1	Stand Up and Bless the Lord, Ye people of his choice
25	1	Stand up & bless the Lord your God with heart & soul & voice
25	4	Stand up and bless the Lord, The Lord your God adore
25	4	Stand up and bless his glorious name Henceforth for evermore
26	1	Sons of every land, Humbly now before him stand
41	1	Active and watchful, stand we all before thee
60	1	We stand to bless thee ere our worship cease
92	4	Enfolded deep in thy dear love, Held in thy law, I stand
96	3	Here shall my stand be taken
105	4	His name shall stand forever, That name to us is Love
107	1	And with fear and trembling stand
144	2	And lo, the eastern sages stand to read in heaven
160	T,1	Beneath the Cross of Jesus I fain would take my stand
185	4	But today amidst the twelve Thou didst stand, bestowing
257	3	Round the whole earth and never stand
269	2	I love thy Church, O God, Her walls before they stand
270	T,1	Built on the Rock the Church doth stand
270	1	the Church doth stand Even when steeples are falling
286	2	Thou at the table, blessing, yet dost stand
293	1	Who dares stand idle on the harvest plain
297	1	The shrines our fathers founded stand
309	2	They stand, those halls of Zion, All jubilant with song
339	2	Love doth stand At his hand, Joy doth wait on his command
346	2	Who steadfast stand at God's right hand
354	3	In all the strife of mortal life Our feet shall stand
354	3	Our feet shall stand securely
354	3	Until we stand at thy right hand Through Jesus' saving merit
356	1	I sink in life's alarms When by myself I stand
372	2	I'll strengthen thee, help thee, and cause thee to stand
373	2	Though hosts encamp around me, Firm in the fight I stand
380	3	In keenest strife, Lord, may we stand, Upheld
384	2	Stand, then, in his great might
384	2	Ye may o'ercome through Christ alone & stand entire at last
385	T,1	Stand Up, Stand Up for Jesus, Ye soldiers of the cross
385	2	Stand Up, stand up for Jesus, The trumpet call obey
385	3	Stand up, stand up for Jesus, Stand in his strength alone
385	4	Stand up, stand up for Jesus, The strife will not be long
397	2	O strengthen me, that while I stand firm on the rock
432	1	Through whose deep purpose stranger thousands stand Here
432	1	stand Here in the borders of our promised land
445	2	Races and peoples, lo, we stand divided
454	1	hand By which supported still we stand
470	5	And stand at last with joy before thy face
477	1	Thy Church shall stand as stands thy word
490	3	But give us grace to stand Decided, brave, and strong

496	2	O thus be it ever when free men shall stand
496	2	stand Between their loved homes and the war's desolation
502	1	Forever ready at thy service stand
562	8	let the whole earth stand in awe of him

standard

| 268 | 1 | With the cross our only standard Let us sing |
| 345 | 5 | Still lift your standard high, Still march in firm array |

standest

| 46 | 3 | Within all shadows standest thou |
| 509 | 3 | Within the shadows standest thou |

standeth

28	2	Thy Church ... standeth sure while earth and time endure
441	3	behind the dim unknown, Standeth God within the shadow
446	3	man hath defied thee, Yet to eternity standeth thy word

standing

26	2	Standing fast to the last, By his hand our lives are stayed
329	T,1	O Jesus, Thou Art Standing Outside the fast-closed door
329	1	O shame, thrice shame upon us To keep his standing there
439	1	Standing in the living present, Memory and hope between

stands

47	5	Thy kingdom stands, and grows forever
76	4	His goodness stands approved Down to the present day
78	3	Supreme in wisdom as in power The Rock of ages stands
82	2	Forever firm thy justice stands
82	2	firm thy justice stands As mountains their foundations keep
261	4	Unharmed upon the eternal rock The eternal city stands
264	4	Unshaken as eternal hills, Immovable she stands
270	2	High above earth his temple stands
308	4	High above the restless tides Stands their city on the hill
312	3	There David stands with harp in hand As master of the choir
356	3	It only stands unbent Amid the clashing strife
361	3	Have faith in God, my soul, His cross forever stands
431	2	Still stands thine ancient sacrifice ... a contrite heart
477	1	Thy Church shall stand as stands thy word

star

43	1	Day-spring from on high be near, Day-star in my heart appear
89	1	Thy glory flames from sun and star
89	2	Star of our hope, thy softened light Cheers
108	2	Her star is risen, her light is come
109	1	See that glory-beaming star
109	2	Higher yet that star ascends
117	3	Ye have seen his natal star
119	T,1	As With Gladness Men of Old Did the guiding star behold
119	4	Bring our ransomed souls at last Where they need no star
119	4	need no star to guide, Where no clouds thy glory hide
123	3	Hail the star That from far Bright with hope is burning
126	1,5	Star of the east, the horizon adorning
136	3	God's bright star, o'er his head, Wise men three to him led
141	2	They looked up and saw a star Shining in the east
141	3	And by the light of that same star Three wise men came

141	3	And to follow the star wherever it went
141	4	This star drew nigh to the northwest
143	R	star of wonder, star of night, Star with royal beauty bright
144	T,1	What Star Is This, With Beams So Bright
144	2	From Jacob shall a star proceed
144	3	O Jesus, while the star of grace Impels us
145	T,1	O Morning Star, How Fair and Bright
152	T,1	We Would See Jesus, Lo, His Star Is Shining
178	1	The star is dimmed that lately shone
198	1	The day-star clear and bright Of every man and nation
257	1	In every star thy wisdom shines
294	T,1	Eternal God, Whose Power Upholds Both flower & flaming star
378	1	Star of our night, and hope of every nation
460	2	He paints the wayside flower, He lights the evening star
498	2	O God, thou star of dawning day

starlight

| 53 | 2 | all the heavenly splendor Breaks forth in starlight tender |

starring

| 458 | 2 | Starring all the land with flowers |

starry

227	3	And all the twinkling starry host, Jesus shines brighter
419	1	Whose purpose binds the starry spheres
419	1	binds the starry spheres In one stupendous whole
433	1	almighty hand Leads forth in beauty all the starry band
433	1	starry band Of shining worlds in splendor through the skies

stars

8	2	Stars and angels sing around thee, Center of unbroken praise
8	4	Mortals, join the happy chorus Which the morning stars began
13	1	Praise him, all ye stars of light
45	3	When forever from our sight Pass the stars ... day ... night
52	2	Soon as dies the sunset glory, Stars of heaven shine out
52	2	Stars ... shine out above, Telling still the ancient story
52	2	Stars ... Telling ... Their Creator's changeless love
52	3	As the darkness deepens o'er us, Lo, eternal stars arise
65	3	Stars that have no voice to sing Give ... glory to our King
66	2	Hill & vale, and tree & flower, Sun & moon & stars of light
68	1	The moon shines full at his command, And all the stars obey
69	1	Sun & moon, uplift your voice, Night & stars, in God rejoice
72	2	Whilst all the stars that round her burn ... confirm
74	1	Bringing suns and stars to birth
74	2	Moon and stars, thy power displayed
75	2	Moon and stars with silvery light Praise him
86	1	Whose stars serenely burn Above this earth's confusion
113	T,1	Creator of the Stars of Night
134	1	Above thy deep and dreamless sleep The silent stars go by
134	2	O morning stars, together Proclaim the holy birth
137	1	The stars in the sky looked down where he lay
197	2	Thrones and dominations, Stars upon their way
257	3	Sun, moon, and stars convey thy praise Round the whole earth
351	5	sun, moon, and stars forgot, Upward I fly
496	1	Whose broad stripes & bright stars through the perilous fight

starving

417	1	The nations sleep starving on heaps of gold

state

127	4	Till man's first heavenly state again takes place
135	1	Our lowly state to make thine own
434	2	laws and habits of the state
434	4	These are the bulwarks of the state

statesman's

253	1	Statesman's, teacher's, hero's treasure

station

203	4	Jesus takes the highest station

statutes

255	3	statutes of the Lord are truth And righteousness ... pure
517	T,1	Teach me, O Lord, the way of thy statutes

stay

14	3	His love shall be our strength and stay, While ages roll
33	3	Lest from thee we stray abroad, Stay our wayward feet,O Lord
60	4	Our balm in sorrow, and our stay in strife
85	3	the Lord thy shade On thy right hand doth stay
91	2	I of the Lord my God will say, He is my refuge and my stay
137	2	And stay by my cradle till morning is nigh
141	4	stop and stay, Right over the place where Jesus lay
153	1	Teach us ... to mourn our sins, And close by thee to stay
167	IV-2	In the darkness be our stay, Hear us, holy Jesus
169	5	Here might I stay and sing, No story so divine
209	3	Who like thyself my guide and stay can be
256	3	Our anchor and our stay
290	4	O Jesus, ever with us stay
305	3	Flow thou to every nation, Nor in thy richness stay
305	3	Stay not till all the lowly Triumphant reach their home
305	3	Stay not till all the holy Proclaim, The Lord is come
342	2	I need thee every hour, Stay thou near by
368	3	Not forever by still waters Would we idly rest and stay
371	2	No foes shall stay his might, Though he with giants fight
401	2	A man that looks on glass On it may stay his eye
418	2	Teach me the wayward feet stay
433	2	Be thou our ruler, guardian, guide, and stay

tayed

26	2	Standing fast to the last, By his hand our lives are stayed
210	2	All my trust on thee is stayed ... my help from thee I bring
381	2	Unstayed by pleasures, still they bent Their zealous course
541	1	Whose mind is stayed on thee

teadfast

86	1	Thine is the mighty plan, The steadfast order sure
100	5	Unto such as keep his covenant And are steadfast in his way
261	2	One holy Church, one army strong, One steadfast high intent
346	2	Who steadfast stand at God's right hand
434	3	God send us men of steadfast will, Patient, courageous
444	2	The quiet of a steadfast faith, Calm of a call obeyed

465 2   assurance Of tender charity and steadfast faith
491 1   Keep us, we pray thee, steadfast and unerring

steadfastly
419 2   And steadfastly pursue the way Of thy commandments still

steadfastness
392 2   Teach us to bear the hope in youth With steadfastness
392 2   With steadfastness and careful truth

steady
161 2   On all, the judgment of the cross Falls steady, clear & sure
325 1   New thorns to pierce that steady brow
459 2   His steady counsels change the face Of the declining year

steal
51   1   Shadows of the evening Steal across the sky (also 510-1)

stealing
173 2   O word of comfort, through the silence stealing

steals
306 5   Steals on the ear the distant triumph song
508 1   And evening steals o'er earth and sky

steel
388 3   They met the tyrant's brandished steel, The lion's gory mane
494 2   Ribbed with the steel that time and change doth mock

steep
42   4   What though the hill be steep, Strength's in the sun
50   2   My wearied eyelids gently steep
368 2   But the steep and rugged pathway May we tread rejoicingly
376 4   However rough and steep the path may be
388 4   They climbed the steep ascent of heaven

steeples
270 1   the Church doth stand Even when steeples are falling

steeps
230 3   We may not climb the heavenly steeps
311 1   armies of the ransomed saints throng up the steeps of light

stem
131 T,1 Lo, How a Rose E'er Blooming From tender stem hath sprung
195 2   Extol the stem of Jesse's rod

step
215 1   one step enough for me
238 1   O'er every thought and step preside
334 2   And thou hast made each step an onward one
396 4   But all my life, in every step, Be fellowship with thee

Stephen
493 T,1 When Stephen, Full of Power and Grace
493 1   When Stephen ... Went forth throughout the land

| 493 | 2 | Stephen preached against the laws & by those laws was tried |
| 493 | 3 | When Stephen, young and doomed to die, Fell crushed |

stepping

| 387 | 1 | Stepping fearless through the night |

steps

31	2	Guiding thy steps as may best for thee be
119	2	As with joyful steps they sped To that lowly manger-bed
127	4	Treading his steps, assisted by his grace
129	3	Who toil along the climbing way With painful steps and slow
259	2	Darkling our great forefathers went The first steps
259	2	The first steps of the way
324	4	Savior, where'er thy steps I see ... I follow thee
351	3	There let the way appear Steps unto heaven
354	2	Thy rod and staff shall keep us safe, And guide our steps
354	2	And guide our steps forever
362	2	Forget the steps already trod, And onward urge thy way
381	2	I have a guide, and in his steps When travelers have trod
405	3	Some dews of mercy shed, Some wayward footsteps led
410	2	Follow with reverent steps the great example Of him

stern

315	3	The foe is stern and eager, The fight is fierce and long
417	2	And the meekest of saints may find stern work to do
440	2	pilgrim feet, Whose stern, impassioned stress

stewards

| 308 | 2 | Faithful stewards of the word |
| 413 | 2 | We but stewards of thy bounty, Held in solemn trust for thee |

still

14	2	In prophet's words he spoke of old He speaketh still
16	2	Praise him, still the same forever
21	3	And pray that thou still our defender wilt be
23	3	Take what he gives And praise him still
23	3	praise him still Through good and ill, Who ever lives
26	3	Enter now his holy gate, Let our burdened hearts be still
29	1	With countless gifts of love, And still is ours today
36	3	New treasures still, of countless price, God will provide
36	3	New treasures still ... God will provide for sacrifice
37	T,1,3	Still, Still With Thee
37	3	A fresh and solemn splendor still is given
52	2	Stars ... shine out above, Telling still the ancient story
55	6	Thy touch has still its ancient power
61	2	Daily manna still provide you
74	2	Yet thy love doth seek him still
77	T,1,3	Be still my soul
77	2	the waves and winds still know his voice
78	5	they who wait upon the Lord In strength shall still increase
79	4	Thy rod and staff my comfort still
81	1	The praises of my God shall still My heart and tongue employ
83	2	Only be still, and wait his leisure in cheerful hope
84	3	thy rod And staff me comfort still
92	3	Thy calmness bends serene above, My restlessness to still
93	2	Strong Deliverer, Be thou still my strength and shield

96	1	I will be still, whate'er he doth
99	5	Still more in resurrection light We read the fullness
100	5	Unto those who still remember His commandments and obey
112	1	I am with you, still he sayeth
129	2	Still through the cloven skies they come
129	2	still their heavenly music floats O'er all the weary world
134	T,1	O Little Town of Bethlehem, How still we see thee lie
134	3	still The dear Christ enters in
143	R	Westward leading, still proceeding
150	3	By words and signs and actions, thus Still seeking
150	3	Still seeking not himself but us
152	5	Still as of old he calleth, Follow me
162	4	See his anguish ... faith, Love triumphant still in death
167	II-2	May we, in our guilt and shame Still thy love & mercy claim
167	V-2	Thirst for us in mercy still, All thy holy work fulfil
173	2	O infinite compassion, still revealing ... forgiveness
205	3	Still he calls mankind his own
206	2	And still he is nigh, his presence we have
209	4	I triumph still if thou abide with me
210	1	While the nearer waters roll ... the tempest still is high
210	2	Leave, ah, leave me not alone, Still support and comfort me
213	2	When thou sayest to them, Be still
214	3	Still to the lowly soul He doth himself impart
215	3	sure it still Will lead me on O'er moor and fen
218	2	O Let me hear thee speaking In accents clear and still
219	2	Thee would I sing, thy truth is still the light
219	3	Yes, thou art still the Life, thou art the Way
220	4	Our brotherhood still rests in him, The brother of us all
220	4	o'er the centuries still we hear The Master's winsome call
222	3	Still have peace within
222	3	Still in thee lies purest pleasure, Jesus priceless treasure
227	2	Fair are the meadows, Fairer still the woodlands
227	3	Fair is the sunshine, Fairer still the moonlight
229	3	And through this desert land, Still keep me near thy side
230	4	And faith has still its Olivet, And love its Galilee
236	5	Flow still in the prophet's word And the people's liberty
249	3	To thee we owe the peace that still prevails
249	5	Pray we that thou wilt hear us, still imploring Thy love
252	2	And still that light she lifteth O'er all the earth to shine
252	3	'Mid mists, and rocks, and quicksands Still guides
252	3	Still guides, O Christ, to thee
253	3	Those whose wisdom still directs us
259	3	The valleys passed, ascending still
270	1	Bells still are chiming and calling
272	4	But we shall still be joined in heart
286	2	Faith still receives the cup as from thy hand
287	3	Here let me feast, and, feasting, still prolong
287	4	thou art here, Nearer than ever, still my shield and sun
289	2	Save it from evil, guard it still
292	3	Most patient Savior who canst love us still
303	4	And still with haughty foes must cope
308	2	Long forgotten, living still
312	2	They triumph still, they still rejoice
322	4	Still he calls in cares and pleasures
324	4	O let thy hand support me still
325	1	And still our wrongs may weave thee now New thorns

327	3	Blessed Jesus, Thou hast loved us, love us still
332	4	Lord, thy mercy still entreating
335	3	Precious Savior, still our refuge
339	T,1	All My Hope on God Is Founded, He doth still my trust renew
339	3	Still from man to God eternal Sacrifice of praise be done
341	4	Drop thy still dews of quietness, Till ... strivings cease
341	5	O still, small voice of calm
345	4	Yes, on through life's long path, Still chanting as ye go
345	5	Still lift your standard high, Still march in firm array
351	1	Still all my song would be, Nearer, my God, to thee
351	5	Still all my song shall be, Nearer, my God, to thee
352	4	Still shall those hearts respond, with full accord
363	1	For still our ancient foe Doth seek to work us woe
363	4	The body they may kill, God's truth abideth still
365	1	living still In spite of dungeon, fire, and sword
365	2	Our fathers, chained in prisons dark, Were still ... free
365	2	Were still in heart and conscience free
368	3	Not forever by still waters Would we idly rest and stay
370	1	Whate'er I do, where'er I be, Still 'tis God's hand
370	1	Still 'tis God's hand that leadeth me
372	2	For I am thy God, and will still give thee aid
376	1	And doubts appall, and sorrows still increase
377	T,1	Lift Thy Head, O Zion, Weeping, Still the Lord thy Father is
377	2	Though untroubled still he sleep Who thy hope is on the deep
380	1	cast to flame, Still made their glory in thy name
381	1	I'll travel on, and still be stirred by silent thought
381	2	Unstayed by pleasures, still they bent Their zealous course
389	T,1	O God of Bethel, by Whose Hand Thy people still are fed
390	3	Hope still, and thou shalt sing The praise of him
391	4	Still be my vision, O Ruler of all
398	2	Still let thy Spirit unto us be given
400	3	This still its prayer shall be, More Love, O Christ, to thee
406	4	And still to things eternal look
418	3	Teach me thy patience, still with thee In closer
419	2	And steadfastly pursue the way Of thy commandments still
423	4	The cup of water given for thee Still holds the freshness
423	4	Still holds the freshness of thy grace
431	2	Still stands thine ancient sacrifice ... a contrite heart
435	2	Still the weary folk are pining for the hour
438	2	Thy blessing came, and still its power Shall onward
441	2	Thy must upward still and onward Who would keep ... truth
445	3	Nation by nation still goes unforgiven
451	1	Still wilt not hear thine inner God proclaim
454	1	hand By which supported still we stand
454	2	By day, by night, at home abroad, Still we are guarded
454	2	Still we are guarded by our God
463	1-3	For his mercies still endure, Ever faithful, ever sure
466	2	With heart still undefiled, Thou didst to manhood come
467	3	Low in the heart faith singeth still her song
468	2	With thee is hidden still their life
472	5	Still may these courts proclaim the glory of thy name
476	4	rich in art, made richer still The brotherhood of duty
481	3	There are hundreds of thousands still
494	T,1	We Would Be Building temples still undone
496	1	Gave proof through the night that our flag was still there
540	1	Still our minds with truth's conviction

stille
139   T,1-3 Stille Nacht, Heilige Nacht

stilled
325   4   Our pride is dust, our vaunt is stilled

stilling
249   3   Stilling the rude wills of men's wild behavior

stillness
129   1   The world in solemn stillness lay To hear the angels sing

stills
  20   1   And every faithless murmur stills
213   2   As a mother stills her child, Thou canst hush the ocean wild

sting
181   4   From death's dread sting thy servants free
182   2   Where, O death, is now thy sting
189   2   The grave has lost its triumph And death has lost its sting
193   2   For her Lord now liveth, Death hath lost its sting
209   4   Where is death's sting, where, grave, thy victory

stir
482   T,1   Little Jesus, Sweetly Sleep, do not stir

stirred
212   1   Let our hearts and souls be stirred
259   1   No, let a new and better hope Within our hearts be stirred
381   1   I'll travel on, and still be stirred by silent thought
381   1   stirred By silent thought or social word
492   2   for friends who stirred The fragile wills of youth

stirring
375   2   not with swords' loud clashing Nor roll of stirring drums
491   T,1   O God of Youth, Whose Spirit in our hearts is stirring

stone
128   1   Earth stood hard as iron, Water like a stone
193   1   Angels in bright raiment Rolled the stone away
299   3   Till hearts of stone begin to beat
325   2   Till not a stone was left on stone
351   2   Darkness be over me, My rest a stone
401   5   This is the famous stone That turneth all to gold
403   1   Raise the stone and thou shalt find me
494   1   waiting till love can raise the broken stone

stones
424   2   All our lives are building stones
493   3   Fell crushed beneath the stones
493   4   that the stones of earthly shame A jewelled crown may seem

stony
351   4   Out of my stony griefs Bethel I'll raise

tood

1	3	Before the hills in order stood, Or earth received her frame
4	4	His truth at all times firmly stood
128	1	Earth stood hard as iron, Water like a stone
290	2	Thy truth unchanged hath ever stood
380	1	Who 'gainst enthroned wrong Stood confident and bold
420	3	city that hath stood Too long a dream, whose laws are love

toop

| 232 | 1 | Stoop to my weakness, mighty as thou art |

tooped

| 302 | 2 | Tell how he stooped to save his lost creation |

top

| 141 | 4 | stop and stay, Right over the place where Jesus lay |

tore

6	3	The earth with its store of wonders untold
50	4	With blessings from thy boundless store
98	4	I thank thee, Lord, that thou hast kept The best in store
322	3	worship Of the vain world's golden store
404	4	Take my love, my Lord I pour At thy feet its treasure store
461	3	But the fruitful ears to store In his garner evermore
463	3	Praise him for our harvest store

tored

| 252 | 2 | It is the golden casket Where gems of truth are stored |
| 443 | 1 | where the grapes of wrath are stored |

tores

462	2	All the stores the gardens yield
462	2	All that liberal autumn pours From her rich ... stores
462	2	From her rich o'erflowing stores
464	2	For the stores our gardens yield
464	3	All that liberal autumn pours From her rich ... stores
464	3	From her rich o'erflowing stores

tories

| 371 | 2 | Who so beset him round With dismal stories |

torm

6	2	And dark is his path on the wings of the storm
22	2	Through life's storm and tempest our guide hast thou been
87	1	He plants his footsteps in the sea And rides upon the storm
210	1	Hide me, O my Savior, hide, Till the storm of life is past
343	1	The storm may roar without me, My heart may low be laid
360	1	When tossed by storm and flood
413	3	Hush the storm of strife and passion
477	1	Nor fear the storm, nor dread the shock

torms

218	2	Above the storms of passion, the murmurs of self-will
222	2	Sin and hell ... With their heaviest storms assail us
222	3	Though the storms may gather, Still have peace within
258	3	When the storms are o'er us And dark clouds before us

337	1	Through waves and clouds and storms He gently clears the way
417	T,1	The Day of the Lord Is at Hand, Its storms roll up the sky
461	1	All is safely gathered in Ere the winter storms begin
462	1	All is safely gathered in Ere the winter storms begin

stormy
1	1	Our shelter from the stormy blast, And our eternal home
42	2	So, o'er the hills of life, Stormy, forlorn
249	3	And calming passion's fierce and stormy gales
410	3	Then shall all shackles fall, the stormy clangor Of ... war

story
17	2	All that hath life and breath, tell the story
17	2	tell the story In accent strong, with voices free
20	4	All ye who own his power, proclaim Aloud the wondrous story
52	2	Stars ... shine out above, Telling still the ancient story
72	2	nightly, to the listening earth, Repeats the story
72	2	Repeats the story of her birth
117	1	Ye who sang creation's story Now proclaim Messiah's birth
127	3	Amazed, the wondrous story they proclaim
157	1,5	All the light of sacred story Gathers round its head sublime
169	5	Here might I stay and sing, No story so divine
249	1	Thy love has blessed the wide world's wondrous story
253	2	Til they came, who told the story Of the Word
253	2	story Of the Word, and showed his glory
317	T,1	I Love to Tell the Story Of unseen things above
317	1	I love to tell the story, Because I know it's true
317	R	I love to tell the story, 'Twill be my theme in glory
317	R	To tell the old, old story Of Jesus and his love
317	2	I love to tell the story, For those who know it best
317	2	'Twill be the old, old story That I have loved so long
366	1	Crown thine ancient church's story
422	5	Living again the eternal gospel story
476	1	The fathers named in story
483	T,1	I Think When I Read That Sweet Story of old

stout
| 381 | 1 | My faith, it is a weapon stout, The soldier's trusty blade |

straight
104	3	Make ye straight what long was crooked
127	3	To Bethlehem straight the enlightened shepherds ran
156	2	Thy road is ready, and thy paths made straight
367	2	Run the straight race through God's good grace

strain
30	1	Bright seraphs, cherubim and thrones, Raise the glad strain
30	1	Raise the glad strain, Alleluia
35	5	In heaven's eternal bliss The loveliest strain is this
47	3	Nor dies the strain of praise away
65	2	Saints in light the strain prolong
185	T,1	Come, Ye Faithful, Raise the Strain Of triumphant gladness
186	T,1	Come, Ye Faithful, Raise the Strain (same words as no. 185)
220	T,1	We Bear the Strain of Earthly Care, But bear it not alone
271	3	Ye saints to come, take up the strain
341	4	Take from our souls the strain and stress

387	3	One the strain that lips of thousands Lift as from the heart
418	1	Tell me thy secret, help be bear The strain of toil
418	1	The strain of toil, the fret of care
449	2	The calm that endeth strain and strife
457	2	God's praises in their loving strain Unconsciously they sing

strains

116	1	And the mountains in reply Echo back their joyous strains
116	2	Shepherds, why this jubilee, Why your joyous strains prolong
178	4	Unheard by mortals are the strains That sweetly soothe
185	3	Welcomes in unwearied strains Jesus' resurrection
504	2	Hosanna in the highest strains The Church on earth can raise

strand

438	1	And when they trod the wintry strand ... they worshipped

strange

74	2	Mixture strange of good and ill
169	2	But men made strange
235	4	That we may love not doctrines strange
369	1	God's Glory ... Most strange in all its ways
484	1	In strange and lovely cities, Or roam the desert sands

stranger

44	2	They could not let the Stranger go
432	1	Through whose deep purpose stranger thousands stand Here

stray

33	3	Lest from thee we stray abroad, Stay our wayward feet,O Lord
238	3	Nor let us from his precepts stray
255	T,1	Most Perfect Is the Law of God, Restoring those that stray
256	1	Our path when wont to stray
321	1	That I from thee no more may stray
324	3	If in this darksome wild I stray
348	3	Nor let me every stray From thee aside

strayed

9	2	And when, like wandering sheep we strayed, He brought us
79	3	Perverse and foolish oft I strayed

straying

332	3	Hearts that far from thee were straying

stream

1	5	Time, like an ever-rolling stream, Bears all its sons away
93	2	fountain, Whence the healing stream doth flow
138	2	Glories stream from heaven afar
256	1	Stream from the fount of heavenly grace
348	4	When death's cold, sullen stream Shall e'er me roll

streaming

157	3	From the cross the radiance streaming
496	1	O'er the ramparts we watched were so gallantly streaming

streams

6	4	It streams from the hills, it descends to the plain

79	2	Where streams of living water flow
99	3	We read thee ... In the seas that swell & streams that flow
161	1	Across our restless living The light streams from his cross
210	3	Let the healing streams abound, Make and keep me pure within
267	2	See ... streams of living waters Springing from eternal love
388	1	His blood-red banner streams afar
390	T,1	As Pants the Hart for cooling streams
459	2	The liquid streams forbear to flow, In icy fetters bound

street

312	5	With blessed saints, whose harmony In every street doth ring
420	2	greed for gain In street and shop and tenement Wring gold
426	2	No field or mart is silent, No city street is dumb

streets

| 134 | 1 | Yet in thy dark streets shineth The everlasting Light |
| 423 | 5 | O tread the city's streets again |

strength

14	3	His love shall be our strength and stay, While ages roll
25	3	God is our strength and song, And his salvation ours
28	2	Thy Church doth in thy strength rely
33	2	Strength unto our souls afford From thy living Bread, O Lord
78	5	they who wait upon the Lord In strength shall still increase
83	1	He'll give thee strength whate'er betide thee
86	4	Inspire us from above With joy and strength for duty
93	2	Strong Deliverer, Be thou still my strength and shield
103	2	Israel's strength and consolation
145	2	Fill me with joy and strength to be Thy member
153	2	O give us strength in thee to fight, In thee to conquer sin
164	4	In this dread act your strength is tried
168	2	Yet give us strength to trust the sweet assurance
207	3	And all our substance and our strength receive
207	3	And give us strength in every trying hour
207	5	That in thy strength we evermore endure
217	2	Your strength in our hearts, Lord, at the noon of the day
232	3	All, all thine own, soul, heart, and strength, and mind
244	1	To strength and gladness wake us
253	T,1	Book of Books, Our People's Strength
274	2	Happy, whose strength in thee doth hide
274	3	They journey on from strength to strength
281	1	Day by day with strength supplied Through the life of him
281	1	strength supplied through the life of him who died
287	5	My strength is in thy might, thy might alone
298	3	March we forth in the strength of God
300	1	Give heart and soul and mind and strength To serve
300	3	Her strength unequal to her task, Rise up and make her great
318	2	In thee my strength renew, Give me thy work to do
334	1,3	revealing Of trust and strength and calmness from above
348	2	May thy rich grace impart Strength to my fainting heart
354	2	Thy strength shall never fail us
363	2	Did we in our own strength confide, Our striving would be
364	1	In the strength that cometh By the holy cross
367	1	Christ is thy strength, and Christ thy right
368	1	But for strength that we may ever Live ... courageously
368	4	Be our strength in hours of weakness

397   2   and strong in thee, I may stretch out a loving hand

stretching
439   1   Stretching far o'er land and sea

strew
169   3   Sometimes they strew his way, And his sweet praises sing
184   2   Bring flowers of song to strew his way

strife
2   1   The strife at last is ended
33   3   Be our guard in sin and strife, Be the leader of our life
42   2   Out of the cloud and strife Sunrise is born
53   3   And grope in faithless strife
60   4   Our balm in sorrow, and our stay in strife
110   4   Bid envy, strife and quarrels cease
161   1   The meaning of our eager strife Is tested by his Way
165   3   Here in o'erwhelming final strife the Lord ... hath victory
175   4   Thy last and fiercest strife is nigh
181   T,1   Alleluia, The Strife is O'er, the battle done
193   3   Life is nought without thee, Aid us in our strife
199   3   And rose victorious in the strife For those he came to save
237   3   And cleanse them of their hate and strife
244   2   Let thy dear word 'mid doubt and strife
304   4   When o'er the strife of nations sounding clear Shall ring
306   5   And when the strife is fierce, the warfare long
314   2   Amid the battle's strife
315   3   O cheering voice of Jesus, Which comes to aid our strife
340   4   peace of God, it is no peace, But strife closed in the sod
347   5   Kept peaceful in the midst of strife, Forgiving and forgiven
354   3   In all the strife of mortal life Our feet shall stand
356   3   It only stands unbent Amid the clashing strife
365   4   love Both friend and foe in all our strife
380   3   In keenest strife, Lord, may we stand, Upheld
385   4   Stand up, stand up for Jesus, The strife will not be long
398   2   To heal earth's wounds and end her bitter strife
403   2   dwells within the market strife
409   2   Thou ... Dwellest in the daily strife
413   3   Hush the storm of strife and passion
423   1   Above the noise of selfish strife
439   4   From the strife of class and faction Make our nation free
440   3   O beautiful for heroes proved In liberating strife
441   1   decide In the strife of truth with falsehood, For the good
444   4   Bring to our world of strife Thy sovereign word of peace
449   2   The calm that endeth strain and strife
465   3   Grant them the peace which calms all earthly strife
468   2   Released from earthly toil and strife
491   2   never Falter or fail however long the strife

strike
359   2   in the darkest battlefield Thou shalt know where to strike
427   3   Strike, let every nerve and sinew Tell on ages, tell for God

strikes
112   3   Comes the Lord when strikes the hour

| 422 | 3 | Strikes for a kingdom and his King's arriving |

strings

| 19 | 4 | Strings and voices, hands and hearts ... bear your parts |

stripes

| 181 | 4 | Lord, by the stripes which wounded thee |
| 496 | 1 | Whose broad stripes & bright stars through the perilous fight |

strive

240	2	In vain we tune our formal songs, In vain we strive to rise
242	3	By thee may I strongly live, Bravely bear, and nobly strive
346	2	And strive to serve him well
452	3	we strive in vain To save ourselves without thine aid

striven

| 378 | 4 | or after we have striven, Peace in thy heaven |

striving

161	3	Yet humbly, in our striving, O God, we face its test
363	2	Did we in our own strength confide, Our striving would be
363	2	Our striving would be losing
364	2	Striving, tempting, luring, Goading into sin
411	3	Rest for the soul, and strength for all man's striving
422	3	When in the depths the patient miner striving

strivings

| 341 | 4 | Drop thy still dews of quietness, Till ... strivings cease |
| 341 | 4 | Till all our strivings cease |

stroke

| 91 | 3 | When fearful plagues around prevail, No fatal stroke shall |
| 91 | 3 | No fatal stroke shall thee assail |

strong

17	1	While o'er my life his strong arm he raises I shall sing
17	2	tell the story In accent strong, with voices free
30	3	Ye holy twelve, ye martyrs strong ... raise the song
58	2	Strong through thee whate'er befall us, O God most wise
64	2	Thou rushing wind that art so strong
92	1	I feel thy strong and tender love, And all is well again
93	2	Strong Deliverer, Be thou still my strength and shield
95	5	wonders great By thy strong hand are done
97	3	When we are strong, Lord, leave us not alone, Our refuge be
99	T,1	O Love of God, How Strong and True, Eternal and yet ever new
105	2	To help the poor and needy, And bid the weak be strong
217	2	Whose strong hands were skilled at the plane and the lathe
235	3	Thou strong Defense, thou holy Light
239	3	And so the yearning strong With which the soul will long
261	2	One holy Church, one army strong, One steadfast high intent
264	2	We mark her goodly battlements, And her foundations strong
268	1	Making strong our company
291	1	Thou alone, our strong defender Liftest up thy people's head
306	5	And hearts are brave again, and arms are strong
308	3	strong in heart and hand and brain
308	3	strong, yet battling for the weak

315	3	But thou hast made us mighty, And stronger than the strong
328	2	The Lord is glorious and strong, Our God is very high
334	3	Now make us strong, we need thy deep revealing
336	4	A strong, desiring confidence To hear thy voice and live
337	2	How wise, how strong his hand
345	2	Strong men and maidens meek
345	3	With voice as full and strong As ocean's surging praise
354	T,1	Who Trusts in God, a Strong Abode
354	1	strong abode In heaven and earth possesses
355	T,1	Who Trusts in God, a Strong Abode (words same as no. 354)
356	1	Imprison me within thine arms, And strong shall be my hand
357	T,1	Strong Son of God, Immortal Love
373	T,1	God Is My Strong Salvation, What foe have I to fear
375	1	Through days of preparation Thy grace has made us strong
380	1	Like those strong men of old
380	3	March on, O soul, with strength, As strong the battle rolls
384	1	Strong in the strength that God supplies
384	1	Strong in the Lord of hosts, And in his mighty power
397	2	and strong in thee, I may stretch out a loving hand
405	2	Daily our lives would show Weakness made strong
411	2	Strong Son of God, whose work was his that sent thee
418	3	In work that keeps faith sweet and strong
419	2	spirit's sword to shield The weak against the strong
429	T,1	Eternal Father, Strong to Save
433	3	Be thy strong arm our ever sure defense
434	3	strong and true, With vision clear and mind equipped
439	4	Strong as when her life began
441	3	Though the cause of evil prosper ... truth alone is strong
450	2	They shall be gentle, brave, and strong
450	2	strong To spill no drop of blood
467	3	And in our weakness thou dost make us strong
470	3	Anoint them priests, Strong intercessors they For pardon
476	2	Praise we the wise and brave and strong
481	2	And his love made them strong
485	3	though the wrong seems oft so strong, God is the ruler yet
487	2	Through him we are strong, Sing our harvest song
489	1	I would be strong, for there is much to suffer
490	3	But give us grace to stand Decided, brave, and strong
521	2	Make strong our faith, increase our light

stronger

162	3	When for stronger faith I seek
315	3	But thou hast made us mighty, And stronger than the strong
470	1	Make each one nobler, stronger than the last

strongly

242	3	By thee may I strongly live, Bravely bear, and nobly strive

strowed

175	1	With palms and scattered garments strowed

struggle

306	4	We feebly struggle, they in glory shine

struggles

232	4	Teach me the struggles of the soul to bear

struggling
46 2 May struggling hearts that seek release Here find the rest
509 2 May struggling hearts that seek release Here find the rest

stumble
376 3 Blindly we stumble when we walk alone
386 1 night Through which we blindly stumble to the day

stumbling
219 2 Stumbling and falling in disastrous night

Stund'
139 3 Da uns schlagt die rettende Stund'

stupendous
419 1 binds the starry spheres In one stupendous whole

subdue
39 4 To guide whate'er we nobly do, With love all envy to subdue
197 5 In your hearts enthrone him, There let him subdue All

subdued
229 2 joyful news ... Of hell subdued and peace with heaven

sublime
199 4 Creator of the rolling spheres, Ineffably sublime
261 T,1 City of God, How Broad and Far Outspread thy walls sublime
266 4 Fulfill thy task sublime
424 2 All must aid alike to carry Forward one sublime design
427 1 In an age on ages telling, To be living is sublime
448 3 The prophecy sublime, The hope of all the years
577 1 power supreme, thy love sublime

submissive
429 2 The winds and waves submissive heard

subside
93 3 Bid my anxious fears subside

substance
207 3 And all our substance and our strength receive
406 3 Thee ... Whose eyes my inmost substance see

subtle
386 2 The subtle darkness that we love so well

succeeding
389 2 God of our fathers, be the God Of their succeeding race

succeeds
298 T,1 God Is Working His Purpose Out, As year succeeds to year

success
246 2 Come, and thy people bless, And give thy word success
440 3 Till all success be nobleness, And every gain divine

successive
| 202 | 1 | sun Doth his successive journeys run |

succor
105	2	He comes with succor speedy To those who suffer wrong
258	5	Word of mercy, giving Succor to the living
377	2	Though thou cry, with heart atremble, O my Savior, succor me
426	1	Whom shall I send to succor My people in their need

such
24	1	No mortal eye hath seen, No mortal ear hath heard such
24	1	No mortal ear hath heard such wondrous things
100	5	Unto such as keep his covenant And are steadfast in his way
101	1	no place ... earth's failing Have such kindly judgment given
108	3	No vision ever brought ... such great glory
108	3	No ear hath ever caught Such great glory
140	2	Why lies he in such mean estate Where ox and ass are feeding
177	3	Did e'er such love and sorrow meet
267	2	Who can faint, while such a river Ever flows
279	1	Let the little ones be given Unto me, of such is heaven
330	2	How can I tell such love
340	1	Such happy, simple fisher-folk, Before the Lord came down
343	1	And safe is such confiding, For nothing changes here
402	2	Such ever bring thee where they come
431	4	Such boastings as the Gentiles use Or lesser breeds
466	3	In all our hearts such love increase, That every home

sudden
| 232 | 2 | No sudden rending of the veil of clay |

suddenly
42	3	Suddenly breaks on earth Light from the sky
117	4	Suddenly the Lord, descending, In his temple shall appear
228	3	Suddenly return, and never, Nevermore thy temples leave

sue
| 166 | 2 | Savior, for our pardon sue, When our sins thy pangs renew |

suffer
83	T,1	If Thou but Suffer God to Guide Thee
105	2	He comes with succor speedy To those who suffer wrong
148	2	Fasting with unceasing prayer, Glad with thee to suffer pain
154	T,1	O thou Who Through This Holy Week Didst suffer for us all
187	1	Who did once upon the cross ... Suffer to redeem our loss
222	1	I will suffer nought to hide thee
374	1	Nor for fear or favor Suffer me to fall
385	1	Lift high his royal banner, It must not suffer loss
417	2	And those who can suffer can dare
449	3	To joy and suffer not alone
489	1	I would be strong, for there is much to suffer

suffered
160	2	see The very dying form of one Who suffered there for me
162	4	There behold his agony, Suffered on the bitter tree
170	2	What thou, my Lord, hast suffered, Was all for sinner's gain
171	2	But we believe it was for us He hung and suffered there

sufferer
  51 4   Comfort every sufferer Watching late in pain

suffering
  153 4   Abide with us, that so, this life Of suffering overpast
  154 3   Thy feet the path of suffering trod
  158 2   Shun not suffering, shame, or loss
  162 2   See that suffering friendless one Weeping, praying ... alone
  178 1   'Tis midnight, in the garden now The suffering Savior
  178 1   The suffering Savior prays alone

sufferings
  167 VI-1   By thy sufferings perfect made, Hear us, holy Jesus

suffers
  419 3   One in the love that suffers long To seek, & serve & save

sufficed
  128 2   In the bleak midwinter A stable place sufficed
  128 2   A stable place sufficed The Lord God almighty, Jesus Christ
  403 1   thus the gift of love sufficed

sufficient
    1 2   Sufficient is thine arm alone, And our defense is sure
  103 4   By ... all-sufficient merit Raise us to thy glorious throne
  372 4   My grace, all-sufficient, shall be thy supply
  412 3   with the task sufficient strength, Show us thy will, we ask

suggest
  32 4   Direct, control, suggest, this day All I design or do or say

suit
  580 3   For mercy, Lord, is all my suit, O let thy mercy spare

sullen
  348 4   When death's cold, sullen stream Shall e'er me roll

sultry
  484 2   Some work in sultry forests Where apes swing to and fro

sum
  411 4   How good thy thoughts toward us, how great their sum

summer
  457 T,1   The Summer Days Are Come Again
  457 1   And deepening shade of summer woods, And glow of summer air
  457 3   The summer days are come again, The birds are on the wing
  457 2   For summer joy in field and wood We lift our song to him
  458 3   Praise him for his summer rain
  462 2   All the fruits in full supply Ripened 'neath the summer sky
  478 3   The cold wind in the winter, The pleasant summer sun
  487 1   Spring wind, summer rain, Then the harvest grain
  579 T,1   Summer Ended, Harvest O'er, Lord, to thee our song we pour

summer's
  455 4   O God, who givest the winter's cold As well as summer's

455   4   As well as summer's joyous rays

summoned
  316 1   Summoned forth its fruit and flower

summons
   63 3   Glad thy summons to obey
  426 T,1   The Voice of God Is Calling Its summons unto men
  426 3   We heed, O Lord, thy summons, And answer, Here are we

sun
    8 1   Opening to the sun above
   13 1   Sun and moon, rejoice before him
   16 4   Sun and moon, bow down before him
   16 4   Sun and moon ... Dwellers in all time and space
   32 T,1   Awake, My Soul, and With the Sun
   33 T,1   As the Sun Doth Daily Rise Bright'ning all the morning skies
   34 2   See how the giant sun soars up, Great lord of years and days
   39 2   O thou true Sun, on us thy glance Let fall
   42 4   What though the hill be steep, Strength's in the sun
   43 1   Sun of righteousness arise, Triumph o'er the shades of night
   47 4   The sun that bids us rest is waking Our brethren
   50 T,1   Sun of My Soul, Thou Savior Dear
   54 1   Our heavenly Sun, our glorious Light
   55 T,1   At Even, Ere the Sun Was Set
   58 2   When the constant sun returning Unseals our eyes
   64 1   Thou burning sun with golden beam
   66 2   Hill & vale, and tree & flower, Sun & moon & stars of light
   68 1   I sing the wisdom that ordained The sun to rule the day
   69 1   Sun & moon, uplift your voice, Night & stars, in God rejoice
   70 3   He the golden-tressed sun Caused all day his course to run
   72 1   The unwearied sun, from day to day ... power display
   72 1   sun ... Does his creator's power display
   85 3   moon by night thee shall not smite, Nor yet the sun by day
   89 1   Thy glory flames from sun and star
   89 2   Sun of our life, thy quickening ray Sheds
  120 3   Hail the Sun of righteousness
  152 4   At even-tide before the sun was set
  157 3   When the sun of bliss is beaming Light and love upon my way
  165 2   E'en though the sun witholds its light
  185 2   And from three days' sleep in death As a sun hath risen
  188 1   The sun shone out with fair array
  201 2   But crowned with glory like the sun
  201 2   like the sun That lights the morning sky
  202 T,1   Jesus Shall Reign Where'er the Sun
  202 1   sun Doth his successive journeys run
  224 3   The solemn shadow of thy cross Is better than the sun
  244 1   Sun of the soul, thou Light divine
  247 3   from morn to set of sun Through the Church the song goes on
  257 2   The rolling sun, the changing light, And nights and days
  257 3   Sun, moon, and stars convey thy praise Round the whole earth
  257 4   That see the light or feel the sun
  259 2   And grow it shall, our glorious sun More fervid rays afford
  287 4   thou art here, Nearer than ever, still my shield and sun
  288 R   When I fall on my knees with my face to the rising sun
  293 4   glad sound comes with the setting sun, Well done, well done

296	1	The sun that lights its shining folds
304	4	Church ... binds the ransomed nations 'neath the sun
351	2	Though like the wanderer, The sun gone down
351	5	sun, moon, and stars forgot, Upward I fly
391	4	May I reach heaven's joys, O bright heaven's Sun
392	6	And love to all men 'neath the sun
419	1	Whose life ... is freely poured On all beneath the sun
420	3	where the sun that shineth is God's grace for human good
448	T,1	Thy Kingdom Come, O Lord, Wide-circling as the sun
459	2	he bids the sun cut short his race, And wintry days appear
478	3	The cold wind in the winter, The pleasant summer sun
480	1	Jesus saw The same bright sun that shines today
486	1	Comes the eastern sun Like a man of brawn
506	2	Gladly hail the sun returning

sung

11	1	Let the Redeemer's name be sung through every land
11	1	sung Through every land, by every tongue
131	1	Of Jesse's lineage coming As men of old have sung
235	2	This to thy praise, O Lord, be sung
383	2	Poets sung its glory, Heroes for it died

sunlight

38	3	Mine is the sunlight, Mine is the morning

sunlit

38	2	Sweet the rain's new fall Sunlit from heaven

sunrise

42	2	Out of the cloud and strife Sunrise is born
165	T,1	Sunset to Sunrise Changes Now
198	2	the whole round world complete, From sunrise to its setting

suns

11	2	Till suns shall rise and set no more
74	1	Bringing suns and stars to birth

sunset

52	2	Soon as dies the sunset glory, Stars of heaven shine out
165	T,1	Sunset to Sunrise Changes Now
478	2	The sunset, and the morning That brightens up the sky

sunshine

101	2	And our lives would be all sunshine (102-4)
160	3	I ask no other sunshine than The sunshine of his face
209	3	Through cloud and sunshine, O abide with me
227	3	Fair is the sunshine, Fairer still the moonlight
422	4	Flames out the sunshine of the great tomorrow
460	1	The breezes and the sunshine, And soft, refreshing rain

sunshine's

67	2	Thy love is in the sunshine's glow
399	2	That in thy sunshine's blaze its day May brighter, fairer be

sunward

8	4	Joyful music leads us sunward, In the triumph song of life

sup
280   2   There sup with us in love divine, Thy body and thy blood

supernal
30   4   O friends, in gladness let us sing, Supernal anthems echoing
259   3   And look down from supernal heights On all the by-gone time

supper
558   5   Till thou return and we shall eat The marriage supper
558   5   The marriage supper of the Lamb

supplication
333   1   Answer in love thy children's supplication
378   1   Hear and receive thy Church's supplication,
519   T,1   To My Humble Supplication, Lord give ear and acceptation

supplied
281   1   Day by day with strength supplied Through the life of him
281   1   strength supplied through the life of him who died
461   1   God, our Maker, doth provide For our wants to be supplied
462   1   God, our Maker, doth provide For our wants to be supplied

supplies
70   5   His full hand supplies their need
281   2   Vine of heaven, thy love supplies ... blest cup of sacrifice
384   1   Strong in the strength that God supplies
384   1   God supplies Through his eternal Son
492   1   whose constant care Supplies our golden days

supply
167   VII-3 May thy life and death supply Grace to live and grace to die
267   2   Well supply thy sons and daughters
372   4   My grace, all-sufficient, shall be thy supply
462   2   All the fruits in full supply Ripened 'neath the summer sky

supplying
258   5   Word of life, supplying Comfort to the dying

support
210   2   Leave, ah, leave me not alone, Still support and comfort me
324   4   O let thy hand support me still
576   4   And my support thy power divine

supported
454   1   hand By which supported still we stand

supports
76   2   While providence supports, Let saints securely dwell
78   4   He ... Supports the fainting heart

supreme
78   3   Supreme in wisdom as in power The Rock of ages stands
424   1   Justice reigns supreme o'er all
577   1   Make manifest in this dread time Thy power supreme
577   1   power supreme, thy love sublime

sure
1	2	Sufficient is thine arm alone, And our defense is sure
4	4	His mercy is forever sure
26	4	Yea, his law is sure, In his light we walk secure
28	2	Thy Church ... standeth sure while earth and time endure
70	R	For his mercies aye endure, Ever faithful, ever sure
86	1	Thine is the mighty plan, The steadfast order sure
87	4	Blind unbelief is sure to err And scan his work in vain
207	T,1	I Greet Thee, Who My Sure Redeemer Art
207	5	Lord, give us peace, and make us calm and sure
215	3	sure it still Will lead me on O'er moor and fen
255	1	His testimony is most sure, Proclaiming wisdom's way
263	T,1	Christ Is Made the Sure Foundation
267	1	On the Rock of Ages founded, What can shake thy sure repose
269	5	Sure as thy truth shall last, To Zion shall be given
308	4	Lord and light of every age, By thy same sure counsel led
354	1	Our great and sure salvation
356	2	It has no spring of action sure, It varies with the wind
363	3	His rage we can endure, For lo, his doom is sure
383	1	Manifold the service, One the sure reward
433	3	Be thy strong arm our ever sure defense
463	1-3	For his mercies still endure, Ever faithful, ever sure
497	1	In all his words most wonderful, Most sure in all his ways
565	2	Be ye sure that the Lord he is God
579	2	For the promise ever sure that, while heaven & earth endure

surely
15	3	Surely his goodness and mercy here daily attend thee
84	5	Goodness and mercy all my life Shall surely follow me
123	2	All you need I will surely give you
270	2	Surely in temples made with hands, God ... is not dwelling
298	1,4	Nearer & nearer draws the time ... time that shall surely be
328	2	thou shalt surely feel His wind, that bloweth healthily
354	3	For thou shalt guard us surely
377	4	Thou his people art, & surely He will fold his own securely
414	3	Who serves my Father as a son Is surely kin to me

surge's
261	4	In vain the surge's angry shock, In vain the drifting sands

surging
14	2	His spirit floweth free, High surging where it will
252	3	It is the chart and compass That o'er life's surging sea
345	3	With voice as full and strong As ocean's surging praise

surpasses
142	2	But the very beasts could see that he all men surpasses

surpassing
312	4	There Mary sings Magnificat With tune surpassing sweet

surprise
360	5	I know not what the future hath Of marvel or surprise

surround
8	2	All thy works with joy surround thee

| 504 | 1 | And praise surround the throne |

surrounded

170	1	Now scornfully surrounded With thorns thy only crown
267	1	With salvation's walls surrounded, Thou may'st smile
445	3	In wrath and fear, by jealousies surrounded

surrounding

| 3 | 2 | See the crowds the throne surrounding |

survey

68	2	If I survey the ground I tread or gaze upon the sky
177	T,1	When I Survey the Wondrous Cross
362	2	A cloud of witnesses around Hold thee in full survey
442	2	When all our lack thou dost survey

surveys

| 94 | T,1 | When All Thy Mercies, O My God, My rising soul surveys |

sustain

2	4	Do thou in faith sustain us
128	2	Our God, heaven cannot hold him, Nor earth sustain
207	3	Sustain us by thy faith and by thy power
334	2	Thou wilt sustain us till its work is done

sustained

| 158 | 2 | Love to man his soul sustained |

sustaineth

| 15 | 2 | Shelters thee under his wings, yea, so gently sustaineth |

sware

| 568 | 6 | To perform the oath which he sware to our forefather Abraham |
| 568 | 6 | sware ... that he would give us |

swathing

| 146 | 4 | All meanly wrapped in swathing bands, And in a manger laid |

sway

18	3	The world is with the glory filled Of thy majestic sway
47	5	grows ... Till all thy creatures own thy sway
75	4	To thy sway all creatures bow
106	2	He comes to reign with boundless sway
198	1	New life, new hope awakes Where'er men own his sway
207	2	So come, O King, and our whole being sway
224	1	We own thy sway, we hear thy call
337	2	Leave to this sovereign sway To choose and to command
432	3	from the breeds of earth thy silent sway Fashions the nation

sways

| 441 | 3 | Yet that scaffold sways the future |

sweat

| 422 | 4 | When on the sweat of labor and its sorrow |

sweeping
422	5	Sweeping the shavings from his workshop floor

sweeps
305	1	Each breeze that sweeps the ocean Brings tidings from afar
401	4	Who sweeps a room, as for thy laws
401	4	Who sweeps a room ... Makes that and the action fine

sweet
23	2	in his light with sweet delight Ye do abound
35	2	The powers of darkness fear, When this sweet chant they hear
37	1	lovelier ... Dawns the sweet consciousness, I am with thee
38	2	Sweet the rain's new fall Sunlit from heaven
50	2	Be my last thought how sweet to rest Forever on my Savior's
51	2	Jesus, give the weary Calm and sweet repose
56	3	And with sweet sleep mine eye-lids close
58	1	Slumber sweet thy mercy send us
76	3	And sweet refreshment find
123	2	Hark, a voice from yonder manger, Soft and sweet
135	T,1,2	O Jesu Sweet, O Jesu Mild
137	1	The little Lord Jesus laid down his sweet head
140	1	Whom angels greet with anthems sweet
155	1,3	To whom the lips of children Made sweet hosannas ring
168	2	Yet give us strength to trust the sweet assurance
169	3	Sometimes they strew his way, And his sweet praises sing
169	4	Sweet injuries
169	5	In whose sweet praise I all my days Could gaily spend
202	2	His name like sweet perfume shall rise With every morning
212	1	By thy teachings sweet and holy
221	T,1	How Sweet the Name of Jesus Sounds In a believer's ear
230	4	But warm, sweet, tender, even yet A present help is he
236	2	Thine is every time & place, Fountain sweet of heart & mind
247	2	Fill the heavens with sweet accord, Holy, holy, holy Lord
260	4	And mystic sweet communion With those whose rest is won
268	2	Sweet the psalm and sweet the carol When our song is raised
269	4	Her sweet communion, solemn vows, Her hymns of love & praise
271	3	The same sweet theme endeavor
275	3	One in our love of all things sweet and fair
292	3	And by this food, so aweful and so sweet Deliver us
309	4	O sweet and blessed country, The home of God's elect
309	4	O sweet and blessed country, that eager hearts expect
312	4	There Mary sings Magnificat With tune surpassing sweet
322	1	Day by day his sweet voice soundeth
349	3	Return, O holy Dove, return, Sweet messenger of rest
354	1	In thee alone, dear Lord, we own Sweet hope and consolation
375	2	And holiness shall whisper The sweet amen of peace
405	T,1	Master, No Offering Costly and Sweet
418	3	In work that keeps faith sweet and strong
423	4	Yet long these multitudes to see The sweet compassion
423	4	The sweet compassion of thy face
437	1	Sweet land of liberty, Of thee I sing
437	3	And ring from all the trees Sweet freedom's song
470	4	Theirs, by sweet love, for Christ a kingdom won
483	T,1	I Think When I Read That Sweet Story of old
493	3	prayer That God, in sweet forgiveness' name ... spare
493	3	God, in sweet forgiveness' name, Should understand and spare

510	2	Jesus, give the weary Calm and sweet repose
539	2	possess in sweet communion Joys which earth cannot afford
542	T,1	Sweet Savior, Bless Us Ere We Go

sweeten
| 402 | 4 | To strengthen faith and sweeten care |

sweeter
46	3	Give sweeter songs than lips can sing
225	1	But sweeter far thy face to see, And in thy presence rest
225	2	Nor can the memory find A sweeter sound than thy blest name
262	3	A sweeter song shall then be heard
405	1	Yet may love's incense rise, Sweeter than sacrifice
509	3	Give sweeter songs than lips can sing

sweetest
| 123 | 1 | As I hear, Far and near, Sweetest angel voices |
| 202 | 3 | Dwell on his love with sweetest song |

sweetly
6	4	And sweetly distills in the dew and the rain
116	T,1	Angels We Have Heard on High Sweetly singing o'er the plains
178	4	Unheard by mortals are the strains That sweetly soothe
178	4	That sweetly soothe the Savior's woe
476	3	The singers sweetly gifted
482	T,1	Little Jesus, Sweetly Sleep, do not stir
482	2	Mary's little baby, sleep, sweetly sleep
525	T,1	Come, & Let Us Sweetly Join Christ to praise in hymns divine

sweetness
38	2	Praise for the sweetness Of the wet garden
101	2	In the sweetness of our Lord (102-4)
225	1	thought of thee With sweetness fills my breast
402	3	Here to our waiting hearts proclaim The sweetness
402	3	The sweetness of thy saving name

swell
99	3	We read thee ... In the seas that swell & streams that flow
247	3	Prophets swell the glad refrain
262	4	That song shall swell from shore to shore
437	3	Let music swell the breeze
460	1	he sends the snow in winter, The warmth to swell the grain
508	2	And through the swell of chanting voices

swelling
| 106 | 4 | Unvisited, unblest, Break forth to swelling song |
| 463 | 2 | Praise him ... he gave the rain To mature the swelling grain |

swerving
| 411 | 1 | purpose never swerving Leads toward the day of Jesus Christ |

swift
16	2	same forever, Slow to chide and swift to bless
42	2	Swift grows the light for us, Ended is night for us
209	2	Swift to its close ebbs out life's little day
217	3	Your hands swift to welcome your arms to embrace

266	3	And feet on mercy's errands swift Do make her pilgrimage
308	3	True and faithful to command, Swift and fearless to obey
404	2	Take my feet and let them be Swift and beautiful for thee
443	1	He hath loosed the fateful lightning of his ... swift sword
443	1	lightning of his terrible swift sword
443	3	O be swift, my soul, to answer him, be jubilant, my feet

swiftly
| 129 | 3 | Look now, for glad and golden hours Come swiftly on the wing |
| 293 | 2 | Redeem the time, its hours too swiftly fly |

swing
| 484 | 2 | Some work in sultry forests Where apes swing to and fro |

sword
198	2	To plough-share beat the sword, To pruning-hook the spear
229	4	Thy scepter and thy sword, Thy reigning grace I sing
246	2	Gird on thy mighty sword, Our prayer attend
308	2	Warriors wielding freedom's sword
356	1	Force me to render up my sword, And I shall conqueror be
365	1	living still In spite of dungeon, fire, and sword
381	3	My faith, it is a trusty sword, May falsehood find it keen
419	2	And lift the spirit's sword
419	2	spirit's sword to shield The weak against the strong
422	3	Holding his pick more splendid than the sword
435	3	Cleave our darkness with thy sword
436	2	From sale and profanation Of honor and the sword
436	3	Lift up a living nation, A single sword to thee
439	2	Not for battleship and fortress ... conquests of the sword
443	1	lightning of his terrible swift sword
446	1	Thunder thy clarion, the lightning thy sword
470	4	Theirs not a jeweled crown, a blood-stained sword
493	1	And on his lips a sword Wherewith he smote and overcame
493	4	Let me, O Lord, thy cause defend, A knight without a sword

swords
| 436 | 1 | The walls of gold entomb us, The swords of scorn divide |

swords'
| 375 | 2 | not with swords' loud clashing Nor roll of stirring drums |

sworn
| 427 | 3 | Sworn to yield, to waver, never, Consecrated, born again |
| 427 | 3 | Sworn to be Christ's soldiers ever |

symbols
| 287 | 4 | Too soon we rise, the symbols disappear |

sympathizing
| 272 | 3 | And often for each other flows The sympathizing tear |

Syrian
| 341 | 2 | In simple trust like theirs who heard, Beside the Syrian sea |

systems
| 357 | 4 | Our little systems have their day |

tabernacles

274	1	how dear The pleasant tabernacles are Where thou dost dwell

table

79	5	Thou spread'st a table in my sight
84	4	My table thou hast furnished In presence of my foes
280	1	Savior, abide with us, and spread Thy table in our heart
286	2	Thou at the table, blessing, yet dost stand
287	3	This is the heavenly table spread for me
458	4	Each the table of our God
558	4	Meet at my table and record The love of your departed Lord

take

4	2	And for his sheep he doth us take
23	3	Take what he gives And praise him still
50	5	ere through the world our way we take
64	4	Forgiving others, take your part, O sing ye, Alleluia
83	2	with heart content To take whate'er thy Father's pleasure
87	2	Ye fearful saints, fresh courage take
96	2	And take, content, What he hath sent
101	2	We should take him at his word (102-4)
105	1	To take away transgression, And rule in equity
150	1	God, the Son of God, should take Our mortal form
150	1	take out mortal form for mortals' sake
160	T,1	Beneath the Cross of Jesus I fain would take my stand
160	3	I take, O cross, thy shadow For my abiding place
168	2	our weak endurance Make us unworthy here to take our part
168	3	Which thou didst take to save our souls from loss
169	1	O who am I, That for my sake My Lord should take Frail flesh
169	1	take Frail flesh and die
175	4	Then take, O Christ, thy power, and reign
205	2	Take the King of glory in
207	1	I pray thee from our hearts all cares to take
210	3	Thou of life the fountain art, Freely let me take of thee
228	2	Take away the love of sinning
228	4	Till in heaven we take our place
232	2	But take the dimness of my soul away
238	4	holiness, the road That we must take to dwell with God
271	3	Ye saints to come, take up the strain
284	2	Thy testamental cup I take, And thus remember thee
311	3	Fill up the roll of thine elect, Then take thy power & reign
335	2,3	Take it to the Lord in prayer
335	3	In his arms he'll take and shield thee
341	4	Take from our souls the strain and stress
348	1	Take all my guilt away
359	4	dares to take the side that seems Wrong to man's ... eye
384	2	And take, to arm you for the fight, The panoply of God
384	3	Take every virtue, every grace, And fortify the whole
392	+1	When we are grown and take our place As men and women
398	4	Take thou our lives and use them as thou wilt
402	2	And going take thee to their home
404	T,1	Take My Life and Let It Be Consecrated, Lord, to thee
404	1	Take my moments and my days
404	3	Take my will, and make it thine, It shall be no longer mine
404	3	Take my heart, it is thine own, It shall be thy royal throne
404	4	Take my love, my Lord I pour At thy feet its treasure store

404	4	Take myself, and I will be Ever, only, all for thee
404	2	Take my hands and let them move At the impulse of thy love
404	2	Take my feet and let them be Swift and beautiful for thee
426	4	Take us, and make us holy, Teach us thy will and way
436	1	Take not thy thunder from us, But take away our pride
461	3	For the Lord our God shall come And shall take his harvest
461	3	And shall take his harvest home
490	2	But take as from thy hands our tasks And glorify them all
528	2	and take not thy Holy Spirit from me
531	1	And take not thy Holy Spirit from us
533	1	And take not thy Holy Spirit from us
576	4	If I the wings of morning take

taken

| 96 | 3 | Here shall my stand be taken |

takes

72	2	Soon as the evening shades prevail The moon takes up .. tale
72	2	The moon takes up the wondrous tale
109	3	Traveler, darkness takes its flight
127	4	Till man's first heavenly state again takes place
203	4	Jesus takes the highest station

takest

554	5	That takest away the sins of the world, have mercy upon us
554	6	that takest away the sins of the world, receive our prayer
555	T,1	O Lamb of God, that takest away the sins of the world
556	1	that takest away the sins of the world

taketh

| 343 | 2 | He knows the way he taketh, And I will walk with him |

tale

| 72 | 2 | The moon takes up the wondrous tale |

talents

| 316 | 3 | Offering talents, time and treasure, For the mercy |

tales

| 424 | 1 | Wondrous tales of it are told |

talk

| 124 | 2 | It is wrong to talk so loud |

tares

| 461 | 2 | Wheat and tares together sown, Unto joy or sorrow grown |
| 461 | 3 | Give his angels charge at last In the fire the tares to cast |

tarries

| 300 | 2 | His kingdom tarries long |

tarry

| 446 | 3 | Falsehood and wrong shall not tarry beside thee |

task

| 36 | 5 | The trivial round, the common task, Will furnish all |

task

36	5	the common task, Will furnish all we ought to ask
58	2	Gird us for the task that calls us
152	2	Shining revealed through every task most lowly
220	1	Beside us walks our brother Christ, & makes our task his own
266	4	Fulfill thy task sublime
300	3	Her strength unequal to her task, Rise up and make her great
370	3	And when my task on earth is done
406	2	task thy wisdom hath assigned, O let me cheerfully fulfill
409	3	Every task, however simple, Sets the soul that does it free
412	3	O thou who didst the vision send And gives to each his task
412	3	with the task sufficient strength, Show us thy will, we ask
424	2	Whether humble or exalted, All are called to task divine
470	1	Each age its solemn task may claim but once

tasks

220	3	The tasks he gives are those he gave Beside the restless sea
395	T,1	Behold Us, Lord, a Little Space From daily tasks set free
490	2	But take as from thy hands our tasks And glorify them all

taste

287	2	Here taste afresh the calm of sin forgiven
557	2	Here taste afresh the calm of sin forgiven

tastes

94	3	Nor in the least a cheerful heart that tastes those gifts
94	3	That tastes those gifts with joy

taught

150	3	For us he prayed, for us he taught
380	2	The sons of fathers we By whom our faith is taught
380	2	taught To fear no ill, to fight The holy fight they fought
395	6	prayer, by thee inspired and taught, Itself with work be one
409	1	By thy patience and thy courage, Thou hast taught us
409	1	Thou has taught us toil is good

tea

481	3	In church, or in trains, or in shops, or at tea

teach

8	3	Teach us how to love each other
74	3	Teach us more of human pity, That we in thine image grow
153	1	Teach us ... to mourn our sins, And close by thee to stay
173	4	Teach us to know our sin which needs forgiving
173	4	Teach us to know the love which can forgive
174	4	Teach me by that bitter cry In the gloom to know thee nigh
232	3	I see thy cross -- there teach my heart to cling
232	4	Teach me to feel that thou art always nigh
232	4	Teach me the struggles of the soul to bear
232	4	Teach me the patience of unanswered prayer
232	5	Teach me to love thee as thine angels love
235	3	Teach us to know our God aright
252	4	O teach thy wandering pilgrims By this their path to trace
277	2	Give to all who teach and guide them Wisdom and humility
316	1	Teach our hearts to love thee only
318	3	Cleanse it from guilt and wrong, Teach it salvation's song
336	1	Lord, teach us how to pray

269	3	For her my tears shall fall, For her my prayers ascend
282	1	Look on the tears by sinners shed
305	1	The sons of earth are waking To penitential tears
329	2	And thorns thy brow encircle, And tears thy face have marred
337	1	God hears thy sighs and counts thy tears
348	3	Wipe sorrow's tears away
358	2	Could my zeal no respite know, Could my tears forever flow
405	3	Some balm of peace for eyes Blinded with tears
420	1	And where the tears are wiped from eyes That shall not weep
423	2	We catch the vision of thy tears
424	3	Oft with bleeding hands and tears
440	4	Thine alabaster cities gleam, Undimmed by human tears
452	4	For us his tears and blood were spent

teeming

| 340 | 3 | Peter, who hauled the teeming net, Head down was crucified |
| 352 | 3 | Low lie the bounding heart, the teeming brain |

tell

4	1	Him serve with mirth, his praise forth tell
6	2	O tell of his might, O sing of his grace
17	2	All that hath life and breath, tell the story
17	2	tell the story In accent strong, with voices free
19	2	Earth to heaven, and heaven to earth ...tell his wonders
19	2	Tell his wonders, sing his worth
104	1	Tell her that her sins I cover, And her warfare now is over
109	T,1-3	Watchman, Tell Us of the Night
134	4	We hear the Christmas angels The great glad tidings tell
167	IV-3	Tell our faith that God is near, Hear us, holy Jesus
171	2	We may not know, we cannot tell What pains he had to bear
174	1	None can tell what pangs unknown Hold thee silent and alone
192	T,1	The Day of Resurrection, Earth, tell it out abroad
258	4	Who can tell the pleasure, Who recount the treasure
302	1	To tell to all the world that God is light
302	2	Tell how he stooped to save his lost creation
308	2	All thy servants tell thy praise
317	T,1	I Love to Tell the Story Of unseen things above
317	1	I love to tell the story, Because I know it's true
317	R	I love to tell the story, 'Twill be my theme in glory
317	R	To tell the old, old story Of Jesus and his love
317	2	I love to tell the story, For those who know it best
328	3	The Lord is wonderful and wise, As all the ages tell
330	2	That thou shouldst bear our sin and shame, How can I tell
330	2	How can I tell such love
346	2	Faithful are all who ... dare the truth to tell
359	3	The instinct that can tell That God is on the field
397	4	Thy love to tell, thy praise to show
418	1	Tell me thy secret, help be bear The strain of toil
427	3	Strike, let every nerve and sinew Tell on ages, tell for God
428	R	Tell old Pharaoh, To let my people go
470	5	Forth may they go to tell all realms thy grace
488	T,R	Go, Tell It on the Mountain, Over the hills and everywhere
488	R	Go, tell it on the mountain That Jesus Christ is born

telling

| 52 | 2 | Stars ... shine out above, Telling still the ancient story |

temptation
168	1	In all the conflict of thy sore temptation
373	1	In darkness and temptation My light, my help is near

temptation's
197	5	Crown him as your captain In temptation's hour
354	3	Temptation's hour shall lose its power

temptations
150	2	For us temptations sharp he knew
335	2	Have we trials and temptations, Is there trouble anywhere
342	2	Temptations lose their power When thou art nigh

tempted
55	5	Thou hast been troubled, tempted, tried
148	1	Forty days and forty nights Tempted, and yet undefiled

tempter
150	2	For us the tempter overthrew

tempter's
158	T,1	Go to Dark Gethsemane, Ye that feel the tempter's power
167	VII-2	Guard us from the tempter's power
209	3	What but thy grace can foil the tempter's power

tempting
364	2	Striving, tempting, luring, Goading into sin
398	3	Walk thou beside us lest the tempting byways Lure us away

ten
9	4	earth, with her ten thousand tongues Shall fill thy courts
94	3	Ten thousand precious gifts My daily thanks employ
311	T,1	Ten Thousand Times Ten Thousand, In sparkling raiment bright
312	3	Ten thousand times that man were blest ... this music hear

tend
275	2	As one with thee, to whom we ever tend, As one with him

tended
506	2	God hath tended With his care thy helpless hours

tender
6	5	Thy mercies how tender, how firm to the end
53	2	all the heavenly splendor Breaks forth in starlight tender
64	4	And all ye men of tender heart
92	1	I feel thy strong and tender love, And all is well again
94	2	Unnumbered comforts to my soul Thy tender care bestowed
131	T,1	Lo, How a Rose E'er Blooming From tender stem hath sprung
138	1	Holy infant so tender and mild, Sleep in heavenly peace
167	III-2	And enjoy thy tender care, Hear us, holy Jesus
230	4	But warm, sweet, tender, even yet A present help is he
327	1	Much we need thy tender care
342	1	No tender voice like thine Can peace afford
423	3	From tender childhood's helplessness
465	2	assurance Of tender charity and steadfast faith
568	11	Through the tender mercy of our God

tenderest
51	2	With thy tenderest blessing May our eyelids close
333	2	Tenderest guide, in ways of cheerful duty, Lead us
510	2	With thy tenderest blessing May our eyelids close

tenderly
277	2	Thou didst receive the children to thyself so tenderly

tenderness
31	3	Truth in its beauty, and love in its tenderness

tending
471	4	Tending with care the lambs within the fold

tends
16	3	Father-like he tends and spares us

tenement
420	2	greed for gain In street and shop and tenement Wring gold

tents
375	1	Henceforth in fields of conquest Thy tents shall be our home

terrestrial
72	3	Move round the dark terrestrial ball
113	4	things celestial thee shall own ...terrestrial, Lord alone
195	4	Let every kindred, every tribe, On this terrestrial ball

terrible
443	1	lightning of his terrible swift sword

terror
109	3	Doubt and terror are withdrawn
373	2	What terror can confound me With God at my right hand
387	2	Chasing far the gloom and terror
436	2	From all that terror teaches, From lies of tongue and pen

terrors
91	5	No nightly terrors shall alarm
446	2	Bid not thy wrath in its terrors awaken

test
161	3	Yet humbly, in our striving, O God, we face its test
224	1	We test our lives by thine

testamental
284	2	Thy testamental cup I take, And thus remember thee

tested
161	1	The meaning of our eager strife Is tested by his Way

testified
383	2	Prophets have proclaimed it, Martyrs testified

testimony
255	1	His testimony is most sure, Proclaiming wisdom's way

tether

291	3	Draw us in the Spirit's tether
436	3	Tie in a living tether The prince and priest and thrall

thank

2	1	O thank him for his goodness
29	T,1	Now Thank We All Our God With heart and hands and voices
47	2	We thank thee that thy Church, unsleeping
98	T,1	My God, I Thank Thee, Who Hast Made The earth so bright
98	2	I thank thee, too, that thou hast made Joy to abound
98	3	I thank thee more that all our joy Is touched with pain
98	4	I thank thee, Lord, that thou hast kept The best in store
170	3	What language shall I borrow To thank thee, dearest friend
253	2	Thank we those who toiled in thought
268	T,1	Lord, We Thank Thee for Our Brothers
289	T,1	Father, We Thank Thee Who Hast Planted
412	1	We thank thee for thy boyhood faith
421	T,1	We Thank Thee, Lord, Thy Paths of Service
460	R	Then thank the Lord, O thank the Lord For all his love
460	3	We thank thee, then, O Father, For all things bright & good
479	T,1	Father, We Thank Thee for the Night
492	2	We thank thee, Father, for each word
500	1	We thank thee for thy gift of light

thankful

9	4	We'll crowd thy gates with thankful songs
144	4	And endless song of thankful praise
276	1	we come With thankful hearts to worship thee
460	3	And, what thou most desirest, Our humble, thankful hearts
461	T,1	Come, Ye Thankful People, Come
462	T,1	Come, Ye Thankful People Come (different vs. 2-3)
462	3	Come, then, thankful people, come, Raise the song of harvest
565	3	be thankful unto him, and speak good of his name

thankfulness

26	3	Let our lives express Our abundant thankfulness

thanks

2	2	We praise, we worship thee, we trust and give thee thanks
2	2	we trust And give thee thanks forever
17	1	thanks to God, my light, Who life and soul hath given me
29	3	All praise and thanks to God The Father now be given
53	1	Let us, as night is falling ... Give thanks to him
63	2	Thanks we give and adoration For thy Gospel's joyful sound
94	3	Ten thousand precious gifts My daily thanks employ
204	1	Rejoice, give thanks, and sing, And triumph evermore
206	4	And thanks never ceasing and infinite love
303	T,1	Creation's Lord, We Give Thee Thanks
303	1	thanks That this thy world is incomplete
303	1	thanks ... That battle calls our marshaled ranks
303	1	thanks ... That work awaits our hands and feet
345	T,1	Rejoice, Ye Pure in Heart, Rejoice, give thanks and sing
345	R	Rejoice, rejoice, Rejoice, give thanks and sing
363	4	No thanks to them, abideth
416	3	Give him thanks in humble zeal
439	2	But for conquests of the spirit Give we thanks ... O Lord

439	3	For all heroes of the spirit, Give we thanks to thee, O Lord
501	1	Our humble thanks we pay
548	T,1	Thanks Be to Thee, O Christ, for this thy holy gospel
552	1	Let us give thanks unto the Lord our God
554	2	we glorify thee, we give thanks to thee for thy great glory

thanksgiving

111	3	Hymn & chant and high thanksgiving And unwearied praises be
439	1	Lord, we would with deep thanksgiving Praise thee most for
562	2	Let us come before his presence with thanksgiving
565	3	O go your way into his gates with thanksgiving

theme

23	1	Assist our song, For else the theme Too high doth seem
271	3	The same sweet theme endeavor
317	R	I love to tell the story, 'Twill be my theme in glory

themselves

| 169 | 4 | Yet they at these Themselves displease, And 'gainst him rise |
| 371 | 2 | Do but themselves confound, His strength the more is. |

thereby

| 313 | 1 | not because I hope for heaven thereby |

therefore

24	1	Therefore with joy our song shall soar In praise to God
69	1	Heaven & earth, awake & sing, God is good and therefore King
108	3	Therefore will we, eternally, Sing hymns of joy and praise
163	4	Therefore, kind Jesus, since I cannot pay thee
559	11	we therefore pray thee, help thy servants

therein

| 192 | 3 | The round world keep high triumph, And all that is therein |
| 328 | 3 | with his light thou shalt be blest, Therein to work and live |

these

46	1	We gather in these hallowed walls
153	T,1	Lord, Who Throughout These Forty Days
153	3	through these days of penitence, & through thy passion-tide
169	4	Yet they at these Themselves displease, And 'gainst him rise
240	1	Kindle a flame of sacred love In these cold hearts of ours
244	T,1	O Holy Spirit, Enter In, Among these hearts thy work begin
279	1	Now these children come to thee As thou biddest
284	4	when these failing lips grow dumb, And mind and memory flee
310	4	Through whom, the Spirit, with these ever One
322	4	Christian, love me more than these
324	1	O burst these bonds, and set it free
336	5	Give these, and then thy will be done
366	2	Grant us wisdom ... courage For the living of these days
394	1	All these were thine, Lord, thou didst give them all to me
423	4	Yet long these multitudes to see The sweet compassion
423	5	Make haste to heal these hearts of pain
423	5	Among these restless throngs abide
434	4	These are the patriots nations need
434	4	These are the bulwarks of the state
438	4	Till these eternal hills remove

thick

thief

thine

170	3	O make me thine forever, And should I fainting be
174	1	Darkness veils thine anguished face
174	4	That thine own might ne'er be left
188	3	From every weapon death can wield Thine own ... shield
188	3	Thine own redeemed forever shield
193	T,1	Thine is the Glory
222	1	Thirsting after thee, Thine I am, O spotless Lamb
222	2	In thine arm I rest me
224	1	We test our lives by thine
229	4	Thine is the power
232	3	All, all thine own, soul, heart, and strength, and mind
232	5	Teach me to love thee as thine angels love
233	3	Til I am wholly thine
233	4	But live with thee the perfect life Of thine eternity
236	2	Thine is every time & place, Fountain sweet of heart & mind
239	1	And visit it with thine own ardow glowing
249	4	Thine is the quickening power that gives increase
266	4	O living Church, thine errand speed
268	1	Glory, glory, thine the kingdom
268	2	Glory, glory, thine the power As in heaven thy will be done
268	3	Glory, glory, thine the glory Through the ages evermore
269	T,1	I Love Thy Kingdom, Lord, The house of thine abode
269	2	Dear as the apple of thine eye, And graven on thy hand
277	1	Let thine arms around them be
278	1	So give this child of thine, we pray Thy grace and blessing
286	1	Nay, let us be thy guests, the feast is thine
286	1	Thyself at thine own board make manifest in ...our sacrament
287	5	I have no help but thine, nor do I need Another arm
287	5	Another arm save thine to lean upon
289	1	Thine is the power, be thine the praise
292	1	That only offering perfect in thine eyes
292	3	In thine own service make us glad and free
294	1	send us forth ... prophets true, To make all lands thine own
306	4	Yet all are one in thee, for all are thine
311	3	Fill up the roll of thine elect, Then take thy power & reign
311	3	Appear, Desire of nations, Thine exiles long for home
312	6	see Thine endless joy, and of the same Partaker ever be
316	1	Man, created in thine image, Lives nor breathes without
316	1	Lives nor breathes without thine aid
318	T,1	Draw Thou My Soul, O Christ, Closer to thine
318	2	Lead forth my soul, O Christ, One with thine own
321	T,1	My God, Accept My Heart This Day, And make it always thine
321	3	Anoint me with thy heavenly grace, Adopt me for thine own
322	5	Give our hearts to thine obedience
327	1	Blessed Jesus, Thou hast bought us, thine we are
327	2	We are thine, do thou befriend us
330	5	Then keep me safe, for so, O Lord Thou keepest but thine own
336	3	Give, what thine eye delights to see, Truth
342	1	No tender voice like thine Can peace afford
347	3	And kindness in our bosoms dwell As free and true as thine
347	4	Then, like thine own, be all our aim To conquer them by love
348	1	Oh, let me from this day Be wholly thine
356	1	Imprison me within thine arms, And strong shall be my hand
356	3	My will is not my own Till thou hast made it thine
357	3	Our wills are ours to make them thine
362	3	'Tis his own hand presents the prize To thine aspiring eye

366	1	Crown thine ancient church's story
367	2	Lift up thine eyes, and seek his face
373	3	His truth be thine affiance, When faint and desolate
377	1	Thou art daily in his keeping, And thine every care is his
394	1	All these were thine, Lord, thou didst give them all to me
395	4	Thine are the loom, the forge, the mart, The wealth of land
395	4	Thine are ... the wealth of land and sea
399	1	that in thine ocean depths its flow May richer, fuller be
404	3	Take my will, and make it thine, It shall be no longer mine
404	3	Take my heart, it is thine own, It shall be thy royal throne
413	1	For thine own dost ever plead
413	2	Thine the gold and thine the silver
413	2	Thine the wealth of land and sea
416	3	Let thine alms be hope and joy
426	3	Send us upon thine errand, Let us thy servants be
427	2	Up, it is Jehovah's rally, God's own arm hath need of thine
431	2	Still stands thine ancient sacrifice ... a contrite heart
432	2	Thine ancient might destroyed the Pharaoh's boast
432	2	thou hast brought thine own
433	4	And glory, laud, and praise be ever thine
435	3	Crown, O God, thine own endeavor
440	2	America, America, God mend thine every flaw
440	4	Thine alabaster cities gleam, Undimmed by human tears
451	1	Still wilt not hear thine inner God proclaim
452	3	we strive in vain To save ourselves without thine aid
461	4	Come, with all thine angels, come
466	1	Who dost in love proclaim Each family thine own
468	1	All souls are thine
468	2	Thine are their thoughts, their works, their powers
468	2	All thine, and yet most truly ours
468	3	Beyond thy voice, thine arm, thy care
469	1	Safe in thine own eternity Our dead are living unto thee
469	2	All souls are thine, and here or there They rest
472	1	Building for thine employ This house of prayer
472	2	Thine evermore to be
473	2	For judgments thine are known
475	2	May be in very deed thine own
475	3	The gold and silver, make them thine
475	4	We but present thee with thine own
477	4	And we, as living temples, thine
501	2	O let heaven's eternal day Be thine eternal praise
508	2	Thine ear discerns, thy love rejoices When hearts rise up
535	T,1	We Give Thee But Thine Own, Whate'er the gift may be
535	1	All that we have is thine alone, A trust, O Lord, from thee
536	1	and of thine own have we given thee
537	T,1	All Things Are Thine
537	1	Thine own before thy feet we lay
557	3	I have no help but thine, nor do I need Another arm
557	3	Another arm save thine to lean upon
559	6	thine adorable, true and only Son
559	13	O Lord, save thy people and bless thine heritage
576	4	The hand that leadeth me is thine

thing

310	2	Nor the thing prayed for come short of the prayer
330	3	Ah, did not he the heavenly throne A little thing esteem

435	3	Cleanse the body of this nation Through the ... Lord
466	3	every home, by this release, May be the dwelling place
468	1	From this our world of flesh set free, We know them living
471	2	Here on thy servant in this solemn hour
472	1	Building for thine employ This house of prayer
472	1	Our willing offerings brought This work to share
472	2	Come, thou, O Lord divine, Make this thy holy shrine
472	3	May this new temple prove True witness of thy love
472	3	May all who seek this door, And saving grace implore
472	4	Thy cross we lift on high This house to glorify
475	2	Grant that all we, who here today ... this foundation lay
475	2	Rejoicing this foundation lay
477	2	For thee this house of praise we rear
477	4	Accept, O God, this earthly shrine
485	T,1-3	This Is My Father's World
491	2	To right the wrongs that shame this mortal life
492	3	Companion of this sacred hour, Renew
496	2	And this be our motto, In God is our trust
499	1	Let us adore And own how solemn is this place
501	2	Let this day praise thee, O Lord God
503	1	O how blessed is this place
504	T,1	This Is the Day the Lord Hath Made
506	1	Come to him who made this splendor
544	1	and incline our hearts to keep this law
548	T,1	Thanks Be to Thee, O Christ, for this thy holy gospel
558	3	'This is my body, broke for sin
558	4	Do this, he cried, till time shall end
559	15	Vouchsafe, O Lord, to keep us this day without sin
575	4	That through the ages all along This may be our endless song
577	1	Make manifest in this dread time Thy power supreme
579	3	Have mercy, now, upon my soul, Hear this my humble prayer

thorn

326	4	But with mocking scorn and with crown of thorn they bore

thorns

98	3	That shadows fall on brightest hours, That thorns remain
170	1	Now scornfully surrounded With thorns thy only crown
177	3	Or thorns compose so rich a crown
200	T,1	The Head That Once Was Crowned With Thorns
325	1	By thorns with which they crowned thee
325	1	And still our wrongs may weave thee now New thorns
325	1	New thorns to pierce that steady brow
329	2	And thorns thy brow encircle, And tears thy face have marred

thorny

77	1	thy best, thy heavenly friend Through thorny ways leads
77	1	Through thorny ways leads to a joyful end

thoroughfare

440	2	A thoroughfare for freedom beat Across the wilderness

though

25	2	Though high above all praise, Above all blessing high
42	4	What though the hill be steep, Strength's in the sun
44	2	And though their Lord they failed to know

72	3	What though, in solemn silence, all Move
72	3	What though no real voice nor sound ... be found
83	3	though undeserving, Thou yet shalt find it true for thee
84	3	Yea, though I walk in death's dark vale
86	2	Though we who fain would find thee
96	1	Though dark my road, He holds me that I shall not fall
96	3	Though sorrow, need, or death be mine, Yet am I not forsaken
106	1	Though absent long, your Lord is nigh
165	2	E'en though the sun witholds its light
167	IV-3	Though no Father seems to hear .. no light our spirits cheer
168	2	We would not leave thee, though our weak endurance
205	3	Though returning to his throne
208	2	Though what I dream and what I do
222	2	Though the earth be shaking, Every heart be quaking
222	3	Though the storms may gather, Still have peace within
251	3	Holy, holy, holy, though the darkness hide thee
251	3	Though the eye of sinful man thy glory may not see
264	3	Though earth-quake shocks are threatening her
287	4	The feast, though not the love is past and gone
303	4	What though the kingdom long delay
315	4	Which calls us, very sinners, Unworthy though we be
319	2	Just as I am, though tossed about
351	1	E'en though it be a cross That raiseth me
351	2	Though like the wanderer, The sun gone down
354	2	Though Satan's wrath beset our path
361	2	Have faith in God, my mind, Though oft thy light burns low
363	3	And though this world, with devils filled
363	3	though this world ... Should threaten to undo us
371	2	No foes shall stay his might, Though he with giants fight
373	2	Though hosts encamp around me, Firm in the fight I stand
372	5	That soul, though all hell should endeavor to shake
377	2	Though the sea his waves assemble And in fury fall on thee
377	2	Though thou cry, with heart atremble, O my Savior, succor me
377	2	Though untroubled still he sleep Who thy hope is on the deep
377	3	Though the hills & vales be riven God created with his hand
377	3	Though the moving signs of heaven Wars presage in every land
377	4	Though in chains thou now art grieving
377	4	Though a tortured slave thou die
396	3	Poor though I be and weak
441	3	Though the cause of evil prosper ... truth alone is strong
442	3	Though by our fault confounded
442	3	Though selfish, mean, & base we be, Thy justice is unbounded
450	4	Though pain and passion may not die
455	3	And though abroad the sharp winds blow
467	1	Dark though the night, joy cometh with the morrow
467	4	Patient, O heart, though heavy be thy sorrows
472	5	Lord, though these hours of praise ... soon be o'er
472	5	though ... all our earthly days Will soon be o'er
485	3	Oh, let me ne'er forget That though the wrong seems oft
485	3	though the wrong seems oft so strong, God is the ruler yet
487	1	Though our work is hard, God gives us reward

thought

14	1	The First, the Last, beyond all thought His timeless years
32	3	Guard my first springs of thought and will
36	1	Restored to life and power and thought

37	4	Shall rise the glorious thought, I am with thee
50	2	Be my last thought how sweet to rest Forever on my Savior's
92	1	The thought of thee is mightier far than sin and pain
99	1	Beyond all knowledge and all thought
147	2	Thou cam'st to us in lowliness of thought
150	1	How passing thought and fantasy
162	1	Then in thought I go to thee, Garden of Gethsemane
221	4	Weak is the effort of my heart, And cold my warmest thought
225	T,1	Jesus, the Very Thought of Thee
225	1	thought of thee With sweetness fills my breast
226	T,1	Jesus, the Very Thought of Thee (same words as no. 225)
236	3	Nerving simplest thought and deed
238	1	O'er every thought and step preside
253	2	Thank we those who toiled in thought
321	4	Let every thought, and work, and word To thee be ever given
324	2	Hallow each thought, let all within Be clean
337	2	Far, far above thy thought His counsel shall appear
370	T,1	He Leadeth Me, O Blessed Thought
381	1	I'll travel on, and still be stirred by silent thought
381	1	stirred By silent thought or social word
391	1	Thou my best thought, by day or by night
392	5	cannot seek By deed or thought, to hurt the weak
397	4	heart o'erflow In kindling thought and glowing word
411	2	One with the Father, thought and deed and word
434	1	But to live out the laws of Christ In every thought
434	1	In every thought and word and deed
465	T,1	O Perfect Love, all human thought transcending
467	2	Comes with its calm the thought that thou art o'er us
477	4	Be thou our rock, our life, our thought
485	1	I rest me in the thought Of rocks and trees, of skies & seas
490	3	And let us not for one short hour An evil thought endure
538	1	Ours is the faith, the will, the thought

thoughts

36	2	New thoughts of God, new hopes of heaven
59	2	Let evil thoughts and spirits flee before us
59	3	Let our last thoughts be thine when sleep o'ertakes us
59	3	Our earliest thoughts be thine when morning wakes us
66	4	For all gentle thoughts and mild
86	2	we ... Have tried, with thoughts uncouth ... to bind thee
98	2	So many gentle thoughts and deeds Circling us round
222	3	Hence, all thoughts of sadness
255	4	The thoughts within my heart, Accept, O Lord
332	2	Sinful thoughts & words unloving Rise against us one by one
351	4	Then, with my waking thoughts Bright with thy praise
378	3	Peace, in our hearts, our evil thoughts assuaging
394	1	Plans and my thoughts and everything I ever do are dependent
411	4	How good thy thoughts toward us, how great their sum
457	2	winging thoughts, and happy moods Of love and joy and prayer
468	2	Thine are their thoughts, their works, their powers
492	3	grant us power That worthy thoughts in deeds may flower
499	2	To him may all our thoughts arise In never-ceasing sacrifice

thousand

1	4	A thousand ages in thy sight Are like an evening gone
9	4	earth, with her ten thousand tongues Shall fill thy courts

94	3	Ten thousand precious gifts My daily thanks employ
223	T,1	O for a Thousand Tongues to Sing My great Redeemer's praise
264	1	Lord, thy Church is praying yet, A thousand years the same
305	2	And thousand hearts ascending In gratitude above
311	T,1	Ten Thousand Times Ten Thousand, In sparkling raiment bright
311	2	What ringing of a thousand harps Bespeaks the triumph nigh
312	3	Ten thousand times that man were blest ... this music hear

thousands

387	3	One the strain that lips of thousands Lift as from the heart
432	1	Through whose deep purpose stranger thousands stand Here
481	3	There are hundreds of thousands still

thrall

| 436 | 3 | Tie in a living tether The prince and priest and thrall |

threaten

| 363 | 3 | though this world ... Should threaten to undo us |

threatening

| 61 | 4 | Smite death's threatening wave before you |
| 264 | 3 | Though earth-quake shocks are threatening her |

threatens

| 394 | 2 | He can give me victory o'er all that threatens me |

three

30	4	To God the Father, God the Son ... the Spirit Three in One
64	5	And praise the Spirit, three in One
136	3	God's bright star, o'er his head, Wise men three to him led
141	3	And by the light of that same star Three wise men came
141	3	Three wise men came from country far
141	5	Then entered in those wise men three
164	3	And all three hours his silence cried for mercy on the souls
174	2	Silent through those three dread hours
181	3	The three sad days are quickly sped
185	2	And from three days' sleep in death As a sun hath risen
246	4	To the great One in Three Eternal praises be Hence evermore
247	4	Holy Father, holy Son, Holy Spirit, Three we name thee
251	1,4	God in three persons, blessed Trinity
260	4	Yet she on earth hath union With God, the Three in One
263	4	Laud and honor to the Spirit, Ever Three and ever One
291	3	For when humbly, in thy name, Two or three are met together
425	3	slaves who dare not be In the right with two or three
463	4	Glory to the Father, Son, And blest Spirit, Three in One

threefold

589	T	Threefold Amen
590	T	Threefold Amen
593	T	Threefold Amen

threshold

| 329 | 1 | In lowly patience waiting To pass the threshold o'er |

thresholds
423 2   On shadowed thresholds dark with fears

thrice
329 1   O shame, thrice shame upon us To keep his standing there
359 3   Thrice blest is he to whom is given The instinct

thrills
437 2   My heart with rapture thrills Like that above

thro'
500 2   Thro' heaven's great day of evermore

throb
450 3   In every heart and brain shall throb the pulse of one

throbbing
456 2   Life mounts in every throbbing vein

throne
1 2   Under the shadow of thy throne Thy saints have dwelt secure
3 2   See the crowds the throne surrounding
9 T,1   Before Jehovah's Awful Throne
10 T,1   Before Jehovah's Awful Throne (same as Hymn No. 9)
19 1   Angels round his throne above
20 4   Cast each false idol from his throne
24 1   partake ... With angels round thy throne of light
28 4   All nations to thy throne shall throng
47 5   So be it, Lord, thy throne shall never ... pass away
68 3   clouds arise, and tempests blow, By order from thy throne
76 3   Haste to your heavenly Father's throne
78 1   firm remains on high The everlasting throne of him
78 1   throne of him Who formed the earth and sky
89 4   Before thy ever-blazing throne We ask no luster of our own
103 4   By ... all-sufficient merit Raise us to thy glorious throne
105 4   O'er every foe victorious, He on his throne shall rest
108 3   In praises round thy glorious throne
135 1   For thou hast left thy heavenly throne
169 2   He came from his blest throne, salvation to bestow
197 4   To the throne of God-head, To the Father's breast
199 T,1   Crown Him With Many Crowns, The Lamb upon his throne
205 3   Though returning to his throne
206 3   Salvation to God who sits on the throne
214 3   for his dwelling and his throne Chooseth the pure in heart
250 2   Who descended from his throne And for us salvation won
272 2   Before our Father's throne We pour our ardent prayers
309 3   There is the throne of David, And there, from care released
321 3   That I may see thy glorious face, And worship at thy throne
326 T,1   Thou Didst Leave Thy Throne and thy kingly crown
330 3   Ah, did not he the heavenly throne A little thing esteem
332 1   Low before thy throne we fall
332 5   Hearken from thy throne on high
349 4   Help me to tear it from thy throne, And worship only thee
356 3   If it would reach a monarch's throne It must ... resign
358 4   See thee on thy judgment throne
364 4   And the end of sorrow Shall be near my throne

28	3	Through her shall every land proclaim the sacred might
29	2	O may this bounteous God Through all our life be near us
35	6	Be this the eternal song Through all the ages long
36	1	Through sleep and darkness safely brought
41	3	glory, gleaming and resounding Through all creation
44	1	bold To crave thy presence through the night
45	1	night Sets her evening lamps alight Through all the sky
47	2	Through all the world her watch is keeping
50	5	ere through the world our way we take
58	2	Strong through thee whate'er befall us, O God most wise
60	3	Grant us thy peace, Lord, through the coming night
63	1	O refresh us, Traveling through this wilderness
67	1	Thy present life through all doth flow
75	2	See the glorious orb of day Breaking through the clouds
75	2	Breaking through the clouds his way
75	2	Praise him through the silent night
77	1	thy best, thy heavenly friend Through thorny ways leads
77	1	Through thorny ways leads to a joyful end
79	6	so through all the length of days thy goodness faileth never
81	T,1	Through All the Changing Scenes of life
82	1	Thy truth shall break through every cloud That veils
83	1	And hope in him through all thy ways
83	1	And bear thee through the evil days
86	3	The deep-toned organ blast That rolls through arches dim
93	1	Pilgrim through this barren land
93	2	Let the fire & cloudy pillar Lead me all my journey through
94	4	Through all eternity to thee A joyful song I'll raise
97	T,1	God of Our Life, Through All the Circling Years
97	3	God of the coming years, through paths unknown we follow
129	2	Still through the cloven skies they come
143	5	Alleluia, alleluia, Sounds through the earth and skies
152	2	Shining revealed through every task most lowly
153	3	through these days of penitence, & through thy passion-tide
154	T,1	O thou Who Through This Holy Week Didst suffer for us all
157	4	Joys that through all time abide
159	2	Till through our pity & our shame Love answers love's appeal
168	T,1	Lord, Through This Holy Week of our salvation
173	1	O voice, which, through the ages interceding
173	2	O word of comfort, through the silence stealing
174	2	Silent through those three dread hours
174	3	peals aloud Upward through the whelming cloud
183	3	through Christendom it rings That the Lamb is King of kings
185	1	Led them with unmoistened foot Through the Red Sea waters
193	3	Make us more than conquerors, Through thy deathless love
193	3	Bring us safe through Jordan To thy home above
197	4	Through all ranks of creatures, To the central height
199	1	And hail him as thy matchless King Through all eternity
209	3	Through cloud and sunshine, O abide with me
209	5	Shine through the gloom, and point me to the skies
220	2	Through din of market, whirl of wheels
220	2	Through ... thrust of driving trade We follow
223	2	spread through all the earth abroad The honors of thy name
225	5	Jesus, be thou our glory now, And through eternity
229	3	And through this desert land, Still keep me near thy side
230	6	Through him the first fond prayers are said
232	1	Wean it from earth, through all its pulses move

247	3	from morn to set of sun Through the Church the song goes on
249	2	Through seas dry-shod, through weary wastes bewildering
256	3	Pillar of fire through watches dark, & radiant cloud by day
257	4	Till through the world thy truth has run
261	3	How gleam thy watch-fires through the night
266	T,1	One Holy Church of God Appears Through every age and race
268	3	Glory, glory, thine the glory Through the ages evermore
281	1	Day by day with strength supplied Through the life of him
281	1	strength supplied through the life of him who died
297	4	give us grace, through ampler years
310	4	Of whom, and in whom, and through whom are all
310	4	Through whom, the Spirit, with these ever One
314	3	Through darkness and perplexity Point thou the heavenly way
318	1	Ever, O Christ, through mine Let thy life shine
318	2	Joyful to follow thee Through paths unknown
318	2	Through me thy truth be shown, Thy love made known
331	3	My ransomed soul ... Through all eternity Offered to thee
334	2	Lord, we have wandered forth through doubt and sorrow
337	1	Through waves and clouds and storms He gently clears the way
339	1	Me through change and chance he guideth
341	5	Breathe through the pulses of desire Thy coolness & thy balm
341	5	Speak through the earthquake, wind and fire
344	2	Lone and dreary, faint and weary, Through the desert
344	2	Through the desert thou didst go
345	4	Yes, on through life's long path, Still chanting as ye go
345	5	As warriors through the darkness toil
347	2	Help us, through good report & ill, Our daily cross to bear
354	3	Until we stand at thy right hand Through Jesus' saving merit
363	3	His truth to triumph through us
363	4	The Spirit and the gifts are ours Through him
363	4	Through him who with us sideth
365	3	And through the truth that comes from God Mankind ... free
367	2	Run the straight race through God's good grace
368	4	Through endeavor, failure, danger, Father, be ...at our side
370	3	Since God through Jordan leadeth me
372	3	When through the deep waters I call thee to go
372	4	When through fiery trials thy pathway shall lie
375	1	Through days of preparation Thy grace has made us strong
376	1	Lead us through Christ, the true and living Way
376	4	Through joy or sorrow, as thou deemest best
382	4	This through countless ages Men and angels sing
383	T,1-3	Forward Through the Ages
384	1	God supplies Through his eternal Son
384	2	Ye may o'ercome through Christ alone & stand entire at last
386	1	night Through which we blindly stumble to the day
387	T,1	Through the Night of Doubt and Sorrow
387	1	Clear before us through the darkness Gleams ... light
387	1	Stepping fearless through the night
388	4	They climbed ... Through peril, toil, and pain
389	1	Who through this earthly pilgrimage Hast all our fathers led
389	3	Through each perplexing path of life
392	+2	Head, heart, and hand through the years to be
399	3	O Joy that seekest me through pain
399	3	I trace the rainbow through the rain
401	2	Or if he pleaseth through it pass, And then the heaven espy
412	1	boyhood faith That shone thy whole life through

422	T,1	When Through the Whirl of Wheels, and engines humming
422	2	When through the night the furnace fires aflaring
432	1	Through whose deep purpose stranger thousands stand Here
432	2	And, all the ages through, past crumbling throne
433	1	starry band Of shining worlds in splendor through the skies
435	3	Cleanse the body of this nation Through the ... Lord
435	3	Through the glory of the Lord
438	2	onward through all ages bear The memory of that holy hour
445	1	Through the thick darkness covering every nation
446	4	Through the thick darkness thy kingdom is hastening
454	4	Adored through all our changing days
455	1	Through leafless boughs the sharp winds blow
455	4	And keep us through life's wintry days
456	2	Burn brighter through the cold
464	1	Singing thus through all our days
471	5	Fit him to follow thee through pain and loss
471	5	Serving the world, until through every trial
480	3	He is my Father, who will keep His child through every day
484	1	Where children wade through rice fields
484	1	wade through rice fields And watch the camel trains
486	1	Through the earth and sky God's great mercies flow
487	2	Through him we are strong, Sing our harvest song
490	1	Through all our days, in all our ways, Our ... Father's will
491	3	And through life's darkness, danger, and disaster
496	1	Whose broad stripes & bright stars through the perilous fight
496	1	Gave proof through the night that our flag was still there
500	2	Praise him through time, till time shall end
502	2	By whom, through whom, in whom all beings are
508	2	And through the swell of chanting voices
542	1	Through life's long day and death's dark night
558	2	What love through all his actions ran
568	11	Through the tender mercy of our God
575	4	That through the ages all along This may be our endless song

throughout

18	5	The holy Church throughout the world, O Lord, confesses thee
60	4	Grant us thy peace throughout our earthly life
100	6	All throughout his vast dominion Bless the Father, O my soul
112	2	For e'en now the reign of heaven Spreads throughout
112	2	heaven Spreads throughout the world like leaven
153	T,1	Lord, Who Throughout These Forty Days
199	4	Thy praise shall never, never fail Throughout eternity
298	3	May shine throughout the world
414	1	fellowship of love Throughout the whole wide earth
414	4	one in him throughout the whole wide earth
447	1	Make wars throughout the world to cease
488	1	Behold throughout the heavens There shone a holy light
493	1	When Stephen ... Went forth throughout the land
559	5	holy Church throughout all the world doth acknowledge thee
570	5	mercy is on them that fear him throughout all generations

thrown

| 325 | 2 | a nation's pride o'erthrown, Went down to dust beside thee |
| 483 | 2 | That his arm had been thrown around me |

thrust

220	2	Through ... thrust of driving trade We follow
380	1	Who, thrust in prison or cast to flame

thunder

142	5	Alpha and Omega be, Let the organ thunder
436	1	Take not thy thunder from us, But take away our pride
446	1	Thunder thy clarion, the lightning thy sword

thyself

32	2	Wake and lift up thyself, my heart
32	3	And with thyself my spirit fill
34	3	To spend thyself nor count the cost
43	3	More and more thyself display, Shining to the perfect day
67	4	Thine image and thyself are there, The indwelling God
86	2	Thou art thyself the truth
147	3	Humbling thyself to death on Calvary
188	2	Do thou thyself our hearts possess
209	3	Who like thyself my guide and stay can be
212	3	Glorious Lord, thyself impart
277	2	Thou didst receive the children to thyself so tenderly
286	1	Thyself at thine own board make manifest in ...our sacrament
313	2	But as thyself hast loved me, O everloving Lord
316	2	Shown thyself in saint and seer
336	1	The path of prayer thyself hast trod
352	3	Lift every gift that thou thyself hast given
412	2	Who shapest man to God's own law, Thyself the fair design
456	3	Thyself the vision passing by In crystal and in rose
466	2	O Christ, thyself a child Within an earthly home
530	1	path of prayer thyself hast trod, Lord, teach us how to pray
559	8	Thou didst humble thyself to be born of a virgin

tibi

133	3	Jesu, tibi sit gloria

tide

105	4	The tide of time shall never His covenant remove
122	4	This holy tide of Christmas Doth bring redeeming grace
236	2	Never was to chosen race That unstinted tide confined
395	2	Around us rolls the ceaseless tide Of business, toil, & care

tides

308	4	High above the restless tides Stands their city on the hill

tidings

72	2	And all the planets in their turn, Confirm the tidings
72	2	Confirm the tidings as they roll
115	1	Come then and hearken, for he brings Glad tidings
115	1	Glad tidings from the King of kings
116	2	Say what may the tidings be Which inspire your heavenly song
121	1	Glad tidings of great joy I bring
122	R	O tidings of comfort and joy
122	2	And unto certain shepherds Brought tidings of the same
127	1	With them the joyful tidings first begun
127	1	tidings first begun of God incarnate and the Virgin's Son
127	2	Behold, I bring good tidings of a Savior's birth

134	4	We hear the Christmas angels The great glad tidings tell
144	1	Glad tidings of our God to bring
146	2	Glad tidings of great joy I bring To you and all mankind
302	R	Publish glad tidings, Tidings of peace
302	R	Tidings of Jesus, Redemption and release
305	1	Each breeze that sweeps the ocean Brings tidings from afar
411	3	O Prince of peace, thou bringer of good tidings

tie

272	T,1	Blest Be the Tie That Binds Our hearts in Christian love
273	T,1	Blest Be the Tie That Binds (same words as no. 272)
436	3	Tie in a living tether The prince and priest and thrall

til

233	3	Til I am wholly thine
253	2	Til they came, who told the story Of the Word
378	4	Grant us thy help til backward they are driven

till

11	2	Till suns shall rise and set no more
17	1	Praise him from morn till fall of night
23	4	Let all thy days Till life shall end ... filled with praise
23	4	Till life shall end, Whate'er he send, Be filled with praise
43	2	Joyless is the day's return Till thy mercy's beams I see
43	2	Till they inward light impart Glad my eyes and warm my heart
47	5	grows ... Till all thy creatures own thy sway
50	3	Abide with me from morn till eve
50	5	Till in the ocean of thy love we lose ourselves in heaven
61	T,1	God Be With You Till We Meet Again (also vs. 1-4)
62	T,1	God Be With You Till We Meet Again (same words as No. 61)
86	2	Till truth from falsehood part, Our souls can find no rest
89	5	Till all thy living altars claim One holy light
93	1	Bread of heaven, Feed me till I want no more
113	2	Till thou, Redeemer, shouldest free Thine own
123	1	Till the air Everywhere Now with joy is ringing
127	4	Till man's first heavenly state again takes place
137	2	And stay by my cradle till morning is nigh
159	2	Till through our pity & our shame Love answers love's appeal
167	VI-3	Till we pass to perfect day, Hear us, holy Jesus
168	3	Let us go also, till we see thee pleading
174	2	Till the appointed time is nigh ... the Lamb of God may die
202	1	Till moons shall wax and wane no more
210	1	Hide me, O my Savior, hide, Till the storm of life is past
212	2	Till thy Spirit breaks our night With the beams of truth
215	3	o'er crag and torrent, till The night is gone
222	1	Long my heart hath panted, Till it well-nigh fainted
228	4	Till in heaven we take our place
228	4	Till we cast our crowns before thee
237	2	Till wilderness and town One temple for thy worship be
239	2	O let it freely burn, Till earthly passions turn To dust
239	3	For none can guess its grace, Till he become the place
252	4	Till, clouds and darkness ended, They see thee face to face
257	4	Till through the world thy truth has run
257	4	Till Christ has all the nations blest
260	3	Till with the vision glorious, Her longing eyes are blest
269	3	Till toils and cares shall end

274	3	Till all before our God at length In Zion do appear
293	4	No time for rest, till glows the western sky
293	4	Till the long shadows o'er our pathway lie
294	2	Till greed and hate shall cease
294	3	Till Christ is formed in all mankind And every land is thine
298	4	Vainly we hope for the harvest-tide Till God gives life
298	4	Till God gives life to the seed
299	3	Breathe thou abroad like morning air Till hearts ... beat
299	3	Till hearts of stone begin to beat
299	4	The name of Jesus glorify Till every kindred call him Lord
304	2	Till saint and martyr sped the venture bold
305	3	Stay not till all the lowly Triumphant reach their home
305	3	Stay not till all the holy Proclaim, The Lord is come
318	3	Till earth, as heaven, fulfill God's holy will
325	2	Till not a stone was left on stone
325	3	Till in the night of hate and war We perish as we lose thee
334	2	Thou wilt sustain us till its work is done
341	4	Drop thy still dews of quietness, Till ... strivings cease
341	4	Till all our strivings cease
345	5	toil Till dawns the golden day
352	3	Low lies the best till lifted up to heaven
352	3	Till, sent from God, they mount to God again
356	2	It cannot freely move Till thou hast wrought its chain
356	3	My will is not my own Till thou hast made it thine
365	R	We will be true to thee till death
375	2	Lead on, O King eternal, Till sin's fierce war shall cease
383	2	For it we must labor, Till our faith is sight
385	1	Till every foe is vanquished, And Christ is Lord indeed
386	3	Till clearer light our slumbering souls awake
389	4	Till all our wanderings cease
405	4	Thus, in thy service, Lord, Till eventide Closes the day
405	4	Till eventide Closes the day of life, May we abide
406	4	And still to things eternal look
411	1	Armed with thy courage, till the world is won
423	6	Till sons of men shall learn thy love
423	6	Till glorious from thy heaven above Shall come the city
438	4	Till these eternal hills remove
439	4	Till it find its full fruition In the brotherhood of man
440	3	Till all success be nobleness, And every gain divine
448	4	Till rise in ordered plan On firm foundations broad
451	3	Nor till that hour shall God's whole will be done
454	1	That mercy crowns it till it close
471	3	Till, from the shadows to thy presence reaching, He sees
484	1	Or farm the mountain pastures, Or till the endless plains
484	3	Till all the distant people In every foreign place
486	2	Jesus at my side Till the day is done
494	1	waiting till love can raise the broken stone
500	2	Praise him through time, till time shall end
500	2	Till psalm and song his name adore
558	4	Do this, he cried, till time shall end
558	5	Till thou return and we shall eat The marriage supper

time

1	5	Time, like an ever-rolling stream, Bears all its sons away
16	4	Sun and moon ... Dwellers in all time and space
28	2	Thy Church ... standeth sure while earth and time endure

105	1	Hail, in the time appointed, His reign on earth begun
105	4	The tide of time shall never His covenant remove
120	2	Late in time behold him come, Offspring of the Virgin's womb
157	1,5	Towering o'er the wrecks of time
157	4	Joys that through all time abide
158	3	Mark that miracle of time, God's own sacrifice complete
174	2	Till the appointed time is nigh ... the Lamb of God may die
199	4	Crown him the Lord of years, The potentate of time
236	2	Thine is every time & place, Fountain sweet of heart & mind
236	3	Freshening time with truth and good
259	3	And look down from supernal heights On all the by-gone time
262	2	in time to be Shall one great temple rise to thee
266	2	From oldest time, on farthest shores
266	4	Redeem the evil time
293	2	Redeem the time, its hours too swiftly fly
293	4	No time for rest, till glows the western sky
294	1	To whom there is no here nor there, No time, no near nor far
297	2	Emerge the gifts that time has proved
298	1	God is working his purpose out, And the time is drawing near
298	1,4	Nearer & nearer draws the time ... time that shall surely be
316	3	Offering talents, time and treasure, For the mercy
332	4	From henceforth, the time redeeming, May we live to thee
333	3	No place can part, nor hour of time remove us
337	1	Wait thou his time, so shall this night Soon end
392	2	That in our time, thy grace may give the truth
427	T,1	We Are Living, We Are Dwelling In a grand and aweful time
441	2	Time makes ancient good uncouth
446	1-3	Give to us peace in our time, O Lord
446	4	Thou will give peace in our time, O Lord
448	3	Speed, speed the longed-for time Foretold by raptured seers
460	3	seed-time and the harvest, Our life, our health, our food
494	2	Ribbed with the steel that time and change doth mock
500	2	Praise him through time, till time shall end
558	4	Do this, he cried, till time shall end
577	1	Make manifest in this dread time Thy power supreme
579	2	Seed-time, harvest, cold, and heat shall their yearly round

time's

189	2	Now let the earth be joyful In spring-time's bright array

timeless

14	1	The First, the Last, beyond all thought His timeless years
444	1	Come with thy timeless judgment now

times

4	4	His truth at all times firmly stood
97	2	God of our past, our times are in thy hand, With us abide
112	3	Not for us ... to know the times and seasons
160	2	Upon that cross of Jesus Mine eye at times can see
164	3	Seven times he spake, seven words of love
311	T,1	Ten Thousand Times Ten Thousand, In sparkling raiment bright
312	3	Ten thousand times that man were blest ... this music hear

tincture

401	3	Which with this tincture, For thy sake, Will not grow bright

tiny
458	3	Praise him for his tiny seed, Holding all his world ... need
478	1	He made their glowing colors, He made their tiny wings
482	1	See the fur to keep you warm, Snugly round your tiny form

tireless
| 297 | 2 | From out their tireless prayer and toil Emerge the gifts |

tires
| 387 | 2 | One the faith which never tires |

title
| 203 | 3 | Own his title, praise his name |

today
29	1	With countless gifts of love, And still is ours today
125	1	Give ye heed to what we say, Jesus Christ is born today
125	1	Christ is born today
134	4	Cast out our sin and enter in, Be born in us today
161	T,1	Before the Cross of Jesus Our lives are judged today
182	T,1	Christ the Lord Is Risen Today
184	4	And sing today with one accord
185	2	'Tis the spring of souls today, Christ hath burst his prison
185	4	But today amidst the twelve Thou didst stand, bestowing
187	T,1	Jesus Christ Is Risen Today, Alleluia
191	1	O'er death today rose triumphing
263	2	Come, O Lord of hosts, today
293	1	And to each servant does the Master say, Go work today
352	2	O Lord of light, lift all our hearts today
475	2	Grant that all we, who here today ... this foundation lay
480	1	Jesus saw The same bright sun that shines today
537	1	And hence with grateful hearts today
582	T,1	Christ the Lord Is Risen Today (as no. 182 with descant)

together
21	T,1	We Gather Together to ask the Lord's blessing
134	2	O morning stars, together Proclaim the holy birth
164	1	O come, together let us mourn
288	T,1	Let us Break Bread Together on our knees
288	2	Let us drink wine together on our knees
288	3	Let us praise God together on our knees
291	3	For when humbly, in thy name, Two or three are met together
383	3	Move we on together to the shining goal
403	2	Where the many work together, they with God himself abide
436	3	Bind all our lives together, Smite us and save us all
461	2	Wheat and tares together sown, Unto joy or sorrow grown

toil
23	3	Ye saints who toil below, Adore your heavenly King
58	1	Who the day for toil hast given, For rest the night
129	3	Who toil along the climbing way With painful steps and slow
219	3	And they who dearest hope and deepest pray Toil
219	3	Toil by the truth, life, way that thou hast given
260	3	'Mid toil and tribulation, And tumult of her war
297	2	From out their tireless prayer and toil Emerge the gifts
303	4	A field for toil and faith and hope

tomb

143	4	Sealed in a stone-cold tomb
149	3	know not how that Joseph's tomb Could solve death's mystery
179	3	Were you there when they laid him in the tomb
191	2	their way To seek the tomb where Jesus lay
193	2	Lo, Jesus meets thee, risen from the tomb

tomb's

185	4	Neither might the gates of death, Nor the tomb's dark portal

tomorrow

422	4	Flames out the sunshine of the great tomorrow

tone

108	3	With harp and cymbal's clearest tone
397	1	speak In living echoes of thy tone
508	1	In perfect love and faultless tone

toned

86	3	The deep-toned organ blast That rolls through arches dim

tongue

6	4	Thy bountiful care, what tongue can recite
11	1	sung Through every land, by every tongue
23	1	Too high doth seem For mortal tongue
24	T,1	Now Let Every Tongue Adore Thee
81	1	The praises of my God shall still My heart and tongue employ
111	2	Let no tongue on earth be silent
147	4	Let every tongue confess with one accord
197	1	Every tongue confess him King of glory now
202	3	People and realms of every tongue Dwell on his love
225	4	Ah, this Nor tongue nor pen can show
229	2	Great Prophet of my God, My tongue would bless thy name
235	2	Thou in the faith dost men unite of every land ... tongue
302	2	Proclaim to every people, tongue & nation ... God ...is love
388	2	Like him, with pardon on his tongue, In midst of mortal pain
436	2	From all that terror teaches, From lies of tongue and pen

tongues

9	4	earth, with her ten thousand tongues Shall fill thy courts
223	T,1	O for a Thousand Tongues to Sing My great Redeemer's praise
240	2	Hosannas languish on our tongues, And our devotion dies
262	1	The wrangling tongues that mar thy praise
268	2	Many tongues of many nations Sing the greater unity
299	2	Give tongues of fire and hearts of love
422	2	Shooting out tongues of flame like leaping blood
431	4	If drunk with sight of power, we loose Wild tongues
431	4	Wild tongues that have not thee in awe
437	3	Let mortal tongues awake, Let all that breathe partake
445	3	Envious of heart, blind-eyed, with tongues confounded
464	1	Let thy praise our tongues employ

tonight

50	4	Be every mourner's sleep tonight Like infants' slumbers

tont
139 2   Tont es laut von fern und nah, Christ der Retter ist da

took
141 4   O'er Bethlehem it took its rest
204 2   When he had purged our stains, he took his seat above
408 2   'Twas not so much that I on thee took hold, As thou
558 2   Before the mournful scene began, He took the bread
558 2   He took the bread and blest and brake
558 3   Then took the cup and blessed the wine
578 2   'Twas not so much that I on thee took hold As thou

tookest
559 8   When thou tookest upon thee to deliver man

torch
124 1   Bring a Torch, Jeannette, Isabella
124 1   Bring a torch, to the cradle run
297 3   The torch of their devotion lent, Lightens the dark
399 2   I yield my flickering torch to thee

torrent
73 3   Troubled torrent, madly rushing
215 3   o'er crag and torrent, till The night is gone

tortured
377 4   Though a tortured slave thou die

toss
417 1   All dreamers toss and sigh

tossed
295 2   The wayward and the lost, By restless passions tossed
319 2   Just as I am, though tossed about
360 1   When tossed by storm and flood

tossing
51 3   Guard the sailors tossing On the deep blue sea
256 3   When waves o'erwhelm our tossing bark

touch
55 6   Thy touch has still its ancient power
129 1   To touch their harps of gold
230 5   touch him in life's throng and press, And we are whole again
276 1   And pray that this may be our home Until we touch eternity
287 1   Here would I touch and handle things unseen
291 3   Touch we now thy garment's hem
292 3   Deliver us from every touch of ill
401 5   that which God doth touch and own cannot for less be told
421 3   We've felt thy touch in sorrow's darkened way
557 1   Here would I touch and handle things unseen

touched
98 3   I thank thee more that all our joy Is touched with pain
257 3   So when thy truth began its race, It touched and glanced on
257 2   It touched and glanced on every land

touching

| 45 | T,1 | Day is Dying in the West, Heaven is touching earth with rest |

toward

74	4	Thou whose purpose moves before us Toward the goal
74	4	Toward the goal that thou hast planned
113	3	When the old world drew on toward night, Thou camest
145	2	Toward thee longing Doth possess me, turn and bless me
411	1	purpose never swerving Leads toward the day of Jesus Christ
411	4	How good thy thoughts toward us, how great their sum

towards

| 554 | 1 | and on earth peace, good will towards men |

tower

412	2	Build us a tower of Christ-like height
412	2	Build us a tower ... That we the land may view
477	3	Our God, our Strength, our King, our Tower

towering

| 157 | 1,5 | Towering o'er the wrecks of time |

towers

261	3	How rise thy towers, serene & bright To meet the dawning day
445	3	Building proud towers which shall not reach to heaven
494	2	O Master, lend us sight To see the towers gleaming
494	2	To see the towers gleaming in the light

town

134	T,1	O Little Town of Bethlehem, How still we see thee lie
146	3	To you, in David's town, this day Is born of David's line
237	2	Till wilderness and town One temple for thy worship be

trace

19	3	Praise the Lord, his mercies trace
33	4	Quickened by the Spirit's grace All thy holy will to trace
78	3	him thou canst not see, nor trace the working of his hands
127	4	trace we the babe, Who hath retrieved our loss
127	4	Trace we the babe ... his poor manger to his bitter cross
174	1	None its lines of woe can trace
252	4	O teach thy wandering pilgrims By this their path to trace
256	T,1	Lamp of Our Feet, Whereby We Trace Our path
297	1	And where the higher gain appears, We trace ... thy hand
297	1	We trace the working of thy hand
399	3	I trace the rainbow through the rain

track

236	4	Consecrating art and song, Holy book and pilgrim track
441	2	By the light of burning martyrs, Jesus' ... feet I track
441	2	Jesus' bleeding feet I track, Toiling up new Calvaries ever

trade

| 220 | 2 | Through ... thrust of driving trade We follow |

tragic

| 451 | 2 | Age after age their tragic empires rise |

train
247	3	Lo, the apostolic train Joins thy sacred name to hallow
388	1,2	Who follows in his train
388	1	Who patient bears his cross below, He follows in his train
388	2	Who follows in his train
388	3	Who follows in their train
388	4	O God, to us may grace be given To follow in their train

trains
481	3	In church, or in trains, or in shops, or at tea
484	1	wade through rice fields And watch the camel trains

trampling
443	1	He is trampling out the vintage where the grapes of wrath

transcending
465	T,1	O Perfect Love, all human thought transcending

transfigured
424	3	It will live and shine transfigured In the final reign

transfigures
443	4	With a glory in his bosom that transfigures you and me

transgression
105	1	To take away transgression, And rule in equity
170	2	Mine, mine was the transgression, But thine the deadly pain

transgressions
100	2	Who forgiveth thy transgressions, Thy diseases all who heals

transient
348	4	When ends life's transient dream

translate
434	2	God send us men alert and quick ... precepts to translate
434	2	His lofty precepts to translate

transport
79	5	O what transport of delight From thy pure chalice floweth

transported
94	1	Transported with the view, I'm lost in wonder, love & praise

traute
139	1	Nur das traute, hochheilige Paar

travail
113	2	To thee the travail deep was known
113	2	travail ... That made the whole creation groan

travail's
168	4	Until thou see thy bitter travail's ending

travailed
198	3	The world has waited long, Has travailed long in pain

travel
381 1   I'll travel on, and still be stirred by silent thought

traveler
109 1   Traveler, o'er yon mountain's height See
109 1   traveler, yes, it brings the day, Promised day of Israel
109 2   Traveler, blessedness and light ... its course portends
109 2   Traveler, ages are its own, See it bursts o'er all the earth
109 3   Traveler, darkness takes its flight
109 3   Traveler, lo, the Prince of peace ... Son of God is come

traveler's
256 1   Brook by the traveler's way
381 1   faith ... The traveler's well-loved aid

travelers
381 2   I have a guide, and in his steps When travelers have trod

traveling
63 1   O refresh us, Traveling through this wilderness

traverse
143 T,1   We Thee Kings of Orient Are, Bearing gifts we traverse afar

treacherous
213 1   Hiding rock and treacherous shoal

tread
68 2   If I survey the ground I tread or gaze upon the sky
78 6   They with unwearied feet shall tread the path of life divine
93 3   When I tread the verge of Jordan
300 4   Lift high the cross of Christ Tread where his feet have trod
308 4   In their footsteps will we tread
344 2   Thou didst tread this earth before us
348 3   While life's dark maze I tread, And griefs around me spread
368 2   But the steep and rugged pathway May we tread rejoicingly
384 3   Tread all the powers of darkness down
387 2   Brightening all the path we tread
409 2   who tread the path of labor Follow where thy feet have trod
410 3   Love shall tread out the baleful fire of anger
423 5   O tread the city's streets again

treading
127 4   Treading his steps, assisted by his grace
382 2   Brothers, we are treading Where the saints have trod

treason
163 2   Alas, my treason, Jesus, hath undone thee

treasure
222 T,1   Jesus, Priceless Treasure, Source of purest pleasure
253 1   Statesman's, teacher's, hero's treasure
258 4   Who can tell the pleasure, Who recount the treasure
316 3   Offering talents, time and treasure, For the mercy
343 3   My Savior has my treasure, And he will walk with me
391 3   High King of heaven, my treasure thou art

404　4　　　Take my love, my Lord I pour At thy feet its treasure store

treasures
　36　3　　　New treasures still, of countless price, God will provide
　36　3　　　New treasures still ... God will provide for sacrifice
119　3　　　All our costliest treasures bring, Christ, to thee
119　3　　　treasures bring, Christ, to thee, our heavenly King
374　2　　　Or its sordid treasures Spread to work me harm
475　4　　　To thee they all belong　...　treasures of the earth and sea

treat
329　3　　　I died for you, my children, And will ye treat me so

tree
　　7　3　　　We blossom and flourish as leaves on the tree
　53　T,1　　The Duteous Day Now Closeth, Each flower and tree reposeth
　66　2　　　Hill & vale, and tree & flower, Sun & moon & stars of light
112　2　　　Like the sheltering tree that groweth, Comes the life
162　4,　　　There behold his agony, Suffered on the bitter tree
174　T,1　　Throned Upon the Awful Tree
179 ′2　　　Were you there when they nailed him to the tree
292　1　　　love That bought us, once for all, on Calvary's tree
326　3　　　In the shade of the forest tree
410　3　　　And in its ashes plant the tree of peace
468　3　　　Not left to lie like fallen tree, Not dead, but living
579　1　　　For the valley's golden yield ... fruits of tree and field

trees
437　3　　　And ring from all the trees Sweet freedom's song
485　1　　　I rest me in the thought Of rocks and trees, of skies & seas

tremble
179　R　　　Oh, Sometimes it causes me to tremble, tremble, tremble
363　3　　　The prince of darkness grim, We tremble not for him
364　2　　　Christian, never tremble, Never be downcast

trembled
488　2　　　The shepherds feared and trembled When lo, above the earth

trembleth
275　3　　　One with the grief that trembleth into prayer

trembling
107　1　　　And with fear and trembling stand
228　1　　　Visit us with thy salvation, Enter every trembling heart

tressed
　70　3　　　He the golden-tressed sun Caused all day his course to run

trial
　81　3　　　Oh make but trial of his love, Experience will decide
167　VII-2　　Keep us in that trial hour, Hear us, holy Jesus
374　T,1　　In the Hour of Trial, Jesus, plead for me
471　5　　　Serving the world, until through every trial

trials
250	3	Who upholds and comforts us in all trials, fears, and needs
335	2	Have we trials and temptations, Is there trouble anywhere
372	4	When through fiery trials thy pathway shall lie

tribe
195	4	Let every kindred, every tribe, On this terrestrial ball

tribes
175	1	Hark, all the tribes hosanna cry
311	2	O day, for which creation And all its tribes were made

tribulation
21	3	Let thy congregation escape tribulation
260	3	'Mid toil and tribulation, And tumult of her war

tribute
16	1	To his feet thy tribute bring
22	1	In grateful devotion our tribute we bring
188	2	That we may give thee all our days the willing tribute
188	2	The willing tribute of our praise
505	1	Your morning tribute bring

tried
55	5	Thou hast been troubled, tempted, tried
86	2	we ... Have tried, with thoughts uncouth ... to bind thee
86	2	we ... Have tried ... In feeble words to bind thee
164	4	In this dread act your strength is tried
301	1	While on earth her faith is tried
493	2	Stephen preached against the laws & by those laws was tried

trimmed
340	3	Young John who trimmed the flapping sail

trinity
41	3	All holy Father, Son and equal Spirit, Trinity blessed
150	5	The Trinity whom we adore For ever and for evermore
250	3	Blest and Holy Trinity, Praise forever be to thee
251	1,4	God in three persons, blessed Trinity
429	4	O Trinity of love and power, Our brethren shield

triumph
8	4	Joyful music leads us sunward, In the triumph song of life
23	4	My soul, bear thou thy part, Triumph in God above
43	1	Sun of righteousness arise, Triumph o'er the shades of night
63	1	Let us each, thy love possessing Triumph
63	1	Triumph in redeeming grace
120	1	Joyful, all ye nations rise, Join the triumph of the skies
156	1	Ride on in triumph, Lord
181	1	The victory of life is won, The song of triumph has begun
184	1	Now is the triumph of our King
189	2	The grave has lost its triumph And death has lost its sting
192	3	The round world keep high triumph, And all that is therein
193	2	Let his church with gladness Hymns of triumph sing
204	1	Rejoice, give thanks, and sing, And triumph evermore
205	2	There the glorious triumph waits

206	2	The great congregation his triumph shall sing
209	4	I triumph still if thou abide with me
306	5	Steals on the ear the distant triumph song
309	3	The shout of them that triumph, The song of them that feast
311	2	What ringing of a thousand harps Bespeaks the triumph nigh
312	2	They triumph still, they still rejoice
363	3	We will not fear, for God hath willed His truth to triumph
363	3	His truth to triumph through us
382	4	Blend with ours your voices In the triumph song
383	3	In each loss or triumph Lose or triumph all
471	5	He learns at length the triumph of the cross
496	2	And the star-spangled banner in triumph shall wave

triumphant

21	3	We all do extol thee, thou leader triumphant
30	3	All saints triumphant raise the song, Alleluia
132	T,1	O Come, All Ye Faithful, joyful and triumphant
162	4	See his anguish ... faith, Love triumphant still in death
182	5	Thee we greet triumphant now ... Hail, the Resurrection thou
185	T,1	Come, Ye Faithful, Raise the Strain Of triumphant gladness
187	1	Our triumphant holy day
197	4	Bore it up triumphant, With its human light
201	1	And light triumphant breaks
203	4	Hark, those loud triumphant chords
305	3	Stay not till all the lowly Triumphant reach their home
388	1	Who best can drink the cup of woe, Triumphant over pain

triumphantes

133	1	Laeti triumphantes, Venite, venite in Bethlehem

triumphed

180	2	Christ has triumphed, & we conquer By his mighty enterprise
199	3	Crown him the Lord of life, Who triumphed o'er the grave

triumphing

191	1	O'er death today rose triumphing

triumphs

175	2	O Christ, thy triumphs now begin
175	2	thy triumphs now begin O'er captive death and conquered sin
182	1	Raise your joys and triumphs high
223	1	The glories of my God and King, The triumphs of his grace
299	4	The triumphs of the cross record
301	5	May she holy triumphs win, Overthrow the hosts of sin
325	4	O love that triumphs over loss, we bring our hearts
418	3	In trust that triumphs over wrong

Triune

17	2	servants of the Triune God, Father and Son and Spirit laud
180	3	Alleluia, Alleluia, To the Triune Majesty
249	5	O Triune God, with heart and voice adoring

trivial

36	5	The trivial round, the common task, Will furnish all

trod

trophies

trouble

troubled

troubles

true

468   2   All thine, and yet most truly ours

trumpet
352   4   Then, as the trumpet call, in after years
385   2   Stand Up, stand up for Jesus, The trumpet call obey
417   2   True hearts will leap at the trumpet of God
422   1   Peals like a trumpet promise of his coming
443   3   He has sounded forth the trumpet
443   3   trumpet that shall never call retreat

trust
2   2   We praise, we worship thee, we trust and give thee thanks
2   2   we trust And give thee thanks forever
6   5   In thee do we trust, nor find thee to fail
26   2   By him we are made, So we trust him unafraid
76   1   And trust his constant care
83   3   So do thine own part faithfully, And trust his word
87   3   But trust him for his grace
91   2   To him for safety I will flee, My God ... my trust shall be
91   6   Because thy trust is   God alone ... no evil shall ... come
97   1   We trust in thee
122   3   free all those who trust in him From Satan's power and might
152   3   The blessedness which simple trust has found
168   2   Yet give us strength to trust the sweet assurance
171   4   And trust in his redeeming blood, And try his works to do
207   1   My only trust and savior of my heart
210   2   All my trust on thee is stayed ... my help from thee I bring
217   1   Whose trust, ever child-like, no cares could destroy
235   4   But Jesus for our Master own, And put our trust in him alone
328   2   O trust in him, trust now in him, And have security
334   1,3   revealing Of trust and strength and calmness from above
334   2   And we will ever trust each unknown morrow
339   T,1   All My Hope on God Is Founded, He doth still my trust renew
341   2   In simple trust like theirs who heard, Beside the Syrian sea
357   5   And yet we trust it comes from thee
360   1   To one fixed trust my spirit clings, I know that God is good
361   T,1   Have Faith in God, my heart, Trust and be unafraid
367   3   Trust, and thy trusting soul shall prove Christ is its life
385   3   The arm of flesh will fail you, Ye dare not trust your own
386   4   We trust to find thee when the night is past
413   2   We but stewards of thy bounty, Held in solemn trust for thee
418   3   In trust that triumphs over wrong
431   5   For heathen heart that puts her trust In reeking tube
447   3   Whom shall we trust but thee, O Lord
465   2   With child-like trust that fears nor pain nor death
468   4   To thee we leave them, Lord, in trust
469   3   Shall rise our psalm of grateful trust
489   T,1   I Would Be True, for there are those who trust me
496   2   And this be our motto, In God is our trust
535   1   All that we have is thine alone, A trust, O Lord, from thee
540   1   Calm with trust each anxious heart
559   16   O Lord, let thy mercy be upon us, as our trust is in thee

trusted
83   3   God never yet forsook at need the soul that trusted him
83   3   The soul that trusted him indeed

252	2	It is the golden casket Where gems of truth are stored
253	1	Bringing freedom, spreading truth
254	2	Bless thou the truth, dear Lord, To me, to me
255	3	statutes of the Lord are truth And righteousness ... pure
257	3	So when thy truth began its race, It touched and glanced on
257	4	Till through the world thy truth has run
258	1	Who its truth believeth Light and joy receiveth
259	T,1	We Limit Not the Truth of God To our poor reach of mind
259	R	The Lord hath yet more light and truth To break forth
266	3	The truth is her prophetic gift
269	5	Sure as thy truth shall last, To Zion shall be given
270	3	His truth doth hallow the temple
275	3	free To follow truth, and thus to follow thee
276	4	May thy whole truth be spoken here
290	2	Thy truth unchanged hath ever stood
298	3	That the light of the glorious gospel of truth May shine
301	4	May she one in doctrine be, One in truth and charity
318	2	Through me thy truth be shown, Thy love made known
336	T,1	O Thou by Whom we Come to God, The Life, the Truth, the Way
336	3	Give, what thine eye delights to see, Truth
336	3	Truth in the inward parts
346	2	Faithful are all who love the truth
346	2	Faithful are all who ... dare the truth to tell
363	3	We will not fear, for God hath willed His truth to triumph
363	3	His truth to triumph through us
363	4	The body they may kill, God's truth abideth still
365	3	And through the truth that comes from God Mankind ... free
373	3	His truth be thine affiance, When faint and desolate
376	2	Lead us, O Father, in the paths of truth
378	4	Grant them thy truth, that they may be forgiven
392	2	With steadfastness and careful truth
392	2	That in our time, thy grace may give the truth
392	2	The truth whereby the nations live
394	2	Thou art the Way, the Truth, thou art the Life
395	3	In truth and patience wrought
413	T,1	Son of God, Eternal Savior, Source of life and truth & grace
419	3	One in the truth that makes men free
425	3	Rather than in silence shrink From the truth
425	3	shrink From the truth they needs must think
430	3	And keep his truth for evermore
434	4	All truth to love, all wrong to hate
438	3	Laws, freedom, truth, and faith in God Came with those
441	1	decide In the strife of truth with falsehood, For the good
441	2	Thy must upward still and onward Who would keep ... truth
441	2	Who would keep abreast of truth
441	3	Though the cause of evil prosper ... truth alone is strong
441	3	Truth forever on the scaffold, Wrong forever on the throne
443	1	His truth is marching on
443	R	Glory, glory, Hallelujah ... His truth is marching on
446	4	Yet shall to freedom and truth be restored
448	2	The service glad and free Of truth and righteousness
453	4	Ring in the love of truth and right
471	3	Be in his mind, the truth of all his teaching
484	2	The truth that comes from Jesus, The glory of his Word
492	2	Each thought-revealing truth
508	2	O Light all clear, O Truth most holy

508	2	When hearts rise up to thee in truth
521	1	And let thy truth within us shine
530	T,1	O Thou by Whom We Come to God, The Life, the Truth, the Way
562	9	judge ... the peoples with his truth
565	4	his truth endureth from generation to generation

ruth's

| 427 | 3 | O let all the soul within you For the truth's sake go abroad |
| 540 | 1 | Still our minds with truth's conviction |

ruthful

| 245 | 2 | Truthful Spirit, dwell with me, I myself would truthful be |

ry

| 171 | 4 | And trust in his redeeming blood, And try his works to do |

rying

| 207 | 3 | And give us strength in every trying hour |

ube

| 431 | 5 | For heathen heart that puts her trust In reeking tube |
| 431 | 5 | In reeking tube and iron shard |

umult

46	4	Life's tumult we must meet again
260	3	'Mid toil and tribulation, And tumult of her war
322	T,1	Jesus Calls Us, O'er the Tumult
322	1	tumult Of our life's wild, restless sea
323	T,1	Jesus Calls Us, O'er the Tumult (same words as no. 322)
429	3	Who bad'st its angry tumult cease
431	2	The tumult and the shouting dies

umults

| 445 | 2 | By wars and tumults love is mocked, derided |

une

| 240 | 2 | In vain we tune our formal songs, In vain we strive to rise |
| 312 | 4 | There Mary sings Magnificat With tune surpassing sweet |

uned

| 23 | 4 | And with a well-tuned heart Sing thou the songs of love |

urn

39	4	To make ill-fortune turn to fair
60	3	Turn thou for us its darkness into light
68	2	Lord, how thy wonders are displayed, Where'er I turn my eye
72	2	And all the planets in their turn, Confirm the tidings
86	T,1	Our God, to Whom We Turn, When weary with illusion
96	2	His hand can turn my griefs away
105	2	To give them songs for sighing, their darkness turn to light
145	2	Toward thee longing Doth possess me, turn and bless me
158	1	Turn not from his griefs away
162	5	Then to life I turn again, Learning all the worth of pain
239	2	O let it freely burn, Till earthly passions turn To dust
256	5	to its heavenly teaching turn With simple, child-like hearts
290	1	From the best bliss that earth imparts, We turn unfilled

290	1	We turn unfilled to thee again
343	2	Wherever he may guide me, No want shall turn me back
348	3	Be thou my guide, Bid darkness turn to day
395	2	And scarcely can we turn aside For one brief hour of prayer
451	T,1	Turn Back, O Man, Forswear Thy Foolish Ways
477	2	To thee with longing hearts we turn
580	T,1	O Lord, Turn Not Thy Face From Them, Who lie in woeful sta

turned
| 198 | 1 | Freedom her bondage breaks, And night is turned to day |
| 322 | 2 | Turned from home and toil and kindred |

turnest
| 92 | 4 | Thou ... turnest my mourning into praise |

turneth
| 401 | 5 | This is the famous stone That turneth all to gold |

turning
| 74 | 2 | From thy ways so often turning, Yet thy love doth seek him |

turns
42	1	Black turns to gray, Bird-song the valley fills
92	3	Thy providence turns all to good
441	2	With the cross that turns not back

twelve
30	3	Ye holy twelve, ye martyrs strong ... raise the song
185	4	But today amidst the twelve Thou didst stand, bestowing
388	3	Twelve valiant saints, their hope they knew

twilight
162	2	There I walk amid the shades While the ... twilight fades
162	2	While the lingering twilight fades
422	4	Toiling in twilight flickering and dim

twilight's
| 496 | 1 | What so proudly we hailed at the twilight's last gleaming |

twinkling
| 227 | 3 | And all the twinkling starry host, Jesus shines brighter |

twixt
| 213 | 3 | 'Twixt me and the peaceful rest |
| 441 | 1 | choice goes by forever 'Twixt that darkness and that light |

two
44	1	Two walked with thee in waning light
160	2	And from my smitten heart with tears Two wonders I confess
208	2	what I dream ... do ... In all my days are often two
291	3	For when humbly, in thy name, Two or three are met togethe
425	3	slaves who dare not be In the right with two or three

twofold
| 586 | T | Twofold Amen |
| 587 | T | Twofold Amen |

unchanged
252 1   O Truth unchanged, unchanging, O Light of our dark sky
266 1   Unwasted by the lapse of years, Unchanged by changing place
290 2   Thy truth unchanged hath ever stood

unchanging
83 1   Who trusts in God's unchanging love Builds on the rock
252 1   O Truth unchanged, unchanging, O Light of our dark sky

uncheered
376 2   And age comes on uncheered by faith and hope

unclouded
212 2   With the beams of truth unclouded

uncomprehended
99 1   Uncomprehended and unbought

unconsciously
457 2   God's praises in their loving strain Unconsciously they sing

uncouth
86 2   we ... Have tried, with thoughts uncouth ... to bind thee
441 2   Time makes ancient good uncouth

uncowed
392 4   That we, with thee, may walk uncowed By fear
392 4   uncowed By fear or favor of the crowd

unction
79 5   Thy unction grace bestoweth
231 2   blessed unction from above Is comfort, life and fire of love
299 2   Give power and unction from above
575 2   blessed unction from above Is comfort, life and fire of love

undaunted
451 3   Peals forth in joy man's old undaunted cry

undefiled
121 3   Make thee a bed, soft, undefiled Within my heart
148 1   Forty days and forty nights Tempted, and yet undefiled
255 3   The fear of God is undefiled And ever shall endure
392 1   That they may build from age to age An undefiled heritage
466 2   With heart still undefiled, Thou didst to manhood come

under
1 2   Under the shadow of thy throne Thy saints have dwelt secure
15 2   Shelters thee under his wings, yea, so gently sustaineth
100 6   Bless the Father, all his creatures, Ever under his control
392 5   That, under thee, we may possess Man's strength to comfort

undergo
207 1   Who pain didst undergo for my poor sake

underlies
360 5   Assured alone that life and death His mercy underlies

understand
112 1   Do you yet not understand
154 2   We cannot understand the woe Thy love was pleased to bear
484 3   Shall understand his kingdom And come into his grace
493 3   God, in sweet forgiveness' name, Should understand and spare

understanding
393 T,1   God Be in My Head, And in my understanding
543 T,1   God Be in My Head, and in my understanding

undertake
77   2   thy God doth undertake To guide the future as ... the past

undeserving
83   3   though undeserving, Thou yet shalt find it true for thee

undeterred
381 1   By all my perils undeterred, A soldier-pilgrim staid

undimmed
440 4   Thine alabaster cities gleam, Undimmed by human tears

undismayed
337 T,1   Give to the Winds Thy Fears, Hope and be undismayed

undivided
247 4   While in essence only One, Undivided God we claim thee

undo
363 3   though this world ... Should threaten to undo us

undone
163 2   Alas, my treason, Jesus, hath undone thee
208 2   Help me, oppressed by things undone
332 2   Good that we have left undone
494 T,1   We Would Be Building temples still undone

undying
185 2   From his light, to whom we give Laud and praise undying

unending
153 4   An Easter of unending joy We may attain at last
263 4   One in might, and One in glory, While unending ages run
264 2   We hear within the solemn voice Of her unending song

unequal
300 3   Her strength unequal to her task, Rise up and make her great

unerring
454 2   By his incessant bounty fed, By his unerring counsel led
491 1   Keep us, we pray thee, steadfast and unerring

unfailing
2   4   O Holy Spirit, precious Gift, Thou Comforter unfailing
61   3   Put his arms unfailing round you
494 2   The unfailing purpose of our noblest creed

unfaith

325   3   From old unfaith our souls release To seek the kingdom

unfathomed

456   3   O thou from whose unfathomed law The year in beauty flows

576   2   Unfathomed depth, unmeasured height

unfilled

290   1   From the best bliss that earth imparts, We turn unfilled

290   1   We turn unfilled to thee again

unfit

330   T,1   One Who Is All Unfit to Count As scholar in thy school

unfold

8   1   Hearts unfold like flowers before thee

248   3   Thou to the meek and lowly Thy secrets dost unfold

304   1   years Wherein God's mighty purposes unfold

456   2   O'er white expanses sparkling pure The radiant morns unfold

unfolding

427   2   Now, the blazoned cross unfolding

unforgiven

445   3   Nation by nation still goes unforgiven

unfurled

129   2   With peaceful wings unfurled

252   3   It floateth like a banner Before God's hosts unfurled

298   3   March we forth ... With the banner of Christ unfurled

unguarded

384   3   Leave no unguarded place, No weakness of the soul

unharmed

261   4   Unharmed upon the eternal rock The eternal city stands

unhasting

7   2   Unresting, unhasting, and silent as light

unheard

178   4   Unheard by mortals are the strains That sweetly soothe

unheeding

159   1   Is this thy sorrow naught to us Who pass unheeding by

unhelped

376   2   Unhelped by thee, in error's maze we grope

union

260   4   Yet she on earth hath union With God, the Three in One

539   2   Thus may we abide in union with each other and the Lord

unite

24   1   Let harps and cymbals now unite

198   3   One Lord, in one great name Unite us all who own thee

235	2	Lord, by the brightness of thy light ... men unite
235	2	Thou in the faith dost men unite of every land ... tongue
289	2	Perfect it in thy love, unite it

united
22	3	With voices united our praises we offer
41	2	Bring us to heaven, where thy saints united Joy
286	3	One Church united in communion blest
499	2	Him day and night The united choirs of angels sing

unity
207	4	That we may dwell in perfect unity
268	2	Many tongues of many nations Sing the greater unity
466	3	O spirit, who dost bind Our hearts in unity

universe
| 45 | 2 | Lord of life, beneath the dome Of the universe, thy home |

unknown
49	2	Father of might unknown
53	2	splendor ...From myriad worlds unknown
97	3	God of the coming years, through paths unknown we follow
167	IV-1	Jesus, whelmed in fears unknown With our evil left alone
169	T,1	My Song Is Love Unknown, My Savior's love to me
174	1	None can tell what pangs unknown Hold thee silent and alone
213	1	Unknown waves before me roll
294	1	No alien race, no foreign shore, No child unsought, unknown
318	2	Joyful to follow thee Through paths unknown
334	2	And we will ever trust each unknown morrow
339	1	God unknown, He alone Calls my heart to be his own
358	4	When I soar to worlds unknown
441	3	behind the dim unknown, Standeth God within the shadow
454	3	The future, all to us unknown, We to thy guardian care commit
465	3	And to life's day the glorious unknown morrow that dawns
468	3	Not wandering in unknown despair Beyond thy voice
508	1	In vaster worlds unseen, unknown

unless
| 298 | 4 | All we can do is nothing worth Unless God blesses the deed |

unloving
| 332 | 2 | Sinful thoughts & words unloving Rise against us one by one |

unmeasured
| 576 | 2 | Unfathomed depth, unmeasured height |

unmoistened
| 185 | 1 | Led them with unmoistened foot Through the Red Sea waters |

unmoved
| 381 | 2 | Unmoved by pain, they onward went |

unnumbered
| 94 | 2 | Unnumbered comforts to my soul Thy tender care bestowed |
| 385 | 2 | Ye that are men now serve him Against unnumbered foes |

unobserved
112 2 Unobserved, and very near, Like the seed when no man knoweth

unresting
7 2 Unresting, unhasting, and silent as light

uns
139 3 Da uns schlagt die rettende Stund'

unseal
521 2 Unseal our lips to sing thy praise

unseals
58 2 When the constant sun returning Unseals our eyes

unseen
192 3 Let all things seen and unseen Their notes of gladness blend
266 2 One unseen Presence she adores, With silence, or with psalm
287 1 Here would I touch and handle things unseen
317 T,1 I Love to Tell the Story Of unseen things above
439 1 Praise thee most for things unseen
508 1 In vaster worlds unseen, unknown
557 1 Here would I touch and handle things unseen

unshadowed
330 2 Thou dwellest in unshadowed light, All sin and shame above

unshaken
264 4 Unshaken as eternal hills, Immovable she stands

unsleeping
47 2 We thank thee that thy Church, unsleeping

unsought
92 4 Thou leadest me by unsought ways
294 1 No alien race, no foreign shore, No child unsought, unknown

unspent
236 T,1,5 Life of Ages, Richly Poured, Love of God unspent and free
297 3 Help us to pass it on unspent Until the dawn lights up
381 2 They cared not, but with force unspent ... they onward went

unspoken
333 1 Hear thou our prayer, the spoken and unspoken

unstayed
381 2 Unstayed by pleasures, still they bent Their zealous course

unstinted
236 2 Never was to chosen race That unstinted tide confined

unswerving
83 3 Sing, pray, and keep his ways unswerving
163 4 Think on thy pity and thy love unswerving, Not my deserving

unthinkable

248	2	Ineffable in loving, Unthinkable in might

unthinking

332	2	Acts unworthy, deeds unthinking

until

110	1	mourns in lonely exile here Until the Son of God appear
114	4	Thy Holy Spirit guide us on Until the glorious crown be won
168	4	Until thou see thy bitter travail's ending
233	2	Until my heart is pure
233	2	Until with thee I will one will To do and to endure
233	3	Until this earthly part of me Glows with thy fire divine
276	1	And pray that this may be our home Until we touch eternity
297	3	Help us to pass it on unspent Until the dawn lights up
297	3	Until the dawn lights up the skies
301	2	Seek the lost until she find
354	3	Until we stand at thy right hand Through Jesus' saving merit
356	2	My heart is weak and poor Until it master find
361	4	Grant me no resting place Until I rest ... The captive
361	4	Until I rest, heart, mind and soul, The captive of thy grace
376	4	Until our lives are perfected in thee
397	4	fill me with thy fullness Lord, Until my very heart o'erflow
411	4	Until in all the earth thy kingdom come
430	2	Until thou see God's kingdom come
434	2	Until the laws of Christ become The laws and habits of
471	5	Serving the world, until through every trial
494	3	O grant enduring worth Until the heavenly kingdom comes
494	3	Until the heavenly kingdom comes on earth

untired

324	4	Dauntless, untired, I follow thee

unto

4	3	Approach with joy his courts unto
33	2	Strength unto our souls afford From thy living Bread, O Lord
37	3	Breathe each day nearness unto thee and heaven
65	3	Silent powers and angels' song ... All unto our God belong
66	5	For each perfect gift of thine Unto us so freely given
91	4	His faithfulness shall ever be a shield & buckler unto thee
100	5	Unto such as keep his covenant And are steadfast in his way
100	5	Unto those who still remember His commandments and obey
121	4	God ... Who unto men his son hath given
122	2	And unto certain shepherds Brought tidings of the same
142	T,1	Unto Us a Boy Is Born, The King of all creation
142	4	Lead us all with hearts aflame Unto the joys above us
187	2	Unto Christ, our heavenly King
191	3	angel clad in white they see, Who sat & spake unto the three
192	1	From death to life eternal, From earth unto the sky
197	3	From the lips of sinners, Unto whom he came
244	2	That we be faithful unto death
271	T,1	We Come Unto Our Father's God, Their Rock is our salvation
271	2	Their joy unto their Lord we bring
276	T,1	Unto Thy Temple, Lord, We Come
279	1	Let the little ones be given Unto me, of such is heaven
289	2	Cleansed and conformed unto thy will

315	T,1	Come Unto Me, Ye Weary, And I will give you rest
315	2	Come unto me, ye wanderers, And I will give you light
315	3	Come unto me, ye fainting, And I will give you life
351	3	There let the way appear Steps unto heaven
365	3	Shall will all nations unto thee
382	4	Glory, laud and honor Unto Christ the King
385	1	From victory unto victory His army shall he lead
394	T,1,2	Heart and Mind, Possessions, Lord, I offer unto thee
394	1	Wondrous are thy doings unto me
394	1	I commit my spirit unto thee
398	2	Still let thy Spirit unto us be given
426	T,1	The Voice of God Is Calling Its summons unto men
456	3	Day unto day doth utter speech, And night to night proclaim
461	2	Fruit unto his praise to yield
461	2	Wheat and tares together sown, Unto joy or sorrow grown
468	1	We know them living unto thee
468	2	well we know where'er they be, Our dead are living unto thee
468	3	Not dead, but living unto thee
468	4	Where all are living unto thee
469	1	Safe in thine own eternity Our dead are living unto thee
483	2	Let the little ones come unto me
501	1	And unto thee we dedicate The first fruits of the day
503	2	Come thou also unto me
516	1	Thy word is a lamp unto my feet And a light unto my path
517	1	teach me ... the way ... And I shall keep it unto the end
526	T,1	O Thou Who Hearest Prayer, Give ear unto our cry
552	T,1	Lift Up Your Hearts. We lift them up unto the Lord
552	1	Let us give thanks unto the Lord our God
562	T,1	O Come, Let Us Sing unto the Lord
565	3	be thankful unto him, and speak good of his name
568	10	To give knowledge of salvation unto his people

untold

| 6 | 3 | The earth with its store of wonders untold |
| 430 | 3 | He shall forgive thy sins untold |

untrodden

| 308 | 3 | Valiantly o'er sea and land Trod they the untrodden way |

untroubled

| 377 | 2 | Though untroubled still he sleep Who thy hope is on the deep |

unveiled

| 468 | 1 | in whose eyes Unveiled thy whole creation lies |

unvisited

| 106 | 4 | Unvisited, unblest, Break forth to swelling song |

unwasted

| 266 | 1 | Unwasted by the lapse of years, Unchanged by changing place |

unwearied

20	2	That men may hear the grateful song My voice unwearied raise
32	2	angels ... Who all night long, unwearied, sing
72	1	The unwearied sun, from day to day ... power display

78	6	They with unwearied feet shall tread the path of life divine
111	3	Hymn & chant and high thanksgiving And unwearied praises be
185	3	Welcomes in unwearied strains Jesus' resurrection

unworthiness

160	2	The wonders of his glorious love And my unworthiness

unworthy

168	2	our weak endurance Make us unworthy here to take our part
315	4	Which calls us, very sinners, Unworthy though we be
330	3	And not unworthy for my sake A mortal body deem
332	2	Acts unworthy, deeds unthinking
425	1	Are ye not base slaves indeed, Slaves unworthy to be freed

up

25	T,1	Stand Up and Bless the Lord, Ye people of his choice
25	1	Stand up & bless the Lord your God with heart & soul & voice
25	4	Stand up and bless the Lord, The Lord your God adore
25	4	Stand up and bless his glorious name Henceforth for evermore
32	2	Wake and lift up thyself, my heart
33	1	So to thee with one accord Lift we up our Hearts, O Lord
34	2	See how the giant sun soars up, Great lord of years and days
42	4	Bid then farewell to sleep Rise up and run
64	1	Lift up your voice and with us sing Alleluia, Alleluia
66	6	Offering up on every shore Her pure sacrifice of love
72	2	Soon as the evening shades prevail The moon takes up .. tale
72	2	The moon takes up the wondrous tale
74	1	Lifting up our hearts in praise
76	2	hand which bears all nature up Shall guide his children well
92	2	But let me only think of thee And then new heart springs up
101	1	where earth's sorrows Are more felt than up in heaven (102-2
108	1	He comes, O Church, lift up thine eyes
108	1	Rise up, with willing feet Go forth, the Bridegroom meet
114	T,1	Lift Up Your Heads, Ye Mighty Gates
141	2	They looked up and saw a star Shining in the east
150	4	For us gave up his dying breath
154	1	sick to cure, the lost to seek, To raise up them that fall
167	VII-1	Yielding up thy soul at last, Hear us, holy Jesus
189	T,1	Lift Up Your Hearts, Ye People, In songs of glad accord
190	T,1	Life Up Your Hearts, Ye People (same words as no. 189)
197	4	Bore it up triumphant, With its human light
204	R	Lift up your heart, lift up your voice
210	3	Spring thou up within my heart, Rise to all eternity
245	3	Ever by a mighty hope, Pressing on and bearing up
271	3	Ye saints to come, take up the strain
291	1	Thou alone, our strong defender Liftest up thy people's head
297	3	Help us to pass it on unspent Until the dawn lights up
297	3	Until the dawn lights up the skies
300	T,1-3	Rise Up, O Men of God
300	3	Her strength unequal to her task, Rise up and make her great
300	4	As brothers of the Son of man Rise up, O men of God
304	1	Lift up your hearts in jubilant accord
311	1	armies of the ransomed saints throng up the steeps of light
311	3	Fill up the roll of thine elect, Then take thy power & reign
337	1	God shall lift up thy head
341	2	Let us, like them, without a word, Rise up and follow thee

upon

559	14	O Lord, have mercy upon us
559	16	O Lord, let thy mercy be upon us, as our trust is in thee
579	3	Have mercy, now, upon my soul, Hear this my humble prayer

upper

286	2	We meet, as in that upper room they met

upraise

35	4	Let mortals, too, upraise, Their voice in hymns of praise

uprising

36	T,1	New Every Morning Is the Love Our wakening & uprising prove

upward

174	3	peals aloud Upward through the whelming cloud
259	3	Upward we press, the air is clear, & the sphere-music heard
351	5	sun, moon, and stars forgot, Upward I fly
377	4	Upward gaze and happy be, God hath not forsaken thee
441	2	Thy must upward still and onward Who would keep ... truth

urge

362	2	Forget the steps already trod, And onward urge thy way

use

114	2	Make it a temple set apart From earthly use
114	2	set apart From earthly use for heaven's employ
144	3	The guidance of thy light to use
327	1	For our use thy folds prepare
398	4	Take thou our lives and use them as thou wilt
426	3	But thou canst use our weakness To magnify thy power
431	4	Such boastings as the Gentiles use Or lesser breeds
452	5	And use the lives thy love sets free

used

480	2	The same white moon, with silver face ... He used to see
480	2	He used to see in Galilee, And watch it with delight

useful

449	4	That useful labor yet may build Its homes with love

usher

118	1	And usher in the morning

utmost

106	4	Shores of the utmost West, Ye that have waited long
298	2	utmost east to utmost west, Where'er man's foot hath trod

utter

72	3	And utter forth a glorious voice
94	4	For, oh, eternity's too short To utter all thy praise
456	3	Day unto day doth utter speech, And night to night proclaim

vain

87	4	Blind unbelief is sure to err And scan his work in vain
92	T,1	I Look to Thee in Every Need And never look in vain
177	2	All the vain things that charm me most

182	3	Death in vain forbids him rise
209	5	Heaven's morning breaks, and earth's vain shadows flee
230	3	In vain we search the lowest deeps
240	2	In vain we tune our formal songs, In vain we strive to rise
261	4	In vain the surge's angry shock, In vain the drifting sands
322	3	Jesus calls us from the worship of the vain world's
322	3	worship Of the vain world's golden store
342	3	Come quickly, and abide Or life is vain
374	2	With forbidden pleasures Would this vain world charm
399	3	And feel the promise is not vain that morn shall tearless be
416	4	Freest faith assailed in vain
420	2	Cry, Christ hath died in vain
447	3	None ever called on thee in vain
452	3	we strive in vain To save ourselves without thine aid
467	2	When the vain cares that vex our life increase
467	4	Be not cast down, disquieted in vain

vainly

126	4	Vainly we offer each ample oblation
126	4	Vainly with gifts would his favor secure
167	IV-2	When we vainly seem to pray, And our hope seems far away
224	3	Apart from thee all gain is loss, All labor vainly done
298	4	Vainly we hope for the harvest-tide Till God gives life

vale

8	2	Field and forest, vale and mountain ... call us to rejoice
66	2	Hill & vale, and tree & flower, Sun & moon & stars of light
75	3	Hill & vale & fruited land, All things living show his hand
79	4	In death's dark vale I fear no ill
84	3	Yea, though I walk in death's dark vale

vales

377	3	Though the hills & vales be riven God created with his hand

valiant

310	1	Crown for the valiant, to weary ones rest
371	T,1	He Who Would Valiant Be 'Gainst all disaster
388	3	Twelve valiant saints, their hope they knew
431	5	All valiant dust that builds on dust
453	5	Ring in the valiant man and free
491	2	Give us the valiant spirit that shall never Falter

valiantly

17	2	exalt the glory Of him whose arm doth valiantly
308	3	Valiantly o'er sea and land Trod they the untrodden way

valley

42	1	Black turns to gray, Bird-song the valley fills
105	3	And righteousness, in fountains, From hill to valley flow
106	1	Valley and lowland, sing

valley's

579	1	For the valley's golden yield ... fruits of tree and field

valleys

104	2	Let the valleys rise to meet him

259	3	The valleys passed, ascending still
458	4	Praise for hills and valleys broad
459	1	And corn in valleys grow

vanguard

| 107 | 3 | Rank on rank the host of heaven   Spreads its vanguard |
| 107 | 3 | Spreads its vanguard on the way |

vanish

| 107 | 3 | powers of hell may vanish As the darkness clears away |

vanquished

| 205 | 2 | Christ hath vanquished death and sin |
| 385 | 1 | Till every foe is vanquished, And Christ is Lord indeed |

vanquisher

| 148 | 3 | Thou, his vanquisher before, Grant we may not faint nor fail |

varies

| 356 | 2 | It has no spring of action sure, It varies with the wind |

various

| 55 | 2 | we, Oppressed with various ills, draw near |

vast

9	5	Vast as eternity thy love
86	3	Hints of the music vast Of thine eternal hymn
100	6	All throughout his vast dominion Bless the Father, O my soul
167	VII-1	Jesus, all thy labor vast, All thy woe and conflict past
247	1	Infinite thy vast domain, Everlasting is thy reign

vaster

| 508 | 1 | In vaster worlds unseen, unknown |

vault

| 203 | 2 | While the vault of heaven rings |

vaunt

| 325 | 4 | Our pride is dust, our vaunt is stilled |

veil

107	4	Veil their faces to the presence
97	1	With each new day, when morning lifts the veil
232	2	No sudden rending of the veil of clay
459	1	And waters veil the sky

veiled

| 120 | 2 | Veiled in flesh the God-head see, Hail the incarnate Deity |
| 468 | 1 | in whose eyes Unveiled thy whole creation lies |

veiling

| 7 | 4 | Thine angels adore thee, all veiling their sight |

veils

| 82 | 1 | Thy truth shall break through every cloud That veils |
| 81 | 1 | That veils and darkens thy designs |

174	1	Darkness veils thine anguished face
493	2	God's daybreak to proclaim And rend the veils of night

vein

73	3	From the mountain's deep vein poured
456	2	Life mounts in every throbbing vein

vengeance

493	4	No shield I ask, no faithful friend, No vengeance, no reward

vengeful

493	3	had no curse nor vengeful cry For those who broke his bones

venite

133	1	Laeti triumphantes, Venite, venite in Bethlehem
133	R	Venite, adoremus ... Dominum

venture

304	2	Till saint and martyr sped the venture bold

verbum

133	3	Patris aeterni Verbum caro factum

verdant

79	2	where the verdant pastures grow With food celestial feedeth

verge

93	3	When I tread the verge of Jordan

very

55	5	Thy kind but searching glance can scan the very wounds
55	5	The very wounds that shame would hide
112	2	Unobserved, and very near, Like the seed when no man knoweth
142	2	But the very beasts could see that he all men surpasses
160	2	see The very dying form of one Who suffered there for me
225	T,1	Jesus, the Very Thought of Thee
226	T,1	Jesus, the Very Thought of Thee (same words as no. 225)
315	4	Which calls us, very sinners, Unworthy though we be
328	T,1	The Lord Is Rich and Merciful, The Lord is very kind
328	2	The Lord is glorious and strong, Our God is very high
364	3	Thou art very weary, I was weary, too
397	4	fill me with thy fullness Lord, Until my very heart o'erflow
475	2	May be in very deed thine own

vesper

46	1	vesper hymn and vesper prayer rise mingling on the holy air
52	1	Let our vesper hymn be blending With the holy calm around
509	1	vesper hymn and vesper prayer Rise mingling on the holy air

vesture

107	2	Lord of lords, in human vesture, In the body and the blood

vex

467	2	When the vain cares that vex our life increase

vexed

408	2	I walked and sank not on the storm-vexed sea
578	2	I walked and sank not on the storm-vexed sea

vexing

148	3	And if Satan, vexing sore, Flesh or spirit should assail

victor

192	2	His own all hail & hearing May raise the victor-strain

victor's

200	1	A royal diadem adorns The mighty victor's brow
203	1	Crowns become the victor's brow
203	3	Spread abroad the victor's fame
306	3	And win with them the victor's crown of gold
380	4	Look up, the victor's crown at length
385	4	This day the noise of battle, The next the victor's song

victorious

7	1	Almighty, victorious, thy great name we praise
13	2	God hath made his saints victorious
24	1	Where we partake through faith victorious with angels
105	4	O'er every foe victorious, He on his throne shall rest
108	2	In grace arrayed, by truth victorious
145	1	Thou art holy, Fair and glorious, all victorious
197	3	Brought it back victorious, When from death he passed
199	3	And rose victorious in the strife For those he came to save
201	3	O brighter than the rising morn When he, victorious, rose
203	1	From the fight returned victorious
206	1	The name, all victorious, of Jesus extol
246	1	Father, all glorious, O'er all victorious
260	3	And the great Church victorious Shall be the Church at rest
302	3	Pour out thy soul for them in prayer victorious
398	5	O Christ, o'er death victorious

victors

8	4	Ever singing march we onward, Victors in the midst of strife
311	1	Fling open wide the golden gates, And let the victors in

victory

28	4	nations ... raise on high the victory song
106	1	He judgment brings and victory
111	3	Honor, glory, and dominion, And eternal victory, Evermore
153	2	As thou with Satan didst contend, And didst the victory win
154	3	Thy hand the victory won
164	4	And victory remains with love, For he, our Lord is crucified
165	3	Here in o'erwhelming final strife the Lord ... hath victory
165	3	Lord of life hath victory
180	3	Alleluia to the Savior Who has won the victory
181	1	The victory of life is won, The song of triumph has begun
182	2	Where thy victory, O grave
184	3	Praise we in songs of victory That love
189	1	For he hath won the victory O'er sin and death's dark night
192	1	Our Christ hath brought us over With hymns of victory
193	1,R	Endless is the victory Thou o'er death hast won
209	4	Where is death's sting, where, grave, thy victory

304	4	Shall ring love's gracious song of victory
326	5	angels sing At thy coming to victory
346	4	And grant us in thy love To sing the songs of victory
346	4	To sing the songs of victory With faithful souls above
362	4	crowned with victory, at thy feet I'll lay my honors down
385	1	From victory unto victory His army shall he lead
391	4	High King of heaven, my victory won
394	2	He can give me victory o'er all that threatens me
496	2	Blest with victory and peace, may the heaven-rescued land

victory's
| 370 | 3 | When, by thy grace, the victory's won |

videte
| 133 | 1 | Natum videte Regem angelorum |

view
94	1	Transported with the view, I'm lost in wonder, love & praise
146	4	babe ... To human view displayed
165	1	On the Redeemer's thorn-crowned brow ... that dawn we view
165	1	The wonders of that dawn we view
349	2	Where is the soul-refreshing view Of Jesus and his word
412	2	Build us a tower ... That we the land may view

vigor
78	5	Mere human power shall fast decay, And youthful vigor cease
362	1	And press with vigor on
422	3	Feels in his arms the vigor of the Lord

vigorous
| 56 | 3 | Sleep that may me more vigorous make To serve my God |

village
| 124 | 1 | It is Jesus, good folk of the village |
| 152 | 2 | Light of the village life from day to day |

vine
| 281 | 2 | Vine of heaven, thy love supplies ... blest cup of sacrifice |

vintage
| 443 | 1 | He is trampling out the vintage where the grapes of wrath |

virgin
122	3	This day is born a Savior, Of a pure virgin bright
131	2	With Mary we behold it, The Virgin Mother kind
138	1	All is calm, all is bright Round yon virgin mother and child
559	8	Thou didst humble thyself to be born of a virgin

virgin's
| 120 | 2 | Late in time behold him come, Offspring of the Virgin's womb |
| 127 | 1 | tidings first begun of God incarnate and the Virgin's Son |

virgins
| 312 | 4 | And all the virgins bear their part, Sitting about her feet |

virtue

| 384 | 3 | Take every virtue, every grace, And fortify the whole |

virtues

| 30 | 1 | Cry out ... Virtues, archangels, angels' choirs, Alleluia |

virtuous

| 365 | 4 | By kindly words and virtuous life |

visage

| 170 | 1 | How does that visage languish Which once was bright as morn |

visible

| 199 | 2 | Rich wounds, yet visible above, In beauty glorified |

vision

97	2	And faith's fair vision changes into sight
108	3	No vision ever brought ... such great glory
260	3	Till with the vision glorious, Her longing eyes are blest
277	2	Vision true to keep them noble
303	3	We see the beckoning vision flame
304	2	When prophets' glowing vision lit the way
310	2	Vision of peace, that brings joy evermore
391	T,1	Be Thou My Vision, O Lord of my heart
391	4	Still be my vision, O Ruler of all
412	3	O thou who didst the vision send And gives to each his task
419	3	One in the vision of thy peace, The kingdom yet to be
423	2	We catch the vision of thy tears
434	3	strong and true, With vision clear and mind equipped
449	3	Give us the peace of vision clear To see our brother's good
456	3	Thyself the vision passing by In crystal and in rose

visions

| 51 | 3 | Grant to little children Visions bright of thee |
| 117 | 3 | Brighter visions beam afar |

visit

43	3	Visit, then, this soul of mine
228	1	Visit us with thy salvation, Enter every trembling heart
239	1	And visit it with thine own ardor glowing

visitant

| 232 | 2 | No angel visitant, no opening skies |

visited

| 568 | 1 | for he hath visited and redeemed his people |
| 568 | 11 | whereby the Dayspring from on high hath visited us |

voice

4	1	Sing to the Lord with cheerful voice
13	1	Worlds his mighty voice obeyed
20	3	That men may hear the grateful song My voice unwearied raise
26	1	Raise your voice and rejoice In the bounty of his hand
28	3	And all rejoice with Christian heart and voice
34	2	Come, let thy voice be one with theirs
35	4	Let mortals, too, upraise, Their voice in hymns of praise

123	1	As I hear, Far and near, Sweetest angel voices
180	T,1	Alleluia, Alleluia, Hearts to Heaven and voices raise
191	5	On the most holy day of days, Our hearts and voices, Lord
202	3	And infant voices shall proclaim their early blessings
237	4	Earth's bitter voices drown In one deep ocean of accord
249	1	To thee all knees are bent, all voices pray
310	3	While for thy grace, Lord, their voices of praise
382	4	Blend with ours your voices In the triumph song
458	1	Hearts, bow down, & voices, sing Praises to the glorious One
458	6	Hearts, bow down and voices, sing Praise and love
492	2	For prophet voices gladly heard, For daring dreams
505	1	Now lift your hearts, your voices raise
508	2	And through the swell of chanting voices

volume
| 257 | 2 | But the blest volume thou hast writ Reveals thy justice |

vouchsafe
170	2	Look on me with thy favor, vouch-safe to me thy grace
263	3	Here vouchsafe to all thy servants What they ask of thee
559	15	Vouchsafe, O Lord, to keep us this day without sin

vouchsafes
| 475 | 1 | And yet vouchsafes in Christian lands To dwell in temples |

vow
| 331 | 1 | In love my soul would bow, My heart fulfill its vow |

vows
32	3	Lord, I my vows to thee renew
269	4	Her sweet communion, solemn vows, Her hymns of love & praise
389	2	Our vows, our prayers, we now present Before thy throne
462	3	And for these our souls shall raise Grateful vows
462	3	Grateful vows and solemn praise
464	2	Lord, for these, our souls shall raise Grateful vows
464	2	Grateful vows and solemn praise
471	1	For saints of old, who made their vows before thee

wacht
| 139 | 1 | Alles schlaft, eisam wacht |

wade
| 484 | 1 | Where children wade through rice fields |
| 484 | 1 | wade through rice fields And watch the camel trains |

waging
| 378 | 3 | Peace, when the world its busy war is waging |

wait
23	T,1	Ye Holy Angels Bright, Who wait at God's right hand
26	3	In the sacred silence wait, As we seek to know his will
45	1	Wait and worship while the night sets her evening lamps
60	1	Then, lowly kneeling, wait thy word of peace
69	2	All who work & all who wait, Sing, The Lord is good & great
78	5	they who wait upon the Lord In strength shall still increase

83	2	Only be still, and wait his leisure in cheerful hope
96	2	And patiently I wait his day
156	2	with longing expectation seem to wait The consecration
300	3	The Church for you doth wait
325	4	We wait thy revelation
329	2	O love that passeth knowledge, So patiently to wait
337	1	Wait thou his time, so shall this night Soon end
339	2	Love doth stand At his hand, Joy doth wait on his command
360	4	And so beside the silent sea I wait the muffled oar
373	3	Place on the Lord reliance, My soul, with courage wait
452	1	We wait thy liberating deed To signal hope and set us free
520	1	and bless all souls that wait before thee

waited
106	4	Shores of the utmost West, Ye that have waited long
198	3	The world has waited long, Has travailed long in pain

waiting
304	3	And from his waiting Church new hopes arise
329	1	In lowly patience waiting To pass the threshold o'er
402	3	Here to our waiting hearts proclaim The sweetness
477	2	For thee our waiting spirits yearn
494	1	waiting till love can raise the broken stone

waits
104	1	Speak ye to Jerusalem Of the peace that waits for them
114	1	Behold the King of glory waits
205	2	There the glorious triumph waits
260	3	She waits the consummation Of peace for evermore
503	1	Where my soul in joyful duty Waits for him who answers
503	1	Waits for him who answers prayer

wake
32	2	Wake and lift up thyself, my heart
50	5	Come near and bless us when we wake
242	1	Wake my spirit, clear my sight
244	1	To strength and gladness wake us
451	2	Would man but wake from out his haunted sleep

waken
124	2	Lest your noise should waken Jesus

wakening
36	T,1	New Every Morning Is the Love Our wakening & uprising prove

wakes
42	1	Mists fold away, Gray wakes to green again
59	3	Our earliest thoughts be thine when morning wakes us
108	2	She wakes, she rises from her gloom
294	2	O God of love, whose spirit wakes In every human breast

waketh
37	1	When the bird waketh, and the shadows flee
37	4	morning, When the soul waketh and life's shadows flee
343	2	His wisdom ever waketh, His sight is never dim

waking

37	3	So does this blessed consciousness, awaking, Breathe
47	4	The sun that bids us rest is waking Our brethren
217	1	Be there at our waking
305	1	The sons of earth are waking To penitential tears
351	4	Then, with my waking thoughts Bright with thy praise
391	1	Waking or sleeping, thy presence my light
427	1	Hark, the waking up of nations, Hosts advancing to the fray
506	T,1	Come, My Soul, Thou Must Be Waking

walk

26	4	Yea, his law is sure, In his light we walk secure
84	2	me to walk doth make Within the paths of righteousness
84	3	Yea, though I walk in death's dark vale
162	2	There I walk amid the shades While the ... twilight fades
248	3	I walk secure and blessed In every clime or coast
343	2	He knows the way he taketh, And I will walk with him
343	3	My Savior has my treasure, And he will walk with me
349	T,1	O For a Closer Walk With God, A calm and heavenly frame
349	5	So shall my walk be close with God, Calm and serene my frame
350	T,1	O for a Closer Walk With God (same words as no. 349)
376	3	Blindly we stumble when we walk alone
392	4	That we, with thee, may walk uncowed By fear
398	3	Walk thou beside us lest the tempting byways Lure us away
408	3	I find, I walk, I love, but oh, the whole Of Love
418	T,1	O Master, Let Me Walk With Thee
430	3	Walk in his way, his word adore
578	3	I find, I walk, I love, but O the whole Of love is

walked

44	1	Two walked with thee in waning light
408	2	I walked and sank not on the storm-vexed sea
578	2	I walked and sank not on the storm-vexed sea

walkedst

429	2	Who walkedst on the foaming deep

walks

91	5	Nor pestilence that walks by night
220	1	Beside us walks our brother Christ, & makes our task his own
421	1	And he who journeys in them walks with thee

wall

171	T,1	There Is a Green Hill Far Away, Without a city wall
424	1	Only righteous men and women Dwell within its gleaming wall

walls

46	1	We gather in these hallowed walls
261	T,1	City of God, How Broad and Far Outspread thy walls sublime
263	2	And thy fullest benediction Shed within its walls alway
267	1	with salvation's walls surrounded, Thou may'st smile
269	2	I love thy Church, O God, Her walls before they stand
377	3	Lo, his wings are walls around thee
395	3	those are not the only walls Wherein thou mayst be sought
402	2	thou, within no walls confined, Inhabitest the humble mind
420	1	Within whose four-square walls shall come No night

436   1   The walls of gold entomb us, The swords of scorn divide
452   2   High walls of ignorance around
494   1   O'er crumbling walls their crosses scarcely lift
509   1   We gather in these hallowed walls

wander
218   1   Now wander from the pathway If thou wilt be my guide

wandered
334   2   Lord, we have wandered forth through doubt and sorrow

wanderer
331   2   Some wanderer sought and won, Something for thee
351   2   Though like the wanderer, The sun gone down

wanderers
315   2   Come unto me, ye wanderers, And I will give you light

wandering
9   2   And when, like wandering sheep we strayed, He brought us
252   4   O teach thy wandering pilgrims By this their path to trace
389   3   Our wandering footsteps guide
398   3   Showing to wandering souls the path of light
468   3   Not wandering in unknown despair Beyond thy voice

wanderings
109   3   Watchman, let thy wanderings cease
368   4   In our wanderings be our guide
389   4   Till all our wanderings cease

wane
202   1   Till moons shall wax and wane no more
382   3   Crowns and thrones may perish, Kingdoms rise and wane

waning
44   1   Two walked with thee in waning light

want
84   T,1   The Lord's My Shepherd, I'll not want
93   1   Bread of heaven, Feed me till I want no more
202   4   The weary find eternal rest & all the sons of want are blest
219   1   To call thy brethren forth from want and woe
267   2   And all fear of want remove
343   2   Wherever he may guide me, No want shall turn me back
353   T,1   Lord, I Want to Be a Christian
353   2   Lord, I want to be more loving
353   3   Lord I want to be more holy
353   4   Lord I want to be like Jesus

wanting
7   2   Nor wanting, nor wasting, thou rulest in might
385   3   Where duty calls, or danger, Be never wanting there

wanton
366   3   Shame our wanton, selfish gladness

wants

81	4	He'll make your wants his care
83	2	Nor doubt our inmost wants are known To him
461	1	God, our Maker, doth provide For our wants to be supplied
462	1	God, our Maker, doth provide For our wants to be supplied
486	2	Simple wants provide, Evil let he shun

war

260	3	'Mid toil and tribulation, And tumult of her war
305	1	Of nations in commotion, Prepared for Zion's war
325	3	Till in the night of hate and war We perish as we lose thee
375	2	Lead on, O King eternal, Till sin's fierce war shall cease
378	3	Peace, when the world its busy war is waging
380	4	Not long the conflict, soon The holy war shall cease
382	T,1,R	Onward, Christian Soldiers, Marching as to war
388	T,1	The Son of God Goes Forth to War, A kingly crown to gain
410	3	Then shall all shackles fall, the stormy clangor Of ... war
410	3	clangor Of wild war music o'er the earth shall cease
439	4	God of justice, save the people From the war of race & creed
444	4	That war may haunt the earth no more And desolation cease

war's

433	3	From war's alarms, from deadly pestilence
496	2	stand Between their loved homes and the war's desolation

warfare

104	1	Tell her that her sins I cover, And her warfare now is over
306	5	And when the strife is fierce, the warfare long
380	4	Faith's warfare ended, won The home of endless peace
449	4	Let woe and waste of warfare cease

warm

43	2	Till they inward light impart Glad my eyes and warm my heart
230	4	But warm, sweet, tender, even yet A present help is he
276	2	And warm and bright and good to all
348	2	O may my love to thee Pure, warm and changeless be
348	2	Pure, warm, and changeless be, A living fire
482	1	See the fur to keep you warm, Snugly round your tiny form
542	1	And make our luke-warm hearts to glow With lowly love

warmer

455	3	And warmer glows her light within
459	3	He calls the warmer gales to blow And bids the spring return

warmest

221	4	Weak is the effort of my heart, And cold my warmest thought

warmly

455	4	Us warmly in thy love enfold

warmth

64	3	That givest man both warmth and light
89	4	Whose light is truth, whose warmth is love
460	1	he sends the snow in winter, The warmth to swell the grain

warning

| 104 | 2 | Oh, that warning cry obey, Now prepare for God a way |
| 118 | 1 | But hear the angel's warning |

warring

| 106 | 2 | Pent be each warring breeze, Lulled be your restless waves |
| 366 | 3 | Cure thy children's warring madness |

warriors

69	2	Warriors fighting for the Lord
308	2	Warriors wielding freedom's sword
345	5	As warriors through the darkness toil
380	2	Heroic warriors, ne'er from Christ ... enticed

wars

377	3	Though the moving signs of heaven Wars presage in every land
445	2	By wars and tumults love is mocked, derided
447	1	Make wars throughout the world to cease

wash

| 324 | 2 | Wash out its stains, refine its dross |
| 358 | 3 | Foul, I to the fountain fly, Wash me, Savior, or I die |

waste

| 91 | 5 | Nor plagues that waste in noonday light |
| 449 | 4 | Let woe and waste of warfare cease |

wastes

| 106 | 2 | And makes your wastes his great highway |
| 249 | 2 | Through seas dry-shod, through weary wastes bewildering |

wasting

| 7 | 2 | Nor wanting, nor wasting, thou rulest in might |

watch

1	4	Short as the watch that ends the night Before the rising sun
47	2	Through all the world her watch is keeping
50	4	Watch by the sick, enrich the poor with blessings
59	2	The morning cometh, watch, Protector, o'er us
134	2	While mortals sleep, the angels keep Their watch
134	2	Their watch of wondering love
140	1	While shepherds watch are keeping
158	1	Watch with him one bitter hour
174	1	King of grief, I watch with thee
289	2	Watch o'er thy Church, O Lord, in mercy
333	3	Father of mercy, from thy watch & keeping No place can part
364	2	Gird thee for the battle, Watch and pray and fast
406	4	And every moment watch and pray
441	3	God within the shadow Keeping watch above his own
480	2	He used to see in Galilee, And watch it with delight
484	1	wade through rice fields And watch the camel trains

watched

| 146 | T,1 | While Shepherds Watched Their Flocks by night |
| 496 | 1 | O'er the ramparts we watched were so gallantly streaming |

watchers
| 30 | T,1 | Ye Watchers and Ye Holy Ones |
| 185 | 4 | Nor the watchers, nor the seal Hold thee as a mortal |

watches
| 89 | 2 | Cheers the long watches of the night |
| 256 | 3 | Pillar of fire through watches dark, & radiant cloud by day |

watchfires
| 261 | 3 | watchfires ... With never fainting ray |
| 443 | 2 | have seen him in the watchfires of a hundred circling camps |

watchful
20	2	His watchful eye ne'er sleepeth
41	1	Active and watchful, stand we all before thee
127	2	Then to the watchful shepherds it was told
471	4	Patient and watchful when thy sheep are roving

watching
51	4	Comfort every sufferer Watching late in pain
117	2	Watching o'er your flocks by night
117	4	Watching long in hope and fear
488	1	While shepherds kept their watching O'er silent flocks

watchman
109	T,1-3	Watchman, Tell Us of the Night
109	1	Watchman, does its beauteous ray ... joy or hope foretell
109	2	Watchman, will its beams alone Gild the spot
109	3	Watchman, let thy wanderings cease

watchmen
| 108 | 1 | The watchmen on the heights are crying |
| 108 | 2 | Zion hears the watchmen singing |

water
64	3	Thou flowing water, pure and clear
79	2	Where streams of living water flow
128	1	Earth stood hard as iron, Water like a stone
260	1	She is his new creation By water and the word
358	1	Let the water & the blood, From thy riven side which flowed
423	4	The cup of water given for thee Still holds the freshness
468	3	Not spilt like water on the ground

watered
| 460 | 1 | But it is fed and watered By God's almighty hand |

waters
84	1	he leadeth me The quiet waters by
167	V-3	Where the healing waters flow, Hear us, holy Jesus
185	1	Led them with unmoistened foot Through the Red Sea waters
210	1	While the nearer waters roll ... the tempest still is high
267	2	See ... streams of living waters Springing from eternal love
298	1-4	As the waters cover the sea
328	1	Like flowing waters cool
333	2	To pastures green beside the peaceful waters
368	3	Not forever by still waters Would we idly rest and stay

372	3	When through the deep waters I call thee to go
456	1	The flowing waters sealed
459	1	And waters veil the sky

wave

61	4	Smite death's threatening wave before you
345	1	Your festal banner wave on high, The cross of Christ
370	3	E'en death's cold wave, I will not flee
429	1	Whose arm doth bind the restless wave
467	4	Where now he ploweth, wave with golden grain
496	1	O say does that star-spangled banner yet wave
496	2	And the star-spangled banner in triumph shall wave

waver

| 374 | 1 | When thou seest me waver, With a look recall |
| 427 | 3 | Sworn to yield, to waver, never, Consecrated, born again |

waves

77	2	the waves and winds still know his voice
106	2	Pent be each warring breeze, Lulled be your restless waves
213	1	Unknown waves before me roll
213	2	Boisterous waves obey thy will
256	3	When waves o'erwhelm our tossing bark
293	1	While all around him waves the golden grain
337	1	Through waves and clouds and storms He gently clears the way
377	2	Though the sea his waves assemble And in fury fall on thee
429	2	O Savior, whose almighty word, The winds and waves ... heard
429	2	The winds and waves submissive heard
438	3	Came with those exiles o'er the waves
440	T,1	O Beautiful for Spacious Skies, For amber waves of grain
460	2	The winds and waves obey him, By him the birds are fed

wax

| 202 | 1 | Till moons shall wax and wane no more |

way

20	3	Then all my gladsome way along, I sing aloud thy praises
29	1	Who, from our mothers' arms, Hath blessed us on our way
50	5	ere through the world our way we take
60	2	Grant us thy peace upon our homeward way
75	2	Breaking through the clouds his way
87	T,1	God Moves in a Mysterious Way His wonders to perform
88	T,1	God Moves in a Mysterious Way (same words as No. 87)
100	5	Unto such as keep his covenant And are steadfast in his way
104	2	Oh, that warning cry obey, Now prepare for God a way
107	3	Spreads its vanguard on the way
119	4	Holy Jesus, every day Keep us in the narrow way
129	3	Who toil along the climbing way With painful steps and slow
152	2	The Christ of God, the Life, the Truth, the Way
156	1	behold we lay Our passions, lusts, & proud wills in thy way
157	3	When the sun of bliss is beaming Light and love upon my way
160	1	A home within the wilderness, A rest upon the way
161	1	The meaning of our eager strife Is tested by his Way
167	VI-3	Brighten all our heavenward way With an ever holier ray
168	3	Along that sacred way where thou art leading
169	3	Sometimes they strew his way, And his sweet praises sing

184	2	Bring flowers of song to strew his way
191	2	their way To seek the tomb where Jesus lay
197	2	Thrones and dominations, Stars upon their way
219	2	light Which guides the nations groping on their way
219	3	Yes, thou art still the Life, thou art the Way
219	3	The holiest know - Light, Life, and Way of heaven
219	3	Toil by the truth, life, way that thou hast given
221	3	My Lord, my Life, my Way, my End, Accept the praise I bring
229	3	Nor rove, nor seek the crooked way
237	1	Too long the darkened way we've trod
238	2	And make us know and choose thy way
238	3	Lead us to Christ, the living Way
255	1	His testimony is most sure, Proclaiming wisdom's way
256	1	Brook by the traveler's way
258	3	Then its light directeth, And our way protecteth
259	2	The first steps of the way
275	1	round Of circling planets singing on their way
302	3	Give of thy wealth to speed them on their way
304	2	When prophets' glowing vision lit the way
305	3	Blest river of salvation, Pursue thy onward way
308	3	Valiantly o'er sea and land Trod they the untrodden way
314	3	Through darkness and perplexity Point thou the heavenly way
315	2	Our hearts are filled with sadness, And we had lost our way
324	3	Be thou my light, be thou my way
327	2	Be the guardian of our way
336	T,1	O Thou by Whom we Come to God, The Life, the Truth, the Way
336	2	And, when to meet thee we prepare, Lord, meet us by the way
337	2	So shalt thou, wondering, own his way
343	2	He knows the way he taketh, And I will walk with him
351	3	There let the way appear Steps unto heaven
362	2	Forget the steps already trod, And onward urge thy way
367	2	Life with its way before us lies
368	2	Not forever in green pastures Do we ask our way to be
368	3	From the rocks along our way
376	1	Lead us through Christ, the true and living Way
386	1	send thy light To set our footsteps in the homeward way
394	2	Thou art the Way, the Truth, thou art the Life
399	2	O Light that followest all my way
403	1	who love and ... labor follow in the way of Christ
418	2	And guide them in the homeward way
418	4	Far down the future's broadening way
419	2	And steadfastly pursue the way Of thy commandments still
421	3	We've felt thy touch in sorrow's darkened way
426	4	Take us, and make us holy, Teach us thy will and way
430	3	Walk in his way, his word adore
433	2	Thy word our law, thy paths our chosen way
433	4	Refresh thy people on their toilsome way
491	3	Teach us to know the way of Jesus Christ, our Master
517	T,1	Teach me, O Lord, the way of thy statutes
517	1	teach me ... the way ... And I shall keep it unto the end
524	1	make thy way plain before my face
530	T,1	O Thou by Whom We Come to God, The Life, the Truth, the Way
565	3	O go your way into his gates with thanksgiving
568	12	and to guide our feet into the way of peace

ways

26	3	All our days, all our ways, shall our Father's love confess
74	1	Marveling at thy mystic ways
74	2	From thy ways so often turning, Yet thy love doth seek him
77	1	thy best, thy heavenly friend Through thorny ways leads
77	1	Through thorny ways leads to a joyful end
83	1	And hope in him through all thy ways
83	3	Sing, pray, and keep his ways unswerving
92	4	Thou leadest me by unsought ways
110	3	knowledge show, And cause us in her ways to go
194	3	He guideth you on all your ways
262	T,1	Forgive, O Lord, Our Severing Ways
269	4	Beyond my highest joy I prize her heavenly ways
274	2	And in their hearts thy ways
295	4	The new-born souls, whose days Reclaimed from error's ways
333	2	Tenderest guide, in ways of cheerful duty, Lead us
341	T,1	Dear Lord and Father of Mankind, Forgive our foolish ways
366	2	hosts of evil round us Scorn thy Christ assail his ways
369	1	God's Glory ... Most strange in all its ways
396	1	That my whole being may proclaim Thy being and thy ways
405	2	Toilsome and gloomy ways Brightened with song
420	3	Whose ways are brotherhood
423	T,1	Where Cross the Crowded Ways of Life
446	2	earth hath forsaken Thy ways all holy, and slighted thy word
451	T,1	Turn Back, O Man, Forswear Thy Foolish Ways
469	3	Thy word is true, thy ways are just
473	1	Just, King of saints, and true thy ways
490	1	Through all our days, in all our ways, Our ... Father's will
497	1	In all his words most wonderful, Most sure in all his ways
568	9	shalt go before the face of the Lord to prepare his ways
576	1	And all my ways are in thy hand

wayside

460	2	He paints the wayside flower, He lights the evening star

wayward

33	3	Lest from thee we stray abroad, Stay our wayward feet,O Lord
295	2	The wayward and the lost, By restless passions tossed
405	3	Some dews of mercy shed, Some wayward footsteps led
418	2	Teach me the wayward feet stay
443	4	God, give thy wayward children peace

weak

78	4	He gives the conquest to the weak
93	1	I am weak, but thou art mighty
105	2	To help the poor and needy, And bid the weak be strong
118	1	This child, now weak in infancy, Our confidence ... shall be
162	T,1	When My Love to God Grows Weak
162	3	When my love for man grows weak
168	2	We would not leave thee, though our weak endurance
168	2	our weak endurance Make us unworthy here to take our part
221	4	Weak is the effort of my heart, And cold my warmest thought
293	3	No arm so weak but may do service here
308	3	strong, yet battling for the weak
334	1	For we are weak, and need some deep revealing
335	3	Are we weak and heavy laden, Cumbered with a load of care

356	2	My heart is weak and poor Until it master find
366	5	Save us from weak resignation to the evils we deplore
392	5	Teach us the strength that cannot seek ... to hurt the weak
392	5	cannot seek By deed or thought, to hurt the weak
396	3	Poor though I be and weak
419	2	spirit's sword to shield The weak against the strong
425	3	They are slaves who fear to speak For the fallen & the weak

weakness

41	2	Banish our weakness, health and wholeness sending
232	1	Stoop to my weakness, mighty as thou art
335	2	Jesus knows our every weakness
344	2	All our weakness thou dost know
368	4	Be our strength in hours of weakness
384	3	Leave no unguarded place, No weakness of the soul
405	2	Daily our lives would show Weakness made strong
426	3	But thou canst use our weakness To magnify thy power
467	3	And in our weakness thou dost make us strong
489	2	I would be humble, for I know my weakness

wealth

31	3	slenderness Of the poor wealth thou wouldst reckon as thine
249	4	Our plenty, wealth, prosperity, and peace
302	3	Give of thy wealth to speed them on their way
316	2	May we offer for thy service All our wealth & all our days
395	4	Thine are the loom, the forge, the mart, The wealth of land
395	4	Thine are ... the wealth of land and sea
413	2	Thine the wealth of land and sea
457	1	One more the glad earth yields Her golden wealth
457	1	golden wealth of ripening grain And breath of clover fields

wean

| 232 | 1 | Wean it from earth, through all its pulses move |

weapon

188	3	From every weapon death can wield Thine own ... shield
381	1	My faith, it is a weapon stout, The soldier's trusty blade
493	1	He bore no shield before his face, No weapon in his hand

wear

| 425 | 2 | share All the chains our brothers wear |

wearied

| 50 | 2 | My wearied eyelids gently steep |

weariness

| 287 | 1 | And all my weariness upon thee lean |
| 557 | 1 | And all my weariness upon thee lean |

wearing

| 49 | 1 | The eternal splendor wearing, Celestial, holy, blest |

weary

| 51 | 2 | Jesus, give the weary Calm and sweet repose |
| 76 | 3 | Why should this anxious load Press down your weary mind |

78	2	can an all-creating arm Grow weary or decay
86	T,1	Our God, to Whom We Turn, When weary with illusion
129	2	still their heavenly music floats O'er all the weary world
129	3	O rest beside the weary road, And hear the angels sing
160	1	The shadow of a mighty rock Within a weary land
202	4	The weary find eternal rest & all the sons of want are blest
221	2	'Tis manna to the hungry soul, And to the weary, rest
249	2	Through seas dry-shod, through weary wastes bewildering
310	1	Crown for the valiant, to weary ones rest
315	T,1	Come Unto Me, Ye Weary, And I will give you rest
344	2	Lone and dreary, faint and weary, Through the desert
364	3	Thou art very weary, I was weary, too
399	1	I rest my weary soul in thee
435	2	Still the weary folk are pining for the hour
510	2	Jesus, give the weary Calm and sweet repose

weave

325	1	And still our wrongs may weave thee now New thorns

week

154	T,1	O thou Who Through This Holy Week Didst suffer for us all
168	T,1	Lord, Through This Holy Week of our salvation

weep

420	1	And where the tears are wiped from eyes That shall not weep
420	1	That shall not weep again
451	2	Built while they dream, and in that dreaming weep

weeping

162	2	See that suffering friendless one Weeping, praying ... alone
377	T,1	Lift Thy Head, O Zion, Weeping, Still the Lord thy Father is

weeps

178	3	The Man of Sorrows weeps in blood

weighed

170	1	With grief and shame weighed down

weight

209	4	Ills have no weight, and tears no bitterness
352	2	The mire of sin, the weight of guilty fears

welcome

155	3	Hosanna, welcome to our hearts
217	3	Your hands swift to welcome your arms to embrace
315	4	O welcome voice of Jesus, Which drives away our doubt
319	4	Wilt welcome, pardon, cleanse, relieve

welcomes

185	3	Welcomes in unwearied strains Jesus' resurrection
471	3	Give him the faith that welcomes all the light

welfare

403	2	Lo, the Prince of common welfare dwells within the market

well

2	2	'Tis well thou art our ruler
16	3	Well our feeble frame he knows
55	3	And some have never loved thee well
92	1	I feel thy strong and tender love, And all is well again
267	2	Well supply thy sons and daughters
293	4	glad sound comes with the setting sun, Well done, well done
328	3	O learn of him, learn now of him, Then with thee it is well
346	2	And strive to serve him well
357	6	That mind and soul, according well, May make one music
386	2	The subtle darkness that we love so well
438	2	Thou heard'st well pleased, the song, the prayer
455	4	O God, who givest the winter's cold As well as summer's
455	4	As well as summer's joyous rays
466	1	Bless thou all parents, guarding well, With constant love
466	1	guarding well ... The homes in which thy people dwell
468	2	well we know where'er they be, Our dead are living unto thee

went

55	1	O in what diverse pains they met ... what joy they went away
141	3	And to follow the star wherever it went
150	5	For us he went on high to reign
155	1	The people of the Hebrews With palms before thee went
168	1	salvation Which thou has won for us who went astray
191	2	That Easter morn at break of day, The faithful women went
259	2	Darkling our great forefathers went The first steps
264	T,1	O Where Are Kings and Empires Now Of old that went and came
325	2	a nation's pride o'erthrown, Went down to dust beside thee
381	2	They cared not, but with force unspent ... they onward went
381	2	Unmoved by pain, they onward went
493	1	When Stephen ... Went forth throughout the land

west

45	T,1	Day is Dying in the West, Heaven is touching earth with rest
100	3	Far as east from west is distant He hath put away our sin
106	4	Shores of the utmost West, Ye that have waited long
106	5	Lo, from the North we come, From East, and West, and South
298	2	utmost east to utmost west, Where'er man's foot hath trod
304	4	To east and west his kingdom bringing near
414	T,1	In Christ There Is No East or West, In him no South or North
414	4	In Christ now meet both East and West
415	T,1	In Christ There Is No East or West (words as no. 414)

western

47	4	Our brethren 'neath the western sky
293	4	No time for rest, till glows the western sky

westward

143	R	Westward leading, still proceeding

wet

34	1	The fields are wet with diamond dew, The worlds awake to cry
38	2	Praise for the sweetness Of the wet garden

whate'er

2	2	Thou dost whate'er thy will ordains

324   4   Savior, where'er thy steps I see ... I follow thee
370   1   Whate'er I do, where'er I be, Still 'tis God's hand
375   3   For gladness breaks like morning Where'er thy face appears
402   T,1   Jesus, Where'er Thy People Meet
402   1   Where'er they seek thee, thou art found
468   2   well we know where'er they be, Our dead are living unto thee
469   T,1   O Lord of Life, Where'er They Be
490   2   Teach us where'er we live, To act as in thy sight
576   T,1   Lord, Thou Hast Searched Me and dost know Where'er I rest
576   1   Where'er I rest, where'er I go

whereby
256   T,1   Lamp of Our Feet, Whereby We Trace Our path
392   2   The truth whereby the nations live
568   11   whereby the Dayspring from on high hath visited us

wherefore
96   1   Wherefore to him I leave it all

wherein
239   3   the place Wherein the Holy Spirit makes his dwelling
256   2   Our guide & chart, wherein we read Of realms beyond the sky
304   1   years Wherein God's mighty purposes unfold
395   3   those are not the only walls Wherein thou mayst be sought

whereof
121   1   joy I bring, Whereof I now will say and sing

whereon
127   1   morn Whereon the Savior of the world was born
256   2   Bread of our souls, whereon we feed

wheresoe'er
429   4   Protect them wheresoe'er they go

wherever
141   3   And to follow the star wherever it went
343   2   Wherever he may guide me, No want shall turn me back

wherewith
493   1   And on his lips a sword Wherewith he smote and overcame

whether
381   2   Whether beneath was flinty rock Or yielding grassy sod
424   2   Whether humble or exalted, All are called to task divine

whirl
220   2   Through din of market, whirl of wheels
422   T,1   When Through the Whirl of Wheels, and engines humming

whisper
375   2   And holiness shall whisper The sweet amen of peace
400   3   Then shall my latest breath Whisper thy praise

whispers
230   6   The last low whispers of our dead Are burdened with his name

white

124	3	How he is white, his cheeks are rosy
191	3	angel clad in white they see, Who sat & spake unto the three
309	3	Forever and forever Are clad in robes of white
456	2	O'er white expanses sparkling pure The radiant morns unfold
480	2	The same white moon, with silver face ... He used to see
485	2	morning light, the lily white, Declare their Maker's praise

whiten

464	2	Flocks that whiten all the plain

whither

576	3	Or whither from thy presence flee

whole

65	1	Let the whole creation cry
69	T,1	Let the Whole Creation Cry, Glory to the Lord on high
110	4	Fill the whole world with heaven's peace
113	2	travail ... That made the whole creation groan
129	4	the whole world send back the song Which now the angels sing
177	4	Were the whole realm of nature mine
194	T,1	The Whole Bright World Rejoices Now
198	2	the whole round world complete, From sunrise to its setting
207	2	So come, O King, and our whole being sway
221	2	It makes the wounded spirit whole
230	1	Forever shared, forever whole, A never-ebbing sea
230	5	touch him in life's throng and press, And we are whole again
241	2	Let our whole soul an offering be To our Redeemer's name
257	3	Sun, moon, and stars convey thy praise Round the whole earth
257	3	Round the whole earth and never stand
276	4	May thy whole truth be spoken here
361	4	Lord Jesus, make me whole
383	3	Bound by God's far purpose In one living whole
384	3	Take every virtue, every grace, And fortify the whole
396	1	That my whole being may proclaim Thy being and thy ways
408	3	I find, I walk, I love, but oh, the whole Of Love
408	3	the whole Of love is but my answer, Lord, to thee
412	1	boyhood faith That shone thy whole life through
414	1	fellowship of love Throughout the whole wide earth
414	4	one in him throughout the whole wide earth
419	1	binds the starry spheres In one stupendous whole
420	4	bids us seize the whole of life And build its glory there
451	3	Nor till that hour shall God's whole will be done
468	1	in whose eyes Unveiled thy whole creation lies
481	2	followed ... The whole of their good lives long
562	8	let the whole earth stand in awe of him
578	3	I find, I walk, I love, but O the whole Of love is
578	3	the whole Of love is but my answer, Lord, to thee

wholeness

41	2	Banish our weakness, health and wholeness sending

wholesome

461	2	Lord of harvest, grant that we Wholesome grain & pure may be

wholly

55	4	none, O Lord, have perfect rest, For none are wholly free
55	4	none are wholly free from sin
233	3	Til I am wholly thine
348	1	Oh, let me from this day Be wholly thine

whosoever

315	4	And whosoever cometh I will not cast him out

why

4	4	For why, the Lord our God is good
76	3	Why should this anxious load Press down your weary mind
116	2	Shepherds, why this jubilee, Why your joyous strains prolong
140	2	Why lies he in such mean estate Where ox and ass are feeding
169	4	Why, what hath my Lord done, What makes this rage and spite
174	3	Thou dost ask him -- can it be, Why has thou forsaken me
357	2	Thou madest man, he knows not why
390	3	Why restless, why cast down, my soul
481	2	not any reason ... Why I shouldn't be one too
485	3	Why should my heart be sad
495	4	If you love him, why not serve him

wicked

21	1	The wicked oppressing now cease from distressing
95	3	This wicked earth redress
150	4	For us to wicked men betrayed

wide

9	5	Wide as the world is thy command
114	2	Fling wide the portals of your heart
114	3	Redeemer, come, I open wide My heart to thee
249	1	Thy love has blessed the wide world's wondrous story
296	1,3	let it float Sky-ward and sea-ward, high and wide
296	4	wide and high, Sea-ward and sky-ward, let it shine
311	1	Fling open wide the golden gates, And let the victors in
316	1	Thou who formed the earth's wide reaches
410	2	So shall the wide earth seem our Father's temple
414	1	fellowship of love Throughout the whole wide earth
414	4	one in him throughout the whole wide earth
435	1	Solace all its wide dominion With the healing of thy wings
580	2	A gate which opens wide to those That do lament their sin

widely

16	3	praise him Widely as his mercy flows

wideness

101	T,1	There's a Wideness in God's Mercy (102-T,1)
101	1	God's mercy, Like the wideness of the sea (102-1)
102	T,1	There's a Wideness in God's Mercy (same as No. 101 in 4 vs.)

widening

432	1	from dawn of days Hast led thy people in their widening ways

wider

383	2	Wider grows the kingdom, Reign of love and light

wie

| 139 | 3 | Gottes Sohn, o wie lacht |

wield

| 188 | 3 | From every weapon death can wield Thine own ... shield |

wielding

| 308 | 2 | Warriors wielding freedom's sword |

wild

53	1	Shade creeps o'er wild and wood
148	T,1	Forty Days and Forty Nights Thou wast fasting in the wild
249	3	Stilling the rude wills of men's wild behavior
322	1	tumult Of our life's wild, restless sea
324	3	If in this darksome wild I stray
410	3	clangor Of wild war music o'er the earth shall cease
431	4	If drunk with sight of power, we loose Wild tongues
431	4	Wild tongues that have not thee in awe
453	T,1	Ring Out, Wild Bells, to the wild sky
453	1	Ring out, wild bells, and let him die
481	2	And one was slain by a fierce wild beast

wilderness

63	1	O refresh us, Traveling through this wilderness
160	1	A home within the wilderness, A rest upon the way
237	2	Till wilderness and town One temple for thy worship be
276	3	Like fountains in the wilderness
440	2	A thoroughfare for freedom beat Across the wilderness

will

2	1	God showeth his good-will to men
2	2	Thou dost whate'er thy will ordains
14	2	His spirit floweth free, High surging where it will
21	1	He chastens and hastens his will to make known
26	3	In the sacred silence wait, As we seek to know his will
26	4	In his will our peace we find, In his service, liberty
31	2	High on his heart he will bear it for thee
32	3	Guard my first springs of thought and will
33	4	Quickened by the Spirit's grace All thy holy will to trace
36	3	New treasures still, of countless price, God will provide
36	3	New treasures still ... God will provide for sacrifice
36	4	Old friends, old scenes, will lovelier be
36	5	The trivial round, the common task, Will furnish all
36	5	the common task, Will furnish all we ought to ask
59	1	For he will shield us
59	4	But thy dear presence will not leave them lonely
59	4	will not leave them lonely Who seek thee only
61	1-4	God be with you will be meet again
74	4	'Tis thy will our hearts are seeking
77	1	In every change he faithful will remain
81	3	Oh make but trial of his love, Experience will decide
84	3	Yet will I fear no ill, For thou art with me
85	T,1	I to the Hills Will Lift Mine Eyes
85	2	nor will He slumber that thee keeps
85	4	Henceforth thy going out and in God keep forever will
87	4	God is his own interpreter, And he will make it plain

91	2	I of the Lord my God will say, He is my refuge and my stay
91	2	To him for safety I will flee, My God ... my trust shall be
92	3	Around me flows thy quickening life, To nerve my ... will
92	3	To nerve my faltering will
93	3	songs of praises, I will ever give to thee
95	T,1	The Lord Will Come and Not Be Slow
96	1	His holy will abideth
96	1	I will be still, whate'er he doth
96	2	He never will deceive me, He leads me by the proper path
96	2	I know he will not leave me
107	2	He will give to all the faithful His own self
108	3	Therefore will we, eternally, Sing hymns of joy and praise
109	2	Watchman, will its beams alone Gild the spot
121	1	joy I bring, Whereof I now will say and sing
123	2	All you need I will surely give you
129	1	Peace on the earth, good will to men
134	3	Where meek souls will receive him ... Christ enters in
135	1	Thy Father's will thou hast fulfilled
146	6	Good will henceforth from heaven to men Begin & never cease
161	2	Our will to dare great things for God
161	3	We crave the power to do thy will With him who did it best
163	4	I do adore thee, and will ever pray thee
167	V-2	Satisfy thy loving will, Hear us, holy Jesus
167	VI-1	Jesus, all our ransom paid, All thy Father's will obeyed
168	4	The world redeemed, the will of God complete
197	5	Let his will enfold you In its light and power
213	2	Boisterous waves obey thy will
213	3	May I hear thee say to me, Fear not, I will pilot thee
215	2	and, spite of fears, Pride ruled my will
215	3	sure it still Will lead me on O'er moor and fen
218	2	Above the storms of passion, the murmurs of self-will
222	1	I will suffer nought to hide thee
222	1	I will ... Ask for nought beside thee
222	2	Jesus will not fail us
227	1	O thou of God and man the Son, Thee will I cherish
227	1	Thee will I honor, Thou, my soul's glory, joy and crown
233	2	Until with thee I will one will To do and to endure
239	3	And so the yearning strong With which the soul will long
242	3	Holy Spirit, Power divine, Fill and nerve this will of mine
256	4	Word of the ever-living God, Will of his glorious Son
265	1	Thy will from none withholds Full liberty
268	2	Glory, glory, thine the power As in heaven thy will be done
284	1	This will I do, my dying Lord, I will remember thee
284	3	Yea, while a breath, a pulse remains, Will I remember thee
289	2	Cleansed and conformed unto thy will
293	3	By feeblest agents may our God fulfill His righteous will
294	3	By whom thy will was done
302	3	And all thou spendest Jesus will repay
303	2	As sons who know the Father's will
308	4	Evermore their life abides Who have lived to do thy will
308	4	In their footsteps will we tread
313	3	E'en so I love thee and will love
313	3	And in thy praise will sing
315	T,1	Come Unto Me, Ye Weary, And I will give you rest
315	2	Come unto me, ye wanderers, And I will give you light
315	3	Come unto me, ye fainting, And I will give you life

315	4	And whosoever cometh I will not cast him out
318	1	Breathe into every wish Thy will divine
318	3	Till earth, as heaven, fulfill God's holy will
327	3	Early let us seek thy favor, Early let us do thy will
329	3	I died for you, my children, And will ye treat me so
334	2	And we will ever trust each unknown morrow
335	2	Who will all our sorrows share
336	5	Give these, and then thy will be done
342	4	I need thee every hour, Teach me thy will
343	2	He knows the way he taketh, And I will walk with him
343	3	Bright skies will soon be o'er me
343	3	My Savior has my treasure, And he will walk with me
347	2	Like thee, to do our Father's will
354	2	While thou art near we will not fear
356	3	My will is not my own Till thou hast made it thine
361	1	God will fulfil in every part Each promise he has made
363	3	We will not fear, for God hath willed His truth to triumph
365	R	Faith of our fathers, holy faith, We will be true to thee
365	R	We will be true to thee till death
365	3	Shall will all nations unto thee
365	4	Faith of our fathers, we will love Both friend and foe
367	3	His boundless mercy will provide
370	3	E'en death's cold wave, I will not flee
371	2	He will make good his right To be a pilgrim
372	2	For I am thy God, and will still give thee aid
372	3	For I will be near thee, thy troubles to bless
373	4	Mercy thy days shall lengthen, The Lord will give thee peace
372	5	I will not, I will not desert to his foes
377	1	Soon again his arms will fold thee To his loving heart
377	4	Thou his people art, & surely He will fold his own securely
382	3	But the Church of Jesus Constant will remain
385	3	The arm of flesh will fail you, Ye dare not trust your own
385	4	Stand up, stand up for Jesus, The strife will not be long
394	1	are dependent on thy will and love alone
401	3	Which with this tincture, For thy sake, Will not grow bright
401	3	Will not grow bright and clean
403	1	Jesus says to those who seek him, I will never pass thee by
404	3	Take my will, and make it thine, It shall be no longer mine
404	4	Take myself, and I will be Ever, only, all for thee
406	2	And prove thy good and perfect will
409	2	They who work without complaining Do the holy will of God
412	3	with the task sufficient strength, Show us thy will, we ask
413	4	grant our hope's fruition, Here on earth thy will be done
416	3	Learning all his will to feel
417	2	True hearts will leap at the trumpet of God
419	2	One in the patient company Of those who heed thy will
422	5	Then will he come with meekness for his glory
424	3	Will not perish with our years
424	3	It will live and shine transfigured In the final reign
424	3	It will pass into the splendors Of the city of the light
425	3	They are slaves who will not choose Hatred, scoffing & abuse
426	4	Take us, and make us holy, Teach us thy will and way
427	2	Will ye play then, will ye dally Far behind the battle line
430	1	His will obey, him serve aright
432	4	For faith, and will to win what faith shall see
434	3	God send us men of steadfast will, Patient, courageous

434	3	mind equipped His will to learn, his work to do
445	1-4	Thy kingdom come, O Lord, thy will be done
446	4	Thou will give peace in our time, O Lord
451	3	Nor till that hour shall God's whole will be done
456	2	And clearer sounds the angel hymn, Good will to men on earth
468	4	Thy word is true, thy will is just
471	5	Be in his will, his strength for self denial
472	5	though ... all our earthly days Will soon be o'er
480	3	He is my Father, who will keep His child through every day
481	3	saints Who love to do Jesus' will
482	1	We will lend a coat of fur, We will rock you
482	2	Sleep in comfort, slumber deep, We will rock you
482	2	We will serve you all we can, Darling, darling little man
490	1	Our heavenly Father's will
494	3	And all the pride of sinful will departs
538	1	Ours is the faith, the will, the thought
542	1	With lowly love and fervent will
554	1	and on earth peace, good will towards men

willed

| 135 | 2 | Help us to do as thou hast willed |
| 363 | 3 | We will not fear, for God hath willed His truth to triumph |

willest

| 413 | 4 | thou who willest That thy people should be one |

willing

108	1	Rise up, with willing feet Go forth, the Bridegroom meet
119	2	So may we with willing feet Ever seek thy mercy seat
188	2	That we may give thee all our days the willing tribute
188	2	The willing tribute of our praise
229	4	behold I sit In willing bonds before thy feet
302	1	he who made all nations is not willing One soul ... perish
472	1	Our willing offerings brought This work to share

wills

156	1	behold we lay Our passions, lusts, & proud wills in thy way
249	3	Stilling the rude wills of men's wild behavior
357	3	Our wills are ours, we know not how
357	3	Our wills are ours to make them thine
416	2	Arm their faltering wills to fight
445	2	His conquering cross no kingdom wills to bear
492	2	for friends who stirred The fragile wills of youth

wilt

21	3	And pray that thou still our defender wilt be
22	2	When perils o'ertake us, thou wilt not forsake us
218	1	Now wander from the pathway If thou wilt be my guide
225	5	Jesus, our only joy be thou, As thou our prize wilt be
249	5	Pray we that thou wilt hear us, still imploring Thy love
319	4	Just as I am, thou wilt receive
319	4	Wilt welcome, pardon, cleanse, relieve
334	2	Thou wilt sustain us till its work is done
335	3	Thou wilt find a solace there
357	2	Thou wilt not leave us in the dust
398	4	Take thou our lives and use them as thou wilt

117	1	Wing your flight o'er all the earth
129	2	Above its sad and lowly plains They bend on hovering wing
210	2	Cover my defenseless head With the shadow of thy wing
351	5	Or if on joyful wing Cleaving the sky
397	3	And wing my words, that they may reach The hidden depths
457	3	The summer days are come again, The birds are on the wing

winged

| 107 | 4 | At his feet the six-winged seraph |
| 175 | 3 | The winged squadrons of the sky Look down |

winging

| 73 | 4 | Each glad soul its free course winging |
| 457 | 2 | winging thoughts, and happy moods Of love and joy and prayer |

wings

6	2	And dark is his path on the wings of the storm
15	2	Shelters thee under his wings, yea, so gently sustaineth
56	1	O keep me, King of kings Beneath thine own almighty wings
61	2	'Neath his wings protecting hide you
91	4	Beneath his wings shalt thou confide
120	3	Risen with healing in his wings
129	2	With peaceful wings unfurled
241	3	Come as the dove, and spread thy wings
241	3	The wings of peaceful love
377	3	Lo, his wings are walls around thee
389	4	Oh, spread thy covering wings around
435	1	Solace all its wide dominion With the healing of thy wings
478	1	He made their glowing colors, He made their tiny wings
576	4	If I the wings of morning take

winning

21	2	So from the beginning the fight we were winning
301	4	Winning all to faith in thee
418	2	move By some clear, winning word of love
491	4	Winning the world to that last consummation

winsome

| 220 | 4 | o'er the centuries still we hear The Master's winsome call |

winter

128	T,1	In the bleak Midwinter, Frosty wind made moan
128	1	In the bleak midwinter, Long ago
128	2	In the bleak midwinter A stable place sufficed
131	1	It came, a floweret bright, Amid the cold of winter
185	2	All the winter of our sins, Long and dark, is flying
455	T,1	'Tis Winter Now, the Fallen Snow
460	1	he sends the snow in winter, The warmth to swell the grain
461	1	All is safely gathered in Ere the winter storms begin
462	1	All is safely gathered in Ere the winter storms begin
478	3	The cold wind in the winter, The pleasant summer sun

winter's

141	1	On a cold winter's night that was so deep
455	4	O God, who givest the winter's cold As well as summer's
458	5	Praise him for the winter's rest

wintry

438	1	And when they trod the wintry strand ... they worshipped
455	4	And keep us through life's wintry days
459	2	he bids the sun cut short his race, And wintry days appear

wipe

348	3	Wipe sorrow's tears away

wiped

420	1	And where the tears are wiped from eyes That shall not weep

wisdom

26	2	Know ye ... the Lord is King, All his works his wisdom prove
33	4	While we daily search thy Word, Wisdom true impart, O Lord
68	1	I sing the wisdom that ordained The sun to rule the day
78	3	Supreme in wisdom as in power The Rock of ages stands
110	3	O come, thou Wisdom from on high
206	4	All glory and power, all wisdom and might
229	T,1	Join All the Glorious Names Of wisdom, love, and power
244	2	In thy pure love & holy faith From thee true wisdom learning
245	2	with wisdom kind and clear Let thy life in mine appear
252	T,1	O Word of God Incarnate, O Wisdom from on high
253	1	Wisdom comes to those who know thee
253	3	Praise we God, who hath inspired Those whose wisdom
253	3	Those whose wisdom still directs us
256	5	Lord, grant us all aright to learn The wisdom it imparts
257	1	In every star thy wisdom shines
277	2	Give to all who teach and guide them Wisdom and humility
304	3	Low lies man's pride and human wisdom dies
343	2	His wisdom ever waketh, His sight is never dim
366	1	Grant us wisdom ... courage, For the facing of his hour
366	2	Grant us wisdom ... courage For the living of these days
366	3	Grant us wisdom ... courage, Lest we miss thy kingdom's goal
366	4	Grant us wisdom ... courage, That we fail not man nor thee
366	5	Grant us wisdom ... courage, Serving thee whom we adore
386	2	darkness ... Which shrouds the path of wisdom from our feet
391	2	Be thou my wisdom, and thou my true word
406	2	task thy wisdom hath assigned, O let me cheerfully fulfill
449	1	Let there be wisdom on the earth
471	2	Endue him with thy wisdom, love, and power

wisdom's

255	1	His testimony is most sure, Proclaiming wisdom's way

wise

2	2	O Father, that thy rule is just And wise, and changes never
7	T,1	Immortal, Invisible, God only Wise
58	2	Strong through thee whate'er befall us, O God most wise
82	2	Wise are the wonders of thy hands
136	3	God's bright star, o'er his head, Wise men three to him led
141	3	And by the light of that same star Three wise men came
141	3	Three wise men came from country far
141	5	Then entered in those wise men three
328	3	The Lord is wonderful and wise, As all the ages tell
337	2	How wise, how strong his hand
451	2	Earth might be fair and all men glad and wise

341	2	Let us, like them, without a word, Rise up and follow thee
343	1	The storm may roar without me, My heart may low be laid
376	1	Without thy guiding hand we go astray
409	2	They who work without complaining Do the holy will of God
431	4	Or lesser breeds without the law
452	3	we strive in vain To save ourselves without thine aid
493	4	Let me, O Lord, thy cause defend, A knight without a sword
511	1	world without end
512	1	world without end
513	1	world without end
559	14	we worship thy name ever, world without end
559	15	Vouchsafe, O Lord, to keep us this day without sin
562	R	world without end
565	R	world without end
568	7	might serve him without fear
568	R	world without end

witness
112	3	Ours to bear the faithful witness
112	3	witness Which can shape the world to fitness
246	3	Thy sacred witness bear In this glad hour
316	2	Borne thy witness in all ages
472	3	May this new temple prove True witness of thy love
472	3	witness of thy love, To all men free

witnesses
| 301 | 3 | Blameless witnesses for thee |
| 362 | 2 | A cloud of witnesses around Hold thee in full survey |

woe
123	2	Doth entreat, Flee from woe and danger
154	2	We cannot understand the woe Thy love was pleased to bear
162	3	Hill of Calvary, I go To thy scenes of fear and woe
167	V-3	May we thirst thy love to know, Lead us in our sin and woe
167	VII-1	Jesus, all thy labor vast, All thy woe and conflict past
174	1	None its lines of woe can trace
178	4	That sweetly soothe the Savior's woe
219	1	To call thy brethren forth from want and woe
344	2	Thou didst feel its keenest woe
345	4	From youth to age, by night and day, In gladness and in woe
363	1	For still our ancient foe Doth seek to work us woe
372	3	The rivers of woe shall not thee overflow
374	3	Should thy mercy send me Sorrow, toil, or woe
388	1	Who best can drink the cup of woe, Triumphant over pain
449	4	Let woe and waste of warfare cease

woeful
| 227 | 2 | Jesus is purer, Who makes the woeful heart to sing |
| 580 | T,1 | O Lord, Turn Not Thy Face From Them, Who lie in woeful stat |

woes
2	4	Avert our woes and calm our dread
55	3	A Savior Christ, our woes dispel
157	2	When the woes of life o'ertake me
166	T,1	Jesus, in Thy Dying Woes, Even while thy life-blood flows
167	T,1	Jesus, in Thy Dying Woes (part I same as 166 but VII parts)

272	3	We share each other's woes, Each other's burdens bear
311	2	O joy, for all its former woes, A thousand-fold repaid
351	4	So by my woes to be Nearer, my God, to thee
354	1	Our shield from foes, our balm for woes

woman's

| 423 | 3 | From woman's grief, man's burdened toil |

womb

| 120 | 2 | Offspring of the Virgin's womb |

women

69	3	Men and women, young and old, Raise the anthem manifold
191	2	That Easter morn at break of day, The faithful women went
392	+1	When we are grown and take our place As men and women
392	+1	As men and women with our race
424	1	Only righteous men and women Dwell within its gleaming wall
484	3	God bless the men and women Who serve him over-sea

won

114	4	Thy Holy Spirit guide us on Until the glorious crown be won
145	1	thou hast won My heart to serve thee solely
154	3	Thy hand the victory won
168	1	salvation Which thou has won for us who went astray
173	2	revealing The infinite forgiveness won for man
180	3	Alleluia to the Savior Who has won the victory
181	1	The victory of life is won, The song of triumph has begun
182	3	Fought the fight, the battle won
189	1	For he hath won the victory O'er sin and death's dark night
193	1,R	Endless is the victory Thou o'er death hast won
250	2	Who descended from his throne And for us salvation won
256	4	Without thee how could earth be trod, Or heaven ... be won
260	4	And mystic sweet communion With those whose rest is won
318	1	Raised my low self above, Won by thy deathless love
331	2	Some wanderer sought and won, Something for thee
370	3	When, by thy grace, the victory's won
380	4	Faith's warfare ended, won The home of endless peace
391	4	High King of heaven, my victory won
405	2	Some deeds of kindness done, Some souls by patience won
411	1	Armed with thy courage, till the world is won
470	4	Theirs, by sweet love, for Christ a kingdom won

wonder

74	T,1	O How Glorious, Full of Wonder
74	1	full of wonder Is thy name o'er all the earth
94	1	Transported with the view, I'm lost in wonder, love & praise
123	3	Here let all, Great and small, Kneel in awe and wonder
127	3	ran To see the wonder God had wrought for man
143	R	star of wonder, star of night, Star with royal beauty bright
228	4	Lost in wonder, love and praise
456	3	In ever changing words of light, The wonder of thy name
458	1	All his year of wonder done
458	6	For his year of wonder done Praise to the all-glorious One

wonderful

| 206 | 1 | And publish abroad his wonderful name |

328	3	The Lord is wonderful and wise, As all the ages tell
330	1	Thou of thy love hast named a friend, O kindness wonderful
478	R	All things wise and wonderful, The Lord God made them all
497	1	In all his words most wonderful, Most sure in all his ways

wonderfully

| 101 | 2 | heart of the Eternal Is most wonderfully kind   (102-3) |

wondering

134	2	Their watch of wondering love
175	3	Look down with sad and wondering eye To see
337	2	So shalt thou, wondering, own his way

wonders

6	3	The earth with its store of wonders untold
19	2	Earth to heaven, and heaven to earth ...tell his wonders
19	2	Tell his wonders, sing his worth
68	2	Lord, how thy wonders are displayed, Where'er I turn my eye
74	3	Thou hast given man dominion o'er the wonders of thy hand
75	4	Lord, great wonders workest thou
82	2	Wise are the wonders of thy hands
87	T,1	God Moves in a Mysterious Way His wonders to perform
95	5	wonders great By thy strong hand are done
130	3	And wonders of his love
160	2	And from my smitten heart with tears Two wonders I confess
160	2	The wonders of his glorious love And my unworthiness
165	1	The wonders of that dawn we view
447	2	The wonders that our fathers told
471	1	And told the world the wonders of thy grace
485	1	His hand the wonders wrought

wondrous

20	4	All ye who own his power, proclaim Aloud the wondrous story
24	1	No mortal ear hath heard such wondrous things
29	1	Who wondrous things hath done, In whom his world rejoices
47	4	lips are making Thy wondrous doings heard on high
72	2	The moon takes up the wondrous tale
74	4	O how wondrous, O how glorious is thy name in every land
99	3	wide-embracing, wondrous love, We read thee in the sky above
127	3	Amazed, the wondrous story they proclaim
127	4	O may we keep and ponder in our mind God's wondrous love
127	4	God's wondrous love in saving lost mankind
134	3	How silently, how silently The wondrous gift is given
177	T,1	When I Survey the Wondrous Cross
213	2	Wondrous Sovereign of the Sea, Jesus, Savior, pilot me
249	1	Thy love has blessed the wide world's wondrous story
270	3	His wondrous mercy forth telling
345	2	God's wondrous praises speak
369	T,1	God's Glory Is a Wondrous Thing
394	1	Wondrous are thy doings unto me
424	1	Wondrous tales of it are told
473	T,1	O Lord, Almighty God, Thy Works Both great and wondrous be
558	2	What wondrous words of love he spake
576	2	O wondrous knowledge, awful might

318	2	In thee my strength renew, Give me thy work to do
321	4	Let every thought, and work, and word To thee be ever given
328	3	with his light thou shalt be blest, Therein to work and live
331	2	That each departing day Henceforth may see Some work of love
331	2	Some work of love begun, Some deed of kindness done
334	2	Thou wilt sustain us till its work is done
337	2	When fully he the work hath wrought that caused thy ... fear
363	1	For still our ancient foe Doth seek to work us woe
364	2	Christian, dost thou feel them, How they work within
374	2	Or its sordid treasures Spread to work me harm
395	3	On homeliest work thy blessing falls
395	6	Work shall be prayer, if all be wrought As thou wouldst
395	6	prayer, by thee inspired and taught, Itself with work be one
403	2	Where the many work together, they with God himself abide
409	2	They who work without complaining Do the holy will of God
409	3	Jesus, thou divine companion, Help us all to work our best
410	2	example Of him whose holy work was doing good
411	2	Strong Son of God, whose work was his that sent thee
411	4	We work with thee, we go where thou wilt lead us
412	1	Did ye not know it is my work My Father's work to do
412	2	And see like thee our noblest work Our Father's work to do
412	3	That it may be our highest joy Our Father's work to do
416	1	Raise thy work and life anew
417	2	And the meekest of saints may find stern work to do
418	3	In work that keeps faith sweet and strong
424	3	And the work that we have builded
434	3	mind equipped His will to learn, his work to do
472	1	Our willing offerings brought This work to share
477	4	Accept the work our hands have wrought
479	2	In all we do in work or play To grow more loving every day
480	1	It gave him light to do his work, And smiled upon his play
484	2	Some work in sultry forests Where apes swing to and fro
487	1	Though our work is hard, God gives us reward
492	1	Whose joyous fellowship we share At work, at rest
492	1	At work, at rest, in play and prayer
538	1	Bless thou the work our hearts have planned

worker

| 403 | 2 | But the lonely worker also finds him ever at his side |

workers

| 409 | 1 | By thy lowly human birth Thou hast come to join the workers |
| 409 | 1 | workers, Burden-bearers of the earth |

workest

| 75 | 4 | Lord, great wonders workest thou |

working

78	3	him thou canst not see, nor trace the working of his hands
261	2	One working band, one harvest song, One King omnipotent
297	1	We trace the working of thy hand
298	T,1	God Is Working His Purpose Out, As year succeeds to year
298	1	God is working his purpose out, And the time is drawing near

workman

| 359 | 2 | Workman of God, O lose not heart, But learn what God is like |

412　T,1　O Master Workman of the Race, Thou Man of Galilee

workman's
422　5　God in a workman's jacket as before

works
8　2　All thy works with joy surround thee
26　2　Know ye ... the Lord is King, All his works his wisdom prove
150　3　For us his daily works he wrought
171　4　And trust in his redeeming blood, And try his works to do
251　4　All thy works shall praise thy name in earth and sky and sea
360　2　No offering of my own I have, Nor works my faith to prove
406　2　In all my works thy presence find
406　3　And labor on at thy command, And offer all my works to thee
425　1　If ye do not feel the chain when it works a brother's pain
447　2　Remember, Lord, thy works of old
468　2　Thine are their thoughts, their works, their powers
473　T,1　O Lord, Almighty God, Thy Works Both great and wondrous be
474　T,1　O Lord, Almighty God, Thy Works　(same words as no. 473)

workshop
422　5　Sweeping the shavings from his workshop floor

world
9　5　Wide as the world is thy command
18　3　The world is with the glory filled Of thy majestic sway
18　5　The holy Church throughout the world, O Lord, confesses thee
29　1　Who wondrous things hath done, In whom his world rejoices
29　2　And free us from all ills In this world and the next
47　2　Through all the world her watch is keeping
49　3　Thee ... O Most High, The world doth glorify
49　3　Thee ... The world doth glorify And shall exalt forever
50　5　ere through the world our way we take
54　2　And for thy truth the world endure
56　2　That with the world, myself and thee, I ... at peace may be
63　3　when thy love shall call us, Savior, from the world away
70　2　Filled the new-made world with light
86　1　plan ... in which the world began, Endures, and shall endure
110　4　Fill the whole world with heaven's peace
111　T,1　Of the Father's Love Begotten, Ere the world began to be
112　2　heaven Spreads throughout the world like leaven
112　3　witness Which can shape the world to fitness
113　3　When the old world drew on toward night, Thou camest
114　1　The Savior of the world is here
115　3　And fill the world with love divine
127　1　morn Whereon the Savior of the world was born
129　1　The world in solemn stillness lay To hear the angels sing
129　2　still their heavenly music floats O'er all the weary world
129　4　the whole world send back the song Which now the angels sing
130　T,1　Joy to the World, The Lord Is Come
130　3　He rules the world with truth and grace
134　3　No ear may hear his coming, But in this world of sin
142　1　Came he to a world forlorn, the Lord of every nation
149　2　know not how ... Calvary's cross A world from sin could free
160　3　Content to let the world go by, To know no gain nor loss
165　1　For God doth make his world anew

world's

180	1	He who on the cross as Savior For the world's salvation bled
198	T,1	Christ Is the World's True Light, Its captain of salvation
249	1	Thy love has blessed the wide world's wondrous story
262	3	Confessing, in a world's accord, The inward Christ
322	3	Jesus calls us from the worship of the vain world's
322	3	worship Of the vain world's golden store
344	1	lead us O'er the world's tempestuous sea

worldly

354	2	And worldly scorn assail us

worlds

13	1	Worlds his mighty voice obeyed
34	1	The fields are wet with diamond dew, The worlds awake to cry
34	3	To serve right gloriously The God who gave all worlds
34	3	The God who gave all worlds that are, And all that are to be
53	2	splendor ...From myriad worlds unknown
358	4	When I soar to worlds unknown
395	4	The worlds of science and of art, Revealed and ruled by thee
427	2	Worlds are charging, heaven beholding
433	1	starry band Of shining worlds in splendor through the skies
508	1	In vaster worlds unseen, unknown

worn

295	1	Sinsick and sorrow-worn, Whom Christ doth heal

worship

2	2	We praise, we worship thee, we trust and give thee thanks
6	T,1	O Worship the King, All Glorious Above
22	2	We worship thee, God of our fathers, we bless thee
22	3	And gladly our songs of true worship we raise
28	T,1	We Worship Thee, Almighty Lord
31	T,1	Worship the Lord in the Beauty of Holiness
45	1	Wait and worship while the night sets her evening lamps
60	1	We stand to bless thee ere our worship cease
64	5	And worship him in humbleness
69	3	let children's happy hearts In this worship bear their parts
117	R	Come and worship, Worship Christ, the new-born King
143	3	Prayer & praising, all men raising, Worship him, God on high
206	3	Fall down on their faces and worship the Lamb
237	2	Till wilderness and town One temple for thy worship be
265	1	All men have equal right To worship thee
276	1	we come With thankful hearts to worship thee
308	1	Source & giver of all good, Lord, we praise, we worship thee
321	3	That I may see thy glorious face, And worship at thy throne
322	3	Jesus calls us from the worship of the vain world's
322	3	worship Of the vain world's golden store
349	4	Help me to tear it from thy throne, And worship only thee
386	3	To all the gods we ignorantly make And worship
386	3	And worship, dreaming that we worship thee
407	3	Clean hands in holy worship raise
410	1	To worship rightly is to love each other
416	3	And thy worship God's employ
473	2	For nations all shall worship thee
521	2	Our souls to thee in worship raise

554	2	We praise thee, we bless thee, we worship thee
559	1	All the earth doth worship thee, The Father everlasting
559	14	we worship thy name ever, world without end
562	6	O come, let us worship and fall down
562	8	O worship the Lord in the beauty of holiness

worshiped
| 438 | 1 | And when they trod the wintry strand...they worshiped |
| 438 | 1 | With prayer and psalm they worshiped thee |

worshipped
| 128 | 3 | his mother ... Worshipped the beloved With a kiss |

worst
| 181 | 2 | The powers of death have done their worst |
| 442 | 2 | In best and worst reveal us |

worth
19	2	Tell his wonders, sing his worth
26	1	Praise him with a glad accord and with lives of noblest worth
162	5	Then to life I turn again, Learning all the worth of pain
229	1	All are too mean to speak his worth
298	4	All we can do is nothing worth Unless God blesses the deed
330	5	If there is aught of worth in me, It comes from thee alone
494	3	O grant enduring worth Until the heavenly kingdom comes

worthless
| 392 | 3 | That we may bring, if need arise, no ... worthless sacrifice |
| 392 | 3 | No maimed or worthless sacrifice |

worthy
| 492 | 3 | grant us power That worthy thoughts in deeds may flower |

would
7	4	All praise we would render, O help us to see
25	2	Who would not fear his holy name, And laud and magnify
33	5	Thee would we with one accord Praise and magnify, O Lord
44	1	As night descends, we too would pray
55	4	they who fain would serve thee best Are conscious most
55	5	The very wounds that shame would hide
86	2	Though we who fain would find thee
101	2	And our lives would be all sunshine (102-4)
126	4	Vainly with gifts would his favor secure
128	4	If I were a shepherd, I would bring a lamb
128	4	If I were a wiseman, I would do my part
132	3	we would embrace thee, with love and awe
132	3	Who would not love thee, loving us so dearly
136	2	Ox and ass beside him From the cold would hide him
152	T,1	We Would See Jesus, Lo, His Star Is Shining
152	2	We would see Jesus, Mary's son most holy
152	3	We would see Jesus, on the mountain teaching
152	4	We would see Jesus, in his work of healing
152	5	We would see Jesus in the early morning
160	T,1	Beneath the Cross of Jesus I fain would take my stand
168	1	We would continue with thee day by day
168	2	We would not leave thee, though our weak endurance

169	2	and none The longed-for Christ would know
208	1	All that I would, but fail, to be
219	2	Thee would I sing, thy truth is still the light
222	2	Foes who would molest me Cannot reach me here
228	3	Thee we would be always blessing
229	2	Great Prophet of my God, My tongue would bless thy name
245	T,1	Gracious Spirit, Dwell With Me, I myself would gracious be
245	1	with words that help and heal Would thy life in mine reveal
245	1	with actions bold and meek Would for Christ my Savior speak
245	2	Truthful Spirit, dwell with me, I myself would truthful be
245	3	Mighty Spirit, dwell with me, I myself would mighty be
245	4	Holy Spirit, dwell with me, I myself would holy be
245	4	Separate from sin, I would Choose & cherish all things good
259	3	Our souls would higher climb
275	3	We would be one in hatred of all wrong
287	1	Here would I touch and handle things unseen
287	2	Here would I feed upon the bread of God
287	2	Here would I lay aside each earthly load
316	3	We would give our lives to thee
316	3	Now in grateful dedication Our allegiance we would own
317	1	It satisfies my longings As nothing else would do
322	3	From each idol that would keep us
331	1	In love my soul would bow, My heart fulfill its vow
332	4	We with shame our sins would own
334	1	Fain would our souls feel all thy kindling love
351	1	Still all my song would be, Nearer, my God, to thee
356	3	If it would reach a monarch's throne It must ... resign
363	2	Did we in our own strength confide, Our striving would be
363	2	Our striving would be losing
365	2	And blest would be their children's fate If they ... die for
368	3	Not forever by still waters Would we idly rest and stay
368	3	But would smite the living fountains From the rocks
359	5	To doubt would be disloyalty, To falter would be sin
370	R	His faithful follower I would be For by his hand he leadeth
370	2	Lord, I would clasp thy hand in mine
371	T,1	He Who Would Valiant Be 'Gainst all disaster
374	2	With forbidden pleasures Would this vain world charm
398	5	We would be faithful to thy gospel glorious
405	2	Daily our lives would show Weakness made strong
417	2	Who would sit down and sigh for a lost age of gold
417	2	Who would ... While the Lord of all ages is here
439	1	Lord, we would with deep thanksgiving Praise thee most for
441	2	Thy must upward still and onward Who would keep ... truth
441	2	Who would keep abreast of truth
451	2	Would man but wake from out his haunted sleep
489	T,1	I Would Be True, for there are those who trust me
489	1	I would be pure, for there are those who care
489	1	I would be strong, for there is much to suffer
489	1	I would be brave, for there is much to dare
489	2	I would be friend of all, the foe, the friendless
489	2	I would be giving, and forget the gift
489	2	I would be humble, for I know my weakness
489	2	I would look up, and laugh, and love, and lift
494	T,1	We Would Be Building temples still undone
494	1	We would be building, Master,
494	1	let thy plan Reveal the life that God would give to man

557	1	Here would I touch and handle things unseen
557	2	Here would I feed upon the bread of God
557	2	Here would I lay aside each earthly load
568	6	sware ... that he would give us

wouldst

31	3	slenderness Of the poor wealth thou wouldst reckon as thine
233	1	And do what thou wouldst do
395	6	Work shall be prayer, if all be wrought As thou wouldst
395	6	As thou wouldst have it done
490	2	And do what thou wouldst have us do With radiant delight
507	1	thou Wouldst be our guard and keeper now

wounded

170	T,1	O Sacred Head, Now Wounded
181	4	Lord, by the stripes which wounded thee
221	2	It makes the wounded spirit whole
325	4	O wounded hands of Jesus, build In us thy new creation

wounds

55	5	Thy kind but searching glance can scan the very wounds
55	5	The very wounds that shame would hide
167	V-1	While thy wounds thy life-blood drain
199	2	Rich wounds, yet visible above, In beauty glorified
221	1	It soothes his sorrows, heals his wounds
281	2	'Tis thy wounds our healing give
398	2	To heal earth's wounds and end her bitter strife

wrangling

| 262 | 1 | The wrangling tongues that mar thy praise |

wrapped

| 146 | 4 | All meanly wrapped in swathing bands, And in a manger laid |
| 468 | 3 | Not wrapped in dreamless sleep profound |

wraps

| 487 | 2 | God's care like a cloak Wraps us country folk |

wrath

6	2	His chariots of wrath the deep thunder-clouds form
354	2	Though Satan's wrath beset our path
443	1	He is trampling out the vintage where the grapes of wrath
443	1	where the grapes of wrath are stored
445	3	In wrath and fear, by jealousies surrounded
446	2	Bid not thy wrath in its terrors awaken
447	1	The wrath of sinful man restrain

wreaths

| 455 | 2 | And clothes the boughs with glittering wreaths |

wrecks

| 157 | 1,5 | Towering o'er the wrecks of time |

wrestle

| 384 | 3 | From strength to strength go on, Wrestle and fight and pray |

wrestlers
397 2   a loving hand To wrestlers with the troubled sea

wrestles
178 2   The Savior wrestles lone with fears

wrestling
174 2   Wrestling with the evil powers

wretched
319 3   Just as I am, poor, wretched, blind

wretchedness
423 2   In haunts of wretchedness and need

wring
420 2   greed for gain In street and shop and tenement Wring gold
420 2   Wring gold from human pain

writ
14   2   law ... Deep writ upon the human heart, On sea, or land
257 2   But the blest volume thou hast writ Reveals thy justice

write
75   4   Write thou deeply in my heart What I am, and what thou art
544 1   and write all these thy laws in our hearts, we beseech thee

wrong
55   4   who serve thee best .... Are conscious most of wrong within
105 2   He comes with succor speedy To those who suffer wrong
124 2   It is wrong when the child is sleeping
124 2   It is wrong to talk so loud
166 3   When with wrong our spirits bleed, Hear us, holy Jesus
198 3   To heal its ancient wrong, Come, Prince of peace, and reign
224 2   The wrong of man to man on thee Inflicts a deeper wrong
236 4   Hurling floods of tyrant wrong From the sacred limits back
275 3   We would be one in hatred of all wrong
300 2   Bring in the day of brotherhood, And end the night of wrong
318 3   Cleanse it from guilt and wrong, Teach it salvation's song
359 4   dares to take the side that seems Wrong to man's ... eye
359 4   seems Wrong to man's blindfold eye
380 1   Who 'gainst enthroned wrong Stood confident and bold
388 2   He prayed for them that did the wrong
418 3   In trust that triumphs over wrong
419 2   One in the holy fellowship Of those who challenge wrong
424 1   Wrong is banished from its borders
434 4   All truth to love, all wrong to hate
441 3   Truth forever on the scaffold, Wrong forever on the throne
446 3   Falsehood and wrong shall not tarry beside thee
476 2   Who helped the right and fought the wrong
485 3   Oh, let me ne'er forget That though the wrong seems oft
485 3   though the wrong seems oft so strong, God is the ruler yet
490 3   The lovers of all holy things, The foes of all things wrong

wrong's
303 3   Beyond ... Wrong's bitter, cruel, scorching blight

wrongs

39	4	And give us grace our wrongs to bear
325	1	And still our wrongs may weave thee now New thorns
380	3	'Gainst lies and lusts & wrongs, Let courage rule our souls
413	1	Heal our wrongs, and help our need
491	2	To right the wrongs that shame this mortal life

wrought

74	1	Thou who wrought creation's splendor
127	3	ran To see the wonder God had wrought for man
147	2	And by thy death was God's salvation wrought
150	3	For us his daily works he wrought
250	1	By whose mighty power alone All is made and wrought and done
337	2	When fully he the work hath wrought that caused thy ... fear
356	2	It cannot freely move Till thou hast wrought its chain
395	3	In truth and patience wrought
395	6	Work shall be prayer, if all be wrought As thou wouldst
456	1	The hand that shaped the rose hath wrought The ... snow
472	1	As we thy help have sought, With labor long have wrought
477	4	Accept the work our hands have wrought
485	1	His hand the wonders wrought

yea

15	2	Shelters thee under his wings, yea, so gently sustaineth
26	4	Yea, his law is sure, In his light we walk secure
84	3	Yea, though I walk in death's dark vale
132	4	Yea, Lord, we greet thee, born this happy morning
153	3	Yea, evermore, in life and death, Jesus, with us abide
222	3	Yea, whate'er we here must bear
284	3	Yea, while a breath, a pulse remains, Will I remember thee
319	3	Yea, all I need in thee to find
430	2	Yea, love with thee shall make his home

year

121	4	A glad new year to all the earth
298	T,1	God Is Working His Purpose Out, As year succeeds to year
453	1	The year is dying in the night
453	2	The year is going, let him go
454	1	The opening year thy mercy shows
456	3	O thou from whose unfathomed law The year in beauty flows
458	1	All his year of wonder done
458	6	For his year of wonder done Praise to the all-glorious One
459	2	His steady counsels change the face Of the declining year

yearly

579	2	Seed-time, harvest, cold, and heat shall their yearly round
579	2	Shall their yearly round complete

yearn

44	2	Did not their spirits inly yearn
290	3	Our restless spirits yearn for thee
334	3	Our spirits yearn to feel thy kindling love
477	2	For thee our waiting spirits yearn

yearning

74	2	Child of earth, yet full of yearning

98	4	A yearning for a deeper peace Not known before
123	3	Love him who with love is yearning
239	3	And so the yearning strong With which the soul will long

years

1	T,1,6	Our God Our Help In Ages Past, our hope for years to come
1	3	From everlasting thou art God, To endless years the same
9	5	thy truth must stand When rolling years shall cease to move
14	1	The First, the Last, beyond all thought His timeless years
34	2	See how the giant sun soars up, Great lord of years and days
97	T,1	God of Our Life, Through All the Circling Years
97	3	God of the coming years, through paths unknown we follow
97	3	Our heart's true home when all our years have sped
111	1	And that future years shall see, Evermore and evermore
129	4	with the ever-circling years Comes round the age of gold
134	1	The hopes and fears of all the years Are met in thee tonight
199	4	Crown him the Lord of years, The potentate of time
215	2	remember not past years
264	1	Lord, thy Church is praying yet, A thousand years the same
266	1	Unwasted by the lapse of years, Unchanged by changing place
297	T,1	O God, Above the Drifting Years
297	4	give us grace, through ampler years
304	T,1	Rejoice, O People, in the Mounting Years
304	1	years Wherein God's mighty purposes unfold
304	2	Rejoice, O people, in the years of old
308	1	Whose forgotten resting place Rolling years have buried deep
352	2	Above the level of the former years
352	4	Then, as the trumpet call, in after years
392	+1	Our love and toil in the years to be
392	+2	Head, heart, and hand through the years to be
413	3	By thy patient years of toiling, By thy silent hours of pain
424	3	Will not perish with our years
426	3	Our strength is dust and ashes, Our years a passing hour
440	4	O beautiful for patriot dream That sees beyond the years
448	3	The prophecy sublime, The hope of all the years
490	4	And be by thee prepared For larger years to come

yellow

| 464 | 2 | Yellow sheaves of ripened grain |

yes

109	1	traveler, yes, it brings the day, Promised day of Israel
219	3	Yes, thou art still the Life, thou art the Way
345	4	Yes, on through life's long path, Still chanting as ye go

yesterday

| 431 | 3 | Lo, all our pomp of yesterday Is one with Nineveh and Tyre |

yet

74	2	Child of earth, yet full of yearning
74	2	From thy ways so often turning, Yet thy love doth seek him
74	2	Yet thy love doth seek him still
79	3	But yet in love he sought me
83	3	though undeserving, Thou yet shalt find it true for thee
83	3	God never yet forsook at need the soul that trusted him
84	3	Yet will I fear no ill, For thou art with me

85	3	moon by night thee shall not smite, Nor yet the sun by day
89	1	Yet to each loving heart how near
96	3	Though sorrow, need, or death be mine, Yet am I not forsaken
98	4	We have enough, yet not too much To long for more
99	T,1	O Love of God, How Strong and True, Eternal and yet ever new
103	3	Born thy people to deliver, Born a child, and yet a king
106	4	High raise the note, that Jesus died, Yet lives and reigns
106	4	Yet lives and reigns, the Crucified
107	2	King of kings, yet born of Mary, As of old on earth he stood
109	2	Higher yet that star ascends
112	1	Do you yet not understand
128	4	Yet what I can I give him - Give my heart
134	1	Yet in thy dark streets shineth The everlasting Light
148	1	Forty days and forty nights Tempted, and yet undefiled
161	3	Yet humbly, in our striving, O God, we face its test
168	2	Yet give us strength to trust the sweet assurance
169	4	Yet they at these Themselves displease, And 'gainst him rise
178	3	Yet he that hath in anguish knelt Is not forsaken
191	4	And yet whose faith hath constant been
199	2	Rich wounds, yet visible above, In beauty glorified
205	3	Yet he loves the earth he leaves
219	2	Yet hoping ever for the perfect day
230	4	But warm, sweet, tender, even yet A present help is he
259	R	The Lord hath yet more light and truth To break forth
259	2	'Twas but the dawning yet to grow Into the perfect day
260	2	Elect from every nation, Yet one o'er all the earth
260	4	Yet she on earth hath union With God, the Three in One
264	1	Lord, thy Church is praying yet, A thousand years the same
270	2	Yet he whom heavens cannot contain Chose to abide on earth
286	2	Thou at the table, blessing, yet dost stand
286	2	This is my body, so thou givest yet
297	4	give us grace ... To build the kingdom yet to be
303	2	thou hast not yet finished man ...we are in the making still
306	4	Yet all are one in thee, for all are thine
308	3	strong, yet battling for the weak
313	1	Nor yet because who love thee not Are lost eternally
326	5	Let thy voice call me home, saying, Yet there is room
343	3	Green pastures are before me, Which yet I have not seen
344	1	Yet possessing every blessing, If our God our Father be
351	2	Yet in my dreams I'd be Nearer, my God, to thee
357	5	And yet we trust it comes from thee
377	3	Yet, O Zion, have no fear, Ever is thy helper near
405	1	Yet may love's incense rise, Sweeter than sacrifice
419	3	One in the vision of thy peace, The kingdom yet to be
421	2	Beheld thee fairer yet while serving thee
421	4	A splendor greater yet while serving thee
423	4	Yet long these multitudes to see The sweet compassion
431	1,2	Lord God of hosts, be with us yet, Lest we forget
431	3	Judge of the nations, spare us yet, Lest we forget
431	4	Lord God of hosts, be with us yet, Lest we forget
441	3	Yet that scaffold sways the future
446	3	man hath defied thee, Yet to eternity standeth thy word
446	4	earth by thy chastening Yet shall ... be restored
446	4	Yet shall to freedom and truth be restored
449	4	That useful labor yet may build Its homes with love
451	1	Yet thou, her child, whose head is crowned with flame

455	2	And yet God's love is not withdrawn
467	4	Yet shall thou praise him, when these darkened furrows
468	2	All thine, and yet most truly ours
475	1	And yet vouchsafes in Christian lands To dwell in temples
484	2	Remember all God's children Who yet have never heard
485	3	though the wrong seems oft so strong, God is the ruler yet
496	1	O say does that star-spangled banner yet wave

yield
59	1	And 'neath his shadow here to rest we yield us
126	3	Say, shall we yield him, in costly devotion
147	1	Didst yield the glory that of right was thine
269	5	brightest glories earth can yield & brighter bliss of heaven
399	2	I yield my flickering torch to thee
427	3	Sworn to yield, to waver, never, Consecrated, born again
461	2	Fruit unto his praise to yield
462	2	All the stores the gardens yield
464	2	For the stores our gardens yield
579	1	For the valley's golden yield ... fruits of tree and field

yielding
167	VII-1	Yielding up thy soul at last, Hear us, holy Jesus
316	3	Naught withholding, freely yielding
381	2	Whether beneath was flinty rock Or yielding grassy sod

yields
297	2	And seed laid deep in sacred soil Yields harvests
297	2	Yields harvests rich in lasting good
457	1	One more the glad earth yields Her golden wealth

yoke
| 185 | 1 | Loosed from Pharaoh's bitter yoke Jacob's sons and daughters |
| 406 | 4 | Give me to bear thy easy yoke |

yon
| 109 | 1 | Traveler, o'er yon mountain's height See |
| 138 | 1 | All is calm, all is bright Round yon virgin mother and child |

yonder
117	2	God with man is now residing, Yonder shines the infant light
123	2	Hark, a voice from yonder manger, Soft and sweet
123	3	Come, then, let us hasten yonder
143	1	Field and fountain, moor and mountain, Following yonder star
195	5	O that, with yonder sacred throng, We at his feet may fall

yore
| 26 | 4 | Evermore, as of yore, Shall his changeless truth endure |

young
69	3	Men and women, young and old, Raise the anthem manifold
270	1	Calling the young and old to rest
293	2	To young and old the gospel gladness bear
340	3	Young John who trimmed the flapping sail
340	3	Young John ... Homeless, in Patmos died
471	4	Make him a shepherd, kind to young and old
493	3	When Stephen, young and doomed to die, Fell crushed

youth

345	2	Bright youth and snow-crowned age
345	4	From youth to age, by night and day, In gladness and in woe
376	2	While passion stains and folly dims our youth
392	2	Teach us to bear the hope in youth With steadfastness
412	1	Who with the eyes of early youth Eternal things did see
490	T,1	Now in the Days of Youth, When life flows fresh and free
491	T,1	O God of Youth, Whose Spirit in our hearts is stirring
492	2	for friends who stirred The fragile wills of youth
508	2	The blended notes of age and youth

youthful

78	5	Mere human power shall fast decay, And youthful vigor cease

zeal

295	1	With loving zeal
348	2	My zeal inspire
358	2	Could my zeal no respite know, Could my tears forever flow
362	1	A heavenly race demands thy zeal, And an immortal crown
416	3	Give him thanks in humble zeal
491	2	Fill thou our hearts with zeal in every brave endeavor

zealous

381	2	Unstayed by pleasures, still they bent Their zealous course
381	2	they bent Their zealous course to God

Zion

108	2	Zion hears the watchmen singing
156	3	for here Thou hast a temple, too, as Zion dear
248	2	High in the heavenly Zion Thou reignest God adored
267	T,1	Glorious Things of Thee Are Spoken, Zion, city of our God
269	5	Sure as thy truth shall last, To Zion shall be given
274	3	Till all before our God at length In Zion do appear
302	T,1	O Zion, Haste, Thy Mission High Fulfilling
309	2	They stand, those halls of Zion, All jubilant with song
310	3	Safely the anthems of Zion shall sing
377	T,1	Lift Thy Head, O Zion, Weeping, Still the Lord thy Father is
377	2	Zion, calm the breast that quaketh
377	3	Yet, O Zion, have no fear, Ever is thy helper near
377	4	Zion, if thou die believing, Heaven's path shall open lie
426	1	As once he spake in Zion, So now he speaks again
503	T,1	Open Now Thy Gates of Beauty, Zion, let me enter there

Zion's

263	1	Holy Zion's help forever, And her confidence alone
305	1	Of nations in commotion, Prepared for Zion's war

PILGRIM HYMNAL NUMBERS COMPARED WITH E & R NUMBERS

PH	E&R	PH	E&R	PH	E&R
1	63	114	92	210	316
2	2	115	95	211	317
3	29	116	105	212	26
4	24	117	104	213	468
6	10	119	123	214	249
8	21	120	102	215	315
10	25	121	114	218	271
12	386	123	119	220	279
14	61	125	116	222	240
16	3	126	121	223	181
22	19	127	115	225	274
29	72	129	107	227	182
30	9	130	120	228	272
35	43	132	112	230	242
37	50	134	108	234	191
39	48	137	109	236	82
41	44	138	101	242	188
45	481	139	101	244	186
48	54	141	118	245	192
50	55	145	122	246	4
51	56	146	106	249	197
53	58	149	241	251	1
55	57	152	456	252	199
57	59	153	141	253	203
60	32	155	135	254	204
63	35	157	164	257	71
64	15	158	144	260	322
66	12	160	161	261	330
67	68	161	261	263	324
70	77	164	146	264	326
72	66	170	142	266	325
75	45	172	149	269	329
77	87	175	133	271	361
79	304	177	158	273	280
83	300	178	145	276	328
86	64	180	174	280	339
87	75	181	173	282	337
89	(74)	182	167	285	338
93	80	185	169	287	(341)
96	309	187	166	290	335
100	83	192	165	291	344
101	(85)	195	184	292	340
103	89	196	185	294	367
104	90	199	176	295	(372)
105	366	202	371	296	381
107	336	203	180	297	377
108	96	205	175	299	190
109	91	206	(11)	300	389
110	88	207	277	302	380
111	13	209	51	305	384

parentheses indicate different tune

E & R HYMNAL NUMBERS COMPARED WITH PILGRIM NUMBERS

E&R	PH	E&R	PH	E&R	PH
1	251	80	93	173	181
2	2	82	236	174	180
3	16	83	100	175	205
4	246	85	(101)	176	199
7	345	87	77	180	203
9	30	88	110	181	223
10	6	89	103	182	227
11	(206)	90	104	184	195
12	66	91	109	185	196
13	111	92	114	186	244
15	64	95	115	188	242
19	22	96	108	190	299
21	8	101	138	191	234
22	562	101	139	192	245
22	563	102	120	197	249
22	564	104	117	198	551
23	503	105	116	199	252
24	4	106	146	203	253
25	10	107	129	204	254
26	212	108	134	205	418
27	352	109	137	206	318
28	521	112	132	207	322
29	3	114	121	211	329
32	60	115	127	213	580
35	63	116	125	214	319
36	539	118	141	216	332
43	35	119	123	217	358
44	41	120	130	218	359
45	75	121	126	220	344
46	506	122	145	221	348
48	39	123	119	222	347
50	37	126	326	225	357
51	209	131	412	226	341
54	48	133	175	227	333
55	50	135	155	228	395
56	51	141	153	237	(408)
57	55	142	170	240	222
58	53	144	158	241	149
59	57	145	178	242	230
61	14	146	164	243	356
63	1	149	172	249	214
64	86	158	177	253	404
65	485	160	374	256	397
66	72	161	160	258	535
68	67	164	157	261	161
71	257	165	192	265	421
72	20	166	187	266	411
74	(89)	167	182	271	218
75	87	167	582	272	228
77	70	169	185	274	225

parentheses indicate different tune

WRITE-IN INDEX FOR USE WITH OTHER HYMNALS

PH /	PH /	PH /	PH /	PH /
1 _____	51 _____	101 _____	151 _____	201 _____
2 _____	52 _____	102 _____	152 _____	202 _____
3 _____	53 _____	103 _____	153 _____	203 _____
4 _____	54 _____	104 _____	154 _____	204 _____
5 _____	55 _____	105 _____	155 _____	205 _____
6 _____	56 _____	106 _____	156 _____	206 _____
7 _____	57 _____	107 _____	157 _____	207 _____
8 _____	58 _____	108 _____	158 _____	208 _____
9 _____	59 _____	109 _____	159 _____	209 _____
10 _____	60 _____	110 _____	160 _____	210 _____
11 _____	61 _____	111 _____	161 _____	211 _____
12 _____	62 _____	112 _____	162 _____	212 _____
13 _____	63 _____	113 _____	163 _____	213 _____
14 _____	64 _____	114 _____	164 _____	214 _____
15 _____	65 _____	115 _____	165 _____	215 _____
16 _____	66 _____	116 _____	166 _____	216 _____
17 _____	67 _____	117 _____	167 _____	217 _____
18 _____	68 _____	118 _____	168 _____	218 _____
19 _____	69 _____	119 _____	169 _____	219 _____
20 _____	70 _____	120 _____	170 _____	220 _____
21 _____	71 _____	121 _____	171 _____	221 _____
22 _____	72 _____	122 _____	172 _____	222 _____
23 _____	73 _____	123 _____	173 _____	223 _____
24 _____	74 _____	124 _____	174 _____	224 _____
25 _____	75 _____	125 _____	175 _____	225 _____
26 _____	76 _____	126 _____	176 _____	226 _____
27 _____	77 _____	127 _____	177 _____	227 _____
28 _____	78 _____	128 _____	178 _____	228 _____
29 _____	79 _____	129 _____	179 _____	229 _____
30 _____	80 _____	130 _____	180 _____	230 _____
31 _____	81 _____	131 _____	181 _____	231 _____
32 _____	82 _____	132 _____	182 _____	232 _____
33 _____	83 _____	133 _____	183 _____	233 _____
34 _____	84 _____	134 _____	184 _____	234 _____
35 _____	85 _____	135 _____	185 _____	235 _____
36 _____	86 _____	136 _____	186 _____	236 _____
37 _____	87 _____	137 _____	187 _____	237 _____
38 _____	88 _____	138 _____	188 _____	238 _____
39 _____	89 _____	139 _____	189 _____	239 _____
40 _____	90 _____	140 _____	190 _____	240 _____
41 _____	91 _____	141 _____	191 _____	241 _____
42 _____	92 _____	142 _____	192 _____	242 _____
43 _____	93 _____	143 _____	193 _____	243 _____
44 _____	94 _____	144 _____	194 _____	244 _____
45 _____	95 _____	145 _____	195 _____	245 _____
46 _____	96 _____	146 _____	196 _____	246 _____
47 _____	97 _____	147 _____	197 _____	247 _____
48 _____	98 _____	148 _____	198 _____	248 _____
49 _____	99 _____	149 _____	199 _____	249 _____
50 _____	100 _____	150 _____	200 _____	250 _____

PH / ____	PH / ____	PH / ____	PH / ____	PH / ____
251 ____	301 ____	351 ____	401 ____	451 ____
252 ____	302 ____	352 ____	402 ____	452 ____
253 ____	303 ____	353 ____	403 ____	453 ____
254 ____	304 ____	354 ____	404 ____	454 ____
255 ____	305 ____	355 ____	405 ____	455 ____
256 ____	306 ____	356 ____	406 ____	456 ____
257 ____	307 ____	357 ____	407 ____	457 ____
258 ____	308 ____	358 ____	408 ____	458 ____
259 ____	309 ____	359 ____	409 ____	459 ____
260 ____	310 ____	360 ____	410 ____	460 ____
261 ____	311 ____	361 ____	411 ____	461 ____
262 ____	312 ____	362 ____	412 ____	462 ____
263 ____	313 ____	363 ____	413 ____	463 ____
264 ____	314 ____	364 ____	414 ____	464 ____
265 ____	315 ____	365 ____	415 ____	465 ____
266 ____	316 ____	366 ____	416 ____	466 ____
267 ____	317 ____	367 ____	417 ____	467 ____
268 ____	318 ____	368 ____	418 ____	468 ____
269 ____	319 ____	369 ____	419 ____	469 ____
270 ____	320 ____	370 ____	420 ____	470 ____
271 ____	321 ____	371 ____	421 ____	471 ____
272 ____	322 ____	372 ____	422 ____	472 ____
273 ____	323 ____	373 ____	423 ____	473 ____
274 ____	324 ____	374 ____	424 ____	474 ____
275 ____	325 ____	375 ____	425 ____	475 ____
276 ____	326 ____	376 ____	426 ____	476 ____
277 ____	327 ____	377 ____	427 ____	477 ____
278 ____	328 ____	378 ____	428 ____	478 ____
279 ____	329 ____	379 ____	429 ____	479 ____
280 ____	330 ____	380 ____	430 ____	480 ____
281 ____	331 ____	381 ____	431 ____	481 ____
282 ____	332 ____	382 ____	432 ____	482 ____
283 ____	333 ____	383 ____	433 ____	483 ____
284 ____	334 ____	384 ____	434 ____	484 ____
285 ____	335 ____	385 ____	435 ____	485 ____
286 ____	336 ____	386 ____	436 ____	486 ____
287 ____	337 ____	387 ____	437 ____	487 ____
288 ____	338 ____	388 ____	438 ____	488 ____
289 ____	339 ____	389 ____	439 ____	489 ____
290 ____	340 ____	390 ____	440 ____	490 ____
291 ____	341 ____	391 ____	441 ____	491 ____
292 ____	342 ____	392 ____	442 ____	492 ____
293 ____	343 ____	393 ____	443 ____	493 ____
294 ____	344 ____	394 ____	444 ____	494 ____
295 ____	345 ____	395 ____	445 ____	495 ____
296 ____	346 ____	396 ____	446 ____	496 ____
297 ____	347 ____	397 ____	447 ____	497 ____
298 ____	348 ____	398 ____	448 ____	498 ____
299 ____	349 ____	399 ____	449 ____	499 ____
300 ____	350 ____	400 ____	450 ____	500 ____

PH / _____   PH / _____

501 _____	551 _____
502 _____	552 _____
503 _____	553 _____
504 _____	554 _____
505 _____	555 _____
506 _____	556 _____
507 _____	557 _____
508 _____	558 _____
509 _____	559 _____
510 _____	560 _____
511 _____	561 _____
512 _____	562 _____
513 _____	563 _____
514 _____	564 _____
515 _____	565 _____
516 _____	566 _____
517 _____	567 _____
518 _____	568 _____
519 _____	569 _____
520 _____	570 _____
521 _____	571 _____
522 _____	572 _____
523 _____	573 _____
524 _____	574 _____
525 _____	575 _____
526 _____	576 _____
527 _____	577 _____
528 _____	578 _____
529 _____	579 _____
530 _____	580 _____
531 _____	581 _____
532 _____	582 _____
533 _____	583 _____
534 _____	594 _____
535 _____	595 _____
536 _____	
537 _____	
538 _____	
539 _____	
540 _____	
541 _____	
542 _____	
543 _____	
544 _____	
545 _____	
546 _____	
547 _____	
548 _____	
549 _____	
550 _____	

SERVICE MUSIC

DESCANT VERSIONS:

AMENS